TEXT, CASES AND MATERIALS ON EUROPEAN UNION LAW

Fourth Edition

John Tillotson, BA, LLM, PGCE
Formerly Course Director and Lecturer, School of Law,
University of Manchester

and

Nigel Foster, BA, LLM, Dip German
Jean Monnet Professor of European Law,
Cardiff Law School

Cavendish
Publishing
Limited

London • Sydney • Portland, Oregon

Fourth edition first published in Great Britain 2003 by
Cavendish Publishing Limited, The Glass House,
Wharton Street, London WC1X 9PX, United Kingdom
Telephone: + 44 (0)20 7278 8000   Facsimile: + 44 (0)20 7278 8080
Email: info@cavendishpublishing.com
Website: www.cavendishpublishing.com

Published in the United States by Cavendish Publishing
c/o International Specialized Book Services,
5824 NE Hassalo Street, Portland,
Oregon 97213-3644, USA

Published in Australia by Cavendish Publishing (Australia) Pty Ltd
45 Beach Street, Coogee, NSW 2034, Australia
Telephone: + 61 (2)9664 0909   Facsimile: +61 (2)9664 5420

British Library Cataloguing in Publication Data
Tillotson, John
European Union law – 4th ed
1 Law – European Union countries
2 Law – European Union countries – cases
I Title II Foster, Nigel G
341.2'422

Library of Congress Cataloguing in Publication Data
Data available

ISBN 1-85941-777-9

1 3 5 7 9 10 8 6 4 2

Printed and bound in Great Britain

PREFACE

The overriding purpose of this text, cases and materials book is to provide students with a clear and manageable guide to the main constitutional, institutional, administrative and substantive features of European Community law within the framework of European Union law as a whole. The European Community has for over 10 years been but one 'pillar' of the European Union, albeit by far the most substantial one in legal terms. EC law is therefore part of EU law but, dating back to the formation of the Community in 1957, the most highly developed part. The EC Treaty remains the basis for those elements of the law of the Union which have the most significant impact in the Member States.

The importance of this subject is undeniable. It is a compulsory foundation subject for undergraduate students on qualifying law degrees. It is studied on other undergraduate and postgraduate courses for both lawyers and others, particularly in the fields of politics and business. It is a subject of a diverse and dynamic character embracing political, economic and social issues and aspirations of which we all – as individuals and lawyers – are a part.

In this country, we have played and continue to play a part in the rapid development of this new – 50 year old – legal system which, in turn, continues to flow back, permeate and change not only the operation of our political and legal institutions, but also the way we engage in business and other affairs, as, for example, employers, employees and consumers.

No book, no course (particularly one of a single semester nature) could hope to cover all aspects of this wide-ranging and dynamic subject. Although in this fourth edition we have endeavoured to cover all the significant developments of the last three years, and both revised and widened the scope of the text, the treatment remains selective, whilst falling within the guidelines outlined by the Law Society and the Council for Legal Education in 1993.

The book falls into four overlapping parts: (1) The European Community and Union and Law in the Union; (2) The Nature and Effect of Community Law; (3) Aspects of Community Economic and Social Law; and (4) Remedies and the Enforcement of Community Law. Efforts have been made throughout to set the law in its political, economic and social context, particularly by the use of appropriate materials from a wide variety of sources, including the writings of specialist academic and other commentators. The subject is inevitably of an interdisciplinary nature.

Key provisions of the EC Treaty and the Treaty on European Union are reproduced together with discussion of the nature and effect of amendments since the original EEC Treaty was signed in Rome in 1957. Account is also taken of key Community legislative acts and policy making, particularly in the substantive fields of the free movement of goods, the free movement of persons, gender equality and competition policy. Decisions of the Court of Justice, the Court of First Instance and other courts are similarly dealt with, where necessary in some depth.

Since publication of the third edition in 2000, major decisions have been made at the highest level, the full effects of which will not emerge until at least the next Intergovernmental Conference in 2004. The Nice Treaty has prepared the way and the Union is due to increase its membership to 25 Member States. A new Convention on the Future of Europe is presently preparing a draft Constitutional Treaty and considering the status of the EU Charter of Fundamental Rights.

Important decisions by the Community Courts have developed the concept of Union citizenship, clarified questions concerning collective dominance and brought closer together the rules on Community and State liability. A CFI decision has brought to a head criticism of the restricted rights of private parties when challenging Community legislation. Modernising reform of competition law and policy continues.

Our thanks go again to Law Librarian Sue Bate and to Lilian Bloodworth, who has done another magnificent job in processing the book. We are finally happy to acknowledge a continuing working relationship *par excellence* with Jeremy Stein and all at Cavendish Publishing.

John Tillotson
Nigel Foster
June 2003

NOTE ON TREATY RENUMBERING

The Treaty of Amsterdam (ToA), which came into force in 1999, 'simplified' and renumbered the Articles of the Treaty on European Union (TEU) and the European Community Treaty (EC). This 'simplification' is 'anything but' for the student and the teacher of the subject.

Prior to the change, the case law and legislation obviously made reference to the 'old' pre-1999 numbers, and it is only in a gradual and piecemeal way that 'new' numbers are applicable in practice. The only solution is to use both numbers, that is, pre- and post-ToA. Depending on the context, you will therefore find, for example: Article 25 (formerly 12) EC or Article 173(2) (now 230(4)) EC or Article D (now 4) TEU. Where this method would complicate the text too much, you will find, for example, 25 (12) or 173(2) (230(4)) or even, where this should not confuse, the old or new number on its own.

CONTENTS

PART FOUR
REMEDIES AND THE ENFORCEMENT OF COMMUNITY LAW
AT COMMUNITY AND NATIONAL LEVELS

TABLE OF CASES (CHRONOLOGICAL)

EUROPEAN COURT OF JUSTICE

COURT OF FIRST INSTANCE

TABLE OF CASES (ALPHABETICAL)

Q

TABLE OF TREATIES AND CONVENTIONS

TABLE OF OTHER LEGISLATION

TABLE OF ABBREVIATIONS

AC ....Appeal Cases
ACP States ....African, Caribbean and Pacific States
AG ....Advocate General
All ER ....All England Law Reports
All ER (EC) ....All England Law Reports (European Cases)
BYIL ....British Yearbook of International Law
CA ....Court of Appeal
CAP ....Common Agricultural Policy
CFI ....Court of First Instance
CFSP ....Common Foreign and Security Policy
Ch ....Chancery
CLP ....Current Legal Problems
CMLR ....Common Market Law Reports
CML Rev ....Common Market Law Review
COREPER ....Committee of Permanent Representatives
DC ....Divisional Court
DG ....Directorate General
EAT ....Employment Appeal Tribunal
EC ....Economic Community
ECB ....European Central Bank
ECJ ....European Court of Justice
ECLR ....European Competition Law Review
ECR ....European Court Reports
ECSC ....European Coal and Steel Community
ECU ....European Currency Unit (formerly unit of account, now the Euro)
EEA ....European Economic Area
EEC ....European Economic Community
EFTA ....European Free Trade Association
EIPR ....European Intellectual Property Review
ELJ ....European Law Journal
EL Rev ....European Law Review
EMS ....European Monetary System
EMU ....Economic and Monetary Union
EPC ....European Political Co-operation
EPL ....European Public Law
ERM ....Exchange Rate Mechanism
ESCB ....European System of Central Banks
EU ....European Union
Euratom ....European Atomic Energy Community
FLR ....Family Law Reports
FSR ....Fleet Street Reports
GATT ....General Agreement on Tariffs and Trade
HL ....House of Lords
ICLQ ....International and Comparative Law Quarterly
ICR ....Industrial Court Reports
IGC ....Intergovernmental Conference
ILJ ....Industrial Law Journal
ILO ....International Labour Organisation
IRLR ....Industrial Relations Law Reports

JBL . . . . .Journal of Business Law
JCMS . . . . .Journal of Common Market Studies
JCPC . . . . .Judicial Committee of the Privy Council
JHA . . . . .Judicial and Home Affairs
JLS . . . . .Journal of Law and Society
LIEI . . . . .Legal Issues of European Integration
LQR . . . . .Law Quarterly Review
MCR . . . . .Merger Control Regulation
MEP . . . . .Member of the European Parliament
MLR . . . . .Modern Law Review
NLJ . . . . .New Law Journal
OEEC . . . . .Organisation for European Economic Co-operation
OJ . . . . .Official Journal
OJLS . . . . .Oxford Journal of Legal Studies
PJCC . . . . .Police and Judicial Co-operation in Criminal Matters
PL . . . . .Public Law
QBD . . . . .Queen's Bench Division
QMV . . . . .Qualified Majority Voting
SAD . . . . .Single Administrative Document
SEA . . . . .Single European Act
TEU . . . . .Treaty of European Union
ToA . . . . .Treaty of Amsterdam
WTO . . . . .World Trade Organization
YEL . . . . .Yearbook of European Law

PART ONE

EUROPEAN COMMUNITY AND UNION
AND LAW IN THE UNION

CHAPTER 1

THE EMERGENCE AND DEVELOPMENT OF THE EUROPEAN COMMUNITY AND UNION

INTRODUCTION

Indeed, when considering perspective, the shortcomings are also apparent if the current situation is compared to the aspirations of the founding fathers. Their motivation was not the price of eggs, bacon or steel, but rather a revolution in international behaviour [Nicoll and Salmon, *Understanding the European Communities*].

Considering that world peace can be safeguarded only by creative efforts commensurate with the dangers that threaten it ... Resolved to substitute for age-old rivalries the merging of their essential interests; to create, by establishing an economic community, the basis for a broader and deeper community among peoples long divided by bloody conflicts [Preamble to the European Coal and Steel Community Treaty 1951].

In March 1957, six sovereign Western European States signed a legal document binding themselves to the creation of an economic community. The signing in Rome of the Treaty Establishing the European Economic Community (EEC) by its six original Member States (France, West Germany, Italy, Belgium, the Netherlands and Luxembourg) was an act which represents a unique and practical conjunction of the political, the legal and economic. The aims of 'the Six' in coming together in this way were outlined in the Preamble to the Treaty:

Determined to lay the foundations of an ever closer union among the peoples of Europe,

Resolved to ensure the economic and social progress of their countries by common action to eliminate the barriers which divide Europe,

Affirming as the essential objective of their efforts the constant improvement of the living and working conditions of their peoples,

Recognizing that the removal of existing obstacles calls for concerted action in order to guarantee steady expansion, balanced trade and fair competition,

Anxious to strengthen the unity of their economies and to ensure their harmonious development by reducing the differences existing between the various regions and the backwardness of the less favoured regions,

Desiring to contribute, by means of a common commercial policy, to the progressive abolition of restrictions on international trade,

Intending to confirm the solidarity which binds Europe and the overseas countries and desiring to ensure the development of their prosperity, in accordance with the principles of the Charter of the United Nations,

Resolved by thus pooling their resources to preserve and strengthen peace and liberty, and calling upon the other peoples of Europe who share their ideal to join in their efforts,

Have decided to create a European Economic Community ...

The main, most clearly defined objective in this preliminary statement is that of the maintenance of 'economic and social progress'. Such progress is to be achieved by 'common action to eliminate the barriers which divide Europe'. This process of integration must, however, be seen in the context of the first stated aim: '... an ever closer union among the peoples of Europe.' As such, it can be argued that the drafters of the Treaty of Rome can be taken as envisaging, at some future date, a Community in which economic solidarity has merged with political solidarity.

It is clear from the Preamble (the wording of which, but for the deletion of 'Economic' in the last line, is the same now as when originally drafted) that the Community is open to new members – there are now 15, and more countries are waiting to join – and that it takes its place within the world economic (and political) order as an upholder of peace, liberty and a free market economy.

The Treaty of Rome therefore indicates that European integration has many dimensions. To be understood properly, it should be appreciated that it may, or must, be viewed from a variety of perspectives: the global, the supranational (or federal), the Member State and last, but certainly not least, from the viewpoint of the individual.

The EEC Treaty, although of tremendous significance, is, however, but one of several treaties underpinning the process of European integration. The first such treaty was the Treaty of Paris 1951 which established the European Coal and Steel Community (ECSC). The Euratom Treaty, the legal basis of the European Atomic Energy Community, was designed at the same time as the Treaty of Rome in 1957. Under the Maastricht Treaty on European Union 1992 (TEU), the European Economic Community was significantly renamed the European Community and the amended EEC Treaty accordingly became the EC Treaty. The 1997 Treaty of Amsterdam (ToA), which came into effect in May 1999, introduced further changes to the TEU and the three Community Treaties. The reform process, considered by some to be too slow and over-cautious, continued with the signing of the Treaty of Nice in early 2001 and, with a view to further strengthening and increased democratisation of an enlarged Union, yet more measures are currently under discussion which will bring about additional treaty amendments, probably in 2005.

The European Union presently comprises three internationally recognised legal persons, the EC, the ECSC and Euratom, making up the first pillar of the Union, together with two further 'policies and forms of co-operation': Common Foreign and Security Policy (CFSP) and Police and Judicial Co-operation in Criminal Matters (PJCC) (formerly known as Co-operation in the Fields of Justice and Home Affairs (JHA) under the Maastricht Treaty), which form the second and third pillars (see the diagram on page 17).

In this book, we will concentrate almost exclusively on the EC Treaty, which is not to be regarded merely as an international agreement but, in the words of the European Court of Justice, as 'the constitutional charter of a Community based on the rule of law'.

DEVELOPMENTS: 1945 TO THE PRESENT DAY

As already indicated, no study of European Community law can be pursued in an effective manner without taking account of the political, social and economic forces with which it is inextricably intertwined. This is the case whether one is dealing with the relationship between the EC and the Member States, with trade regulation within a Single European Market, with environmental issues or with questions of equal pay or pension rights.

Any account of the establishment and continuing development of the EC must be approached along the same interrelated lines. The history of European integration, as one might expect with such an immense undertaking, is one of considerable complexity and neither the theory nor the practice is free from controversy. This opening chapter merely serves to draw attention to the more significant milestones and signposts along the way:

> The European Economic Community is an outgrowth of the European movement, a complex composite of political, social and economic forces which have come to the fore in strength since World War II. By the end of the war, national government structures in Continental Europe were weakened to the point of collapse. Europe, devastated and enfeebled by war and the loss of colonies, faced the two emergent giants, the United States and the Soviet Union. Its division by trade barriers underlined its weakness. Determined to build on pre-war ideas of a united Europe, on the feeling of the people that there must be no more internecine European wars, and on a variety of special national interests favouring such a movement, a small group of individuals pressed for new institutions to advance unification of Europe. The process of institution-building was marked from the beginning by a pervasive ambiguity. Should new institutions be built so as to preserve the nation state with all its trappings of national loyalties and rivalries, or should there be new transnational institutions which would dilute or supersede the nation state and provide a constitutional foundation for a unified Europe? Today the ambiguity is still with us [Stein, Hay and Waelbroeck, *European Community Law in Perspective*, 1976].

At the present time, that 'pervasive ambiguity' remains, not least in the shape of a recent British Prime Minister. In 1946, another Conservative leader, Winston Churchill, in his famous 'United States of Europe' speech in Zurich, spoke of a unified and democratic 'greater Europe'. However, according to his Private Secretary:

> He never for one moment during or after the war contemplated Britain submerging her sovereignty in that of a United States of Europe or losing her national identity ... In January 1941, at Ditchley, he went so far as to say that there must be a United States of Europe and that it should be built by the English: if the Russians built it there would be communism and squalor; if the Germans built it there would be tyranny and brute force. On the other hand, I knew he felt that while Britain might be the builder and Britain might live in the house, she would always preserve her liberty of choice and would be the natural, undisputed link with the Americans and the Commonwealth [John Colville, *The Fringes of Power*, 1985].

In 1947, in order to assist in the reconstruction of post-war Europe amid fears of Soviet expansion westwards in Europe beyond what became known as the Iron Curtain, the then US Secretary of State, George Marshall, initiated a 13 billion dollar Economic Recovery Programme. However, in the words of a State Department memorandum of the time, it was imperative that the recovery of Europe be tied to:

... a European plan which the principal European nations ... should work out. Such a plan should be based on a European economic federation on the order of the Belgian-Netherlands-Luxembourg Customs Union. Europe cannot recover from this war and again become independent if her economy continues to be divided into many small watertight compartments as it is today.

The result was the establishment in 1948 of the intergovernmental Organisation for European Economic Co-operation (OEEC) consisting of 18 European (but not Eastern bloc) countries. In the required spirit of 'continuous and effective self-help and mutual aid', the OEEC worked with considerable success in the field of trade liberalisation through the gradual removal of quota restrictions, and, through its European Payments Union, it provided a clearing mechanism for multilateral settlement of trading accounts. However, by 1949, speedier progress towards 'an integration of the Western European economy' was being urged at an OEEC meeting:

> The substance of such integration would be the formation of a single large market within which quantitative restrictions on the movement of goods, monetary barriers to the flow of payments and, eventually, all tariffs are permanently swept aside.

Within a matter of months, these aspirations began to take practical shape. The Schuman Declaration of 9 May 1950 was based on a plan devised by another Frenchman, Jean Monnet. In part, it read:

> Europe will not be made all at once, or according to a single plan. It will be built through concrete achievements which first create a *de facto* solidarity. The coming together of the nations of Europe requires the elimination of the age-old opposition of France and Germany. Any action taken must in the first place concern these two countries.

> With this aim in view, the French Government proposes to take action immediately on one limited but decisive point. It proposes to place Franco-German production of coal and steel as a whole under a common higher authority, within the framework of an organisation open to the participation of the other countries of Europe.

> The pooling of coal and steel production should immediately provide for the setting up of common foundations for economic development as a first step in the federation of Europe, and will change the destinies of those regions which have long been devoted to the manufacture of munitions of war, of which they have been the most constant victims.

> The solidarity in production thus established will make it plain that any war between France and Germany becomes not merely unthinkable, but materially impossible. The setting up of this powerful productive unit, open to all countries willing to take part and bound ultimately to provide all the member countries with the basic elements of industrial production on the same terms, will lay a true foundation for their economic unification.

The European Coal and Steel Community

In 1951, the EUROPEAN COAL AND STEEL COMMUNITY (ECSC) was established under the terms of the Treaty of Paris. Six countries subscribed to the principles of the Schuman Plan: France, West Germany, Italy and the three Benelux countries. It is important to appreciate the following points regarding the ECSC:

(a) The primary motive underlying this integrative initiative was political rather than economic.

(b) It was seen merely as a first step in the integrative process – a sectoral scheme providing guidelines for a more general form of economic union later.

(c) Great weight was attached to the creation of new, European institutions, in particular a *supranational* High Authority, under the executive control of which the coal and steel production of the Member States was placed.

(d) The *independence* of the non-elected High Authority was balanced by a Council of Ministers (from the Member States), and a Common Assembly (later, Parliament) with the power to dismiss the High Authority.

(e) The Community was firmly set in a *legal* framework with a Court of Justice charged with the duty of ensuring the observance of the law in the interpretation and application of the Treaty.

Represented though they were in the Council of Ministers, the Member States nevertheless relinquished and transferred a large measure of their national sovereignty and therefore control in the coal and steel sectors when they signed the Treaty, in as much as the supranational High Authority possessed the power to take decisions binding on national enterprises requiring the approval of governments.

This direct linking of the institutional control of the High Authority to economic sectors located in different countries involved jettisoning the traditional intergovernmental approach to international co-operation. The basis of this novel strategy is to be found in what was called the *functionalist* approach to integration: a method which has been described as one 'which would ... overlay political divisions with a spreading web of international activities and agencies, in which and through which the interests and life of all nations would be gradually integrated': David Mitrany, 1933.

The integrative cornerstone of the ECSC was a Common Market which combined elements of the concept of free movement of goods and a competitive market system with a minimum of institutional intervention in the market:

ECSC Treaty

Article 1

By this Treaty, the High Contracting Parties establish among themselves a EUROPEAN COAL AND STEEL COMMUNITY, founded upon a Common Market, common objectives and common institutions.

Article 2

The European Coal and Steel Community shall have as its task to contribute, in harmony with the general economy of the Member States and through the establishment of a Common Market as provided in Article 4, to economic expansion, growth of employment and a rising standard of living in the Member States.

The Community shall progressively bring about conditions which will of themselves ensure the most rational distribution of production at the highest possible level of productivity, while safeguarding continuity of employment and taking care not to provoke fundamental and persistent disturbances in the economies of Member States ...

Article 4

The following are recognised as incompatible with the Common Market for coal and steel and shall accordingly be abolished and prohibited within the Community, as provided in this Treaty:

a   import and export duties, or charges having equivalent effect, and quantitative restrictions on the movement of products;

b   measures or practices which discriminate between producers, between purchasers or between consumers, especially in prices and delivery terms or transport rates and conditions, and measures or practices which interfere with the purchaser's free choice of supplier;

c   subsidies or aids granted by states, or special charges imposed by states, in any form whatsoever;

d   restrictive practices which tend towards the sharing or exploiting of markets.

Article 5

The Community shall carry out its task in accordance with this Treaty, with a limited measure of intervention.

To this end the Community shall:

–   provide guidance and assistance for the parties concerned, by obtaining information, organising consultations and laying down general objectives;

–   place financial resources at the disposal of undertakings for their investment and bear part of the cost of readaptation;

–   ensure the establishment, maintenance and observance of normal competitive conditions and exert direct influence upon production or upon the market only when circumstances so require;

–   publish the reasons for its actions and take the necessary measures to ensure the observance of the rules laid down in this Treaty.

The institutions of the Community shall carry out these activities with a minimum of administrative machinery and in close co-operation with the parties concerned.

Regarding the outcome of this amalgam of free market and *dirigisme*, it has been said that:

> The High Authority emerged from the negotiations presiding over a highly imperfect single market in raw materials and manufactures, with powers to interfere in transport, with the capacity to make some decisions of its own about capital investment, and presiding over a common labour market which existed only in theory. Where the economic distortions of the nation state were replaced, it was less by the neutral, anonymous efficiency of the free market, or of an expert technocratic decision making body, than by a set of complex regulations arising from the careful balancing and adjustment of the interests of the various nation states to allow them to achieve particular national objectives. The future political economy of the Treaty of Rome, the analysis of which by any neo-classical formulations is likely to reduce the analyst only to a state of bewildered despair, had already taken shape.

> Yet in many respects this was a big improvement on what had gone before. It not only made a set of economic issues which had been closely intermingled with the causes of war and peace the subject of permanent government regulation but it provided a permanent international governmental organisation, with some public appearance of neutrality, to regulate them [Alan Milward, 1984].

Later in the 1950s, following the failure of attempts to establish a European Defence Community (and European Army containing West German elements) and a European Political Community possessing institutions with supranational authority, it became increasingly evident that economic integration would have to precede political integration. Planning moved away from the idea of progressive integration of the European economy by sectors towards the creation of a wide-ranging economic union. In 1955, the Foreign Ministers of the six members of the ECSC declared their intention to:

> ... pursue the establishment of a United Europe through the development of common institutions, a progressive fusion of national economies, the creation of a Common Market and harmonisation of social policies.

Over a nine month period beginning in June 1955, an Intergovernmental Committee presided over by the Belgian Foreign Minister, Paul-Henri Spaak, worked on the preparation of treaties which would lay down the legal basis of such goals. Britain was invited to participate in this planning but her contribution was minimal and short lived. Her ties with the Commonwealth and the USA, together with a preference for traditional intergovernmental co-operation and a less advanced form of integration based on a free trade area, all militated at this time against joining the *'relance européenne'*.

The European Economic Community and Euratom

The Spaak Report was adopted by the Foreign Ministers of 'the Six' in May 1956 and became the basis for the treaties establishing the EUROPEAN ECONOMIC COMMUNITY (EEC) and the EUROPEAN ATOMIC ENERGY COMMUNITY (EURATOM) signed in Rome in March 1957 (effective 1 January 1958).

The aims and principal features of the report were to be found in Part One: Principles, Articles 1–8 of the EEC Treaty (since amended):

EEC TREATY

Article 1

By this Treaty, the High Contracting Parties establish among themselves a EUROPEAN ECONOMIC COMMUNITY.

Article 2

The Community shall have as its task, by establishing a Common Market and progressively approximating the economic policies of Member States, to promote throughout the Community a harmonious development of economic activities, a continuous and balanced expansion, an increase in stability, an accelerated raising of the standard of living and closer relations between the States belonging to it.

Article 3

For the purposes set out in Article 2, the activities of the Community shall include, as provided in this Treaty and in accordance with the timetable set out therein:

a   the elimination, as between Member States, of customs duties and of quantitative restrictions on the import and export of goods, and of all other measures having equivalent effect;

b   the establishment of a common customs tariff and of a common commercial policy towards third countries;

c   the abolition, as between Member States, of obstacles to freedom of movement for persons, services and capital;

d   the adoption of a common policy in the sphere of agriculture;

e   the adoption of a common policy in the sphere of transport;

f   the institution of a system ensuring that competition in the Common Market is not distorted;

g   the application of procedures by which the economic policies of Member States can be co-ordinated and disequilibria in their balances of payments remedied;

h   the approximation of the laws of Member States to the extent required for the proper functioning of the Common Market;

i   the creation of a European Social Fund in order to improve employment opportunities for workers and to contribute to the raising of their standard of living;

j   the establishment of a European Investment Bank to facilitate the economic expansion of the Community by opening up fresh resources;

k   the association of the overseas countries and territories in order to increase trade and to promote jointly economic and social development.

Article 4

1   The tasks entrusted to the Community shall be carried out by the following institutions:

an ASSEMBLY [later, the PARLIAMENT],

a COUNCIL,

a COMMISSION,

a COURT OF JUSTICE.

Each institution shall act within the limits of the powers conferred upon it by this Treaty.

2   The Council and the Commission shall be assisted by an Economic and Social Committee acting in an advisory capacity.

Article 5

Member States shall take all appropriate measures, whether general or particular, to ensure fulfilment of the obligations arising out of this Treaty or resulting from action taken by the institutions of the Community. They shall facilitate the achievement of the Community's tasks.

They shall abstain from any measure which could jeopardise the attainment of the objectives of this Treaty.

Article 6

1   Member States shall, in close co-operation with the institutions of the Community, co-ordinate their respective economic policies to the extent necessary to attain the objectives of this Treaty.

2   The institutions of the Community shall take care not to prejudice the internal and external financial stability of the Member States.

Article 7

Within the scope of this Treaty, and without prejudice to any special provisions contained therein, any discrimination on grounds of nationality shall be prohibited.

The Council may, on a proposal from the Commission and in co-operation with the European Parliament, adopt, by a qualified majority, rules designed to prohibit such discrimination.

Article 8

1   The Common Market shall be progressively established during a transitional period of twelve years.

This transitional period shall be divided into three stages of four years each; the length of each stage may be altered in accordance with the provisions set out below.

2   To each stage there shall be assigned a set of actions to be initiated and carried out concurrently ...

At the time of the signing of the Rome Treaties, a Convention was concluded which provided for a single Court of Justice and a single Parliamentary Assembly for all three Communities. By 1965, it was also found necessary by means of the so called Merger Treaty to establish a single Commission of the European Communities (replacing the ECSC High Authority and the EEC and Euratom Commissions) and a single, and now more powerful, Council of Ministers.

Even before the entry into force of the EEC Treaty, an attempt (initiated by the UK) was made to create an OEEC free trade area including the EEC as an economic unit. When this was strongly rejected by France as constituting a potential dilution of the integrative process, seven OEEC countries (the UK, Denmark, Norway, Sweden, Austria, Switzerland and Portugal) signed a treaty in Stockholm in 1960 establishing the EUROPEAN FREE TRADE ASSOCIATION (EFTA) to be run on an intergovernmental basis.

Britain's eventual accession to the European Community (together with Ireland and Denmark) on 1 January 1973 came about after two French-inspired rejections of applications made by the Macmillan government in 1961 and the Wilson government in 1967. In the intervening years, the UK had come to realise that its economic future lay in Europe. However, then as now, the true extent of her commitment to the progress of economic and political integration in Europe remains somewhat an open question:

Treaty of Accession

Article 1

1   The Kingdom of Denmark, Ireland, the Kingdom of Norway* and the United Kingdom of Great Britain and Northern Ireland hereby become members of the European Economic Community and of the European Atomic Energy Community and Parties to the Treaties establishing these Communities as amended or supplemented.**

2   The conditions of admission and the adjustments to the Treaties establishing the European Economic Community and the European Atomic Energy Community necessitated thereby are set out in the Act annexed to this Treaty. The provisions of that Act concerning the European Economic Community and the European Atomic Energy Community shall form an integral part of this Treaty.

---

*   Following a national referendum, Norway did not accede.
**   The new Member States acceded to the ECSC Treaty at the same time.

3   The provisions concerning the rights and obligations of the Member States and
     the powers and jurisdiction of the institutions of the Communities as set out in
     the Treaties referred to in paragraph 1 shall apply in respect of this Treaty ...

Act of Accession

...

Article 2

From the date of accession, the provisions of the original Treaties and the acts adopted
by the institutions of the Communities shall be binding on the new Member States
and shall apply in those States under the conditions laid down in those Treaties and in
this Act.

Prior to the 1973 enlargement, the Community had in 1965 experienced a serious crisis
when, mainly in protest against a 'federalist-inspired' Commission proposal that the
Community raise its own budgetary resources from agricultural levies and tariffs on
goods from non-EEC countries, instead of being reliant on contributions from the
Member States, France (in the form of General de Gaulle) withdrew from the Council,
the Community's main legislative body under the Treaty of Rome, and hence from its
decision making process for a period of seven months. This impasse was only broken
after the Council adopted the so called *Luxembourg Accords*, which redefined and
reduced the Commission's role in the decision making process and, in practice,
extended the unanimity requirement in the Council at a time when, under the terms of
the Treaty, the Member States were scheduled to move to more qualified majority
voting (see Article 205(2) EC to see how this procedure operates), with the intended
effect of *reducing* the power of individual Member States:

The Luxembourg Accords

...

(b) Majority voting procedure
     I   Where, in the case of decisions which may be taken by majority vote on a
          proposal of the Commission, very important interests of one or more partners
          are at stake, the Members of the Council will endeavour, within a reasonable
          time, to reach solutions which can be adopted by all the Members of the
          Council while respecting their mutual interests and those of the Community,
          in accordance with Article 2 of the Treaty.
     II   With regard to the preceding paragraph, the French delegation considers that
          where very important interests are at stake the discussion must be continued
          until unanimous agreement is reached.
     III The six delegations note that there is a divergence of views on what should be
          done in the event of a failure to reach complete agreement.
     IV   The six delegations nevertheless consider that this divergence does not
          prevent the Community's work being resumed in accordance with the normal
          procedure.

The effect of this agreement to disagree was to slow down the pace of decision
making, and hence the process of integration, until a new impetus was found in the
mid-1980s for the completion of the *Internal Market* by the end of 1992. Further internal
and external, political and economic difficulties from the late 1960s to the early 1980s
(for example, the energy crises, inflation, world recession and prolonged differences

over the UK contribution to the Community budget) were all instrumental in that period in creating a weakening of the political resolve of the Member States towards finding Community based solutions and implementing new common policies.

Nevertheless, tentative first steps were taken in this period in several fields including *economic and monetary union* (1969–71) and *European Political Co-operation* (1970). Some of the advances as were forthcoming did, however, have the effect of further diluting the concept of supranationality and the aims of European federalists. For example, the basis for European Political Co-operation was laid by means of regular *intergovernmental* meetings of the Foreign Ministers of the Member States plus the President of the Commission. Similarly, it was decided in 1974 to institutionalise the Summit Conferences of Heads of State or Government which had been held since 1969. In this way, the *European Council* was established, a development which elicited this comment from Jean Monnet:

> We were wrong in 1952 to think that Europe would be built with the High Authority of the Coal and Steel Community as a supranational government. What matters now is that the Heads of national governments meet together regularly in the European Council. That's where the authority is. It's a very big change.

In its *Solemn Declaration on European Union* (1983), the European Council outlined its role in the following terms:

2.1   The European Council

2.1.1 The European Council brings together the Heads of State or Government and the President of the Commission assisted by the Foreign Ministers of the Member States and a member of the Commission.

2.1.2 In the perspective of European Union, the European Council:

provides a general political impetus to the construction of Europe;

defines approaches to further the construction of Europe and issues general political guidelines for the European Communities and European Political Co-operation;

deliberates upon matters concerning European Union in its different aspects with due regard to consistency among them;

initiates co-operation in new areas of activity;

solemnly expresses the common position in questions of external relations.

2.1.3 When the European Council acts in matters within the scope of the European Communities, it does so in its capacity as the Council within the meaning of the Treaties.

It should be noted that both the European Council and European Political Co-operation in the field of foreign policy were later provided with a legal basis by the Single European Act of 1986.

Other major developments in the 1970s were the establishment in 1977 of the *exchange rate mechanism* (ERM) for the stabilisation of currencies within the Community (the UK did not join until 1990 and suspended membership in 1992 following turbulence in the international money markets), and the first *direct elections* to the European Parliament in 1979 – an event of great significance for European federalists, not many of whom were to be found in the UK, where voter turnout was only 32.6 per cent (the lowest in the Community). Members of the European Parliament (MEPs) are no longer merely delegates from national legislatures but the elected representatives of 'Euro-constituencies' and political parties from within the Member States. The legal basis for direct elections in the EEC Treaty was Article 138(3) as replaced by Council Decision 76/787 and Act of 20 September 1976 on Direct Elections. The originally envisaged uniform electoral procedure is still not in existence: see now Article 190(4) EC.

Also in the 1970s, on the basis of the Budgetary Treaties of 1970 and 1975, the EEC (and Euratom) did eventually move from a system whereby revenue was raised by direct financial contributions from the Member States to one based on the fiscal federalist concept of the Communities' *'own resources'* (that is, its own tax revenue). Since 1988, 'true' own resources have been made up of customs duties levied under the Common Customs Tariff on imports from non-member countries and agricultural levies and duties charged on imports and on some internal agricultural over-production. These sources are supplemented by the application of a 1.4 per cent contribution from Member States' value added tax (VAT) assessments and further, variable contributions from Member States depending on Community needs and Member States' ability to pay. An important feature of the Budgetary Treaty 1970 was the measure of control over the EEC budget that was granted to the Parliament. This was necessary to the extent that own resources no longer passed through Member States' budgets subject to control by their Parliaments.

The years 1965 to 1975 thus witnessed a somewhat hesitant progress in the development of the Community, during a period when what has been termed 'the dialectics of co-operation or integration' were markedly on display. What, for federalists, were regarded as regressive steps back towards intergovernmentalism (the Luxembourg Accords, Political Co-operation and the European Council) were later matched by developments of a federal nature ('own resources' and direct elections to the European Parliament). As we have seen, these years also saw the first enlargement of the Community from six to nine Member States.

Enlargement of the Community to 15 Member States came about through the accession of Greece in 1981, Spain and Portugal in 1986 and Austria, Sweden and Finland in 1995. However, the most significant development of the 1980s was the Commission's proposal in 1985 of a programme for a *Single European (or Internal) Market* to be achieved by the end of 1992. Not that considerable progress had not already been made in this direction. The Commission had announced the creation of a customs union (see Chapter 2) between the original 'Six' in 1968 and between 'the Nine' in 1977. However, many non-tariff barriers and national tax differentials remained to hinder the free movement of goods and uneven progress had been made as regards removing obstacles to the achievement of the other freedoms essential to the establishment of the Common Market to be found in Article 3(c) of the Treaty of Rome, that is, the free movement of persons (including the right of establishment for firms), of services and of capital.

In February 1986, the 12 Member States signed the SINGLE EUROPEAN ACT (amending the EEC Treaty) so giving legal effect to the Commission's proposals. A new Article 7a of the Treaty of Rome (now Article 14 EC following renumbering brought into effect by the Treaty of Amsterdam (ToA) in 1999) stated in part that:

> The Community shall adopt measures with the aim of progressively establishing the internal market over a period expiring on 31 December 1992 ... The internal market shall comprise an area without internal frontiers in which the free movement of

goods, persons, services and capital is ensured in accordance with the provisions of this Treaty.

However, the Single European Act was not important merely in terms of '1992'. The Preamble noted 'the results achieved in the fields of economic integration and political co-operation and *the need for new developments*' (emphasis added). In this light, the Preamble went on to express the will of the Member States 'to transform relations as a whole among their States into a European Union, in accordance with the solemn Declaration of Stuttgart of 19 June 1983' (see above). Further, the Preamble drew attention to the 'Conference in Paris from 19 to 21 October 1972 [at which] the Heads of State or of Government approved the objective of the progressive realisation of Economic and Monetary Union'.

In the result, and in a renewed drive towards an as yet undefined 'European Union', the Single European Act amended the EEC Treaty to introduce new, or rather to develop existing but unrealised, policies in the fields of, for example, economic and monetary 'convergence', social policy and the environment. It also, as will be seen, improved the Parliament's position as regards the Community's law making process by means of a new 'co-operation procedure' between the Council and the Parliament, and it extended the permitted range of qualified majority voting in the decision making process of the Council. This last change was particularly significant in respect of a new Article 100a EEC (now Article 95 EC) concerning the adoption of Community Directives, the purpose of which was the approximation (usually known as harmonisation) of national laws affecting the establishment or functioning of the Internal Market.

Although the cornerstone of the Single European Act was the Internal Market programme and the elimination of barriers to trade, so making the Act attractive to 'free market' Conservatives in the UK, it seemingly took Mrs Thatcher a little time to grasp those features of the Act which strengthened the Commission, weakened the position of individual Member States in the Council – and so altered yet again the political balance in the Community – and which, on the basis of strengthened Community competences, gave added weight to the 'social dimension' in Europe.

In the early 1990s, with the completion of the Internal Market arguably on course, the main focus of attention and debate switched away from the first of the Community's 'tasks' in Article 2 of the 1957 Treaty – the establishment of a Common Market – to the second – the progressive approximation of the economic policies of the Member States. The next 'Great Debate' began in Rome in December 1990 at the Intergovernmental Conferences on Economic and Monetary Union and on Political Union.

At the conclusion of these conferences in the Dutch city of Maastricht in December 1991, the European Council adopted a Treaty on Political Union and a Treaty on Economic and Monetary Union, the whole making up the Treaty on European Union (TEU). The Treaty was signed in February 1992 and it was intended that it would enter into force on 1 January 1993 following ratification by all 12 Member States in accordance with their respective constitutional requirements. However, a negative vote in the Danish referendum on the Treaty in June 1992 cast serious doubts as to its future. Following concessions to the Danes, a second referendum in May 1993 resulted in a 'Yes' vote and the Treaty entered into force in November 1993. Various reservations, however, were expressed in a number of Member States, particularly

Germany, regarding the further steps towards 'an ever closer union' (particularly monetary union) that the new Treaty represented: see Chapter 3.

EUROPEAN UNION AND EUROPEAN COMMUNITY

The three foundation Treaties (subject to various amendments) were incorporated into the structure of the Maastricht Treaty on European Union (TEU). By this Treaty, the Member States established among themselves a European Union: Title I 'Common Provisions', Article A TEU (see now Article 1 TEU following ToA renumbering). Throughout the Treaty, the term 'European Economic Community' was replaced by the term 'European Community': Title II 'Amending the EEC Treaty', Article G (now 8) TEU.

Structure of the TEU: the Three 'Pillars'

The TEU was made up of seven titles. Title I 'Common Provisions' set out the basic objectives of the Union; it did not amend the three foundation Treaties in any way. Such amendments were found in Titles II, III and IV applying to the EEC, ECSC and Euratom Treaties respectively. These four titles constituted the first pillar of the Union: *The European Communities*. The second pillar was to be found in Title V on *Common Foreign and Security Policy* and the third in Title VI covering *Justice and Home Affairs*: (see the diagram on page 17). Title VII contained final provisions, followed by protocols to the Treaty and declarations.

Common Provisions (Title I, Articles A–F (now Articles 1–7 TEU))

Avoiding the use of the word 'federal', Article A (now 1) TEU stated: 'This Treaty marks a new stage in the process of creating an ever closer union among the peoples of Europe, in which decisions are taken as closely as possible to the citizen.' This last point was a reference to the new principle of *subsidiarity*, which also found a place in Article B(2) (now 2(2)) TEU: 'The objectives of the Union shall be achieved as provided in this Treaty ... while respecting the principle of subsidiarity as defined in Article 3b of the Treaty establishing the European Community': see below and Chapter 3.

Article A (now Article 1) TEU identified the three pillars: 'The Union shall be founded on the European Communities, supplemented by the policies and forms of co-operation established by this Treaty.' These policies were, as indicated above, co-operation on Common Foreign and Security Policy (formerly European Political Co-operation under the Single European Act) and co-operation on Justice and Home Affairs. These policies were not incorporated into the EC Treaty (formerly the EEC Treaty). Although it was agreed that further steps would be taken towards more intensive co-operation and, if necessary, joint action in these fields, it was also agreed at Maastricht that such co-operation was initially to proceed on an *intergovernmental* and not a strictly Community basis.

As regards foreign and security policy, the European Council was given the responsibility of defining its principles and general guidelines and the Council of Ministers (Foreign and Defence in particular) the responsibility of taking decisions – generally unanimous decisions – for the implementation of policy: Title V, Article J.8

EUROPEAN UNION: THE THREE PILLARS

EUROPEAN UNION*

established by the Maastricht Treaty on European Union 1992

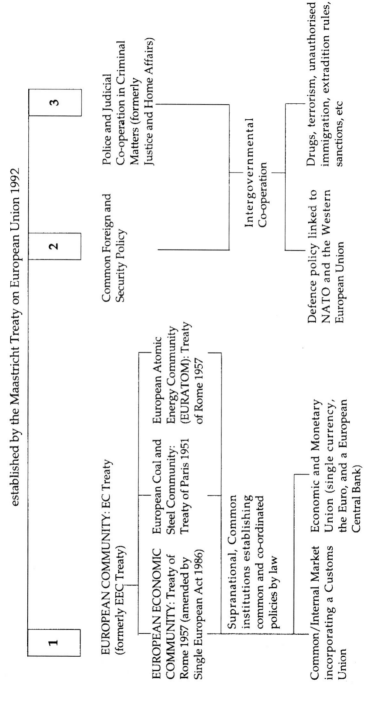

1

EUROPEAN COMMUNITY: EC Treaty (formerly EEC Treaty)

EUROPEAN ECONOMIC COMMUNITY: Treaty of Rome 1957 (amended by Single European Act 1986)

European Coal and Steel Community: Treaty of Paris 1951

European Atomic Energy Community (EURATOM): Treaty of Rome 1957

Supranational, Common institutions establishing common and co-ordinated policies by law

Common/Internal Market incorporating a Customs Union

Economic and Monetary Union (single currency, the Euro, and a European Central Bank)

2

Common Foreign and Security Policy

Intergovernmental Co-operation

Defence policy linked to NATO and the Western European Union

3

Police and Judicial Co-operation in Criminal Matters (formerly Justice and Home Affairs)

Drugs, terrorism, unauthorised immigration, extradition rules, sanctions, etc

* The Union currently has 15 members: the original six – France, West Germany (now Germany), Italy, Belgium, the Netherlands and Luxembourg plus the United Kingdom, Ireland, Denmark, Greece, Spain, Portugal, Sweden, Finland and Austria.

(now 18) TEU. 'European' policy was, however, neither common nor effective with respect to the Gulf War or the wars in the former Yugoslavia, and disagreement still exists over the creation of a European army.

The areas of activity listed in Title VI, Article K.1 (now 29) TEU as being of 'common interest' in terms of co-operation on Justice and Home Affairs included asylum and immigration policy, the combating of drug addiction and international fraud, judicial co-operation, and customs and police co-operation in the fight against terrorism and drug trafficking. Provision was made for these matters to be transferred to the Community pillar without the need to amend the Treaty: Article K.9 (now 37) TEU. Indeed, under the Amsterdam Treaty, following further realisation that many of these important policy areas involved questions of fundamental human rights and free movement, parts of this third pillar, renamed *Police and Judicial Co-operation in Criminal Matters*, were reworked and incorporated into the first pillar of the Union.

The Union's Main Objective

The first stated objective of the Union in Article B (now 2) TEU was indicative of what had already been achieved and what remained to be achieved:

— to promote economic and social progress which is balanced and sustainable, in particular through the creation of an area without internal frontiers, through the strengthening of economic and social cohesion and through the establishment of economic and monetary union, ultimately including a single currency ...

Underlying Principles

Fundamental principles underlying the Union included, in particular, respect for the *national identities* of its Member States and for *fundamental rights* as general principles of Community law: Article F (now 6) TEU, and also respect for the principle of *subsidiarity*: Article B (now 2) TEU. As discussed in Chapter 3, the purpose of this latter principle is, in broad terms, to provide a practical basis on which decisions can be made as to whether it is better for Community action to be taken on a particular issue or whether the Member States are better placed to achieve the objectives in question. Some issues, by reason of scale or effects, are better suited to Community action than others. The principle is therefore to be seen as a counterweight to the federalist and centralising tendencies of the TEU.

It was also established under Article C (now 3) TEU that the Union shall be served by a *single institutional framework* which will build upon the *acquis communautaire* (the existing body of Community law). However, the role of the institutions under the second and third intergovernmental pillars is, at present, much reduced: see Article E (now 5) TEU.

Arrangements under the two new Maastricht pillars, focusing as they did on co-operation and common action between the Member States, clearly diluted the federal nature of the Union, although, as seen below, the ToA has partially reversed this trend and developments regarding economic and monetary union within the EC pillar may be said to have more than offset this effect in the 'fledgling' areas and greatly advanced the concept of central control at the expense of national sovereignty.

The European Community – Maastricht Amendments to the EEC Treaty: Extension of Powers

As compared with the original Article 3 of the EEC Treaty (see above), the list of common policies or activities of the new European Community (EC) in Article 3 of the amended Treaty shows a further *strengthening or expansion of Community powers* (legal bases) in a number of economic, monetary and social fields. Building in part on advances recognised by the Single European Act in 1986, these include the strengthening of economic and social cohesion (aid to poorer regions) and environmental policy and the promotion of research and technology, consumer protection and education and training. The new list also includes the establishment and development of trans-European transport networks, health protection, culture and (overseas) development co-operation.

Economic and Monetary Union

It will be recalled that the two means by which the Community's objectives would be achieved in Article 2 of the original EEC Treaty were the establishment of a Common Market and progressive approximation of the economic policies of the Member States. In the TEU, the first of these means remained (the '1992' Internal Market programme bringing the concept much closer to a reality) but the second, closely related, means became the establishment of 'an economic and monetary union' (EMU).

The origins of EMU go back to 1969, but progress was thwarted for many years by both economic and political problems. The European Council laid down the basis for a *European Monetary System* (EMS) in 1979, the central features of which were the *exchange rate mechanism* (ERM) for the stabilisation of exchange rates between Member States' currencies and the recognition of the *European Currency Unit* (the ECU) to replace national currencies for an increasing number of purposes. As we have seen, the Single European Act re-emphasised the need for the 'convergence' of the Member States' economic and monetary policies.

As progress proceeded towards the completion of the Internal Market in the late 1980s, the European Council came to accept a three stage plan for the attainment of EMU as proposed by a committee chaired by Jacques Delors, the President of the Commission. The legal basis for EMU was in a new Article 3a (now Article 4) EC:

1   For the purposes set out in Article 2, the activities of the Member States and the Community shall include, as provided in this Treaty and in accordance with the timetable set out therein, the adoption of an economic policy which is based on the close coordination of Member States' economic policies, on the internal market and on the definition of common objectives, and conducted in accordance with the principle of an open market economy with free competition.

2   Concurrently with the foregoing, and as provided in this Treaty and in accordance with the timetable and the procedures set out therein, these activities shall include the irrevocable fixing of exchange rates leading to the introduction of a single currency, the ECU, and the definition and conduct of a single monetary policy and exchange-rate policy the primary objective of both of which shall be to maintain price stability and, without prejudice to this objective, to support the general economic policies in the Community, in accordance with the principle of an open market economy with free competition.

3   These activities of the Member States and the Community shall entail compliance
     with the following guiding principles: stable prices, sound public finances and
     monetary conditions and a sustainable balance of payments.

The complex Economic and Monetary Policy provisions of the TEU were to be found
in Part Three 'Community Policies', Title VI beginning at Article 102a EC (now Article
98), and the three stage timetable for the realisation of the 'Delors Plan' for EMU was
set out in Article 109e–m EC (now Articles 116–24).

Stage One was assumed to have been in existence since mid-1990 when its
requirements were met: (i) virtually all restrictions on currency and capital
movements between Member States had been removed; (ii) closer co-ordination of
Member States' economic policies had been achieved; (iii) co-operation between
central banks had been strengthened; (iv) Member States were adhering to the
Exchange Rate Mechanism.

Stage Two began on 1 January 1994 and was set within a prescribed framework of a
high level of economic convergence on the part of the Member States. Four
'convergence criteria' were monitored by the Commission and a new European
Monetary Institute: price stability (a low level of inflation), a sound government
financial position (no excessive budget deficit), stable exchange rates within the ERM
and low interest rates.

Preparations were also made during this stage for the establishment of a European
System of Central Banks (ESCB), which in the third stage would 'define and
implement the monetary policy of the Community', and for a new, similarly
independent institution, the European Central Bank (ECB) which would have law
making powers within the monetary field: see now Articles 8 and 107(2) EC.

Stage Three was scheduled to begin, if a majority of Member States fulfilled the
convergence criteria, at a date to be set by the European Council. If no date had been
fixed by the end of 1997, the third stage would, according to the Maastricht timetable,
begin on 1 January 1999 for those Member States which did fulfil the criteria. At this
time, the ECB and the ESCB would become fully operational. The ECU (or, as later
announced, the Euro) would become the single currency for such Stage Three Member
States.

Nevertheless, considerable uncertainty remained regarding the future
development of EMU and the single currency. At Maastricht itself, the UK and
Denmark were unable to give a firm commitment to full participation in the third
stage. The UK negotiated the right 'not to be obliged or committed to move to the
third stage of economic and monetary union without a separate decision to do so by
its government and Parliament'. In 1992, intense speculation in international money
markets created a crisis in the ERM. The UK, Italy and Greece were forced to
withdraw and the bands within which the other currencies were allowed to fluctuate
against each other were widened.

Most significantly, reservations and indeed antagonism with respect to EMU and a
single currency were encountered in the 1990s in most Member States. Protagonists
argued that the lack of a single currency, and the machinery to manage it through a
Community Central Bank, were major weaknesses of the Single Market. They were
firm in the view that there was a need to establish a strong Euro-currency in order to
eliminate currency speculation, money market turbulence and foreign exchange risks

for firms operating across the Community. In other words, a zone of monetary stability needed to be created that would encourage economic growth and investment.

However, those who tended to see the Community merely as a free trade area were not prepared to cede further sovereignty (legal competence) to the Community in matters of monetary, budgetary and fiscal policy. They regarded such a step as a 'dangerous' advance towards political union and one to be resisted.

In May 1998, the Heads of State and Government, on the basis of a report from the EMI and the recommendation of the Commission, decided that 11 Member States could be regarded as having met the required convergence criteria and could proceed to Stage Three. The few excluded or non-qualifying States were the UK, Denmark, Sweden and Greece. An EMU comprising the 11 States came into effect on 1 January 1999. These States adopted the Euro as a common currency – for accounting and financial purposes but not as yet as an issued currency – and the ESCB and ECB, based in Frankfurt, came into operation at the same time. The ECB's operational independence as regards monetary policy within the Union is, however, balanced by its accountability for its actions to the directly elected European Parliament.

On 1 January 2002, Euro-denominated coins and notes came into circulation as legal tender, alongside national currencies, within a 'Euro-zone' of 12 Member States (the original 11, plus Greece). National notes and coins were withdrawn seven months later. Sweden and Denmark remain as 'Member States with a derogation' (Article 122 EC) who will join the 'Euro-zone' as soon as their economic policies allow. UK membership of EMU probably depends on the outcome of a referendum on the Euro and a parliamentary vote on joining the single currency.

From these developments, two points in particular emerge. In economic terms, the Community has been divided into an inner 'core' of Member States surrounded by a satellite ring of States unable to affect policy in the field but in practical terms closely affected by the advent of the single currency. The 'playing field' is not level and, in the Community jargon, a severe case of 'variable geometry' has been created. Secondly, although there are sound economic arguments for a central bank with a high degree of independence from national governments and the other Community institutions – so long as it commands respect and its policy pronouncements are taken as authoritative – the other side of the coin is a loss of democratic control. The ECB should be accountable and the appropriate body is the European Parliament.

The Maastricht Social Policy Protocol

At Maastricht, at UK insistence, new 'deepening' social policy measures concerning 'the promotion of employment, improved living and working conditions, proper social protection', etc, were left out of the main Treaty. The other 11 Member States, however, committed themselves to the harmonisation of their policies within these fields in a separate Protocol annexed to the EC Treaty.

The UK opted out on grounds of cost, the need to combat inflation and the maintenance of a right to create jobs within its own particular market conditions free of 'interference' from Brussels. This was, of course, another case of 'variable geometry', the effect of which could be diminished if the policy measures in the Protocol could to some extent be achieved on the basis of an existing Treaty base (for example, the then Article 118 (now Article 137) EC on minimum health and safety standards for workers).

However, as will be seen, this further example of differential advancement of the process of integration was removed under the terms of the ToA.

Further Issues

The changes brought about by the Maastricht, Amsterdam and Nice Treaties to the institutional system and the law making processes of the Community will be examined in due course in Chapter 5. However, it is important to note at this early stage that, although the powers of the European Parliament have gradually been increased as regards its participation in the legislative process (and in other matters also), its role still remains of lesser importance than that of the Council – the final decision maker – and the Commission, the prime initiator of legislation and the body charged with the implementation of rules laid down by the Council.

To this extent, the so called 'democratic deficit' has not therefore been appreciably reduced. The Parliament has for many years sought a major role as co-legislator with the Council, a function which it does now exercise but not, as will be seen, 'across the board' but within certain, albeit expanding, policy areas. The people's representatives in the Parliament therefore remain somewhat subordinate to those of the Member State governments in the Council.

This issue, together with that of subsidiarity, is of obvious significance to those in the Member States who insist that national governments retain as many powers as possible – as opposed to 'losing' them to the Council where they rarely have veto powers. This view tends also to find favour with those who advocate the *broadening* of the Union through the accession of new Member States, rather than a *deepening*, whereby the process of economic and political integration will lead inexorably, so it is argued, to some form of European federal structure in which the central institutions exercise extensive powers.

Enlargement of the Union

The Union continues to develop despite crucial questions of size, institutional structure and uniformity in the speed of change. In legislative terms at least, the Internal Market for goods, persons, services and capital was substantially completed on time at the end of 1992.

In 1994, the Agreement on the European Economic Area (EEA) came into force signifying a partial 'common market' merger between the EC and all but one (Switzerland) of the EFTA countries: Austria, Sweden, Finland, Iceland, Norway and Liechtenstein. Close economic ties had existed between the EC and EFTA for many years and the nature of this further integrative step has been outlined as follows:

> The idea behind the EEA is to give the EFTA countries all the free-trade advantages of EC membership, without making them part of the EC political system. All the rules of Community law regarding free movement of goods (but only as regards products originating in the Contracting States), persons, services and capital apply – with only slight modifications – to the EFTA countries, as do the rules of EC law relating to competition and state aid. This has great attractions, but also serious drawbacks. In

particular, it means that the EFTA countries will have to apply a system of rules in the making of which they will have virtually no say [Hartley].

In Opinion 1/91 *Re the Draft Treaty on a European Economic Area*, the Court of Justice raised certain objections to the Agreement. The Court was particularly concerned to preserve the autonomy and homogeneity of the Community legal order, the position of the Court of Justice within that legal order as established by Article 164 EEC (now Article 220 EC), and the binding nature of its decisions. In its Opinion 1/92, following revisions of the EEA text, the Court was satisfied that the Agreement was compatible with Community law.

At the same time that this development was taking place, five EFTA countries, not content with 'satellite status' under the EEA arrangements, applied for membership of the Community: Austria (1989), Sweden (1991), Switzerland, Finland and Norway (1992). Of these, Austria, Sweden and Finland left EFTA and joined the Union in 1995.

Following a referendum in Switzerland, that country's membership of the EEA was rejected and its application for membership of the Union was put on hold. The Norwegian government also decided not to join the Union after a negative vote in a national referendum (52 per cent of the population was opposed to membership). The end result of these developments has been to weaken the significance of the EEA concept, EFTA being left with only four members: Norway, Iceland, Switzerland and Liechtenstein.

However, several other countries are at present waiting to join the Union. Amongst the Mediterranean applicants, Turkey applied for membership in 1987 but concerns over human rights and economic dislocation have long delayed that country's accession. (A customs union with Turkey came into effect at the end of 1995.) Cyprus and Malta applied for membership in 1990 and they will be in a position to join the Union shortly.

Since freeing themselves of Communist control in 1989, most of the countries of Central and Eastern Europe have also become candidate members. (Following unification with West Germany, the territory of the former East Germany came within the Community without the need for any treaty amendments.) Poland, Hungary, the Czech Republic and Slovakia all formally applied for membership and these countries (the Visegrad Group) in 1993 established a Central European Free Trade Area of which Slovenia became a member at the end of 1995. Estonia, Latvia, Lithuania, Romania and Bulgaria also applied for membership. Closer economic and political ties with these countries were established by the EU through association agreements known as 'Europe Agreements', which place particular emphasis on the dismantling of trade barriers and on competition law. (As regards the accession of these countries, see the section on the Nice Treaty, below.)

The Commission's pre-accession strategy in these cases involves a deepening of the relationship, the creation of the appropriate legal and institutional basis, the enhancement of trade and the provision of economic aid. Bearing in mind the political regimes these countries endured for more than 40 years and the inefficient, centralised 'command' economies foisted on them during that time, it requires a tremendous effort of will for them to acquire sufficient knowledge, skills and legal expertise to be able to cope with the transition to full membership.

Any State which applies for membership of the European Union must satisfy the three basic conditions of respect for human rights, democracy and the rule of law:

Article 6(1) TEU. The obligations of membership also presuppose a functioning competitive market economy and an adequate legal and administrative framework in the public and private sectors. An applicant State must obviously also accept the Community legal system and be in a position to implement it. This entails a commitment to the *acquis communautaire*, the existing body of Community law, which includes the Treaties (as amended), all Community legislation adopted in implementation of the Treaties, all adopted declarations and resolutions and all international agreements entered into by the Community. (This is subject to any transitional measures that might be agreed in accession negotiations.)

The procedure under which new States become members of the Union is now to be found in Article 49 (formerly TEU O):

> Any European State which respects the principles set out in Article 6(1) may apply to become a Member of the Union. It shall address its application to the Council, which shall act unanimously after consulting the Commission and after receiving the assent of the European Parliament, which shall act by an absolute majority of its component members.

> The conditions of admission and adjustments to the Treaties on which the Union is founded which such admission entails shall be the subject of an agreement between the Member States and the applicant State. This agreement shall be submitted for ratification by all the contracting States in accordance with their respective constitutional arrangements.

The Intergovernmental Conference of 1996

The implications and complexities of the Union's position in the mid-1990s were wide-ranging. In Pinder's opinion:

> Enlargement may, then, carry membership beyond twenty states, and eventually even to thirty or more. The implications of this prospect for Community institutions are profound. How could unanimous agreement on difficult questions be reached among so many and such diverse governments? How, indeed, could a basically intergovernmental system function effectively or democratically among them? In any or all of the cases of possible future enlargement, the European Parliament's right to refuse accession is likely to be used to secure that widening is accompanied by deepening, in the form of strengthening and democratising the Community's institutions; and it will have some support from member states. By the time that the accession of new applicants would bring the number of members up to twenty or so, the Parliament and at least some member states are likely to withhold their consent unless the institutions are given a federal form.

Perhaps the first of the many interrelated questions which arose was whether the common and co-ordinated policies which had provided the cohesive basis of Community integration would give way even further to an increasingly inconsistent state of differentiated integration, leading not to an 'ever closer union' but an à la carte Union characterised by a 'variable geometry'.

As we have already seen, initially only 11, later 12, proceeded to the third stage of EMU. (Again, we have noted that two other Member States initially failed to meet the necessary convergence criteria for entry into the third, single currency stage.) The UK also opted out of the Maastricht Social Policy measures, which were therefore at that time merely annexed to the TEU. There was insufficient consensus within the second pillar of intergovernmental foreign and security policy for real progress and the Union still has no common identity on the international scene in that sphere. The Justice and Home Affairs pillar, which covered controls on people crossing EU external borders (with obvious implications for immigration and security), had not enabled the Union to secure full free movement of persons, as envisaged by Article 7a EC, through the removal of internal border controls.

It was against the background of delay in securing this key element of the 1992 Internal Market Programme that, outside the TEU and on the basis of the intergovernmental 1985 Schengen Agreement and its implementing Convention, six Member States (the Benelux countries, Germany, Spain and Portugal) agreed to abolish all border controls at internal land, sea and air frontiers within their 'Schengen Area'. A range of accompanying measures were designed to maintain a high level of security in the frontier-free area and to combat drug trafficking. The Treaty has now been signed (but not necessarily brought into force) by all the Member States, apart from the UK and Ireland, and its provisions integrated into the EU regime by the ToA.

It can be argued that as the integration process advances into the realms of 'high politics', and as some governments resist further transfers of sovereignty over such fundamental issues as finance, security and voting powers in the Council of Ministers, that compromises are inevitable. However, although in terms of practical politics this is inevitable, and is now legally recognised as the case (see below), it has resulted in what has been described as an increasingly tangled EU constitutional and legal order.

In a more positive vein, it can be claimed that the cumulative force of the integration process over the last 50 years and the ever increasing interdependence of the Member States in the economy, in security and in the environment will lead them to resolve current differences and so secure, as a next but not final step, a further acceptable degree of concordance on the road to 'ever closer union'.

There was little doubt, however, in the months prior to the 1996 Intergovernmental Conference that the Union could not be seen as a cohesive legal unit. The Member States were formally committed to a 'widening' of the Union, but would they agree to a 'deepening' of institutional powers and policies, which many considered to be a necessary corollary of the expected enlargement? Would they agree to a further enhanced role in the law making process for the European Parliament, so reducing what is perceived as the Union's 'democratic deficit'?

The Intergovernmental Conference of 1996 and subsequent amendments to the TEU and its three component treaties were anticipated by 'consolidating' provisions in the Maastricht document itself. Article N(2) referred to the extent to which the policies and forms of co-operation in place might need to be revised to ensure 'the effectiveness of the mechanisms and the institutions of the Community'. Together with issues raised in Article N(2) itself, recommendations and reports from the Community institutions eventually presented the Conference with a weighty agenda.

Of particular importance were, first, questions regarding widening the scope of the Council–Parliament 'co-decision' law making procedure, and related but more general concerns about the complexity and lack of transparency in the decision making process as a whole. Secondly, it was felt that the time had come for the putting into place of appropriate institutional arrangements to ensure that the Union would operate smoothly in the event of enlargement. Third was the need for more effective decision making in the second pillar's field of foreign and security policy.

The Treaty of Amsterdam

The Treaty of Amsterdam (ToA), signed in October 1997, came into force in May 1999. It represented no great leap forward. Institutional changes, particularly reform of the Council and Commission, needed to prepare for enlargement were not addressed but instead deferred. Some of the changes, which affected all three EU pillars, have been referred to already and some will be dealt with in subsequent chapters, for example, the amendments to the institutional law making process (Chapter 5) and to elements of social policy (Chapter 13). Other changes are of only peripheral significance bearing in mind the scope of this book. A brief overall survey is presented at this point.

Legislative Procedures

A significant widening of the use of the Council–Parliament 'co-decision' procedure was agreed at the expense of the institutional co-operation procedure. This was itself a clear strengthening of the Parliament's legislative powers, which is reinforced by a simplification of the 'co-decision' procedure enabling the Parliament more easily to veto a legislative measure: see Article 251 (formerly 189b) EC and also Chapter 5.

Flexible Action

New provisions within the first and third pillars allow, as a last resort in achieving certain Union objectives, a 'vanguard group' of eight or more Member States to move to closer integration amongst themselves in specified areas. These 'Provisions on Closer Co-operation', based on Article 11 EC and Article 40 TEU, thus provide the Treaty base for a degree of 'variable geometry' within an enlarged Union, subject to conditions and an authorisation procedure.

Flexible action must respect the principles of the Treaty and the *acquis communautaire* (the established body of Community law) and is more likely to operate under the third, revamped Police and Judicial Co-operation in Criminal Matters pillar (formerly Justice and Home Affairs) in moves to establish an area of 'freedom, security and justice'.

Freedom, Security and Justice – a New Level Playing-field?

Provisions on visas, asylum, immigration and other policies concerning the free movement of persons were moved from the third pillar to the EC Treaty: Articles 61–69. Provisions on police and criminal judicial co-operation remained in the third pillar.

The primary aim of the provisions relating to the free movement of persons was to achieve the Internal Market objective within five years. (One should recall the current special provisions in Article 69 and its related Protocol regarding UK and Irish retention of frontier controls and Schengen Area developments referred to above.) Free movement within the Union is matched by tighter controls at its external borders (see Chapter 13), although concern regarding illegal immigrants and terrorism have increased in the last few years.

Police and Judicial Co-operation in Criminal Matters

Police co-operation may be between competent national authorities or through Interpol. Key targets are drug trafficking and addiction, terrorism, unauthorised immigration, international fraud and organised crime. Racism and xenophobia are also subject to 'common action'. Judicial co-operation includes compatibility of extradition rules, prevention of conflicts of jurisdiction and harmonisation of penalties. Although still on an intergovernmental basis, procedures and instruments have been changed to accord more closely with those under the EC Treaty (the first pillar), and the European Court of Justice now has a limited jurisdiction regarding the validity and interpretation of certain measures taken in the field and may similarly review certain measures on the initiative of the Commission or a Member State (see Chapter 7).

Common Foreign and Security Policy

Detailed treatment of this second pillar of the TEU lies outside the scope of this book. The new Article 17 TEU (formerly J.7) TEU discusses closer relations with the Western European Union defence organisation as a provider of 'operational capability'. More significantly, it recognised that some Member States 'see their common defence realised in NATO'.

Fundamental Rights and Non-discrimination

As seen above, insofar as the Court of Justice now has jurisdiction under the third pillar (much of which has been transferred in any case to the EC pillar where it has had jurisdiction since 1958) to review acts of the institutions in this field, Article 46 (formerly L) TEU enables it to examine such acts as regards their compliance with the provisions of Article 6(2) (formerly F(2)) TEU which expressly declares that the Union is founded on respect for human rights.

Political control over the Member States in this respect was also secured by Article 7 TEU (formerly Article F.1) which allowed for the suspension of a Member State guilty of a serious and persistent breach of the principles of liberty, democracy, respect for human rights and fundamental freedoms or the rule of law. Suspension could involve the Member State's rights under both the TEU and EC Treaty (for example, as to voting). It was unlikely that this provision, as it stood, would be triggered except in a case of collapse of democratic government in a Member State. Consequently, as a response to concern in 2000 regarding the inclusion of extreme right-wing elements in a new Austrian coalition government – concern which was eventually allayed – Article 7 was reworded by the Treaty of Nice to accord more closely to political reality. It now involves a 'softer', two stage approach covering (a) 'a clear risk of a serious breach' and appropriate action that can be taken by the Council of Ministers, and (b) 'the existence of a serious and persistent breach' and provision for action by both the Council of Ministers and the European Council.

Under a new Article 13 (formerly 6a) EC, a unanimous Council may legislate to combat discrimination based on sex, racial or ethnic origin, religion or belief, disability, age or sexual orientation. This provision is without prejudice to other Treaty provisions such as Article 12 (formerly 6) EC on discrimination according to nationality or Article 141 (formerly 119) EC on sex discrimination (see Chapter 14).

Social Policy

The UK 'opted in' to the provisions originally set out in the Agreement on Social Policy annexed to Protocol No 14 to the TEU. These 'deepening' provisions were re-enacted in Articles 136–43 (formerly 117–20) EC and the Protocol is repealed. To this extent, a level playing field replaces 'variable geometry' or differentiated integration in this policy area.

Subsidiarity

The ToA's Protocol on the Application of the Principles of Subsidiarity and Proportionality is dealt with in Chapter 3.

The Treaty of Nice

In December 2000, following a year's preparatory work by the Intergovernmental Conference, the European Council, charged as we have seen with providing the necessary political impetus for the Union's development, met in Nice for further revision of the Treaties. Although the Heads of State or Government called for a 'deeper and wider debate about the future of the European Union', the substantive decisions reached centred mainly on what have been called 'the Amsterdam leftovers'. The Treaty revisions were therefore restricted to those considered necessary in order to complete 'the institutional changes necessary for the accession of the new Member States'. Since Nice, two candidate States, Romania and Bulgaria, have been found, as yet, unable to meet the strict EU entry requirements, so enlargement planned for 2004 will be to a Union of 25 Member States. Ireland, following a second referendum, was the last of the existing Member States to ratify the Treaty, which will come into effect in early 2003.

At this early stage, only the broad nature of the most significant changes made – or impending (as in the next section) – is outlined and further details are dealt with, in context, in the chapters indicated.

Enlargement and the Political Institutions

In Protocol A (attached to the Treaties), Article 2 concerning the European Parliament, for which the next elections take place in 2004, states that on 1 January 2004, Article 190(2) EC, which lists the Member States and the number of MEPs for each of them, will be replaced. A new list shows reductions in the number of MEPs for most existing Member States, and published figures give MEP allocations for Poland, (Romania), the Czech Republic, Hungary, (Bulgaria), Slovakia, Lithuania, Latvia, Slovenia, Estonia, Cyprus and Malta. It is stated that the total number of MEPs will eventually rise from the 700 set by the ToA to around 732.

Article 3 of the Protocol indicates changes of a similar nature to Article 205(2) EC to be made from 1 January 2005 regarding Member State voting rights in an enlarged

Council of Ministers. Article 4 of the Protocol deals with changes to the Commission, including the number of Members (Commissioners) and their allocation within a Union of 27 Member States. (For further details of these changes, see Chapter 5.)

The Judicial Structure

The continually increasing caseload of the European Court of Justice since the 1970s was only partially met by the establishment of the Court of First Instance (CFI) in 1988. However, the problem of delay in the handing down of judgments remains and will be exacerbated by the accession of the new Member States and the ever increasing scope and complexity of Community/Union law. Pressure from the Courts, which, however, produced no answers at Amsterdam, was reapplied prior to Nice. The Courts proposed that in order to improve the situation, the European Council should deal exclusively with amendments of a procedural and jurisdictional nature.

The jurisdictional relationship between the two Courts involves more than a simple appeal system from the CFI to the Court of Justice. The jurisdictional division between them has changed since 1988 with more classes of actions being transferred to the CFI, and this trend was continued at Nice. Under a new Article 225 EC, the CFI will have jurisdiction, within certain limits, to hear and determine questions referred from *national* courts and tribunals for a *preliminary ruling* 'in specific areas' (see Article 234 EC). This jurisdiction, previously the sole preserve of the Court of Justice, involves the laying down of authoritative rulings on the interpretation and validity of points of Community law arising in proceedings at national level, so enabling a decision to be reached by the referring court or tribunal. The particular 'specific areas' of such CFI jurisdiction will be determined by the Council of Ministers and will involve amendments to the Statute of the Court of Justice (which will cover both Courts: see Protocol B attached to the Treaties at Nice) and the detailed Rules of Procedure of the two Courts. In future, such amendments will generally be more easily secured, without recourse to Treaty revision and ratification, by means of Council qualified majority decisions.

Declaration 12 adopted at Nice suggests that the jurisdiction of the CFI regarding the hearing of *direct actions at Community level* (see Chapter 7) may also be extended. These moves can be seen as making the CFI, the membership of which may well be increased, a full partner of the Court of Justice (see the new Article 220 EC), unless they are seen as leading to a situation where the Court of Justice becomes the Union's Supreme Court, dealing only with cases of particular constitutional significance.

A further prospective change to the judicial structure is to be found in a new Article 225a EC enabling the creation of 'judicial panels to hear and determine at first instance certain classes of action or proceeding brought in specific areas'. Declaration 15 makes it clear that the first use of such panels will be to decide disputes 'between the Community and its servants', a function at present of the CFI, to whom appeals may be made. (All these points and others are discussed further in Chapter 7.)

Legislative Procedures

At Nice, the Council–Parliament co-decision legislative procedure and qualified majority voting in the Council were extended to a variety of Treaty provisions though not, as a result of strong opposition from certain Member States, to contentious, 'high politics' areas such as taxation and social security.

Enhanced (formerly 'Closer') Co-operation

This 'flexible action' policy, a new element of 'variable geometry' introduced by the ToA (see above) and now available to groups of eight or more Member States, within all three pillars of the EU, initially proved a failure owing to the strict conditions imposed and the right of veto of each of the Member States. The Nice Treaty modified Article 11 EC and Articles 40, 43–45 TEU including the removal of the right of veto. The new Article 40 relating to Police and Judicial Co-operation in Criminal Matters speaks of 'the aim of enabling the Union to develop more rapidly into an area of freedom, security and justice'. The Treaty has extended the field of enhanced co-operation to the second Common Foreign and Security pillar, a new Article 27a TEU stating the aim as that of 'safeguarding the values and serving the interests of the Union as a whole by asserting its identity as a coherent force on the international scene'.

EU Charter of Fundamental Rights

The short history of this proposed Charter, 'combining in a single test the civil, political, economic, social and societal rights hitherto laid down in a variety of international, European and national sources', is to be found in Chapter 10.

In 2000, a majority of the Member States in the Council of Ministers refused to agree to the incorporation of the Charter into the Treaty. Since the early 1970s, the Court of Justice has 'borrowed' provisions of the Strasbourg Council of Europe's Convention for the Protection of Human Rights and Fundamental Freedoms of 1950 in appropriate cases. This is a legally binding constitutional instrument, accepted by all 15 EU Member States and many other European countries. At Nice, the Charter was 'welcomed' by the European Council and the question of its status – legally binding or declaratory – will be considered by a new Intergovernmental Conference in 2004.

The Future of the European Union

The relatively minor 'institutional' changes made at Nice contrast strongly with what have been called the 'constitutional visions' of certain leading European politicians. At Nice itself, the Summit Conference's Declaration 23 on the Future of the Union, which called for a 'deeper and wider debate', stated that the process of discussion at a combined Union and national level leading up to 2004 should focus on the following four issues:

(a) how to establish and monitor a more precise delimitation of powers between the EU and the Member States, reflecting the principle of subsidiarity;

(b) the status of the EU Charter of Fundamental Rights;

(c) a simplification of the Treaties with a view to making them clearer and better understood without changing their meaning;

(d) the role of national parliaments in the European architecture.

Most significantly, the Declaration stated that in addressing these issues, 'the Conference recognizes the need to improve and to monitor the democratic legitimacy and transparency of the Union and its institutions, in order to bring them closer to the citizens of Europe'. How will this gap between the Union and its citizens be closed? Discussion of 'Europe' by national politicians and the press through a filter of perceived national interests too often distorts the picture.

Rather, as Wouters proposes, 'bridging the wide gap ... will not be achieved through Treaty amendments ... European and national politicians will need to invest more seriously in explaining the European Union and its policies to their citizens and engaging in an interactive dialogue with them'.

The question of 'a more precise limitation of powers' is highly contentious and complex. Wouters is of the view that:

> The theme is a Pandora's box since undoubtedly some Member States would hope to use it in order to strengthen the European Union's competences, but most others may well want to seize the occasion to strip the European Union of certain competences. Too strict a delimitation of competence would fly in the face of the dynamic nature of the European integration process. This dynamism has been rendered possible through a step-by-step approach based on a Treaty method which assigns objectives to the Community/European Union, confers powers upon them and specifies the tools of action and limitations in the relevant Treaty chapter. By the same token, one should not overlook the delimitation function of existing provisions such as Article 5 EC. Above all, in many fields of activity in which the European Union intervenes, the interwovenness of decision-making and implementing levels (international, Community, national, regional) is such that purely from the point of view of efficiency it is almost absurd to delineate spheres of competence rigidly.

> The question may be raised whether, instead of focusing on delimitation of powers, the post-Nice debate would not do better to look at ways to establish smoother and more loyal cooperation between the different political levels within the European Union and, if necessary, develop further institutional arrangements for this purpose. Rather than strictly demarcating spheres of competence, the European Union should be further developed as a multilevel governance system in which, depending on each policy sphere, tasks and – even more so – responsibilities are attributed to different layers and in which the different players are linked together by efficient arrangements while preserving a sufficient degree of autonomy [see also Chapter 3].

In furtherance of the need for a 'deeper and wider debate,' the European Council in its 'Laeken Declaration' of December 2001 re-introduced the 'Convention formula' adopted in the preparation of the Charter of Fundamental Rights. A constitutional Convention on the Future of Europe was established in March 2002 as a 'drafting and proposals forum'. It is headed by a Praesidium of 12 comprising the Chairman, former French president Giscard d'Estaing, together with two former prime ministers, representatives of the governments holding the Council Presidency during the Convention (Spain, Denmark and Greece) and representatives of national parliaments, the European Parliament and the Commission. Further representatives of the governments and national parliaments of the existing Member States, of the Commission and of the candidate Member States (including Turkey) make up the Convention's total composition. The EC Economic and Social Committee, the Committee of the Regions and the Court of Justice have observer status, together with other interested parties reflecting public opinion who may make their views known. The Convention's remit is based on the four issues set down in Nice Declaration 23, which aims at improvement of the democratic nature and efficiency of the process (including that applying to the Intergovernmental Conference itself) that is scheduled to produce Treaty reforms in 2004. At Laeken, the Heads of State and Government agreed that 'the Union needs to become more transparent', that is, more accessible to public scrutiny and more open to inquiry and investigation.

Two particular points demand serious consideration. The continuing and increasing flurry of intergovernmental, initiatory activity (on paper at least), particularly since Nice, highlights the ever-growing role and power of the European Council – and a weakening of the position of the supranational Commission, the so called 'engine room' of the Community. However, in 1974, at the time of the institutionalisation of the European Council, Monnet himself, the creator of the Commission, conceded, as we have seen, that 'what matters now is that the Heads of national governments meet regularly in the European Council. That's where the authority is. It's a very big change'.

Secondly, the question of 'a more precise delimitation of powers' between the EU and the Member States is directly related to what is known as the constitutionalisation of the Treaties, a process which, with respect to the EC Treaty, has to a large extent been initiated and developed through its case law by the Court of Justice since the early 1960s: see Chapters 4 and 7.

Will fundamental constitutional changes come about in the near future? A Common Market Law Review 'Editorial Comment' in mid-2001 stated that:

> Whatever views one holds about Europe, the essential question is to determine which level of government is best suited to making public policies, given that we want such policies to be economically efficient, socially just and decided by institutional methods respectful of the requirements of democratic legitimacy and transparency. In this respect there is no difference between those who advocate a federal form for the European Union and those who are not prepared to surrender additional powers for the purpose of allowing the Union to move beyond the stage which it has reached now, ie a highly complex, multi-layered, sophisticated, innovative and dynamic form of international organization. In fact, in our opinion, it is not very likely that the time is ripe for this very original structure to undergo important changes in 2004. After all is said and done, the Intergovernmental Conference must decide on treaty reforms by unanimous vote and all national parliaments must approve the proposed amendments. This rigid amending formula entrenches the role of the Member States as 'Herren der Vertäge' and ensures that the system is not susceptible of radical changes. Under those circumstances, forms of enhanced cooperation or speculation about 'vanguard' groups of States is inevitable.

On 6 February 2003, the *Praesidium* presented to the Convention a 'Draft of Articles 1–16 of the Constitutional Treaty' based on a draft structure published in October 2002. The draft text is based on reports from Convention Working Groups (Annex 1) and is supported by an explanatory note (Annex 2). Details can be found on the Convention website: http://european-convention.eu.int.

The sixteen Articles cover:

Title I Definition and objectives of the Union:

1. Establishment of the Union; 2. The Union's values; 3. The Union's objectives; 4. Legal personality.

Title II Fundamental rights and citizenship of the Union:

5. Fundamental rights; 6. Non-discrimination on grounds of nationality; 7. Citizenship of the Union.

Title III The Union's competences:

8. Fundamental principles; 9. Application of fundamental principles; 10. Categories of competence; 11. Exclusive competences; 12. Shared competences; 13. The co-ordination of economic policies; 14. The common foreign and security policy; 15. Areas for supporting action; 16. Flexibility clause.

Article 5(1) states that, 'The Charter of Fundamental Rights shall be an integral part of the Constitution ...' and Article 5(2) that, 'The Union may accede to the European Convention for the Protection of Human Rights and Fundamental Freedoms'. Are these alternate strategies? See Chapter 10.

Article 8(1) states that, 'The limits and use of Union competencies are governed by the principles of conferral, subsidiarity, proportionality and loyal co-operation': see Chapter 3.

On 16 April 2003, the heads of government of the 10 incoming Member States signed a joint treaty of accession to the European Union in Athens. A further treaty governing an EU of 25 Member States will come into effect after its signing in Rome, probably in May 2004.

REFERENCES AND FURTHER READING

Corbett, R, *The Treaty of Maastricht*, 1993.

Curtin, D, 'The constitutional structure of the Union: a Europe of bits and pieces' (1993) 30 CML Rev 17.

Duff, A (ed), *The Treaty of Amsterdam*, 1997.

Editorial Comments, 'Preparing for 2004: the post-Nice process' (2001) 38 CML Rev 493.

Holland, M, *European Integration from Community to Union*, 1993.

Kennedy, D and Webb, D, 'The limits of integration' (1993) 30 CML Rev 1095.

Maresceau, M and Montaguti, E, 'The relations between the European Union and Central and Eastern Europe: a legal appraisal' (1995) 32 CML Rev 1327.

Mayne, R, 'The contribution of Jean Monnet' (1967) Government and Opposition 349.

Millward, Alan S, *The Reconstruction of Western Europe 1945–51*, 1984, Chapters XII and XIII.

O'Keefe, D and Twomey, P (eds), *Legal Issues of the Amsterdam Treaty*, 1999.

Peers, S, 'An ever closer waiting room?: the case for East European accession to the European Economic Area' (1995) 32 CML Rev 187.

Pinder, J, *The Building of a European Union*, 1998.

Shaw, J, 'The Treaty of Nice: legal and constitutional implications' (2001) 7 EPL 195.

Shaw, J, 'The interpretation of European Union citizenship' (1998) 61 MLR 293.

Shonfield, A, *Europe – Journey to an Unknown Destination*, 1973.

Urwin, D, *The Community of Europe (A History of European Integration since 1945)*, 1995.

Weiler, J, 'The transformation of Europe' (1991) 100 Yale LJ 2403.

Wouters, Jan, 'Institutional and constitutional challenges for the European Union – some reflections in the light of the Treaty of Nice' (2001) 26 EL Rev 342.

CHAPTER 2

THE EVOLVING PROCESS OF EUROPEAN INTEGRATION

European integration differs markedly from other attempts to create a common market, or, more commonly, a free trade area. Its goal is political. Its instruments may be economic [Juliet Lodge, *Towards a Political Union*].

The European Union is a unique structure which cannot be related to any known model of government nor to any single theory of inter-State relations. In consequence, the process of economic and political integration by which the Community has proceeded and continues to develop represents a journey to an unknown, or at least disputed, destination. The early 2000s may reveal more clearly what is meant by 'European Union' and the degree of consensus among the Member States as to how far they wish to go together in that direction. What seems certain is that further progress will only be achieved in a gradual way (as has been the case in the past) by a series of practical measures. As always, the central issue is: how many more steps are to be taken? Is the ultimate aim some form of United States of Europe or a somewhat looser pattern of economic and political integration or co-operation involving the Member States and the Community institutions?

The history of European integration over the last 40 years or so is littered with concepts and theories such as interdependence, convergence, approximation, harmonisation, common market, union, federal finality, subsidiarity and sovereignty. In order to understand the nature of the integration process over this period, it is necessary to familiarise ourselves with these concepts and theories, their political, economic and legal dimensions, and by doing so we will be able to establish clearer guidelines to the future.

In her September 1988 speech in Bruges, Mrs Thatcher declared that the Community was 'not an institutional device to be constantly modified according to the dictates of some abstract theory'. The then Prime Minister's adherence to free market policies and the deregulatory Internal Market aspects of European integration surely owed something to economic theory, and in what follows differences between the theories and models may well show up in the differences of approach displayed by the politicians and practitioners of integration. In so far as the Union is still only part of the way down the integrative road, the theories have a predictive value reflecting, for example, the 'ever closer union' of the Preamble to both the Treaty of Rome and the Maastricht Treaty or the 'willing and active co-operation between independent sovereign States' of the Bruges speech.

REGIONAL ECONOMIC CONCEPTS, INTEGRATION AND THE TREATY OF ROME

Integration is the combination of parts into a whole, and union is a whole resulting from the combination of parts ... Negative and positive integration together comprise economic integration, whose end is economic union [John Pinder, 1968].

As we have already seen, the Preamble to the Treaty of Rome expressed this process in similar terms: '... ever closer union ... common action to eliminate barriers ... by pooling their resources ...'

Integration is therefore a process: parts/nations proceeding in political, economic and legal terms from positions of (relative) independence to some form of union. The process has been divided by economists into two constituent processes: negative integration involving the removal of restrictive and discriminatory barriers between the parts/nations, and positive integration which calls for further necessary common action in order that union can be attained.

In the 1950s, a number of international economists (Tinbergen, Pinder and others) paid particular analytical attention to a number of regional economic concepts, each of which can be seen as representing a recognisable stage in an integrative process.

The first stage is the FREE TRADE AREA in which a group of sovereign nations abolishes all customs duties (tariffs) and quantitative restrictions on mutual trade, but each member retains its own customs duties and quota system as regards trade with other countries. A regional arrangement of this type, whether covering all products or (as with the European Free Trade Association) only industrial goods, represents only a modest form of negative economic integration and it does not necessarily advance political integration.

The members of a free trade area may, as a matter of policy, decide against further integration or, more likely, either extend the scope of free trade through bilateral agreements with other countries (as is the case with EFTA and the Central European Free Trade Area) or proceed to a further stage of economic integration (as is the case with the EFTA–EC creation of the European Economic Area and the decision of some former EFTA members to join the EC).

A problem with the basic form of free trade area can be illustrated as follows:

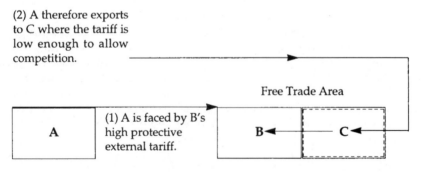

(2) A therefore exports to C where the tariff is low enough to allow competition.

Free Trade Area

A

(1) A is faced by B's high protective external tariff.

B ◄   C ◄

(4) B therefore imposes a certificate of origin requirement for imports and imposes a differential tariff on A's goods at the border with C to equal her external tariff.

(3) A's goods are re-exported from C to B (no tariffs between C and B) so avoiding B's high external tariff.

The solution to this problem would be for the member countries to form a CUSTOMS UNION with a *common* external tariff wall. Article 23(1) (formerly 9(1)) EC states that:

> The Community shall be based on a customs union which shall cover all trade in goods and which shall involve the prohibition between Member States of customs duties on imports and exports and of all charges having equivalent effect, and the adoption of a common customs tariff in their relations with third countries [NB Customs duties and tariffs are the same in this context].

Agreement on a uniform level of external tariffs, on its enforcement and on the destination and use of the revenue which accrues as goods cross the wall all involve some loss of the member countries' sovereignty (in terms of their competence or legal control over international trade) which passes to a central authority composed of all member countries.

Following the political dissolution of the Czechoslovak State in 1993, the newly constituted Czech and Slovak Republics agreed to retain close economic ties particularly by the formation of a joint customs union. Conversely, the Benelux countries had already formed a customs union before their accession to the EEC in 1957 and if we refer back to the development of the European Community as discussed in Chapter 1, it is clear that the original EEC Treaty (see Articles 2 and 3) embodied the concept of a Common Market, later to be completed by the Internal Market Programme, of which, in terms of the free movement of goods, *a customs union, originally for 'the Six', was an integral part.*

Thus, returning to the theory of a *developing* integrative process, a customs union becomes a COMMON MARKET when, apart from the removal of restrictions on the free movement of goods (including agricultural products) – and services such as banking and insurance – restrictions are also removed on the movement between the Member States of the factors of production: labour, capital and enterprise, and, in particular, a system is established to ensure that competition within the Common Market is not distorted: Article 3(c) and (f) (which has become Article 3(c) as amended and (g) EC) in which the concept of Internal Market, rather than Common Market, is referred to. The 'across the board' negative economic integration involved in the establishment of a Common Market (beyond that applying to goods in a customs union) clearly involves further transfers of sovereignty/competence – in the case of the EC to Community institutions, whose rules will apply in the economic markets in question in all the Member States.

Apart from the United States, the European Community's Common Market is the most highly developed in the world. Others, such as Mercosur, the Southern Cone Common Market (comprising Argentina, Brazil, Paraguay and Uruguay) and the Caribbean Community and Common Market aspire to common market status but have, as yet, barely established free trade areas.

Nearly 30 years ago, the ultimate steps in the process of *economic* integration from Common Market to ECONOMIC UNION were described by the economist, Professor FR Root, in the following terms:

> The completion of the final stage of economic union involves a full integration of the member economies with supranational authorities responsible for economic policy making. In particular, an economic union requires a single monetary system and central bank, a unified fiscal system, and a common foreign economic policy. The task of creating an economic union differs significantly from the steps necessary to

establish the less ambitious forms of economic integration. A free trade area, a customs union, or a common market mainly result from the abolition of restrictions, whereas an economic union demands a positive agreement to transfer economic sovereignty to new supranational institutions.

As already pointed out, it is perfectly acceptable for economic theory to present the integration process as a series of models each in turn embodying a greater degree of integration. However, it is already clear that it would be a mistake to conclude that in practice, the Community has followed this precise sequence. In 1957, the Community's legal base, the Treaty of Rome, established the framework for both a customs union and a common market together with, arguably, an indication of ultimate economic union. This Treaty can, as we will see, therefore be seen as laying down the ground rules for both the abolition of restrictions (negative integration) and for '*positive* agreement' on other common and co-ordinated policies.

From 1958, actual progress in the 'negative' sphere was much faster than in the 'positive' for reasons that will be discussed, but it was not a case of negative integration of necessity preceding positive integration as the theory might suggest. Additionally, and most importantly, the Treaty (and the ECSC Treaty before it) also established supranational institutions (the Commission, Council, Parliament and Court) at the time the integrative enterprise was first launched. Indeed, some theories of integration have concentrated less on economic analysis and more on institutional and policy making considerations. For example, Ernest Haas, the founder of one of the most influential theories (neofunctionalism), described integration as the 'process whereby political actors in several distinct national settings are persuaded to shift their loyalties, expectations and political activities towards a new and larger setting'.

However, it is essential, in order to gain real insight into the nature and structure of the EEC Treaty (and the post-Maastricht EC Treaty), that we pursue further an analysis based on the concepts of negative and positive integration. A Common Market Law Review editorial of 1989 on the Commission's November 1988 report on the half-way point in the 'Completion of the Internal Market' programme stated that:

> The bonds between negative and positive integration are manifold, but the framework for action created by the Single Act and the 'new momentum' is basically confined to securing the free flow of goods, persons, services and capital in an area without frontiers.

NEGATIVE INTEGRATION, COMMON MARKET AND THE EEC TREATY

It will be recalled that the two basic means in Article 2 of the Treaty of Rome for achieving the Community's economic, social (and political?) objectives were *the establishment of a common market and the progressive approximation of the economic policies of the Member States*. These two means are different in nature, but they are complementary – and both are essential for the attainment of 'unity'.

Elaborating on the distinction made earlier between negative and positive integration, Pinder explains that: 'Negative and positive integration together comprise economic integration, whose end is economic union ... negative integration unaccompanied by positive integration may be called a common market.' Negative integration is again used here to signify 'the removal of discrimination' and by this Pinder primarily means the removal by the Member States, as part of their Treaty obligations, of discriminatory and restrictive national legal measures applied by them to a wide variety of inter-Member State business transactions (involving goods, services, labour and capital) and arising in large part from protectionist national policies designed to safeguard home-based industries and employment levels against foreign competition. (Companies themselves must also comply with Community rules against restrictive and monopolistic practices as we will see in Chapter 14.)

A direct relationship therefore clearly exists between negative integration and the establishment of a Common Market. What needs to be shown is, firstly, the relationship between Pinder's 'removal of discrimination' and more specific indications in the Treaty as to how the Common Market is to be established and, secondly, the connection between the basic means in Article 2 EEC described as 'the progressive approximation of the economic policies of Member States' and the other side of the integrative coin, positive integration. This he defined (not very helpfully) as:

> The formation and application of co-ordinated and common policies in order to fulfil economic and welfare objectives other than the removal of discrimination.

Thirdly, it is necessary to indicate the nature of the 'bonds between negative and positive integration' – two means to form an indissoluble unity.

Article 3 EEC[1] stated that, for the purposes set out in Article 2, the Community was to engage in a number of 'activities', including the following which relate to Pinder's definition of negative integration – and to the regional economic concepts analysis above:

Article 3

(a) the elimination, as between Member States, of customs duties and quantitative restrictions on the import and export of goods, and of all other measures having equivalent effect;

(b) the establishment of a common custom tariff and a common commercial policy towards third countries;

(c) the abolition, as between Member States, of obstacles to freedom of movement of persons,* services and capital;

(d) the adoption of a common policy in the sphere of agriculture;

(e) the adoption of a common policy in the sphere of transport;

(f) the institution of a system ensuring that competition in the common market is not distorted;

...

(h) the approximation of the laws of the Member States to the extent required for the proper functioning of the common market;

...

[*The freedom of establishment in other Member States of, for example, companies (legally created persons) should be considered here.]

---

1 As this chapter focuses on developments prior to the Maastricht Treaty, references to the Treaty refer to 'old' numbering.

Writing in 1991, VerLoren van Themaat confirmed this Common Market listing when discussing the developing case law of the Court of Justice:

> In this consistent case law, it used the notion of a Common Market also as a link between the 'five freedoms' provided for concerning goods, persons, services, capital and payments, the rules of competition (Articles 85–94), the common policies for agriculture, transport and external trade, Articles 95–98 on fiscal discrimination and the provisions on harmonisation of legislation.

The fundamental legal principles underpinning the Common (and the Internal) Market are those of *freedom and equality*. This can be seen in particular as regards the 'four fundamental freedoms' (the free movement of goods, persons, services and capital – omitting payments) and the maintenance of free and equal competitive conditions (the 'level playing-field').

The economic and legal concept of the Internal Market (Article 8A EEC introduced by the Single European Act of 1986) is the particular creation of the Community. As noted in Chapter 1, the Internal Market Programme 1986–92 involved an accelerated continuation and completion of those Common Market activities that had fallen badly behind schedule. (The Common Market should have been completed by the end of 1969: Article 8(1) EEC.) Internal Market measures, as will be discussed in Chapter 11, relate largely to certain aspects of Article 3(a), (c), (e) and (h) as listed above. In essence, therefore, the Common (in the sense of 'single') and the Internal Market are one and the same; the later Internal Market Programme was required to be more intensive but not as comprehensive as that originally laid down for the Common Market.

Some commentators on the Treaty have omitted agriculture and transport – Article 3(d) and (e) – from the concept of the Common Market. However, the Spaak Report of 1956 (see Chapter 1) stated that: 'One cannot conceive the establishment of a Common Market in Europe without the inclusion of agriculture' and this was confirmed by Article 38(1) which stated that: 'The common market shall extend to agriculture and trade in agricultural products.' The Common Agricultural Policy (CAP) (and the same generally applies to the other sectoral policies: transport, coal and steel and atomic energy) is, nevertheless, as much concerned with interventionist market management and control as with the removal of discrimination. The prices of agricultural products are fixed on a common Community basis within a complex system of Community import levies and subsidies to producers. (The CAP has been described as 'merely a complicated kind of customs union'.) One of the prime aims of the common policy is to stabilise agricultural product markets, as referred to in Article 39(1)(c), and the rules relating to the free movement of goods and competition apply to the production and distribution of agricultural products only to a limited extent.

The approximation (better known now as *harmonisation*) of the national laws of Member States referred to in Article 3(h) above is a key element of the *legal integration* which underpins economic integration. Differences between Member States' laws embodying discriminatory obstacles to free movement (for example, differing national rules or standards relating to the contents or packaging of products which hinder free movement and make imports more expensive, or differing national rules concerning professional qualifications which hinder the free movement of persons) are removed by means of judicial decisions or this Community based legislative process of harmonisation which will be examined in Chapter 5 and elsewhere. However, harmonisation measures do not relate solely to the removal of discrimination as between Member States. Measures concerning equal pay and equal treatment for men and women in employment, which remove discrimination by gender *within* Member States, also have an impact on the costs and therefore the competitive position of a Member State's industries vis à vis those of the other Member States, but equal pay policy is *primarily* an element of Community Social Policy, which comes within the scope of *other* 'economic and welfare objectives', that is, positive integration. (Consider also the harmonisation of national environmental and VAT laws.) Approximation (harmonisation) of national laws is therefore included within *both* negative and positive integration.

POSITIVE INTEGRATION, ECONOMIC AND SOCIAL POLICIES AND THE EEC TREATY

We must first of all add to Pinder's 1968 definition of positive integration his bases of positive integration in the Community, remembering that positive integration advances the integration process beyond the Common Market on towards full economic (and political?) union. We find, therefore – as well as and beyond 'the removal of discrimination' – the necessity for 'co-ordinated and common policies in order to fulfil [other] economic and welfare objectives', in particular:

(i)   major common policies at Community level ... including regional, social, monetary and fiscal policies ...; and

(ii) the co-ordination of monetary, budgetary and incomes policies of the Member States.

This is a formulation similar to Professor Root's description above of the essential elements of the final stage of economic union. It will readily be noted that some of these policies (monetary, fiscal and social) are the subject-matter of current controversy and it will be recalled that Root explained that 'economic union demands a positive agreement to transfer economic sovereignty to new supranational institutions'.

What indications of such 'positive' policies do we find in the original 1957 version of the Treaty?:

Article 3

(g) the application of procedures by which the economic policies of Member States can be co-ordinated and disequilibria in their balances of payments remedied;

(h) the approximation of the laws of Member States ...;

(i)   the creation of a European Social Fund in order to improve employment opportunities for workers and to contribute to the raising of their standards of living;

(j)   the establishment of a European Investment Bank to facilitate the economic expansion of the Community by opening up fresh resources;

(k) the association of the overseas countries and territories in order to increase trade and to promote jointly economic and social development.

The most significant difference between Article 3 activities which relate to negative integration and those associated with positive integration was, at least until 1986, that whereas the former were developed in detail in the body of the Treaty (and in secondary legislation), so giving rise to ease of legal implementation (for example, in the fields of the free movement of goods and competition policy), this was generally not the case for positive agreement on common policies dealing predominantly with economic and social issues other than the removal of restrictions and discrimination. In the period prior to the new impetus established by the Single European Act in 1986, the programme of policies and procedures for positive integration was variously described as 'vague', 'feeble' and 'permissive instead of definite and mandatory' (for example, no time limits were laid down). What were the reasons for this difference?

One view of the reasons for slow progress was expressed by Stuart Holland in 1980:

> It is conceivable that governments with a predominantly liberal capitalist ideology should try to establish economic union on negative integration lines through a process of harmonisation of national policies which downgrades their differences to a lowest common denominator [but equally that such an ideological base] accounts for some of the major handicaps experienced in achieving planned policies for positive integration.

During the economically difficult 1975–85 period, faced with a choice between concerted action or a search for solutions along national lines, Member States exhibited little European will. The concept of supranationality flattered to deceive; Community progress was attributable less to the capacity of its institutions to function 'above' governments than to their small success in managing to stimulate their co-operation.

However, as seen in Chapter 1, the Single European Act was concerned not merely with completion of the Internal Market programme but also with a determination to 'improve the social and economic situation by extending common policies and pursuing new objectives'. Subsequent to the Act, Treaty of Rome provisions to be identified with the process of positive integration were to be found between Articles 102a and 136 EEC. These Articles still rested in the main on Article 3(g)–(k) of the Treaty (or parts thereof) which was itself amended (in part) and supplemented by the Act. For the most part, they were only 'new' policies in as much as they now specifically featured in the (amended) Treaty. The groundwork for them had in fact proceeded previously, albeit slowly, over a number of years and in some cases indirectly, in a legal sense, on the basis of other Treaty Articles. By far the most important of these new Articles applied to:

(1) *Co-operation in Economic and Monetary Policy*: Article 102a provided that 'convergence' of the Member States' policies in these fields 'shall take account ... of the European Monetary System and ... the ECU'. Here was the Treaty basis of the Delors Plan for Economic and Monetary Union (and see now Title VII of the EC Treaty: 'Economic and Monetary Policy').

(2) New *Social Policy* provisions under Articles 118a and b to which should be linked the Commission's 'Social Charter' of 1989, which aimed to protect workers' wage levels, bargaining rights and conditions of employment in the more competitive market of post-1992 Europe (and see now Title XI of the EC Treaty: 'Social Provisions').

(3) Provisions concerning *Economic and Social Cohesion* introduced for the purpose of 'reducing the disparities between various regions and the backwardness of the least favoured regions': Article 130a. Article 130b established that: 'The

Community shall support the achievement of these objectives by the action it takes through the Structural Funds (European Agricultural Guidance and Guarantee Fund, Guidance Section; European Social Fund; European Regional Development Fund), the European Investment Bank and other existing financial instruments.' (See now Title XVII of the EC Treaty.)

Thus, for example, in early 1994, the Commission announced EAGGF funding of ECU 4,631 million (the ECU is now the Euro and presently equals £0.61) in support of restructuring required under the reform of the Common Agricultural Policy. The assistance was geared to assist young farmers, improve farm management, provide hardship payments for hill farmers and support co-operatives.

A further, Maastricht based development was the creation of a Cohesion Fund to support economic infrastructure and environmental projects.

Massive economic, technical and training programmes also provide assistance to non-EU countries under, for example, PHARE (Aid and Assistance for the Restructuring of the Economy in Central and Eastern Europe) and TACIS (Technical Assistance to the former Soviet Union).

(4) *Research and Technological Development* which serves to strengthen the scientific and technological base of European industry in order to make it more competitive at the international level: Article 130f–q. (See now Title VIII of the EC Treaty.)

(5) *Environmental Policy* under new Article 130r–t which directed the Community towards improvement of the quality of the environment, the protection of human health, and prudent and rational utilisation of natural resources. Policy in this field dates back to 1973 even though protection of the environment did not appear as an express objective in the Treaty of Rome. Measures were, however, taken as elements of free trade policy, competition policy or agricultural policy, and in 1985 the Court of Justice held that environmental protection was indeed an essential objective of the Community: see Article 2 EEC in which a qualitative dimension was implied into the 'raising of the standard of living'. (See now Article XIX of the EC Treaty.)

(6) *Foreign Policy Co-operation* under Article 30 of the Single European Act (not incorporated into the EEC Treaty) was, as seen, yet again not a totally new development but the continuation of political moves dating back to 1970: see Article 1 of the Act. Whether this and further steps taken throughout the 1990s and to the present day will help to bring forth a more definite and influential European 'voice' in international relations remains to be seen. This issue has been discussed in Chapter 1 in relation to the Maastricht second pillar: Title V of the TEU on Common Foreign and Security Policy.

THE BONDS BETWEEN NEGATIVE AND POSITIVE INTEGRATION

It will have been noticed that the dividing line between negative and positive integration is not as neat in practice as in theory (for example, as regards sectoral policies). Pinder recognised this when, for example, he stated that 'the Rome Treaty employs the term common market ambiguously, sometimes including, and sometimes excluding, some of the fruits of positive integration'. And, in 1989, he stressed that: 'While the distinction between positive and negative integration should not be pressed too far, it is useful in helping to show why the SEM [Single European Market] brings the need for other common objectives and policies in its train.' These two points – that blurring can occur between negative and positive integration and that negative integration acts as a motor for further, positive, integration – can be illustrated in the following ways.

For example, the Common Commercial Policy of Article 3(b) which covers Community trade relations with the rest of the world is a necessary corollary to the establishment of the Common Customs Tariff and therefore an essential feature of the customs union and hence the Common Market: see Article 110 EEC (now Article 131 EC). However, Common Commercial Policy has increasingly been used solely as an instrument of the Community's external trade relations and not as a guarantee for the proper operation of the Common Market. Nevertheless, in the context of the Uruguay Round of GATT (General Agreement on Tariffs and Trade) talks in the early 1990s on the liberalisation of world trade, the Community came under extreme pressure from the United States to bring about drastic reductions in measures operating within the CAP to protect Community farmers from the rigours of world trade in agricultural products. (GATT is now known as the World Trade Organization, the WTO.)

As regards the second point, as Pinder himself has explained:

> When the EC determines a standard for car exhausts, it is both removing the distortion whereby the differing standards previously fragmented the market; and is taking a view as to the sort of environment it wants to have ... When the EC establishes a monetary union, it is both removing the distortions of variable exchange rates and providing itself with the instruments for a common macroeconomic policy which also implies objectives beyond that of removing distortions [Pinder, 'The Single Market: a step towards European Union', in Lodge (ed)].

The process of linking the economic concepts of negative and positive integration to the EEC Treaty (as successively amended) has enabled us to sketch the outlines of the *economic and social law* of the Community. Nor have these references to the substance of policies (in economic and legal terms) ignored – they have at times been inevitably linked to – questions of economic management and the respective roles of the Community's political institutions and the Member States. These are the issues which, from a legal viewpoint, comprise the remainder of this book.

In the meantime, however, having identified the integral Treaty elements of, and the relationship between, negative and positive integration – and recalling that the ultimate aim of the integration process is 'union' – an attempt must be made to say what is currently understood by that term in practice.

EUROPEAN UNION

As seen in Chapter 1, Article A of Title I (Common Provisions) of the Maastricht Treaty (now Article 1 TEU) provided that the then 12 Member States of the European Community 'establish among themselves a European Union'. No definition of this Union was provided, references to a 'federal structure' were deleted, and Article A merely continued by stating that the Treaty marked 'a new [not a final] stage in the process of creating an ever closer union among the peoples of Europe'.

Commenting on the expression 'ever closer union', which of course first appeared in the Preamble to the Treaty of Rome in 1957, Wellenstein argues that:

> The sense of the term is still the same, that of a political objective of a general nature. In order to give it a specific substantive meaning, one has to opt for specific common approaches to specific practical problems and to devise institutions and procedures to cope with them, like in 'custom union' [Article 9 EEC: '1 The Community shall be based on a customs union ... etc'].

From this, it is clear that 'union' remains an undefined objective; it remains to be achieved. That part of it which has been achieved can be identified only by singling out those 'specific practical problems' (for example, customs union, equal pay, competition, the environment, monetary union, etc) which have from time to time been agreed as constituting proper Community/Union concerns, and which have been established (coped with) on a common (or almost common) basis through the agency of the European institutions and their procedures.

The original list of common policies and activities in Article 3 EEC has been expanded not only by the Single European Act in 1986 but later at Maastricht to encompass new, mainly positive, objectives of an economic and social nature. Article 3 EC now comprises a list of 22 'activities' including, other than those discussed, the protection of health, education and training, consumer protection, tourism and development co-operation with overseas territories. Economic and monetary union now finds its place, as we have seen, in an amended Article 2 and in Article 4 EC and recognises, *as it must*, its constituent negative and positive elements, in particular the internal market, free competition and the conduct of a single monetary policy.

In conclusion, what was said about the nature of, or aspirations for, European Union in the 1990s and beyond? For Pinder, writing in 1991:

> If it is true that negative integration brings with it the need for positive integration, a completed single market after 1992 is not likely to rest in stable equilibrium. Either, if the needs for positive integration are not met, it will tend to become less integrated again, as the Community market did in the 1970s. Or the Community will, with more positive integration, move farther towards Union on federal lines. The Maastricht Treaty included a number of steps in that direction. If the new technologies, and the specialization that goes with them, continue to press the European economies towards integration, the cost of resisting movement towards such a Union could be high.

In 1992, Wellenstein said:

> So there we are. We have (that is to say, after ratification [of the TEU] we will have) a Union without real unity, a building half-built with an institutional 'géométrie variable' and a 'rendez-vous' in 1996 to try to improve on what was achieved in Maastricht. Between today and 1996, the world, especially the European world, will remain in constant turmoil.

And, in 1993, Lodge, stressing that the Member States are engaged in a continuing process of integration, also warned that, as the Member States were not agreed on the 'end' or 'the common good':

> The weakness of seeing integration as a process rather than an end lies in the potential to regress from as well as to progress to an assumed common interest in closer, deeper co-operation.

REFERENCES AND FURTHER READING

George, S, *Politics and Policy in the European Union*, 1996, particularly Chapter 2, 'European integration in theory and practice'.

Haas, E, *The Uniting of Europe: Political, Social and Economic Forces*, 1958.

Holland, M, *European Integration from Community to Union*, 1993.

Holland, S, *Uncommon Market*, 1980.

Lodge, J (ed), *The European Community and the Challenge of the Future*, 1993, particularly Chapter 1.

Mandel, E, 'International capitalism and supranationality', in Radice (ed), *International Firms and Modern Imperialism*, 1969.

Molle, W, *The Economics of European Integration (Theory, Practice, Policy)*, 2001.

Pinder, J, 'Positive integration and negative integration: some problems of Economic Union in the EEC', *The World Today*, March 1968; also in Denton, GR (ed), *Economic Integration in Europe*, 1969.

Pinder, J, 'Economic integration versus national sovereignty: differences between Eastern and Western Europe' (1989) Government and Opposition 309.

Root, FR, *International Trade and Investment – Theory, Policy Enterprise*, 1973 (now 1994).

Webb, C, 'Theoretical perspectives and problems', in Wallace, Wallace and Webb (eds), *Policy Making in the European Community*, 1983.

Wellenstein, EP, 'Unity, Community, Union – what's in a name?' (1992) 29 CML Rev 205.

Williams, R, 'The EC's technology policy as an engine for integration' (1989) Government and Opposition 158.

CHAPTER 3

FEDERALISM, SOVEREIGNTY, COMPETENCE AND SUBSIDIARITY

While the idea of limiting sovereignty in a united Europe was widespread, some influential figures were more precise. They envisaged a federal constitution for Europe, giving powers over trade, money, security, and related taxation to a federal parliament, government and court, leaving all other powers to be exercised by the institutions of the Member States [John Pinder, *European Community: The Building of a Union*].

The debate on federalism in Europe is hopelessly confused, as nobody cares to define its subject and purpose. As a result, politicians and journalists feel free to tell us that federalism is synonymous with 'centralized bureaucracy', although every beginning student of federalism knows that the very aim of federal systems is to avoid centralization [Koopmans, 1992].

A FEDERAL PATTERN

Taking the United States as a model, in the constitution of that federal State, sovereignty (political power and legal competence) is divided between the central, federal government and the governments of the associated States:

The Constitution of the United States establishes an association of states so organized that powers are divided between a general government which in certain matters – for example, the making of treaties and the coining of money – is independent of the governments of the associated states, and, on the other hand, state governments which in certain matters are, in their turn, independent of the general government. This involves, as a necessary consequence, that general and regional governments both operate directly upon the people; each citizen is subject to two governments. It is not always easy to say what matters are within the spheres of the general and the regional governments respectively [Wheare, *Federal Government*, 1964].

Neither the European Union nor its strongest pillar, the European Community, is a federal State. The European institutions do not comprise a European government. Within the EC's first pillar institutional structure and legislative processes, there are both supranational and intergovernmental elements. The second Common and Security Policy pillar and, since the ToA, the remainder of the third Police and Judicial Co-operation in Criminal Matters pillar of the EU operate merely on the basis of Member State intergovernmental co-operation. From a different perspective, although since Maastricht there is Treaty recognition of European citizenship, a concept which is being developed mainly from 'the top', there is at 'the bottom' no sufficiently 'integrated' sense of such citizenship to form the basis of a meaningful democratic European State.

The competences of the European Community have always been based on conferrals of power to the institutions by the Treaty as duly amended; that is, by the Member States themselves. Where the Community has neither express nor implied powers to act, competence remains with the Member States. Competence is indeed shared in many policy areas.

As regards the legislative processes at European level, the more important the role of the Commission, the wider the scope of the co-decision and veto powers of the directly elected European Parliament, and the more extensive the use of majority voting at the expense of unanimity in the Council (a body of an intergovernmental nature made up of ministers from the Member States), the more supranational or federal the EC/EU can be regarded. Majority voting signals the end of the single State veto of Community legislation. The judicial activism of the Court of Justice, with 'its own view of Europe', has also contributed to the shift in power away from the Member States.

However, it has also been argued that the separation of powers within the Community, as a federal structure in the making – which as an eventual Union will absorb its intergovernmental elements – does not correspond to the requirements of a democratic State. Although Article 6 TEU states that the Union, and therefore the Community, is founded, amongst other things, on the principles of democracy, concern regarding democratic legitimacy intensifies.

Attention has already been drawn to the fact that legislative powers still rest primarily with, not the European Parliament, which has no independent legislative status, but with a shifting body (depending on the subject matter of the legislation) of government ministers who, although checked at national level, have not been elected at European level. The legislative powers of this body, the Council of Ministers – and the *political* powers of the European Council – have increased with successive transfers of competence from the Member States. This 'executive dominance' has only in part been offset by the increasing participation of the European Parliament in the legislative process as it has grown from its 'talking shop' origins to a position of directly elected co-decision maker with respect to the majority of Community legislation. This is not an argument that can be advanced for the national parliaments – who in any event can be said to exercise control over legislative 'executive dominance' at national level only rarely.

The 'democratic deficit' debate frequently focuses on the role of the Commission within the legislative process. It is a non-elected body but exists to serve the Community interest and the advancement of Community policies. Its right of legislative initiative – the drafting of Community legislation for consideration by the Council and the Parliament – normally embraces wide consultation with appropriate bodies, including pressure groups, at both Community and national level. Its powers, delegated to it by the Council, regarding the putting into effect of adopted legislation concern the formulation of detailed secondary rules which 'flesh out' the measures passed to it for this purpose. The position is akin to that concerning secondary legislation and its control – or lack of it at national level. The Commission (and the Council to some extent) is responsible in many ways to its European partner, the Parliament, which caused it to resign *en bloc* in 1999.

The Court of Justice, the supreme arbiter on Community legal issues, is made up of members, one from each Member State at present, delegated by national parliaments. The Court's role in the reduction of the 'democratic deficit' through the operation of its case law is considered in Chapter 7.

It is in the legal rather than the political sphere that the EC most clearly demonstrates its supranational or federal character. It was the Court of Justice which established in the early days the primacy of Community law over national law, together with the principle of direct effect – the creation for individuals of EC law rights which prevail over national provisions in a two-tier structure. The Court, as already noted in Chapter 1, has increasingly recognised the Treaty as the EC constitution rather than an international agreement.

The European Community/Union is then, at present, a hybrid – a federation in the making perhaps, moving towards some form of United States of Europe, but only if the combined political will can come to see that goal as a desirable and democratically achievable 'end' within the process of integration. It is perhaps best described as a half-way house, being based, since the creation of the ECSC, on a *federal pattern*:

> It is important to remember that with the ratification of the European treaties, concessions of sovereignty to autonomous European institutions have already occurred. An embryonic federal structure is in place, even if its powers are confined to certain areas ... [Peter Sutherland (former EC Commissioner), 1988].

It will be recalled that the prime motive behind the Community concept in the first place was to *reduce the power of the nation State* and thus the central cause of war. Therefore, over the last 50 years or so, the integrative process has led to an increasing shift in the balance of power from the Member States to the Community institutions. In 1951, 1957, 1986, 1992, 1997 and 2002, under the original Treaty and successive amendments, the Member States have themselves established and successively widened Community competence and, therefore, correspondingly reduced the scope of their own sovereignty. However, as we have said, this does not mean we now have a federal Europe.

In 1989, Pinder explained the question of successive accretions to Community powers not only in terms of the 'bonds' between negative and positive integration (economic 'spill-over') but also in terms of the links between economic and political integration (political 'spill-over'):

> ... the closer the interdependence, the less effective the Member States' policies become ... Member States' policies are replaced or supplemented by common policies for the Community as a whole. But positive integration is harder to achieve than the removal of distortions. The making and execution of laws and policies are, after all, the task of governance, so we are expecting the Community's institutions to be capable of governance ...

> ... If the single market implies, in turn, the need for further stages of policy integration such as an economic and monetary union, it is hard to escape the conclusion that federal structures of government for the Community will be required. Intergovernmental co-operation would be unable to produce effective policies or democratically legitimate laws.

A European federal structure is emerging gradually, step by step, but not without opposition from those who wish to see national governments retain their sovereignty in key areas of economic policy. As Pinder explained:

> This sequence of events has given rise to a neo-federalist analysis of Community development, which sees the second half of the 20th century as a period in which federal structures and competencies, instead of being established by a single constituent act, are being created by a series of steps ... envisaging institutions of government beyond the nation state. It differs from the neo-functionalists ... by considering what institutions and competencies are adequate for the democratic governance of a single economy; and unlike the neo-functionalists, it treats each step

as a political struggle between forces favouring integration and the reactions of national sovereignty, in which it is not certain which of the two will prevail.

For the 'Euro-sceptics' of the various Member States, federation means centralism, hence their stiff opposition to the Maastricht Treaty. As Anatole Kaletsky, writing in *The Times* prior to the Maastricht summit, stated:

Whether or not the dreaded word 'federal' appears in the treaties, the virtual certainty of a deal on EMU [economic and monetary union] makes some form of federalism inevitable. For once monetary sovereignty is removed from the nations of the European Union, the other attributes of the state are bound to follow, regardless of what provisions on political union may or may not be agreed next week.

What is clear is that these developments bring about a changing relationship between the Community and the Member States which is underpinned by the Treaties (the legal acts of the Member States) and thus by the rule of Community law. In a 1986 article, Hartley stressed, in terms similar to those above, that 'it is precisely those parts of the Community constitution [the Treaties] which are concerned with the legal and judicial system [as opposed to the political system] that are most federal'. In reply to the question, 'What are the essential features of a federation, as far as the courts and legal system are concerned?', he stated that:

First, obviously, there must be a federal constitution which delimits the respective spheres of the federation and the units (states, provinces, etc).

...

The Community Treaties fulfil most of the requirements of a constitution in that they establish the legislative, executive and judicial organs of the Community and grant them their powers. They do not, however, grant any powers to the Member States: it is assumed (quite correctly) that the Member States already have their powers from another source. The consequence of this is that all powers not granted to the Community remain with the Member States.

This attribution of powers by the Treaties was examined by the European Court of Justice in 1963 in the *Van Gend en Loos* case. Here, the Court spoke of the establishment by the Treaty of Rome of 'institutions endowed with sovereign rights, the exercise of which affects Member States and their citizens'. It also stated that 'the States have limited their sovereign rights, albeit within limited fields'. (This case will be examined in more detail in the next chapter.)

Similarly, in litigation before the Court of Appeal in 1989, Kerr LJ stated that:

... there is equally no doubt that the EEC exercises powers and functions which are analogous to those of sovereign states ... the EEC enjoys certain sovereign powers to the extent to which these have been ceded to it by its members under the various EEC treaties and from this cession it has derived its own legislative, executive and judicial organs whose acts and decisions take effect within the member states. On the other hand, the EEC differs from sovereign states in that it has no sovereignty over territory as such and no nationals or citizens [*JH Rayner (Mincing Lane) Ltd v Department of Trade and Industry* (1989)].

If we draw together the main points from the foregoing discussion, the following picture emerges. *Transfers* of sovereignty from the Member States to the Community have taken place within certain economic and social fields. Although only partial, these transfers have assumed greater proportions as wider powers have been granted to the Community institutions by the Member States under successive agreements. The purpose of this *pooling of sovereignty* is to enable the Community to achieve those economic, social and political objectives laid down in the Treaties for the benefit of the Member States and their citizens. These are policies which are considered better achievable at Community rather than Member State level, but they require the involvement and co-operation of all the Member States.

Such co-operation from Member States' governments has not followed as a matter of course over the years. Disputes between Member States and the Community concerning the scope and outer limits of Community competence, concerning unwarranted and allegedly invalid intrusions into national sovereignty have occurred with some frequency. Taking just one prime example (others will be discussed in later chapters), *Brunner v The EU Treaty*, decided by the German Federal Constitutional Court in 1993, considered the claimant's constitutional complaint regarding Germany's ratification of the Maastricht Treaty. The challenge was rejected but in the course of its ruling, the Constitutional Court gave what has been called 'a courteous but clear warning' with respect to Community institutional practice at the margins of its powers.

In particular, the German court expressed concern over what it perceived as overactive interpretation of the Community's expressly stated Treaty powers by 'Community institutions and agencies' (including no doubt the Court of Justice) in so far as the use of the doctrine of implied powers had spilled over in effect into Treaty amendments. Such amendments can of course only be made by the Member States acting unanimously and with the effect of agreed limitations on national sovereignty where they operate as extensions of Community sovereignty. Such limitations, affecting individual constitutional rights, cannot be brought about by Community institutions alone as they lack the necessary democratic legitimacy. The Constitutional Court warned that:

> ... in future it will have to be noted as regards the interpretation of enabling provisions by Community institutions and agencies that the Union Treaty as a matter of principle distinguishes between the exercise of a sovereign power conferred for limited purposes and the amending of the Treaty, so that its interpretation may not have effects that are equivalent to an extension of the Treaty. Such an interpretation of enabling rules would not produce any binding effects for Germany.

The federal or supranational nature of the Community legal (as opposed to its political) system rests on the extent to which Community law, comprising the Treaties and the law enacted by the Community institutions, is directly binding in the Member States and has primacy over national law. Lasok and Bridge summed up the position in the following terms:

> In the terms of the EEC Treaty, the States endeavour to build Community institutions and to create a body of law to regulate the economic activities of the members. Although surrender of a certain portion of sovereignty is necessary in order to achieve these objectives, the pooling of sovereignty is not explicit enough to create a federal State or a federal government of the Community. Therefore, at this stage of its development, the Community is merely an association of sovereign States with a federal potential.

Although written some years ago, the position as stated here still holds good.

NATIONAL SOVEREIGNTY, COMMUNITY POWERS AND SUBSIDIARITY

The political tug-of-war between those who advocate further integration and the upholders of national sovereignty is a phenomenon which Jean Monnet himself foresaw in 1978, when he warned that the Community process 'would stop where the frontiers of political power began. Then something new would have to be invented'. A response to those who seek to stop the process of integration is to ask to what extent nowadays do national governments independently exercise control over their economies in any case:

> The massive growth of international trade and its accompanying huge capital flows, and the emergence of multinational corporations, with annual turnovers often in excess of the gross national products of independent countries, have made the whole world economically interdependent. As a result countries that try to isolate themselves by erecting barriers against the outside pay a heavy price in economic stagnation and backwardness, while the rest of the world moves ahead. These dramatic changes in the nature of global society have thrown up new problems that can no longer be tackled by individual countries merely looking after their own interests. Unfettered national sovereignty is obsolete, and economic and political independence is giving way to growing interdependence between nation states. The major task for the world today is to devise policies to deal with global problems and create appropriate political structures to ensure that the policies are put into effect. The same applies to individual continents or major regions within them that are affected by common problems. Amongst these, for instance, pollution, disease, crime and terrorism know no frontiers and can no longer by tackled by individual countries in isolation, but require international solutions [Wistrich].

MacCormick, writing in 1993 under the title *Beyond the Sovereign State*, asks:

> ... whether there actually are any sovereign states now. My answer is to be a negative one so far as concerns Western Europe, and is so notwithstanding the *Daily Telegraph's* first leader on the day of this lecture's first delivery. In this leading article, the Chancellor of the Exchequer, Mr Lamont, was praised for his absolute adherence to the principle of 'fiscal sovereignty' while exhibiting sensible flexibility about some process of harmonisation of taxes to a sensible degree within the Community.

> Taking the view of the sovereign State which I suggested, or any reasonable variant on its terms, it seems obvious that no state in Western Europe any longer is a sovereign State. None is in a position such that all the power exercised internally in it, whether politically or legally, derives from purely internal sources. Equally, of course, it is not true that all the power which is exercised either politically or normatively is exercised by, or through, or on the grant of, one or more organs of the European Community. Nor has the Community as such the plenitude of power politically or normatively that could permit it remotely to resemble in itself a sovereign State or sovereign federation of States ... Where at some time past there were, or may have been, sovereign States, there has now been a pooling or a fusion within the communitarian normative order of some of the states' powers of legislation, adjudication and implementation of law in relation to a wide but restricted range of subjects. Some matters fall to be handled within one normative system or normative order, while other parts remain rooted or based in other normative systems or normative orders, with arrangements designed (so far, rather successfully) to prevent incompatibility in areas of overlap.

It is therefore appropriate to ask to what extent it is true to say that sovereignty is 'lost' or 'surrendered' to Brussels. When competence is 'lost', where does it come to rest? What precisely happens when an exclusive right to legislate is ceded to a superior law making body? The answers to these questions depend upon the view one takes of the legislative process in the Community. Monsieur Delors (the former President of the Commission) said that 'it is the Council not the Commission which takes the real decisions' – the Commission merely proposes. As such, it is therefore the representatives of the Member States themselves constituting the Council of Ministers, together now with the European Parliament, who are the Community's legislators.

On this view, there is no real 'surrender' of sovereignty (a word with, it is said, emotional connotations suggesting coercion on the Community's part) rather a pooling of sovereignty, jointly exercised by the Member States in order to achieve objectives which they could not attain on an individual basis:

> The Council stands at the crossroads of two kinds of sovereignty, national and supranational. While it must safeguard the national interests of member states, it must not regard this as its paramount task. Its paramount task is to promote the interests of the Community; and, unless it does so, the Community will not develop [Konrad Adenauer, West German Chancellor, 1951].

> The Community is based not on a loss of sovereignty but on a pooling of sovereignty, on its exercise jointly in the common good rather than its exercise separately – often selfishly and to the detriment of other people [Lord Cockfield, EC Commissioner in charge of the Internal Market programme, in an address to the Swiss Institute of International Affairs in Zurich, October 1988].

Nevertheless, 'lukewarm' Europeans still perceive two particular threats to national interests, arising from a different view of the Community's legislative process. First, they point out that the Commission, the guardian of the Community interest, puts forward detailed proposals to a Council that has a limited right of amendment, unanimity being required in certain circumstances (see Chapter 5). Secondly, to a reply that the Commission always works within the (widening) scope of Community competence as established by the Treaties – a contention that is itself sometimes disputed (as in the *Brunner* case, above) – critics observe that the return to majority voting in the Council on an increasingly wide range of issues in the Single European Act and the TEU has resulted in the demise of the national interest: in such cases the power of veto, as we have seen, has been lost.

For example: is vocational training for young people a matter of national education policy or one which falls within Community competence as a question of social policy? In an action which arose prior to the Maastricht Treaty, the Court of Justice rejected a UK claim that a Council Decision on this question lacked a sufficient legal base – Article 128 EEC which allowed for a simple majority vote in the Council:

> The Council shall, acting on a proposal from the Commission and after consulting the Economic and Social Committee, lay down general principles for implementing a common vocational training policy capable of contributing to the harmonious development both of the national economies and of the common market.

The Court would not accept the argument that Article 235 EEC (now Article 308 EC), a general residual provision which requires unanimity, must be added. This Article states that:

If action by the Community should prove necessary to attain, in the course of operation of the common market, one of the objectives of the Community and this Treaty has not provided the necessary powers, the Council shall, acting unanimously on a proposal from the Commission and after consulting the European Parliament, take the appropriate measures.

However, it is of further interest to note that, following Maastricht, Article 128 EEC became Article 127 EC (and now Article 150 EC) and, in conformity with the principle of subsidiarity, merely states that EC vocational policy 'shall support and supplement the action of the Member States, while fully respecting the responsibility of the Member States for the content and organisation of vocational training'.

Competence and Subsidiarity

As integration proceeds towards union and power passes increasingly to the Community institutions, a further question arises: when transfers of sovereignty occur, do the Member States lose *all* their powers within the areas concerned?

It is contended that the division of powers should be seen not in terms of a separation but rather as a sharing of responsibilities based on the concepts of solidarity and co-operation as found in Article 10 (formerly 5) and Article 234 (formerly 177) of the EC Treaty. Nevertheless, it remains the case that, in terms of the 'moving boundary' between the Community and the Member States, the transfer of powers from the latter to the former is a continuing process with the Community increasingly in the 'driving seat'.

The principle of *subsidiarity*, which, as seen in Chapter 1, found its first formal expression in the TEU, is designed to go to the heart of the question of transfers of sovereignty and hence to the sharing of legislative and administrative powers within the Community. It can only be properly understood in the context of a federal structure. But what type of federal structure? In the UK, it is often stated that a fully federal Europe will inevitably and speedily lead to a concentration of 'real' power at the centre. There is talk of a 'super-State' located in Brussels. However, federalism has a different meaning for many continental Europeans, one which is reflected in the principle of subsidiarity in Article 5 (formerly 3b) EC. On the basis of this principle, which came into effect in late 1993, the Community should take action only to the extent to which Treaty objectives can be accomplished more effectively at Community level than at national (or regional or local) level. Decisions should be taken 'as closely as possible to the citizen': Article 1 (formerly A) TEU.

However, the second paragraph of Article 5 states that the principle only applies in areas which do *not* fall within the Community's exclusive competence. Within the Community, competence is seen as taking three different forms:

(a) *Exclusive Community powers* (transferred from the Member States under the Treaties) in particular policy areas. In such areas, unilateral national action or competence is not allowed.

(b) *Exclusive powers* retained by the Member States in other policy areas (in which the Community has potential competence).

(c) *Concurrent (also known as non-exclusive or shared) powers* in further policy areas where Community and Member State powers co-exist. In such areas, powers have been transferred to the Community but (as yet) they have not been exercised (acted upon), or they have been exercised but not to their full extent, or they have been exercised in such a way as to authorise the exercise of some part of the Community powers by national authorities in the Member States.

A major problem arising from this division of powers is that nowhere in the Treaty can be found any explicit statement as to which policy areas (those in Article 3) fall under which heading – exclusive or concurrent. As Weatherill has said:

> So the dividing line between Community and national competence – which must in theory exist [see the discussion of federalism in the early part of this chapter] – is in practice hard to discern and, critically, is not static. It shifts under the influence of Treaty amendments, legislation invading unexpected areas, and also because of the Court's own activism. And that shift has been essentially in one direction only – in favour of enhanced Community competence, cutting down the realms in which the Member States retain an exclusive national competence.

The scope of *exclusive* Community competence is a matter of debate but the weight of opinion (but not the Commission's) is that it is of an exceptional nature. Where it exists, it denies unilateral action (legislation) by the Member States. State powers have been 'pre-empted' and the Community has 'occupied the field', although the Community may delegate powers, normally of an administrative nature back to the Member States. In other words, national law may operate but only if authorised by the Community. Bieber takes the view that:

> ... the Community has exclusive powers if it can clearly be deduced from the wording of the Treaties that such powers have been conferred upon it or if a provision cannot be properly applied if this were not the case (for example, the setting up of the Common Customs Tariff in accordance with Article 21(2) EEC [and] provisions concerning the institutional system).

Court of Justice rulings have certainly established Community exclusive competence in the external relations sphere particularly as regards the implementation of the Common Commercial (External Trade) Policy based on Article 133 (formerly 113) EC, and also in the field of fisheries conservation: see also Case 22/70 *Commission v Council (ERTA)* in Chapter 6. Some, particularly early, Internal Market Directives relating to the manufacturing and marketing of goods insisted on the adoption of *uniform* rules by the Member States but the trend now is to allow flexibility by merely setting minimum required standards: see Case 60/86 *Commission v UK (Re Dim-Dip Headlights)* in Chapter 12.

In cases of concurrent or shared competence, Steiner has argued that 'there are few areas of activity in which Member States do not retain some degree of competence – national rules must not conflict with Community rules'. If so, the fundamental supremacy principle means that the former must give way to the latter: see the next chapter. EC legislation may be introduced which eats away national competence and 'occupies the field' in question to that extent. Otherwise the Member States may act to exercise their concurrent powers, but in so acting must in no way harm the Community interest: Article 10 (formerly 5) EC, which states that the Member States 'shall abstain from any measure which could jeopardise the attainment of the objectives of the Treaty'.

The case law of the Court of Justice shows this to be the position within the common organisation of agricultural product markets (cereals, beef, dairy products, etc) within the CAP. This policy area also demonstrates that, as in areas of exclusive competence, within the vastly wider field of concurrent competence, powers may be returned to appropriate national authorities (for example, DEFRA) which are authorised and required to adopt implementing or supplementary national measures in order to make the underlying Community measures fully effective in an operational sense in the Member States. In this way, integrative aims can be secured through continuing co-operation between Community institutions and national authorities.

The Principle of Subsidiarity

An isolated example of the principle was introduced into the EEC Treaty, pre-Maastricht, by the Single European Act in 1986. Article 130r(4) EEC (now Article 174(4) EC) relating to environmental protection was a clear illustration of the express conferral of concurrent Community powers:

> The Community shall take action relating to the environment to the extent to which the objectives referred to in paragraph 1 can be attained better at Community level than at the level of the individual Member States.

Since Maastricht, this paragraph now states that 'within their respective spheres of competence, the Community and the Member States shall co-operate with third countries and with the competent international organisations', and Article 130s(4) EEC (now Article 175(4) EC) provides that 'the Member States, shall finance and implement the environment policy'.

The principle of subsidiarity, referred to in Article 2 (formerly B) TEU and in Article 5 (formerly 3b) EC, is in three parts:

> The Community shall act within the limits of the powers conferred upon it by this Treaty and of the objectives assigned to it therein.

> In the areas which do not fall within its exclusive competence, the Community shall take action, in accordance with the principle of subsidiarity, only if and in so far as the objectives of the proposed action cannot be sufficiently achieved by the Member States and can therefore, by reason of the scale or effects of the proposed action, be better achieved by the Community.

> Any action by the Community shall not go beyond what is necessary to achieve the objectives of this Treaty.

Article 5(1) embodies the *principle of conferred (attributed or assigned) powers*. Such powers have, as we have seen, expanded over the years as Treaty amendments have extended the Community's Article 3 activities. Objectives, originally couched in vague terms, have been translated into specific powers which have been duly acted upon. As we have also seen, the Community's powers include not only express Treaty based powers but also, according to the Court of Justice, such further implied powers as are necessary for the institutions to achieve their objectives. In addition, Article 235 EEC (now Article 308 EC) has been used to enable the Community to act to achieve 'one of the objectives of the Community' where the Treaty 'has not provided the necessary powers'.

The *subsidiarity principle* itself is to be found in Article 5(2) EC. As stated, it does not apply to areas of exclusive competence and therefore only applies in areas of concurrent competence. However, in such areas, the competence of the Member States ends once the Community has *exercised* its powers – 'every new Community measure creates a new area of exclusive competence': Temple Lang. Similarly, Emiliou states that:

> ... the Court has taken the view that whenever the Treaty gives the Community a power to enact binding measures, and the Community exercises that power by adopting legislation or entering into an international agreement, that area is regarded as falling within the exclusive competence of the Community. In other words, once the Community has 'occupied the field', the original power of the Member States has been transferred to the Community. If the Court were to follow the same line of reasoning with regard to Article 3b [now 5], any given area would be regarded as falling within the exclusive jurisdiction of the Community once the Community had occupied the field; consequently subsidiarity would be applicable only when the Community legislated for the first time in a new area.

Article 5(2) covers the *need* for action on the basis of a 'comparative efficiency' test. It provides that the Community shall act if 'by reason of the scale or effects of the proposed action', it can be shown that better results can thereby be achieved in terms of the objectives in question. The phrase 'scale or effects' indicates a transnational dimension to the issue in hand. Thus, for example, an environmental or animal health problem will probably involve such a cross-border dimension. The very character of the Community means that many proposed actions will be of this nature.

Article 5(3) goes to *the means employed* and embodies the *principle of proportionality*, whereby any action taken is no more than is *appropriate and necessary* to achieve its designed purpose. Thus: 'Any action by the Community shall not go beyond what is necessary to achieve the objectives of this Treaty.' (On proportionality, see also Chapter 10.) As Steiner has pointed out: 'The proportionality test thus acts both to control the scope of legislation (avoiding excessively detailed prescription) and to determine the most appropriate (that is, the least intrusive) means for its implementation.'

It is important to recognise that the principle of proportionality applies to 'any action' of the Community whether taken in the field of concurrent or exclusive competence. As regards the *means employed* for achieving objectives, the Commission has itself analysed Article 5(3) in terms of the best instrument, proposing the use of Directives rather than Regulations, together with the use of flexible non-binding instruments such as recommendations or codes of conduct.

A Protocol on the Application of the Principles of Subsidiarity and Proportionality attached to the ToA examines the practical implementation of the principle particularly in terms of the need for Commission justification of draft legislation. If Council or Parliament amendments to measures entail greater Community intervention, justification in terms of Article 5 must similarly be submitted. The Protocol also lays down guidelines for determining when the conditions for Community action are met:

(a) the issue under consideration has transnational aspects which cannot be satisfactorily regulated by action by Member States;

(b) actions by Member States alone or lack of Community action would conflict with the requirements of the Treaty (such as the need to correct distortion of competition or avoid disguised restrictions on trade or strengthen economic and social cohesion) or would otherwise significantly damage Member States' interests;

(c) action at Community level would produce clear benefits by reason of its scale or effects compared with action at the level of the Member States.

A final question: is the Court of Justice prepared to declare Community measures invalid for infringement of the principle of subsidiarity? The Court can be asked to interpret the principle in Article 5 or to apply it, for example, on a request from a national court for a preliminary ruling (see Chapter 9) or in a direct action at Community level – an action for annulment of a binding Community measure under Article 230 (formerly 173) EC (see Chapter 19).

It can be argued that as subsidiarity lies at the heart of difficult socio-economic policy decisions of a discretionary nature taken by political institutions, the Court, a non-elected body, should not engage in 'second guessing' those institutions. Nevertheless, the Court, as a constitutional court has, as we will see, not infrequently decided clear political issues (in disputes between the Community institutions themselves or between a Member State and the Community), albeit disguising the fact by ruling in 'narrow' legal terms.

Two cases concerning direct challenges to EC legislation brought by Member States and involving the principle of subsidiarity failed to impress the Court on that score. In Case C-84/94 *UK v Council*, the UK requested the Court to annul Council Directive 93/104 on Working Time (or parts thereof) on the grounds that:

(a) although it purported to be a health and safety measure which could properly be based on Article 118a (now 138) EC, the regulatory system put in place by the Directive went beyond the Council's competence under Article 118a when read in conjunction with the first paragraph of Article 3b (now 5); and

(b) having regard to the requirements of Article 118a, and the principles of subsidiarity and proportionality, the Council had manifestly acted unlawfully in enacting the Working Time Directive.

In this case, the UK was attempting to preserve a veto by arguing that the Directive had the wrong Treaty base (Article 118a) which required only a majority vote whereas it should have been based on a Treaty Article requiring a unanimous vote. The Court held that Article 118a was the correct basis for Council Community-wide action in terms of the improvement of health and safety at work.

In Case C-233/94 *Germany v Parliament and Council*, the applicant sought annulment of a banking Directive on various grounds, including breach of the duty to state reasons for the measure under Article 190 (now 253) EC. The claim was that the recitals in the contested Directive made no reference to the principle of subsidiarity even though the Federal Republic drew attention to the omission during the Council's deliberations. The Court held on this procedural issue that express reference to the principle was not required provided that the recitals to the legislation contained a clear justification for Community action.

The question of subsidiarity arose again in 2000 in a further challenge by Germany, this time to the adoption under, *inter alia*, Article 100a (1) (now 95(1)) EC of a co-decision Internal Market harmonisation Directive. However, the Court of Justice, which annulled the Directive as being adopted on the wrong Treaty basis, was able to avoid the need to examine this issue directly. (The Advocate General – see Chapter 7 – was of the opinion that the Directive fell within a field of exclusive competence of the Community, a view that has not gone unchallenged.)

Nevertheless, this highly significant decision by the Court covered key constitutional matters discussed throughout this chapter. It may be seen as a response by the Court to the concerns expressed by the German Federal Constitution Court in the *Brunner* case, above.

Case C-376/98 *Germany v Parliament and Council (Tobacco Advertising Directive)*

Directive 98/43 on tobacco advertising and sponsorship, based primarily on Article 100a(1) (now 95(1)), laid down harmonised rules the effect of which was to ban such promotion of the product, with only minor exceptions. Germany had voted against the measure in the Council but it was adopted by a qualified majority vote.

In challenging the Directive under Article 173 (now 230), the German government argued (a) that the national rules subject to the Directive had no appreciable effect on the operation of the Internal Market: the characteristics of the tobacco product market were not such as to make it suitable for harmonisation as the effects of tobacco advertising were limited to highly specific national markets, with negligible inter-Member State trading in advertising media – both static (posters, cinema advertising, ashtrays, etc) and non-static (newspapers, magazines, etc); (b) that the Directive was in fact a public health policy measure; (c) that Article 100a(1) was therefore not the correct legal basis for its adoption; (d) that the measure was beyond the Community's competence, it being excluded from adopting harmonisation measures in the (concurrent competence) public health field by the terms of Article 129(4) (now 152(4)).

The Court stated that the harmonisation measures referred to in Article 100a(1) were intended to improve the conditions for the establishment and functioning of the Internal Market. The competence conferred upon the Community legislature by that Article did not however allow, as in this case, overly broad legislation going beyond the removal of specific obstacles to the free movement of goods and services or the elimination of appreciable distortions of competition. It did not vest in the legislature a general power to regulate the Internal Market as this would be contrary to the Treaty's basic provisions in Article 3(c) (now 6) and Article 7a (now 14) on free movement – and incompatible with the principle of Article 3b (now 5) that the powers of the Community were limited to those conferred upon it and the objectives assigned to it.

The Court did nevertheless grant that Article 100a could be relied upon as the basis for Internal Market harmonisation of national rules 'where public health protection is a decisive factor'. (Article 95(3) (formerly 100a(3)) provides that Commission harmonisation proposals which concern health 'will take as a base a high level of protection, taking into account in particular of any new development based on scientific facts'.) However, this was only so where the measure in question was genuinely intended to improve conditions in the Internal Market; it could not be an attempt to avoid the express exclusion of harmonisation measures (as in Article 129(4)), in which event competence would be absent.

In addition, in terms of effect, the measure must also ensure that an actual improvement in the establishment and functioning of the Internal Market was achieved.

The Court ruled that the Directive's ban did not in fact facilitate inter-Member State trade in the services and products concerned and that any distortion of competition caused by differences in the relevant national rules had only a minimal effect within the Internal Market. As the ban did not contribute to the enhancement of Internal Market conditions, the Court annulled the Directive in its entirety.

The Court's explicit reference to the conferred powers principle in Article 5(1) shows, as Weatherill has explained, that the Court is 'sending a message to national courts that it, the European Court, is serious about patrolling the limits of Community competence' – that national courts should refrain from considering performing (as in *Brunner*) 'their own national-level constitutional check'.

Article 220 EC states that the Court (and post-Nice, the CFI) shall ensure that 'the law is observed', and the political institutions, including the Parliament, must act within the bounds of limited Community competences – difficult though it may be to establish where the boundary lies.

TRANSFERS OF SOVEREIGNTY AND PARLIAMENTARY SOVEREIGNTY

Sovereignty is a word of many meanings. In the UK, the expression *parliamentary* sovereignty refers to the constitutional doctrine that there are no legal limits to the legislative power of Parliament except that Parliament cannot limit its own powers for the future. Thus, in *national* law, there is nothing that a statute properly enacted cannot do and therefore no act is irreversible. Now, as Collins points out:

> It is only in the sense last mentioned that the word has any useful meaning in relation to the national law of the United Kingdom. In the international sphere and in the political sphere there may have been a limitation of sovereignty but there is no reason to believe that there has yet been any limitation on the sovereignty of the United Kingdom Parliament [Collins, *European Community Law in the United Kingdom*, 1990].

Therefore, as regards transfers of national sovereignty as discussed earlier, it is agreed that whereas this involves the removal of legislative powers from the UK Parliament by *limiting* its authority, such transfers do not amount (at least in theory) to an encroachment upon the doctrine of *parliamentary* sovereignty:

> The stage has now been reached where the current legal and political reality is that there has been a transfer of powers to the Community. It has already been suggested that the traditional rule that Parliament may not bind its successors is not necessarily irreconcilable with the concept of a transfer of powers to another authority. It may further be suggested that whilst the political reality remains membership of the Community, such powers are unlikely in practice to be recovered, and at least to that extent the transfer can be regarded as irreversible [Usher, 1981].

For an international treaty to be binding and enforceable at the domestic level, UK law, which regards international law and domestic law as separate systems of law, requires the treaty to be incorporated into the national legal system by means of an enabling Act. The European Communities Act 1972, which provides for the incorporation of Community law into the law of the UK, whilst recognising in sections 2 and 3 the supremacy of Community law (as established by the European Court of Justice), also lays down a rule of interpretation to the effect that Parliament is to be presumed not to intend any statute to override Community law. Community law will therefore always prevail over national law unless Parliament expressly states in a future statute that it is to override Community law.

In this way, the remote possibility that Parliament might some day wish to repeal the 1972 Act is not excluded and the ultimate sovereignty of Parliament is upheld:

> We have all been brought up to believe that, in legal theory, one Parliament cannot bind another and that no Act is irreversible. But legal theory does not always march alongside political reality ... What are the realities here? If Her Majesty's Ministers sign this Treaty and Parliament enacts provisions to implement it [the 1972 Act], I do not envisage that Parliament would afterwards go back on it and try to withdraw from it. But if Parliament should do so, then I say we will consider that event when it happens [Lord Denning in *Blackburn v Attorney General* (1971)].

Lord Denning is here referring to the unlikely eventuality of this country withdrawing from the Community. (The EC Treaty contains no provisions for withdrawal.)

The reality, however, is that while the UK is a member of the Community, the constitutional doctrine of parliamentary sovereignty cannot be relied upon in the face of directly enforceable rules of Community law. Although in 1983, Sir Robert Megarry VC stated in *Manuel v Attorney General* that, 'once an instrument is recognised as being an Act of Parliament, no English court can refuse to obey it or question its validity', this statement must certainly now be modified to read 'once an instrument is recognised as being an Act of Parliament and is compatible with enforceable Community law, no English court can refuse to obey it or question its validity'. That this is the present state of the law in this country was expressed in the clearest terms and on the highest judicial authority by Lord Bridge in the *Factortame (No 2)* case (see Chapter 20):

> Some public comments on the decision of the European Court of Justice, affirming the jurisdiction of the courts of Member States to override national legislation if necessary to enable interim relief to be granted in protection of rights under Community law, have suggested that this was a novel and dangerous invasion by a Community institution of the sovereignty of the United Kingdom Parliament. But such comments are based on a misconception. If the supremacy within the European Community of Community law over the national law of Member States was not always inherent in the EEC Treaty it was certainly well established in the jurisprudence of the European Court of Justice long before the United Kingdom joined the Community. Thus, whatever limitation of its sovereignty Parliament accepted when it enacted the European Communities Act 1972 was entirely voluntary. Under the terms of the Act of 1972, it has always been clear that it was the duty of a United Kingdom court, when delivering final judgment, to override any rule of national law found to be in conflict with any directly enforceable rule of Community law ... Thus, there is nothing in any way novel in according supremacy to rules of Community law in those areas to which they apply and to insist that, in the protection of rights under Community law, national courts must not be inhibited by rules of national law from granting interim relief in appropriate cases is no more than a logical recognition of that supremacy.

The *Factortame* litigation involved the disapplication of certain provisions of an Act of Parliament pending a decision by the Court of Justice on the question of whether the legislation was in breach of Community law and the directly enforceable Treaty rights of a number of Spanish private parties. The Court later held that the statute did infringe Community law and the private parties concerned brought an action for damages against the government department responsible for the legislation on the basis of what is known as the *Francovich* principle of State liability (see Chapter 20). This *Factortame* damages litigation has only recently been settled at national level, but the following passages from the Advocate General's Opinion at an earlier stage are of particular relevance in the context of the continuing developing relationship between Community law and national law:

It is beyond argument that the State should not incur liability for legislative action except in exceptional circumstances. The freedom of the legislature must not be trammelled by the prospect of actions for damages ... The 'power to express the sovereignty of the people' justifies the legislature's immunity in relation to the general rule of liability ...

State liability for breach of Community law and State liability in domestic law for legislative action do not have the same basis. The first type of liability is necessarily founded on illegality: breach of a higher ranking rule of law and therefore of the principle of primacy ...

Respect for primacy requires not only that legislation contrary to Community law should be disapplied. It requires also that damage resulting from its application in the past should be made good ...

Refuge can no longer be taken behind the supremacy or unchallengeability of legislation ... the bringing of an action for damages against the State for the legislature's failure to act is perfectly permissible where the State's liability is based on a breach of Community law, as *Francovich* shows, whereas this is hardly conceivable in domestic law.

As Lord Bridge explained in the judgment delivered after the Court had given its judgment in *Factortame II*, by ratifying the Treaty of Rome (or, in the United Kingdom's case, by adopting the 1972 European Communities Act), the Member States accepted that the legislative sovereignty of their Parliaments was limited by the principle of the primacy of Community law.

REFERENCES AND FURTHER READING

Beaud, M, 'The nation State questioned' (1989) Contemporary European Affairs: *1992 and After*, Vol 1, 1989, No 1/2.

Bieber, R, 'On the mutual completion of overlapping legal systems: the case of the European Communities and the national legal orders' (1988) 13 EL Rev 147.

Bradley, AW, 'Sovereignty of Parliament', in Jowell and Oliver (eds), *The Changing Constitution*, 2000.

Campbell, D and Young, J, 'The metric martyrs and the entrenchment jurisprudence of Lord justice Laws' (parliamentary sovereignty and EC law) [2002] PL 399.

Cass, D, 'The word that saves Maastricht? The principle of subsidiarity ...' (1992) 29 CML Rev 1107.

Cockfield (Lord), 'National sovereignty and the European Community' (1986) 39 Studia Diplomatica 649.

Dashwood, A, 'The limits of European Community powers' (1996) 21 EL Rev 113.

Emiliou, N, 'Subsidiarity: panacea or fig leaf?', in O'Keefe and Twomey (eds), *Legal Issues of the Maastricht Treaty*, 1994.

Koopmans, T, 'Federalism: the wrong debate' (1992) 29 CML Rev 1047.

Layton, C, 'The sharing of sovereignty', in 'One Europe, One World' (1986) Journal of World Trade Law, Special Supplement No 4.

Lenaerts, K, 'Constitutionalism and the many faces of federalism' (1990) 38 American Journal of Comparative Law 205.

Lenaerts, K and Desomer, M, 'Bricks for a constitutional treaty of the European Union: values, objectives and means' (2002) 27 EL Rev 377.

MacCormick, N, 'Beyond the sovereign State' (1993) 56 MLR 1.

Pinder, J, 'European Community and nation State: a case for a neo-federalism?' (1986) International Affairs 41.

Steiner, J, 'Subsidiarity under the Maastricht Treaty', in O'Keefe and Twomey (see above).

Temple Lang, J, 'European Community constitutional law: the division of powers between the Community and the Member States' (1988) 39 NILQ 209.

Toth, A, 'A legal analysis of subsidiarity', in O'Keefe and Twomey (see above).

Turpin, C, *British Government and Constitution*, 2002 (sections on 'Parliamentary sovereignty' and 'Sovereignty and the European Community').

Usher, J, *European Community Law and National Law: The Irreversible Transfer?*, 1981.

Weatherill, S, *Law and Integration in the European Union*, 1995 (Chapter 2: 'The competence of the Union'; and Chapter 5: 'Pre-emption and competence in a wider and deeper union').

Wistrich, E, *After 1992 – The United States of Europe*, 1989.

PART TWO

THE NATURE AND EFFECT
OF COMMUNITY LAW

CHAPTER 4

THE NATURE AND MAIN SOURCES OF COMMUNITY LAW

THE SOURCES OF COMMUNITY LAW

... all Community law by one route or another must find its roots and its authority in a written text, that of the Treaties themselves. The bulk of Community law, as the reported cases demonstrate, is concerned with the interpretation and validity of further written texts, Community 'acts' such as directives, regulations or decisions [Lord Mackenzie Stuart, former President of the European Court of Justice].

The three major formal (as opposed to economic or social) sources of European Community law are to be found in Lord Mackenzie Stuart's statement:

(a) The Constitutional Treaties of the Community (which are acts of the Member States).

(b) The law making acts of the Community's political institutions.

(c) The decisions of the Court of Justice (and the general principles of law and fundamental rights recognised and developed by that court).

The Treaties form the basis of the Community legal order. They are *primary* sources from which *secondary* sources are derived. Thus, Community acts (Regulations, Directives and Decisions) must establish themselves upon the correct legal base from within the Treaties. This applies also to the many and varied international agreements with non-Member States (and international organisations) concerning association, trade, development aid and other forms of co-operation.

The Founding Treaties

The constitutional, rather than international, nature of the EC (formerly EEC) Treaty has been discussed in the preceding chapters. Although the Treaty was signed by the Member States as High Contracting Parties (see Article 1), it is clear that it does not merely create reciprocal rights and duties between the Member States. As seen, the original Treaty established the autonomous legislative, executive and judicial organs of the Community – each of which is granted specific powers (see, for example, Article 4 (now Article 7) EC) which regulate the activities of the Member States, business organisations, individuals – and the Community itself.

The three founding Treaties were:

- The Treaty of Paris Establishing the European Coal and Steel Community, 1951 (in force 1952, expired 2002 and reintegrated within the EC Treaty).

- The Treaty of Rome Establishing the European Economic Community, 1957 (in force 1958).

- The Treaty of Rome Establishing the European Atomic Energy Community (Euratom), 1957 (in force 1958).

Revisions of the founding Treaties have been discussed, the main ones being:

- The Treaty Establishing a Single Council and a Single Commission of the European Communities (the Merger Treaty), 1965 (in force 1967).

- The Treaties of Accession of new Member States: The First Accessions (Denmark, Ireland and the UK) of 1972 (in force 1973); The Second Accession (Greece) of 1979 (in force 1981); The Third Accessions (Spain and Portugal) of 1985 (in force 1986); and the Fourth Accessions (Austria, Sweden and Finland) of 1994 (in force 1995).

- The Single European Act of 1986 (in force 1987).

- The Treaty on European Union, agreed at Maastricht in December 1991 and signed in February 1992 (in force November 1993).

- The Treaty of Amsterdam, agreed in June 1997, formally signed in October 1997 (in force May 1999).

- The Treaty of Nice, formally signed in February 2001 (in force 2003).

The integrative aims of the original EEC Treaty* were, from a legal standpoint, facilitated by the 'self-executing' character of the Treaty. This means that upon ratification, the Treaty of Rome *automatically* became law within the Member States and (subject to amendments) must be directly applied as such by national courts and tribunals. (This point was touched upon in the previous chapter when discussing the supranational character of Community law.) There was no Community *requirement*, as in the case of a 'non-self-executing' treaty (which merely creates obligations of a contractual nature binding on the signatories in international law), for the Treaty to be incorporated into the national law of the Member States by means of implementing legislation to enable it to take effect at the domestic level. However, as seen in the previous chapter, as a consequence of the UK's *dualist* view of international law as being a separate system of law from national law, it became necessary upon accession, from a *national* viewpoint, for the UK to make Community law applicable within the national legal system by means of a special Act, the European Communities Act 1972: see also Chapter 8.

The Treaty took its 'self-executing' character from its legislative form and its constitutional design. The implementation of the Treaty was, by its terms (Article 4 (now 7) EC), placed primarily in the hands of the Community institutions, and the rights and duties which it established exist, as we have seen, not merely between the Member States on a reciprocal, horizontal and international basis, but on the basis of a complex set of legal relationships between the Member States, their *nationals* and the Community institutions: see, in particular, Case 26/62 *Van Gend en Loos*, discussed below, in which the Court of Justice established that certain key provisions of the Treaty were *directly effective*, that is, they created rights for individuals (both natural and legal) which they may invoke in national courts in disputes with their national authorities or with other individuals. The enormous impact of the principle of direct effect, as established and developed by the Court of Justice, in terms of the Community's quasi-federal structure, its integrative goals, and the rights of Community nationals, will be discussed below and in subsequent chapters.

---

*   In line with the earlier explanation of the scope of this book in the Preface, the text, cases and materials will hereafter refer mainly to the European Community (formerly European Economic Community), the first pillar of the Union, and to the EC Treaty (formerly the EEC Treaty).

In broad terms, the content of the (EEC and now the EC) Treaty can be divided into two main parts, although Community case law shows that they are very much interwoven. It embodies the *institutional* organisation of the Community and the powers and duties of the institutions in terms of law making and law enforcement. The Treaty also contains the legal basis for the Community's economic and social policies: the *substantive* law of the Community. On the basis of Articles 2 and 3 (aims, means and objectives), it lays down in varying degrees of detail the legal framework of the interlocking processes of negative and positive integration: for example, the customs union rules, the common agricultural policy, the rules on competition, and economic and monetary union.

Community Law Making Acts (Community Legislation)

The three political institutions, the Brussels Council of Ministers, the Commission and the European Parliament, are responsible for the adoption of binding Community acts (secondary or derived legislation), which amplify the Articles of the Treaty and enable Community law and policy to be brought fully into effect. (The European Central Bank has similar law making powers to enable it to carry out its functions: see now Articles 8 and 110 EC.)

Such acts derive their authority from the fact that they are brought into force by institutions invested with the necessary power, *where specific Articles of the Treaty so provide*: for example, Article 40 (formerly 49) which authorises the Council and the Parliament jointly to issue Directives or make Regulations in order to bring about freedom of movement for workers; or Article 95 (formerly 100a) which grants the Council and the Parliament power to adopt measures for the harmonisation of the laws of the Member States in the course of the establishment and functioning of the Internal Market.

In that they derive their authority from the Treaty (which is an act of the Member States) and so rank below it, Community acts can be compared to delegated legislation. Whereas neither the Community Courts nor national courts have the power to test the validity of the Treaty (which can be regarded as the constitutional document), the validity of Community acts can be challenged either directly before the Court of Justice or the CFI, or indirectly in a national court on the basis of the Court's preliminary rulings jurisdiction under Article 234(1)(b) (formerly 177(1)(b)) (see Chapters 9 and 19).

Article 249 (formerly 189) of the Treaty provides legal definitions of the various Community acts. The first paragraph states that:

> In order to carry out their task and in accordance with the provisions of this Treaty, the European Parliament acting jointly with the Council, the Council and the Commission shall make regulations and issue directives, take decisions, make recommendations or deliver opinions.

The original Article 189(1) was amended by the TEU to take account of the Parliament's power of co-decision with the Council in certain defined areas: see Chapter 5.

Regulations, Directives and Decisions are obligatory acts whereas recommendations and opinions are stated in Article 249(5) to 'have no binding force'. They are therefore non-obligatory and are not legal acts.

Official Journal of the European Communities   475

No L 25712   Official Journal of the European Communities   19.10.68

REGULATION (EEC) No 1612/68 OF THE COUNCIL
of 15 October 1968
on freedom of movement for workers within the Community

THE COUNCIL OF THE EUROPEAN COMMUNITIES,

Having regard to the Treaty establishing the European Economic Community, and in particular Article 49 thereof;

Having regard to the proposal from the Commission;

Having regard to the Opinion of the European Parliament[1];

Having regard to the Opinion of the Economic and Social Committee[2];

Whereas freedom of movement for workers should be secured within the Community by the end of the transitional period at the latest; whereas the attainment of this objective entails the abolition of any discrimination based on nationality between workers of the Member States as regards employment, remuneration and other conditions of work and employment, as well as the right of such workers to move freely within the Community in order to pursue activities as employed persons subject to any limitations justified on grounds of public policy, public security or public health;

Whereas by reason in particular of the early establishment of the customs union and in order to ensure the simultaneous completion of the principal foundations of the Community, provisions should be adopted to enable the objectives laid down in Articles 48 and 49 of the Treaty in the field of freedom of movement to be achieved and to perfect measures adopted successively under Regulation No 15[3] on the first steps for attainment of freedom of movement and under Council Regulation No 38/54/EEC[4] of 25 March 1964 on freedom of movement for workers within the Community;

Whereas freedom of movement constitutes a fundamental right of workers and their families; whereas mobility of labour within the Community must be one of the means by which the worker is guaranteed the possibility of improving his living and working conditions and promoting his social advancement, while helping to satisfy the requirements of the economies of the Member States; whereas the right of all workers in the Member States to pursue the activity of their choice within the Community should be affirmed;

Whereas such right must be enjoyed without discrimination by permanent, seasonal and frontier workers and by those who pursue their activities for the purpose of providing services;

Whereas the right of freedom of movement, in order that it may be exercised, by objective standards, in freedom and dignity, requires that equality of treatment shall be ensured in fact and in law in respect of all matters relating to the actual pursuit of activities as employed persons and to eligibility for housing, and also that obstacles to the mobility of workers shall be eliminated, in particular as regards the worker's right to be joined by his family and the conditions for the integration of that family into the host country;

Whereas the principle of non-discrimination between Community workers entails that all nationals of Member States have the same priority as regards employment as is enjoyed by national workers;

Whereas it is necessary to strengthen the machinery for vacancy clearance, in particular by developing direct co-operation between the central employment services and also between the regional services, as well as by increasing and co-ordinating the exchange of information in order to ensure in a general way a clearer picture of the labour market; whereas workers wishing to move should also be regularly informed of living and working conditions; whereas, furthermore, measures should be provided for the case where a Member State undergoes or foresees disturbances on its labour market which may seriously threaten the standard of living and level of employment in a region or an industry; whereas for this purpose the exchange of information, aimed at discouraging workers from moving to such a region or industry, constitutes the method to be applied in the first place but, where nec-

---

1 ,   OJ No 268, 6.11.1967, p 9.

2   OJ No 298, 7.12.1967, p 10.

3   OJ No 57, 26.8.1961, p 1073/61.

4   OJ No 62, 17.4.1964, p 965/64.

essary, it should be possible to strengthen the results of such exchange of information by temporarily suspending the above mentioned machinery, any such decision to be taken at Community level;

Whereas close links exist between freedom of movement for workers, employment and vocational training, particularly where the latter aims at putting workers in a position to take up offers of employment from other regions of the Community; whereas such links make it necessary that the problems arising in this connection should no longer be studied in isolation but viewed as inter-dependent, account also being taken-of the problems of employment at the regional level; and whereas it is therefore necessary to direct the efforts of Member States toward co-ordinating their employment policies at Community level;

Whereas the Council, by its Decision of 15 October 1968[1] made Articles 48 and 49 of the Treaty and also the measures taken in implementation thereof applicable to the French overseas departments;

HAS ADOPTED THIS REGULATION:

PART I

EMPLOYMENT AND WORKERS' FAMILIES

TITLE I

Eligibility for employment

Article 1

1. Any national of a Member State, shall, irrespective of his place of residence, have the right to take up an activity as an employed person, and to pursue such activity, within the territory of another Member State in accordance with the provisions laid down by law, regulation or administrative action governing the employment of nationals of that State.

2. He shall, in particular, have the right to take up available employment in the territory of another Member State with the same priority as nationals of that State.

Article 2

Any national of a Member State and any employer pursuing an activity in the territory of a Member State may exchange their applications for and offers of employment, and may conclude and perform contracts of employment in accordance with the provisions in force laid down by law, regulation or administrative

action, without any discrimination resulting therefrom.

Article 3

1. Under this Regulation, provisions laid down by law, regulation or administrative action or administrative practices of a Member State shall not apply:

— where they limit application for and offers of employment, or the right of foreign nationals to take up and pursue employment or subject these to conditions not applicable in respect of their own nationals; or

— where, though applicable irrespective of nationality, their exclusive or principal aim or effect is to keep nationals of other Member States away from the employment offered.

This provision shall not apply to conditions relating to linguistic knowledge required by reason of the nature of the post to be filled.

2. There shall be included in particular among the provisions or practices of a Member State referred to in the first subparagraph of paragraph 1 those which:

(a) prescribe a special recruitment procedure for foreign nationals;

(b) limit or restrict the advertising of vacancies in the press or through any other medium or subject it to conditions other than those applicable in respect of employers pursuing their activities in the territory of that Member State;

(c) subject eligibility for employment to conditions of registration with employment offices or impede recruitment of individual workers, where persons who do not reside in the territory of that State are concerned.

Article 4

1. Provisions laid down by law, regulation or administrative action of the Member States which restrict by number or percentage the employment of foreign nationals: in any undertaking, branch of activity or region, or at a national level, shall not apply to nationals of the other Member States.

2. When in a Member State the granting of any benefit to undertakings is subject to a minimum percentage of national workers being employed, nationals of the other Member States shall be counted as national workers, subject to the provisions of the Council Directive of 15 October 1963.[2]

---

1   OJ No L 257, 19.10.1968, p 1.

2   OJ No 159, 2.11.1963, p 2661/63.

Regulations

Under Article 249(2):

> A regulation shall have general application. It shall be binding in its entirety and directly applicable in all Member States.

The 'general application' of a Regulation is indicative of its legislative character and it is the main instrument for uniformity throughout the Community. The Court of Justice in Case 6/68 *Zuckerfabrik Watenstedt v Council* stated: 'It is applicable ... to objectively determined situations and involves legal consequences for categories of persons viewed in a general and abstract manner.' For example, see *Council Regulation 1612/68 on Freedom of Movement for Workers within the Community*, Official Journal, Special Edition 1968(II), 475, the first part of which is reproduced on pages 70 and 71. (Note its Treaty base: Article 49 (now 40) as it stood in 1968.)

In Article 249(2), the provisions of Regulations are stated to be 'directly applicable'; that is, they penetrate into the legal order of the Member States *without the need for any national implementing measures* (cf Treaty Articles). Also, as will be seen, Regulations normally have *direct effect*, creating rights for individuals (for example, workers) that must be protected by national courts: see Chapter 8. However, this is not the case where a Regulation states that certain of its provisions are to be implemented by the national authorities: for example, as regards the creation of new criminal offences in Case 128/78 *Commission v UK (Re Tachographs)*.

Directives

Under Article 249(3):

> A directive shall be binding, as to the result to be achieved, upon each Member State to which it is addressed, but shall leave to the national authorities the choice of form and methods.

Unlike a Regulation which is binding in every respect, a Directive is only binding 'as to the result to be achieved' for each Member State to which it is addressed. A Directive may be addressed to all the Member States (for example, Internal Market harmonisation Directives issued under Article 95 (formerly 100a)) or perhaps to only one. It is therefore not necessarily of 'general application':

> ... while the principal subjects governed by Regulations are agriculture, transport, customs and social security of migrant workers, Community authorities resort to Directives when they intend to harmonise national laws on such matters as taxes, banking, equality of the sexes, protection of the environment, employment contracts and the organisation of companies. Plain cooking and haute cuisine, in other words. The hope of seeing Europe grow institutionally, in matters of social relationships and in terms of quality of life, rests to a large extent on the adoption and implementation of Directives [Mancini].

An addressee Member State is under an obligation (see Article 10 (formerly 5)) to achieve the aim or purpose of a Directive but has a discretion as to the type of measure and procedure adopted at national level to achieve that result. A Directive is not therefore directly applicable. Under the scheme envisaged by Article 249(3), individuals within the scope of the Directive *will acquire* rights on the basis of the national implementing measure. However, where national authorities *fail to implement*

Directives properly, or within the time limit laid down, rights for individuals may nevertheless accrue, that is, Directives may have direct effect: see Chapter 8.

On pages 74 and 75 is an example of a Directive within the field of social policy. It was based in 1975 on Article 100 EEC relating to harmonisation of national laws (now Article 94 EC) and it implemented in more specific terms the principle of equal pay in Article 119 (now 141). Most Directives are issued now by the Council following the co-decision procedure.

Decisions

Under Article 249(4):

> A decision shall be binding in its entirety upon those to whom it is addressed.

Community law is normally applied in *specific* cases by means of Decisions. They are binding in every respect upon their addressees who may be Member States, individuals or corporations. In Case 54/65 *Compagnie des Forges de Châtillon v High Authority*, the Court of Justice defined a decision (so distinguishing it from a non-binding communication, opinion or recommendation: see Article 249(5)) as:

> A measure emanating from the competent authority, intended to produce legal effects and constituting the culmination of procedure within that authority, whereby the latter gives its final ruling in a form from which its nature can be identified.

The binding nature of a Decision means that there is no room for any discretion as to the manner in which it is to be carried out. Clearly, Decisions may be adopted (as institutional acts) for a wide variety of purposes. Commission Decisions in the field of competition policy are of a quasi-judicial nature. Such a Decision may, on the basis of Article 82 (formerly 86) and implementing Council Regulation 17/62, find an *undertaking* to be abusing its dominant position on a product market and impose a large fine. To take a further example, at the time of one of the 'mad cow disease' (BSE) scares in the UK, the Commission adopted Decision 89/469 concerning 'certain protective measures relating to bovine spongiform encephalopathy in the United Kingdom'. It was based on Council Directive 64/432 on 'animal health problems affecting intra-Community trade in bovine animals and swine', which was in turn based on the appropriate Treaty Article: see page 77.

What has been called the bicephalous or two-headed nature of Community law making, the fact that both the political and judicial institutions have powers to act, requires some elaboration. For the most part, the Commission's powers are delegated to it by the Council: see Article 202 (formerly 145) and, more particularly, Article 211 (formerly 155). As noted earlier, in these cases the Council lays down general principles, for example in a Regulation, and delegates to the Commission the task of implementing those general principles by means of detailed rules in a further measure: see Case 25/70 *Köster*, in which, acting on the basis of agriculture policy Article 43(2) (now 37(2)), the Council brought into effect a Regulation establishing the general principles for the organisation of a common market in cereals. The Regulation provided for detailed rules to be laid down in measures (for example, Regulations) to be adopted by the Commission.

Article 190 (amended by the TEU to take account of the Council and Parliament acting jointly) presently provides (as Article 253) that:

19. 2. 75   Official Journal of the European Communities   No L 45/119

II

(Acts whose publication is not obligatory)

COUNCIL

COUNCIL DIRECTIVE
of 10 February 1975

on the approximation of the laws of the Member States relating to the application of the principle of equal pay for men and women

(75/117/EEC)

THE COUNCIL OF THE EUROPEAN COMMUNITIES,

Having regard to the Treaty establishing the European Economic Community, and in particular Article 100 thereof;

Having regard to the proposal from the Commission;

Having regard to the Opinion of the European Parliament ([1]);

Having regard to the Opinion of the Economic and Social Committee ([2]);

Whereas implementation of the principle that men and women should receive equal pay contained in Article 119 of the Treaty is an integral part of the establishment and functioning of the common market;

Whereas it is primarily the responsibility of the Member States to ensure the application of this principle by means of appropriate laws, regulations and administrative provisions;

Whereas the Council resolution of 21 January 1974([3]) concerning a social action programme, aimed at making it possible to harmonise living and working conditions while the improvement is being maintained and at achieving a balanced social and economic development of the

Community, recognized that priority should be given to action taken on behalf of women as regards access to employment and vocational training and advancement, and as regards working conditions, including pay;

Whereas it is desirable to reinforce the basic laws by standards aimed at facilitating the practical application of the principle of equality in such a way that all employees of the Community can be protected in these matters;

Whereas differences continue to exist in the various Member States despite the efforts made to apply the resolution of the conference of the Member States of 30 December 1961 on equal pay for men and women and whereas, therefore, the national provisions should be approximated as regards application of the principle of equal pay,

HAS ADOPTED THIS DIRECTIVE:

Article 1

The principle of equal pay for men and women outlined in Article 11 9 of the Treaty, hereinafter called 'principle of equal pay', means, for the same work or for work to which equal value is attributed, the elimination of all discrimination on grounds of sex with regard to all aspects and conditions of remuneration.

In particular, where a job classification system is used for determining pay, it must be based on the same criteria for both men and women and so drawn up as to exclude any discrimination on grounds of sex.

---

(1) OJ No C S5, 13. 5. 1974, p 43.

(2) OJ No C 88, 26. 7. 1974, p 7.

(3) OJ No C 13, 12. 2. 1974, p 1.

No L 45/20   Official Journal of the European Communities   19.2.75

Article 2

Member States shall introduce into their national legal systems such measures as are necessary to enable all employees who consider themselves wronged by failure to apply the principle of equal pay to pursue their claims by judicial process after possible recourse to other competent authorities.

Article 3

Member States shall abolish all discrimination between men and women arising from laws, regulations or administrative provisions which is contrary to the principle of equal pay.

Article 4

Member States shall take the necessary measures to ensure that provisions appearing in collective agreements, wage scales, wage agreements or individual contracts of employment which are contrary to the principle of equal pay shall be, or may be declared, null and void or may be amended.

Article 5

Member States shall take the necessary measures to protect employees against dismissal by the employer as a reaction to a complaint within the undertaking or to any legal proceedings aimed at enforcing compliance with the principle of equal pay.

Article 6

Member States shall, in accordance with their national circumstances and legal systems, take the measures necessary to ensure that the principle of equal pay is applied. They shall see that effective means are avail able to take care that this principle is observed.

Article 7

Member States shall take care that the provisions adopted pursuant to this Directive, together with the relevant provisions already in force, are brought to the attention of employees by all appropriate means, for example at their place of employment.

Article 8

1. Member States shall put into force the laws, regulations and administrative provisions necessary in order to comply with this Directive within one year of its notification and shall immediately inform the Commission thereof.
2. Member States shall communicate to the Commission the texts of the laws, regulations and administrative provisions which they adopt in the field covered by this Directive.

Article 9

Within two years of the expiry of the one-year period referred to in Article 8, Member States shall forward all necessary information to the Con-mission to enable it to draw up a report on the application of this Directive for submission to the Council.

Article 10

This Directive is addressed to the Member States.
Done at Brussels, 10 February 1975.

For the Council

The President

G FITZGERALD

Regulations, directives and decisions adopted jointly by the European Parliament and the Council, and such acts adopted by the Council and Commission shall state the reasons on which they are based and shall refer to any proposals or opinions which were required to be obtained pursuant to this Treaty.

In Case 18/62 *Barge*, Advocate General Lagrange submitted with reference to Regulations that they must be reasoned, indicating in general terms the aims pursued, the reasons justifying them and the outline of the system adopted. Article 190 (now 253) does not therefore impose a mere formal requirement:

In imposing upon the Commission the obligation to state the reasons for its decisions, Article 190 is not taking mere formal considerations into account but seeks to give an opportunity to the parties of defending their rights, to the Court of exercising its supervisory functions and to Member States and to all interested nationals of ascertaining the circumstances in which the Commission has applied the Treaty [Court of Justice in Case 24/62 *Germany v Commission (Brennwein)*].

An absence of sufficient reasons may lead the Court to nullify an act under Article 230 (formerly 173) on the grounds of the infringement of an essential procedural requirement. This was also the case where the Council failed to obtain the opinion of the Parliament as required by the then relevant Treaty provision: Case 138/79 *Roquette Frères v Council*.

As seen in the last chapter, the Commission should also consider justification of a proposed measure in terms of the principle of subsidiarity.

Article 254 (formerly 191) lays down rules regarding the publication of Community acts. The following must be published: all Regulations; Directives adopted under the Council–Parliament co-decision procedure, Council or Commission Directives addressed to all Member States; and Decisions adopted under the co-decision procedure. They are published in the Official Journal, 'L' series. Other Directives and Decisions must be notified to those to whom they are addressed and they will probably be published in the Official Journal as well. Community acts normally take effect on the date specified in them or upon notification.

The foregoing description of Community acts suggests, in Hartley's words, 'a fairly neat and tidy system ... Unfortunately, things are not as simple as this'. First, although exceptionally, the formal designation of an act is not always an accurate guide to its contents. For example, a Directive may leave very little discretion to Member States as to the choice of form and methods for its implementation. It may therefore take on the character (although not the legal status) of a Regulation. A Regulation may, at least in part, lose its general and objective character and, in deciding a specific issue, become what the Court has termed a 'disguised decision'. (As will be seen in Chapter 19, this is significant in that under Article 230 (formerly 173), natural and legal persons may within certain limits challenge the validity of Decisions but not Regulations – except in certain exceptional cases.) It is the function of an act rather than its label which is of primary importance.

It is also significant that in Case 22/70 *Commission v Council (ERTA)*, the Court of Justice ruled that the list of acts in Article 189 (now 249) was *not exhaustive*. It was decided in this case (discussed more fully in Chapter 6) that a Council 'resolution' concerning the negotiating procedure for the European Road Transport Agreement was intended to have, and in practice did have, legal effects on relations between the Community and the Member States and on the relations between the institutions. The 'resolution' was held to be an act *sui generis*.

3. 8. 89   Official Journal of the European Communities   No L 225/51

COMMISSION DECISION
of 28 July 1989

concerning certain protection measures relating to bovine spongiform encephalopathy in the United Kingdom

(89/469/EEC)

THE COMMISSION OF THE EUROPEAN COMMUNITIES,

Having regard to the Treaty establishing the European Economic Community,

Having regard to Council Directive 64/432/EEC of 26 June 1964 on animal health problems affecting intra-Community trade in bovine animals and swine ('), as last amended by Directive 89/360/EEC(²), and in particular Article 9 thereof,

Whereas several outbreaks of bovine spongiform encephalopathy have occurred throughout the territory of the United Kingdom;

Whereas this disease can be considered to be a new serious contagious or infectious animal disease whose presence may constitute a danger to cattle in other Member States;

Whereas a significant risk may be considered to exist in respect of live animals; whereas however, this risk is considered to exist only for cattle born before 18 July 988 or born to affected cows, in view of the epidemiology and pathogenesis of the disease;

Whereas the United Kingdom authorities have given certain guarantees to certain Member States to prevent the spread of the disease; whereas therefore these measures should be applied to intra-Community trade to all Member States;

Whereas the measures provided for in this Decision are in accordance with the opinion of the Standing Veterinary Committee,

HAS ADOPTED THIS DECISION:

Article 1

The United Kingdom shall not send to other Member States live cattle born before 18 July 1988 or born to

females in which bovine spongiform encephalopathy is suspected or has been officially confirmed.

Article 2

The health certificate provided for in Directive 64/432/EEC accompanying cattle sent from the United Kingdom must be completed by the following:
'animals in accordance with Commission Decision 89/469/EEC of 28 July 1989 concerning bovine spongiform encephalopathy'.

Member States shall amend the measures which they apply to trade so as to bring into compliance with this Decision three days after its notification. They shall immediately inform the Commission thereof.

Article 4

The Commission will follow developments in the situation. This Decision may be amended in the light of such developments.

Article 5

This Decision is addressed to the Member States.

Done at Brussels, 28 July 1989.

For the Commission

Ray MACSHARRY

Member of the Commission

---

(1)   OJ No 121, 29. 7. 1964, p 1977/64.

(2)   OJ No L 153, 6. 6. 1989, p 29.

In a further development, which was significant in the light of the European Parliament's continuing campaign for real legislative powers, the Court recognised the Parliament's capacity to adopt legally binding acts in Case 294/83 *Partie Ecologiste Les Verts v Parliament*. The Court's ruling came within the context of a Article 173 (now 230) challenge to a decision of the Parliament in connection with direct elections and was justified on the basis of the Parliament's enhanced status and power to pass measures which could affect the rights of third parties (see also Chapter 6).

Decisions of the Court of Justice

Decisions of the Court of Justice constitute a secondary source of Community law by providing authoritative *interpretations* of the Treaty and acts of the institutions made thereunder. The Treaty is a *'traité cadre'*, a framework Treaty, the wording of which is much removed from the precise, tightly drafted provisions of an English statute. In the course of explaining the Treaty (and derived legislation) over several decades, the Court has complemented and filled in gaps in the Community legal system in a way which has considerably enhanced the process of economic and legal integration.

In particular, in a number of highly important decisions, the Court has gone some way beyond interpretation in the normal sense of the term and, as a policy maker, has established, refined and developed several *basic principles* which can be said to be implied within the Treaty. In the cases discussed in the section which follows can be found the interrelated principles of the autonomy, supremacy (or primacy), direct applicability and direct effect of Community law. While establishing and clarifying the relationship between Community law and national law, the Court has, in its use of these principles, also done much to increase the scope and effectiveness of Community law, not least as regards the availability of rights for individuals within the Community legal order.

A further major contribution, closely linked to the final point made above, has come about through the Court's recognition and development of *general principles of Community law* (referred to in the Treaty as 'general principles common to the laws of the Member States' in Article 288 (formerly 215)). The jurisprudence of the Court in this field has been variously described as 'a creative act of judicial legislation' and 'naked law making'. Some of these principles are to be found in the Treaty itself, for example, solidarity in Article 10 (formerly 5) and non-discrimination on the grounds of nationality in Article 12 (formerly 6, and earlier 7), and see also the wider phrased new Article 13 covering racial discrimination, etc, but in the main they have been taken by the Court from the national legal traditions of the Member States and adapted to the Community context. They include *equality* (or non-discrimination as a general principle), *fundamental human rights* (to which before Maastricht, the Treaty made no express reference) and *proportionality*.

The principle of proportionality, already discussed in the context of subsidiarity, means that economic burdens may be placed on individuals (or corporations) for purposes of the general Community interest (that is, in the furtherance of Community policy) only to the extent that they are appropriate and strictly necessary for the attainment of such purposes: a question of means and ends. This definition, and the clear purpose of the other principles mentioned, indicates that the main, but not sole, function of these general principles (they may also provide a bedrock aid to interpretation) lies in the field of Community administrative law. They may be invoked by individuals and corporations and Member States in the course of challenges to action, or inaction, on the part of the Community institutions (see Chapters 10 and 19).

THE COURT OF JUSTICE AND THE PRINCIPLES OF SUPREMACY AND DIRECT EFFECT OF COMMUNITY LAW

It follows from the very concept of integration, of common and co-ordinated policies, and not least from the need for the establishment and maintenance of the Common Market and economic and monetary union (EMU) by institutions charged with these duties by the Treaty itself (that is, by the agreement of the Member States), that Community law must have a uniform meaning and effect in all the Member States and that *supremacy or primacy* must be accorded to Community law within the national legal orders of the Member States. The Community would not be able to function properly if Member States had the power to annul Community law by adopting, or giving precedence to, national law. If this were possible, Community law would lose its essential character and the legal basis of the Community would be radically impaired. The continuing development of Community policies, in the search for the attainment of the objectives and activities of Articles 2 and 3, must of necessity also involve the provision of new or enhanced legal rights for individuals (that is, for both natural and legal persons) within the widening ambit of the Community's economic and social jurisdiction. The duty of the Member States under Article 10 (formerly 5) to fulfil the obligations imposed on them by the Treaty and Community legislation entails not only the possibility of an action brought against them, by the Commission under Article 226 (formerly 169), for breach of these obligations, but also a duty which rests on their national courts to recognise and protect those *directly effective* rights which Community law confers on individuals (private parties) and which they seek to enforce against national authorities or other individuals. These rights, as we have indicated and shall discuss in more detail in due course, may arise under the Treaty itself or from specific provisions of the binding Community acts defined in Article 249 (formerly 189), that is, Regulations, Directive and Decisions.

Neither the supremacy of Community law nor its capability to give rise to individual rights is to be found in the Treaty, except in the case of supremacy by way of the definition of a Regulation in Article 249 (formerly 189). These fundamental principles, lying at the heart of the Community legal system and its relationship with the law of the Member States, were established and elucidated by the Court of Justice in some of its earlier judgments. The nature and supremacy of Community law is more fully spelt out in the following policy decision.

Case 6/64 *Costa v ENEL*

In 1962, the Italian government nationalised private electricity undertakings and transferred their assets to ENEL. Costa, a lawyer and former shareholder in one of the undertakings, objected to the nationalisation measures. When presented with an electricity bill for £1 by ENEL, he refused to pay it and on being sued he pleaded, amongst other things, that the nationalisation legislation was incompatible with various Treaty Articles.

The Milanese magistrate sought guidance from the Court of Justice under the then Article 177 preliminary rulings procedure. The Italian authorities argued that the matter was to be settled by domestic law alone and that the magistrate's request was 'absolutely inadmissible'. The Court of Justice ruled that:

> The Italian Government submits that the request of the Giudice Conciliatore is 'absolutely inadmissible', inasmuch as a national court which is obliged to apply a national law cannot avail itself of Article 177.

> By contrast with ordinary international treaties, the Treaty has created its own legal system which, on the entry into force of the Treaty, became an integral part of the legal systems of the Member States and which their courts are bound to apply.

> By creating a Community of unlimited duration, having its own institutions, its own personality, its own legal capacity and capacity of representation on the international plane and, more particularly, real powers stemming from a limitation of sovereignty or a transfer of powers from the States to the Community, the Member States have limited their sovereign rights, albeit within limited fields, and have thus created a body of law which binds both their nationals and themselves.

> The integration into the laws of each Member State of provisions, which derive from the Community and more generally the terms and the spirit of the Treaty, make it impossible for the States, as a corollary, to accord precedence to a unilateral and subsequent measure over a legal system accepted by them on a basis of reciprocity. Such a measure cannot therefore be inconsistent with that legal system. The executive force of Community law cannot vary from one State to another in deference to subsequent domestic laws, without jeopardising the attainment of the objectives of the Treaty set out in Article 5(2) and giving rise to the discrimination prohibited by Article 7.

> The obligations undertaken under the Treaty establishing the Community would not be unconditional, but merely contingent, if they could be called in question by subsequent legislative acts of the signatories. Wherever the Treaty grants the States the right to act unilaterally, it does this by clear and precise provisions ...

> The precedence of Community law is confirmed by Article 189, whereby a regulation 'shall be binding' and 'directly applicable in all Member States'. This provision, which is subject to no reservation, would be quite meaningless if a State could unilaterally nullify its effects by means of a legislative measure which could prevail over Community law.

> It follows from all these observations that the law stemming from the Treaty, an independent source of law, could not, because of its special and original nature, be overridden by domestic legal provisions, however framed, without being deprived of its character as Community law and without the legal basis of the Community itself being called into question.

> The transfer by the States from their domestic legal system to the Community legal system of the rights and obligations arising under the Treaty carries with it a permanent limitation of their sovereign rights, against which a subsequent unilateral act incompatible with the concept of the Community cannot prevail. Consequently Article 177 is to be applied regardless of any domestic law, whenever questions relating to the interpretation of the Treaty arise ...

These statements are based on the Court's view or interpretation of the Treaty as the legal vehicle whereby the *objectives* of the Community may be achieved. It may be cited as an example of what is known as the teleological or purposive method of interpretation. However, as Hartley has explained:

... the court prefers to interpret texts on the basis of what it thinks they should be trying to achieve; it moulds the law according to what it regards as the needs of the Community. This is sometimes called the 'teleological method of interpretation' but it really goes beyond interpretation properly so-called: it is decision making on the basis of policy.

It will be noticed that in the course of this ruling, which concerned Treaty Articles, the Court confirms the precedence of 'independent' Community law by reference to the direct applicability of Regulations. Not only may no unilateral national legislative measure nullify a Regulation, but no such measure is required to implement or transpose a Regulation into national law. Gormley has put the position in the following terms:

> The Court of Justice, however, on the basis of the Community legal order takes a quite different position from the current conception of international law, a conception which leaves the regulation of the internal effect of rules of international law to constitutional law. As a matter of fact, it appears from the case-law of the Court that Treaty provisions ... penetrate into the internal legal order without the aid of any national measure, to the extent that their character makes this appropriate ... Such provisions, like regulations (which are by nature and function in the system of Community sources of law directly applicable) must be applied by the national courts without the intervention of a legal measure designed to transpose Community law ... into domestic law.

Similarly, in Case 34/73 *Variola*, the Court of Justice stated that:

> In the fourth and fifth questions, the Court is, in effect, asked to determine whether the disputed provisions of the Regulations can be introduced into the legal order of Member States by internal measures reproducing the contents of Community provisions in such a way that the subject-matter is brought under national law, and the jurisdiction of the Court is thereby affected.

> The direct application of a Regulation means that its entry into force and its application in favour of or against those subject to it are independent of any measure of reception into national law.

> By virtue of the obligations arising from the Treaty and assumed on ratification, Member States are under a duty not to obstruct the direct applicability inherent in Regulations and other rules of Community law.

> Strict compliance with this obligation is an indispensable condition of simultaneous and uniform application of Community Regulations throughout the Community.

Direct applicability, which strictly speaking only applies to Regulations, relates to how provisions of Community law enter the legal order of the Member States. The principle of direct effect on the other hand concerns the effectiveness of provisions of Community law once they enter the national legal systems. Although closely related, the two principles should be considered separately.

In *Costa v ENEL*, the Court of Justice stated that Community law binds both Member States and individuals and also that the national courts of the Member States are bound to apply Community law. As we have seen when examining the definitions of the binding Community acts in Article 249 (formerly 189), such acts may well create rights for individuals which may be relied upon by them in national courts. And, if this is so as regards Community legislation (a secondary source), then, although the

Treaty does not state as such, it must also be the case as regards Treaty provisions themselves (a primary source).

In the famous *Van Gend en Loos* case in 1963, the principle of direct effect, the clearest legal indicator of supranationality, was fully explained by the Court of Justice. In the course of answering questions regarding the nature and effect of one of the Treaty's customs union rules (Article 12 (now 25)) put to it by a Dutch court called upon to decide a case brought by a Dutch company against the national customs authorities, the Court ruled that this provision of Community law 'produces direct effects and creates individual rights which national courts must protect'. The Court stressed the constitutional nature of the Treaty – 'this Treaty is more than an agreement which merely creates mutual obligations between the contracting States' – and thus a consequent need to provide 'direct legal protection of the individual rights of ... nationals'. These rights find their Community law corollary in *obligations* which rest upon others – in this case the Dutch State. Because the Article in question was 'ideally adapted to produce direct effects in the legal relationship between Member States and their subjects', it enabled the plaintiff company, financially threatened by the breach of its Treaty obligations by the Dutch State, to assert its rights before the national court.

As Brown and Jacobs have explained:

> The notion of the direct effect of Community law, coupled with the jurisdiction of the Court to give preliminary rulings and so to determine the scope of the individual's rights and obligations, is a more powerful weapon [than Articles 169 and 170 (now 226 and 227)]. The individual has no direct remedy, before the Court, against the default of a State. The remedy lies with the national court, with the use of Article 177 where necessary. In this way, the national courts enforce, if necessary against their own State, the rights conferred on the individual by the Treaty.

Case 26/62 *Van Gend en Loos*

In September 1960, VG imported into the Netherlands from West Germany a quantity of a chemical product known as ureaformaldehyde.

In December 1959, a Dutch statute had been passed which brought into force modifications of the Benelux tariff system as a result of acceptance of the Brussels Nomenclature, a measure designed to secure international unification of the classification of goods for customs purposes. Regrouping of goods under the nomenclature resulted in an increase in the amount of duty payable on ureaformaldehyde to 8 per cent on an *'ad valorem'* basis.

However, Article 12 EEC had come into force as regards intra-Community trade on 1 January 1958:

> Article 12: Member States shall refrain from introducing between themselves any new customs duties on imports or exports or any charges having equivalent effect, and from increasing those which they already apply in their trade with each other.

VG contended that on 1 January 1958 the duty payable under Dutch law on the product in question was 3 per cent and they objected to paying the additional 5 per cent.

The Customs Inspector having rejected their claim, VG appealed to the Dutch Tariefcommissie (Customs Court) in Amsterdam. Under Article 177, the

Tariefcommissie certified two questions to the Court of Justice in Luxembourg regarding the nature of Article 12:

1   Does Article 12 have the effect of national law as claimed by VG, and may individuals derive rights from it which a national court must protect?

2   If the answer is affirmative, has there been an unlawful increase in customs duties or merely a reasonable modification of the duties which, although bringing about an increase, is not prohibited by Article 12?

The governments of Belgium, West Germany and the Netherlands, and the EEC Commission filed additional memoranda with the Court. All three governments argued that Article 12 merely created obligations for Member States and did not therefore create rights for individuals. A claim might be brought against a Member State which broke its Treaty obligations under Article 169 or 170 EEC.

The Court ruled as follows:

> The first question of the Tariefcommissie is whether Article 12 of the Treaty has direct application [that is, direct effect, as explained earlier and in the sense actually used by the Court here] in national law in the sense that the nationals of Member States may on the basis of this Article lay claim to rights which the national court must protect.
>
> To ascertain whether the provisions of an international treaty extend so far in their effects, it is necessary to consider the spirit, the general scheme and the wording of those provisions.
>
> The objective of the EEC Treaty, which is to establish a Common Market, the functioning of which is of direct concern to interested parties in the Community, implies that this Treaty is more than an agreement which merely creates mutual obligations between the contracting states. This view is confirmed by the preamble to the Treaty which refers not only to governments but to peoples. It is also confirmed more specifically by the establishment of institutions endowed with sovereign rights, the exercise of which affects Member States and also their citizens. Furthermore, it must be noted that the nationals of the states brought together in the Community are called upon to co-operate in the functioning of this Community through the intermediary of the European Parliament and the Economic and Social Committee.
>
> In addition, the task assigned to the Court of Justice under Article 177, the object of which is to secure uniform interpretation of the Treaty by national courts and tribunals, confirms that the states have acknowledged that Community law has an authority which can be invoked by their nationals before those courts and tribunals.
>
> The conclusion to be drawn from this is that the Community constitutes a new legal order of international law for the benefit of which the states have limited their sovereign rights, albeit within limited fields, and the subjects of which comprise not only Member States but also their nationals. Independently of the legislation of Member States, Community law therefore not only imposes obligations on individuals but is also intended to confer upon them rights which become part of their legal heritage. These rights arise not only where they are expressly granted by the Treaty, but also by reason of obligations which the Treaty imposes in a clearly defined way upon individuals as well as upon the Member States and upon the institutions of the Community.
>
> With regard to the general scheme of the Treaty as it relates to customs duties and charges having equivalent effect it must be emphasised that Article 9, which bases the Community upon a customs union, includes as an essential provision the

prohibition of customs duties and charges. This provision is found at the beginning of the part of the Treaty which defines the 'Foundations of the Community'. It is applied and explained by Article 12.

The wording of Article 12 contains a clear and unconditional prohibition which is not a positive but a negative obligation. This obligation, moreover, is not qualified by any reservation on the part of states which would make its implementation conditional upon a positive legislative measure enacted under national law. The very nature of this prohibition makes it ideally adapted to produce direct effects in the legal relationship between Member States and their subjects.

The implementation of Article 12 does not require any legislative intervention on the part of the states. The fact that under this Article it is the Member States who are made the subject of the negative obligation does not imply that their nationals cannot benefit from this obligation.

In addition, the argument based on Articles 169 and 170 of the Treaty put forward by the three Governments which have submitted observations to the Court in their statements of the case is misconceived. The fact that these Articles of the Treaty enable the Commission and the Member States to bring before the Court a state which has not fulfilled its obligations does not mean that individuals cannot plead these obligations, should the occasion arise, before a national court, any more than the fact that the Treaty places at the disposal of the Commission ways of ensuring that obligations imposed upon those subject to the Treaty are observed, precludes the possibility, in actions between individuals before a national court, of pleading infringements of these obligations.

A restriction of the guarantees against an infringement of Article 12 by Member States to the procedures under Article 169 and 170 would remove all direct legal protection of the individual rights of their nationals. There is the risk that recourse to the procedure under these Articles would be ineffective if it were to occur after the implementation of a national decision taken contrary to the provisions of the Treaty.

The vigilance of individuals concerned to protect their rights amounts to an effective supervision in addition to the supervision entrusted by Articles 169 and 170 to the diligence of the Commission and of the Member States.

It follows from the foregoing considerations that, according to the spirit, the general scheme and the wording of the Treaty, Article 12 must be interpreted as producing direct effects and creating individual rights which national courts must protect.

...

It follows from the wording and the general scheme of Article 12 of the Treaty that, in order to ascertain whether customs duties or charges having equivalent effect have been increased contrary to the prohibition contained in the said Article, regard must be had to the customs duties and charges actually applied at the date of the entry into force of the Treaty.

Further, with regard to the prohibition in Article 12 of the Treaty, such an illegal increase may arise from a re-arrangement of the tariff resulting in the classification of the product under a more highly taxed heading and from an actual increase in the rate of customs duty.

It is of little importance how the increase in customs duties occurred when, after the Treaty entered into force, the same product in the same Member State was subjected to a higher rate of duty.

The application of Article 12, in accordance with the interpretation given above, comes within the jurisdiction of the national court which must enquire whether the dutiable product, in this case ureaformaldehyde originating in the Federal Republic of Germany, is charged under the customs measures brought into force in the Netherlands with an import duty higher than that with which it was charged on 1 January 1958.

The Court has no jurisdiction to check the validity of the conflicting views on this subject which have been submitted to it during the proceedings but must leave them to be determined by the national courts ...

The costs incurred by the Commission of the EEC and the Member States which have submitted their observations to the Court are not recoverable, and as these proceedings are, in so far as the parties to the main action are concerned, a step in the action pending before the Tariefcommissie, the decision as to costs is a matter for that court.

On those grounds,

Upon reading the pleadings,

Upon hearing the report of the Judge-Rapporteur,

Upon hearing the opinion of the Advocate General,

Having regard to Articles 9, 12, 14, 169, 170 and 177 of the Treaty establishing the European Economic Community,

Having regard to the Rules of Procedure of the Court of Justice of the European Communities,

THE COURT in answer to the questions referred to it for a preliminary ruling by the Tariefcommissie by decision of 16 August 1962, hereby rules:

1   Article 12 of the Treaty establishing the European Economic Community produces direct effects and creates individual rights which national courts must protect.

2   In order to ascertain whether customs duties or charges having equivalent effect have been increased contrary to the prohibition contained in Article 12 of the Treaty, regard must be had to the duties and charges actually applied by the Member State in question at the date of the entry into force of the Treaty.

   Such an increase can arise both from a re-arrangement of the tariff resulting in the classification of the product under a more highly taxed heading and from an increase in the rate of customs duty applied.

3   The decision as to costs in these proceedings is a matter for the Tariefcommissie.

The decision in *Van Gend en Loos* dramatically increased the impact and effectiveness of Community law in the Member States. It is a decision which ultimately rests on two related factors: first, on the Court's perception of the federal and constitutional (as opposed to international) nature of the Treaty, key provisions of which bear directly upon the individual and, secondly, on the Court's clear appreciation that the establishment of the customs union was a key element of negative integration within the Community – and that Community law must be fully effective in that respect. It is 'undoubtedly the richest and most creative of all Community cases, and one in which virtually every later development can – at least with hindsight – be seen to have its germ' (Rudden).

Thus, the case law of the Court of Justice clearly shows that a *directly effective* provision of Community law, whether of the Treaty or a legally binding secondary act, always prevails (takes precedence) over a conflicting provision of national law. In such cases, individual Community rights must be protected irrespective of whether the Community provision takes effect before, or after, the national provision. The case which follows concerns the impact of a Community Regulation within Italian national law. A Regulation, as we have seen, is directly applicable. The Court of Justice assumes that it is therefore 'a direct source of rights and duties for all those affected thereby', that is, that direct effect is the norm for Regulations. (On this point and possible confusion between direct applicability and direct effect, see also Chapter 8.)

Case 106/77 *Amministrazione delle Finanze v Simmenthal*

S imported a consignment of beef from France into Italy. In accordance with an Italian statute of 1970, the company was charged fees for veterinary and public health inspections made at the frontier. S sued for the return of their money in the Italian courts, pleading that the charges were contrary to EEC law. Following an Article 177 reference, the Court of Justice held that the inspections were contrary to Article 30, being measures having an equivalent effect to a quantitative restriction, and the fees were contrary to Article 12 being charges equivalent to customs duties. The Court also held that this question of animal and public health had been governed by EC Regulations since 1964 and 1968.

In consequence, the national court ordered the Italian Finance Ministry to repay the fees charged. The Ministry, however, pleaded the national statute of 1970 and argued that, under the Italian Constitution, this bound them until such time as it was set aside by the Constitutional Court. Following a further reference, the Court held:

> The main purpose of the first question is to ascertain what consequences flow from the direct applicability of a provision of Community law in the event of incompatibility with a subsequent legislative provision of a Member State.

> Direct applicability in such circumstances means that rules of Community law must be fully and uniformly applied in all Member States from the date of their entry into force and for so long as they continue in force.

> These provisions are therefore a direct source of rights and duties for all those affected thereby, whether Member States or individuals, who are parties to legal relationships under Community law.

> This consequence also concerns any national court whose task it is as an organ of a Member State to protect, in a case within its jurisdiction, the rights conferred upon individuals by Community law.

> Furthermore, in accordance with the principle of the precedence of Community law, the relationship between provisions of the Treaty and directly applicable measures of the institutions on the one hand and the national law of the Member States on the other is such that those provisions and measures not only by their entry into force render automatically inapplicable any conflicting provision of current national law but – in so far as they are an integral part of, and take precedence in, the legal order applicable in the territory of each of the Member States – also preclude the valid adoption of new national legislative measures to the extent to which they would be incompatible with Community provisions.

> Indeed, any recognition that national legislative measures which encroach upon the field within which the Community exercises its legislative power or which are otherwise incompatible with the provisions of Community law had any legal effect would amount to a corresponding denial of the effectiveness of obligations undertaken unconditionally and irrevocably by Member States pursuant to the Treaty and would thus imperil the very foundations of the Community.

The same conclusion emerges from the structure of Article 177 of the Treaty which provides that any court or tribunal of a Member State is entitled to make a reference to the Court whenever it considers that a preliminary ruling on a question of interpretation or validity relating to Community law is necessary to enable it to give judgment.

The effectiveness of that provision would be impaired if the national court were prevented from forthwith applying Community law in accordance with the decision or the case law of the Court.

It follows from the foregoing that every national court must, in a case within its jurisdiction, apply Community law in its entirety and protect rights which the latter confers on individuals and must accordingly set aside any provision of national law which may conflict with it, whether prior or subsequent to the Community rule.

Accordingly any provision of a national legal system and any legislative, administrative, or judicial practice which might impair the effectiveness of Community law by withholding from the national court having jurisdiction to apply such law the power to do everything necessary at the moment of its application to set aside national legislative provisions which might prevent Community rules from having full force and effect are incompatible with those requirements which are the very essence of Community law.

This would be the case in the event of a conflict between a provision of Community law and a subsequent national law if the solution of the conflict were to be reserved for an authority with a discretion of its own, other than the court called upon to apply Community law, even if such an impediment to the full effectiveness of Community law were only temporary.

The first question should therefore be answered to the effect that a national court which is called upon, within the limits of its jurisdiction, to apply provisions of Community law is under a duty to give full effect to those provisions, if necessary refusing of its own motion to apply any conflicting provision of national legislation, even if adopted subsequently, and it is not necessary for the court to request or await the prior setting aside of such provision by legislation or other constitutional means ...

It follows from the answer to the first question that national courts must protect rights conferred by provisions of the Community legal order and that it is not necessary for such courts to request or await the actual setting aside by the national authorities empowered so to act of any national measures which might impede the direct and immediate application of Community rules ...

The need for national courts to set aside the law of their own country when it is found to conflict with directly effective Community law is a point which will be seen to arise in many of the cases which follow, for example, *Factortame*, discussed in Chapter 3 and Chapter 20. Such national law must be repealed by the national legislature and the failure to do so amounts to a breach of Article 10 (formerly 5) of the Treaty.

Reaction in the Member States

As these cases illustrate, some Member States, at least initially, encountered difficulties in accepting the supremacy of directly effective Community law in their courts. That the Court of Justice would brook no interference with the requirement that Community rules be uniformly applied by national courts throughout the Member States is thrown into sharp relief in the following German case. It concerns the question of a possible conflict between a provision of a Regulation (secondary Community law) and fundamental human rights provisions of the West German Constitution. The case also illustrates the point that the validity of Community law may not be tested against provisions of national law.

Case 11/70 *Internationale Handelsgesellschaft*

In order to export certain agricultural products an export licence was required. If the products were not exported during the period of the licence's validity, the exporter forfeited a deposit. The company, having lost a deposit of DM 17,000, claimed that this Community system, based on two Community Regulations and operated through the West German National Cereals Intervention Agency, was contrary to the fundamental human rights provisions of the German Constitution. In particular, it was in breach of the principle of *proportionality*: it imposed obligations (relating to deposits) on individuals that were not necessary for the attainment of the intended objective (the regulation of the cereals market).

The question of the validity of one of the Regulations was referred to the Court of Justice under Article 177(1)(b) (now 234(1)(b)) by the Frankfurt Administrative Court. The Court stated that the validity of Community measures could not be judged according to the principles of national law; Community criteria only might be applied.

The Court continued:

> Recourse to the legal rules or concepts of national law in order to judge the validity of measures adopted by the institutions of the Community would have an adverse effect on the uniformity and efficiency of Community law. The validity of such measures can only be judged in the light of Community law. In fact, the law stemming from the Treaty, an independent source of law, cannot because of its very nature be overridden by rules of national law, however framed, without being deprived of its character as Community law and without the legal basis of the Community itself being called in question. Therefore the validity of a Community measure or its effect within a Member State cannot be affected by allegations that it runs counter to either fundamental rights as formulated by the constitution of that State or the principles of a national constitutional structure.

> However, an examination should be made as to whether or not any analogous guarantee inherent in Community law has been disregarded. In fact, respect for fundamental rights forms an integral part of the general principles of law protected by the Court of Justice.

> The protection of such rights, whilst inspired by the constitutional traditions common to the Member States, must be ensured within the framework of the structure and objectives of the Community. It must therefore be ascertained, in the light of the doubts expressed by the Verwaltungsgericht, whether the system of deposits has infringed rights of a fundamental nature, respect for which must be ensured in the Community legal system ...

> It follows from all these considerations that the system of licences involving an undertaking, by those who apply for them, to import or export, guaranteed by a deposit, does not violate any right of a fundamental nature. The machinery of deposits constitutes an appropriate method, for the purposes of Article 40(3) of the Treaty, for carrying out the common organisation of the agricultural markets and also conforms to the requirements of Article 43.

However, the referring Frankfurt court *did not apply* the Court's ruling that the Regulation did not contravene the Community concept of human rights. Instead, it made a reference to the West German Federal Constitutional Court which, drawing attention to the absence of a 'codified catalogue of human rights' at Community level, allowed the reference and held that Community measures were *subject to the fundamental rights provisions of the German Constitution*. Nevertheless, it ruled that the Community Regulation in issue was not contrary to the Constitution. Thus, although the Federal Constitutional Court refused to acknowledge the absolute supremacy of Community law, an open rift with the Court of Justice was averted.

By 1986, however, the Federal Constitutional Court felt sufficiently confident regarding the protection of human rights at Community level that in *Wünsche Handelsgesellschaft* it reversed its previous decision in the following terms:

> Since 1974, the Community has advanced convincingly in the protection of human rights both in the adoption in a legally significant manner of texts whereby the institutions agree to be guided as a legal duty by respect for fundamental rights and by the development of case law by the European Court. The consequent connection of human rights guarantees in the national constitutions and European Convention on Human Rights on the one hand and the general principles of Community law on the other obviates the continuing need for a catalogue of fundamental rights. In view of these developments, it is now the position that, so long as the European Communities and particularly the case law of the European Court generally ensure an effective protection of fundamental rights as against the sovereign powers of the Community which is to be regarded as substantially similar to the protection required unconditionally by the German Constitution, and in so far as they generally safeguard the essential content of fundamental rights, the German Federal Constitutional Court will no longer exercise its jurisdiction to decide on the applicability of secondary Community law cited as the legal basis for any acts of German courts or authorities within the sovereign jurisdiction of the Federal Republic of Germany; and it will no longer review such legislation by the standard of the fundamental rights contained in the German Constitution. References to the Constitutional Court under Article 100(1) of the Constitution for that purpose are therefore inadmissible.

On the strength of this development, together with similar ones in other Member States, it is possible to say that the courts (if not some politicians) of the Member States have now accepted the doctrine of the supremacy of directly effective Community law. Following the *Factortame* direct effect decision, the Master of the Rolls, Sir Thomas Bingham, stated that: 'The supremacy of Community law has been accepted by the English courts with a readiness, and applied with a loyalty, which, if equalled in one or two other Member States, has probably been exceeded in none.'

In the light of these (at one time) controversial cases on direct effect, it is important to consider the attention they direct towards the role of the Member States in the development of the Community and the duty of solidarity which rests on them by virtue of Article 10 of the Treaty.

The Community, principally through the exercise of its Treaty powers by the Commission, is concerned to achieve full and effective implementation of the policies within its competence. However, in many cases, the Commission, as seen in the discussion of competence in the previous chapter, must, in order to achieve its aims, work with and through one of a variety of national authorities (government departments, customs authorities, agricultural intervention agencies, etc). Within this working relationship, Member States and their agencies are required to adopt certain courses of action or to refrain from doing so. This can involve an obligation to adopt new legislation (or secondary legislation), to revise existing legislation or to repeal existing legislation.

Similarly, national courts, often in co-operation with the Court of Justice through the medium of the preliminary rulings procedure of Article 234 (formerly 177), have a duty, based again on Article 10, to ensure the full effectiveness of Community law within the scope of their jurisdictions. Where there is a Community dimension to a case, national courts and tribunals are obliged to interpret Community law (or request an interpretation from the Court of Justice), to apply Community law and to enforce it.

Interpretations of Community law by the Court of Justice are definitive in the courts and tribunals of the Member States. It may also, as seen, be called upon to assess the validity of the acts of the Community institutions. It may not exceed its powers as laid down in the Treaty but it does not look to a Parliament as supreme law maker. It is not bound by its own decisions but frequently cites such decisions to indicate a consistent line of reasoning. Its crucial role in the development of the Community will become increasingly apparent in succeeding chapters.

REFERENCES AND FURTHER READING

Collins, L, *European Community Law in the United Kingdom*, 2000, Chapter 1, 'Introduction'.

Gormley, LW (ed), *Kapteyn and VerLoren van Themaat's Introduction to the Law of the European Communities*, 1998, Chapters 2, 3 and 5.

Hartley, TC, *The Foundations of European Community Law*, 1998, Chapters 3 and 4.

Mackenzie Stuart (Lord), *The European Communities and the Rule of Law*, 1977, Chapter 1.

Mancini, F, 'The making of a constitution for Europe' (1989) 26 CML Rev 595.

Rudden, B, *Basic Community Cases*, 1997, Part 1.

Sorensen, M, 'Autonomous legal orders' (1983) 32 ICLQ 559.

Usher, J, *European Community Law and National Law: The Irreversible Transfer*, 1981, comments on *Van Gend en Loos*, etc.

Weiler, J, 'The Community system: the dual character of supranationalism' (1981) 1 YEL 267.

Weiler, J, 'Community, Member States and European integration: is the law relevant?' (1982) 21 JCMS 39.

Wyatt, D, 'New legal order, or old?' (1982) 7 EL Rev 147.

CHAPTER 5

LAW MAKING AND THE COMMUNITY'S POLITICAL INSTITUTIONS

INTRODUCTION

Although the ECSC, the EEC and Euratom were originally endowed with separate institutions, following changes in the structure in the intervening years (as seen in Chapter 1), by the time the Single European Act came into effect in 1987, it was correct in both a practical and formal sense to say that there was a single institutional framework comprising the European Parliament, the Council, the Commission and the Court of Justice: Article 4 EEC. The Maastricht Treaty preserved this unitary framework (Article 4 (now 7) EC) and added the Court of Auditors, first established in 1975, as a fifth Community institution within the first pillar.

Article 7 (formerly 4) also provides that: 'Each institution shall act within the limits of the powers conferred upon it by this Treaty.' Their powers are therefore only those which have been expressly (or impliedly) conferred upon, or *attributed* to, them by the Member States under the Treaties. Thus, any allegedly invalid legislative act of any of the three main *political* institutions (the Council, Commission and Parliament), for example, an act of the Council adopted upon an allegedly incorrect Treaty base, can become the basis for an action for annulment under Article 230 (formerly 173) (see Chapter 19).

Since 1958, the Council and the Commission have been assisted in an advisory capacity by the *Economic and Social Committee* and, in a further move towards the decentralisation of policy making, the TEU created a similar *Committee of the Regions*: see now Article 7(2). The *European Central Bank*, with law making powers within the field of monetary policy, has since been established under Article 8 (formerly 4a) and the Luxembourg based *European Investment Bank*, which has acted since 1958 as a prime source of investment finance for Community projects, is accorded further legal recognition in Article 9 (formerly 4b).

The Community's four main institutions (the three political institutions and the Court of Justice), acting within their powers, are responsible for the performance of the legislative, executive and judicial functions of the Community. However, as should already be appreciated, and contrary to basic notions of the 'separation of powers', the legislative function still rests *primarily* with the Council of Ministers, although the powers of the Parliament within this field have, as we have seen, steadily increased since 1958. This has been most clearly significant where, since Maastricht, the Article 251 (formerly 189b) EC co-decision legislative procedure applies – a procedure effective from 1993 in an ever increasing number of Treaty policy Articles following further Treaty amendments.

The Commission, which represents the Community interest (in contrast to the Council's identification with the interests of the Member States), is not only 'the guardian of the Treaties', overseeing and if necessary enforcing (particularly vis à vis the Member States) the execution of existing Community policies, but it is also both the main proposer of new Community policy initiatives (in the form of draft legislation) for consideration by the Council and Parliament, and the body entrusted by the Council with the implementation of such policies as have been adopted by means of legislative powers delegated to it by the Council: Article 202 (formerly 145), indent three.

Commenting on the institutional structure in 1989, Gormley has said:

> The institutional structure is of decisive importance for the balance of power within the Community. The two most important actors are undoubtedly the Council of Ministers and ... the Commission. It is on the co-operation of these two Institutions that the implementation of the Treaties is largely dependent ...

> At the outset the European Parliament – the Institution which involves the peoples of the Member States in the activities of the Community – played only a modest role. Since 1979 the Parliament has been directly elected and its role has grown in importance. The Court of Justice also plays an important part in the institutional structure as it has to ensure the observance of the law in the implementation of the Treaty by the Institutions and the Member States. Its jurisdiction enables the Court to contribute to the maintenance of the balance of rights and duties both amongst the Institutions themselves and between them and the Member States. The Court is also in the position of being able to ensure the legal protection of private parties, which is of great importance because of the limited nature of parliamentary supervision of the behaviour of the institutions.

At the present time, however, as regards the political institutions, it can be said that the Community's legislative function and powers are divided between the three of them.

Over and above this view of the Community's institutional structure as based on Article 7, it is also essential to take due account (as in the historical survey of the Community's development in Chapter 1) of a further, all important political body, the European Council.

THE EUROPEAN COUNCIL

The summit conferences of Community leaders which began in 1969 were put on a formal basis in 1974 and brought within the framework of Community law by virtue of Article 2 of the Single European Act. Article 4 (formerly D) of the TEU states that:

> The European Council shall provide the Union with the necessary impetus for its development and shall define the general political guidelines thereof. The European Council shall bring together the Heads of State or of Government of the Member States and the President of the Commission. They shall be assisted by the Ministers for Foreign Affairs of the Member States and by a member of the Commission ...

The European Council, which meets at least twice a year and is presided over by the Member State which holds the presidency of the Council of Ministers, is not itself normally engaged in formal Treaty legislative and political co-operation processes, and the adoption of its policy guidelines (within the institutional, economic, social and foreign policy or security fields) rests largely with the Council of Ministers in Brussels unless Treaty amendments are involved. In terms of 'impetus', the European Council has been heavily involved, amongst other things, in the establishment of the European Monetary System in 1979, the introduction of direct elections to the European Parliament in the same year, and successive enlargements of the Community/Union. At the Maastricht Summit of December 1991, crucial questions concerning further economic and political integration – EMU, common foreign and security policy, the admission of new Member States and the reform of the institutions – all lay on the European Council's table. As the following extract from an article by Adrian Hamilton, published in *The Observer* in October 1991, indicates, a complex mixture of national interests and priorities will often make for difficult decisions in the Council and, perhaps inevitably, for trade-offs and compromises:

EC's EMBRACE OF NEW ORDER LACKS POLITICAL PASSION

One immediate victim of the collapse of Communism may be the drive towards a tighter Europe. That at any rate is what John Major seems to believe and President François Mitterrand to fear, judging by their meeting last week.

They have their own reasons for voicing their separate views, of course. With little to offer at home, Mitterrand is anxious to show himself still the master of a new Europe, just as Major, with a party conference in view, would be happy to see the contentious issue of European federalism disappear into the sands of a fragmenting Soviet Union.

What is more curious is that Major seems to have been so surprised that his French host should have reaffirmed so publicly both his federalism and his suspicions that the British would try to undermine them.

The French and the British see these things differently. To the French – as to others – the European Community is very much a political association and events in Eastern Europe and the Soviet Union make it all the more imperative to accelerate the integration of its existing members.

There are good hard commercial reasons why the French should be reluctant to open up the Common Market to Polish fruit or to share too much of the wealth of the Twelve with the poorer neighbours to the east. But there are also good political reasons why the French should see in an integrated Europe a means of tying down the Germans to a common policy.

To John Major and to his Foreign Secretary, Douglas Hurd, on the other hand, the EC is primarily an economic, not a political ideal.

Despite the obvious differences with his predecessor on the style of discussion with our European colleagues (and the real differences on ERM entry), on this Mr Major and Mrs Thatcher are as one. The Common Market should be just that. On defence, the British remain Atlanticists; on foreign policy, both Hurd and Major are essentially pragmatic nationalists who see the Community as a balance of bilateral arrangements shifting from issue to issue.

In that vision, a wider Europe makes more sense than a narrower one. Not for them Delors' [the then French President of the Commission] vision of a tighter grouping of the existing 12 in which majority voting is the 'tiger in the tank' ...

Although it may be argued that the existence of the intergovernmental European Council has diluted the supranational character of the Community/Union, it will be recalled that Jean Monnet himself conceded that the way forward lay with the Council, as that was where 'authority' resided as the questions and answers moved into the realms of 'higher politics'. In any event, the Commission fought hard in the late 1970s for a full voice within the Council (see Jenkins in References and Further Reading at the end of the chapter) and, as the Internal Market programme illustrated, the Commission and the European Council have often forged successful partnerships.

At Nice in late 2000 (as seen in Chapter 1), the European Council in large part restricted itself to measures considered necessary for 'preparing the institutions of the European Union to function in an enlarged Union'. Steps were taken concerning the composition, size, appointments and functioning of the institutions, in particular the voting rights governing the adoption of legislative decisions. The main aim was to enhance the operational efficiency and democratic legitimacy of the Union. These matters are dealt with in the following pages – and as regards the judicial system in Chapter 7.

THE COUNCIL OF THE EUROPEAN UNION
(THE COUNCIL OF MINISTERS):
ARTICLES 202–10 (FORMERLY 145–54)

Introduction

The Council of the European Union (formerly of the European Communities) is the principal political and legislative organ of the Community/Union. Often referred to as the Council of Ministers, it is based in Brussels (although some meetings are held in Luxembourg) and consists of representatives of the Member States. Article 203 (formerly 146) states that:

> The Council shall consist of a representative of each Member Sate at ministerial level, authorized to commit the Government of that Member State ...

The main function of the Council is 'to take decisions' (Article 202 (formerly 145), indent two), that is, in the main to decide whether or not to adopt Community legislation.

It is *not* a fixed body but whoever the representatives in attendance in Brussels are and whatever their responsibilities, the powers of the Council remain the same. When foreign and security policy, general institutional and other broad policy matters are on the agenda, the Foreign Ministers of the Member States make up what is called the General Affairs Council. For other more specialist matters, for example, economic and financial affairs (the Ecofin Council), agriculture, transport or social security, the appropriate ministers will attend for the legislative and other business in hand. A representative of the Commission also takes part in Council proceedings, but does not have a vote.

The Presidency of the Council presently rotates among the Member States at six-monthly intervals, but this system will certainly require revision following enlargement. Although the President has the role of honest broker in the search for agreement between the Member States, he or she will usually be keen to achieve the maximum progress during his or her term of office. The latter ambition may defeat the former function as the Dutch discovered in the period leading up to the crucial decisions on further 'positive' integration scheduled for December 1991. See the following article, which was reported in *The Times* on 2 October of that year:

LUBBERS LICKS EC TREATY WOUNDS

from George Brock in Brussels

Ruud Lubbers, the Dutch prime minister, conferred yesterday with Hans van den Broek, his foreign minister, on how to pick up the pieces after EC foreign ministers rejected their draft for federal union by 10:2 on Monday. His government was mauled by yesterday morning's Dutch papers. 'One of the worst political blunders ever', thundered the conservative *De Telegraaf*.

But with the return to the Luxembourg treaty draft, the pressure on Britain also returns. Jacques Delors, the federalist president of the European Commission, has treated the whole fuss over the Dutch text in a lofty 'much ado about nothing' manner and pointed out that agreement on several key points is in sight.

The outlines of a monetary union treaty are nearly all agreed. Norman Lamont, the Chancellor, plainly believes his officials have helped write a treaty which both keeps Britain in and allows it to stay out. No such flexibility exists in the talks on political union. There has so far been no real meeting of minds – let alone the unanimity which would allow treaty drafting – on several questions of principle.

The EC has not agreed how to handle foreign policy. Thanks to the disappearance of the Dutch text, foreign policy is unlikely to be integrated into the central system. But most EC countries want, or say they want, majority voting in foreign policy. Britain wants co-operation decided by unanimity. Should the EC have a defence policy and armed forces independent of the United States? Britain, Germany and France have come nowhere near agreeing on this question, which will also confront them at the Nato summit next month.

Britain will probably concede that the EC should start to make policy in areas where Brussels has no law making power at the moment. Some extension of the EC's power to set Community wide standards for education, health, welfare and transport is likely.

But the extension of majority voting is a far more sensitive issue. On that and on new powers for the European Parliament, Britain does not look set to yield very much.

Although the Maastricht summit does not open until 9 December, the effective deadline for settling contentious points is the middle of November, so that the treaty text can be completely ready for Maastricht. The Dutch government has scheduled a three day meeting of EC foreign ministers in the North Sea resort of Noordwijk on 13 November. That meeting will decide the treaty's fate.

Council Working Parties and COREPER

Article 207 (formerly 151) states that:

(1) A committee consisting of the Permanent Representatives of the Member States shall be responsible for preparing the work of the Council and for carrying out the tasks assigned to it by the Council ...

Before a Commission proposal reaches the Council, it will usually be examined in detail first by a Council working party of national technical experts. When agreement is reached, the proposal goes forward to the Committee of Permanent Representatives of the Member States in Brussels (COREPER), as it does in the absence of agreement in the hope that it will be forthcoming at the higher level. COREPER itself is divided into two bodies, deputy Permanent Representatives (COREPER I) for technical, economic issues and Permanent Representatives (COREPER II) for more political questions.

Proposals agreed by a working party receive formal approval and proceed to Part A of a Council agenda. They will normally be adopted by the Council without further discussion. Proposals not yet agreed may be agreed by a COREPER committee and proceed as outlined above. If COREPER fails (even with Commission involvement) to agree, the matter is placed on Part B of the Council agenda. Agreement may then be reached in the Council, possibly on the basis of a 'package deal' in which several decisions are put together so that concessions made by a Member State on one issue are balanced against gains on another. Proposals on which there is failure to agree are passed back to the working party.

Decision Making and Voting

Article 202 (formerly 145) provides that:

> To ensure that the objectives set out in this Treaty are attained, the Council shall, in accordance with the provisions of this Treaty:
>
> – ensure co-ordination of the general economic policies of the Member States;
>
> – have power to take decisions;
>
> – confer on the Commission, in the acts which the Council adopts, powers for the implementation of the rules which the Council lays down.
>
> The Council may impose certain requirements in respect of the exercise of these powers ...

Indent one assumed increasing importance, as seen in Chapter 1, as the Community (or the larger part of it) moved through the third stage necessary for the achievement of EMU. This is a task which clearly requires the co-operation of the Member States: see Article 4 (formerly 3a). Indent three establishes that power to implement acts of the Council is conferred on the Commission (see below). It is the deceptively simply worded indent two which confers on the Council its key role (together with the Parliament) regarding the adoption of legislation, based upon and developing the framework established by the Treaty itself. This legislative process, voting in the Council and the relationship of the Council to the other political institutions and other bodies within that process will be examined later in this chapter.

THE EUROPEAN COMMISSION: ARTICLES 211–19 (FORMERLY 155–63)

Composition

Article 9 of the Merger Treaty of 1965 stated that:

> A Commission of the European Communities ... is hereby established. This Commission shall take the place of the High Authority of the European Coal and Steel Community, the Commission of the European Economic Community and the Commission of the European Atomic Energy Community.

The Commission (since 1993, the European Commission), whose headquarters are in Brussels, presently consists of 20 members (Commissioners) 'whose independence is beyond doubt' and who shall in the performance of their duties, 'neither seek nor take instructions from any government or from any other body': see Article 213 (formerly 157). The pre-Nice *composition* of the Commission was of two Commissioners from each of the five largest Member States (Germany, the UK, France, Italy and Spain) and one from each of the remainder. A ToA Protocol anticipated that upon enlargement of the Union, no Member State should have two Commissioners – subject to modifications to the weighting of votes in the Council (see below) in favour of States losing a Commissioner, conditional upon the agreement of all (old and new) Member States.

Article 4(1) of the Nice Treaty's Enlargement Protocol states that when the new Commission takes office in January 2005, the Commission will have the same number of members as there are Member States. The five largest States will lose their second Commissioner and each new Member State may nominate a Commissioner. Upon the accession of the twenty-seventh (now twenty-fifth) Member State, a new rotation system enabling each Member State to nominate a Commissioner will come into effect. It will be 'based on the principle of equality' as laid down by the Council acting unanimously: Article 4(2). This process will reduce the size of the Commission to what will be considered optimum size, but it will certainly cause controversy and prove difficult to operate, particularly as Article 4(3) provides that each college of Commissioners must reflect 'the demographic and geographical range of all the Member States of the Union'. These changes will necessitate amendments to Article 213 EC.

The Nice Treaty itself amends Article 214 EC regarding the *appointment* of the Commission with effect from January 2005. The nominee President is chosen by the Council (at Heads of State and Government level) by a qualified majority and with Parliament approval. Remaining Commissioners are to be selected from 'the list ... drawn up in accordance with the proposals made by each Member State' and in agreement with the nominee President. The Commission will then be appointed by a qualified majority of the Council subject to parliamentary approval.

A new version of Article 217 EC gives additional power to the President of the Commission 'to ensure that it acts consistently, efficiently and on the basis of collegiality'. He may reshuffle the allocation of Commission responsibilities (policy portfolios) and a Commissioner 'shall resign if the President so requests, after obtaining the approval of the College'.

The Commission's current president, Romano Prodi, is from Italy and the UK's two members are Neil Kinnock, a Vice President and former Labour Party leader, and Christopher Patten, a former Conservative MP and later Governor of Hong Kong, now in charge of the External Relations portfolio.

The Commission itself is divided into 24 departments known as Directorates General (for example, DG I External Relations; DG IV Competition Policy), each of which is headed by a Director General who is responsible to the relevant Commissioner. DGs are divided into Directorates which in turn are divided into Divisions. In addition, there are a number of specialised services including the Legal Service. The Commission now has a total staff of 16,000, over 3,000 of whom are involved with translation and interpretation duties.

Each Commissioner is assisted by his private office or *Cabinet*, a group of officials appointed by the Commissioner and responsible to him. The *Chefs de Cabinet* meet at regular intervals to co-ordinate activities and prepare for Commission meetings.

Commission decisions are made on a collegiate basis either by decisions taken at its weekly meetings or by a written procedure whereby proposals are circulated to all Commissioners. If no objections are notified within a stated period, the proposal is deemed to have received assent. Objections are referred to a full Commission meeting where decisions are taken by a simple majority vote.

Functions and Powers

The Commission embodies the Community interest and the classic description of the Commission's role identifies three distinct functions: to initiate proposals for legislation, to act as 'guardian of the Treaties', and to execute policies and actions.

The Commission's functions are set out in Article 211 (formerly 155) EC which is indicative of the Commission's central role within the Community order:

> In order to ensure the proper functioning and development of the Common Market, the Commission shall:
>
> – ensure that the provisions of this Treaty and the measures taken by the institutions pursuant thereto are applied;
>
> – formulate recommendations or deliver opinions on matters dealt with in this Treaty, if it expressly so provides or if the Commission considers it necessary;
>
> – have its own power of decision and participate in the shaping of measures taken by the Council and by the European Parliament in the manner provided for in this Treaty;
>
> – exercise the powers conferred on it by the Council for the implementation of the rules laid down by the latter.

(1) The first of these functions, which operate within the context of the proper functioning and development of the Community, places the Commission in the role of *guardian and enforcer of the Treaty*. In order to secure observance of the Treaty and legislative measures taken in pursuance of it, the Commission has the power to initiate proceedings not only against Member States but also against other Community institutions (but not the Court), and against individuals and legal persons, particularly business undertakings.

As regards an action against a *Member State* alleged to be in breach of its Treaty obligations (see Article 10), for example, it has failed to implement a Directive or has placed a ban on intra-Community trade, the Commission may proceed on the basis of Article 226 (formerly 169):

> If the Commission considers that a Member State has failed to fulfil an obligation under this Treaty, it shall deliver a reasoned opinion on the matter after giving the State concerned the opportunity to submit its observations.
>
> If the State concerned does not comply with the opinion within the period laid down by the Commission, the latter may bring the matter before the Court of Justice.

It will be seen that the Commission gives Member States ample opportunity to remedy infringements and at present less than a third of the reasoned opinions issued have lead to Court of Justice rulings. As will be discussed later, the

Commission also has a role to play under Article 227 (formerly 170) (actions between Member States), and further special enforcement proceedings are available to it in relation to, for example, hindrances to the establishment of the internal market: Article 95 (formerly 100a).

Proceedings against *other Community institutions* may now be taken by the Commission under Article 230 (formerly Article 173, as extended by the TEU) against the Council and Parliament jointly, the Council, the Parliament and the Central Bank. Such proceedings are for the purpose of enabling the Court of Justice *to review the legality of binding acts* of these bodies. (Commission acts may similarly be challenged.) An important Commission direct action for the annulment of a Council act, in Case 22/70 *Commission v Council (ERTA)*, will be examined in Chapter 6. Under Article 232 (formerly 175), the Commission may also challenge a *failure to act* by the Council or Parliament and, again, the Commission's own omissions may, in certain circumstances, be similarly challenged.

These inter-institutional conflicts indicate quite clearly the operation of the Rule of Law within the Community: the law makers are also bound by it themselves and, in Hartley's words, 'the legality of government action should be subject to determination by an independent, impartial adjudicatory body ... the European Court'. Articles 230 and 232 will be discussed more fully in later chapters.

Proceedings brought by the Commission against individuals or, more probably, business undertakings (for example, corporations) for violations of the Treaty arise within the sphere of Community *competition policy* under Article 81 (formerly 85) (restrictive trading agreements), Article 82 (formerly 86) (abuse of a dominant position on a product market) and under the 1989 Merger Regulation. Within this field, the Commission's enforcement role is supplemented *by its own decision making powers* (of a quasi-judicial nature) granted to it by the Council under Article 83 (formerly 87) of the Treaty. As will be seen in Chapter 17, the Commission may impose large fines on business undertakings engaging in anti-competitive behaviour. All such Decisions made by the Commission are, however, subject to review by the Court of First Instance under Article 230 (see Chapter 7).

(2) The second of the Commission's functions under Article 211 (formerly 155) concerns its right to '*formulate recommendations or deliver opinions* on matters dealt with in the Treaty'. The initial policy impetus may have come from the European Council. Although under Article 249 (formerly 189), such recommendations and opinions are not binding, this power to initiate and formulate Community policy is of great importance. Each year, numerous policy proposals are put to the Council. In 1984, a proposal introducing discipline in agricultural spending was accepted by the Council; in 1985, the Commission produced its White Paper on *Completing the Internal Market*; and, in 1989, the Commission's 'Social Charter' was adopted by the European Council and later formed the basis of the 'social chapter' in the original draft of the TEU (finally being added as a Protocol, following the UK's failure to approve it, and thus binding at that time only on the remaining 11 signatory States).

In 1991, the Commission proposed, in a recommendation to the Council, what was reported as 'a swingeing energy tax that would cut emissions of global warming gases, but raise some fuel costs by up to 60 per cent'. This recommendation was seen as an unprecedented attempt by the Commission to determine the tax policies of Member States and to add flames to sovereignty arguments within the Community before and since the Maastricht summit meeting. Although welcomed by environmentalists, the proposal has yet to find draft legislative form. The energy tax proposal is, however, revealing on the subject of the relationship between the Commission and the Member States. It has been said that:

> ... though the Commission is an independent force in its own right, it cannot fulfil its functions without the co-operation of national governments. Consequently, it is very much concerned with national interests and one of its most important tasks is the reconciliation of national policies with Community objectives [Hartley].

Linked to the Commission's role as an initiator of policy is the crucial part it plays as the initial drafter of Community legislation.

(3) This further role for the Commission is to be found in the third indent of Article 211, which speaks not only of that body's 'own power of decision' but also of the Commission's participation *'in the shaping of measures taken by the Council and by the European Parliament'*. Although, as we have seen, the Council of Ministers or the Council and the Parliament acting jointly take the final decision on Community legislation, the normal procedure is for the Council or the joint bodies to act on a proposal – draft legislation – formulated by the 'European' institution.

The Commission's right of initiative in this respect is drawn from the many provisions of the Treaty which empower the Council or the joint bodies to act on a proposal from the Commission. For example, Article 40 (formerly 49), as amended by the TEU, relating to the free movement of workers (as seen in the last chapter) now reads as follows:

Article 40

> The Council shall, acting in accordance with the procedure referred to in Article 251 [formerly 189b] and after consulting the Economic and Social Committee, issue directives or make regulations setting out the measures required to bring about freedom of movement for workers ...

Article 189b (now 251) EC, which established under the Maastricht Treaty in 1991 the Council–Parliament co-decision legislative procedure, stated (and still states) that:

> 1 Where reference is made in this Treaty to this Article for the adoption of an act, the following procedure shall apply.
>
> 2 The Commission shall submit a proposal to the European Parliament and the Council ...

Although, as previously indicated, the initiative may have originally come from the European Council (or on the basis of a 'request' from the Council under Article 208 (formerly 152), or the Parliament under Article 192 (formerly 138b), the Commission's role as the formulator of draft legislation, within an annual programme largely of its own devising, places it at the heart of policy making within the EC pillar. In this respect, it is seen as the 'motor of integration'. At no time was this more apparent than in the Delors Commission's policy initiative and 1986–92 legislative programme for the establishment of the Internal Market:

COMMUNITY INSTITUTIONS AND LAW MAKING

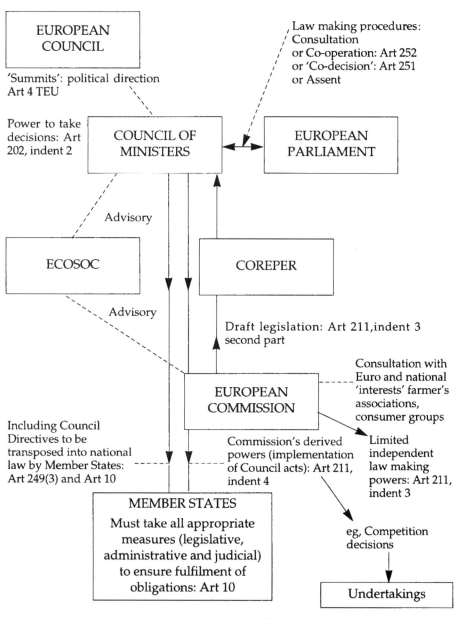

Latest status of Internal Market proposals:

In November 1989, the latest status of the Internal Market legislative Programme was as follows:

– 279 proposals currently comprise the programme;
– 134 proposals have been finally adopted by the Council;
– 7 proposals have been partially adopted by the Council;
– 6 proposals have reached the stage of a Council Common Position;
– 116 proposals of the Commission are with the Council;
– 29 proposals are still to be presented by the Commission.

By 1991, Weiler, writing of the 'Transformation of Europe', was of the view that:

> ... it has become clear that 1992 and the SEA do constitute an eruption of significant proportions ... for the first time since the early days of the Community, if ever, the Commission plays the political role clearly intended for it by the Treaty of Rome. In stark contrast to its nature during the foundational period in the 1970s and early 1980s, the Commission in large measure both sets the Community agenda and acts as a power broker in the legislative process.

Contrary to common belief, the Commission does not act in isolation as the proposer of Community legislation. The appropriate Directorate General, say DG V responsible for Employment, Industrial Relations and Social Affairs will first work on a proposal (for example, draft Directive) in consultation with interested parties including other relevant DGs, government departments in the Member States, consultative committees, national experts (for example, the UK Equal Opportunities Commission) and the Commission's Legal Service. Once a firm proposal has been formulated, it is circulated to the other DGs for comment and possible amendment. It will finally be submitted to the College of Commissioners for approval (by simple majority) before being presented to the Council (or Council and Parliament).

The Commission's role in the legislative process does not stop at this point. Article 211 speaks of the Commission's participation 'in the shaping of measures'. The Commission is represented at all meetings within the Council (for example, in COREPER) and in the Parliament (for example, at its Social Affairs Committee) which involve Commission proposals by a Commissioner who is thereby in a position to act to resolve difficulties or a deadlock in the legislative process, in particular by amending the proposal in order for the required vote in the Council to be achieved. (Details of the various legislative procedures and voting requirements are considered later in this chapter.)

(4) With regard to the provision in Article 211 that the Commission shall 'have its own power of decision', we are concerned here with the Commission's power to bring legislation into effect in its own right. As will be seen in (5) below, the vast majority of Commission acts (Regulations, Directives and Decisions) stem from derived powers and are of a delegated nature. They are issued on the basis of Council legislation and deal with its detailed implementation by means of specific rules.

However, the role of the Commission as an independent legislator (as opposed to the Council, the representative of the Member States) causes some concern for some Member States, despite the fact that the extent of the express Treaty basis for its autonomous legislative competence is not extensive.

Cases 188–90/80 *France, Italy and UK v Commission*

Article 90 (now 86) of the Treaty is concerned with the application of the competition policy rules to public undertakings. In 1980, the Commission adopted Directive 80/723 on the transparency of financial relations between Member States and public undertakings. The aim was to establish the extent to which public funds were being made available to public undertakings and the uses to which they were being put. The legal base for this measure was Article 90(3) which states that: 'The Commission shall ensure the application of the provisions of this Article and shall, where necessary, address appropriate directives or decisions to Member States.' The Directive was part of a more vigorous policy adopted by the Commission in applying the Treaty rules to state involvement in economic activity, and it was challenged under Article 173 (now 230) by the three Member States with the largest public sectors.

The UK argued on a separation of powers basis that all original law making power was vested in the Council; the Commission's powers being confined to 'surveillance and implementation' (that is, executive powers). France and Italy argued that even if Article 90(3) did confer a general law making power on the Commission, its exercise was precluded where the rules in question could have been adopted by the Council.

The Court drew attention to the Commission's 'own power of decision' under Article 155 (now 211). In rejecting the applicants' arguments, it stated that:

> The limits of the powers conferred on the Commission by a specific provision of the Treaty are to be inferred not from a general principle, but from an interpretation of the particular wording of the provision in question ... analysed in the light of its purpose and place in the Treaty.

The power conferred on the Commission by Article 90(3):

> ... thus operates in a specific field of application and under conditions defined by reference to the particular objective of that Article. It follows that the Commission's power to issue the contested directive depends on the needs inherent in its duty of surveillance provided for in Article 90 and that the possibility that rules might be laid down by the Council, by virtue of its general power under Article 94 (now 89), containing provisions impinging upon the specific sphere of aids granted to public undertakings does not preclude the exercise of that power by the Commission.

In a later decision, the Court held, as seen in Chapter 3, that whenever the Treaty of Rome confers a *specific task* on the Commission, it *impliedly* confers on the Commission the powers, including legislative powers, necessary to carry out that task.

Cases 281, 283–85 and 287/85 *Germany, France, the Netherlands, Denmark and the UK v Commission*

By Decision 85/381 the Commission required Member States to enter into a prior communication and consultation procedure with the Commission with regard to their policies on immigration from non-Member States. It was to cover such matters as entry, residence and equal treatment.

The decision was based on Article 118 EEC (now Article 140 EC):

> Without prejudice to the other provisions of this Treaty and in conformity with its general objectives, the Commission shall have the task of promoting close co-operation between Member States in the social field, particularly in matters relating to:

- employment;
- labour law and working conditions ...

It is clear that, on the face of it, this Article is not concerned with immigration, nor does it confer any legislative power on the Commission.

The Court held:

(a) Immigration from non-Member States (for example, 'guest workers') can affect employment and working conditions in the Community.

(b) On the basis of the doctrine of implied powers:

> Where an Article of the EEC Treaty – in this case Article 118 – confers a specific task on the Commission it must be accepted, if that provision is not to be rendered wholly ineffective, that it confers on the Commission necessarily and *per se* the powers which are indispensable in order to carry out that task.

In 1988, Hartley made the following observations on this outcome:

> The consequences of this ruling could be far reaching. There are many provisions in the EEC Treaty conferring tasks on the Commission, one of the most important being that in Article 155 EEC [now Article 211 EC] of ensuring that Community law is applied. This task of acting as Community policeman could in theory entitle the Commission to adopt the most extensive measures. Are we now on the threshold of an expansion of Commission competence comparable to the expansion of Community treaty making power that occurred in the 1970s? Has the European Court adopted the policy of enhancing Commission legislative power as its answer to the continuing difficulty of getting measures through the Council? The answers to these questions are not yet clear but they open up intriguing possibilities.

However, in 1998, as Hartley himself has recognised, this decision remains 'potentially significant' and has not, as yet, introduced 'an era of increased Commission law making'. Statements made by the German Federal Constitutional Court in the *Brunner* case in 1992 in this context, as discussed in Chapter 3, should also be recalled.

(5) The final indent of Article 211 states that the Commission shall 'exercise the powers conferred on it by the Council for the implementation of the rules laid down by the latter'. Additionally, and crucially, Article 202 (formerly 145), as we have seen, states that:

> ... the Council shall ... confer on the Commission, in the acts which the Council adopts, powers for the implementation of the rules which the Council lays down. The Council may impose certain requirements in respect of the exercise of these powers. The Council may also reserve the right in specific cases, to exercise directly implementing powers itself ...

On the basis of this provision, the Council delegates to its 'European partner' powers of an implementing and executive nature which are necessary for the carrying out of 'decisions' taken by the Council on the basis of Article 202. The amount of legislation emanating from the Commission under these delegated or secondary powers is enormous, but it is largely made up of detailed rules of policy implementation, not least in the field of agriculture. This is apparent from a typical list of the contents of an issue of the Official Journal: see page 108.

Although the Council's power to delegate in the legislative field extends only to the implementation of rules, it is clear from the case law of the Court that considerable discretionary powers may be delegated to the Commission provided the empowering Council provision establishes the basic principles in issue.

It will be seen that Article 202 lays down that the Council 'may impose certain requirements' of a procedural nature in respect of the Commission's subordinate powers. Thus, the Council may provide for the establishment of committees of representatives of the national governments to which the Commission must submit drafts of measures it intends to adopt under its derived authority. The degree of control which the Council exercises over the Commission via these advisory, management and regulatory committee procedures varies considerably. However, it would appear that the system generally operates to the Commission's satisfaction, but see Case 302/87 *Parliament v Council (Comitology)* in the next chapter.

THE EUROPEAN PARLIAMENT: ARTICLES 189–201 (FORMERLY 137–44)

The European Parliament was known until 1962 as the Assembly and the change of name was not officially recognised until the coming into effect of the Single European Act in 1987. The history of the European Parliament is a history of gradual and hard-won accretions of power within the institutional structure.

Article 189 (formerly 137) states that the Parliament 'shall consist of representatives of the peoples of the States brought together in the Community', but its members were appointed by and from national parliaments until 1979, the year of the first direct elections, now held every five years. Direct elections by universal suffrage constituted an important step towards increasing the Parliament's legitimacy and therefore authority and also towards reducing the 'democratic deficit' within the Community. Article 137 (now 189) originally stated that the Parliament 'shall exercise the advisory and supervisory powers which are conferred upon it by this Treaty'. As amended by the TEU, the words 'advisory and supervisory' disappeared from this Article. The deletion of these words is indicative of the considerable efforts the Parliament had made in the intervening years to expand its sphere of influence and power. Earlier, in 1988, Davidson and Freestone had explained the Parliament's position as follows:

> ... the EP is not a Parliament in the sense that Westminster is a parliament. It does not pass legislation, nor is the executive drawn from its members. As we have seen, the legislative and executive functions are performed by the Council and the Commission ... Built into the Treaties are specific powers which indicate that the drafters intended the EP to provide an important element of democratic accountability within the legislative and executive system ... Members of the European Parliament (MEPs) are increasingly assertive in their demands for increased influence over, and indeed share in, the legislative and executive processes of the Community.

The most important additions to the Parliament's powers over the years relate to the Community budget (under the Budgetary Treaties of 1970 and 1975) and to its more influential role in the legislative process: from mere *consultation* under the original Treaty of Rome to selective introduction of *co-operation* and *assent* procedures under the Single European Act in 1986 and *co-decision* under the Maastricht, Amsterdam and Nice Treaties.

Official Journal

ISSN 0378-6978

L 32

Volume 42

of the European Communities

5 February 1999

. English edition   ## Legislation

Contents

1

(Continued overleaf)

EN

Acts whose titles are printed in light type are those relating to day-to-day management of agricultural matters, and are generally valid for a limited period.
The titles of all other acts are printed in bold type and preceded by an asterisk.

Seats and Political Parties

The European Parliament was originally based in Luxembourg but its permanent seat is now the *Palais de l'Europe* in Strasbourg, where it meets each month in plenary sessions for one week. Additional plenary sessions are also held in a new Parliament building in Brussels.

The make-up of the Parliament in 1998 in terms of its transnational political groups, and group membership by nationality is shown in the chart on page 110. Article 191 (formerly 138a) states that:

> Political parties at European level are important as a factor for integration within the Union. They contribute to forming a European awareness and to expressing the political will of the citizens of the Union.

MEPs represent almost 100 European national political parties. At Union level, this vast range of political opinion is reduced into large 'political groups' which, on the basis of ideological affinities between their members, represent the major divisions in European politics: for further details, see Nugent in the References and Further Reading at the end of this chapter.

It will be seen that the total number of MEPs is currently 626. Prior to the reunification of Germany, the four largest Member States (West Germany, France, Italy and the UK) each had 87 members.

Article 2 of the Enlargement Protocol annexed to the Nice Treaty, which is scheduled to replace Article 190(2) EC, makes provision for a revised allocation of seats for the elected representatives of the existing Member States. This reallocation envisages a total of 732 MEPs (see also the amended Article 189 EC) at the start of the 2004/09 parliamentary term. Germany retains its 99 seats but all the others (except Luxembourg) have a reduced figure. The full list is as follows: Germany 99 seats, the UK, France and Italy 72, Spain 50, the Netherlands 25, Portugal, Belgium and Greece 22, Sweden 18, Austria 17, Denmark and Finland 13, Ireland 12 and Luxembourg 6.

The new Article 190(2) sets a total of 732 MEPs for a Union of 27 Member States on 1 January 2004, that is, 535 plus, according to figures to be found in Declaration 20 annexed to the Final Act of the Nice Treaty, an allocation for 12 new Member States as follows: Poland 50 seats, (Romania 33), Czech Republic and Hungary 20, (Bulgaria 17), Slovakia 13, Lithuania 12, Latvia 8, Slovenia 7, Estonia and Cyprus 5, Malta 4.

These allocations did not meet with general approval and they are dependent on 12 accession treaties being signed before 1 January 2004. If this is not the case, the new Article 190(2) states that 'a *pro rata* correction shall be applied to the number of representatives to be elected in each Member State, so that the total number is as close as possible to 732 ...'. The failure of Romania and Bulgaria to meet entry requirements by the above date means that a revision will have to be made for a Union of 25 Member States.

Most of the Parliament's work is presently done in 17 Standing Committees (Agriculture and Rural Development, Budget, Economic and Monetary Affairs, Legal Affairs and Internal Market, Employment and Social Affairs, etc) where issues are considered and reported before being debated. Resolutions of the Parliament do not have any legal effect, although the Parliament may well seek in this way to bring pressure to bear on the Commission and the Council to take appropriate action with regard to not only Community, but also to international matters of concern.

		B	DK	D	EL	E	F	IRL	I	L	NL	A	P	FIN	S	UK	Total
PES	Group of party of European Socialists	6	4	40	10	21	16	1	18	2	7	6	10	4	7	61	213
EPP	Group of the European People's Party	7	3	47	9	30	11	4	15	2	9	7	9	4	5	18	180
UFE	Union for Europe Group				2		18	7	24		2		3				56
ELDR	Group of Liberal Democratic and Reformist Party	6	5			2	1	1	4	1	10	1		5	3	2	41
EUL/NGL	Confederal Group of the European United Left/Nordic Green Left				4	9	7		5				3	2	3	1	34
Green	Green Group in the European Parliament	2		12					4		1	1		1	4	1	28
ERA	Group of the European Radical Alliance	1				2	12	2	2	1							20
I-EdN	Group of Independents for a Europe of Nations		4				11				2					1	18
Ind	Non-attached	3					11		15			6				1	36
	Total	25	16	99	25	64	87	15	87	6	31	21	25	16	22	87	626

Source: DG I. 21.3.1998

Functions and Powers

Apart from its growing participation in the law making process – as established in the Treaty base of the act in question (consultation, co-operation, co-decision or assent) – the Parliament's other main powers relate to the Community budget and its supervision of the Commission.

A significant increase in the Parliament's budgetary powers came about in 1975 under the second Budgetary Treaty, as a result of which the Parliament now exercises joint control of the Community budget with the Council. Although the Commission draws up the draft budget and the Council ultimately determines 'compulsory' expenditure (approximately 55 per cent of the total annual budget and mainly spent on the CAP), the Parliament has, within certain constraints, the final decision on 'non-compulsory' expenditure, relating in the main to social and regional policy, research and, significantly in recent years, aid to non-Community countries such as the Central and Eastern European Countries and Russia.

When, in 1985, the Parliament refused to abide by limits placed on 'non-compulsory' expenditure, the Council obtained a ruling that the decision of the President of the Parliament, declaring the 1986 budget adopted, was invalid: see Case 34/86 *Council v Parliament* in Chapter 6. It is, however, agreed, at least in a political sense, that the Council and the Parliament will co-operate on budgetary matters (Joint Declarations of the Parliament, the Council and Commission, 1975 and 1982) and, since 1988, that they will do so within a framework of 'budgetary discipline'. Since 1977, the Parliament has possessed the power under Article 272(8) (formerly 203(8)) to reject the draft budget in its entirety. It has exercised this power twice, in 1979 and 1984. (In such circumstances, until the matter is settled, the Community proceeds on the basis of the preceding year's budget allocations.)

The Commission is responsible for the implementation of the Community budget in accordance with financial regulations and subject to control by the Parliament and the Council as assisted by the Court of Auditors.

As regards the Parliament's *supervisory powers*, under Article 197 (formerly 140), the Commission (and, in practice, the Council) is required to answer questions from MEPs either orally or in writing: see the Official Journal, 'C' series. Roy Jenkins was President of the Commission from 1977 to 1980. In his 'European Diary' for 10 May 1978 whilst in Strasbourg, he noted:

> Then into the Chamber, luckily as little Fellermaier without any notice got up on a complicated point of order which turned out to be a justified complaint about the very poor attendance and performance of the Commission at question period the previous day. Only Burke and Vredeling had been there. We had discussed this at the Commission meeting that morning, deciding that we must strengthen the team for Thursday and in the future. I therefore had an answer, but felt I had to change my plans, stay in Strasbourg and do Thursday questions myself.

The Commission is also required by Article 200 (formerly 143) to submit to the Parliament for public debate an annual general report.

Article 201 (formerly 144) provides that the Parliament can obtain the *en bloc* resignation of the Commission by a vote of censure passed by a two-thirds majority of votes cast, representing a majority of all members. This power has in fact never been used by the Parliament against its most pro-European ally, although, as seen in

Chapter 1, in order to avoid a motion of censure regarding charges of inefficiency and malpractice, the Commission resigned in March 1999.

New supervisory powers introduced by the TEU included the right to set up Committees of Inquiry to investigate 'alleged contraventions or maladministration in the implementation of Community law' (except where the matter is *sub judice*): Article 193 (formerly 138c). The Parliament now also has the power to appoint an Ombudsman empowered to receive complaints concerning instances of maladministration in the activities of the Community's political institutions. Established cases of maladministration will be reported to the Parliament and the institution concerned, the complainant being informed of the outcome: Article 195 (formerly 138e).

THE COURT OF AUDITORS
ARTICLES 246–48 (FORMERLY 188(a–c))

Established in 1975, the Luxembourg based Court of Auditors (which is not a court in the legal sense) was added to the list of Community institutions in Article 4 (now 7) EC by the TEU. Its composition and powers are to be found in Articles 246–48. Under Article 247 (as amended at Nice), the Court consists of one national from each Member State.

Although now an institution, the Court has no Treaty power to adopt Community acts under Article 249 (formerly 189) and so, it would seem, cannot be subject to annulment proceedings before the Court of Justice under Article 230 (formerly 173) (but see Cases 193 and 194/87 *Maurissen v Court of Auditors* in which, exceptionally, the Court of Justice allowed such an action). However, it does now have a limited power to challenge in judicial review proceedings acts adopted by the other institutions: Article 230(3).

The Court's main functions are to examine the annual accounts of all Community revenue and expenditure (as drawn up by the Commission), to provide a statement as to the reliability of the accounts and the legality of the underlying transactions, and to examine the soundness of the financial management involved. It must provide an annual financial report, which, together with the replies to its observations from the institutions under audit, is published in the Official Journal. It is often highly critical of the management and control of Community finances. The Court of Auditors may also submit special reports on specific questions (for example, agricultural fraud, budgetary discipline).

The Court of Auditors is the Community's financial watchdog, exercising control and supervision over the implementation of the budget and providing the Parliament with the documentation necessary for it to give discharge to the Commission in respect of the budget.

OTHER COMMUNITY BODIES

The *Economic and Social Committee*, established under the Treaty of Rome (see now Article 7 EC) acts, as numerous Treaty Articles testify, in an advisory capacity to both the Council and the Commission in the law making process: see now, for example, Article 95 (formerly 100a) relating to Internal Market harmonisation measures and Article 37 (formerly 43) on the establishment of common organisations of the markets for agricultural products.

Where the Treaty provides for such consultation, a failure to take the Committee's advice amounts to a breach of an essential procedural requirement invalidating the resultant Community measure.

Under Article 257 (formerly 193), as amended by the Treaty of Nice:

> ... The Committee shall consist of representatives of the various economic and social components of organised civil society, and in particular, representatives of producers, farmers, carriers, workers, dealers, craftsmen, professional occupations, consumers and the general interest.

The Committee is based in Brussels and members are appointed by the Council on the basis of national allocations from lists provided by the Member States. Although appointed in their personal capacity, they are generally representative of employers, trade unions, consumers, farmers and professional bodies. The number of members shall not exceed 350, a figure which takes into account the appointment of members from the new Member States: Article 258 (formerly 194), as amended at Nice.

Article 258 also provides that the members of the Committee shall be 'completely independent in the performance of their duties, in the general interest of the Community'. In addition to Treaty based mandatory consultation, the Council, the Commission and the Parliament may also consult the Committee on other matters as they see fit. The Committee also produces advisory opinions on its own initiative.

A *Committee of the Regions* was established by the Maastricht Treaty (see now Article 7 EC) to act in a similar advisory capacity. Article 265 (formerly 198c) provides that:

> The Committee of the Regions shall be consulted by the Council or by the Commission where this Treaty so provides and in all other cases, in particular those which concern cross border cooperation, in which one of these two institutions considers it appropriate.

Treaty provisions which provide a need to consult the Committee of the Regions include those relating to Public Health, Trans-European Networks for transport, telecommunications and energy and the Regional Development Fund.

Under Article 263 (formerly 198a), the Committee, which is again based in Brussels, is made up of representatives of 'regional and local bodies', so providing, in furtherance of a general policy that decisions be taken 'as closely as possible to the people', a direct link between the Community institutions and representatives of, for example, the German *Länder* and, presumably, such Spanish regions as Catalonia and the Basque country as well as local authority representatives. A Nice amendment to Article 263 states that the representatives of the 'regional and local bodies' must hold an 'electoral mandate' or be 'politically accountable to an elected assembly'. The maximum number of members of the Committee is now 350.

Attention has already been drawn to other important Community bodies: the European Investment Bank in Luxembourg (see now Articles 266 and 267) and the European Central Bank, which has its seat in Frankfurt (Article 8 and the new Articles on Economic and Monetary Policy). Of the other new decentralised agencies established post-Maastricht, the following are of particular interest: the European Monetary Institute (the forerunner of the European Central Bank and established in Frankfurt), the European Environment Agency (Copenhagen), the European Agency for the Evaluation of Medicinal Products (London), the Office for Veterinary and Plant Health Inspection and Control (Dublin), Europol (The Hague), the European Monitoring Centre for Drugs and Drug Addiction (Lisbon) and the Translation Centre (Luxembourg).

THE COMMUNITY LAW MAKING PROCESS

It will already be apparent that there is no single Community law making process; no single procedure whereby Community institutional acts (Regulations, Directives and Decisions) are adopted and come into effect. At the simplest level, it is said that 'the Commission proposes and the Council disposes'. Although correct in a general sense (at least prior to the TEU coming into force), the Commission's legislative powers being as we have seen mainly of a derived nature, this remark fails to take any account of the varying roles of the European Parliament in Community decision making. Not only therefore is there no single procedure, as we have seen, but no one institution which can be called the Community legislature.

The only safe way of determining the procedure necessary for putting into effect a particular Community policy, or element of it, is to refer to the Treaty Article, or Articles, which form its base. For example, in Chapter 4 in the section on Community acts, attention was drawn to Council Regulation 1612/68 on freedom of movement for workers. The preamble to that act indicates that it is based on Article 49 EEC which at that time (1968) required that the Council had regard 'to the Opinion of the European Parliament'. When Article 49 was amended by the Single European Act of 1986, the Council was then required to act 'in co-operation with the European Parliament'. Following the coming into force of the TEU, as seen earlier in this chapter, a further amendment came into effect and measures based on Article 49 EC were to be adopted by the Council 'acting in accordance with the procedure referred to in Article 189b', the co-decision procedure. (ToA renumbering means that Article 49 is now Article 40 and Article 189b is Article 251.) This single Article is therefore indicative not only of three of the Parliament's possible roles in the legislative process but also of that institution's growing legislative status.

Indeed, one way of beginning to understand the complexities of the legislative process is through such an historical approach. In the original 1957 EEC Treaty, the Parliament's role in the process was, as seen above, for the most part purely of a *consultative* nature – with no *obligation* for the Council or the Commission to take account of its opinions. Very few Treaty Articles now remain which provide for such a procedure. For example, in an Article concerning taxation:

Article 93 (formerly 99) EC

The Council shall, acting unanimously on a proposal from the Commission and after consulting the European Parliament and the Economic and Social Committee, adopt provisions for the harmonisation of legislation concerning turnover taxes, excise duties and other forms of indirect taxation to the extent that such harmonisation is necessary to ensure the establishment and the functioning of the internal market ...

It should be noted that unanimity in the Council is required in this Article dealing with the highly contentious political question of taxation at the national level.

Returning to 1957, in most cases in a six Member State Community, the Council took its decisions on the basis of unanimity and the 1966 'Luxembourg Accords' (see Chapter 1) operated to check the introduction of qualified majority voting (see Article 205(2)) as envisaged by the Treaty when it first came into effect. As Nugent has explained:

> The Luxembourg Compromise did not ... replace a system of majority voting by one of unanimous voting. On the contrary, before 1966 majority voting was rare ... From 1966 the norm became one not of unanimous voting but one of no voting at all. Decisions came to be made by letting issues run until an agreement finally emerged ... the preference for unanimity, which still exists ... was not, and is not, just a consequence of an unofficial agreement made over twenty five years ago [now over thirty-five]. There are strong positive reasons for acting on the basis of unanimity. In many ways the functioning and development of the Community is likely to be enhanced if policy-making processes are consensual rather than conflictual.

We have seen in Chapter 1 that it was not until the mid-1980s and the Commission's Internal Market initiative that, in a 12 Member State Community, it became imperative, in the interests of progress free of a single Member State veto, to move as far as expedient and politically possible to qualified majority voting. In 1986, the Single European Act introduced the legislative *co-operation procedure*, which enabled this move to be made and, albeit in small measure, enhanced the Parliament's legislative role. The adoption of the many harmonisation measures (Directives) necessary for the completion of the Internal Market was facilitated by the Single European Act through the introduction of a new Article 100a EEC to which the co-operation procedure and qualified majority voting in the Council of Ministers applied:

Article 100a EEC (now 95 EC)

1   ... The Council shall, acting by a qualified majority on a proposal from the Commission in co-operation with the European Parliament and after consulting the Economic and Social Committee adopt the measures for the approximation of the provisions laid down by law, regulation or administrative action in Member States which have as their objective the establishment and functioning of the internal market.

2   ... Paragraph 1 shall not apply to fiscal provisions ... [see Article 93 (formerly 99) above].

The co-operation procedure, having supplanted consultation in many policy areas throughout the Treaty, has since 1993 been itself successively superseded by the co-decision procedure. This has come about of course through the Treaty amendments made first at Maastricht and then at Amsterdam and Nice. Although the TEU significantly enhanced the Parliament's legislative role, it cannot be said that it has become the main actor in the process nor even an equal partner with the Council. Macrae (in *Legal Issues of the Maastricht Treaty*) states that it is 'innaccurate to refer to co-decision since the Parliament's power is a negative one: it cannot force the Council to adopt a measure that the Council does not want. Parliament can only block the measure'. However, it is as co-decision that the process has come to be known. The increasingly extended use of this procedure in a Treaty of wider and wider scope makes it by far the most important process of those to be found in the EC Treaty and as such represents an important step taken by the Member States to enhance the democratic legitimacy of the Union.

The co-operation procedure can still be found in the Treaty as a basis for institutional acts (it applies in Articles relating to Economic and Monetary Policy), but it no longer applies, for example, to Article 95:

Article 95 EC (formerly 100a EEC)

1. ... The Council shall, acting in accordance with the procedure referred to in Article 251 [co-decision] and after consulting the Economic and Social Committee, adopt the measures for the approximation of the provisions laid down by law, regulation or administrative action in Member States which have their object the establishment and functioning of the internal market.

2. Paragraph 1 shall not apply to fiscal provisions ... [see Article 93 EC (formerly 99) above].

Although co-decision is now the most significant and widely used procedure, it will be more easily understood by first examining the two earlier established methods.

The following steps can be identified with the basic *consultative* procedure:

(a) Draft legislation (a proposal) is prepared by the relevant policy area Directorate General of the Commission assisted by an advisory working group of persons nominated by the Member State governments.

(b) The proposal is submitted to the Council by the Commission.

(c) The Council sends the proposal for its opinion to the European Parliament (which will utilise the services of its appropriate standing committee) and, if required by the Treaty Article upon which the proposal is based, to the Economic and Social Committee or the Committee of the Regions or both.

(d) The *Parliament's opinion* may be to accept, reject or seek amendments to the proposal. The Council and the Commission are under *no obligation* to follow the Parliament's opinion or other advice.

(e) A COREPER working group of national officials prepares a report for the Council. Amendments to the proposal may be accepted by the Commission representatives. However, if an amendment is *one of substance* and not in line with the Parliament's wishes, that institution must be consulted again: Case C-65/90 *Parliament v Council (Road Haulage Services)*.

(f) If full agreement is reached in COREPER, the proposal will be adopted by the Council without debate.

(g) Where this is not the case, deadlock may be broken by the national Ministers and Commission representatives in the Council. However, if the Ministers cannot obtain the required vote (for example, the unanimity in Article 93, above) to agree to the proposal as it stands and cannot obtain the unanimity to amend the proposal as required under Article 250 (formerly 189a), the impasse can be broken by the Commission altering its proposal to enable the vote for adoption to be obtained: Article 250(2).

As seen in Chapter 4, under this procedure, the Council must respect the Parliament's right to be consulted, otherwise the act may be annulled: Case 138/79 *Roquette Frères v Council*.

Where a Treaty Article (the act's Treaty base) provides that the *co-operation procedure* be used, it is now expressed as 'the procedure referred to in Article 252' (formerly 189c). Although only applying now in limited circumstances, a grasp of the steps involved is helpful in understanding the even more complex co-decision procedure.

Building on the consultation procedure, where the Council would under that procedure be in a position to adopt the act in question, the Council instead is required to adopt a *common position*. It is reached on the basis of a qualified majority vote and is sent back to the Parliament with the reasons which led to its adoption and a statement of the Commission's position. The Parliament therefore has a second opportunity (a second reading) to consider the draft measure and react to it. The Parliament may approve the Council's position, in which case, the Council will adopt the act.

Alternatively, the Parliament may reject or, more likely, prepare amendments to the common position, in either case by an absolute majority. If its draft has been rejected, the Council can maintain it at a second reading only by a unanimous vote. It is unlikely that unanimity will be achieved where the common position was originally adopted by a qualified majority. The minority will in all probability maintain their dissenting position and the Parliament's rejection will in effect become a veto: for example, the demise of the Commission's proposed Directive on sweeteners for use in foodstuffs of September 1990: see Earnshaw and Judge in 'References and Further Reading' at the end of the chapter.

In the case of Parliament amendments, the *Commission* will examine them and forward a new proposal to the Council, together with the amendments, whether accepted or not. The Council may then, acting by a qualified majority, adopt the proposal as re-examined by the Commission. Otherwise, if the Council wishes to amend this proposal or adopt Parliament amendments not accepted by the Commission, it must act on a unanimous basis. If it fails to take a decision within a deadline, the proposal fails.

The *co-decision procedure* – 'the procedure referred to in Article 251' (formerly 189b) – follows the pattern of the co-operation procedure, except that the Commission's original proposal is submitted to both the Council *and the Parliament*, up to the point where the Parliament at its second reading, either approves, rejects or seeks to amend the Council's common position:

(a) If the Parliament approves, the Council adopts the act.

(b) If the Parliament rejects the common position by an absolute majority, the proposed act shall be deemed *not to have been adopted*.

(c) If the Parliament proposes amendments, then, following reconsideration by the Council and Commission, the Council, if it approves all the amendments, can proceed to *adopt the act as amended* by a qualified majority. However, it must act unanimously on amendments on which the Commission has delivered a negative opinion. If the position becomes one where the Council does not approve all the amendments, the President of the Council and the President of the Parliament shall appoint a *Conciliation Committee* made up of equal representatives of these two institutions. The Committee, with the Commission acting as honest broker, will attempt to agree a joint text on the basis of a qualified majority of the Council representatives and a majority of the Parliament representatives.

(d) An agreed joint text will become *the basis of an adopted act*, the Council acting by qualified majority and the Parliament by absolute majority within a stipulated time period. If the Conciliation Committee cannot reach agreement, the proposed act will be deemed *not to have been adopted*.

Two other legislative processes, of relatively minor significance, can be found in the EC Treaty. As seen, on the basis of the third indent of Article 211 (formerly 155), the Commission has autonomous legislative powers but they are granted in a very limited number of areas, for example, under Article 86 (formerly 90) regarding public undertakings and under Article 39 (formerly 48) concerning free movement of workers.

Also, in certain areas, the Council is empowered by the Treaty to act on a Commission proposal and decide (in accordance with the voting requirement laid down in the relevant Article) *without any requirement to consult the Parliament*, although it may choose to do so, for example, Article 26 (formerly 28) on the common customs tariff and Article 133 (formerly 113) on the Common Commercial Policy.

The TEU contains two further special procedures. Under the assent procedure, originally introduced by the Single European Act, the Council may only adopt a Commission proposal after having obtained the formal approval of the Parliament. (A conciliation procedure, introduced by the Parliament, is available.) This procedure applies, amongst other matters, to decisions under Article 49 (formerly O) TEU regarding applications for membership of the Union and to decisions concerning certain international agreements.

The special procedures involved in dealing with 'a clear risk of a serious breach by a Member State' of fundamental rights principles and 'the existence of a serious and persistent breach by a Member State' of such principles (see Chapter 1) are now, following the Nice Treaty, to be found in Article 7 TEU.

Voting in the Council

Article 205(1) (formerly 148(1)) EC provides that:

> Save as otherwise provided in this Treaty, the Council shall act by a majority of its members.

However, as will already be apparent, the vast majority of the Treaty Articles which lay down a voting procedure do provide otherwise. It can be said that, with few exceptions (for example, taxation), qualified majority voting (QMV) has become the pattern for decision making on the more important EC policies.

For QMV purposes, the Treaty establishes for each Member State a number of votes determined or *weighted* mainly on the basis of the size of its population. Article 3 of the Nice Treaty's Protocol on the Enlargement of the European Union provides for a change in the weighting of votes in Article 205(2) for the present Member States from 1 January 2005, and the number of votes assigned to the candidate countries in a Union of 27 Member States is to be found in Declaration 20 annexed to the Final Act of the Nice Treaty. The position regarding the respective weighting attributed to each Member State and the threshold for attaining a qualified majority (and blocking minority) in the light of these anticipated future developments can be shown as follows (although some revision of the figures will now be required following the inability of Romania and Bulgaria to meet the entry requirements):

(1) *The position prior to 1 January 2005*

Germany, France, Italy, UK	10 votes each
Spain	8 votes
Belgium, Greece, Netherlands and Portugal	5 votes each
Austria and Sweden	4 votes each
Denmark, Ireland and Finland	3 votes each
Luxembourg	2 votes

On this basis, where the Council is acting, as is normally the case, on a proposal from the Commission, the required minimum vote for a qualified majority represents 71.26 per cent of the total number of votes, that is, 62 out of 87. The minimum population required is 58.16 per cent. A blocking minority is 26 votes. Thus, for example, the 'Big Five' need the support of two of the Member States with 5 votes and one with 4 votes to secure a qualified majority. At least eight of the 15 Member States must vote in favour of the proposal.

(2) *The position on 1 January 2005: 15 Member States*

Germany, France, Italy, UK	29 votes each
Spain	27 votes
Netherlands	13 votes
Belgium, Greece and Portugal	12 votes each
Austria and Sweden	10 votes each
Denmark, Ireland and Finland	7 votes each
Luxembourg	4 votes

These figures assume that no new Member States will have joined the Union by this date. On this basis, the number of votes needed for a qualified majority rises to 169 out of 237 (71.31 per cent). A blocking minority is 69 votes. Thus, for example, the 'Big Five' would require the votes of any three Member States, excepting the four smallest, to secure a qualified majority. As before, at least eight States must vote in favour of adoption. Article 3 of the Enlargement Protocol also states that 'any member of the Council may request verification that the qualified majority comprises at least 62 per cent of the total population of the Union'.

(3) *The position for a Union of 27 Member States*

Enlargement Declaration 20 sets out what was seen at Nice to be the QMV weighting system for a Union of 27 Member States. The figures for 'the fifteen' are as in Table 2 above. The votes assigned to the new Member States are as follows:

Poland	27 votes
(Romania	14 votes)
Czech Republic and Hungary	12 votes each
(Bulgaria	10 votes)
Slovakia and Lithuania	7 votes each
Latvia, Slovenia Estonia and Cyprus	4 votes each
Malta	3 votes

A qualified majority would require 258 votes out of the total of 345 and represent 74.78 per cent of the votes. A blocking minority would be 88 votes. However, Declaration 21 states that the Member States agree to increase the blocking minority to 91 when all the 12 candidate States have acceded. This would lower the qualified majority threshold to 255 or 73.91 per cent of the votes. This is inconsistent with the further statement that the maximum qualified majority requirement, regardless of the pace of accession, will be 73.4 per cent of the votes.

This and other sources of confusion, plus the unknown pace of accession, make it as yet impossible to see how the position will unfold.

COMMENTS: THE WIDER PICTURE

Students of politics, or even constitutional law, will not need to be told that this Treaty based examination of the Community's law making process tells only part of the real story. Thus, for example, 'identifying the policy context' in 1983, Carole Webb observed that:

> ... the Community institutions themselves represent but the tip of an iceberg. When all the facts of the wider consultative and implementative processes are exposed, and the inputs from the national systems and, on occasions, the international system, are taken into account, a much more dense network emerges.

Illustrations of the 'wider consultative' process abound in Roy Jenkins' 'European Diary'. During his four year period as President of the Commission (1977–80), and in his search for progress towards economic and monetary union (the European Monetary System (EMS) was created in 1978), he discussed, debated and decided issues at informal and formal levels with a wide variety of individuals and institutions, for example: the Italian Minister of the Treasury, the Ecofin Council, German Chancellor Schmidt, within the Commission itself, Swiss Central Bank governors, the US Secretary of the Treasury, British bankers and businessmen, International Monetary Fund officials, the European Parliament (plenary sessions and the Economic and Monetary Affairs Committee), COREPER and the European Council, etc.

From a different angle, Nugent draws attention to a wide range of 'interests' to be found within the wider context of the Community's decision making process. Their main target is naturally the Commission as the main initiator of economic and social legislation. They include regional and local authorities, individual companies and corporations and their representative bodies such as the Confederation of British Industries (CBI), national interest groups such as environmentalists, and Euro-groups such as the European Trade Union Confederation (ETUC).

Helen Wallace, speaking of 'Negotiation, Conflict and Compromise' in 1983, concluded that:

> The Community process is both diverse and intricate ... the character of Community negotiations puts pressure on the member governments to aggregate their policy priorities and so defend them in Brussels. The public visibility of Council sessions emphasises the apparent importance of overall national interests and presents an illusory image of monolithic governments, bargaining with each other, especially the governments of the larger members.

However, despite the attempt by governments to set up gatekeeping mechanisms, transnational networks of policy making elites have emerged and become increasingly significant ...

During the 1970s, a crucial change took place in the EC policy process. A less benign economic context, enlargement, and the international environment were met by disputes over the policy agenda of the EC. There is no longer a ready consensus on what should constitute the core of collaboration within the enlarged Community comparable to the initial list of priorities to which the Treaties committed the founder members. Instead there is controversy over both the content and order of the policy agenda combined with demands for policies that are difficult to satisfy, given the limitation of resources and authority at the Community level. Inevitably, therefore, the bargaining on which agreement depends has become more tortuous and competitive, while the challenge of accommodating diverse interests subjects the output of policies to more public scrutiny than hitherto. The Community has thus begun to tread the tortuous path from a policy process largely concerned with issues of regulation and adjudication towards the harsher world of distributional policies, but without a policy making system with authority and legitimacy commensurate to the task.

Later in the 1980s, the Member States discovered a 'core of collaboration', the completion of the Internal Market, and a system and process, strengthened institutional co-operation and qualified majority voting, with which to achieve it. Greater efforts have also been geared to distributional policies, particularly through the operation of the Community's Structural Funds (the Social Fund, the Regional Development Fund, the Agricultural Funds and the new Cohesive Fund).

From Maastricht and beyond, the Union's decision making process has operated regularly and most visibly at the intergovernmental, European Council level. In terms of the further progress of the integrative process, the outcome of the Amsterdam and Nice deliberations in practical terms has, as yet, been less than dramatic. The candidate States are still in the waiting room.

Where unanimity has been unattainable, opt-outs have been allowed, as was the case in the field of social policy and remains the case for economic and monetary union. Closer, now 'enhanced' co-operation between 'progressive' groupings of Member States is now firmly within the Treaties (with relaxed conditions) – if not yet in practice. 'Variable geometry' is thus accepted as one way to progress along the 'tortuous path' to further deepening of the integrative process – since Nice, even in the field of foreign policy.

On the other side of this integrative coin, that of the widening of the Union, the decisions made may before too long appear, in a wider historical context, as dramatic.

These political decisions regarding both widening and deepening raise as we have seen, crucial questions as to system, means and process. The Treaty of Nice, within the Amsterdam remit, focused attention on such matters as the balance of institutional power within the Union, on the question of democratic legitimacy, and on the relative representation and strengths of the Member States within the European Parliament and the Brussels Council. However, this is not to say that such focus reveals satisfactory results in terms of process. Kieran Bradley, commenting on the QMV issue at Nice, reveals the long standing tension between national and Community/Union interests:

The *numberfest* at Nice provides proof, if any were needed, that the Nation-State, jealous of its place in the world and somewhat forgetful of the long-term benefits of integration, is alive and well and living in the South of France. Considerations of national advantage dominated the debate, with not even lip-service being paid to other political values, such as the long-term efficiency of the future decision-making process, or the transparency of its operation. If the larger Member States were motivated to copper-bottom their own position, the smaller Member States could but follow suit, and so on in a downward spiral. The IGC was reported to have spent so much time and energy on the question of re-weighting that it was unable properly to negotiate the extension of qualified majority voting, leaving the way free for the defenders of pet national vetoes. It has been suggested that the question was so hotly debated because it raised issues of national pride, as much as that of the capacity of the individual Member State to influence the content of policy decisions within the Union.

Bradley also refers to a Commission study which indicates that the application of the new weighting system would not, over the three year period covered, have changed the result of a single decision. Writing in more general terms, concerning the Treaty as 'an exercise in institutional design', he concludes that:

In concentrating so much attention on national 'representation' in the composition of the institutions, the IGC ignored other dimensions of proper political concern, such as the legitimacy of the Community/Union, and the democratic character of its operation.

Whether these shortcomings will be satisfactorily addressed by Giscard d'Estaing's Convention and the 'deeper and wider debate about the future of Europe' remains to be seen.

REFERENCES AND FURTHER READING

Bradley, K St C, 'Legal developments in the European Parliament' (1992) 12 YEL 505.

Bradley, K St C, 'Institutional design in the Treaty of Nice' (2001) 38 CML Rev 1095.

Bulmer, S and Wesels, W, *The European Council*, 1987.

Curtin, D, 'The constitutional structure of the Union: a Europe of bits and pieces' (1993) 30 CML Rev 17.

Dashwood, A, 'The constitution of the European Union after Nice: law-making procedures' (2001) 26 EL Rev 215.

Dehousse, R (ed), *Europe: The Impossible Status Quo*, 1997.

Earnshaw, D and Judge, D, 'The European Parliament and the sweeteners directive' (1993) 31 JCMS 103.

George, S, *Politics and Policy in the European Community*, 1996.

Jacobs, F, Corbett, R and Shackleton, M, *The European Parliament*, 1995.

Jenkins, R, *European Diary 1977–81*, 1989.

Lenaerts, K, 'Some reflections on the separation of powers in the European Community' (1991) 28 CML Rev 11.

Lodge, J, 'EC policy making: institutional considerations', and 'The European Parliament – from assembly to co-legislature: changing the institutional dynamics', in Lodge, J (ed), *The European Community and the Challenge of the Future*, 1994.

Nugent, N, *The Government and Politics of the European Union*, 1999.

Scharpf, FW, 'The joint decision trap: lessons from German federalism and European integration' (1988) 3 Public Administration 239.

Wallace, Wallace and Webb, *Policy Making in the European Community*, 1983, Chapters 1 and 2.

Weiler, J, 'The transformation of Europe' (1991) 100 Yale LJ 2403.

Westlake, M, *A Modern Guide to the European Parliament*, 1994.

Westlake, M, *The Parliament and the Commission: Partners and Rivals in the European Policy Making Process*, 1994.

CHAPTER 6

COMMUNITY ACTS: TREATY BASIS AND CONSTITUTIONAL CHECKS AND BALANCES

TREATY BASIS

Article 249 (formerly 189) EC provides that the Community's political institutions, acting in their law making capacity, shall make Regulations, issue Directives and take Decisions *'in accordance with the provisions of this Treaty'*, indicative of the fact that the institutions only have 'attributed' powers. Article 253 (formerly 190) states that Community acts 'shall state the reasons on which they are based'. The Council's rules of procedure provide that every Community act which it adopts (and those it adopts jointly with the Parliament) shall contain a reference to the provisions on which the measure is based.

This reference is usually to a particular Treaty Article (or Articles), which authorises the adoption of the act and specifies both the procedure to be followed and the type of act permitted. It is usually found in the first recital of the preamble to the act in question. For example (as seen in Chapter 4), Council Regulation 1612/68 on the free movement of workers was based on Article 49 EEC; Council Directive 75/117 on the approximation of Member State laws relating to the application of the equal pay principle was based on Article 100 EEC. Commission Decision 89/469 concerning BSE ('mad cow disease') in the UK was based on a Council Directive of 1964 on animal health problems, itself based on Articles 43 and 100 EEC.

However, as we have seen in earlier chapters, the scope of Community powers is in practice more extensive than this analysis suggests. First, express law making powers of a more general nature are to be found in Article 94 (formerly 100), 95 (formerly 100a) and 308 (formerly 235).

Aside from Article 99 (now 93) (dealing with national indirect taxation), Article 100 EEC was the original Treaty provision empowering the Council to issue harmonisation Directives in connection with the establishment and functioning of the Common Market. It was in large part overtaken by Article 100a EEC as introduced by the Single European Act:

Article 100a EEC

1   By way of derogation from Article 100 and save where otherwise provided in this Treaty, the following provisions shall apply for the achievement of the objectives set out in Article 8a. The Council shall, acting by a qualified majority on a proposal from the Commission in cooperation with the European Parliament and after consulting the Economic and Social Committee, adopt the measures for the approximation of the provisions laid down by law, regulation or administrative action in Member States which have as their object the establishment and functioning of the internal market ...

(When TEU amendments came into effect, the co-operation procedure was, as we have seen, replaced in this Article by the 'co-decision' procedure. Article 8a(2), defining the Internal Market, is now Article 14(2).)

As the basis for Internal Market harmonisation measures, Article 100a was applied to a vast range of subjects. For example, as regards the removal of differing national rules relating to goods, it was used to introduce new European standards to pressure vessels, children's toys and building materials, and in total Article 100a formed the basis of some 300 measures within the full range of the Single Market '1992' programme.

Article 235 (now 308) is similarly of a general nature, but it serves a totally different purpose:

Article 308

If action by the Community should prove necessary to attain, in the course of the operation of the Common Market, one of the objectives of the Community and this Treaty has not provided the necessary powers, the Council shall, acting unanimously on a proposal from the Commission and after consulting the European Parliament, take the appropriate measures.

This Article, containing a *residual* legislative power, enables the Council to act on policy matters which, whilst falling within the broad objectives of the Community, are not however specifically spelt out in the Treaty.

To illustrate the requirement that this power must be used to attain one of the Community's *objectives*, prior to the introduction of Articles 130r–t (now 174–76) into the Treaty by the Single European Act, environmental protection was brought within Article 2 of the Treaty by regarding a 'continuous and balanced expansion' in a qualitative sense. Environmental action Directives were then based on Article 235 (or Article 100 in connection with the removal of technical barriers to trade which were also detrimental to the environment).

In addition, action must also be 'necessary', which in practice means that a measure of discretion is left to the Council and Commission. Thirdly, although what is now Article 308 states that the objective must be attained in the 'course of the operation of the Common Market', this in effect sometimes meant in practice that the action fell within the context of the Treaty as a whole, so that the Common Market may function more effectively: an institutional practice viewed critically by the German Federal Constitutional Court in the *Brunner* case (see Chapter 3) in the context of unwarranted Treaty 'amendments' – and see also the discussion of implied powers below.

Nevertheless, it is also the case that, in the words of the Court of Justice in Case 45/86 *Commission v Council (Generalised Tariff Preferences)*, 'it follows from the very wording of Article 235 that its use as the legal basis for a measure is justified only where no other provision of the Treaty gives the Community institutions the necessary power to adopt the measure in question'. Thus, it may be that powers are to be found elsewhere in the Treaty, but they are not considered sufficiently effective. In Case 8/73 *Hauptzollamt Bremerhaven v Massey-Ferguson*, a Regulation enacted under Article 235 on uniform rules for the valuation of goods was held to be valid since Article 27 EEC (now repealed) on the same subject only provided for the issue of non-binding recommendations.

Article 235 was used extensively, prior to the Single European Act 1986 amendments of the Treaty, in connection with the establishment of a basis for economic and monetary union and also for the development of common regional, social, environmental, energy, and science and technology policies. Whilst, therefore, the Single European Act and the TEU reduced the significance of Article 235, it still allows the Council to act, where necessary and under the conditions laid down, to the exclusion of Article 236 (now Article 48 TEU) which, in *dealing with Treaty amendments*, calls for a conference of the Member States and the ratification of agreed amendments by each of those States.

Apart from these general powers conferred under the 'old' Articles 100, 100a and 235, when examining the full range of the Community's legislative powers it is also necessary to consider the question of *implied powers*. In a narrow sense, implied powers may be derived from the Council's or Commission's express powers and typically extend to such power as is necessary to permit of a *reasonable application* of such express powers: see Case 8/55 *Fédération Charbonnière de Belgique*. However, in Cases 281, 283–85, 287/85 *Germany et al v Commission*, which was discussed in relation to the Commission's powers in the previous chapter, it was seen that the Court of Justice took a wider view of the theory of implied powers. It will be recalled that the Court held in that case that where a provision of the Treaty conferred a specific task on the Commission, such provision was also to be regarded as impliedly conferring on the Commission 'the powers which are indispensable in order to carry out that task'.

Alleged Defects in the Treaty Basis of Adopted Measures

The legal foundation on which measures of Community legislation are based had, until recently, rarely been a contentious issue in the relations between the Community institutions, nor had alleged defects in the legal basis frequently been pleaded as a ground of invalidity of such measures. Previous literature on the subject of the legal basis of Community legislation has thus largely been confined to the question of the extent of the Community's powers under certain Treaty Articles, in particular, Articles 100 and 235 EEC. The spotlight has been thrown on this issue by the institutional modifications introduced by the Single European Act: the extension of the scope of majority voting within the Council, the setting up of a new legislative procedure for the adoption of measures in certain areas of Community activity and the granting of a right to veto to the European Parliament on proposed accession and association agreements [Bradley, 1988].

Legal basis disputes can arise in a variety of ways and the challenge to an act can be set in several contexts. The *Massey-Ferguson* case (above) was an Article 234 (formerly 177) preliminary ruling validity reference from a national court (see Chapter 9) which questioned the scope of the Community's powers. An allegation of a lack of competence of the adopting *institution*, the Commission, was the fundamental issue in the Article 230 (formerly 173) annulment action brought directly before the Court of Justice by three Member States in Cases 188–90/80 *France, Italy and UK v Commission* (see Chapter 5). However, of increasing significance, for the reasons set out by Bradley, are disputes where it is alleged that the correct institution (the Council or Council and Parliament) has based its measure on the wrong Treaty Article.

Typically, such a challenge arises either as an *intra-Council matter*, the action being brought by a Member State out-voted in the Council at the time the measure was adopted by a qualified majority, or in the course of an *inter-institutional dispute* involving the Commission (the 'European' body) and the Council (representing the interests of the Member States). In the latter situation, an added factor has sometimes been an assertion by the Parliament of its enhanced status within the institutional structure. In short, the cases are about the *division of powers*.

This first case (an intra-Council matter) arose shortly before Article 100a (and its qualified majority procedure) (now Article 95) came into effect.

Case 68/86 *UK v Council (Agricultural Hormones)*

The UK brought proceedings under Article 173(1) (now 230(1) and (2)) for the annulment of Council Directive 85/649 prohibiting the use of natural hormones for fattening purposes in meat production. The UK was opposed to a total prohibition and had voted (with Denmark) against the adoption of the Directive in the Council. It was submitted, *inter alia*, that the Directive had an insufficient legal basis. It had been adopted on the basis of Article 43 (now 37) which requires only a qualified majority; the UK arguing that it should have been based on both Article 43 and Article 100 (now 94), the latter requiring unanimity. (It was claimed that Article 100 was necessary in order to cover the consumer protection aspects of the Directive.) If Article 100 had been required, the Council would not be able to impose the hormone ban at all. The Court of Justice ruled as follows on the issue of legal basis:

> ... Article 43 of the Treaty is the appropriate legal basis for any legislation concerning the production and marketing of agricultural products listed in Annex II to the Treaty which contributes to the achievement of one or more of the objectives of the Common Agricultural Policy set out in Article 39 [now 33] of the Treaty. There is no need to have recourse to Article 100 of the Treaty where such legislation involves the harmonisation of provisions of national law in that field.

> ... even where the legislation in question is directed both to objectives of agricultural policy and to other objectives which, in the absence of specific provisions, are pursued on the basis of Article 100 of the Treaty, that Article, a general one under which directives may be adopted for the approximation of the laws of the Member States, cannot be relied on as a ground for restricting the field of application of Article 43 of the Treaty.

The Court did, however, go on to annul the Directive because the Council had infringed its own rules of procedure. However the Council quickly re-adopted the Directive – only to be met by two more annulment actions.

Further case law of the Court shows that where an institutional act *properly* comes within the areas covered by two Treaty Articles, the correct approach is to apply the most onerous requirement of each aspect of the procedure, for example, unanimity in the Council together with the co-operation procedure. However, in the following case (an inter-institutional dispute), the Court adopted a different approach; preference being given to the Treaty Article which provided an enhanced role for the Parliament.

Case C-300/89 *Commission v Council (Titanium Dioxide Waste)*

The Commission (supported by the Parliament) brought proceedings under Article 173(1) (now 230(1) and (2)) for the annulment of Council Directive 89/428 on procedures for harmonising national programmes for the reduction and elimination of pollution caused by waste from the titanium dioxide industry.

The Commission had proposed that the Directive be based on Article 100a (now 95), which involved the Council acting by a qualified majority in co-operation with the Parliament. However, despite the Parliament's objections, the Council adopted the Directive on the basis of the environmental policy Article 130s (now 175). This Article provided (at the time) for unanimity and merely for consultation of the Parliament.

Although the Directive had the dual objectives of environmental protection and the removal of distortions of competition (by establishing harmonised production conditions), the Court decided that the integrative Single Market Article 100a, which also provided more fully for the Parliament's participation in the legislative process, was the correct legal base.

In what was primarily a policy decision, which did not exclude the future use of Article 130s where waste management was the primary purpose (see Case C-155/91 *Commission v Council (Waste Directive)*), the Court stated that it did not wish to see the co-operation procedure 'compromised'. If that were so, 'the very objective of the co-operation procedure, which was to reinforce the participation of the European Parliament in the legislative process of the Community, would thereby be called into question'.

As a contribution towards a reduction in the Community's 'democratic deficit', the Court concluded that the participation of the Parliament was 'the reflection at the Community level of a fundamental democratic principle, according to which people were to take part in the exercise of power through the intermediary of a representative assembly'.

The wrong Treaty basis decision of the Court in Case C-376/98 *Germany v Parliament and Council (Tobacco Advertising Directive)*, with its message to the Member States that it is mindful of the limits to the Community legislators' competence, has been examined in some detail in Chapter 3. As already seen in earlier chapters, the Court has at times been criticised regarding its 'soft' approach to the review of Community legislation, thereby allowing alleged unwarranted extensions of EC competence at the expense of the Member States. However, it was evident in the above case that the Court had undertaken an in-depth investigation of the Directive, the outcome of which enabled the German government to make a successful challenge to the legislation, which went beyond the bounds set by the Treaty. This case established that the political institutions had no general power to regulate the Internal Market and showed that the interest in public health protection and the interest in free movement and effective competition could collide where Article 95 formed the legal basis of the legislation.

A similar in-depth review was undertaken by the Court in the complex scientific and legal area of biotechnological inventions in Case C-377/98 *Netherlands v Parliament and Council*, in which it was decided that Article 100a (now 95) was, in the particular circumstances, the appropriate legal basis of the Directive at issue. These two cases serve to highlight the expressed aim of the European Council in 2004 to 'address ... how to establish and monitor a more precise delimitation of powers between the EU and the Member States, reflecting the principle of subsidiarity'.

Turning again to questions of public health protection, the Commission's 'tobacco control programme' (in co-operation with the World Health Organization) and its linkage with Internal Market harmonisation of national rules, in the recent Case C-491/01 *R v Secretary of State for Health ex p British American Tobacco and Imperial Tobacco*, the applicant tobacco companies indirectly challenged the validity of Tobacco Directive 2001/37 under Article 234(1)(b):

> Directive 2001/37, based primarily on Article 95, goes beyond previous similar Internal Market harmonisation measures (for example, Directive 90/239) by reducing still further the maximum allowed tar yield of cigarettes manufactured in the Community, by imposing lower maximum yields on nicotine, and by increasing the size of health warnings on cigarettes which may still be produced. The obvious effect is to prohibit some cigarettes previously manufactured and sold in conformity with earlier Community law.

> The applicants argued that the Directive's aim was not to ensure the free movement of goods but to harmonise national rules on the protection of public health – which the

Community had no power to do under the Treaty: see Article 152(4)(c) and the *Tobacco Advertising* case in Chapter 3.

The Court of Justice ruled, *inter alia*, that:

(a) a Directive constituted an act covered by Article 234, even though its period for implementation had not expired;

(b) the Directive genuinely had as its object the improvement of the conditions for the functioning of the Internal Market and, therefore, it was possible for it to be adopted on the basis of Article 95. (The Court spoke of 'the emergence of multifarious development of national laws' in the field.)

(c) Article 95(3) explicitly required that, in achieving harmonisation, a high level of protection of human health should be guaranteed – it could be a decisive factor. The Community legislature had the freedom to amend relevant legislation in order to take account of changes in perceptions or circumstances.

(d) The Directive's objective could not be sufficiently achieved by the Member States and the Directive was not invalid by reason of infringement of the principle of subsidiarity.

CONSTITUTIONAL CHECKS AND BALANCES

In the preceding chapter, we examined the collaborative law making powers of the Community institutions. However, as the foregoing legal basis case shows, this collaborative process can break down, not least on account of differing views held by the Commission (the 'European' body) and the Council (of national ministers) concerning the precise nature and scope of each other's powers within this process. Similarly, as seen, the increased status of the European Parliament within the law making process has added a further dimension to any discussion of the institutional power structure. It is in this context that Rudden has observed that 'it seems as if institutional problems which prove intractable to negotiated political solution are being passed to the Court'.

Within this context, the jurisdiction of the Court of Justice regarding judicial review and annulment of acts of the Community's law makers falls within the concept of Community constitutional law and, as the pre-Maastricht Article 173(1) EEC (on the basis of which all but one of the following cases were decided) demonstrates, it extends beyond inter-institutional disputes:

Article 173(1) EEC (now 230(1) and (2) EC)

The Court of Justice shall review the legality of acts of the Council and Commission other than recommendations or opinions. It shall for this purpose have jurisdiction in actions brought by a Member State, the Council or Commission on grounds of lack of competence, infringement of an essential procedural requirement, infringement of this Treaty or of any rule of law relating to its application, or misuse of powers.

However, from within this wide field of challenge and review, it is appropriate at this point that we confine our attention to those cases (concerning not only challenges to the legal basis of an act but to other matters also) which involve the institutions alone. This will enable us to concentrate upon the development by the Court of the 'interdependent legal accountability' of the institutions: 'The Council, Commission and Parliament collaborate to make laws, but are becoming more and more answerable to the guardian of the law': Rudden. The cases which follow tend to operate on two levels: large political-constitutional issues are decided in narrow, technical terms. All the cases, with one exception, are of an inter-institutional direct challenge nature, but one case contains special features. The applicant, the French Ecology Party, was not a 'privileged plaintiff' under Article 173(1) EEC, and the act challenged was not an act of the Council or the Commission as would appear necessary under that paragraph.

In the first case, the central issue was the distribution of powers between the Community (the Commission) and the Member States (the Council) as regards the negotiation of an international treaty. In Winter's view:

> The position of the two institutions opposing each other in this legal dispute clearly reflected the interests which each has a duty to safeguard: the Commission represented the interests of the Community and its institutions; claiming that the principle of attributed (or enumerated) powers should not be applied with the utmost strictness in the field of the Community's external relations in an area with so many international aspects as transport. The Council, on the other hand, clung to a narrow definition of the Community's external powers and sought to protect the sovereignty of the Member States in the foreign field from an allegedly illegal limitation by the Community.

Case 22/70 *Commission v Council (ERTA)*

In 1962, five Member States and other European countries signed the European Road Transport Agreement [ERTA], which harmonised certain social provisions (composition of crews, rest periods, etc) relating to international road transport. Before it came into force, renegotiations were started in 1967 for its revision.

In October 1969, on the basis of a Commission proposal, Council Regulation 543/69 came into effect. It was based on Article 75 of the Treaty concerning the implementation of the EEC Common Transport Policy and covered much the same ground as ERTA.

In March 1970, the Council decided that the geographically wider based ERTA II negotiations should continue and that the six Member States would co-ordinate their positions. It was on this basis that the six Member States renegotiated and agreed ERTA II.

The Commission claimed that the Council proceedings and resolution of 20 March 1970 were an encroachment by the Council on the Commission's responsibilities and functions in this regard. It therefore brought proceedings against the Council under Article 173(1) to annul the resolution.

The Court held:

(a) The Commission's application for annulment was admissible. Although not within the terms of Article 189, the Council resolution was a reviewable act under Article 173 (see also Chapter 4). It 'had definite legal effects both on relations between the Community and the Member States and on the relationship between institutions'. Not being an act listed in Article 189, it could not be annulled for lack of reasons under Article 190.

(b) The adoption by the Community of Regulation 543/69 in October 1969 as an element of the Common Transport Policy gave rise to a transfer of treaty making power from the Member States to the Community:

> As and when such common rules come into being, the Community alone is in a position to assume and carry out contractual obligations towards third

countries affecting the whole sphere of application of the Community legal system. With regard to the implementation of the provisions of the Treaty the system of internal Community measures may not therefore be separated from that of external relations.

(c) Most of the work on ERTA I and II having been completed, on a Member State basis, in October 1969, 'it was for the two institutions whose powers were directly concerned, namely, the Council and Commission, to reach agreement ... on the appropriate methods of co-operation with a view to ensuring most effectively the defence of the interests of the Community'.

(d) The Council had not acted improperly in continuing the ERTA negotiations on a Member State basis, the Commission having failed to exercise its rights as regards the initiation of such co-operation as provided for in the Treaty.

By means of a skilful use of Article 173 in relation to Article 189 so as to create an act *sui generis* (the Council resolution), and by its application of the doctrine of 'parallelism' (whereby the exercise of *internal* powers gave rise to *external* powers also), the Court was able to increase, at the expense of the Member States, the competence of the Community in the field of external relations. In this important sense, the Commission won the war although it lost this particular battle, because the Court did not wish to throw the long running negotiations with non-Member States into confusion by allowing the Commission to replace the Member States at such a late date.

The Court's powers of review under Article 173(1) (and now 230) enable it to maintain the institutional balance of power, while ensuring that Community activities remain within the boundaries established by the Treaty. It was however also clear from the ERTA decision that, if policy requires it, the Court was prepared to extend those boundaries. (Note, however, the 1992 'warning' from the German Federal Constitutional Court in *Brunner* in Chapter 3; and see also the next chapter on the Court of Justice.) Nowhere is this more apparent than in a series of Article 173 cases involving the European Parliament. At that time, that Article provided that: 'The Court of Justice shall review the legality of acts of the Commission and the Council ...' There was no mention of acts of the Parliament. Nevertheless, in the case which follows, the Court, having reviewed the growth of the Parliament's powers since the Treaty came into force, ruled that to hold it unaccountable as regards measures intended to have legal effects would amount to a failure by the Court to fulfil its duty under Article 164 (now 220) to ensure that the law is observed. Commenting upon this extension by the Court of its own jurisdiction, Hartley has stated that: 'All courts are of course influenced by policy, but in the European Court policy plays a particularly important role: occasionally the Court will ignore the clear words of the Treaty in order to obtain a policy objective.'

Under certain conditions, Article 173(2) EEC (now 230(4) EC) allowed 'any natural and legal person' to challenge a Decision (but not a 'true' Regulation or a Directive).

Case 294/83 *Partie Ecologiste 'Les Verts' v European Parliament*

The Parliament adopted a decision involving the expenditure of budgetary funds which had the effect of subsidising the expenses of parties fighting the forthcoming 1984 direct elections. The method of allocation resulted in the bulk of the money going to parties already represented in the Parliament. The Greens were not such a party and therefore challenged the decision under Article 173(2) EEC as being discriminatory.

Having ruled that the challenge by 'Les Verts' was admissible, the Court stated that acts of the Parliament were not expressly included in the Treaty because at that time (1958) the Parliament merely possessed powers of consultation and political control rather than the power to adopt measures which had legal effects.

In *ERTA*, the Court had expressed the view that the 'general scheme' of the Treaty was to make a direct action available against 'all measures adopted by the institutions ... which are intended to have legal effects'. To exclude acts of the Parliament from the ambit of this statement would, in the Court's view, be contrary to the functions of the Court itself under Article 164 and the Treaty as a whole:

> ... the European Economic Community is a Community based on the rule of law, inasmuch as neither its Member States nor its institutions can avoid a review of the question whether the measures adopted by them are in conformity with the basic constitutional charter, the Treaty.

> ... Measures adopted by the European Parliament in the context of the EEC Treaty could encroach on the powers of the Member States or of the other institutions, or exceed the limits which have been set to the Parliament's powers, without its being possible to refer them for review by the Court. It must therefore be concluded that an action for annulment may lie against measures adopted by the European Parliament intended to have legal effects vis à vis third parties.

The Parliament's act was annulled on the ground that 'in the present state of Community law, the establishment of a scheme for the reimbursement of election campaign expenses ... remains within the competence of the Member States'.

It is noteworthy that the Parliament itself did not claim that the action was inadmissible because it was not a named defendant in Article 173. The logic of this was that if its acts, as this case demonstrates, could be challenged, then at the earliest opportunity the Parliament would seek to become a challenger, although again not so named in Article 173.

At the time of *Les Verts*, another case was in progress in which it was alleged that the Parliament had exceeded the limit set to its budgetary powers.

Case 34/86 *Council v Parliament (Budget)*

In December 1985, the President of the Parliament acting under Article 203(7) (now 272(7)) declared the budget for 1986 to be finally adopted. This was despite increases in non-compulsory expenditure in excess of the maximum rate fixed by the Commission and in the absence of an agreement between the Parliament and the Council on a new rate: Article 203(9) (now 272(9)). The Parliament had expressed the view that the Council had failed to take into account commitments already entered into and the cost of accession of two new Member States – Spain and Portugal.

In Advocate General Mancini's opinion: 'The Parliament's strategy is inspired by the history of Western institutions ... and a basic forecast: the greater its influence in determining the budget becomes the less resistible will be its requests for new powers and, by the same token, for greater democracy in the Community system.' In this Article 173 action brought by the Council, the question of whether the President's declaration was a reviewable act was dealt with by the Court as follows:

> It is the President of the Parliament who formally declares that the budgetary procedure has been brought to a close by the final adoption of the budget and thus endows the budget with binding force vis à vis the institutions and the Member States. In exercising that function the President of the Parliament intervenes by means of a separate legal act of an objective nature at the conclusion of a procedure characterised by the joint action of various institutions.

The Court concluded that the President's declaration had been made before the Parliament and Council had agreed the new rate of increase for non-compulsory expenditure. It was tainted with illegality and therefore annulled. The Court went on to rule that those two institutions as a matter of urgency should, in accordance with their obligation under Article 176 (now 233), take steps to agree the budget.

In 1987, the European Parliament, in an attempt to establish a position as a fully privileged applicant under Article 173(1), challenged a Council Decision relating to the operation of Council regulatory committees acting in conjunction with the Commission, where the Commission is exercising powers conferred on it by the Council for the implementation of rules laid down by the latter: see Chapter 5.

As Weiler argues:

... it was possible (but by no means necessary) to construe the earlier case law on the position of the Parliament before the European Court (most importantly, Case 138/79 *Roquette Frères* ... Case 294/83 *Les Verts*; Case 34/86 *Budget* ...) as being informed by a judicial policy of 'equalising' the jurisdictional status of Parliament to that of the other principal Community institutions. *Comitology* might simply have become the 'logical' continuation of this case law, especially of *Les Verts*. It must have come as a disappointment to Parliament that in its judgment the European Court underscored its interest, already revealed in *Les Verts*, in having all legal acts in the Community order susceptible to judicial review and was less concerned with institutional jurisdictional 'equity'. It might nonetheless be that, in negating any standing to Parliament under Article 173, the European Court left an unacceptable jurisdictional lacuna and compromised the very system of protection it was at pains to complete in *Les Verts*.

Case 302/87 *Parliament v Council (Comitology)*

The Parliament contended that Article 173 should be interpreted in its favour as it had been, against the Parliament, in *Les Verts* and the *Budget* case. Rejecting this argument based on 'balance' and 'equity', the Court refused the Parliament's right to sue under Article 173.

Amongst other things, the Court stated that the Commission was charged with the guardianship of the Treaty under Article 155 (now 211) and so could introduce an action for annulment of acts which endangered the Parliament's prerogatives.

The Court did not follow the compromise put forward by Attorney General Darmon who argued for limited rights for the Parliament under Article 173. In view of the case which follows, it is important to see that he argued that the Parliament should be entitled to challenge Council or Commission acts where its own interests or rights were directly affected, otherwise it would stand in an unfavourable position as compared with the other institutions and Member States under Article 173(1) and with private parties under Article 173(2). The case which follows had been commenced when this argument was put before the Court.

Case C-70/88 *Parliament v Council (Chernobyl)*

The Parliament sought the annulment under Article 173 (and Article 146 Euratom) of Council Regulation 3954/87 which laid down permitted maximum levels of radioactive contamination of food and feeding-stuffs. It claimed that the Regulation should have been based on Article 100a (now 95), which required the opening of the co-operation procedure with the Parliament, and not on Article 31 Euratom which merely required the Parliament to be consulted. The Council's action, it was claimed, amounted to a failure to observe the Parliament's post-Single European Act powers regarding its more influential role in the drawing up of legislation. The Council objected to the admissibility of the action, denying Parliament's standing under Article 173.

The Court of Justice ruled that the action was admissible despite its decision in *Comitology*.

In *Comitology*, the Court had stated that the prerogatives of the Parliament were sufficiently safeguarded by its own rights as a plaintiff under Article 175 (now 232 and regarding an institution's *failure* to act: see Chapter 19) and indirectly by way of Article 177 references concerning an act's validity and Article 173 annulment actions brought by privileged (paragraph 1) and non-privileged (paragraph 2) applicants. Nevertheless, in *Chernobyl*, a differently constituted Court felt that the existence of these other remedies was not sufficient to guarantee in all circumstances the annulment of an act of the Council or Commission which had infringed the prerogatives of the Parliament.

However, in following Attorney General Darmon's compromise in *Comitology*, the Parliament's interest in such proceedings was restricted to situations where an infringement of its prerogatives is in question. Such interest is not the *general* interest of the Council, the Commission or the Member States, and the Court emphasised that proceedings brought by the Parliament in defence of its prerogatives (relating, for example, to its proper participation in the legislative process) were not covered by Article 173, but under a right of action created by the Court to ensure respect for the institutional balance.

Thus, in Case C-295/90 *Parliament v Council*, the Court of Justice annulled Directive 90/366 on the right of residence of students because the Council had based it partly on the 'residual' Article 235 (now 308) which required only consultation of the Parliament, rather than solely on Article 7(2) (now 12) which required use of the co-operation procedure. However, the Parliament was unsuccessful in Case C-187/93 *Parliament v Council (Transfer of Waste)* where, as in its decision in Case C-155/91 *Commission v Council (Waste Directive)* (see above), the Court held that the legislation in question had been properly based on Article 130s (now 175) and consequently there had been no failure to respect the Parliament's prerogatives.

On the basis of its rules of procedure, the Parliament on several occasions challenged the Council, within the context of the simple consultation procedure, following the latter's failure to reconsult the Parliament where the Council had adopted an act, the provisions of which had been substantially modified since the Parliament originally gave its opinion: see page 116 and Case C-21/94 *Parliament v Council*, in which a successful challenge was made to a Council harmonisation Directive concerning vehicle taxation.

If it is argued, however, that the Parliament's interest is that of its constituents, the citizens of the Community, then it may be added that at some future date that view of the Parliament's interest must be recognised. *Chernobyl* nevertheless extended the scope of judicial review of Community acts and institutional 'balance' was in large part achieved.

These developments, and others, were later accepted by the Member States and reflected in Article 173 EC which (now as Article 230) reads, in part, following a Treaty of Nice amendment:

The Court of Justice shall review the legality of acts adopted jointly by the European Parliament and the Council, of acts of the Council, of the Commission and of the ECB [European Central Bank] other than recommendations and opinions, and acts of the European Parliament intended to produce legal effects vis à vis third parties ...

It shall for this purpose have jurisdictions in actions brought by a Member State, *the European Parliament*, the Council or the Commission on the grounds of lack of competence ... [Nice amendment emphasised.]

REFERENCES AND FURTHER READING

Bradley, K St C, 'Maintaining the balance' (1987) 24 CML Rev 41.

Bradley K St C, 'The European Court and the legal basis of Community legislation' (1988) 13 EL Rev 379.

Bradley, K St C, 'Sense and sensibility: *Parliament v Council* continued' (*Chernobyl*) (1991) 16 EL Rev 245.

Bradley, K St C, '"Better rusty than missing"?: institutional reforms of the Maastricht Treaty and the European Parliament', in O'Keefe and Twomey (eds), *Legal Issues of the Maastricht Treaty*, 1994.

Crosby, S, 'The new tobacco control directive: an illiberal and illegal disdain for the law' (2002) 27 EL Rev 177.

Hervey, T, 'Up in smoke? Community (anti)-tobacco law and policy' (2001) 26 EL Rev 101.

McGee, A and Weatherill, S, 'The evolution of the Single Market – harmonisation or liberalisation?'; Part 5, 'Choice of legal base: the Court's role reasserted' (1990) 53 MLR 578.

Page, A, 'Transparency directive upheld' (1981) 6 EL Rev 496.

Rudden, B and Phelan, D, *Basic Community Cases*, 1997, Part IB, 'Inter-institutional balance'.

Weiler, J, 'Pride and prejudice – *Parliament v Council*' (*Comitology*) (1989) 14 EL Rev 334.

Winter, J, 'Annotation on Case 22/70, *Re ERTA*' (1971) 8 CML Rev 550.

CHAPTER 7

THE EUROPEAN COURT OF JUSTICE AND THE COURT OF FIRST INSTANCE (ARTICLES 220–45 (FORMERLY 164–88))

INTRODUCTION

The Convention on Certain Institutions Common to the European Communities, signed in Rome in 1957, provided that the three Communities were to be served by a single Court, the Court of Justice of the European Communities. The Court of Justice, which sits in Luxembourg, is the supreme authority on all aspects of Community law. It should not be confused with the European Court of Human Rights which sits in Strasbourg and which is not a European Community institution.

The Court of First Instance (CFI), established in 1988 under powers laid down in the Single European Act, was originally 'attached' to the Court of Justice. Elements of the Court's jurisdiction were transferred to the CFI at that time, a process which has continued, with the basis for further modifications being laid down in the Treaty of Nice and a Declaration attached to that Treaty. These changes are indicative of the continuing struggle to deliver 'justice' in a successively enlarged Union possessing an ever wider spread of legislative competences.

These jurisdictional shifts are reflected most clearly, following Nice, in a new Article 220 EC which states that: 'The Court of Justice *and the Court of First Instance*, each within its jurisdiction, shall ensure that in the interpretation and application of this Treaty the law is observed.' (Emphasis added to the Nice insertion.)

A new Article 225a also provides, following action by the Council, for the establishment of 'judicial panels to hear and determine at first instance certain classes of action or proceeding brought in specific areas'. The outcome of these most recent changes will be the emergence of a three tier judicial structure – with, of course, national courts (and tribunals) acting as Community courts in disputes coming within the sphere of the Treaties.

This chapter considers questions of structure, jurisdiction and procedure and in particular the role and methodology of the Court of Justice as regards its highly significant part in the constitutionalisation of the Treaty.

THE COMPOSITION AND ORGANISATION OF THE COURT OF JUSTICE

The new, post-Nice Article 221(1) provides that: 'The Court of Justice shall consist of one judge per Member State.' Previously it was merely an expedient convention for each of the 15 Judges to be a national of a different Member State. The Judges are nonetheless *Community* Judges in a European court, with French as its working language.

Article 221(2) and (3) now provides that the Court will either sit in *chambers*, which is the normal practice, each chamber consisting of three or five Judges; or in a *Grand Chamber* of nine or 11 Judges if a Member State or Community institution which is a party to the case so requests; or as a *full Court*, for which a minimum of 11 Judges will be counted as a plenary, in cases considered to be of exceptional importance.

The present position regarding the assignment of cases has come about through successive amendments to the Treaty and to the Statute of the Court. These changes have first of all enabled the Court to sit in chambers, and later given it greater freedom to assign cases to chambers – so helping to alleviate its increasingly heavy caseload. It is now possible for any category of case within the Court's jurisdiction (see below) to be heard by a chamber.

The appointment and status of the Judges (and Advocates General, see below) are covered by Article 223 (formerly 167) which, as slightly modified by the Nice Treaty, states, in part, that:

> The Judges and Advocates General of the Court of Justice shall be chosen from persons whose independence is beyond doubt and who possess the qualifications required for appointment to the highest judicial offices in their respective countries or who are jurisconsults of recognised competence; they shall be appointed by common accord of the governments of the Member States for a term of six years.

> Every three years there shall be a partial replacement of the Judges and Advocates General, in accordance with the conditions laid down in the Statute of the Court of Justice.

> The Judges shall elect the President of the Court of Justice from among their number for a term of three years. He may be re-elected.

> ...

> The Court of Justice shall establish its rules of Procedure. Those Rules shall require the approval of the Council, acting by a qualified majority.

Over the years, the Judges have come from a variety of backgrounds including their national judiciary, legal practice, political or administrative office, university law faculties or some combination of these. The President of the Court of Justice is currently Gil Carlos Rodriguez Iglesias and the UK Judge is David Edward, previously Professor of European Community Law at Edinburgh University.

ADVOCATES GENERAL

Under Article 222 (formerly 166), as modified at Nice:

> The Court of Justice shall be assisted by eight Advocates General. Should the Court of Justice so request, the Council, acting unanimously, may increase the number of Advocates General.

> It shall be the duty of the Advocate General, acting with complete impartiality and independence, to make, in open court, reasoned submissions on cases which, in accordance with the Statute of the Court of Justice, require his assistance.

The change made by the Nice Treaty was to remove the necessity for an Advocate General to give a 'reasoned submission' in every case. In one of the several moves made to expedite the Court's business, the Statute now states that, after hearing the Advocate General, the Court may decide that as 'the case raises no new point of law', it shall be determined without a submission.

There is no equivalent to the Advocate General in the English legal system. As Brown and Kennedy explain:

> ... although a member of the Court, he acts as its independent adviser. Unlike however his counterpart in the French *Conseil d'Etat, the commissaire du gouvernement*, he does not attend the judges' deliberations ... even in a consultative capacity.

Where his assistance is required, the prime function of an Advocate General is to deliver an impartial and reasoned *Opinion*. This Opinion is given after the conclusion of the final submissions of the parties at the oral hearing. It will review the facts, the submissions of the parties and others who have taken part, examine the law (including previous decisions of the Court) and finally express a view as to how the case should be decided.

The Advocate General's Opinion is not binding on the Court, which may or may not follow his or her submissions:

> The advocate general may also see himself as in effect delivering a reserved first instance judgment in a case being taken to appeal, but his opinion, while it may have authority in future cases, does not of course decide the instant case, even provisionally [Brown and Kennedy].

In essence, therefore, an Opinion forms an extremely valuable basis on which the Court, which is still frequently a court of both first and last instance, can arrive at its judgment. (The role of the Advocate General should be distinguished from that of the assigned *Judge Rapporteur*, whose function, following the written proceedings (see below), is to prepare a report for the Court, which normally outlines the facts and the submissions of the principal parties plus, where necessary, the submissions of third parties, such as Member States, who have a sufficient interest in the case.)

Together with the Court's judgment, the submission of the Advocate General, which may be very influential not only in the instant case but in later ones, is published in the Court's Reports.

THE JURISDICTION OF THE COURT OF JUSTICE

Article 220 (formerly 164) EC sets out the role of the Court of Justice (and now the CFI) in, on the face of it, somewhat uninformative terms. It shall 'ensure that in the interpretation and application of this Treaty, the law is observed'. Thus, in a formal sense, the jurisdiction of the Court is that which is conferred upon it by the EC Treaty (a limited or attributed competence). The particular heads of jurisdiction, for example, preliminary rulings under Article 234 (formerly 177) and judicial review actions under Article 230 (formerly 173), are to be found in the Treaty, bearing in mind, as we have seen, that since 1989 certain classes of action have been transferred to the CFI.

Nevertheless, the Court has interpreted Article 220 (formerly 164) very broadly – to such an extent that some commentators have accused it of conferring upon itself a general, inherent jurisdiction. Indeed, at times, the Court has been very 'creative': it has established fundamental principles of a constitutional character which are stated to be 'inherent in the Treaty' (for example, supremacy, direct effect and State liability) and, as will be seen in Chapter 10, it has 'discovered', largely from sources outside the Treaty, general principles of Community law, which form essential elements of the Rule of Law against which both Community and national measures can be tested for their legitimacy. In addition, as has been discussed earlier, it extended its judicial review powers to acts of the Parliament (in *Les Verts*) and allowed that institution to bring such proceedings (in *Chernobyl*) at a time when the Treaty made no provision for such developments. It also dramatically extended the Community's powers within the field of external relations in *ERTA*: see Chapter 6. The Court's 'creativity' will be discussed further in the section on 'Policy'. (What has been regarded as excessive institutional creativity has of course been criticised by, amongst others, the German Federal Constitutional Court in *Brunner*: see Chapters 3 and 6.)

The Court's main heads of jurisdiction, as found in the EC Treaty, can be explained in the following way. The Court's *dispute solving* powers operate within the complex set of relationships that exist between the subjects of Community law: the political institutions, the Member States and private parties (natural and legal persons). Here the Court may be called upon to exercise a jurisdiction of a *constitutional* nature, relating either to the balance of powers between the institutions themselves (for example, the *ERTA* and *Titanium Dioxide Waste* cases) or between the Community and the Member States, for example, an action brought by a Member State against a Community institution for annulment of an act, as in the *Agricultural Hormones* case brought by the UK against the Council or, alternatively, an action brought by the Commission against a Member State for failure to fulfil its Treaty obligations, for example, the *Tachographs* action brought against the UK.

In other disputes concerning the interpretation and application of Community law, the Court exercises a jurisdiction, originally first (and last) instance *and now appellate*, of an *administrative* character. Here its duty is the protection of private parties against illegal acts or omissions of the institutions. Such cases as *Roquette Frères v Council* (1980) and *Les Verts v Parliament* (1988) are examples of direct actions for judicial review brought by private parties to the Court of Justice under Article 173 (now 230). However, in 1993, a two tier system for all actions (not merely under Article 230) brought by natural and legal persons was established by Council Decision and these actions are now dealt with by the CFI, subject to the possibility of an appeal to the Court of Justice on a point of law. It should also be recalled that, for natural and legal persons, an alternative, indirect route from a national court, regarding rulings on the *validity* of acts of the institutions, exists under the preliminary rulings jurisdiction of the Court of Justice: Article 234(1)(b) (formerly 177(1)(b)).

The powers of the Court in relation to the *interpretation* of Community law are of particular significance within the framework of the preliminary rulings jurisdiction under Article 234. Here, the keynote is considered to be one of *co-operation* between Member States (that is, their national courts and tribunals) and the Community (the Court of Justice). The Court is concerned to ensure the *uniformity* of interpretation of Community law in its application by these national courts. These are the courts which first refer questions of interpretation to the Court of Justice and they are the courts which, armed with that Court's interpretative ruling, must ultimately settle the disputes in the actions which have arisen before them. Many of the most important Community law cases in which *constitutional* principles were established are of this kind: *Van Gend en Loos*, *Costa v ENEL*, *Francovich* and many more. They are also the cases which focus on both the legal relations between private parties and the State and between one private party and another within the Community dimension.

Since 1989, the Court's *appellate* jurisdiction – see Article 225 (as amended at Nice) – was originally mainly concerned with appeals from the CFI on points of law brought by undertakings against Court of First Instance decisions upholding original Commission Decisions under the Treaty's competition rules. However, as the jurisdiction of the CFI has been enlarged (see above and the section on that Court), so has the range of appeals in terms of the issues involved.

At Nice, an amendment to Article 225 anticipates a sharing with the CFI of the Court's previously defended exclusive jurisdictional preserve regarding preliminary rulings. A new Article 225(3) states that the CFI shall have jurisdiction to hear and determine questions referred for a ruling under Article 234 in specific areas laid down by the Statute of the Court of Justice (on the basis of an act adopted by the Council). However, if the CFI considers that the case in question requires a decision of principle likely to affect the unity or consistency of Community law, it may pass the case to the Court for a ruling. In similar circumstances, a preliminary ruling by the CFI may exceptionally be subject to review (not appeal) by the Court – probably under an emergency procedure.

Declaration 12 attached to the Nice Treaty calls on the Court and the Commission to give consideration to the division of jurisdiction between the Court and the CFI as regards direct actions. This proposed change, which will not require Treaty amendment, may well be aimed at the transfer, at least in part, of Article 226 (formerly 169) direct actions brought by the Commission against Member States who have failed to fulfil a Treaty obligation - usually a failure to implement a Directive in the specified time.

The main heads of jurisdiction of both the Court of Justice and the CFI are set out in the diagram on page 146 and have been, and will be, discussed in more detail elsewhere.

PROCEDURE BEFORE THE COURT OF JUSTICE

The basis for the required *procedural flexibility* for the Union's judicial system, pressed on the Member States for many years particularly by the Court of Justice itself, was finally established at Nice. To a considerably greater extent, future reform of the two Courts will no longer require Treaty amendment but will fall within the powers of the Council. Only such fundamental matters as the basic structure of the judicature and the jurisdictional scope of the two Courts will remain within Treaty amendment procedures.

The *Statute of the Court of Justice* (which also covers the CFI), annexed at Nice to the TEU and EC and Euratom Treaties, contains in amended form the most important practical elements of the procedure of both Courts. As before Nice, it may be amended under Article 245 EC by unanimous Council Decision – but now to a greater extent. The only exception is Title I of the Statute, which mainly deals with judicial independence.

The more detailed *Rules of Procedure* of the two Courts, necessary for the application of the Statute, can now be established by the Courts (in the CFI's case with the agreement of the Court of Justice) subject to the approval of the Council acting by a qualified majority: see the new Article 223(6).

It has been said that:

A lawyer from the British Isles is likely to find the procedure very strange. The oral and adversary character of English civil procedure (and its Scottish and Irish counterparts) is in marked contrast with the written and inquisitorial features of the Luxembourg procedure ... [Brown and Kennedy].

The procedure falls into two parts: the written procedure, which is the more important, and the oral procedure. The language to be used is determined by the applicant. Only the main features of the procedure are presented here.

A case is brought before the Court by a written application addressed to the Registrar. It must contain the applicant's name and permanent address, the name of the party (or parties) against whom the application is made, the subject matter of the dispute, the form of order sought and a brief statement of the pleas in law on which the application is made. (The procedure where a national court or tribunal requests a preliminary ruling from the Court under Article 234 EC obviously differs.)

The Court may require the parties to produce all documents and to supply all information which the Court considers desirable. It may also require Member States and institutions not parties to the case to supply all information considered necessary. Expert opinions may be obtained.

The application is served on the defendant (often a Community institution or Member State) who must lodge a defence generally within one month, stating, amongst other things, the arguments of fact and law relied upon and evidence offered in support. A reply from the applicant and the defendant's rejoinder may also be submitted within fixed time limits. Further measures of inquiry may be ordered.

Member States and institutions may always *intervene* in cases before the Court. They are deemed to have the necessary *interest* in the outcome of all such cases. However, individuals (private parties or natural or legal persons) must establish an interest in the result of a case before being accorded the same right. Intervention must be limited to supporting the submissions of one of the parties.

In the Article 234 (formerly 177) preliminary ruling procedure, it should be noted, the proceedings are not regarded as contentious – there are no parties before the Court. The national court makes the order for reference to the Court of Justice. Having received copies of the order, the parties to the national proceedings, the Member States, the Commission and, where a Council measure is in issue, the Council may submit written observations to the Court and attend the oral hearing.

The *oral* procedure may begin with the reading of the Judge Rapporteur's 'report for the hearing' with its summary of the facts and legal arguments. Next the legal representatives of the various parties may be heard together with any witnesses and experts. The Court frequently asks questions of the legal representatives. Finally, the Advocate General reads the operative part of his Opinion unless, as seen above, it has been decided (following the change made to Article 222 at Nice) that no submission will be required.

The Judges frame their decision as a single collegiate judgment following secret deliberations in which the aim, according to a close observer of the Court, may in difficult cases be to combine 'diverging arguments into a real synthesis'. There are no dissenting judgments or separate concurring judgments. If necessary, decisions may be reached on a majority basis and, although this will not be apparent on the record, the presence of dissenting voices may well affect the tenor of the judgment.

In due course, at a later date, the operative part of the judgment is read in open Court – the judgment and the Advocate General's Opinion are published in the European Court Reports.

The defendant in most of the cases before the Court is either the Community, or one (or more) of its institutions, or a Member State, or a ministry or department thereof. It is not possible in such cases to obtain execution of the Court's judgment although it is binding on the defendant. Thus, as regards enforcement actions against Member States under Articles 226 and 227 (formerly 169 and 170), Article 228(1) (formerly 171(1)) provides that:

> If the Court of Justice finds that a Member State has failed to fulfil an obligation under this Treaty, the State shall be required to take the necessary measures to comply with the judgment of the Court of Justice.

However, in such a case, where a Member State fails to comply with the Court's judgment, under a new second paragraph to Article 171 introduced at Maastricht, the Commission may bring the case before the Court again and financial penalties may be imposed: see Chapter 20.

Similarly, in cases brought against an institution regarding reviewable acts or failures to act under Articles 230 and 232 (formerly 173 and 175), Article 233 (formerly 176) goes on to state that:

> The institution or institutions whose act has been declared void or whose failure to act has been declared contrary to this Treaty shall be required to take the necessary measures to comply with the judgment of the Court of Justice.

The evidence is that Member States do comply with judgments but it may take them a year or more to do so. When France refused to comply with a judgment of the Court regarding a ban on lamb imports (mainly from Britain) until it received Community concessions which Britain was blocking in the Council, the Commission brought new proceedings and applied for an interim order under Article 186 (now 243) requiring France to admit British exports of lamb. The 'lamb war' was however eventually settled on the political plane by means of trade-off concessions negotiated in the Council.

A final point concerning the practice of the Court of Justice is that although it almost always follows its own previous decisions, it does not operate on the basis of the doctrine of precedent. It cites previous decisions to support its reasoning and occasionally it departs from its previous decisions, for example, in Case C-10/89 *Sucal v Hag* (see Chapter 18) and in Case C-267/91 *Keck*, although in the latter instance the Court did not specify from which earlier decisions it was departing (see Chapter 12).

THE COURT OF JUSTICE: POLICY AND THE PROCESS OF INTEGRATION

The importance of the judicial dimension to the process of integration – to the functioning of the Community – is generally recognised. The Court of Justice has, as a basic policy objective, consistently advanced the process of integration. In its landmark decisions establishing the principles of the supremacy of Community law and direct effect (*Costa v ENEL*, *Van Gend en Loos* and *Simmenthal*, and see now the *Francovich* principle of State liability in the next chapter), it has dramatically increased the scope and effectiveness of Community law within the legal systems of the Member States. In *ERTA* and subsequent competence cases, it has extended the powers of the Community institutions. Its continuing emphasis on the Treaty as the

THE COURT OF JUSTICE AND THE COURT OF FIRST INSTANCE: MAIN HEADS OF JURISDICTION

Judgments — Preliminary Rulings
- Interpretation of Treaty Articles and Community Acts — Article 177 (now 234)
- Direct Effect of EC Law
- Validity of Community Acts

Direct Actions
- Against Member States
  - Brought by Commission — Article 169 (now 226)
  - Brought by Member States — Article 170 (now 227)
- Against Community Institutions — Judicial Review (Actions brought by Member States or by Institutions)
  - Annulment Actions — Article 173 (now 230)
  - Failure to Act — Article 175 (now 232)

Appellate Jurisdiction — On points of law from the COURT OF FIRST INSTANCE — Article 168a (now 225)

Annulment actions and failure to act (Brought by private parties)

Articles 173 and 175 (now 230 and 232)

Review of Commission competition decisions

Articles 173 and 175 (Now 230 and 232)

Non-contractual Liability of the Community (Brought by private parties)

Articles 178 and 215(2) (now 235 and 288(2))

Staff cases

Article 179 (now 236)

Community's 'constitution' rather than an international agreement underpins its policy objectives.

Remarks regarding the role of the Court of Justice attributed to the then British Prime Minister, John Major, in September 1991, drew an interesting response in a letter to the editor of *The Times* from a former President of the Court – a response which was not allowed to go unchallenged:

EC AND THE LAW

from Lord Mackenzie Stuart

Sir, According to your political editor the prime minister regards the Court of Justice of the European Communities 'as a politically motivated body that should have no role in shaping member governments' policies' (report, 26 September, earlier editions). If this accurately represents the prime minister's belief, which would surprise me, then he should be rapidly disabused of this slur on the court's integrity.

The European treaties, which are agreements reached by the governments of the member states, are the result of political choice. So, too, is every act of Parliament. The court plays no part in that choice. Its function, a purely judicial one, as the Treaty of Rome provides, is to see that the law is observed.

This, of course, includes applying the old common law rule that, where possible, a legal document should be given an intelligible meaning rather than that it should be declared a nullity.

To suggest, as does your report, that the court ignores proper judicial standards, is a calumny.

Yours faithfully,

MACKENZIE STUART

(President, Court of Justice of the European Communities, 1984–88), Le Garidel, Gravières, 07140 Les Vans, France. 27 September.

JUDICIAL FUNCTION OF EUROPEAN COURT

From Mr Gavin Smith

Sir, One hesitates to take issue with a jurist of the distinction of Lord Mackenzie Stuart. However, his assertion (October 3) that the function of the European Court of Justice is a purely judicial one cannot go unchallenged.

In the opinion of many objective commentators, the court has since its inception been inspired more by a political urge to achieve European integration than by a desire to 'ensure that in the interpretation and application of the treaties the law is observed', as it is enjoined to do by Article 164 of the Treaty of Rome.

Indeed, of the two most fundamental principles of EC law one (its supremacy over national law) is exclusively and the other (its direct applicability in national proceedings) largely the product of judicial inventiveness, designed to increase the impact of EC law at the expense of national law.

Perhaps Lord Mackenzie Stuart would like to comment on the recent statement made (extra-judicially) by one of his former brethren, Judge Mancini, that 'the main endeavour of the court has been to reduce the differences between the treaties and a constitution; that it 'has sought to "constitutionalise" the treaty ... to fashion a constitutional framework for a federal-type structure in Europe' (*Common Market Law*

Review, 1989). I am not aware that any present or former judges of the court have dissociated themselves from these views.

Probably the most striking recent instance of judicial policy making by the European Court was its decision last year in the *Chernobyl* case (Case 70/88), where it held that the European Parliament could in certain circumstances challenge EC legislation before the court.

The relevant treaty provision (Article 173) can only be construed as denying the parliament this right. However, this 'procedural lacuna' did not prevent the court from ruling, in effect, that since – in its view – the parliament needed such a power, it should be *granted* it.

What is particularly disturbing about that judgment is that the court must have been aware that a European Commission proposal to give the parliament this very power had been rejected by the Member States only five years before, at the last revision of the treaties. [However, the Member States fell in line with the Court at Maastricht in 1992, and see now the renumbered, and as amended at Nice, Article 230(2).]

It is no doubt going too far to accuse the European Court, as did a former prime minister of France, Michel Debré, of suffering from a *mégalomanie maladive.* Nevertheless, concern at the unorthodoxy of the court's approach cannot be dismissed merely as a slur on its integrity.

Perhaps, with the issue of European federalism high on the political agenda, those commentators who display such enthusiasm for criticism of our own judges should apply themselves with equal vigour to analysis of how the European Court performs its judicial function.

Yours faithfully,

GAVIN SMITH

1 Metre Court Buildings, Temple, EC4.

9 October.

Both Lord Mackenzie Stuart and Mr Smith draw particular attention to Article 164 (now 220). Regarding the Court's interpretative function, the former states that the Treaty – 'a legal document' – must be given 'an intelligible meaning'. The latter argues that, rather than engaging in judicial interpretation, the Court, for political reasons, has been more involved in 'judicial inventiveness'. Lord Mackenzie Stuart is saying rather less than he might and Mr Smith is focusing on only a part of the picture – and surely direct effect should be seen as a mechanism whereby Community law operates to protect a subject of that law, the individual, against shortcomings in national law, rather than one which operates 'at the expense of national law'.

The EC Treaty, like its predecessor, is a *traité cadre* – an open-textured framework of evolutionary institutional and socio-economic law agreed by the Member States. At the very least, 'gap-filling' is required and this comes about both by the adoption of Community legislation by the political institutions and by the Court as interpreter of the Treaty on the basis of Article 220. Now, although Article 7 (formerly 4) states that, 'Each institution shall act within the powers conferred upon it by this Treaty', the Court itself is the sole interpreter of its powers within the various heads of jurisdiction conferred upon it (although its powers may be changed by amendment of the Treaty). It is also clear that the Court, operating within the dynamic of the integration process and the goals set out in Article 2, regards itself as a necessary contributor to the integration process.

Article 220 demands that the Community acts on the basis of the *Rule of Law* and, as a matter of *policy*, given its own view of the European Community, the Court has, where it has felt it necessary, taken an activist or creative position regarding the scope and nature of that law. Cappelletti has argued that:

> A court ... especially one dealing with constitutional, federal, or generally transnational matters, has to have the courage to stand against temporary pressures whenever the 'higher law' which it is its mission to enforce so demands ...

> The vision of a great court, of course, should not be arbitrary. Now I have no difficulty in admitting that Rasmussen is right in seeing the European Court's vision as one of furthering European integration. Contrary to Rasmussen, however, I am convinced that such a vision, far from being arbitrary, is fully legitimate, for it is rooted in the text, most particularly in the Preamble and the first Articles of the EEC Treaty ...

The Court's pursuit of the 'higher law' not only regarding integration – both economic and legal – has, as seen in the above quotation, elicited a considerable amount of criticism from legal academics, including Rasmussen, and from politicians. The criticism has focused on what is termed the Court's excessive judicial activism. This accusation amounts to a charge that, as Tridimas explains, the Court 'assumes for itself powers which go beyond its judicial function'. Having established integration as a key facet of policy, and by adopting, where necessary, a decision making approach which will further this purpose, it is argued that the Court has either read too much into, or flaunted the language of, the 'written' law of the Community and 'assumed a quasi-legislative role'.

On the other hand, it can be said that, operating in this way, not only has the Court greatly assisted in the advancement of the integrative process, but it has also increased the effectiveness of the law which underpins the Community, strengthened the rights of individuals, and extended the powers of the Community. There is no better case law example on which to base a view of the two sides of the activism issue than *Van Gend en Loos* (see Chapter 4).

In *Van Gend en Loos*, the Court made it clear that direct effect, a fundamental principle of Community law of a federal nature, was *inherent* in the Treaty, to be gleaned from 'the spirit, the general scheme and the wording of the Treaty', not from any particular provision. Here is 'gap-filling' on a grand scale (so too in the State liability *Francovich* case: see the next chapter) or rather a policy-directed formulation of a basic principle arising on the basis of the ideally suited Article 12 (now 25). Such interpretation, which in the case in question was by no means inevitable, is called *teleological or purposive* interpretation. It is a form of interpretation, or for some commentators, for example, Hartley, 'beyond interpretation properly so called', which furthers Community objectives. Here (as again with *Francovich*), the objective was to increase the scope and effectiveness (immediacy for private parties) of Community law and to secure its uniform application throughout the Member States. Community law must be effective with respect to individual rights and remedies following breaches of that law by the Member States. Additionally, this case, concerned as it was with customs duties and the free movement of goods and therefore with the Common Market, made a significant contribution to the process not only of legal but also economic integration.

Nevertheless, the Court must keep within bounds. It must be mindful of its relationship with the law making political institutions. It resolves their power struggles and similar competence disputes between the Community and the Member States. (Note particularly the TEU's introduction of the principle of subsidiarity in Article 5 (formerly 3b) EC in the latter regard.) As we have seen, the Member States must be able to see the Court's activist developments as legitimate and so be ready to accept them into their legal systems. Over the years, the Court moved very tentatively on the issue of individual rights based on Directives which Member States had failed to implement. Such rights – against the defaulting State – were eventually recognised in Case 41/74 *Van Duyn*, as we will see in the next chapter. However, horizontal rights in such situations, the rights of one private party against another, have been consistently denied, most recently in Case C-91/92 *Faccini Dori*, on the ostensible basis of a *literal* interpretation of Article 189(3) (now 249(3)) EC.

Alternatively, the Court may play a *reactive* role, for example, it may be prompted by a Member State to 'find' the law which is to be observed under Article 220 (formerly 164). This was so in the case of West Germany in the early 1970s with respect to the protection of fundamental human rights, which found no expression in the 1957 Treaty. Such rights and other 'general principles' of Community law have been established by the Court mainly from sources *beyond* the express provisions of the Treaty to ensure that basic democratic values are upheld (see Chapter 10).

The Court took up a clearly activist role, particularly at a time of legislative stagnation in the political institutions from the mid-1970s into the 1980s, in the field of negative integration – the establishment and maintenance of the Common/Internal Market. Here, the Court, mainly on the basis of its preliminary rulings jurisdiction under Article 234 (formerly 177), acted as a prime mover in determining and refining the obligations of the Member States. It did this with respect not only to the free movement of goods (*Van Gend en Loos*, Case 8/74 *Dassonville* and Case 120/78 *Cassis de Dijon*; see Chapter 12) but also to persons (Case 2/74 *Reyners*) and capital (Cases 286/82 and 26/83 *Luisi* and *Carbone*). As Gormley has explained:

> ... the Court has sometimes been obliged with the aid of the systematic teleological method of interpretation to deduce solutions from Community law for concrete problems which should have been dealt with by the Community legislator. This has led to the Court being accused of indulging in judicial policy making. Geelhoed has rightly observed, though, that the systematic teleological method of interpretation binds the judges to the system and aims of Community law and thus limits their freedom of policy choice.

> However, the systematic teleological approach seems to bind the judges less in some areas than in others with the result that the Court's case law acquires a stronger aspect of judicial creativity than lawyers are used to seeing from national judges.

In the 1990s and beyond, following the establishment of the Internal Market, it may be that the Court's influence has diminished and will diminish as the focus switches to positive economic and political integration. For example, in 1994, Gerber was of the view that:

> The Court's methodology has also evolved in accordance with this change in leadership role. The teleological reasoning that the Court relied on so heavily during earlier periods has become less evident, as the Court turns increasingly to the manipulation of narrower principles drawn largely from its own previous decisions. Teleology is an appropriate tool for an aggressive court, while reasoning that relies

primarily on the authority of previous concepts and decisions comports more easily with a more cautious role ... once the 'big' issues have been resolved and the basic conceptual framework has been established, a court has less room to play an aggressive role.

Alternatively, it may be that, the essential nature of the process of integration remaining the same, the same basic questions both of competence and the effectiveness of Community law will remain as questions for the Court to face. Certainly, in terms of effectiveness, the Court's State liability decision in 1991 in *Francovich* has had as great an impact as its 1963 *Van Gend en Loos* direct effect decision as regards the protection of individuals in the face of infringements of Community law by Member States. The establishment of this new principle, 'inherent in the Treaty', elicited the strongest protests from UK 'Euro-sceptics' and (unsuccessful) calls from them pre-Maastricht for the Intergovernmental Conference to agree measures to curb this 'non-elected' body.

THE COURT AND THE TREATY AS A CONSTITUTION

The question of the existence, or the emergence, of a constitution for the European Community and, since Maastricht, of the European Union has been discussed in the law journals, particularly over the last 12 years or so, but chiefly by European continental commentators. By definition, this is a fundamental question, one which can adequately be understood only in the context of the Community/Union as a dynamic organisation. In turn, analysis of this question goes a long way towards the acquisition of the 'big picture' view of a legal system.

A principal argument against the existence of a European constitution has been that a constitution is the basic law of a State, and since neither the Community nor the Union are States but international organisations, neither can be capable of having constitutions. This view is linked to that of sovereignty, which identifies the State as the highest authority within its frontiers. Further, if one turns to the primary source of Community law, one finds of course that it is a treaty (in the first instance the EEC Treaty of 1957), at first sight a creature of international law governing relations between States, and on the standard view of such contracts merely a document creating mutual obligations between those States and not possessing higher law status vis à vis the laws of the contracting powers.

As is well known, that view of the Treaty of Rome, put forward by the Dutch government in Case 26/62 *Van Gend en Loos*, was rejected by the Court of Justice. The Court's reasoning, when stating that the Treaty was 'more than' a standard international treaty, represents its first steps in the making of a constitution for Europe. In doing so, the Court had in mind that definition of a constitution which asserts that its purpose is to establish the fundamental principles or doctrines of a new system of government. Here the Court had regard to what it saw as the intentions of the framers of the Treaty – to 'the spirit, the general scheme and the wording of [its] provisions'. It saw the Treaty's aim as being the bringing together, the integration, of 'interested parties' comprising both governments *and* peoples into a single Community and, later, a Union.

Also, quite clearly, in line with the standard view of a constitution, the Court could find within the Treaty 'the establishment of [Community] institutions endowed with sovereign rights, the exercise of which affects both Member States and also their citizens'; restraints on the exercise by those institutions of their powers through the medium of judicial review 'checks and balances' in Article 173 (now 230); access to Community law by nationals of the Member States via Article 177 (now 234); and the creation of a court inevitably concerned with the settlement of disputes of a constitutional nature.

The conclusion the Court drew from all this was 'that the Community constitutes a new legal order', from which (although not explicitly stated in *Van Gend en Loos* beyond the 'something more' reference to the Treaty) it may be implied that this view of the Treaty as a constitution – as subsequently developed by the Court – would provide the Community with necessary moral authority and legitimacy. The shift of the Court's focus from international agreement to constitution is not without historical precedent. Indeed, Manfred Zuleeg, a former Judge at the Court of Justice, has stated that 'international organizations are not excluded from the number of entities possessing a constitution because of the contractual nature of the founding act, at least if sovereign powers are granted to those organisations'.

Nevertheless, an examination of the original 1957 Treaty in the search for a constitution to underpin this new *'sui generis'* system of law is not particularly rewarding. It set out the objectives and, within the then very limited scope of Article 3, the competence of the Economic Community insofar as transfers of sovereign rights had been made by the six Member States. It laid down certain fundamental rules regarding the operation of the Common Market particularly with respect to free movement and competition. As stated above, it set out the powers of the political and judicial institutions, albeit the *horizontal* division of legislative, executive and judicial powers (recognised by the Court of Justice as early as 1958 in the Coal and Steel Community Case 9/56 *Meroni v High Authority*) must have struck the reader as distinctly odd. In the legislative sphere, the non-directly elected Assembly (later Parliament) had merely a consultative role, the institutions having the key roles within the process being a non-elected body, the Commission, and an intergovernmental body, the Council of Ministers. Furthermore, although the signatories were resolved 'to preserve and protect peace and liberty', the original Treaty contained no guarantees of fundamental rights and only limited, indirect protection of individual rights. Although the founders were 'determined to lay the foundations of an ever closer union between the peoples of Europe', the substance of the 1957 Treaty was essentially economic, revealing the philosophy of the bureaucrat Monnet and a shortfall that became known as the 'democratic deficit'.

In 1991, in its *Opinion on the Draft Agreement on a European Economic Area*, the Court of Justice felt in a position to make the following statement in clear express terms:

> The EEC Treaty, albeit concluded in the form of an international agreement, none the less constitutes the constitutional charter of a Community based on the rule of law. As the Court of Justice has consistently held, the Community treaties established a new legal order for the benefit of which the states have limited their sovereign rights, in ever wider fields, and the subjects of which comprise not only Member States but also their nationals ... The essential characteristics of the Community legal order which has thus been established are in particular its primacy over the law of the Member States and the direct effect of a whole series of provisions which are applicable to their nationals and to the Member States themselves.

In the Court's view therefore, the pre-Maastricht EEC Treaty operated as the constitutional charter of a Community legal system possessing and exercising competence in 'ever wider fields'. Inasmuch as the subjects of the Community legal order were both Member States and their 'nationals' (private parties, that is, human and legal persons), this constitution formed the basis of an upper tier of a two tier system of law. Just two years earlier, Judge Frederico Mancini, speaking extra-judicially, had similarly said that 'the Court has sought to "constitutionalise" the Treaty, that is to fashion a constitutional framework for a federal-type structure in Europe'.

Clearly it is imperative to know what form this fashioning had taken – step by step and to total effect. Other questions arise for us at the present day. What further steps in this direction – if any – have been taken by the Court – or the Member States – since 1991? What, in this context, was the effect of the European Community becoming but one pillar of the new Maastricht Union? And finally, while generally recognised, is the constitutional order of the European order, in Barendt's words, 'complex and flawed'?

The steps taken by the Court of Justice have to be seen first of all in the light of legitimacy, of acceptance by the Member States and their courts. This can be restated in terms of the legitimacy of the Court of Justice acting as a constitutional court. Such acceptance has been forthcoming, sometimes slowly and reluctantly. Some of the steps taken now find their place in the Treaties. Secondly, the steps taken, as Mancini said, have taken the Community legal system along a federal path. As Lenaerts has stated:

> As a system of divided powers, federalism proceeds from the very essence of constitutionalism, which is limited government operating under the rule of law.
>
> ...
>
> Federalism is also present whenever a divided sovereignty is guaranteed by the national or supranational constitution and umpired by the supreme court of the common legal order. Both sovereigns enact laws with direct operation upon those to whom they are addressed.

The Court of Justice formulated (as should be well known) the first and probably the most important basic principle of the European constitution in 1962 in *Van Gend en Loos* itself. This is that clear and unconditional provisions of the Treaty (EEC, now EC) may create *directly effective rights* for individuals enforceable in their national courts. Without the need for national legislation (or in the face of conflicting national legislation), Community law acts as a source of individual protection at national level. Here we find the constitutionalisation of the vertical separation of powers between the Community and the Member States. As discussed above, without an express statement to this effect, the Court was basing its ruling on the Treaty as being in substance a constitution of a central legal order federally related to the legal orders of the Member States. Whether the Court's ruling amounted to an activist use of teleological interpretation of the Treaty provision in question or 'naked law making' is an issue related to that of acceptance.

Since 1962, direct effect has been extended to Regulations (Case 93/71 *Leonesio*, Case 106/77 *Simmenthal*) and, to a limited extent, to Directives (Case 148/78 *Ratti*, Case 152/84 *Marshall*). Additional sources of individual Community rights were found by the Court in the principles of indirect effect (Case 14/83 *Von Colson*) and State liability (Case C-6/90 *Francovich*), in which the Court laid down a principle which, like that in *Van Gend en Loos*, was 'inherent in the Treaty', that 'a Member State is liable to make good damage to individuals caused by a breach of Community law for which it is responsible'.

The protection of individual rights at Community level on the basis of direct effect, indirect effect and State liability rests full square on a further fundamental and 'inherent' principle – that of the supremacy or primacy of Community law as enunciated by the Court in Case 6/64 *Costa v ENEL*. Building on the basis of the Treaty as creating 'its own legal system', on the 'transfer of powers from the States' and the binding and directly applicable nature of Regulations as found in Article 189 (now 244), the Court stated that:

> It follows from these observations that the law stemming from the Treaty, an independent source of law, could not, because of its special and original nature, be overridden by domestic [national] legal provisions, however framed, without being deprived of its character as Community law and without the legal basis of the Community itself being called into question.

This is essentially a question of intention – the purpose and objectives of the Community and the legal basis on which they must be achieved. The integrity or unity of the overall structure must be maintained. Closely related to the question of transfers of sovereignty and the supremacy of Community law is that of *pre-emption*, which has been addressed by the Court of Justice on a number of occasions. According to Cappelleti, pre-emption determines 'whether a whole [EC] policy area has been actually or potentially occupied by the central authority so as to influence the intervention of the States in that area'. Pre-emption goes to the question of whether the Community possesses exclusive or concurrent (together with the Member States) competence in any particular policy area. The Court has determined that national legislation is impermissible (not merely subordinate) in fields where the Community is found to have exclusive competence. This has occurred for example with regard to Community common commercial policy under Article 113 (now 133) which states that the policy should be based on uniform principles: see Opinion 1/75 [1975] ECR 1355; to the establishment of common organisations of agricultural markets under the CAP; and to Internal Market harmonisation Directives which 'occupy the field', setting common standards and abolishing Member State competence to introduce or maintain differing national rules: see, for example, Case 60/86 *Commission v UK (Re Dim-Dip Headlights)*.

Turning to the omission from the Rome Treaty of a Bill of Rights (although the prohibition of various forms of discrimination were expressly covered), it has been said that the creation of an 'unwritten' Bill of Rights in EC law is the Court's greatest contribution to the development of a constitution for Europe. In Case 11/70 *Internationale Handelsgesellschaft*, the Court stated that 'respect for fundamental rights forms part of the general principles of law protected by the Court of Justice'. There being at that time no express reference to such general principles in the Treaty (see now Article 6(2) of the Maastricht Treaty on European Union 1992), the basis of this statement by the Court should primarily be found in the Court's interpretation of Article 164 (now 220) concerning its power to ensure that 'in the interpretation and application of this Treaty *the law is observed*' (emphasis added). In the above case, the West German Constitutional Court declared that as the Treaty made no provision for the protection of fundamental human rights, it lacked a lawful democratic basis. The Court's above response may be seen as another activist development or as a reaction to German promptings.

As the Court has stated on many occasions, the general principles of Community law have two sources. Firstly, the constitutional values common to the Member States. For example, the Constitution of the German Federal Republic opens with a list of basic rights which 'bind the legislature, the executive and the judiciary as directly enforceable law'. Secondly, they draw inspiration from the Council of Europe's Convention on Human Rights and Fundamental Freedoms of 1950. As a result, EC legislation and Member State laws operating within the sphere of EC law must meet human rights standards found in these 'borrowed' sources of law in cases brought to the Court of Justice.

An examination of the Court of Justice, as a constitutional court within a federal-type legal structure, as regards its powers of judicial review raises a number of important issues. Its review jurisdiction was originally laid down in Article 173 (now 230). Its powers were restricted to review of the acts of the Council and the Commission in actions brought by those institutions, by the Member States and, within limits, by 'natural and legal persons'. It had, and has, unlike the US Supreme Court, no power of direct review of Member State legislation.

However, Court of Justice rulings under Article 177 (now 234) on the correct interpretation of Community law enable the Court to indicate that national rules do not comply with the higher law – as in the first *Marshall* case in 1986, which led to an amendment of the Sex Discrimination Act 1975 in order to remove discrimination with respect to retirement ages in line with the *Marshall* ruling. Successful Commission Article 226 (formerly 169) direct actions against Member States can bring about the same result: see, for example, Case 167/73 *Commission v France (French Merchant Seamen)*, in which the Court stated that there is a positive obligation on the Member States to repeal conflicting national legislation even though it is inapplicable. In neither case does the Court declare the non-compliant national rules to be invalid but they cannot stand.

Turning to the institutional structure of the Community and the division and balance of powers within that structure, the Court's judicial review case law reveals its contribution to the lessening of the 'democratic deficit' and its role in the enhancement of the status and powers of the European Parliament, first directly elected (on the basis of a Council Decision) in 1979. The case law is particularly important as regards the Parliament's role in the Community's legislative processes. In the early days of the Parliament's Luxembourg existence it was, as we have seen, commonly regarded as a mere 'talking shop'.

In the *Roquette and Maizena* cases (138 and 139/79), the Court confirmed both the Parliament's right to intervene in its proceedings, in the same way as the other political institutions – and its right to be consulted as part of the legislative process where the Treaty so provides. Later, in Case C-300/89 *Commission v Council (Titanium Dioxide Waste)*, the Court, as seen in the previous chapter, stated that 'the very objective of the cooperation procedure ... was to reinforce the participation of the European Parliament in the legislative process' – participation which reflected a fundamental democratic principle that a people should take part in the exercise of power through the intermediary of a representative assembly.

In Case 294/83 *Les Verts v Parliament*, the Court recognised the need for the Parliament to have the power to adopt legally binding, and therefore challengeable, acts although this involved a 'rewriting' of the then Article 173, and in Case C-70/88 *Chernobyl*, the Court again assumed jurisdiction in permitting the Parliament to bring actions against the other institutions, here the Council, in order to safeguard its own role in the legislative process. It was in the former case that the Court first expressly stated its view of the Treaty as a constitution: 'The European Economic Community is a Community based on the rule of law, inasmuch as neither its Member States nor its institutions can avoid a review of the question whether the measures adopted by them are in conformity with the basic constitutional charter, the Treaty.' It should be remembered that the developments found in *Les Verts* and *Chernobyl* now find their place in the EC Treaty (Articles 230 and 232).

Recent years have also witnessed a significant further example of the Court's proactive approach in the absence of Council action. It has moved to extend the scope of substantive individual rights whilst breathing life into the seemingly unpromising Union citizenship provisions of the post-Maastricht EC Treaty. The Court has achieved this in a series of free movement cases through the use of the *general* prohibition on discrimination on grounds of nationality in the directly effective Article 12 (formerly 6), as opposed to the more specific prohibitions elsewhere, in conjunction with, in particular, Article 18(1) which grants citizens the right to move and reside freely within the territories of the Member States. It has done this in the absence of Council action 'facilitating' the above rights.

The potential force of the constitutional citizenship provisions following this development is shown in Case C-184/99 *Grzelczyk v CPAS* (see Chapter 13) in which the Court stated that:

> Union citizenship is destined to be the *fundamental* status of nationals of the Member States, enabling those who find themselves in the same situation to enjoy the same treatment in law, irrespective of their nationality, subject to such exceptions as are expressly provided for ... a citizen of the European Union, lawfully resident in the territory of a host Member State, can rely on Article 6 [now 12] of the Treaty in all situations which fall within the scope *ratione materiae* of Community law [emphasis added].

It is said that the Court's activist, constitutional role has diminished – or should diminish according to the German Constitutional Court in the *Brunner* case of 1994. Treaty amendments are now regularly considered and put in place by the European Council. The Parliament is increasingly involved in the 'co-decision' process and qualified majority voting (QMV) has become the predominant form for decision making in the Council of Ministers.

However, it is more than doubtful that the Member States alone will settle the difficult questions of the scope and effect of Community law in the future. The rise of QMV has made the question of the relationship between Community and national competence more contentious as the number of challenges by 'minority' Member States bears witness: see, for example, Case C-84/94 *UK v Council (Working Time Directive)*. The introduction into the Treaty of the principle of subsidiarity at Maastricht has not inserted transparency into the matter.

At the end of Chapter 1, attention was drawn to post-Nice developments within the Union. What signs, if any, are there that the Union is now moving closer towards the establishment of a core constitution in some more clearly defined system of three tier governance? This is a question to be asked when the 'big decisions' are being taken by the intergovernmental European Council and when the Union 'architecture' is composed of a highly developed supranational EC pillar and two much less developed intergovernmental pillars on Common Foreign and Security Policy and Police and Judicial Co-operation in Criminal Matters.

A 'wider and deeper' debate is being conducted in a more widely representative and open manner than previously by a constitutional Convention on the Future of Europe in preparation for further reforms in 2004. Its remit is based on the four issues in Nice Declaration 23: clearer delimitation of EU and Member State competence, the status of the EU Charter of Fundamental Rights, simplification of the Treaties and the role of *national* parliaments within the EU structure.

It is possible to see this agenda as representing a wish for further, if tentative, steps towards a constitution of a federal form for the Union, a view which might, for example, be found in Germany but not in other Member States.

Where the Member States remain ambivalent about further political integration, might not the Court of Justice again take the lead in the path towards 'an ever closer union among the peoples of Europe'?

THE COURT OF FIRST INSTANCE

As discussed in the first part of this chapter, the period since the Single European Act of 1986 made provision for the creation of the CFI and Council Decision 88/591 brought it into operation has nevertheless been one of the judicial system attempting, and failing, to keep pace with an ever increasing caseload. This was initially due to the increase in references under Article 234 (formerly 177) as the Community/Union increased to 15 Member States and to case law arising from the mass of legislation adopted to implement the Internal Market Programme. Whether the reforms introduced by the Treaty of Nice will bring respite in the face of enlargement to 25 Member States remains to be seen.

The transfers of jurisdiction from the Court to the CFI from the time when the CFI was first 'attached' to the Court up to the Nice reforms and calls for further action by the institutions have in large part been examined above. The position of the CFI at present in terms of structure and jurisdiction, and of the new judicial panels that are to be established, is as follows:

A new Article 244 states, in part, that:

> The Court of First Instance shall comprise *at least one* Judge per Member State. The number of Judges shall be determined by the Statute of the Court of Justice. The Statute may provide for the Court of First Instance to be assisted by [an] Advocate General [emphasis added].

The rules concerning qualifications and appointment of CFI members and President are similar to those for the Court of Justice. Members of the CFI may be called upon to perform the task of an Advocate General. The Court normally sits in chambers of three or five Judges, in more difficult cases in plenary session, and in cases which do not raise any difficult questions of law or fact a single judge hearing may be sufficient.

As regards jurisdiction, the new Article 225 introduced at Nice provides that:

1   The Court of First Instance shall have jurisdiction to hear and determine at first instance actions or proceedings referred to in Articles 230, 232, 235, 236 and 238, with the exception of those assigned to a judicial panel and those reserved in the

Statute for the Court of Justice. The Statute may provide for the Court of First Instance to have jurisdiction for other classes of action or proceeding.

Decisions given by the Court of First Instance under this paragraph may be subject to a right of appeal to the Court of Justice on points of law only, under the conditions and within the limits laid down by the Statute.

2   The Court of First Instance shall have jurisdiction to hear and determine actions or proceedings brought against decisions of the judicial panels set up under Article 225a.

Decisions given by the Court of First instance under this paragraph may exceptionally be subject to review by the Court of Justice, under the conditions and within the limits laid down by the Statute, where there is a serious risk of the unity or consistency of Community law being affected.

3   The Court of First Instance shall have jurisdiction to hear and determine questions referred for a preliminary ruling under Article 234, in specific areas laid down by the Statute.

Where the Court of First Instance considers that the case requires a decision of principle likely to affect the unity or consistency of Community law, it may refer the case to the Court of Justice for a ruling.

Decisions given by the Court of First Instance on questions referred for a preliminary ruling may exceptionally be subject to review by the Court of Justice, under the conditions and within the limits laid down by the Statute, where there is a serious risk of the unity or consistency of Community law being affected.

We have seen that the CFI hears direct actions brought by *private parties* (natural and legal persons, particularly undertakings). The Articles referred to in paragraph 1 above cover:

(a) Article 230(4) challenges to Community acts (including Commission competition policy Decisions) which may be declared void;

(b) Article 232(3) actions based on the alleged failure of the institutions (including the Commission) to act;

(c) Article 235 (and see also Article 288(2)) actions for damages based on the non-contractual liability of the Community;

(d) Article 236 staff cases concerning disputes between the Community and its employees (which will in all probability be transferred to judicial panels); and

(e) Article 238 contractual arbitration cases.

Article 225(1) also covers the established 'right of appeal to the Court of Justice on points of law only ...'. Appeals may be brought by an unsuccessful party, an intervening Member State or Community institution, or a directly affected natural or legal person. The three available grounds for appeal are:

(i) lack of competence of the CFI;

(ii) breach of procedure which adversely affects the interests of the appellant; and

(iii) any other infringement of Community law by the CFI.

If the Court decides that an appeal is well founded, it is required to quash the CFI's decision and either give final judgment itself or refer the case back to the CFI for judgment.

As yet, therefore, the Nice Treaty has not changed the division of jurisdiction between the CFI and the Court of Justice (see the chart on page 146), but the changes indicated will shortly come about, at least to some degree, as with the splitting of the Article 234 preliminary rulings jurisdiction: see Article 225(3) with its transfer or review provisions where 'the unity or consistency of Community law' is at risk. As indicated earlier, Nice Declaration 12 also envisages further transfers of direct action jurisdiction to the CFI.

The introduction of *judicial panels* attached to the CFI and operating 'in certain specific areas' is signalled in Article 220a. Their establishment depends on a unanimous Decision by the Council following a proposal from the Commission or a request from the Court of Justice. In either case, consultation with the other institutions must take place.

The organisation of the panel and its jurisdiction will be laid down in the Decision. Appeals on points of law (and, if necessary, on matters of fact) go initially to the CFI – in exceptional cases with provision for further *review* by the Court of Justice (see above). Staff cases will be the first to be transferred from the CFI.

REFERENCES AND FURTHER READING

Arnull, A, 'Owning up to fallibility: precedent and the Court of Justice' (1993) 30 CML Rev 247.

Arnull, A, *The European Union and its Court of Justice*, 1999.

Arnull, A, 'Judicial architecture or judicial folly? The challenge facing the European Union' (1999) 24 EL Rev 516.

Brown, N and Kennedy, T, *The Court of Justice of the European Communities*, 2000.

Cappelletti, M, 'Is the European Court of Justice running wild?' (1987) 12 EL Rev 3.

Eleftheriadis, P, 'Aspects of European constitutionalism' (1996) 21 EL Rev 32.

Gerber, D, 'The transformation of Community competition law' (1994) Harvard International LJ 97.

Gormley, L (ed), *Kapteyn and VerLoren Van Themaat's Introduction to the Law of European Communities*, 1998, Chapter IV, Part 3.

Hartley, TC, *The Foundations of European Community Law*, 1998, Chapter 2.

Howe, G, 'Euro-justice: yes or no?' (1996) 21 EL Rev 187.

Johnston, A, 'Judicial Reform and the Treaty of Nice' (2001) 38 CML Rev 499.

Lenaerts, K, 'Constitutionalism and the many faces of federalism' (1990) 38 American Journal of Comparative Law 205.

Mancini, GF, 'The making of a constitution for Europe' (1989) 26 CML Rev 595.

Mancini, GF and Keeling, DT, 'Democracy and the European Court of Justice' (1994) 57 MLR 175.

Millett, T, 'The New European Court of First Instance' (1989) 38 ICLQ 811.

Rasmussen, H, *On Law and Policy in the European Court of Justice*, 1986.

Rasmussen, H, 'Between self-restraint and activism: a judicial policy for the European Court' (1988) 13 EL Rev 28.

Rasmussen, H, 'Remedying the crumbling EC judicial system' (2000) 37 CML Rev 1071.

Rinze, J, 'The role of the Court of Justice as a Federal Constitutional Court' [1993] PL 426.

Tridimas, T, 'The Court of Justice and judicial activism' (1997) 22 EL Rev 199.

Weiler, J, 'The Court of Justice on trial' (Review essay on Rasmussen's book listed above) (1987) 24 CML Rev 555.

Weiler, J, 'Journey to an unknown destination: a retrospective and prospective of the European Court of Justice in the arena of political integration' (1993) JCMS 417.

CHAPTER 8

DIRECT EFFECT, INDIRECT EFFECT AND STATE LIABILITY

THE DIRECT EFFECT OF TREATY ARTICLES

In 1963, in Case 26/62 *Van Gend en Loos* (see Chapter 4), it will be recalled that the Court of Justice stated that the Community constituted a 'new legal order'. The Dutch and other governments' arguments that the 'standstill' on customs duties in Article 12 (now 25) was a Treaty obligation, any violation of which could be invoked only at international level (that is, by an action brought either by the Commission or another Member State – a *dualist* position in international law terms), was rejected by the Court on policy grounds and in *monist* terms:

> The objective of the EEC Treaty, which is to establish a Common Market, the functioning of which is of direct concern to interested parties in the Community, implies that this Treaty is more than an agreement which merely creates mutual obligations between the Contracting States.

Such a view rests on the theory, recognised by many Member States but not the UK, that international law (including in this respect the Treaty of Rome) and municipal law (the internal law of the Member States) are a *single* (monist) system in which the former has primacy, rather than their being separate systems, the former binding States only and having effect in municipal law only when expressly incorporated by, for example, an Act of Parliament.

The Court of Justice therefore concluded that the 'subjects' of the new legal order were 'not only Member States but also their nationals':

> Independently of the legislation of Member States, Community law therefore not only imposes obligations on individuals, but is also intended to confer upon them rights ... These rights arise not only where they are expressly granted by the Treaty, but also by reason of obligations which the Treaty imposes in a clearly defined way upon individuals as well as upon Member States and upon the institutions of the Community.

Thus, not only are provisions of Community law capable by their very nature (the Treaty is of a self-executing character) of direct application in the national courts of the Member States, but such application by national judges is intended to be effective in the sense of the creation of Community rights for individuals.

As we have seen, there is nothing in the Treaty itself to indicate that its provisions may have such *direct effect, that is, the capacity to create directly enforceable rights which may be relied upon by an individual in an action before the national courts*. In Chapter 4, it was argued that the Court wished to assert not only the federal and constitutional nature of the Treaty (individuals being subjects of both Community law and national law, subject to the principle of supremacy) but also the full effectiveness of a provision of substantive Community economic law in a case involving the customs union and an action brought by an undertaking engaged in inter-Member State trade against a national authority. It is clear, as seen in the previous chapter, that the Court was (as it remains) anxious to play its part in the promotion of European economic integration through a policy of increasing the scope and effectiveness of Community law. The

Court's rulings on direct effect, whether based on its interpretative functions under Article 234 (formerly 177) or otherwise, are crucial as regards the compliance of Member States (and, in some cases, private parties, particularly companies) both with the Treaty and, as will be seen, with Community legislation. They are therefore fundamental to the overall coherence and consistency of the law which underpins common and co-ordinated policies.

In *Van Gend en Loos*, the Court considered itself empowered to establish the principle of direct effect on the basis of the 'purpose, spirit and wording' of the Treaty. Except where the Treaty so provides, there must be no transformation of Community law into national law. It must be of *direct* use to Community citizens who, within their national legal orders, are enabled to exercise the 'vigilance of individuals to protect their rights' so securing 'an effective form of supervision of Member States acting in breach of the provisions of the Treaty'.

However, it should not be assumed that all Treaty Articles (or Community legislative provisions) create rights for individuals. In *Van Gend en Loos*, the Court stated that Article 12 was 'ideally adapted to produce direct effects in the legal relationship between Member States and their subjects'. This was so because the provision contained a 'clear and unconditional' prohibition (an obligation *not* to increase customs duties), which was independent of the need for any further action being taken by national (or Community) authorities. Article 12 was therefore appropriate to confer rights on individuals, being in itself 'complete and legally perfect'. While observing the overlapping tests or requirements of clarity and unconditionality in a rather informal way, the view of the Court of Justice has increasingly been that direct effect is the *norm*, and Professor Van Gerven (formerly an Advocate General) has suggested that:

> ... the direct effect of a provision depends mainly on whether the courts and finally the Court of Justice, feel able and sufficiently equipped to apply the provision without any further act by the authorities of the Communities or of its Member States.

The case law of the Court shows that a number of Articles (or paragraphs of an Article) do not create direct effects because they are insufficiently precise or by their nature they are not capable of conferring individual rights (for example, Article 95 (formerly 100a)). However, a fundamentally important Article such as Article 12 (formerly Article 6 EC and earlier Article 7 EEC), which provides that discrimination on the grounds of nationality is prohibited, although of a very general character, can be either directly effective in itself or in conjunction with other Community provisions: see, for example, Case 186/87 *Cowan v Tresor Public*.

Article 141 (formerly 119), which concerns another kind of discrimination and imposes an obligation on Member States to *implement* and maintain the principle of 'equal pay for equal work' for men and women, was also held to be directly effective in Case 43/75 *Defrenne v Sabena (No 2)* once the stated deadline for implementation by the Member States had passed; see also Chapter 14. A further significant feature of *Defrenne* is that, although it is addressed to Member States, Article 141 does not merely apply to public sector (State) employees. The equal pay principle must apply throughout the Community and in so doing, it places *obligations* on *all* employers. Thus, as *Defrenne* and other cases show, an employee can rely on Article 141 against a private sector employer: the legal status of the defendant employer and its relation to the State is irrelevant. Article 141 is therefore an illustration of the availability of a

Community provision for use by one individual against another individual or undertaking; so called *horizontal* direct effect. (Article 39 (formerly 48) concerning the free movement of workers is also both vertically and horizontally directly effective: see, for example, Case C-415/93 *URBSFA v Bosman*.) The use of Article 12 (now 25) in *Van Gend en Loos* against a branch of the Dutch government was a case of *vertical* direct effect. (This is a distinction which is all important when considering the direct effect of Directives.)

Since *Van Gend en Loos*, the case law of the Court on the direct enforceability of Treaty Articles in national courts has extended the list of such Articles not only within the field of the free movement of goods but to other policy areas such as the free movement of workers, the right of establishment, the freedom to provide services, competition policy and equal pay.

However, in *R v Secretary of State for the Home Department ex p Flynn* (1997), the Court of Appeal, without recourse to the preliminary rulings procedure, decided that no individual rights were to be found in Article 7a (now 14) on the Internal Market:

> While travelling from France in 1993, F refused to show his passport at Dover and was detained. He applied for certiorari to quash the maintenance by the Secretary of State of controls on the free movement of persons between the UK and other Member States and for declaratory relief and damages.
>
> He based his claim on Article 7a EC which, as seen, provides for the progressive establishment of the Internal Market over a period expiring on 31 December 1992 and for, amongst other things, the free movement of persons within that area 'without internal frontiers'. At first instance, F's claim failed and he appealed.
>
> The Court of Appeal held that for the appellant to succeed it was necessary to find (i) that Article 7a *required* Member States to abolish all frontier controls by the date stated, and (ii) that the requirement had direct effect. However, on a true construction of Article 7a, the Court felt that it was impossible to find such an obligation imposed on the Community, still less on individual Member States. Article 7a expressed an aim and not an obligation and 31 December 1992 was a target date, not a deadline which created legal obligations. In any event, Article 7a did not meet the criteria necessary for the creation of direct effect. It was not unconditional but contingent upon a great many implementing measures being adopted by the Community institutions and brought into effect by the Member States.
>
> Article 7a was therefore not of direct effect and so did not create enforceable rights which F could enforce against the Secretary of State. (This case should be considered in the context of the Schengen Agreement's frontier-free area and the Protocol on the application of Article 7a (now 14) EC to the UK and Ireland attached by the ToA to the EC Treaty and the TEU: see Chapter 1.)

Before proceeding further, it should be borne in mind that, as the Court of Justice has no jurisdiction over the provisions of the Maastricht second pillar (Common Foreign and Security Policy), the question of the legal effect of those provisions (or of measures adopted under them) does not arise. The position is almost certainly the same as regards the remaining provisions of the third pillar (now Police and Judicial Co-operation in Criminal Matters). What is now Article 34 TEU explicitly states that, although Council legislative decisions in this field shall be binding on the Member States, such decisions 'shall not entail direct effect'.

Also, it should be noted that the discussion of direct effect in this chapter does not extend to the possible direct effect of provisions of international agreements entered into by the Community.

THE DIRECT EFFECT OF COMMUNITY ACTS: REGULATIONS

Regulations, as defined in Article 249(2) (formerly 189(2)), and as seen in Chapter 4, are of general application; they are also binding in their entirety and are directly applicable in all Member States.

Much confusion has existed in relation to the terms 'direct effect' and 'direct applicability'. Regulations are directly applicable in the sense that national legislation is not required to implement and so transpose or incorporate them into the national legal system: see Case 34/73 *Variola* in Chapter 4. The entry into force of a Regulation occurs automatically upon adoption or upon a date laid down by the Council or Commission. As Freestone and Davidson state:

> This system of Community legislation is a vital part of the Community system for regulating such matters as customs tariffs and the control of agricultural products where market structures and prices change rapidly. In order for such a system to work effectively, the legislation must take effect in all Member States at the same time.

Although Regulations are directly applicable, they are not necessarily directly effective in the sense described above, that is, that they confer directly enforceable rights upon individuals. In Case 131/79 *Santillo*, Advocate General Warner stated in his Opinion that:

> Unquestionably, every provision of every regulation is directly applicable, but not every provision of every regulation has direct effect in the sense of conferring on private persons rights enforceable by them in national courts. One can point to numerous examples of provisions of regulations that confer no direct rights on individuals.

A prime source of the confusion between the two terms (in the UK at least) has been the Court of Justice itself where the expressions have been used interchangeably *in the sense* of the creation of Community rights for individuals. (This can be seen in the *Van Gend en Loos* ruling itself.)

Not only is there no need for national measures to be enacted by the Member States in order to incorporate a Regulation into their legal systems but, unless otherwise provided, they are contrary to Article 10 (formerly 5) and improper. This is because they would tend to obscure the essential Community nature of the act, with possible consequences for its meaning and scope, the time it comes into force, and the jurisdiction of the Court of Justice under Article 234 (formerly 177) to give a preliminary ruling on its interpretation or validity.

In the following exceptional case, implementing national measures were, however, obligatory.

Case 128/78 *Commission v UK (Re Tachographs)*

The Commission's action under Article 169 (now 226) concerned the failure of the UK to implement Article 21 of Regulation 1463/70 relating to the introduction, for health and safety reasons, of tachographs in commercial vehicles. Although Article 4 of the

Regulation laid down the date from which use of the equipment became compulsory, Article 21(1) provided that:

> Member States shall, in good time and after consulting the Commission, adopt such laws, regulations or administrative provisions as may be necessary for the implementation of this Regulation. Such measures shall cover, *inter alia*, the reorganisation of, procedure for, and means of carrying out, checks on compliance and the penalties to be imposed in case of breach.

This vague and conditional provision could not become effective and, for example, create any new criminal offence except through specific implementation at national level spelling out the nature of the offence, responsibility for it, penalties and defences.

The Court of Justice ordered the UK to implement the provision as required.

The normal position as regards Regulations is however illustrated by the following case.

Case 93/71 *Leonesio v Italian Ministry of Agriculture*

L brought a claim in the Italian courts for payments due from the national Ministry under Community Regulations relating to a scheme to reduce dairy herds and over-production of dairy products. Although the Community rules established that payments to farmers should be made within two months of their slaughter of dairy cows, the Italian government delayed final implementation of the scheme until the necessary budgetary provision was made to meet that part of the cost falling on the national authorities.

In a preliminary ruling, the Court of Justice held that the Regulations were of direct effect, creating a right in the applicant L to a payment which could not be conditional or altered by national authorities, and which was immediately enforceable in the national courts. The Court referred to Article 5(1) (now 10(1)) of the Treaty: 'Member States shall take all appropriate measures, whether general or particular, to ensure fulfilment of the obligations arising out of this Treaty or resulting from action taken by the institutions of the Community.'

If the objections of the Italian State had been recognised, Italian farmers would have been placed in a less favourable position than those in the other Member States. This would have involved a disregard of the fundamental principle that Regulations must be uniformly applied throughout the whole Community.

In view of the fact that Regulations are of 'general application', it follows, providing that their relevant provisions are sufficiently 'clear and unconditional', that they may be invoked in national courts both against other individuals (that is, horizontally) and against the State (that is, vertically). Additionally, it will be recalled that, as with Treaty Articles, such directly effective provisions of Regulations take priority over conflicting national law: see Case 106/77 *Simmenthal (No 2)* and Case 11/70 *Internationale Handelsgesellschaft* in Chapter 4.

DECISIONS

As we have also seen in Chapter 4, a Decision of the Council or Commission is binding in its entirety upon those to whom it is addressed: Article 249(4) (formerly 189(4)). Unlike a Regulation, which is of 'general application', it may be addressed to a

Member State(s), an individual(s) or an undertaking(s). By definition, Decisions are formal acts imposing rights or obligations on their addressees.

In Case 9/70 *Grad v Finanzamt Traunstein*, the plaintiff haulage contractor challenged a West German transport tax alleged to be in breach of a Council Decision addressed to the Member States providing for the application of the common VAT system to road haulage (and other methods of transporting goods) and a harmonisation Directive which laid down the deadline for the implementation of the Decision. On the question of the Decision having direct effect, and thus creating rights in favour of G, the Court of Justice ruled that Article 189 (now 249) does not prevent individuals from founding their actions in national courts upon Decisions (and Directives) addressed to Member States:

> ... the provision according to which decisions are binding in their entirety on those to whom they are addressed enables the question to be put whether the obligation created by the decisions can only be invoked by the Community institutions against the addressee or whether such a right may possibly be exercised by all those who have an interest in the fulfilment of this obligation. It would be incompatible with the binding effect attributed to decisions by Article 189 to exclude in principle the possibility that persons affected might invoke the obligation imposed by a decision.

In each particular case, stated the Court:

> ... it must be ascertained whether the nature, background and wording of the provision in question are capable of producing direct effects in the legal relationships between the addressee of the act [here, the West German tax authorities] and third parties [such as Grad].

The Court ruled that the obligation imposed in the Decision was sufficiently clear and unconditional to be capable of giving rise to enforceable individual rights

In Case 249/85 *ALBAKO*, a Berlin margarine producer sought an order in the national courts to restrain the German agricultural intervention agency from distributing in West Berlin 900 tonnes of free butter from the EEC 'butter mountain' in accordance with a Commission Decision addressed to the Federal Republic. The applicant claimed that the agency's proposed action was in breach of German competition law. Following an Article 177 (now 234) reference, the Court of Justice observed that the circumstances of the case were different from those in *Grad*. In that case, the Decision in question had required national law to be modified and it had been invoked in order to prevent the application to G of provisions of national law which G claimed had not been amended in accordance with the Decision's requirements.

In *ALBAKO*, the Commission's Decision did not require any rules of general application to be adopted by the Federal Republic which, through its intervention agency, had duly complied with it. Unlike *Grad*, there was consequently no question of protecting a litigant from the adverse consequences of a Member State failing to comply with its obligations under Community law. The Commission's valid Decision obliged the Federal Republic to act and left it no margin of discretion. Its binding character had to be respected by all the organs of the addressee State including its courts. By virtue of the primacy of Community law, national courts had to refrain from giving effect to all provisions of national law the application of which would interfere with the implementation of the Community Decision.

DIRECTIVES: CAN THEY CREATE RIGHTS FOR INDIVIDUALS?

The question of the direct effect of Directives originally aroused a great deal of controversy and considerable case law. It would appear from Article 249 (formerly 189) that no question of direct effect should arise. Article 249(3) provides that:

> A Directive shall be binding, as to the result to be achieved, upon each Member State to which it is addressed, but shall leave to the national authorities the choice of form and methods.

From this provision, several points emerge:

(a) Directives are *not necessarily* of general application: they may be addressed to one or more Member States.

(b) As they are required to be implemented by national authorities, it is clear that they are *not directly applicable* as defined above. *When issued* by the Council or the Commission, Directives are not designed to be law in that form in the Member States.

(c) This being so, they only take effect – *or should take effect* – on the basis of appropriate and properly implemented *national* measures, which will secure for individuals whatever rights the Community measure seeks to confer upon them. Member States to whom a Directive is addressed must implement its provisions within the *time limit* laid down in the Directive: see Article 10 (formerly 5) of the Treaty.

(d) Directives are of a somewhat different character from Regulations; they are in several ways a more flexible instrument. They can be addressed merely to one or more Member States where particular problems are found or, of necessity, to all the Member States, for example, Internal Market harmonisation Directives. Also, directives leave a discretion to the Member States, not as regards 'the result to be achieved', but as to the 'form and methods' by which that result is brought about. They will in all probability be transposed into national law by the Member States at different times.

For example, Article 6 of Council Directive 76/207 on the implementation of the principle of equal treatment for men and women as regards access to employment, promotion, etc, requires all Member States to 'introduce into their national legal systems *such measures as are necessary* to enable all persons who consider themselves wronged' by discrimination 'to pursue their claims by judicial process' (emphasis added). In answer to an Article 177 (now 234) question from a German court as to whether the Directive required certain *specific* sanctions (compulsory engagement or substantial damages), the Court of Justice replied that:

> ... Member States are required to adopt measures which are sufficiently effective to achieve the objective of the Directive ... However, the Directive does not prescribe a specific sanction, it leaves Member States free to choose between the different solutions suitable for achieving its objectives.

Despite the fact that the authors of the Treaty did not intend Directives to have direct effect, *individual rights being provided by the implementing national law*, significant failures by Member States to fulfil their obligations under Article 189(3) (now 249(3)) eventually led the Court of Justice to apply the principle of direct effect, at least to a limited extent, to Directives. Difficulties posed by the wording of the Article's third paragraph regarding the nature of Directives were not to stand in the way of two of the Court's predominant concerns: legal integration and the effectiveness of Community law.

An early major development in a long line of decisions arose in a case involving the questions of (a) the direct effect of a Treaty Article which did not appear to contain an absolute, unqualified rule but rather one incorporating a discretionary element, and (b) the direct effect of a Council Directive which fleshed out that Treaty Article.

Case 41/74 *Van Duyn v Home Office*

Miss D, a Dutch national and scientologist, arrived at Gatwick Airport on 9 May 1973. Her purpose in coming to the UK was to take up a post as secretary at the British headquarters of the Church of Scientology of California. She was refused leave to enter by the immigration authorities on grounds of public policy. In particular, the Home Secretary considered it 'undesirable' to allow anyone to enter the UK on the business or employment of the Church of Scientology. This decision was based on government policy to the effect that the Church's activities, although not illegal, were harmful to the mental health of those involved.

Miss D claimed in the High Court that she was entitled under EEC law to enter and remain in the UK for the purpose of employment. She relied first on Article 48 (now 39) of the Treaty, which grants workers the right of free movement between Member States, subject in paragraph (3) to 'limitations justified on grounds of public policy, public security or public health'. She further relied on Article 3(1) of Directive 64/221 which particularises and limits the powers of the Member States as laid down in Article 48(3). Thus, measures taken by them on public policy grounds must be 'based exclusively on the personal conduct of the individual concerned'. Miss D claimed that this provision was directly effective and gave her the right to enter – her argument being that her exclusion was based on the UK government's declared policy towards the Church of Scientology generally and not on account of any 'personal conduct' on her part. (The UK had not implemented Directive 64/221, relying instead on pre-existing immigration rules which did not, however, state that entry could be refused only on the basis of personal conduct.)

In the first ever Article 177 (now 234) reference from the UK, the High Court put to the Court of Justice questions regarding the direct effect of both the Treaty Article and the Directive.

The Court ruled that Article 48 imposed on Member States a precise and immediate obligation regarding the free movement of workers. A Member State's right to invoke the limitations on that freedom in paragraph (3) of the Article was, as stated in the Directive, 'subject to judicial control' in national courts and it did not prevent the Article from conferring on individuals rights which were enforceable by them.

On the question of the creation of individual rights on the basis of the Directive, the Court's main ground for declaring that Article 3(1) of the Directive was directly effective was not the UK government's failure to implement the Directive (there was, as stated earlier, no provision in national law that entry could be refused only on basis of the 'personal conduct' of a would-be immigrant such as Miss D) but the Court's policy decision that, given the nature, general scheme and wording of the provision, its *effectiveness* would be greater if individuals were entitled to invoke it in national courts. Therefore, Article 3(1) of the Directive was also directly effective.

At the end of the day, however, Miss D lost her case: the Court of Justice ruled that *present association* with an organisation considered socially harmful by a Member State does amount to 'personal conduct'. (Later decisions in this area suggest that 'the Court may have been very indulgent towards the UK'; see Rudden, *Basic Community Cases*.) Miss D could not gain entry to the UK, but could Dutch nationals 'presently associated' be deported? (See the later case of *Adoui and Cornuaille v Belgium*.)

In a broader context, the Court of Justice had established a principle: Directives were capable of creating rights for individuals who might enforce them in national courts. Member States were put on warning regarding their duty under Article 10 (formerly 5) to fulfil their Treaty obligations; here, to transpose Directives into national law so that individuals might secure their Community rights in the manner envisaged by those who had drafted Article 249 (formerly 189). In addition, proper transposition of Directives by Member States would mean that pressure might be taken off the Commission regarding the bringing of enforcement proceedings under Article 226 (formerly 169) against defaulting Member States.

In the case which follows, the Italian State had clearly failed to implement a harmonisation Directive within the time limit laid down in the measure itself.

Case 148/78 *Pubblico Ministero v Ratti*

R, who was in business selling solvents and varnishes, fixed labels to certain dangerous substances in a manner which was in conformity with Directive 73/173, but which contravened the relevant Italian legislation of 1963. Italy had failed to implement the Directive within the time limit laid down (8 December 1974). This would have necessitated amending the national legislation.

R was prosecuted for breach of the Italian labelling law and he pleaded the provisions of the Directive in his defence. The Milan Court, being unsure 'which of the two sets of rules should take precedence', referred the following question to the Court of Justice: 'Does Council Directive 73/173/EEC of 4 June 1973, in particular Article 8 thereof, constitute directly applicable legislation conferring upon individuals personal rights which the national courts must protect?' [Note the use here of the word 'applicable'.]

The Court held that:

> This question raises the general problem of the legal nature of the provisions of a Directive adopted under Article 189 of the Treaty.

> In this regard, the settled case law of the Court ... lays down that, whilst under Article 189 regulations are directly applicable and, consequently, by their nature capable of producing direct effects, that does not mean that other categories of acts covered by that article can never produce similar effects.

> It would be incompatible with the binding effect which Article 189 ascribes to Directives to exclude on principle the possibility of the obligations imposed by them being relied on by persons concerned.

> Particularly in cases in which the Community authorities have, by means of a Directive, placed Member States under a duty to adopt a certain course of action, the effectiveness of such an act would be weakened if persons were prevented from relying on it in legal proceedings and national courts prevented from taking it into consideration as an element of Community law.

> Consequently, a Member State which has not adopted the implementing measures required by the Directive in the prescribed periods may not rely, as

against individuals, on its own failure to perform the obligations which the
Directive entails.

It follows that a national court requested by a person who has complied with the
provisions of a Directive not to apply a national provision incompatible with the
Directive not incorporated into the internal legal order of a defaulting Member
State, must uphold that request if the obligation in question is unconditional and
sufficiently precise.

Therefore the answer to the first question must be that after the expiration of the
period fixed for the implementation of a Directive a Member State may not apply
its internal law – even if it is provided with penal sanctions – which has not yet
been adapted in compliance with the Directive, to a person who has complied
with the requirements of the Directive.

In relation to a second prosecution for the selling of varnishes, improperly labelled
under the national law of 1963, the Court of Justice held that R could not rely on
Directive 77/128 relating to varnishes because the time limit for implementation into
national law (9 November 1977) had not been reached at the relevant time. The
obligation was not then directly effective.

Article 249 (formerly 189) states that a Directive is binding, as to the result to be
achieved, upon a Member State. Thus, where a Member State fails to implement a
Directive within the time limit laid down (or implements it in a defective manner, for
example, beyond the limits of the State's discretion: see Case 51/76 *VNO*) and as a
result deprives individuals of their Community rights, such individuals may,
nevertheless, in the face of conflicting national provisions, rely upon the Directive
(providing its relevant provisions are 'unconditional and sufficiently precise'). In these
circumstances, Directives create enforceable rights for individuals as plaintiffs or
defendants – *against the State* – by means of what has been described as a 'reflex or
ricochet effect rather in the nature of estoppel':

... the European Court of Justice has developed a doctrine which is akin to estoppel. It
works this way. If a citizen sues a Member State in the national courts claiming that
the State has caused him damage by acting in a way which is contrary to the
Directive, and has done so at a time when, if the State had fulfilled its duty under
Community law, national law would have been amended to make such action
unlawful, the State is not permitted to defend itself on the basis that its actions were
lawful in terms of national law. It is otherwise if the defendant is a private person
[*Foster v British Gas, per* Sir John Donaldson MR].

It must be stressed that the cases considered so far have involved a dispute between a
private individual (or undertaking) and the State (that is, State authorities). They
establish that Directives may have vertical direct effect, that is, they may be used as a
sword, to sue a Member State which has failed to implement (properly) a Directive
(see, for example, Case 8/81 *Becker v Finanzamt Münster-Innenstadt*, paragraph 25 of
the judgment) or as a shield against a Member State which seeks to enforce conflicting
national legislation against the individual: *Ratti.*

The next question regarding the attribution of direct effect to Directives was, and
remains, a controversial one. It may be put several ways: is it open to an individual to
rely on a Directive in litigation *not* against a Member State but against another
individual? Can Directives impose *obligations*, and not merely confer rights, on
individuals? Are Directives capable of creating *horizontal* direct effect?

Both provisions of the Treaty – see Case 43/75 *Defrenne* regarding Article 119 (now 141) – and Regulations (which are of 'general application') may, exceptionally, confer rights and impose obligations on private individuals, that is, they may be both vertically and horizontally directly effective. The argument employed by the Court against Directives imposing obligations on individuals is that they are not binding on individuals but on the Member State to whom they are addressed, and a defaulting Member State should not take advantage of its own wrong. This is not an argument that can be employed against individuals. (Nor, however, is this literal approach to Article 249(3) (formerly 189(3)), the approach adopted by the Court in *Defrenne*, above, as regards Article 119 (now 141), which is similarly addressed to Member States.)

There seems little doubt that the Court of Justice was anxious to maximise the *'effet utile'* of Directives in the sense of securing rights for individuals that *should* be available through proper implementation in national law. However, in the face of a serious revolt by some superior national courts to the concept even of the *vertical* direct effect of Directives (see, for example, the French *Conseil d'Etat* in the *Cohn-Bendit* case in 1978, when it refused to follow *Van Duyn* (see Chapter 9), although the attitude of this national court has since changed), the Court of Justice not only did not extend the concept but eventually clearly decided in the *Marshall* case against horizontal direct effect.

Nevertheless, not least because the *Marshall* decision, whilst affirming the vertical direct effect of Directives but denying any horizontal effect, created a serious anomaly, the Court moved later, in the *Von Colson* case, to rectify the position and, by an alternative route, sought to maximise the effect of Directives via national law.

Case 152/84 *Marshall v Southampton and SW Hampshire Area Health Authority*

Miss M was employed by the AHA which had a policy of compulsory retirement for women at 60 and men at 65 (in line with eligibility for State pension). M was dismissed at 62 on the sole ground that she was over the retirement age for women. The Sex Discrimination Act 1975 excluded from the ambit of its prohibition on discrimination by an employer on the ground of sex 'provision in relation to death or retirement'. M, who wished to remain in employment, alleged sex discrimination by the AHA contrary to Council Directive 76/207 (the Equal Treatment Directive).

The UK had adopted the Directive in 1976 but had not amended the 1975 Act as it considered that the Directive permitted discrimination in retirement ages.

The Court of Appeal referred to the Court of Justice questions as to whether the dismissal was an act of unlawful discrimination and whether the Directive could be relied upon by an individual in the national courts.

The Court of Justice answered both these questions in the affirmative:

(a) The different compulsory retirement ages amounted to discrimination on the grounds of sex contrary to Article 5(1) of the Equal Treatment Directive.

(b) Article 5(1) could be relied upon against a State authority acting in its capacity as an employer in order to avoid the application of any national provision (s 6(4) of the Sex Discrimination Act) which did not conform to Article 5(1).

The Court stressed that the defendant Health Authority was a *public* body and that a person in Miss Marshall's position was able to rely on the Directive as against the State regardless of the capacity in which the latter was acting – whether public authority or employer. Thus, while not accepting the UK government's contention that as an employer, the State was no different from a private employer (that is, an individual), the Court did accept that:

> With regard to the argument that a Directive may not be relied upon against an individual, it must be emphasised that according to Article 189 of the EEC Treaty the binding nature of a Directive, which constitutes the basis for the possibility of relying on the Directive before a national court, exists only in relation to 'each Member State to which it is addressed'. It follows that a Directive may not of itself impose obligations on an individual and that a provision of a Directive may not be relied upon as such against such a person.
>
> ...
>
> The argument submitted by the United Kingdom that the possibility of relying on provisions of the Directive against the respondent *qua* organ of the State would give rise to an arbitrary and unfair distinction between the rights of State employees and those of private employees does not justify any other conclusion. Such a distinction may easily be avoided if the Member State concerned has correctly implemented the Directive in national law.

Following Miss Marshall's success, it being conceded when the ruling was remitted that the AHA was a 'public authority', it nevertheless remained the case that where a Directive has not been implemented or has been implemented incorrectly, its effectiveness against the State but not against a private individual (for example, employer) could clearly lead to anomalies. As Morris has said: 'Making the right to rely on a Directive by an employee dependent on the status of his employer seems a remarkably arbitrary criterion for setting the parameters of an important component of Community social law.'

The problems surrounding the 'public/private' dichotomy can be mitigated or removed in several ways. While it may be said that, for the Court to argue that the blame lies with Member States who fail to act correctly and in time is idealistic, the duty so to act certainly exists under Article 10 (formerly 5) of the Treaty. A failure properly to implement a Directive can bring about an Article 226 (formerly 169) action by the Commission, which, as we have seen, is now backed by the possibility of sanctions against a defaulting Member State in the form of financial penalties (not that this is of direct assistance to the individual – but see the *Francovich* principle of State liability at the end of this chapter).

Following *Marshall*, it became clear that the Court of Justice was intent on giving 'the State' the widest possible interpretation.

Case 188/89 *Foster and Others v British Gas plc*

In the Court of Appeal, the appellants, who were former employees of the (then nationalised) British Gas Corporation, claimed discrimination by their employer contrary to Article 5(1) of Council Directive 76/207 on Equal Treatment, in that they had been compulsorily retired at 60 whereas their male colleagues were not required to retire until 65. Their dismissals were not unlawful under the national legislation in force at the time (the Sex Discrimination Act 1975). As in *Marshall*, the domestic rules had not yet been amended to bring them in line with the Directive's insistence on equal treatment in regard to, *inter alia*, the conditions of dismissal. (They were amended in 1986.)

The Court of Appeal held that the Directive was only vertically directly effective, that is, so as to provide rights for an individual employee against the non-compliant State

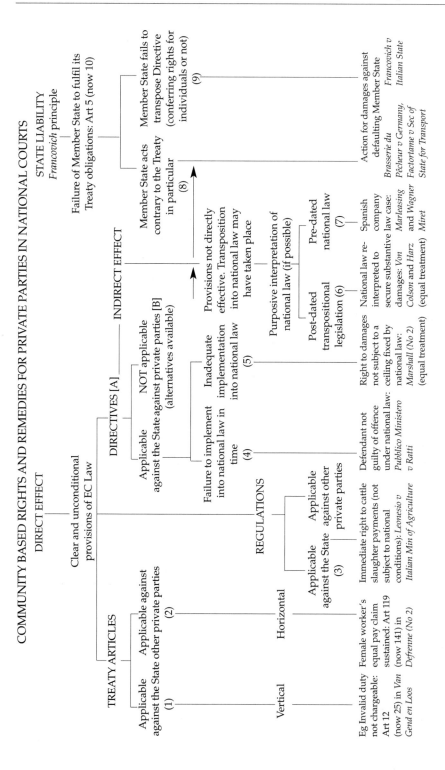

COMMUNITY BASED RIGHTS AND REMEDIES FOR PRIVATE PARTIES IN NATIONAL COURTS

NOTES: [A] Rights/remedies normally in national law transposing the Directive. [B] See *Marshall (No 1)* and *Faccini Dori* (no horizontal direct effect).

(as employer) or any organ or emanation thereof: see *Marshall*, which makes it clear that the task of determining whether a defendant is part of the State rests on national courts. Relying on domestic case law, 'most of it concerning post-war nationalisation measures light years removed from the social policy objectives embodied in the Equal Treatment Directive' (see Morris), the Court held that British Gas was not an organ or emanation of the State. It was therefore not bound by the Directive and the appeal failed.

On further appeal, the House of Lords sought a preliminary ruling under Article 177 (now 234) on the basic question: was British Gas a body of the kind against which the provisions of the Directive could be invoked?

The Court of Justice held that:

(a) (On a preliminary issue) it was the function of the Court of Justice to determine the categories of person against whom a Directive might be relied. It was for national courts to decide if a party fell within one of those categories.

(b) Article 5(1) of the Equal Treatment Directive might be relied upon in a claim for damages against:

> ... a body, whatever its legal form, which has been made responsible, pursuant to a measure adopted by the State, for providing a public service under the control of the State and has for that purpose special powers beyond those which result from the normal rules applicable in relations between individuals is included *in any event* among the bodies against which the provisions of a Directive capable of having direct effect may be relied upon [emphasis added].

Earlier, in Case 222/84 *Johnston v Chief Constable of the Royal Ulster Constabulary*, the Court had observed that the Chief Constable was:

> ... an official responsible for the direction of the police service. Whatever its relations may be with other organs of the State, such a public authority, charged by the State with the maintenance of public order and safety, does not act as a private individual. It may not take advantage of the failure of the State, of which it is an emanation, to comply with Community law.

There was, therefore, following the ruling in *Foster*, little doubt that the appellants in that case would be able to rely on the Equal Treatment Directive when the case returned to the House of Lords. Thus, as Lord Templeman stated in applying the ruling:

> Applying those words, it seems to me that the 1972 Act created a body, the BGC, which provided a public service, the supply of gas to citizens of the State generally under the control of the State, which could dictate its policies and retain its surplus revenue; the BGC was equipped with a special monopoly power which was created and could only have been created by the legislature. The BGC is therefore a body against which the relevant provisions of the equal treatment Directive may be enforced.

The Court of Justice therefore merely established guidance for the referring national court regarding the scope of 'the State'. It did not provide an exhaustive definition of 'the State'. The nationalised body, BGC, came within the terms of the guidance. It should also be appreciated that the wider the definition of 'the State', the weaker becomes the estoppel rationale, that is, that the State cannot rely on its own wrong. An Area Health Authority and, even more so, a nationalised body have no obligation to transpose a Directive into national law: see also *Griffin v South West Water Services Ltd*, below.

In another compulsory retirement case, *Rolls Royce plc v Doughty* (1992), the Court of Appeal, applying the *Foster* guidelines, held (a) that the 100 per cent control exercised over RR by the State as its sole shareholder was irrelevant; albeit (b) the service provided by RR was under control of the State; (c) that RR traded *with* the State at arm's length on a commercial basis (as regards sales of military equipment) and could not be said to have been made responsible, pursuant to a measure adopted by the State, for providing a public service; and (d) that RR had not been granted any special powers. RR was not therefore an appropriate body against which to invoke the Directive and the appeal was dismissed.

That the *Foster* guidelines may point in different directions and make it extremely difficult for the national court to reach a ready conclusion was further borne out in *NUT v Governing Body of St Mary's Church of England (Aided) Junior School*, another Court of Appeal decision in 1997.

INDIRECT EFFECT AND 'SYMPATHETIC' INTERPRETATION

A solution, *at least in some cases*, to problems surrounding the vertical/horizontal, public/private dichotomy was in fact available as a result of earlier decisions of the Court of Justice in two West German references which again involved the Equal Treatment Directive: Case 14/83 *Von Colson* (in which the defendants were the provincial authorities of North-Rhine Westphalia) and Case 79/83 *Harz* (in which the defendant was a private sector company). Contrary to the position in *Marshall* and *Foster*, the Equal Treatment Directive had been implemented in West Germany but the national law did not appear to provide an adequate remedy for the discrimination that had taken place. Could therefore the two plaintiffs have recourse to the Directive?

Case 14/83 *Von Colson v Land Nordrhein-Westfalen*

This case and *Harz* were referred to the Court of Justice from the West German Labour Court. C had been discriminated against on grounds of sex when applying for the post of prison social worker, and H when applying to join a training programme with a commercial company.

The national court considered that it only had power to award nominal damages (travelling expenses) to the plaintiffs under the provisions of the German implementing law. C and H claimed that such implementation of Article 6 of the Equal Treatment Directive failed to achieve that Article's intended aim. Article 6 states that:

> Member States shall introduce into their national legal systems such measures as are necessary to enable all persons who consider themselves wronged by failure to apply to them the principle of equal treatment ... to pursue their claims by judicial process after possible recourse to other competent authorities.

C and H contended that they either had the right to be offered the posts they had applied for or substantial damages (six months' salary). The national court referred questions to the Court of Justice to establish:

(a) whether Directive 76/207 required Member States to provide for particular sanctions or other legal consequences to attach to cases of discrimination on grounds of sex against a person seeking employment;

(b) whether the provisions of Directive 76/207 were directly effective.

The Court replied that the Directive did not impose an obligation on the employer to conclude a contract of employment with a job applicant who had been discriminated against.

Next, in view of the obvious inconsistency that would arise from the public/private dichotomy for two plaintiffs in otherwise identical circumstances, the Court pursued a solution which ignored the question of the vertical, but not horizontal, direct effect of Directives.

The Court did not say that a Directive could be invoked against a private party (the defendant in *Harz*) but it did state that domestic law, particularly that introduced to implement a Directive, must be interpreted by national courts to achieve the result required by the Directive whether the defendant was the State or *a private party.*

In any event, the Court found that Article 6 of the Directive did not include 'any unconditional and sufficiently precise obligation as regards sanctions for discrimination' which could be relied upon by individuals to obtain particular sanctions – these were a matter for national law. Thus, continued the Court:

> It should, however, be pointed out to the national court that although Directive No 76/207/EEC, for the purpose of imposing a sanction for the breach of the prohibition of discrimination, leaves the Member States free to choose between the different solutions suitable for achieving its objective, it nevertheless requires that if a Member State chooses to penalize breaches of that prohibition by the award of compensation, then in order to ensure that it is effective and that it has a deterrent effect, that compensation must in any event be adequate in relation to the damage sustained and must therefore amount to more than purely nominal compensation such as, for example, the reimbursement only of the expenses incurred in connection with the application. It is for the national court to interpret and apply the legislation adopted for the implementation of the Directive in conformity with the requirements of Community law, in so far as it is given discretion to do so under national law.

The duty of the national court to secure an *effective* sanction arose quite apart from direct effects. It rested on Article 249(3) (formerly 189(3)) and the duty of Member States (including their courts) under Article 5 (now 10) of the Treaty to fulfil their obligations regarding the result envisaged by the Directive.

When the case returned to the German Labour Court, it reinterpreted the relevant implementing rules and discovered that it did possess the power to award damages (to both parties) not exceeding six months' gross salary. In this way, *Von Colson* achieves what has been called the *indirect effect* of Directives. The principle enables the equivalent of the horizontal direct effect of a Directive to be achieved; domestic law is to be interpreted in such a way that the Directive is applied indirectly against the State or a private party.

The Court stated that the *Von Colson* principle applied to 'national law and in particular the provisions of a national law specifically introduced in order to implement' the Directive. Thus, not being limited to implementing legislation, the principle could, it appeared, also be applied to national law adopted *before* the Directive. However, placing national courts under a duty to review domestic law enacted prior to a Directive, so as to comply with it, raises difficult questions regarding legal certainty and non-retroactivity. The rights of individuals (defendant private parties) who have arranged their affairs on the basis of such legislation, with a legitimate expectation that it would not suddenly be changed (reinterpreted to their detriment) in this way, must be safeguarded.

In the next case of significance, Case 80/86 *Kolpinghuis Nijmegen*, in addition to national law, the Dutch Public Prosecutor sought to supplement his case against the KN Company by relying on provisions of a Directive that had not yet been implemented although the time limit had expired. Since, following *Marshall*, the Court had stated that Directives could not of themselves, that is, without being transposed into national law, impose obligations on individuals, it was not surprising that in this case, following a reference, the Court of Justice made it clear that there was no corresponding right, not only for an individual but even more so for the State, *directly* to enforce a Directive against an individual in the national court. On this question of *reverse vertical direct effect*, the Court stated that 'a national authority may not rely, as against an individual, upon a provision of a Directive whose necessary implementation in national law has not yet taken place'. On a further question regarding *interpretation* of the existing national law in the light of the non-implemented Directive and its required result, the Court stated that 'a Directive cannot, of itself and independently of a law adopted for its implementation, have the effect of determining or aggravating the liability in criminal law of persons who act in contravention of the provisions of that Directive'. The duty of the national court to sympathetically interpret national law on the basis of the *Von Colson* principle was limited by the general principles of Community law (see Chapter 10), in particular the principles of legal certainty and, in this case, the non-retroactivity of criminal liability: see also Case C-168/95 *Arcaro (Criminal Proceedings)*, below.

In a subsequent case, the Court of Justice reviewed the operation of the *Von Colson* principle in a case involving two private parties and a non-implemented Directive.

Case C-106/89 *Marleasing SA v La Comercial Internacional de Alimentación SA*

M brought a claim in the Spanish courts for a declaration of nullity regarding the founders' contract establishing the defendant company. The claim was based on certain articles of the Spanish Civil Code and alleged that the contract was void on the grounds of 'lack of cause', or whose 'cause was wrongful', being a bogus and fraudulent transaction entered into for the purpose of evading creditors. M had lent money to the company and argued that if its contract of association was void, the company was a nullity and the debt could be recovered personally from those behind the scheme. In reply, the defendants argued that Article 11 of the first Company Directive (Directive 68/151), which exhaustively lists the grounds on which the nullity of a company may be declared, did not include the grounds on which M relied. However, certain provisions of the Spanish Civil Code did provide for the ineffectiveness of contracts for 'lack of cause'.

Directive 68/151 not having been implemented by Spain as required, as from the date of its accession to the European Communities, the Spanish court asked the Court of Justice whether Article 11 of the Directive had direct effect such as to bar a declaration of nullity for reasons other than those listed in Article 11.

The Court drew attention to its consistent line of case law (*Marshall*, etc) denying to Directives any horizontal direct effect: a Directive may not of itself impose obligations on any individual and therefore its provisions might not be relied upon as such against an individual – such as a Spanish public limited company.

Nevertheless, the Court chose to reword the question referred in terms of an obligation to interpret national law in conformity with the provisions of a Directive on the basis of its judgment in *Von Colson*.

The purpose of Directive 68/151 was to co-ordinate safeguards for the protection of members of companies and others – to make such safeguards equivalent throughout the Community – and the Court of Justice informed the Spanish court that it was obliged so far as was possible, to interpret its national law, *whether it pre-dated or post-dated the Directive, in the light of its terms.*

As a result, the Spanish court was placed under a duty to endeavour to interpret the pre-dated Spanish Civil Code (on which Marleasing relied – but which was not clear on the issue) in such a way as to exclude from it a declaration of nullity based on any ground other than those listed in Article 11 of the (unimplemented) Directive.

This 'horizontal' action (between private parties), involving neither criminal nor civil penalties, therefore explicitly confirmed that, even where national law pre-dated the Directive, the non-implemented Directive was to be used by the national court as the guide to the interpretation of that national law. Although, as seen above, the duty of the national court is said to be to interpret the national law 'so far as was possible' and 'to endeavour to interpret the pre-dated' law to comply with the Directive, in another part of its ruling, the Court of Justice appeared to lay down that national courts are *prohibited* from interpreting national law (even pre-dated legislation, which was not introduced to comply with a Directive) inconsistently with a Directive. This could hardly be the case where to do so would be in breach of an individual defendant's legitimate expectations. As we will see shortly, in *Duke v GEC Reliance Ltd* (1988), a sex discrimination case, the House of Lords refused to engage in 'purposive' or 'sympathetic' interpretation of inconsistent pre-dated national law so as to impose obligations contained in a non-implemented Directive upon an individual (company), as this would have necessitated an unwarranted distortion of the national law and been 'unfair' and in breach of the company's legitimate expectations. (Marleasing arguably could not show legitimate expectations under the relevant but unclear Spanish law.)

In any event, the *Von Colson* principle, as elaborated in *Marleasing*, could surely not apply where pre-dated national law was clearly incompatible with the terms of the Directive, that is, where there was no real question of interpretation. This point was later accepted by the Court of Justice in Case C-334/92 *Wagner Miret v Fondo de Garantia Salarial*, another case involving pre-dated Spanish legislation. To apply the principle in such a case would be to stretch the concept of 'purposive' interpretation beyond all bounds. Thus, even the *Von Colson* principle may fail to provide individuals with their Community law rights.

Case C-168/95 *Arcaro (Criminal Proceedings)* aroused considerable comment from 'Court-watchers', including the suggestion that a three-Judge chamber had reversed the Court's policy on indirect effect. In this case, the Court stated that the 'obligation of the national court to refer to the context of the Directive when interpreting the relevant rules of its own national law reaches a limit where such an interpretation leads to the imposition on an individual of any obligation laid down by a Directive which has not been transposed ...'.

In Arnull's view, the correct approach to this statement is as follows:

That passage needs to be understood in the context in which it was delivered. *Arcaro* concerned a prosecution of a businessman for infringing Italian legislation on pollution. It was unclear whether that legislation was consistent with a series of Community Directives it was designed to implement. The Court's judgment makes it clear that the duty of consistent interpretation does not apply where the effect would be to enable a *Member State* to enforce *against an individual* an obligation to which he might not otherwise be subject. Since it is the Member State which is responsible for not having implemented the Directive properly (or at all), it would be unconscionable to allow it to escape the consequences of its default in vertical proceedings of this kind. In horizontal proceedings *between individuals*, that consideration is not relevant and the *Marleasing* principle continues to apply in its full rigour [footnotes omitted].

In a similar vein, Weatherill is of the opinion that: 'An interpretative obligation may be inappropriate where the Member State has completely failed to implement the Directive even after the time limit has expired where it leads to the imposition of an obligation on an individual.'

FURTHER CONTROVERSY REGARDING HORIZONTAL DIRECT EFFECT

A series of cases decided by the Court of Justice in the 1990s has given rise to continuing debate regarding the basis for, and nature of, the effect given by the Court to incorrectly implemented or non-implemented Directives in cases which involve private parties. It will be recalled that in *Marshall*, a case of incorrect implementation, the Court declared that 'a Directive may not of itself impose *obligations* on an individual and that a provision of a Directive may not be *relied upon* as such against such a person' (emphasis added). Later, in Case C-91/92 *Faccini Dori v Recreb*, the Court affirmed this ruling; Miss FD not being able to rely on a non-implemented Directive of 1985 against a private party.

The question which arose from the cases now under discussion was whether the Court of Justice had reversed its position on horizontal direct effect. This has not proved to be the case.

The key to the cases which follow probably rests on a clearer and broader appreciation of the concept of direct effect which has been obscured by excessive concentration on the creation of individual rights. It has been pointed out (see Winter and Pescatore in 'References and Further Reading' at the end of the chapter) that some Community provisions are directly effective only in a 'lesser' sense in that they do not create enforceable individual rights but may serve as a standard for a review of Member State action. As the Court laid down in Case 8/81 *Becker*, the unconditional and sufficiently precise terms of a non-implemented Directive may 'be relied upon as against any national provision which is incompatible with the Directive' (or they may be relied upon 'in so far as the provisions define rights which individuals are able to assert [in this case] against the State'). Van Gerven, commenting on the *Becker* ruling, points to its dual character, its reference to 'the general right, and accompanying remedy, to have a court set aside national measures which conflict with the requirements of a Directive' and 'a specific right which a Directive grants to private persons ...'. This dual character has been present in virtually all the direct effect cases examined earlier in this chapter. As seen, the Court of Justice has no judicial review jurisdiction with regard to national legislation but one result of successful direct effect claims is frequently the need to withdraw or, more likely, amend national rules: for example, Dutch rules regarding rates of import duty payable in *Van Gend en Loos*, section 6(4) of the Sex Discrimination Act in *Marshall*. Here we have a form of indirect judicial review, as referred to in the previous chapter on the Court of Justice.

The recently decided controversial cases would appear to illustrate the point that the directly effective provisions of a Directive may, as stated above, serve only as a standard for a review of Member State action; individual rights and obligations not being created.

Case C-194/94 *CIA Security v Signalson and Securitel*

CIA brought an action against S and S in the Belgian courts in which it requested an order requiring the defendants to cease alleged unfair trading practices. S and S had allegedly libelled CIA by claiming in their sales promotions that alarm systems sold by CIA had not been approved by national technical regulations. CIA conceded that it had not sought approval but argued that the regulations were invalid, not having been notified to the Commission prior to implementation as required by the Technical Standards Directive 83/139.

The Belgian court referred questions to the Court of Justice including (a) whether the national rules should have been so notified; (b) whether the Directive was directly effective; (c) whether a national court should refuse to apply regulations which had not been notified.

The Court of Justice ruled that the Directive's provisions on notification laid down ' a precise obligation on Member States'. They were 'unconditional and sufficiently precise' and could 'be relied upon by individuals before national courts'. The Court then considered the legal consequences to be drawn from the breach of this obligation, in particular whether it rendered the regulations inapplicable and unenforceable against individuals.

The Court upheld CIA's claim, finding that the direct effect of the Directive rendered the non-notified regulations inapplicable to individuals. CIA could rely on the Directive as against a claim based on national rules which were incompatible with it.

The Directive's directly effective provisions concerned the relationship between Member States and the Commission; they did not create any specific identifiable right for individuals. CIA was, however, able to invoke the Directive to its advantage (it had not acted unlawfully in failing to seek approval) and to the probable disadvantage of S and S, in view of CIA's claim against them.

This can be explained by seeing CIA as falling within the category of persons who had a direct interest in the Directive's aim of securing the free movement of technically sound goods. It is true that some effect was given to the Directive in this action between individuals but not, it is contended, such as to amount to the imposition of any legal obligation on the defendants. In Advocate General Elmer's view, this action was brought and the Directive pleaded to test the validity of the national regulations, and the Directive did not 'aim to impose duties on individuals'. The Court's ruling required that action be taken by the State to ensure the validity of the regulations.

In a further case involving private parties, Case C-441/93 *Pafitis and Others v TKE Bank and Others*, existing shareholders in a Greek bank brought proceedings against the bank and new shareholders, claiming that the increase in the bank's capital thus brought about, although valid on the basis of enabling national law, was contrary to directly effective provisions of the Second Banking Directive. This Community measure laid down that a general meeting of (existing) shareholders, which had not been held, was required to decide on any increase in capital.

The Court of Justice ruled in favour of the applicants, holding that the Directive precluded the application of the national law on which the increase in capital was based. The national law being therefore ineffective, the Directive deprived the new shareholders of their status unless the Bank complied with the obligation to hold a meeting at which the increase was agreed.

This ruling can be compared to that in *CIA* in that, it would appear, direct effect only went to the 'general right ... to have a court set aside national measures which conflict with the requirements of a Directive'. This is a process which has been called '*l'invocabilité d'exclusion*', the invoking of the Directive to achieve the 'disapplication' of the national rules. No reference to horizontal direct effect was made in the Court's rulings. The enforcement of the Directive in the national court would nevertheless clearly prevent the bank and the new shareholders from relying on the national law. The steps taken on its basis would have to be retraced and the required meeting would probably act to their disadvantage.

In the third of this line of decisions, in Case C-129/94 *Bernáldez (Criminal Proceedings)*, although B was ordered in criminal proceedings to compensate a third party for damage to property caused by him when driving while drunk, Spanish compulsory insurance rules allowed B's insurance company to exclude themselves from liability to meet this third party claim. Following a reference to the Court under Article 177 (now 234) from the provincial appeal court in Seville, it was held that neither national statutory provisions nor contractual exclusions allowed the insurer to escape liability. This ruling was based on the interpretation of the First Motor Insurance Directive by the Court of Justice. The insurer was therefore directly liable to compensate victims of accidents of the kind in question on the basis of the Directive which took precedence over the national rules.

The crucial question here is whether a *legal obligation* (to pay the third party), which according to the Spanish court of first instance in the main proceedings was not an obligation under domestic law, was being imposed on a private party as a consequence of the reliance by B (and the Public Prosecutor) on the provisions of the Directive. Can the position be realistically distinguished from horizontal direct effect?

The report of the case is not helpful in finding answer to these questions. The fact that the insurer, as the Court pointed out, having paid the third party had a right of recovery against B, the insured, does not amount to a strong case for distinguishing. It has also been argued that, as seen above, this case does not concern the creation of specific individual rights but rests on a requirement, in line with the Seville appeal court's view, that the Spanish law be interpreted in accordance with the Directive.

Like *CIA Security*, the most recent in this line of cases concerned the Technical Standards Directive 83/139 and the ruling in the earlier case was followed.

Case C-443/98 *Unilever Italia v Central Food*

U supplied CF with olive oil which was labelled in compliance with EC law. However, the goods were rejected by CF as they were not labelled in accordance with the relevant Italian law. This law had been notified to the Commission in accordance with the Directive, but was adopted in mid-1998 despite the issue by the Commission of a suspension notice under the terms of the Directive and a notification that the Italian rules would not be enforceable against private parties, as a Commission

Regulation on marketing standards (including labelling) for olive oil was to be adopted – as it was in December 1998.

U argued that the Italian law was inapplicable and sued CF for the price of the goods. Following a reference on the interpretation of the Directive, the Court of Justice ruled that 'application of the Italian rules is liable to hinder Unilever in marketing the extra virgin olive oil which it offers for sale'.

While acknowledging that its own case law (*Faccini Dori*) denies that a Directive can of itself impose obligations on an individual, the Court stated that that case law did not apply where violations of the obligations arising under Directive 83/139 rendered a national measure inapplicable. The violation of the obligation to respect the 'standstill' provision was equated with the violation of the notification provision in *CIA Security*.

The Court declared that the Directive 'does not in any way define the substantive scope of the legal rule on the basis of which the national court must decide the case before it. It creates neither rights not obligations for individuals'.

Directive 83/139 imposes only procedural obligations on a Member State and so its enforcement against contrary provisions of national law cannot of itself impose direct obligations on private parties. In addition, as discussed above, the enforcement of the Directive, while rendering the national law inapplicable, did not create any substantive Community obligations for either of the private parties. Nevertheless, the Italian rules being ineffective, the contract would presumably have to be enforced under other national rules.

The present existence of an uneasy relationship between the *Marshall* and *Faccini Dori* 'no horizontal direct effect' cases and the now clearly flourishing 'incidental horizontal effect' line of cases clearly provides problems for legal certainty. At bottom, the fault lies with Member States who fail to comply with their Community obligations.

It is clear that these cases will not alter the Court's position on horizontal direct effect as expressed in 1994 in *Faccini Dori*, together with its reference in that case to the then newly emerging basis for the enforcement of individual rights under the concept of State liability. This route depends on neither direct effect nor the *Von Colson* principle of 'sympathetic' interpretation. It is an action for damages brought by the individual against the Member State that has deprived that individual of his or her Community law rights.

A FURTHER DEVELOPMENT: THE *FRANCOVICH* PRINCIPLE OF STATE LIABILITY

Marshall, *Foster*, *Von Colson* and *Marleasing* have all played their part in providing avenues to enable individuals to secure rights to be found in Community Directives – in some instances adopted by the Member State in a defective manner (*Marshall* and *Foster*, where existing national law, as claimed, did not meet the terms of the Directive), or implemented in an insufficient manner (*Von Colson*, where national law did not provide an effective remedy), or not implemented at all (*Marleasing*).

At the same time, and particularly since 1986 as the Community has sought, amongst other things, to complete the Internal Market, mainly by the use of

Directives, Member States have continued to fail to fulfil their obligation to implement Directives properly. The TEU introduced penalties, in the amended Article 171 (now 228), to be imposed on Member States which fail to fulfil their Treaty obligations (not merely as regards Directives), but this will not secure compensation for individuals who have thereby suffered loss. That Member States might be liable in damages on a non-contractual (tortious) basis to individuals who have suffered loss as a result of their breach of Community law was discussed in the literature, and hinted at by the Court of Justice, over a number of years. For example, in Case 60/75 *Russo v AIMA*, a Member State introduced national measures in contravention of a CAP regulation. Here the Court, in the operative part of its ruling (but without further clarification), stated that:

> If an individual producer has suffered damage as a result of the intervention of a Member State in violation of Community law it will be for the State, as regards the injured party, to take the consequences upon itself in the context of the provisions of national law relating to the State.

However, it was not until 1991, in *Francovich v Italian State*, that a possibility became rather more than a probability – Directives might be made fully effective by yet another route.

Joined Cases C-6/90 and C-9/90 *Francovich v Italian State* **and** *Bonifaci v Italian State*

Council Directive 80/987 on the protection of employees in the event of the insolvency of their employers requires Member States to ensure that payment of employees' outstanding claims arising from the employment relationship and relating to pay is guaranteed by 'guarantee institutions' financed by employers but independent of them.

In the UK, the Employment Protection (Consolidation) Act 1978 (as amended) meets the Directive's requirements and payments are made out of the Redundancy Fund. However, in Case 22/87 *Commission v Italy*, the Court of Justice held in Article 169 (now 226) proceedings that Italian legislation was insufficient for the proper implementation of the Directive. This was still the position in 1991 when these cases came before the Court.

Mr Francovich was owed 6 million lire by his insolvent employers, CDN Elettronica, and, being unable to enforce judgment against them, he brought an action against the Italian government for sums due in accordance with the terms of Directive 80/987 or for compensation in lieu. (The position of Mrs Bonifaci and others, employees of another insolvent employer, was the same.)

The Italian court referred questions to the Court of Justice for a preliminary ruling which the Court examined on the following basis: (1) whether the provisions of the Directive in relation to payment of the guaranteed debts were directly effective; and (2) whether there was State liability in damages arising from its failure to implement the Directive.

The Court reached the following conclusions:

(a) Interested parties cannot assert their rights to obtain guarantees of payment against the State because the relevant provisions of the Directive did not make it clear that it was the State itself which should guarantee the sums owed by the employer. (Although the beneficiaries of the guarantee and its content could be identified, the discretion allowed by the Directive did not enable the Court to identify the debtor with sufficient clarity.)

(b) It is a general principle 'inherent in the scheme of the Treaty' that 'a Member State is liable to make good damage to individuals caused by a breach of Community law for which it is responsible'.

Liability for failure to take the steps necessary in order to achieve the result required by a Directive depends on the following conditions: (i) the result required by the Directive includes the conferring of rights for the benefit of individuals; (ii) the content of those rights is identifiable by reference to the Directive; and (iii) there exists a causal link between the breach of the State's obligations and the damage suffered by persons affected.

Where these conditions are fulfilled (as they apparently were in these cases) the individual is entitled to damages as a matter of Community law.

Building on its own case law on supremacy and direct effect, the Court stressed that it was necessary to provide full protection of the rights of individuals, in *particular* where those rights were conditional on the Member States taking certain action and where, as a result of a Member State's breach of Community law, such individuals were unable to rely on their Community rights.

It was apparent from this statement of principle regarding State liability and from the Court's reliance on Article 10 (formerly 5) of the Treaty – which requires Member States to take all appropriate measures to ensure the fulfilment of their Treaty obligations including those under Article 249(3) (formerly 189(3)) – that *Francovich* would have an impact beyond the failure to implement Directives. Advocate General Mischo was of the opinion that this principle was 'capable of being extended to cover any failure of Member States to observe Community law ... whether the failure is in breach of the Treaty, Regulations or Directives, whether they have direct effect or not'. Thus, Member States which act in a manner contrary to the Treaty – which are in breach of their fundamental Community obligations, as, for example, was the case with the UK in *Factortame* – now come within the scope of the *Francovich* decision and may be liable for loss caused until such time as the infringement is terminated or relief granted: see also Chapter 20.

The claim for compensation is based on the State's breach of Community law, *such as* its clear failure to implement a Directive. It is not based on direct effect. Where a Directive has not been implemented and either: (i) it is not enforceable against the State owing to its lack of precision (it has no vertical direct effect) as in *Francovich*; or (ii) it is not enforceable against another individual (it has no horizontal effect), as decided in *Marshall* and which was the stumbling block in *Wagner Miret* (1993) above and *Faccini Dori* (1994) below, an individual who nevertheless suffers harm may sue the State as tortfeasor as a result of the State's default so long as the three conditions laid down are met.

However, as Steiner pointed out in 1993: 'The problem with *Francovich* lies not in the decision itself but in its implications.' In *Francovich*, there was a serious failure by the Italian State to fulfil a fundamental Treaty obligation (as decided in Case 22/87). However, given the potential scope of the decision, Steiner asked: 'If Member States are to be liable for breach of any binding Community obligation, under what circumstances will they be liable? This question concerns the nature and gravity of the breach':

... *Francovich* will be invoked to support a claim in respect of other, lesser failures. A failure to fulfil a Community obligation can take many forms, embracing a broad spectrum of culpability. At its most blatant, it can be a deliberate or knowing breach of Community law, for example a clear failure to implement an obligation, as in *Francovich* itself. It may be a partial failure, where implementation measures have been adopted, but they are faulty or inadequate. Such failures may be deliberate, knowing, negligent or innocent. Implementation measures may not have been adopted because existing national law was deemed to be adequate. Here, the failure may be negligent or innocent.

The failures may be legislative or executive. They will normally comprise a wrongful act or omission; the enactment of measures, or failure to amend, repeal or introduce legislation, in breach of Community law ...

It is submitted that even where the other conditions for liability under *Francovich* are met not all the above failures should give rise to non-contractual liability on the part of the State. They would not do so under the majority of laws of Member States, nor under the principles of Community liability [under Article 215(2) (now 228(2)) of the Treaty].

For what kind of failures, then, should a state be liable? On what principles is this to be decided? And are these matters of national or Community law?

Member State courts are now obliged to settle these questions (with or without an Article 234 reference for a preliminary ruling) within the context of national law on State liability and to provide real and effective protection for individuals' Community law rights. Steiner concluded that although 'States should not escape liability for damage caused by any wrongful acts, legislative or otherwise, both the nature of Community law and the principles of certainty and equity demand that States should not, in this context, be liable in the absence of fault'. However:

... whilst all States provide for the non-contractual liability of public authorities, their law, in the vast majority of (perhaps all) cases, will be inadequate to provide effective protection for individual rights under *Francovich*. Moreover, national laws governing the non-contractual liability of public authorities differ considerably from State to State. Thus, if *Francovich* is to be fully and fairly applied in all Member States, it will be necessary to develop a framework of common Community rules.

The implications of *Francovich* can now be clearly discerned and are discussed in Chapter 20. However, one important – and contentious – post-*Francovich* development must finally be examined. It concerns strenuous efforts to persuade the Court of Justice to accept, on various grounds, the horizontal direct effect of defectively implemented or non-implemented Directives. This proposition, rejected by the Court in *Marshall*, as we have seen, would of course mean that the terms of such a Directive could be relied upon by a private party to impose *obligations on another private party* (and note in this regard the discussion of the *CIA Security* and *Unilever Italia* line of decisions discussed above).

However, in Case C-91/92 *Faccini Dori v Recreb Srl*, the Court reiterated its position in *Marshall* and drew particular attention to a private party's new-found rights as established in *Francovich*:

In January 1989, Miss Faccini Dori entered into a contract with an Italian company at Milan Central Station for an English language correspondence course. Four days later she informed the company that she was withdrawing from the contract. In June, the company wrote to her stating that it had assigned its rights to the defendant company, Recreb. Miss Dori wrote to Recreb confirming her cancellation, indicating that she relied on the right of cancellation provided for by Council Directive 85/577 concerning protection of the consumer in respect of contracts negotiated away from business premises. (The 1985 Directive is a harmonisation measure designed to eliminate discrepancies between Member States' rules in the field in question. It allows consumers a right of cancellation for a period of at least seven days to enable them to weigh up the full implications of the obligations arising under the contract. The Directive was transposed into English law by means of the Consumer Protection (Cancellation of Contracts Concluded away from Business Premises) Regulations 1987 which allow cancellations within a period of seven days.)

Recreb next asked the Judge Conciliator in Florence to order Miss Dori to pay the agreed sum with interest and costs. The decision of the court having gone against her, Miss Dori lodged an objection to this order, again pleading the cancellation provisions of the Directive.

However, at the material time, Italy had not transposed the Directive into national law. The period laid down for transposition had expired in December 1987 but Italy had not complied until March 1992. The Judge Conciliator stayed the proceedings and referred a question to the Court of Justice under Article 177 (now 234) regarding the interpretation of the Directive in order to establish whether, even though the Directive had not been transposed into national law at the material time, the national court could nevertheless apply its provisions within the legal relationship between the consumer and the trader.

The Court ruled that the question of the national court's application of the Directive (in favour of Miss Dori) in the circumstances of the case depended on two main issues:

(a) *Whether the relevant provisions of the Directive were unconditional and sufficiently precise.* The Court ruled that the relevant Articles of the Directive, regarding the determination of the persons for whose benefit they were adopted and the minimum period within which notice of cancellation had to be given, were unconditional and sufficiently precise. (It appears clear that Miss Dori was a 'consumer' and that the contract had been entered into 'away from business premises'. Seven days was a clear minimum guarantee.)

(b) *Whether, in the absence of measures transposing the Directive within the prescribed time limit, consumers might derive from the Directive itself a right of cancellation against traders with whom they had concluded contracts and enforce that right before a national court.* The Court ruled that consumers could not in such circumstances derive such a right of cancellation or enforce such a right in a national court.

In denying the horizontal direct effect of the non-transposed Directive (and so opening the door to the national court's upholding of the trader's claim against Miss Faccini Dori), the Court perpetuated the previously noted public/private, vertical/horizontal anomaly. Having cited Article 189(3) (now 249(3)), *Marshall* and similar case law on vertical direct effect, it was stated that:

The effect of extending that case law to the sphere of relations between individuals would be to recognize a power in the Community to enact obligations for individuals with immediate effect, whereas it has competence to do so only where it is empowered to adopt regulations.

This is a remarkable statement. The arguments for the horizontal direct effect of Directives (see, for example, Advocate General Jacobs, below) are put forward on the basis that this effect would only come into play *after* the time limit for their transposition into national law had expired. The period between adoption and final date for implementation, as laid down in each Directive, varies but is normally measured in years.

In his Opinion in *Faccini Dori*, Advocate General Lenz acknowledged the Court's case law on Directives, which 'should be maintained for reasons of legal certainty, in respect of situations of the past'. However, he continued: 'As regards the future, it would seem necessary to acknowledge ... in the interest of a uniform and effective application of Community law, the *general applicability* of the precise and unconditional provisions of a Directive ...' (emphasis added).

While rejecting this proposition, the Court drew attention to the availability of rights for individuals on the basis of its rulings in *Von Colson, Marleasing* and *Wagner Miret* (that is, on indirect effect) and, particularly, 'if the result prescribed by the Directive cannot be achieved by way of interpretation', the availability of individual rights on the basis of *Francovich*. In the Court's view, Miss Faccini Dori's case met the required conditions for the imposition of State liability (see above).

In short, the Court was apparently saying that although Article 189(3) (now 249(3)) does not allow obligations to be imposed on individuals, the case law of the Court had closed the gaps as regards protection for individuals. This is not entirely true. For example, Miss Faccini Dori was not allowed to use direct effect as a 'shield' in the action brought against her in the Italian courts – contrast the position of *Ratti* in the proceedings brought against him by the State. To recover damages, she would have had to institute new proceedings against the State on the basis of *Francovich*.

In Case C-316/93 *Vaneetveld v SA Le Foyer*, Advocate General Jacobs argued for horizontal direct effect of Directives on an imposing array of grounds:

(a) *Marshall (No 1)* (1986) was decided on the basis of the wording of Article 189(3) (now 249(3)) (Directives are binding on the State), but that Article 'does not expressly exclude the possibility of derived obligations arising for persons other than Member States'.

(b) A similar *literal* approach to Article 119 (now 141) of the Treaty would have made it impossible to impose directly effective equal pay obligations on private sector employers in Case 43/75 *Defrenne v SABENA (Defrenne (No 2))*. Article 119 imposed an obligation on the *Member States* to implement an equal pay policy: but see Chapter 14 for the Court's policy decision in this case.

(c) The 'rationale for assigning direct effect to a Directive as against a Member State, namely, that a Member State ought not to be able to rely upon its own failure to implement a Directive, is singularly inapposite in relation to such a body [as the Southampton and South West Hampshire Area Health Authority in *Marshall* or South West Water Services Ltd in *Griffin*, below] which has not responsibility for that failure'.

(d) In any event, it is difficult to justify distinctions between, for example, public sector employers and employers in the private sector.

(e) All other binding provisions of Community law (Treaty Articles, Regulations and Decisions) may impose obligations on individuals.

(f) Following the TEU amendment of Article 191 (now 254), Directives either must be published or, where they need not be, in practice invariably are published.

(g) 'A Directive ... will produce legal effects only after the period which it lays down for its implementation has expired. Regulations and Directives will remain different instruments, appropriate in different situations and achieving their aims by different means ...'

(h) Despite the wording of Article 189(3) (now 249(3)), 'it is no longer accurate to say that Directives are binding only "as to the result to be achieved". The "choice of form and methods" left to the Member States is often illusory because the discretion of the Member States in implementing Directives is severely limited by the detailed, exhaustive nature of much of the legislation now emanating from the Council in the form of Directives. Many of the provisions contained in Directives are in consequence ideally suited to have direct effect'. (In *Van Gend en Loos*, the Court described Article 12 (now 25) of the Treaty as being 'ideally adapted to produce direct effects'.)

(i) Assigning both vertical and horizontal direct effect to Directives would be consistent with the need to ensure the effectiveness of Community law, its uniform application in all Member States and the provision of effective remedies in national courts for the protection of Community rights. At present, distortions result, 'both between and within Member States, if Directives are enforceable, for example, against employers or suppliers of goods or services in the public sector but not in the private sector'. (Note again, however, the *Griffin* decision, below.)

(j) The present case law on Directives has led to legal *uncertainty*, for example, a very broad interpretation of the concept of Member State which covers 'enterprises in which there is no particular element of State participation or control, notwithstanding that those enterprises have no responsibility for the default of the Member States, and notwithstanding that they might be in direct competition with private sector undertakings against which the same Directives are not enforceable'.

In conclusion, but to no avail (the Court did not see it as necessary to address the issue in this case), Advocate General Jacobs stated that:

> ... it seems to me that Directives whose very object is that rights should be conferred on individuals, and that obligations should be imposed on individuals, should be enforceable at the suit of the plaintiff [in the instant case] unless the legitimate expectations of the defendant would thereby be defeated ...

However, at present, it apparently remains the case in this increasing complex area that with respect to Directives, individual rights may be secured on the basis of vertical but not horizontal direct effect (but again recall *CIA Security*, etc), by way of indirect effect (within increasingly unclear limits after *Arcaro*) and under the emerging principle of State liability. In *Francovich*, the Court of Justice stated that State liability for damages is 'required by Community law' and as we have seen, certain conditions were laid down where the Member State's breach consists of failure to implement a Directive.

The Court's important post-*Francovich* decision in Joined Cases C-46/93 and C-48/93 *Brasserie du Pêcheur SA v Germany* and *R v Secretary of State for Transport ex p Factortame and Others*, which modifies the *Francovich* ruling, is examined in Chapter 20 together with other State liability rulings.

DIRECT EFFECT, INDIRECT EFFECT AND THE IMPLEMENTATION OF COMMUNITY LAW IN THE UK

The European Communities Act 1972

In Chapter 4, it was pointed out that the UK approach to international law is of a dualist character. Treaties entered into by the UK do not in themselves affect the law applied in the UK courts. Although binding in international law, a treaty only has effect in the domestic legal system if an Act of Parliament incorporates it. It was on this footing that the European Communities Act 1972 was passed to make provision for UK membership of the Community and to supply the *national* legal basis for enforceable Community rights for individuals, that is, the direct effect of Community law in the UK.

Under section 2(1), what the Act terms 'directly enforceable rights' are given effect within the UK legal system, and the combined effect of section 2(1) and (4) and section 3 is to make the principle of the supremacy of directly effective Community law part of UK law. Thus, on the basis of section 2(4), domestic legislation 'shall be construed and have effect' subject to the principle of supremacy. Section 3(1), as amended, directs national courts to follow the decisions (precedents in domestic terms) of the Court of Justice:

> 3(1) For the purposes of all legal proceedings any question as to the meaning or effect of any of the Treaties, or as to the validity, meaning or effect of any Community instrument, shall be treated as a question of law (and, if not referred to the European Court, be for determination as such in accordance with the principles laid down by and any relevant decision of the European Court or any court attached thereto).

Thus, in the House of Lords in 1983, in a case involving Article 86 (now 82) of the Treaty, a competition policy Article first established as being of direct effect by the Court of Justice in 1974, Lord Diplock said:

> The rights which the Article confers on citizens in the United Kingdom fall within section 2(1) of the 1972 Act. They are without further enactment to be given legal effect in the United Kingdom and enforced accordingly.

Later, in 1990, in the highly controversial and much publicised *Factortame* litigation, Lord Bridge stated that:

> Under the terms of the Act of 1972, it has always been clear that it was the duty of a United Kingdom court, when delivering final judgment, to override any rule of national law found to be in conflict with any directly enforceable rule of Community law ... there is nothing in any way novel in according supremacy to rules of Community law ...

In this series of cases, in which it was eventually decided that provisions of the Merchant Shipping Act 1988 conflicted with the plaintiff's directly enforceable Treaty rights, Lord Bridge concluded that section 2(1) of the 1972 Act had the same effect as if a section had been incorporated into the 1988 Act which in terms laid down that the 1988 Act was to be *without prejudice* to the plaintiffs' (or any other EEC national's) directly effective rights (see also Chapters 3 and 20).

It has often been observed that the 1972 Act does not *expressly* accord supremacy to Community law and that Parliament remains free to repeal the Act itself. Supremacy is recognised by denying effectiveness to UK legislation while we are a member of the Community to the extent that it conflicts with directly effective Community law. Section 2(4) provides that UK legislation shall be construed and have effect subject to the principle of supremacy, leaving open the perhaps theoretical possibility of Parliament *expressly* withdrawing from the Community (see Chapter 3 regarding parliamentary sovereignty).

No question of the construction or interpretation of the Merchant Shipping Act arose in *Factortame*. The Court of Justice declared that the Act was in breach of the plaintiffs' directly effective rights. The House of Lords applied that decision: Community law took priority and in accordance with the *Simmenthal* decision on supremacy (see Chapter 4), the 1988 Act was amended to comply with Community law. Similarly, following the *Marshall* decision on equal treatment regarding retirement ages for men and women, national law was amended in 1986 to make discriminatory retirement ages illegal (but not in time for Mrs Duke: see below).

A survey of the English case law in which the question of the supremacy of directly effective Community law has been the issue shows that our courts have generally been ready and willing to comply with the principle. This has been done in some cases, as in *Factortame*, by a direct application of Community law (following a reference to the Court of Justice on the issue) in the face of the conflicting domestic law.

Earlier, in *Macarthys Ltd v Smith* (1981), an equal pay case discussed in more detail in Chapter 14, following a reference to the Court of Justice regarding the interpretation of Article 119 (now 141) of the Treaty, the Court of Appeal directly applied that Article in S's favour, so giving it priority over restrictive and therefore conflicting provisions of the Equal Pay Act 1970. This approach, which amounts to an indirect review of national legislation by the Court of Justice, is of course in line with the ruling of the Court in Case 106/77 *Simmenthal* (see Chapter 4) which requires the immediate and direct enforcement of directly effective Community law. However, two years later, in a very similar case, the House of Lords adopted instead an *indirect* approach to the enforcement of the directly effective Article 119; 'conflicting' *national* law (the Equal Pay Act again) being subjected to a purposive interpretation, in accordance with section 2(4) of the 1972 Act, in order to secure its compliance.

A purposive or teleological interpretation of national law, as we have seen when discussing the interpretative methods of the Court of Justice, will seek to achieve the purpose or aims of the relevant directly effective Community law. Thus, in 1982, in *Garland v British Rail Engineering*, Lord Diplock stated that:

> The instant appeal does not present an appropriate occasion to consider whether, having regard to the express direction as to the construction of enactments 'to be passed' which is contained in section 2(4), anything short of an express positive statement in an Act of Parliament passed after 1 January 1973, that a particular provision is intended to be made in breach of an obligation assumed by the United Kingdom under a Community treaty, would justify an English court in construing that provision in a manner inconsistent with a Community treaty obligation of the United Kingdom, however wide a departure from the *prima facie* meaning of the language of the provision might be needed in order to achieve consistency.

The House of Lords therefore construed the Equal Pay Act to comply with Article 119 of the Treaty 'without any undue straining of the words' of the Act. Their Lordships did not directly apply Article 119, which, as seen, is capable of both vertical and horizontal direct effect, but instead sought a ruling from the Court of Justice as to whether that Article conferred directly enforceable rights on the facts of this particular case. The Court of Justice ruled that it did (see Chapter 14) and their Lordships then proceeded by way of a 'harmonious construction' of the national law.

In 1989, in *Pickstone v Freemans plc,* concerning a claim for equal pay for work of *equal value,* the Court of Appeal found for the plaintiffs against the defendant company by means of direct enforcement of EC law whereas, on appeal, the House of Lords reached the same conclusion via the indirect *Von Colson* construction approach.

The Equal Pay Act 1970 (operative 1975) did not allow for 'equal value' claims, but it was amended by statutory instrument in 1983, on the basis of section 2(2) of the European Communities Act, in order to comply with the 1975 Equal Pay Directive. The Court of Appeal found it impossible to construe the 1983 amendment (which was in terms of 'outstanding obscurity') in the plaintiff's favour but instead directly applied Article 119 (read in conjunction with the Directive) against the private sector employer. In the House of Lords, however, their Lordships chose to 'interpret' the Equal Pay Act (to the extent of reading certain words into the relevant amended sub-section) in order to achieve a result compatible with the non-directly effective Directive as interpreted by the Court of Justice.

In *Litster v Forth Dry Dock and Engineering Co Ltd* (1990), in an action brought against another private sector employer, the House of Lords, proceeding in line with *Von Colson,* was prepared to interpret national law introduced for the purpose of complying with a Directive in a way which was *contrary* to its *prima facie* meaning. Their Lordships adopted a purposive construction of UK regulations made in 1981 under section 2(2) of the 1972 Act in order to implement a 1977 Council Directive on the protection of employees' rights on the transfer of a business from one employer to another. Additional words were implied into the regulations to ensure that they complied with the obligation in the Directive that it should apply not only to employees who were employed in the business immediately before its transfer, but also to employees who would have been so employed if they had not been unfairly dismissed in contemplation of the transfer. Lord Oliver stated that:

> The critical question, it seems to me, is whether, even allowing for the greater latitude in construction permissible in the case of legislation introduced to give effect to this country's Community obligations, it is possible to attribute to regulation 8(1) when read in conjunction with regulation 5, the same result as that attributed to Article 4 [of the Directive] in the *Bork* case [1989] IRLR 41. Purely as a matter of language, it clearly is not. Regulation 8(1) does not follow literally the wording of Article 4(1) ... If this provision fell to be construed by reference to the ordinary rules of construction applicable to a purely domestic statute and without reference to Treaty obligations, it would, I think be quite impermissible to regard it as having the same prohibitory effect as that attributed by the European Court to Article 4 of the Directive. But it has always to be borne in mind that the purpose of the Directive and of the Regulations was and is to 'safeguard' the rights of employees on a transfer and that there is a mandatory obligation to provide remedies which are effective and not merely symbolic to which the Regulations were intended to give effect. The remedies provided by the Act of 1978 in the case of an insolvent transferor are largely illusory unless they can be exerted against the transferee as the Directive contemplates and I

do not find it conceivable that, in framing Regulations intending to give effect to the Directive, the Secretary of State could have envisaged that its purpose should be capable of being avoided by the transparent device to which resort was had in the instant case. *Pickstone v Freemans Plc* [1989] AC 66 has established that the greater flexibility available to the court in applying a purposive construction to legislation designed to give effect to the United Kingdom's Treaty obligations to the Community enables the court, where necessary, to supply by implication words appropriate to comply with those obligations [see particularly the speech of Lord Templeman, at pp 120–21].

However, in an earlier decision in 1988 involving a claim by a former employee against her private sector employer, a purposive interpretation of national law on behalf of the plaintiff was not embarked upon by their Lordships. It is a decision which should be viewed in the light of both *Von Colson* (1983) and *Marleasing* (1989), and now *Wagner-Miret* (1993).

Duke v GEC Reliance Ltd (1988)

Mrs Duke's equal treatment claim regarding compulsory retirement at 60 was essentially the same as that in the earlier case of *Marshall*. Their Lordships were urged to construe the Sex Discrimination Act 1975 as amended in 1986 to comply with the 1976 Equal Treatment Directive as interpreted by the Court of Justice in *Marshall* to make discriminatory retirement ages unlawful. However, the 1986 amendment had not been made retrospective and D's claim for damages related to a period, as in *Marshall, prior to* the amendment. In addition, her company employers were not, as in *Marshall*, to be regarded as an arm of the State; that is, there was no question of the vertical direct effect of the Directive itself.

It was argued on D's behalf that the effect of section 2(4) of the European Communities Act ('... any enactment passed or to be passed ... shall be construed ...') was to make the Sex Discrimination Act 1975 subject to the ban on discriminatory retirement ages in the 1976 Directive.

It was held that a purposive construction could not be given to legislation *pre-dating* a Directive and which was not enacted to give effect to its provisions. Nor did their Lordships feel obliged to distort the meaning of a domestic statute to comply with a Community provision which was not directly effective as between private parties. Lord Templeman stated that section 2(4) 'does no more than reinforce the binding nature of legally enforceable rights and obligations imposed by appropriate Community law'. Therefore, section 2(4), relating to section 2(1) and to directly effective rights only, had, in their Lordships' view, no application in this case.

The House of Lords felt it would be 'most unfair' to allow this claim against a private sector employer by interpreting the Sex Discrimination Act, which prior to its amendment allowed for differing retirement ages, against its literal meaning so as to comply with the *later* Directive – and certainly not when the 1986 amendment operated prospectively not retrospectively.

Of the various factors at play in this case:

(a) The *raison d'être* of the *Von Colson* principle is that it applies in respect of Community law which is *not* directly effective (not sufficiently clear in *Von Colson* and not enforceable in 'horizontal' situations such as in *Litster*).

(b) The way was therefore open for their Lordships to attempt a purposive interpretation of the pre-dated national law on the basis of *Von Colson* (as explained in *Marleasing*).

(c) Nevertheless, even if their Lordships had felt able to construe section 6(4) of the Sex Discrimination Act 1975 (which excluded retirement ages from the prohibition on discrimination) contrary to its literal meaning so as to comply with the Directive, the powerful point remains that this would have been an infringement of the private employer's legitimate expectation (that the English statute meant what it said and that meaning would not suddenly be changed in a retrospective manner): see Case 80/86 *Kolpinghuis Nijmegen*, above.

In *Webb v EMO* (1995) (see also Chapter 14), the Court of Appeal, following *Duke*, refused to 'distort' the natural meaning of the Sex Discrimination Act 1975 in order to achieve compliance with the later, and non-directly effective, Equal Treatment Directive of 1976 and so enable the applicant female worker to succeed. On appeal, the House of Lords, while supporting the Court of Appeal's approach, referred questions regarding the interpretation of the Directive on the point at issue to the Court of Justice. The Court of Justice's ruling in favour of Webb meant that her dismissal on grounds of unavailability for work due to pregnancy constituted direct sex discrimination in breach of the Directive. The House of Lords, when applying this ruling, interpreted the Act so as to conform to the Directive despite expressing difficulty in doing so.

It is now generally clear that the UK courts will enforce directly effective EC law directly rather than by the section 2(4) 'construction' approach, and they will usually strain to interpret pre-dated national law to comply with non-directly effective provisions of a Directive.

As regards direct effect and supremacy, the UK *'cause célèbre'* was the *Factortame* case, referred to above and dealt with in more detail in Chapter 20. A further development (also dealt with in Chapter 14) came in the case of *Equal Opportunities Commission v Secretary of State for Employment* (1994). In the wake of the *Factortame* litigation, the key features of which were the initial suspension and later disapplication of a statute in the face of the applicants' directly effective Treaty rights, came a ruling by the House of Lords in the *EOC* case which meant that not only could national legislation be disapplied in national courts in the face of a successful claim of directly effective rights (or in a State liability *Francovich* action), but that a body such as the EOC, operating under statutory duties to eliminate sex discrimination, had the capacity and sufficient interest to obtain from the court a declaration that provisions of the relevant legislation, the Employment Protection Act 1978, were incompatible with the Community law and inapplicable. As a result, and for the first time, in applying Community law, English courts were granted new direct powers of legislative review by this decision. (See also the discussion of direct effect and judicial review in the section 'Further Controversy regarding Horizontal Direct Effect', above.)

Attention must also be drawn to *Griffin v South West Water Services Ltd* (1995), a direct effect case which closely relates to *Foster v British Gas plc* and that case's guideline as to what constitutes ' the State' with respect to the direct effect of the provisions of a Directive. Foster's successful claim, as seen above, was against British Gas when it was a nationalised industry operating as a public utility, that is, before the industry was privatised. In general terms, privatisation means that the government divests itself of ownership or control of the economic sector in question (coal, gas and electricity, water, rail services, etc) and returns the industry to the private sector as a commercial enterprise.

The question in *Griffin*, a High Court decision, was whether a privatised utility could nevertheless be classed as an emanation of the State for the purposes of a direct effect claim and the *Foster* guideline. An affirmative answer, which on the face of it seemed unlikely, would mean that obligations in the Directive could be pleaded in the *vertically* direct manner against the *company*. The claim rested on the assertion that SWW should have consulted with the relevant (but unrecognised by SWW) trade union over collective redundancies in accordance with Directive 75/129.

Blackburne J held against the company. Taking the *Foster* guideline step by step, he found (a) that SWW fulfilled the 'special powers' and 'public service' conditions; and (b) that on the facts of the case, the relevant statutory provisions and the conditions of SWW's licence to operate showed that it performed its public service as a water undertaking under the control of the State. SWW's legal form was irrelevant (see the *Foster* test) and it was not necessary to show that the State was able to exercise influence over the company as regards the subject matter of the relevant provision of the particular Directive. The Directive was to be applied. Like *Doughty* above, this is a case which illustrates the difficulty in some cases of drawing the line between 'public' and 'private'.

REFERENCES AND FURTHER READING

Arnull, A, 'Editorial: the incidental effect of Directives' (1999) 24 EL Rev 1.

Barnard, C and Greaves, R, 'The application of Community law in the United Kingdom, 1986–93' (1994) 31 CML Rev 1055.

Bebr, G, 'Case note on *Francovich*' (1992) 29 CML Rev 557.

Coppel, J, 'Rights, duties and the end of *Marshall*' (1994) 57 MLR 859.

Craig, PP, 'Once upon a time in the west; direct effect and the federalization of EEC law' (1992) 12 OJLS 453.

Craig, PP, 'Directives: direct effect, indirect effect and the construction of national legislation' (1997) 22 EL Rev 519.

Curtin, D, 'Effective sanctions and the Equal Treatment Directive: the *Von Colson* and *Harz* cases' (1985) 22 CML Rev 505.

Curtin, D, 'The province of government: delimiting the direct effect of Directives in the common law context' (1990) 15 EL Rev 195.

De Búrca, G, 'Giving effect to European Community Directives' (1992) 55 MLR 215.

Eleftheriadis, P, 'The direct effect of Community law: conceptual issues' (1996) 16 YEL 205.

Hilson, C and Downes, T, 'Making sense of rights: Community rights in EC law' (1999) 24 EL Rev 121.

Lenz, M, Sif Tynes, D and Young, L, 'Horizontal What? Back to basics' (2000) 25 EL Rev 509.

Maltby, N, '*Marleasing*: what is all the fuss about?' (1993) 109 LQR 301.

Morris, PE, 'The direct effect of Directives – some recent developments in the European Court – I and II' (1989) JBL 233 and 309.

Pescatore, P, 'The doctrine of "direct effect": an infant disease of Community law' (1983) 8 EL Rev 155.

Prechal, S, 'Does direct effect still matter?' (2000) 37 CML Rev 1047.

Shaw, J, 'European Community judicial method: its application to sex discrimination' (1990) 19 ILJ 228.

Steiner, J, 'From direct effects to *Francovich*: shifting means of enforcement of Community law' (1993) 18 EL Rev 3.

Van Gerven, W, 'Of rights, remedies and procedures' (2000) 37 CML Rev 501.

Weatherill, S, 'Breach of Directives and breach of contract' (2001) 26 EL Rev 177.

Winter, TA, 'Direct applicability and direct effects' (1972) 9 CML Rev 425.

See also case notes on the cases discussed to be found in the European Law Review, the Common Market Law Review, the Modern Law Review, etc.

CHAPTER 9

REFERENCES FOR PRELIMINARY RULINGS (ARTICLE 234 (FORMERLY 177))

INTRODUCTION

The preliminary rulings procedure, whereby national courts and tribunals refer questions of Community law to the Court of Justice, has featured in many of the cases in the previous chapters. It is through this procedure that disputes at the national level in which, as we have seen, individuals have asserted their Community rights against their Member States that the Court has established and developed such basic concepts as supremacy, direct effect and State liability. Whether the drafters of the Treaty foresaw that Article 177 (now 234) would provide the vehicle for such a fundamentally significant outcome is doubtful.

The nature of the procedure shows that difficult questions regarding the correct interpretation (including that of direct effect) and therefore application of Community law (Treaty Articles, Regulations, Directives and Decisions) are raised not only directly before the Court of Justice, but also in the national courts and tribunals of the Member States in cases with a 'Community dimension'. This latter situation could clearly give rise to an obvious danger: that differing interpretations and therefore applications of Community law would emerge from Member State to Member State. Because it follows from the supremacy of Community law, in the furtherance of common and co-ordinated Community policies, that it must have the same meaning and effect in all the Member States, this is a situation that would be inimical to the proper functioning of the Community. The preliminary rulings procedure is the mechanism provided by the Treaty to avert this danger, providing national courts and tribunals clearly understand their vital role in the way in which the procedure's mechanism is designed to operate.

The procedure has been described as one involving co-operation between national courts and tribunals and the Court of Justice: see the extract from the *CILFIT* case, below. However, it is arguably more realistic to see the relationship in the form of a hierarchical pyramid formed by the Community Court at the apex and national courts and tribunals operating as *Community courts and tribunals* across the base.

At present, the Court of Justice has sole jurisdiction under Article 234 (formerly 177) but, as seen in Chapter 7, a Nice Treaty amendment to Article 225 states in a new Article 225(3) that the CFI shall have jurisdiction 'to hear and determine questions referred for a ruling under Article 234 in specific areas laid down by the Statute of the Court of Justice' on the basis of an act adopted for this purpose by the Council:

Article 234

The Court of Justice shall have jurisdiction to give preliminary rulings concerning:

(a) the interpretation of this Treaty;

(b) the validity and interpretation of acts of the institutions of the Community and of the ECB;

(c) the interpretation of the statutes of bodies established by an act of the Council, where those statutes so provide.

Where such a question is raised before any court or tribunal of a Member State that court or tribunal may, if it considers that a decision on the question is necessary to enable it to give judgment, request the Court of Justice to give a ruling thereon.

Where any such question is raised in a case pending before a court or tribunal of a Member State, against whose decisions there is no judicial remedy under national law, that court or tribunal shall bring the matter before the Court of Justice.

It must be stressed that Article 234 does not provide an appeals procedure. The jurisdiction of the Court of Justice is limited to *preliminary* rulings on specific Community law issues referred to it by a national court or tribunal (not by a party), and the answers given are remitted to the national court or tribunal which must itself *apply* them when finally deciding the case before it.

Therefore, the Court of Justice does not decide the case but provides in its answers to the questions referred a form of interlocutory ruling which binds the national court or tribunal. The ruling is framed in an objective or non-specific manner, although the Court's answers often leave little doubt as to how the national court or tribunal should proceed. The Court of Justice has no jurisdiction under Article 234 (formerly 177) to interpret national law or decide on the validity of a provision of national law – although a direct effect ruling, as seen in earlier chapters – may well result in the need for disapplication of conflicting national legislation.

In the *CILFIT* case, the Court stated, in response to a question raised by an Italian court relating to the correct interpretation of Article 177 (now 234) itself:

In order to answer that question, it is necessary to take account of the system established by Article 177, which confers jurisdiction on the Court of Justice to give preliminary rulings on, *inter alia*, the interpretation of the Treaty and the measures adopted by the institutions of the Community.

...

[The obligation in Article 177(3)] to refer a matter to the Court of Justice is based on cooperation, established with a view to ensuring the proper application and uniform interpretation of Community law in all Member States, between national courts, in their capacity as courts responsible for the application of Community law, and the Court of Justice. More particularly, the third paragraph of Article 177 seeks to prevent the occurrence within the Community of divergences in judicial decisions on questions of Community law.

As regards the types of provisions which may be referred, Article 234 EC and Article 150 Euratom are the same. Article 41 ECSC confers jurisdiction upon the Court only with respect to the validity of acts of the Council or Commission. This was seen as an oversight and, in a 1988 case, the Court held that it has jurisdiction to give preliminary rulings on the interpretation of such acts and the ECSC Treaty itself. The basis of this decision was policy – the uniformity of application of Community law.

The vast majority of rulings concern the EC Treaty and EC institutional acts, but following the ToA, there is an exception concerning Articles 61–69 dealing with 'Visas, Asylum, Immigration and Other Policies Concerning the Free Movement of Persons' as removed by the ToA from the 'old' third pillar on Justice and Home Affairs. Here, Article 68 states that a preliminary ruling on a question of interpretation or validity can only be sought by a national court or tribunal of last resort. Such courts or tribunals *shall*, if they consider that a decision on the question is necessary to enable them to give judgment, request the Court of Justice to give a ruling thereon.

Although, exceptionally, the Council, the Commission and the Member States may request a ruling on issues within these related policy areas, the operation of the procedure as laid down in Article 68 amounts to a dilution of its purpose and the curtailment of the protection of individual rights.

Also, within the remodelled third pillar on Police and Judicial Co-operation in Criminal Matters, Article 35 TEU, as modified by the ToA, in effect provides (as noted in Chapter 1) that the Court has the jurisdiction to give preliminary rulings on the interpretation and validity of certain decisions and other measures adopted in this field, but not on the Treaty provisions themselves, if the Member State involved has accepted the Court's jurisdiction.

THE MAIN PROVISIONS UPON WHICH REFERENCES MAY BE BASED

Article 234(1)(a) covers the interpretation of the EC Treaty, all Treaties amending or supplementing it (except where otherwise provided, for example, as regards the common provisions of the TEU (see Article 35 TEU), and international agreements entered into by the Community). Article 234(1)(b) extends to both the interpretation and *validity* of acts of the Community institutions. The vast majority of these will be acts of the Council and the Commission, and the case of law of the Court shows that they include not only the binding acts of Article 189 (now 249) (whether directly effective or not) but also those which are not binding. In Case C-322/88 *Grimaldi*, in which a Belgian tribunal referred a question relating to the possible direct effect of a *recommendation*, the Court stated that Article 177 (now 234) conferred upon it the jurisdiction to give preliminary rulings on the interpretation and validity of all acts adopted by the institutions. As explained earlier by Advocate General Warner in Case 113/75 *Frecassetti*:

> I do not think it correct to say that the interpretation of a recommendation can never be relevant to an issue before a national court. Where, for example, a national statute has been passed for the express purpose of giving effect to a recommendation the correct interpretation of that statute may well depend on that of the recommendation. Whether it does so depend or not is a matter for the national court concerned.

The Court of Justice may also be asked as a question of interpretation, as seen in *Van Gend en Loos* and many other cases, whether a provision of Community law produces direct effects.

THE COURTS OR TRIBUNALS WHICH MAY OR MUST REFER

Article 234(2) and (3) refers to courts or tribunals of a Member State which may or must request a ruling from the Court of Justice. What is a 'court or tribunal' for this purpose is a matter of Community law, based by the Court of Justice on general criteria against which, however, the rules of national law governing the composition, status and functions of the body in question must be measured.

The Court's test for establishing if a national body is a court or tribunal has become a standard feature of cases which raise this issue. Thus, in the recent case C-182/00 *Lutz GmbH and Others*, the Court stated that:

In order to determine whether a referring body is a court or tribunal within the meaning of Article 234 [formerly 177], which is a question governed by Community law alone, the Court takes account of a number of factors, such as whether the body is established by law, whether it is permanent, whether its jurisdiction is compulsory, whether its procedure is *inter partes*, whether it applies rules of law and whether it is independent.

A good example of the application of this test can be found in the following case in which it was necessary to establish whether the immigration officer was to be regarded as a court or tribunal within the meaning of Article 177 (now 234).

Case C-416/96 *El-Yassini v Secretary of State for the Home Department*

The Court of Justice based its ruling on this point on the following grounds:

(a) The office of immigration adjudicator was established by the Immigration Act 1971 which conferred on the adjudicator jurisdiction to hear and determine disputes on the rights of foreigners to enter and remain in the UK.

(b) Immigration adjudicators constituted a permanent organ; their decisions were to be made in accordance with the Act and in compliance with the Immigration Appeals (Procedure) Rules 1984.

(c) The procedure was *inter partes* in nature.

(d) Adjudicators were required to give reasons for their decisions, which were binding and could in certain circumstances be appealed against to the Immigration Appeal Tribunal.

(e) Adjudicators were appointed for a renewable ten year (full-time) or one year (part-time) term of office. They enjoyed the same guarantees of independence as judges.

The Court ruled that the immigration adjudicator had to be regarded as a court or tribunal within the meaning of Article 177 and therefore the questions referred for a preliminary ruling were admissible.

In a reference from Italy in Case 14/86 *Pretore di Salo v X*, the Court observed that:

... the Pretori are judges who, in proceedings such as those in which the questions referred to the Court in this case were raised, combine the functions of a public prosecutor and an examining magistrate. The Court has jurisdiction to reply to a request for a preliminary ruling if that request emanates from a court or tribunal which has acted in the general framework of its task of judging, independently and in accordance with law, cases coming within the jurisdiction conferred on it by law, even though certain functions of that court or tribunal in the proceedings which give rise to the reference for a preliminary ruling are not, strictly speaking, of a judicial nature.

In essence, the Court will accept a reference from any body which exercises judicial, as opposed to merely investigatory, administrative or advisory functions: that is, a body which, through its relationship to the State, possesses the power to make binding decisions affecting the legal rights and obligations of individuals and others.

Administrative authorities cannot make references under Article 234 nor can a court which is merely performing an administrative function: Case C-111/94 *Job Centre Coop arl*, in which a court in Milan had been requested in the exercise of non-contentious jurisdiction to confirm the articles of association of a company where there was doubt about their entitlement to registration. (The position in the *Lutz* reference, above, was of the same nature.)

In Case 246/80 *Broekmeulen*, concerning a Dutch Appeals Committee for General Medicine which refused B's application to be registered as a doctor in the Netherlands, the question arose as to whether the Committee (which was not a court or tribunal in Dutch law) was a court or tribunal for the purposes of Article 177 (now 234). The Court of Justice concluded that:

> ... in the absence, in practice, of any right of appeal to the ordinary courts, the Appeals Committee, which operates with the consent of the public authorities and with their cooperation, and which, after an adversarial procedure, delivers decisions which are recognised as final, must, in a matter involving the application of Community law, be considered as a court or tribunal of a Member State within the meaning of Article 177 of the Treaty. Therefore, the Court has jurisdiction to reply to the question asked.

In Case 102/81 *Nordsee Deutsche Hochseefischerei*, where the question was whether an arbitrator in a German contract dispute was a 'court or tribunal', it was held that there was an insufficiently close link between the arbitration procedure and the court system.

Under Article 234(3), *subject to a qualification referred to below*, if a question of Community law is raised before 'a court or tribunal of a Member State, against whose decisions there is no judicial remedy under national law', that court or tribunal *must* refer it to the Court of Justice. For such a body, therefore, referral is not, as in Article 234(2), discretionary or 'permissive' but (within the terms of the Article) mandatory so long as a decision on a *question* of Community law is necessary to enable the court or tribunal to give judgment: see, however, *CILFIT*, below.

Case 6/64 *Costa v ENEL*, as seen in Chapter 4 a key decision on supremacy, concerned a reference made by an Italian magistrate in a case involving less than £2. Under Italian law, there was no right of appeal from the magistrate's decision because the amount involved was so small. Although not expressly called upon to rule on the matter, the Court of Justice was of the opinion that:

> By the terms of the Article ... national courts against whose decisions, as in the present case, there is no judicial remedy, must refer the matter to the Court of Justice so that a preliminary ruling may be given upon the 'interpretation of the Treaty' whenever a question of interpretation is raised before them.

On the basis of this statement, it can be said that the *obligation* to refer in Article 234(3) applies to any court or tribunal whose decision *in the particular case* is not subject to appeal (the 'concrete' theory), rather than merely to those courts and tribunals whose decisions are never subject to appeal (the narrower, 'abstract' theory). This view of the matter clearly provides litigants with wider opportunities for references to be made on the *interpretation* of Community law. (However, as will be seen, the position is different as regards questions of validity.)

DISCRETION, OBLIGATION AND THE COURT'S RULING IN *CILFIT*

Under Article 234(2), national courts or tribunals whose decisions are subject to a judicial remedy (basically, an appeal) under national law have a discretion as to whether or not to ask for a preliminary ruling on a point of Community law. Therefore, if a 'necessary' question is one of interpretation and the court decides *not* to refer, the court must interpret the Community provision itself. On possible dangers in taking this course of action, and for questions of *validity*, see below.

The national court will otherwise refer when a question of Community law (for example, on the interpretation of the Equal Treatment Directive) has been raised in the proceedings and the court considers that an answer to that question is necessary to enable it to give judgment. Thus, in Case 166/73 *Rheinmühlen*, the Court of Justice stated that the power to make a reference arises 'as soon as the judge perceives either of his own motion or at the request of the parties that the litigation depends on a point referred to in the first paragraph of Article 177'.

In this case, the Court also ruled that the discretion to refer in Article 177(2) (now 234(2)) could not be fettered by national rules of precedent: '... the existence of a rule of domestic law whereby a court is bound on points of law by the rulings of the court superior to it cannot of itself take away the power provided for by Article 177 of referring cases to the Court of Justice.'

If the national court exercises its discretion in favour of a referral, this does not in itself mean that everything must be thought to hinge on the Community point; rather, it is potentially a determining factor of significance in the final outcome and the Court of Justice is better placed to provide clarification.

Although it is for the national court itself to decide at what stage in the proceedings it is appropriate to refer, in Joined Cases 36 and 71/80 *Irish Creamery Milk Suppliers Association v Ireland*, the Court of Justice stated that:

> The need to provide an interpretation of Community law which will be of use to the national court makes it essential ... to define the legal context in which the interpretation requested should be placed. From that aspect, it might be convenient, in certain circumstances, for the facts in the case to be established and for questions of purely national law to be settled at the time the reference is made to the Court of Justice so as to enable the latter to take cognizance of all the features of fact and of law which may be relevant to the interpretation of Community law which it is called upon to give.

> However, those considerations do not in any way restrict the discretion of the national court, which alone has a direct knowledge of the facts of the case and of the arguments of the parties, which will have to take responsibility for giving judgment in the case and which is therefore in the best position to appreciate at what stage in the proceedings it requires a preliminary ruling from the Court of Justice.

> Hence, it is clear that the national court's decision when to make a reference under Article 177 must be dictated by considerations of procedural organisation and efficiency to be weighed by that court.

> [Note: This extract should now be read in the light of 'Changes to the Reference Process' towards the end of this chapter, in particular, the Court's 1997 'Notes for Guidance on References by National Courts'.]

In the UK, the courts have on various occasions been drawn into a discussion of 'considerations of procedural organisation and efficiency' and attempts have been made to establish guidelines as to how the discretion to ask for a preliminary ruling should be exercised. This will be discussed shortly.

As stated earlier, an Article 234(2) national court may of course decide the interpretative point of Community law itself without seeking any guidance from the Court of Justice. It may well consider exercising its discretion in this way where the correct application of the Community rule appears so clear as to leave no room for doubt. (See, however, the discussion of *CILFIT*, below: what is obvious to one judge, in one Member State, may not be obvious to another.)

In *R v Henn and Darby* (1978), the Court of Appeal (Criminal Division) decided that national legislation banning certain imports was not contrary to Article 30 (now 28) of the Treaty on the ground that the term 'quantitative restrictions' in that Article connotated restrictions 'concerned with quantity' and not total prohibitions. The defendants appealed to the House of Lords, which referred this and other matters to the Court of Justice. There it was found, not surprisingly, that the prohibition was a quantitative restriction.

In the House of Lords, Lord Diplock warned that English judges should not be 'too ready to hold that because the meaning of the English text (which is one of six of equal authority) seems plain to them no question of interpretation can be involved'.

Where a doubt exists, the national court should refer. In *Garland v British Rail Engineering* (1983), the House of Lords, operating under Article 177(3) (now 234(3)) but examining whether there was in reality a 'question' to be referred, did refer on certain equal pay matters despite there not being 'any serious doubt'. This was because there was not, in their Lordships' opinion, in existence at the time:

> ... so considerable and consistent a line of case law of the Court of Justice on the interpretation and direct applicability of Article 119, as would make the answer too obvious and inevitable to be capable of giving rise to what could properly be regarded as a 'question' within the meaning of Article 177 [Lord Diplock].

> [Note: Article 119 is now Article 141 and it would be preferable to refer to its direct effect not its direct applicability.]

From another angle, it should also be borne in mind that the Court of Justice is free to depart from its previous decisions – interpretative or otherwise. Even if the identical point of interpretation has already been ruled upon, the national court may refer.

In Cases 28–30/62 *Da Costa en Schaake*, the Dutch tribunal referred questions on Article 12 (now 25) which were identical to those in the *Van Gend en Loos* ruling which was given a fortnight before the oral hearing in these cases. The Commission argued that no 'question' remained and the request for a ruling should be dismissed for lack of substance.

The Court stated that the fact that an authoritative interpretative ruling had already been given might absolve a national court even from a *duty* to refer if the meaning of the disputed provision was now clear. (The Dutch tribunal was covered by Article 177(3).) However, *no* national court or tribunal could be deprived of the power to refer a question on a provision which had already been interpreted.

This is because:

(a) Article 177/234 always allows a national court whether operating under paragraph (2) or paragraph (3), if it considers it necessary to enable it to reach a decision, to refer questions of interpretation to the Court again (in such circumstances, unless a new argument is raised, the Court will probably merely restate its previous ruling on the point – as it did in *Da Costa*);

(b) the national court may not fully understand, and therefore encounter difficulty in applying, an interpretation already given (for example, the House of Lords reference in the *B & Q* Sunday trading case following the Court's earlier interpretative ruling on Article 30 (now 28) in *Conforama*: see Chapter 12);

(c) the national court may consider the previous ruling to be wrong, and therefore seek a reversal, as in Case C-10/89 *Sucal v Hag*: see Chapter 18; and

(d) Community law is in a continual state of evolvement and should be interpreted not as at the date it came into effect but when it falls to be applied.

A national court or tribunal acting within the area of *discretionary* jurisdiction under Article 234(2), faced with a question of interpretation of Community law, must first ask:

(a) Is an interpretative ruling a *necessary* step in reaching a decision? Only if the answer to this question is in the affirmative does a second question arise.

(b) How should the discretion be exercised? Should a referral be made or should the national court or tribunal provide its own interpretation?

A national court or tribunal acting within (on the face of it) the *mandatory terms* of Article 234(3), that is, 'that court or tribunal shall bring the matter before the Court of Justice', nevertheless, on the basis of the Court's ruling in Case 283/81 *CILFIT v Ministry of Health*, has a discretion in respect of the first question: 'Is an interpretative ruling a *necessary* step in reaching a decision?' If the court (say, the House of Lords) decides that it is not, that there is no doubt as to the meaning of the provision, and that therefore there is no 'question' in terms of Article 234, the court merely proceeds to apply the Community provision. However, as we will see, the Court's ruling on this issue in *CILFIT* was hedged round with various qualifications. As Hartley has pointed out:

> This ... is important only with regard to Article 177(3): since a lower court is not in any case obliged to make a reference, it would be entitled to refrain from doing so on the ground that the provision is sufficiently clear. In the case of a court against whose decisions there is no judicial remedy, however, the question is crucial ...

> ... even a court covered by Article 177(3) is not obliged to make a reference where the answer is 'so obvious as to leave no scope for any reasonable doubt'. [The Court of Justice] qualified this, however, by saying that the national court must be convinced that the answer would be equally obvious to a court in another Member State and to the European Court.

Closer study of the *CILFIT* decision enables us to establish clearly the situations in which an Article 234(3) court or tribunal's obligation (not the power) falls away, and to examine the Court's qualifying guidelines on the matter of 'freedom from doubt' to which not only national courts or tribunals falling under Article 234(3) should pay close attention but also those falling under Article 234(2) when exercising their discretion to refer. The *CILFIT* reference came from the Italian Supreme Court and in reply, the Court of Justice stated that:

> ... it follows from the relationship between the second and third paragraphs of Article 177 that the courts or tribunals referred to in the third paragraph have the same discretion as any other national court or tribunal to ascertain whether a decision on a question of Community law is necessary to enable them to give judgment. Accordingly, those courts or tribunals are not obliged to refer to the Court of Justice a question concerning interpretation of Community law raised before them if that question is not relevant, that is to say, if the answer to that question, regardless of what it may be, can in no way affect the outcome of the case.

If, however, those courts or tribunals consider that recourse to Community law is necessary to enable them to decide a case, Article 177 imposes an obligation on them to refer to the Court of Justice any question of interpretation which may arise.

The question submitted by the Corte di Cassazione seeks to ascertain whether, in certain circumstances, the obligation laid down by the third paragraph of Article 177 might nonetheless be subject to certain restrictions.

It must be remembered in this connection that in its judgment of 27 March 1963 in Joined Cases 28 to 30/62 (*Da Costa v Nederlandse Belastingadministratie* [1963] ECR 31) the Court ruled that: 'Although the third paragraph of Article 177 unreservedly requires courts or tribunals of a Member State against whose decisions there is no judicial remedy under national law ... to refer to the Court every question of interpretation raised before them, the authority of an interpretation under Article 177 already given by the Court may deprive the obligation of its purpose and thus empty it of its substance. Such is the case especially when the question raised is materially identical with a question which has already been the subject of a preliminary ruling in a similar case.'

The same effect, as regards the limits set to the obligation laid down by the third paragraph of Article 177, may be produced where previous decisions of the Court have already dealt with the point of law in question, irrespective of the nature of the proceedings which led to those decisions, even though the questions at issue are not strictly identical.

However, it must not be forgotten that in all such circumstances national courts and tribunals, including those referred to in the third paragraph of Article 177, remain entirely at liberty to bring a matter before the Court of Justice if they consider it appropriate to do so.

Finally, the correct application of Community law may be so obvious as to leave no scope for any reasonable doubt as to the manner in which the question raised is to be resolved. Before it comes to the conclusion that such is the case, the national court or tribunal must be convinced that the matter is equally obvious to the courts of the other Member States and to the Court of Justice.

Thus, a final court may decide that an interpretative question is necessary – or not necessary, that is, not relevant to the outcome. If an interpretative ruling is considered necessary, the obligation to refer arises, subject to three 'limits':

(a) the existence of a previous, authoritative, interpretative ruling by the Court of Justice (a precedent) on the issue especially if arising from a 'materially identical' reference;

(b) the existence of previous decisions of the Court on the point of law irrespective of the nature of the proceedings which gave rise to them; and

(c) situations where the application of the Community law in issue is 'so obvious' to the national court as 'to leave no scope for reasonable doubt'.

In such cases, therefore, *even* an Article 177(3) court or tribunal need not refer.

This relaxation of the terms of Article 177 (now 234) was, as Hartley stated above, 'crucial' (and controversial) in the case of a court against whose decisions there is no judicial remedy. It must be remembered that, as the Court itself has repeatedly stated, the *purpose* of Article 234 is to ensure that Community law is interpreted and applied in a uniform manner in all the Member States, and the particular objective of Article

234(3) is to prevent a body of national case law not in accordance with the rules of Community law from coming into existence in any Member State.

It has been argued that the *CILFIT* decision endangers these primary objectives and has done so by the Court's acceptance that the French administrative law *acte clair* doctrine – an *acte clair* (clear provision) does not need interpretation – is not limited to cases where the point in issue has already been the subject of authoritative interpretation – and extends to final courts and tribunals.

Nevertheless, as stated earlier, the Court hedged round its ruling with a series of qualifications which led Rasmussen to conclude that: 'The real strategy of *CILFIT* is not to incorporate an *acte clair* concept into Community law. It is to call the national judiciaries to circumspection when they are faced with problems of interpretation and application of Community law.' In this respect, what the Court proceeded to say in *CILFIT* was as follows:

> However, the existence of such a possibility [of not referring] must be assessed on the basis of the characteristic features of Community law and the particular difficulties to which its interpretation gives rise.
>
> To begin with, it must be borne in mind that Community legislation is drafted in several languages and that the different language versions are all equally authentic. An interpretation of a provision of Community law thus involves a comparison of the different language versions.
>
> It must also be borne in mind, even where the different language versions are entirely in accord with one another, that Community law uses terminology which is peculiar to it. Furthermore, it must be emphasised that legal concepts do not necessarily have the same meaning in Community law and in the law of the various Member States.
>
> Finally, every provision of Community law must be placed in its context and interpreted in the light of the provisions of Community law as a whole, regard being had to the objectives thereof and to its state of evolution at the date on which the provision in question is to be applied.

An indication of how national courts have viewed their responsibilities within this process can be seen from the following statements by two High Court judges.

In *R v HM Treasury ex p Daily Mail and General Trust* (1987), McPherson J based his decision to refer on the following grounds:

> I do not refer the case simply because a serious point of Community law arises, but I do so for the following reasons:
>
> 1   The relevant facts are not in dispute. The case before me in its written form and the documents before me set out the facts which are substantially, if not wholly, agreed.
>
> 2   The point raised will in my judgement be substantially determinative of the case.
>
> 3   There is no Community authority precisely or indeed in my judgement closely in point.
>
> 4   The point raised and indeed the case itself are both put forward in good faith and without any adverse motive. Of course, the applicants wish to improve their financial and fiscal position. Of course the Revenue wish to maintain this source of tax. Neither of these wishes is improper in any way.
>
> 5   I am convinced that at some stage in its life the case will be or will have to be referred to Europe.

6   I do not find the point free from doubt. And I feel justified in asserting that I am not (in Lord Denning's words) shirking my responsibilities by referring this case. It seems to me to be tailor-made for reference here and now.

In the course of his decision to refer in *Customs and Excise Commissioners v Samex ApS* (1983), Bingham J clearly acknowledges the advantages possessed by the Court of Justice when dealing with Community law matters:

In endeavouring to follow and respect these guidelines, I find myself in some difficulty, because it was submitted by counsel on behalf of the defendant that the issues raised by his client should be resolved by the Court of Justice as the court best fitted to do so, and I find this a consideration which does give me some pause for thought. Sitting as a judge in a national court, asked to decide questions of Community law, I am very conscious of the advantages enjoyed by the Court of Justice. It has a panoramic view of the Community and its institutions, a detailed knowledge of the Treaties and of much subordinate legislation made under them, and an intimate familiarity with the functioning of the Community market which no national judge denied the collective experience of the Court of Justice could hope to achieve. Where questions of administrative intention and practice arise the Court of Justice can receive submissions from the Community institutions, as also where relations between the Community and non-Member States are in issue. Where the interests of Member States are affected, they can intervene to make their views known. That is a material consideration in this case since there is some slight evidence that the practice of different Member States is divergent. Where comparison falls to be made between Community texts in different languages, all texts being equally authentic, the multinational Court of Justice is equipped to carry out the task in a way which no national judge, whatever his linguistic skills, could rival. The interpretation of Community instruments involves very often not the process familiar to common lawyers of laboriously extracting the meaning from words used but the more creative process of supplying flesh to a spare and loosely constructed skeleton. The choice between alternative submissions may turn not on purely legal considerations, but on the broader view of what the orderly development of the Community requires. These are matters which the Court of Justice is very much better placed to assess and determine than a national court.

Later in his judgment, Bingham J drew attention to questions of time and cost:

The reference to the Court of Justice would be unlikely to take longer than appeals have normally taken to reach the Court of Appeal, at least until recently, and unlikely to cost much more. If, at the Court of Appeal stage, a reference were held to be necessary, the delay and expense would be roughly doubled.

The same judge, as Master of the Rolls, in *R v International Stock Exchange ex p Else* (1993) said that, once the facts have been found and it is clear that the Community law issue is 'critical' to the final decision of the national court, the appropriate course is to refer to the Court of Justice, unless the national court can with real confidence resolve the issue itself. Thus, if in doubt, refer. Should the issue of the necessity for a preliminary ruling come on appeal to the House of Lords, Article 234(3) comes into play in the House of Lords. Subject to the *CILFIT* ruling, 'that court ... shall bring the matter before the Court of Justice'.

Although the *CILFIT* guidelines may be taken to extinguish the *obligation* to refer imposed by Article 234(3) on a court or tribunal of last resort in the instant case, such court or tribunal, as we have seen, may in such circumstances nevertheless refer if it considers it desirable, that is, the power to refer remains. On the other hand, if a question of interpretation in, for example, a recently adopted Regulation is important, is novel and is not free from doubt, it would seem clear that the obligation in the third paragraph would remain: a ruling from the Court of Justice on the question would be 'necessary'. (We will deal with questions of validity below.)

Attention has already been drawn to the fact that what is clear to one national court may well be a source of doubt, or be clear in quite a different sense, to another court in the Community, including the Court of Justice. In the case of lower courts, which under Article 234(2) are not obliged to make a reference and which mistakenly decide that a Community provision is 'clear', the matter may be cleared up on the basis of an appeal (as in *R v Henn and Darby* but see also, for example, *R v Inner London Education Authority ex p Hinde,* in which no appeal was made). With regard to final courts and Article 234(3), such a problem, in the light of the requirement of uniform interpretation and proper application of Community law in all the Member States, can obviously result in an irretrievable misapplication of Community law to the detriment of one of the parties. It is for this reason that the Court of Justice subjected the *'acte clair'* principle to so many qualifications in *CILFIT*; qualifications described as being so 'intimidating to an English judge' as to make it seem likely that UK courts will hesitate long before deciding, at least without the aid of a previous line of authority from the Court of Justice, that a Community provision is clear.

This is not to say that there are no instances of courts of last resort failing to meet their responsibilities under Article 234(3). Particularly noticeable are cases where the national court has been faced with the question of the direct effect of a Directive. In *Minister of the Interior v Cohn-Bendit* (1980), C-B ('Red Danny', a leader of student unrest in Paris in 1968) was refused entry when he tried to return to France. He sought to rely on Directive 64/221 on the freedom of movement of persons, which had been held to be directly effective in Case 41/74 *Van Duyn v Home Office* (see Chapter 8). The French *Conseil d'Etat*, the supreme administrative court, was advised that it must either follow *Van Duyn* or refer to the Court of Justice under the then Article 177(3). Instead the court held that Directives could not be invoked by individuals against administrative acts of the government; the Directive was not directly effective.

Similar problems with Directives led the German Federal Constitutional Court to declare that a court operating within Article 177(3), which knowingly deviates from the case law of the Court of Justice and fails to make a reference, is in breach of Article 101 of the German Constitution. In 1989, in *Re Patented Feedingstuffs*, the Constitutional Court stated that it would review an 'arbitrary' refusal to co-operate with the Court of Justice by such a court:

> The main types of case of an arbitrary misconception of the obligation to refer which come into consideration for these purposes are first of all cases in which a court of final instance judging the main issue gives no consideration at all to a reference under Article 177(3) in spite of the relevance (in the court's view) of the question of Community law to its judgment although the court itself entertains doubts as to the correct answer to the question; secondly there are the cases in which the court of final instance deciding the main issue consciously departs in its judgment from the judgments of the European Court on relevant questions in issue and nevertheless does not make a reference or does not make a fresh reference.
>
> The first kind of case constitutes a fundamental misconception of the obligation to make a reference; a case of the second sort must be categorised as being in itself an arbitrary act. Finally, a further kind of arbitrary misconception of the obligation to

make a reference under Article 177(3) ... may occur typically where either there is not as yet any decisive judgment of the European Court on a question of Community law relevant to the issue or where, although such judgment or judgments have been given, they may possibly not have provided an exhaustive answer to the relevant question or there may appear to be a more than remote possibility of a further development of the case law of the European Court on the issue.

In such cases, there is only an arbitrary misconception of the obligation to seek a ruling under Article 177(3) and therefore a breach of Article 101(1), second sentence, of the Constitution if the court of final instance trying the main issue has exceeded to an indefensible extent the scope for its exercise of the discretion which it must necessarily have in such cases; that will occur where there may be contrary views on the relevant question of Community law which should obviously be given preference over the view put forward by the court.

CHANGES TO THE REFERENCE PROCESS

In their comprehensive review of the Article 177 (now 234) reference process, Barnard and Sharpston (see 'References and Further Reading' at the end of the chapter) ask: 'Has the jurisdictional face of Article 177 altered beyond all recognition in recent years? In 20 cases since 1990, the Court has, in fact, declined jurisdiction to hear preliminary questions referred by national courts.' In particular, the writers inquire into the extent to which since that date 'the Court has been prepared to "second guess" the national court making the reference as to whether the matters referred are amenable to answer under Article 177' – what is the reason for the Court's more restrictive approach? Is it purely a matter of case overload and the consequent problem of delays?

Documenting the history of Article 177 (now 234), the writers identify 'a series of phases in the development of the Court's case law'. The first phase was characterised by 'a great willingness to receive references' since the first under Article 177 in 1961. The second phase was marked by a degree of 'interpretation by the Court' in which it began to engage, where it was considered necessary, in a rewriting of the questions referred in order that the required answers could be given. It was also a phase in which, for the first time, the Court declined jurisdiction. This was in the 'non-genuine dispute' referral in Case 104/79 *Foglia v Novello (No 1)*, an issue that has come before the Court on several occasions since. In *Foglia*, the Court took the view that litigation between Italian parties in their national court was an artificial and collusive device designed to obtain a ruling that the law of another Member State was contrary to Community law. (See the arguments for and against this decision in Wyatt and Barav in 'References and Further Reading' at the end of the chapter.) In Hartley's view:

it seems likely that the real reason for its decision in *Foglia v Novello* was one of policy: it did not wish to offend the French by allowing the lawfulness of its taxes to be challenged by such roundabout means, rather than by the more normal route of an enforcement action under Article 169 EC [now 226] (or by means of a reference from a *French* court).

The Court's third phase began with its introduction of the *acte clair* doctrine in Case 283/81 *CILFIT* at a time when it was receiving about 100 references a year from nine Member States. *Acte clair* has been discussed above and it is perhaps only necessary to add Bernard and Sharpston's comment that: 'This move from power (Article 177(2)) and obligation (Article 177(3)) to a perception of no absolute obligation (because of *acte clair*) created doubts as to the real necessity of making a reference even for lower courts.'

Phase four was taken to begin in 1990 and was characterised by 'tighter control by the Court of Justice of its own jurisdiction'. It was the period in which up to 1997 the Court declined jurisdiction in 20 cases. In a number of these cases, there was no question of Community law for the Court to give a ruling on – the Court had no jurisdiction under Article 177 over what it had been asked to consider: see, for example, Case C-167/94 *Grau Gomis*, regarding one of the Maastricht Treaty common provisions on the Union's objectives, and C-307/95 *Max Mara*, regarding a request for a ruling on the interpretation of national law. However, in a line of cases in which Community law had been transposed into national law or in which national law made reference to Community law, the references were usually declared to be admissible: see Case 130/95 *Giloy v HZA Frankfurt*.

In another group of cases, the Court showed continuing and more rigorous concern that all the necessary conditions for a reference had been fulfilled. Was the body making the reference a 'court or tribunal of a Member State'? Was a dispute 'pending' at national level?

A further collection of post-1990 cases illustrated generally what Barnard and Sharpston describe as the Court's 'new tough approach'. Here we find the Court 'refusing to answer questions where the Court perceives either that there is no genuine dispute or that the issue is hypothetical, where it considers that inadequate information has been provided or where it takes the view that the questions referred have no connection with the dispute before the national court'.

In Case C-83/91 *Meilicke v ADV/ORGA FA Meyer*, for example, some 10 pages of questions regarding the compatibility of the West German legal doctrine of disguised non-cash subscriptions of capital (as developed by the German courts) with the Second Company Law Directive were referred by the Hanover Regional Court to the Court of Justice. The Court stated that from the file submitted by the national court it was apparent that it had not been established that the conditions for the application of the theory were present in the action brought by shareholder M against the defendant company. The questions raised were therefore hypothetical, as the Court did not have before it those elements of fact and national law necessary for it to provide a useful answer to the questions. (M was the author of a German law book attacking the doctrine in question.)

In Joined Cases C-320-322/90 *Telemarsicabruzzo*, the inadmissibility of the reference was the consequence of, as described by the Commission, the 'particularly laconic' nature of the question referred in what the Court described as 'the field of competition which is characterized by complex factual and legal situations'.

The Court alluded to the 'risk of error' where the national court had failed to 'define the factual and legislative context of the questions'. (Later, in Case C-157/92 *Banchero (No 1)*, the Court stated that 'the order for reference, in its insufficiently precise account of the situations in law and fact referred to by the national court, does not enable the Court to give an adequate interpretation of Community law'.)

These and other examples from the 1990s can lead to the conclusion that the Court of Justice has 'changed the rules' regarding references; that Article 177, as an instrument of judicial co-operation between the national courts and the Court itself, has, at a time when, for example, 262 references were filed with the Court in 1998, become instead a 'quasi-federal instrument for reviewing the compatibility of national laws with Community law': Mancini and Keeling (1994). Whether or not a reference is necessary is, as we have seen, a matter for the national court, but these recent developments show that the autonomy of such courts in this respect cannot withstand ill-conceived, unprofessional references.

The recent case law therefore reveals that there must be a real and not a hypothetical issue, adequate information must be provided regarding the factual and legal context of the questions referred (or at least the factual basis for them), and that the questions must be relevant to the dispute before the national court. On this last point, the Court has stated on more than one occasion that 'it is essential for the national court to explain the reasons why it considers that a reply to its questions is necessary to enable it to give judgment'.

'Note for Guidance on References by National Courts for Preliminary Rulings' [1997] 1 CMLR 78, [1997] All ER (EC) 1

In 1997, the Court of Justice felt constrained to issue this 'Note for Guidance' in order 'to make co-operation more effective' and to 'help to prevent the kind of difficulties which the Court has sometimes encountered'. After outlining the main features of the preliminary rulings procedure, regarding both questions of interpretation and validity (see below) in the context of leading cases, the Note's guidance takes the following form:

(a) The order of the national court or tribunal referring a question to the Court of Justice for a preliminary ruling may be in any form allowed by national procedural rules. The question of staying proceedings until the Court has given its ruling is also a matter of national law.

(b) The order should be drafted as clearly and precisely as possible as it will have to be translated into the other official languages of the Community; Member States and Community institutions being entitled to submit observations.

(c) The order for reference should include in particular:

(i) a statement of the facts which are essential to a full understanding of the legal significance of the main proceedings;

(ii) an exposition of the national law which may be applicable (but not, somewhat surprisingly, the EC provisions considered relevant);

(iii) a statement of the reasons which have prompted the national court to refer the question or questions to the Court of Justice; and

(iv) where appropriate, a summary of the main arguments of the parties.

(d) The order should be accompanied by copies of any documents needed for a proper understanding of the case, especially the text of the applicable national provisions. However, as the case file or documents annexed to the order are not always translated in full into the other Community official languages, the national court should ensure that the order for reference contains all the relevant information.

The 1997 'Note for Guidance' can be taken as, in Barnard and Sharpston's words, 'encouraging the national courts to take greater responsibility'. A response to the Court's initiative in the UK came in the form of a 'Practice Direction from the English Lord Chief Justice's Court on References to the Court of Justice' (January 1999). In paragraph 3, it is stated that:

The referring court should, in a single document scheduled to the order:

(i) identify the parties and summarise the nature and history of the proceedings;

(ii) summarise the salient facts, indicating whether those were proved or admitted or assumed;

(iii) make reference to the rules of national law (substantive and procedural) relevant to the dispute;

(iv) summarise the contentions of the parties so far as relevant;

(v) explain why a ruling of the European Court was sought, identifying the EC provisions whose effect was in issue;

(vi) formulate, without avoidable complexity, the question(s) to which an answer was requested.

Where the document was in the form of a judgment, as would often be convenient, passages which were not relevant to the reference should be omitted from the text scheduled to the order.

In looking for reasons why the Court of Justice has in recent years moved towards stricter control of its Article 177 (now 234) jurisdiction, the most apparent is its increased case load, not only of references. This is what is known as a *'docket control'* reason. Commentators have not been slow to suggest alternative methods of achieving such control. One is the creation of *additional, specialist, first instance tribunals* with competence to hear references within their particular field (for example, competition, agriculture). This is a development which the Court of Justice opposes as, amongst other things, 'it would raise problems as to the authority of judgment given at first instance and as to the identification of parties entitled to lodge an appeal' (for example, the Commission or a Member State). Kapteyn is of the view that 'the coherence of Community law makes it virtually impossible, and certainly undesirable, to split-off subject matters'.

Another suggestion is to *limit the reference procedure to superior courts* in the Member States. This would of course be contrary to the concept of all national courts being Community courts. The time and expense involved in reaching an appellate court from which a reference might be made is, as seen, a further negative factor. Taking its cue from the US Supreme Court, the House of Lords and other supreme courts is the further idea of a *filter system* to weed out 'inappropriate' cases. A system of this kind, whereby the Court of Justice itself is able to deal quickly, but in a consistent and reasoned manner, with what it considers to be inadmissible references could arguably operate as a step forward.

However, as seen in the introduction to this chapter, the preferred way forward is the Nice initiative whereby the Article 234 jurisdiction is split between the Court of Justice and the CFI, with a likely increase in the membership of the latter.

PRELIMINARY RULINGS ON VALIDITY

It will be recalled that Article 234(1)(b) covers the jurisdiction of the Court of Justice to give preliminary rulings concerning 'the validity ... of acts of the institutions of the Community', but the Article does not expressly give the Court exclusive jurisdiction on this matter. Thus, a 'permissive' reading of Article 234(2) would seemingly give such a national court the power to exercise its discretion so as to declare a Community act, say a Regulation, invalid. Such a result would clearly be contrary to the aim of preventing a body of case law coming into existence in any Member State which is not in accordance with Community law.

This matter was put to rest by the Court of Justice in Case 314/85 *Foto-Frost v Hauptzollamt Lübeck-Ost*, where it was held that a national court cannot declare a Community act invalid; the power to declare such an act invalid is reserved to the Court of Justice. A national court can declare a Community act valid but should a real doubt be raised, providing a decision on the question is necessary, then the matter must be referred. *CILFIT* and the *acte clair* principle are only relevant to questions of interpretation.

In *Foto-Frost*, the Court stated that:

> In enabling national courts against whose decisions there is a judicial remedy under national law to refer to the Court for a preliminary ruling questions on interpretation or validity, Article 177 did not settle the question whether those courts themselves may declare that acts of Community institutions are invalid.

> Those courts may consider the validity of a Community act and, if they consider that the grounds put forward before them by the parties in support of invalidity are unfounded, they may reject them, concluding that the measure is completely valid. By taking that action they are not calling the existence of the Community measures into question.

> On the other hand, those courts do not have the power to declare acts of Community institutions invalid ... the main purpose of the powers accorded to the Court by Article 177 is to ensure that Community law is applied uniformly by national courts. That requirement of uniformity is particularly imperative when the validity of a Community act is in question. Divergences between courts in the Member States as to the validity of Community acts would be liable to place in jeopardy the very unity of the Community legal order and detract from the fundamental requirement of legal certainty.

> The same conclusion is dictated by consideration of the necessary coherence of the system of judicial protection established by the Treaty. In that regard, it must be observed that requests for preliminary rulings, like actions for annulment, constitute means for reviewing the legality of acts of the Community institutions. As the Court pointed out in its judgment of 23 April 1986 (Case 294/83 *Partie Ecologiste 'Les Verts' v Parliament* [1986] ECR 1339), 'in Articles 173 and 184 [now 230 and 241], on the one hand, and in Article 177, on the other, the Treaty established a complete system of legal remedies and procedures designed to permit the Court of Justice to review the legality of measures adopted by the institutions'.

> Since Article 173 gives the Court exclusive jurisdiction to declare void an act of a Community institution, the coherence of the system requires that where the validity of a Community act is challenged before a national court the power to declare the act invalid must also be reserved to the Court of Justice ...

> It should be added that the rule that national courts may not themselves declare Community acts invalid may have to be qualified in certain circumstances in the case of proceedings relating to an application for interim measures; however, that case is not referred to in the national court's question.

> The answer to the first question must therefore be that national courts have no jurisdiction themselves to declare that acts of Community institutions are invalid.

The relationship between Article 177 (now 234) (as regards such indirect challenges to Community acts) and, particularly, Article 173 (now 230) (direct challenges to

Community acts in the Court of Justice) has been noted already and will be examined more closely in Chapter 19.

The qualification referred to by the Court in the penultimate paragraph of the extract from the judgment in *Foto-Frost* regarding an application for interim measures in the national court became of significance in Joined Cases C-143/88 and C-92/89 *Zuckerfabrik Süderdithmarschen* and later in Case C-465/93 *Atlanta v BEF*. In the latter case, following a reference to the Court of Justice by the German court regarding (a) the validity of a Regulation; and (b) the power of a national court to suspend a *national* measure based on the disputed Regulation, the Court stated that, for the protection of a party in the context of an Article 177 reference, a national court should possess such a right of temporary suspension while a decision by the Court is pending on the validity of the Community provision but within strictly defined limits. There must be serious doubts as to the validity of the Community act, the applicant must be at risk of serious and irreparable harm (that is, damages would not be an adequate remedy), and the Community interest regarding the Community act must be taken into account. This case will also be discussed in more detail in Chapter 19.

THE EFFECTS OF PRELIMINARY RULINGS

The ruling given by the Court of Justice under Article 234 is sent back to the national court which originally made the reference. That court must apply the ruling, which is binding upon it, in its resumed proceedings. This may, for example, require the court to refuse to apply conflicting provisions of national law – the point which was at the heart of Case 106/77 *Simmenthal*, a leading case on supremacy: see Chapter 4.

The ruling (on interpretation or validity) should operate as a precedent for *all* national courts in subsequent cases involving the same Community provision: for the UK, see section 3(1) of the European Communities Act, although, as seen, a national court is not precluded from making a further reference.

A ruling that a Community act is invalid will mean that the measure will be treated as void for all purposes unless, in the interests of legal certainty, the Court of Justice limits the effect of its ruling on past transactions: see, for example, Case 66/80 *International Chemical Association*. Similar considerations can, exceptionally, apply to the temporal effect of rulings on interpretation. On a number of occasions, the Court has stated that a preliminary ruling on interpretation:

> ... clarifies and defines where necessary the meaning and scope of that rule as it must or ought to have been understood and applied from the time of its coming into force. It follows that the rule as thus interpreted may, and must, be applied by the courts even to legal relationships arising and established before the judgment ruling on the request for interpretation.

> ... It is only exceptionally that the Court may, in the application of the general principle of legal certainty inherent in the Community legal order and in taking into account the serious effects which its judgments might leave, as regards the past, on legal relationships established in good faith, be moved to restrict for any person concerned the opportunity of relying on the provision as thus interpreted with a view to calling in question those legal relationships.

> Such a restriction may, however, be allowed only in the actual judgment ruling upon the interpretation sought ... it is for the Court of Justice alone to decide upon the

temporal restrictions to be placed on the interpretation which it lays down [Case 61/79 *Denkavit Italiana*].

Thus, in Case 43/75 *Defrenne (No 2)*, the Court decided that its ruling on the direct effect of equal pay Article 119 (now 141) should, 'for important considerations of legal certainty', only apply to future cases and those lodged prior to judgment. Member States had at the time, in the main, not implemented the equal pay principle, perhaps considering that the broad principle in Article 119 required further implementation. However, in spite of warnings from the Commission, no proceedings had been taken against them under Article 169 (now 226). This situation had, in the Court's view, consolidated 'the incorrect impression as to the effects of Article 119' prior to the Court's decision.

It has been argued that to shield *employers* (including the State) in this way from 'an avalanche of similar claims' was at the expense of legal principle:

... if Article 119 was directly effective for Miss Defrenne, it must have been directly effective for all other workers; claims for back pay might be affected by national statutes of limitation, but there was no legal ground for making the date of the judgment in the *Defrenne* case decisive [Hartley].

REFERENCES AND FURTHER READING

Alexander, W, 'The temporal effects of preliminary rulings' (1988) 8 YEL 11.

Anderson, D, 'The admissibility of preliminary references' (1994) 14 YEL 179.

Arnull, A, 'The use and abuse of Article 177 EEC' (1989) 52 MLR 622.

Arnull, A, 'References to the European Court' (1990) 15 EL Rev 375.

Arnull, A, 'The evolution of the Court's jurisdiction under Article 177 EEC' (1993) 18 EL Rev 129.

Barav, A, 'Preliminary censorship? The judgment of the European Court in *Foglia v Novello*' (1980) 5 EL Rev 443.

Barnard, C and Sharpston, E, 'The changing face of Article 177 references' (1997) 34 CML Rev 1113.

Bebr, G, 'Preliminary rulings of the Court of Justice – their authority and temporal effect' (1981) 18 CML Rev 475.

Bebr, G, 'The reinforcement of the constitutional review of Community acts under Article 177 EEC' (*Foto-Frost* and *'Berlin Butter'*) (1988) 25 CML Rev 684.

Demetriou, M, 'When is the House of Lords not a judicial remedy' (Case note on *Chiron v Murex (No 2)*) (1995) 20 EL Rev 628.

Hartley, TC, *The Foundations of European Community Law*, Chapter 9, 'Preliminary references'.

Kennedy, T, 'First steps towards a European certiorari?' (1993) 18 EL Rev 121.

Mancini, G and Keeling, D, 'From *CILFIT* to *ERT*: the constitutional challenge facing the European Court' (1991) 11 YEL 1.

Mancini, G and Keeling, D, 'Democracy and the Court of Justice' (1994) 57 MLR 175.

Rasmussen, H, 'The European Court's *acte clair* strategy in *CILFIT*' (1984) 9 EL Rev 242.

Wyatt, D, 'Following up *Foglia*: why the Court is right to stick to its guns' (1981) 6 EL Rev 447, and see also (1982) 7 EL Rev 186.

PART THREE

ASPECTS OF COMMUNITY ECONOMIC AND SOCIAL LAW

CHAPTER 10

COMMUNITY ECONOMIC AND SOCIAL LAW: ITS NATURE AND THE IMPACT OF GENERAL PRINCIPLES OF COMMUNITY LAW

COMMUNITY ECONOMIC AND SOCIAL LAW

The *original* Treaty foundations for the economic and social policies of the European Economic Community are to be found in the EEC Treaty of 1957 (the Rome Treaty): see Articles 2, 3 and 8 EEC (as developed to varying degrees in subsequent Articles) in Chapter 1. As we have seen, this Treaty has been successively amended by the Single European Act of 1986, the Maastricht Treaty on European Union of 1992 (TEU), the Treaty of Amsterdam of 1997 (ToA) and the Treaty of Nice of 2001. The general cumulative effect of the changes brought about has been to modify overall aims and to increase the scope of the Community's competence by additions to its economic and social policy areas within, since 1992, the first pillar of the Union.

The economic and social objectives as set out in the current Article 2 EC are to promote throughout the Community:

- a harmonious, balanced and sustainable development of economic activities,
- a high level of employment and of social protection,
- equality between men and women,
- sustainable and non-inflationary growth,
- a high degree of competitiveness and convergence of economic performance,
- a high level of protection and improvement of the quality of the environment,
- the raising of the standard of living and quality of life, and
- economic and social cohesion and solidarity among Member States.

The means or methods in Article 2 whereby these objectives are to be achieved are:

- the establishment of a Common Market,
- the establishment of an Economic and Monetary Union, and
- the implementation of the common policies and activities found in Articles 3 and 4 EC.

The most significant parts (for our present purposes) of the EC Treaty are as follows:

Part One – Principles:

Article 2 (number unchanged): Common Market, Economic and Monetary Union (EMU) and common policies.

Article 3 (number unchanged): 21 policy areas or 'activities'.

Article 4 (formerly 3a) : economic and monetary policy.

Article 6 (formerly 3c) : environment protection requirements.

Articles 12 and 13 (formerly 6 and 6a): prohibition of discrimination.

Article 14 (formerly 7a): Internal Market.

Part Two – Citizenship of the Union

Part Three – Community Policies (in particular):

Title I   Free Movement of Goods.

Title II   Agriculture.

Title III Free Movement of Persons, Services and Capital.

Title VI   Common Rules on Competition, Taxation and Approximation (Harmonisation) of Laws.

Title XI   Social Policy, etc.

Article 3 now reads as follows:

1 For the purposes set out in Article 2, the activities of the Community shall include, as provided in this Treaty and in accordance with the timetable set out therein:

(a) the prohibition, as between Member States, of customs duties and quantitative restrictions on the import and export of goods, and of all other measures having equivalent effect;

(b) a common commercial policy [basically external trade policy];

(c) an internal market characterized by the abolition, as between Member States, of obstacles to the free movement of goods, persons, services and capital;

(d) measures concerning the entry and movement of persons in the internal market as provided for in Title IV;

(e) a common policy in the sphere of agriculture and fisheries;

(f) a common policy in the sphere of transport;

(g) a system ensuring that competition in the internal market is not distorted;

(h) the approximation of the laws of Member States to the extent required for the functioning of the common market;

(i) the promotion of coordination between employment policies of the Member States with a view to enhancing their effectiveness by developing a coordinated strategy for employment;

(j) a policy in the social sphere comprising a European Social Fund;

(k) the strengthening of economic and social cohesion;

(l) a policy in the sphere of the environment;

(m) the strengthening of the competitiveness of Community industry;

(n) the promotion of research and technological development;

(o) encouragement for the establishment and development of trans-European networks;

(p) a contribution to the attainment of a high level of health protection;

(q) a contribution to education and training of quality and to the flowering of the cultures of the Member States;

(r) a policy in the sphere of development cooperation;

(s) the association of the overseas countries and territories in order to increase trade and promote jointly economic and social development;

(t) a contribution to the strengthening of consumer protection;

(u) measures in the spheres of energy, civil protection and tourism.

2 In all the activities referred to in this Article, the Community shall aim to eliminate inequalities, and to promote equality, between men and women.

At the heart of Community economic law, by reference to the first of the means in Article 2 and hence to the concept of negative integration (the removal of restrictions and discrimination), lie the rules relating to the establishment and maintenance of the Common Market. As seen in the early chapters, these include the rules governing the free movement across internal frontiers of goods (including the customs union rules), persons (particularly workers, and including the right of establishment of companies and self-employed persons), services (including banking and insurance) and capital flows.

Closely linked to the rules on the free movement of goods and services are the common rules on competition within the Internal Market. Of particular significance are the rules which apply to undertakings which, either jointly or individually, seek to control markets for goods and services and so restrict competition to the detriment of inter-Member State trade.

Sectoral common policies embrace agriculture (and the establishment and maintenance of common organisations of the markets for agricultural products such as cereals, wine and sheepmeat), fisheries, the transport infrastructure, coal and steel (under the Treaty of Paris) and atomic energy (under the Euratom Treaty). Harmonisation of the laws of the Member States proceeds to the extent required for the proper functioning of the Common Market.

As also seen in the early chapters, the second of the then two means in Article 2 – 'the approximation of the economic policies of the Member States' in the Rome Treaty – became the establishment of an 'economic and monetary union' under the Maastricht Treaty of 1992, and a new Article 4 (formerly 3a) EC comprises a broad statement of activities and goals concerning the process of integration as the Community moves towards Union. Picking out the key features of Article 4 enables us to highlight the essential interdependence of the negative and positive sides of the process. In paragraph 1: '... close co-ordination of Member States' economic policies ... internal market ... open market economy with free competition.' In paragraph 2: 'Concurrently with the foregoing ... single currency, the ECU [now renamed the Euro] ... single monetary and exchange rate policy ... price stability ... open market economy with free competition.'

While, therefore, the main thrust of positive integration now centres on economic and monetary union, that is, Article 4, paragraph 2 policies (in Pinder's terms, those co-ordinated and common policies the *main* aim of which is to achieve economic and welfare objectives other than the removal of discrimination), in addition, from the list to be found in Article 3, we must include common commercial (external trade) policy (linked to the Common Market but increasingly positive in nature), policies in the social sphere, the strengthening of economic and social cohesion (aimed at 'reducing disparities between the various regions'), protection of the environment and the promotion of research and technological development, etc.

The social policy measures in Articles 136–53 (formerly 117–129a) EC relate in particular to such issues as a co-ordinated strategy for the promotion of employment, equal pay and treatment for men and women within the field of employment, eligibility for social security benefits for those persons (and their families) who exercise their right of free movement, health and safety at work, education and vocational training, culture, public health and consumer protection.

The policies in some of these fields (for example, equal pay and environmental protection) have both social and economic dimensions and are both negative and positive in integration terms.

As regards the implementation and enforcement of Community economic and social law, it is important to remember that Community law creates a complex of legal relationships involving the Community's policy makers, legislators and policy overseers; a wide range of national authorities engaged in the implementation of Community policies; and business undertakings and individuals who are affected in one way or another by such policies. Consider, for example, the customs union rules and *Van Gend en Loos*, the competition rules directed at undertakings, and equal pay and treatment measures which impact not only on individual employees and employers but also, because of the costs involved, on the economies of the Member States.

Hence, when discussing the concept of the Community law of the economy, Lasok and Bridge stated that:

> The dual role of the law as a force of integration is that of organising the Community and its economy. Therefore, the Community law of the economy is the body of rules addressed to the Member States, individuals and private and public corporations which in their entirety purport to govern the economic and social life both at a state and individual level.

In slightly different terms, the economic and social law of the Community can be seen as encompassing:

(a) policies adopted by the Community institutions for the attainment of economic, social (and political) *objectives*;

(b) *economic management* functions assumed at the Community level, particularly by the Commission, within the 'market and plan' pattern underlying European economic integration;

(c) active participation by competent *authorities within the Member States* (including their courts) in the development of the Community and their involvement in the decision making processes of the Community.

Community law, while assuming a market economy operating on the basis of effective competition, also provides for varying degrees of 'economic *dirigisme*' (economic direction or control) on the part of the Community institutions and the Member States.

As Mertens de Wilmars has pointed out:

> This was already the case in economic systems of the 'Soziale Marktwirtschaft' [Social Market Economy] type where the essential aims of such intervention were, on the one hand, to create the conditions for 'workable competition' and to oblige to abide by the rules regarded as appropriate to ensure self-regulation of the market economy and, on the other hand, to redress, by means of systems involving direct or indirect transfers of income, the socially or culturally unfavourable consequences of market mechanisms.

The legally binding instruments for the implementation (and enforcement) of Community economic and social law are those which were introduced in Chapter 4: Treaty provisions themselves and the secondary legislation derived from them – Regulations, Directives and Decisions of the political institutions. Legal integration goes hand in hand with economic and social integration.

Weatherill summed up the position (some years ago) in the following terms:

> The substance of Community law [at the present stage of its development] concerns market integration and the establishment of a common market ... Because those rules

of law, which permit regulation of the economy, directly affect individuals, the procedures must respect the position of the individual. Community law accordingly contains important principles protecting the individual. The legislative and administrative tasks performed by the Community institutions are subject to review on the basis of these principles.

... The Treaty contains some explicit principles which protect the individual ... *However, the Court has proved vigorous in developing a substantial body of principles independent of explicit Treaty support* [emphasis added].

In the final paragraph of this extract, Weatherill is referring to *general principles of Community law* (introduced in Chapter 4) which in the above context operate as a criterion of the validity of Community legislation. As such, they operate within the procedures whereby the legality of Community acts may be reviewed by the Court of Justice, and since the mid-1990s by the Court of First Instance (CFI), and if necessary annulled at the behest of private parties. They may also be used by the Court as the basis for an award of damages in an action brought by an individual against a Community institution(s) for loss suffered as a result of an invalid act: Article 288(2) (formerly 215(2)). They may additionally be used as a basis for striking down measures taken by a Member State within the Community context. They may be used as well as an aid to the interpretation of Community law. In general terms, they fill gaps in the Community legal order.

GENERAL PRINCIPLES OF COMMUNITY LAW AND FUNDAMENTAL RIGHTS

The 'written' sources of Community law (the Treaties and the acts of the institutions) cannot possibly in themselves provide a solution for every question that comes before the Court of Justice or the CFI. Thus, in the exercise of its jurisdiction under Article 220 (formerly 164) regarding the interpretation and application of Community law, the Court of Justice has developed a form of 'unwritten' law, an independent body of general principles, in order to assist it and the CFI partner in their duties and to fill gaps in the written sources.

The clear relevance of these general principles to the body of Community rules which 'purport to govern the economic and social life both at a state and individual level', and, therefore, their relevance to the vital question of the *protection of the individual* was explained in 1982 by Professor Mertens de Wilmars, a former President of the Court of Justice. He drew attention to the increasingly wide range of interventionary powers of public authorities (including the Community's institutions) in mixed economies and the new economic management methods available to such bodies. Accordingly, 'the problem of controlling the exercise of *discretionary powers* has acquired greater significance and new dimensions'. Such control, particularly through the medium of judicial review, which traces 'the boundary between the lawful and unlawful exercise of a discretionary power', must rest on the basis of 'general criteria which may be transposed from one case to another'. Such criteria are to be 'found in a number of general legal principles whose aim and effect are both to guarantee the freedom of action given to the authority and to place such restrictions on it as are necessary in order to avoid arbitrariness'.

What is meant by 'discretionary powers' in this context? There are no fixed and certain rules for the conduct of economic and social affairs by public authorities, whether at local, national or Community level. Economic and social policy decisions usually involve questions of choice. What is the best way to achieve the economic or social objective in question? One particular course of action is adopted rather than another. It is presumably taken in the general interest, as the policy makers see it, and it is given legal effect. For example, British government energy policy decisions involve the closure of 35 collieries with thousands put out of work. The reduction of a costly Community sugar mountain involves penalties being levied not only against sugar producers but also against isoglucose manufacturers whose product to some extent occupies the same market. Does the general interest outweigh the interests of those harmed by the course of action adopted? Is it possible to challenge the validity of the action taken and to recover loss suffered?

At Community level, such challenges create a dilemma for the Court, and now for the CFI, to which jurisdiction (under Article 230(4) (formerly 173(4))) was transferred from the Court of Justice in the mid-1990s subject to the right of appeal. It is in effect being asked to 'second-guess' the discretionary choices taken by the political institutions. In Cases 197-200/80, etc, *Ludwigshafener Walzmühle Erling KG v Council*, the Court stated that:

> It should be remembered that, in determining their policy in this area, the competent Community institutions enjoy wide discretionary powers regarding not only establishment of the factual basis of their action, but also definition of the objectives to be pursued, within the framework of the provisions of the Treaty, and the choice of the appropriate means of action.

The CFI has two means at its disposal to alleviate the problem when faced by a direct challenge to Community action by an individual under Article 230(4). The first is to restrict the number of applications which it allows to be heard by adopting stringent tests of *standing*, that is, the right to be heard (see Chapter 19). Secondly, if it does allow a review of the validity of enacted discretionary powers, either directly under Article 230 or indirectly, as seen in the previous chapter, under Article 234(1)(b) (formerly 177(1)(b)), it can and does confine itself to an assessment of whether their exercise of those powers by the Community's law making institutions has exceeded, in a manifest and grave manner, the bounds of the margin of discretion at the policy makers' disposal. It is at this point of control that the general principles of Community law can be called in aid to distinguish between the lawful and the unlawful exercise of such discretionary powers.

Legal Basis and Sources of the General Principles and Fundamental Rights

The Treaty basis for the development of these general principles by the Court of Justice, and their incorporation into the body of Community law, can be justified by reference to the following Treaty Articles (emphasis added):

> The Court of Justice and the Court of First Instance [added by the Nice Treaty] shall ensure that in the interpretation and application of this Treaty *the law is observed*: Article 220 [formerly 164]. ['The law' including a body of law beyond the text of the Treaty.]

The Court of Justice shall review the legality of acts adopted jointly by the European Parliament and the Council, of acts of the Council, the Commission and of the ECB ... and of acts of the European Parliament intended to produce legal effects vis à vis third parties ... on grounds of lack of competence, infringement of an essential procedural requirement, infringement of this Treaty *or of any rule of law* relating to its application, or misuse of powers [Article 230(1) (formerly 173(1))].

In the case of non-contractual liability, the Community shall, in accordance with the *general principles common to the laws of the Member States*, make good any damage caused by its institutions ... [Article 288(2) (formerly 215(2))].

It is arguable whether in a technical sense these three Treaty Articles form a solid basis for the general principles of Community law – such as fundamental rights and freedoms, non-discrimination and proportionality established and developed by the Court of Justice. Only the old Article 215(2) refers to 'general principles'. Are there any such principles 'common to the laws of the Member States'? However, in terms of the provision of an EC 'bill of rights' and further protection of the individual, this concern can surely be dismissed, at least to the extent that as a control mechanism the general principles operate, through the case law, to achieve those objectives. This, as will be seen, is another moot point. Where has the dividing line between Community interest and individual interest been drawn?

As regards the sources of the Community's general principles of law, they are partly 'written' and partly 'unwritten' in the case law or judge made sense. They have been derived by the Court from three sources:

(a) The national legal systems and constitutional traditions of the Member States.

(b) The Council of Europe's European Convention for the Protection of Human Rights and Fundamental Freedoms 1950 (ECHR). (See also the EU Charter of Fundamental Rights, below.)

(c) The EC Treaty (as amended).

It was not until 1992 with the signing of the Maastricht Treaty that Community/Union general principles, in particular respect for fundamental rights, received Treaty recognition in Article F(2) (now 6(2)) TEU:

The Union shall respect fundamental rights, as guaranteed by the European Convention for the Protection of Human Rights and Fundamental Freedoms signed in Rome on 4 November 1950 and as they result from the constitutional traditions common to the Member States, as general principles of Community law.

Under a ToA amendment to Article F TEU, a new first paragraph (now 6(1) TEU) states that:

The Union is founded on the principles of liberty, democracy, respect for human rights and fundamental freedoms, and the rule of law, principles which are common to the Member States.

The effect of this is to render this provision justiciable, the Court of Justice having jurisdiction under the EC Treaty and any provision of the other two Union pillars (mainly the pillar) over which it now has jurisdiction under Article 46 TEU, particularly 46(d). This represents a strengthening of the Court's previous powers with respect to the judicial review of institutional acts.

The basis of the ECHR as a source of Community fundamental rights is, according to the Court of Justice, indirect in that its declarations of rights are basic principles to which all the Member States as signatories to the ECHR have subscribed (and all of which have incorporated into their national legal systems).

The 'discovery' of general principles from 'the constitutional traditions common to the Member States' has been said to be:

> ... largely an exercise in comparative law. This use of the comparative technique is not governed by an *a priori* intent to find the highest common denominator: rather it is governed by an intent to trace elements from which Community legal principles and rules can be built up which will offer an appropriate, fair and viable solution for the questions with which the Court is confronted [Gormley].

In the State liability case, Case C-5/94 *R v Ministry of Agriculture, Fisheries and Food ex p Hedley Lomas (Ireland) Ltd*, Advocate General Léger said:

> as far as State liability for legislative action is concerned, there are no general principles which are truly common to the Member States. The principles established by the Court in relation to Article 215 [now 288] of the Treaty have, in fact been those laid down by the systems of domestic law *most protective of individuals* suffering damage through legislative action [emphasis added].

General principles have, as seen above, also been derived or extrapolated from the EC Treaty itself. The Member States' duty of 'solidarity' or 'cooperation' underlies the requirement in Article 10 (formerly 5) that they 'ensure fulfilment of the obligations arising out of this Treaty', for example, the obligation to transpose Directives correctly and in time.

The general principle of non-discrimination (or equality of treatment) is to be found, albeit with varying degrees of scope, in various parts of the Treaty: for example, as regards nationality (Article 12 (formerly 6)), citizenship (Article 18 (formerly 8a)), the free movement of workers (Article 39 (formerly 48)), equal pay for men and women (Article 141 (formerly 119)), opportunities and treatment in matters of employment and occupation generally (Article 137 (formerly 118)), common organisations of agricultural markets (Article 34 (formerly 40)) and the free movement of goods (Articles 25 and 28 (formerly 12 and 30)). In cases involving Treaty provisions such as these, the Court, where appropriate, has held that the provision 'is merely a specific enunciation of the general principle of equality which is one of the fundamental principles of equality'.

In his discussion of general principles, Mertens de Wilmars drew a distinction between the following (although it will be seen that the cases may well cross these boundaries):

(a) Principles borrowed from the foundations of the democratic system: *respect for fundamental rights and freedoms* and the principle of *non-discrimination*.

(b) Principles of sound and proper administration, including the *balancing of interests, proportionality and the protection of legitimate expectations*.

(c) General principles relating to the concept of legal certainty: laws must not be *retroactive* and *vested rights* must be protected.

Respect for Fundamental Rights and Freedoms and the EU Charter

The Treaty of Rome, in which the focus was almost exclusively on economic integration, contained no express reference to fundamental rights and freedoms. For many years, this was a matter of great concern to some Member States, particularly West Germany where, despite or as a consequence of the *Internationale Handelsgesellschaft* case in 1970 (see Chapter 4), this omission for some time posed a threat to the supremacy of Community law. Nevertheless, since that time, the Court of Justice has developed a considerable body of case law on fundamental rights – *within the context of the structure and aims of Community law* Nevertheless, it is clear that the rights which have been recognised by the Court can serve to protect private parties by curtailing the legislative powers both of the Community and the Member States.

The indirect challenge under Article 177(1)(b) (now 234(1)(b)) in Case 11/70 *Internationale Handelsgesellschaft* concerned the validity of a Community measure as implemented by a national agency. The issue was whether the system of forfeitable deposits introduced under Regulation 120/67 was, as the company claimed, contrary to various fundamental rights provisions (including the right of economic liberty and the principle of proportionality) of the German Basic Law. The Court of Justice refused to test the validity of the Community measure against principles of national constitutional law. Instead, it held that respect for such rights formed part of the general principles of law recognised in the *Community* legal order. The Court nevertheless held that the system of forfeitable deposits was justifiable in order to support the effective functioning of the common organisation of the market in cereals: see also *Wünsche* (1987) in Chapter 4. In this case, the German Constitutional Court expressed satisfaction with Community progress in the field of human rights.

In Case 4/73 *Nold KG v Commission*, a direct action for judicial review under Article 173(2) EEC (now Article 230(4) EC), the German national rights at issue related to the protection of commercial interests, discrimination and denial of economic opportunities. While drawing attention to both national constitutional traditions and international treaties such as the ECHR as inspiration for respect for fundamental rights at the Community level, the Court held that the pleas made on behalf of the German undertaking failed when assessed against the market rationalisation scheme pursued under the ECSC Treaty. The Court declared that such rights are not 'unfettered prerogatives' but are subject to limitations 'justified by the overall objectives pursued by the Community'.

Case 4/73 *Nold KG v Commission*

Nold, a West German wholesale coal undertaking, sought the annulment of a Commission Decision which provided that coal wholesalers could not buy Ruhr coal direct from the selling agency unless they agreed to purchase a minimum quantity. Nold was not in a position to meet this requirement and dealing through an intermediary proved more costly.

The Court of Justice ruled:

As to the objection based on an alleged violation of fundamental rights:

The applicant asserts finally that certain of its fundamental rights have been violated, in that the restrictions introduced by the new trading rules authorised by the Commission have the effect, by depriving it of direct supplies, of jeopardizing both the profitability of the undertaking and the free development of its business activity, to the point of endangering its very existence.

In this way, the Decision is said to violate, in respect of the applicant, a right akin to a proprietary right, as well as its right to the free pursuit of business activity, as protected by the Grundgesetz [Basic Law] of the Federal Republic of Germany and by the Constitutions of other Member States and various international treaties, including in particular the Convention for the Protection of Human Rights and Fundamental Freedoms of 4 November 1950 and the Protocol to that Convention of 20 March 1952.

As the Court has already stated, fundamental rights form an integral part of the general principles of law, the observance of which it ensures.

In safeguarding these rights, the Court is bound to draw inspiration from constitutional traditions common to the Member States, and it cannot therefore uphold measures which are incompatible with fundamental rights recognized and protected by the Constitutions of those States.

Similarly, international treaties for the protection of human rights on which the Member States have collaborated or of which they are signatories, can supply guidelines which should be followed within the framework of Community law.

The submissions of the applicant must be examined in the light of these principles.

If rights of ownership are protected by the constitutional laws of all the Member States and if similar guarantees are given in respect of their right freely to choose and practice their trade or profession, the rights thereby guaranteed, far from constituting unfettered prerogatives, must be viewed in the light of the social function of the property and activities protected thereunder.

For this reason, rights of this nature are protected by law subject always to limitations laid down in accordance with the public interest.

Within the Community legal order it likewise seems legitimate that these rights should, if necessary, be subject to certain limits justified by the overall objectives pursued by the Community, on condition that the substance of these rights is left untouched.

As regards the guarantees accorded to a particular undertaking, they can in no respect be extended to protect mere commercial interests or opportunities, the uncertainties of which are part of the very essence of economic activity.

The disadvantages claimed by the applicant are in fact the result of economic change and not of the contested Decision.

It was for the applicant, confronted by the economic changes brought about by the recession in coal production, to acknowledge the situation and itself carry out the necessary adaptations.

This submission must be dismissed for all the reasons outlined above.

The ECHR has also been invoked by the Court of Justice in a number of cases concerning the actions of *national authorities and the administration of justice at Member State level.*

Case 63/83 *R v Kent Kirk*

Captain Kirk, a Danish fisherman, was arrested and prosecuted for fishing on 6 January 1983 within 12 miles of the UK coast contrary to the Sea Fish Order 1982, which was ostensibly a conservation measure. He was fined £30,000 by the magistrate, but appealed to the Crown Court. He argued that as a Community national, he had a right to fish anywhere in EC waters.

Article 100 of the Act of Accession of the UK to the Community had permitted the UK for 10 years, in derogation from other provisions of EC law, to maintain a 12 mile exclusion zone against fishing vessels from certain Member States, including Denmark, until 31 December 1982. On 25 January 1983, Council Regulation 170/83 was adopted permitting the UK to maintain the derogation for another 10 years *as from 1 January 1983* (that is, with retroactive effect). Therefore, at the time he was arrested, K had a right *under Community law* to fish in the 12 mile coastal zone. The Crown Court referred the case to the Court of Justice for a preliminary ruling as to whether the UK had the right to prosecute K under the 1982 Order.

The Court ruled that the purported retroactivity could not have the effect of ex *post facto* validation of the penal provision of the UK Order:

> ... such retroactivity may not, in any event, have the effect of validating *ex post facto* national measures of a penal nature which impose penalties for an act which, in fact, was not punishable at the time it was committed. That would be the case where at the time of the act entailing a criminal penalty, the national measure was invalid because it was incompatible with Community law.

> The principle that penal provisions may not have retroactive effect is one which is common to all the legal orders of the Member States and is enshrined in Article 7 of the European Convention ... as a fundamental right; it takes its place among the general principles of law whose observance is ensured by the Court of Justice.

Consequently, the fine was quashed.

Kent was not a challenge to the validity of the Community Regulation but a challenge to the validity of the UK Order. The Court ruled that the effect in *national* law of applying the retroactive provision of the 1983 Regulation to the 1982 Order was not permissible as it would approve a breach by the UK of the principle of the non-retroactivity of penal liability. On this basis, national measures purporting to be an application of Community law but which breach a fundamental right are invalid.

In Case 222/84 *Johnston v Chief Constable of the Royal Ulster Constabulary* (an employment equal treatment case discussed in detail in Chapter 14), it was argued that a certificate relating to national security and public safety, signed by the Secretary of State for Northern Ireland under the Sex Discrimination (Northern Ireland) Order 1976, prevented the national court from hearing the applicant's discriminatory treatment claim. Mrs Johnston had formerly been a policewoman in Northern Ireland. Following an Article 177 (now 234) reference, the Court of Justice interpreted Article 6 of Council Directive 76/207 on Equal Treatment, which requires Member States 'to enable all persons who consider themselves wronged by discrimination to pursue their claims by judicial process', to the effect that the requirement of *effective judicial control* stipulated by Article 6 reflected a *general principle of law* (as regards access to justice) which underlies the constitutional traditions of the Member States and which is to be found in Article 6 of the ECHR. The Order was an infringement of the Directive and, indirectly, of the Convention.

The following case raised questions concerning the compliance with fundamental rights of national legislation based on allowable derogations from basic Treaty Articles on free movement within the Internal Market.

Case C-260/89 *ERT v DEP and SK*

The Greek State granted exclusive statutory rights to ERT, a Greek radio and TV company, in reliance on Articles 56 (now 46) and 66 (now 55) EC, which allow Member States to derogate from the rules on free movement of services 'on grounds of public policy, public security or public health'. ERT sought an injunction in the national courts against DEP and SK, who had set up a TV station and broadcast programmes in defiance of ERT's exclusive rights. Various defences were raised relating to free movement, competition and Article 10 of the ECHR concerning freedom of expression.

Following a reference by the national court, the Court of Justice ruled, as regards the fundamental rights issue:

1   That the fundamental rights which it upholds are not absolute.

2   It is necessary to review compliance with fundamental rights by Member States when they rely on derogations from basic Treaty provisions for the validity of national rules which are likely to obstruct the freedom to provide services.

3   The national rules in question can fall within the exceptions provided for in Articles 56 and 66 only if they are in compliance with the fundamental rights the observance of which is ensured by the Court, including the general principle of freedom of expression embodied in Article 10 of the European Convention on Human Rights.

This ruling by the Court left the national court with the need to balance respect for the right of freedom of expression against the interests put forward on the basis of the grounds for derogation expressed in the Articles in question, for example, public policy. Weiler and Lockhart have said that 'human rights by definition almost invariably involve a balance between competing interests'.

If, therefore, the national court held that the provisions of the disputed Greek statute were not in compliance with the right to freedom of expression, it would be required to strike them down. (See also Case C-368/95 *Familiapress v Heinrich Bauer* in Chapter 12.)

The welding of respect for fundamental rights and freedoms onto the Community/Union's legal order has not been solely a matter of Court of Justice policy. In 1977, the political institutions' Joint Declaration attached 'prime importance' to the protection of fundamental rights; a statement of principle endorsed by the European Council the following year. In 1986, the Single European Act referred in its preamble to respect for the fundamental rights recognised in the constitutions and laws of the Member States, the ECHR and the European Social Charter.

These developments and its own case law were reviewed by the Court of Justice in March 1996 in Opinion 2/94 *Re Accession by the Community to the European Convention on Human Rights*. This was an Opinion given by the full Court, after hearing all the Advocates General, pursuant to a request by the Council under Article 228(6) (now 300(6)) EC. As regards the competence of the Community to accede to the ECHR, the Court stated that it followed from Article 3b (now 5) of the Treaty, which states that the Community is to act 'within the limits of the powers conferred upon it by this Treaty and of the objectives assigned to it therein', that it had only those powers which had been conferred on it. The Court found that no Treaty provision conferred on the Community institutions any general power to enact rules on human rights or to conclude international conventions in that field.

In the absence of any express or implied powers for that purpose, the Court went on to consider whether Article 235 (now 308) (concerning residual powers) could constitute a legal basis for accession. The Court concluded that Article 235 could not be used as a basis for the adoption of provisions whose effect would be to amend the Treaty. The integration of the provisions of the ECHR into the Community legal order would have, in the Court's view, fundamental institutional implications for the Community and for the Member States. The constitutional significance of such a development was such as to go beyond the scope of Article 235 and could be brought about only by way of Treaty amendment.

This was unlikely because there was as yet no unanimous agreement in the Council on the need for accession. The UK, Ireland, Denmark and Sweden submitted arguments to the Court that the request was inadmissible or, in any event, premature.

The strengthening of the Union's position on human rights brought about at Maastricht and Amsterdam by the new Article 6 TEU has been referred to above. Not only was respect for human rights and fundamental freedoms to be found, for the first time, within the four corners of European Union law, but it had become one of the principles of constitutional status upon which the Union was founded. It had become, as seen in Chapter 1, a principle to be met by any new entrant to the Union and one the 'serious and persistent' breach of which could lead to the suspension of a Member State.

Nevertheless, pressure remained, particularly from the Commission, to put the protection of fundamental rights within the Union on a firmer, more direct footing. However, not unusually, there were differences of opinion as to what form the result of that pressure should take. In mid-1999, at the meeting of the European Council in Cologne, the Member States proposed the establishment of what is now called a European Union Charter of Fundamental Rights. A specially appointed Convention consisting of representatives of the European Parliament, the Court of Justice, the Council, the Commission, national parliaments and governments and other bodies was called upon to prepare a draft Charter. The emphasis was on transparency with debates open to the public and comments called for on successive drafts available on the Convention website.

The final draft received a mixed reception. Political leaders in the Union were reportedly not agreed as to whether the Charter should have legal effect or take the form of a political declaration, and the House of Lords Select Committee on the European Union expressed the view that such a catalogue of rights could have the effect of undermining the ECHR.

At the Nice Summit, the European Council welcomed the Charter, but only as a political declaration and it was solemnly proclaimed as such by the European Parliament, the Council and the Commission on 7 December. A decision as to whether it should take the form of a legally enforceable instrument was left until at least the next IGC Summit in 2004. As a political declaration, the Charter's role in bringing the issue of human rights more clearly and directly to EU citizens is therefore at present limited. It has been *referred to* by the Community Courts in recent rulings (see, for example, Case T-177/02 *Jégo-Quéré & Cie SA v Commission* in Chapter 19) but, at most, it can only be regarded as 'soft law'. In this regard, it must be borne in mind that, as Francis Jacobs stated in a recent lecture:

> ... the European Convention is legally binding. It has the force of a European constitutional instrument. It is accepted by all the European Union Member States – and by twenty-five or so other European States. The Charter, a useful domestic Bill of Rights for the European Union itself, should not be allowed to upstage the Convention. Nor should it preclude the possibility of European Union access to the Convention.

The Charter itself can be found in the Official Journal at (2000) OJ C364/1 of 18 December. It is already clear that the Charter, as it stands and particularly if it eventually takes on an EU constitutional character, raises complex questions regarding its aims and scope of application, its relationship with the ECHR and the existing protection of human rights in the Union. It main aim can be regarded as political and, as a further step in establishing a constitution for the Union, raise fresh fears in some quarters of the creation of an over-centralised 'super State'. Its aims in a legal sense may be seen as creating a unnecessary schism in human rights protection bearing in mind the protection already provided under the Council of Europe's ECHR.

The Charter contains fundamental human, civil, political, economic and social rights within six chapters, using simple, accessible language. A sample of the rights in each chapter is included here:

(a) *Dignity*, including human dignity, the right to life and to integrity of the person, particularly in the fields of medicine and biology;

(b) *Freedoms*, including liberty and security, respect for private and family life, protection of personal data, freedom of expression, freedom of assembly and of association, the right to education, freedom to work and provide services, the right to property, the right to asylum;

(c) *Equality* before the law, including non-discrimination, equality between men and women, the rights of the child and of the elderly;

(d) *Solidarity* including the right of collective bargaining and action, fair and just working conditions; social security and health care, environment protection;

(e) *Citizen's rights* including the right to vote, the right to good administration, the right to access to Parliament, Council and Commission documents, freedom of movement and residence;

(f) *Justice*, including the right to an effective remedy and fair trial, presumption of innocence and the right of defence.

Reviewing the Charter's full list, Lenaerts and De Smijter (see 'References and Further Reading' at the end of the chapter) find that it:

> ... essentially contains new descriptions of existing fundamental rights' [which are set out in the main] in unlimited, unconditional terms and often appear to have a broader scope, resulting from the rights concerned to meet the needs of modern society, or form a combination of similar fundamental rights provisions drawn from different sources, each having *a distinct legal value* [emphasis added].

These 'different' sources include the United Nations Universal Declaration of Human Rights of 1948, the ECHR (the substantive provisions of which have, by and large, been incorporated into the Charter although not in the same wording), the Council's European Social Charter of 1961 (revised in 1996 and ratified by most Member States), and the 1989 Community Charter on the Fundamental Rights of Workers.

As regards 'unlimited, unconditional terms', it is, however, made clear in Article 52 of the EU Charter on 'Scope of Guaranteed Rights' that:

> Any limitation on the exercise of the rights and freedoms recognised by this Charter must be provided for by law and respect the essence of those rights and freedoms. Subject to the principle of proportionality, limitation may be made only if they are necessary and genuinely meet objectives of general interest recognised by the Union or the need to protect the rights and freedoms of others.

> Rights recognised by this Charter which are based on the Community Treaties or the Treaty on European Union shall be exercised under the conditions and within the limits defined by those Treaties.

In so far as this Charter contains rights which correspond to rights guaranteed by the Convention on the Protection of Human Rights and Fundamental Freedoms, the meaning and scope of those rights shall be the same as those laid down by the said Convention. This provision shall not prevent Union law providing more extensive protection.

With respect to the scope of the Charter itself, Article 51 states that:

The provisions of this Charter are addressed to the institutions and bodies of the Union with due regard for the principle of subsidiarity and to the Member States only when they are implementing Union law. They shall therefore respect the rights, observe the principles and promote the application thereof in accordance with their respective powers.

This Charter does not establish any new power or task for the Community or the Union, or modify powers and tasks defined by the Treaties.

Article 51(1) should be read in the light of the principal aim of the drafters to establish the Charter as the constitutional bedrock for the protection of the fundamental rights of EU citizens (and non-EU citizens who are in situations linked to Community law) against actions taken by the Community institutions and by Member States' authorities when they act within the framework of Community law. As such, the Charter would apply at present to EC institutional acts (secondary legislation) and those of the Member States when implementing such acts. It would therefore form a basis for judicial review claims under Articles 230(4) and 234(1)(b) EC and compensation claims under Article 288(2) EC. In addition, the Court of Justice ensures the respect for fundamental rights in relations between private parties governed by Community law.

The role of the Community Courts is, however, somewhat restricted at present with respect to Article 51(1) of the Charter by, as seen above, the terms of Article 46(d) TEU and their duty to enforce and apply Article 6(2) TEU within *the confines of their jurisdiction*. It must also be recalled that the fundamental rights recognised and guaranteed by the Community Courts are, as stated in Case 4/73 *Nold* (see above):

... far from constituting unfettered prerogatives ... [and] are protected by law subject always to limitations laid down in accordance with the public interest. Within the Community legal order it likewise seems legitimate that these rights should, if necessary, be subject to certain limits justified by the overall objectives pursued by the Community, on condition that the substance of these rights is left untouched [see also Article 51(1)].

Of the various types of technical questions and required adaptations raised by the Charter and the current protection of fundamental rights in the Union, of particular interest and value is a form of case study by Lenaerts and De Smijter based on Case C-249/96 *Grant v South West Trains* (see Chapter 14), a case which came in for some criticism:

The preceding analysis may be illustrated by reconsidering the *Grant* judgment delivered by the Court of Justice on 17 February 1998. Ms Grant started proceedings against her employer for not allowing the woman with whom she had a stable relationship to benefit from the travel facilities which partners of the opposite sex of employees did receive. According to Ms Grant, this refusal constituted discrimination on grounds of sexual orientation. Upon examination of the constitutional traditions common to the Member States and certain international standards of protection of human rights, the Court found no basis to prohibit this type of discrimination. It also observed that the Treaty of Amsterdam had introduced Article 13 EC on the basis of which the Council could take the necessary measures, but that provision – which moreover was not yet then in force – could as such not be of any help to Ms Grant. If the case were judged today, would Article 21(1) of the Charter be of any help? As long as the Council does not use its competence under Article 13 EC, the application of Article 21(1) of the Charter is unlimited. Since that provision states that "[a]ny discrimination based on (...) sexual orientation shall be prohibited", the Court would in principle be able to rely on it in order to sanction any behaviour which contradicts the prohibition in question. Such behaviour must, however, fall within the scope of the Charter defined in Article 51(1). It is at this level that Ms Grant would probably continue to face some difficulty, as the discrimination she is complaining of takes place in an employment relationship governed by national law. According to Article 51(1), the provisions of the Charter are addressed "to the Member States only when they are implementing Union law." Consequently, if the case of Ms Grant were considered merely from the standpoint of the prohibition of discrimination on grounds of sexual orientation – as distinct from discrimination on grounds of sex – it would be necessary to construe an appropriate nexus between that prohibition and substantive Union law so as to declare Article 21(1) of the Charter applicable to the legal relationship at issue. This seems hard to do. Furthermore, Article 51(2) makes it clear that the Charter does not create new powers for the Community. Since Article 141 EC is prohibiting discrimination on grounds of sex and not on any other ground the extension of the scope of application of Article 141 to a prohibition of discrimination on grounds other than sex, such as sexual orientation, would have to be regarded as the establishment of new powers for the Community. From the moment, of course, that the Council uses its competence under Article 13 EC, the application of Article 21(1) of the Charter will be determined by the scope of the Community act adopted [footnotes omitted].

It is also worthy of note that in *Grant* it was found that the European Commission on Human Rights did not consider that stable homosexual relationships fell within the scope of the right to respect for family life under Article 8 of the ECHR. However, Article 8 was the key factor in Case C-60/00 *Mary Carpenter v Secretary of State for the Home Department* in which Mrs Carpenter, a national of the Philippines, having been given leave to stay in the UK for six months, overstayed her leave, failed to apply for an extension and married Mr Carpenter. He travelled regularly from the UK to other Member States in the course of providing services to advertisers in those States: see Article 49 (formerly 59) EC. Mrs Carpenter faced deportation by the UK immigration authorities. Following an Article 234 reference, the Court ruled that:

Article 49 EC, read in the light of the fundamental right to respect for family life, was to be interpreted as precluding, in circumstances such as those of the case, a refusal, by the Member State of origin of a provider of services established in that Member State who provided services to recipients established in other Member States, of the right to reside in its territory to that provider's spouse, who was a national of a third country.

What has been described as 'the most controversial example of an apparent conflict between Community law and the Convention' is provided by the ruling of the Court of Justice in Case C-159/90 *Society for the Protection of Unborn Children Ireland v Grogan and Others* and the European Court of Human Rights' decision in *Open Door Counselling and Dublin Well Woman Centre v Ireland* shortly afterwards. As Arnull goes on to explain, in the Community case:

... the Court of Justice was asked about the compatibility with the Treaty rules on services of a national restriction on the publication of information concerning the availability of abortion facilities lawfully provided in another Member State. The Court held that such a restriction fell outside the scope of the relevant provisions of the Treaty where those performing the abortions were not involved in distributing the information. Since the relevant national legislation did not come within the ambit of Community law, the Court said it had no jurisdiction to assess its compatibility with fundamental rights. In *Open Door* ... the Court of Human Rights subsequently held that an injunction granted by the Irish Supreme court in similar circumstances restraining the applicants from imparting or receiving information about abortion facilities available abroad amounted to a breach of Article 10 of the Convention concerning freedom of expression.

... The restrictive view taken by the Court of Justice of the scope of the Treaty rules on services might well have been motivated by a desire to avoid considering a question on the effect of the Convention which was pending before the Court of Human Rights. But there was no overlap, and consequently no inconsistency, between the rulings of the two Courts.

The next important question concerns how a binding EU Charter would relate to the ECHR. Clearly, if the Charter were to become legally binding in its present form, two mandatory but different systems of human rights protection would exist in Europe: that of the Council of Europe and that of the Union. At present, many of the Charter's rights are to be found in the ECHR although most with different wording. The two systems are headed by different Courts and different processes of litigation. The Charter draws on sources other than the ECHR such as the European Social Charter and it creates new 'modern' rights particularly regarding social rights under the heading of 'Solidarity' and in the fields of medicine and biology. Where the Charter corresponds to a fundamental right guaranteed by the ECHR, the ECHR, in accordance with Article 52(3) of the Charter (see above), acts as a minimum in determining 'the meaning and scope' of the right in question, but the Charter may provide more extensive protection.

David Pannick QC has argued that:

It would be a recipe for chaos for the EU to adopt its own legally binding charter that differed in content from the European Convention on Human Rights (which is a part of the domestic law of all Member States) or for the ECJ to be authorised to interpret that Convention, since there would then be rival interpretations of that instrument by the ECJ and by the European Court of Human Rights.

The sensible solution, as advocated by the [House of Lords Select Committee in its European Union – Eighth Report 1999–2000] is for the EU to accede to the European Convention on Human Rights, thereby enabling the Strasbourg Court of Human Rights to act as the external final authority in this context. This would 'secure the Convention as the common code for Europe', and it would 'go a long way in guaranteeing a firm and consistent foundation for fundamental rights in the European Union' [(2000) *The Times*, 20 June].

The Charter cannot be an alternative for the Convention. The Council of Europe has already proposed EU accession to the Convention in order to link the two systems of protection formally. This would seemingly require the Council of Europe to review the contents of the ECHR, particularly to broaden its scope to cover the fundamental social rights to be found in the EU Charter and in the Council's own Social Charter and other 'modern' rights. Such expansion has already been accomplished with respect to environmental rights.

Nevertheless, within the accession argument there are differing views as to whether the European Court of Human Rights should be 'the external final arbiter within a linked system'. Rather, it has been proposed by some within the House of Lords Select Committee that, although there should be 'full and formal integration' of the ECHR 'as part of the directly written Union law', the Court of Justice should 'remain the supreme guardian in respect of Union actions as well as Member State action falling within the scope of Union law'.

Many questions remain to be answered before uniformity and clarity in the protection of fundamental rights in Europe can be achieved and the EU can at that same time secure a binding Bill of Rights.

In the final part of this chapter, attention is paid to particular general principles which feature prominently in the case law of the Community Courts. The preamble to the EU Charter 'reaffirms, with due regard for the powers and tasks of the Community and the Union and the principle of subsidiarity, the rights as they result [amongst other sources] from ... the case law of the Court of Justice of the European Communities ...'.

Non-Discrimination

Referring to the operation of the principle of non-discrimination (as a basis for the judicial review of Community acts), Mertens de Wilmars stated that: 'The principle of non-discrimination is merely the transposition into economic law of the constitutional principle of the equality of citizens before the law and with regard to taxes.'

The principle of non-discrimination (or equality) permeates the whole fabric of Community law. As stated previously, it is to be found (within limited contexts) in several provisions of the Treaty itself and in many provisions of Community legislation. The directly effective Article 7 of the Treaty of Rome (now Article 12 EC) established the principle of non-discrimination on grounds of *nationality* across the whole range of the Treaty, and the principle operates in the case law usually in conjunction with other Treaty Articles to provide rights for individuals: see, for example, Case 186/87 *Cowan v Tresor Public* (Article 59 (now 49) relating to Cowan's freedom, as a cross-border tourist, to receive services; the action being against an arm of the French State), Case 293/83 *Gravier v City of Liège* (Article 128 EEC (now 150 EC) concerning equality of the right to access to vocational training for foreign students studying in Belgium), and Case C-221/89 *R v Secretary of State for Transport ex p Factortame Ltd (No 2)* (Article 52 (now 43) concerning the right of establishment; see Chapter 20). Article 141 (formerly 119) EC provides for equal pay for equal work or work of equal value irrespective of sex, and Directive 76/207 implements the principle of equal treatment for men and women in the field of employment.

The principle of non-discrimination also constitutes a basic element of the Common Market, being an integral part of the concept of free movement. For example, it operates, as has been seen, to strike down national measures which discriminate against and obstruct the free movement of goods imported from other Member States. (Nevertheless, within this context, similar situations may be treated differently on the basis of overriding, objectively justifiable grounds of public concern.

Article 30 (formerly 36) allows for derogation from the principle of free movement of goods for a number of reasons including the protection of the health and life of humans, animals or plants. See also Article 39(3) (formerly 48(3)) as regards the free movement of persons.)

The Court of Justice deduced an 'unwritten' general principle of non-discrimination from these various Treaty provisions. In Case 1/72 *Frilli*, a Belgian State pensions case, it was declared that:

> The absence of any agreement of reciprocity may not ... be validly raised against such a worker, such a condition being incompatible with the rule of equality of treatment, which is one of the fundamental principles of Community law, embodied in this matter in Article 8 of Regulation 3.

The principle in its various applications means that similar situations (a question which can call for careful consideration and judgement) must be treated in the same way; different treatment must not be arbitrary, that is, based on uninformed or random decision, as this will amount to discrimination. In the same way, two essentially different situations treated the same way without objective justification may give rise to an infringement of the principle. Discrimination may be covert or indirect: see the French car tax case of *Humblot* in Chapter 12.

Economic policy decisions of the Community institutions and national agencies regarding the reduction of agricultural surpluses have not infrequently been the subject of challenges by producers on grounds of discrimination: see, for example, Case 114/76, etc, *Bela-Mühle v Grows-Farm* (discussed below in the section on proportionality, a second ground for complaint) and Cases 103 and 145/77 *Royal Scholten-Honig v Intervention Board for Agricultural Produce*. In the latter case, a Regulation imposed an onerous levy on the production of isoglucose, a product which in certain respects competes with sugar, which was in surplus to the extent of creating a 'sugar mountain'. Isoglucose manufacturers indirectly challenged the Regulation in national court proceedings, claiming that it threatened to put them out of business. Following a reference under Article 177(1)(b) (now 234(1)(b)), the Court of Justice held that the provisions of the Regulation 'offend against the general principle of equality of which the prohibition on discrimination set out in Article 40(3) (now 34(2)) of the Treaty is a specific expression'. In *Bela-Mühle*, the Advocate General defined non-discrimination as being 'concerned with the relationship between various groups of persons [for example, isoglucose and sugar manufacturers] and takes the form of equality of treatment by bodies vested with public authority'.

It will be recalled that the ToA introduced a new Article 13 EC which enables the Council to 'take appropriate action to combat discrimination based on sex, racial or ethnic origin, religion or belief, disability, age or sexual orientation'. Council action is therefore required in order to make this provision operative. As seen in the *Grant* case above, no such action had been taken as regards sexual orientation, but this ground for a claim of discrimination is to be found in Article 21(1) of the EU Charter of Fundamental Rights.

The Balancing of Interests and Procedural Rights

It will be recalled that Mertens de Wilmars' second category of general principles concerned *sound and proper administration*. The case law of the Court indicates that the first of these, the balancing of interests, is, in his own words, 'one transposed into the administrative field from the area of legal proceedings: *audi alterem partem'*. Thus:

> Public authorities, when adopting an administrative decision [are obliged] to take into account all the interests involved and in particular not to take decisions which are likely to damage the interests of private individuals without giving them an opportunity to make their views known in advance.

In Case 17/74 *Transocean Marine Paint Association v Commission*, an administrative (quasi-judicial) Decision by the Commission, pursuant to Article 85(3) (now 81(3)) of the competition law rules, renewed, subject to new conditions (one of which TMPA claimed was unduly onerous), an exemption for TMPA from the prohibitions in Article 85(1) (now 81(1)) relating to anti-competitive trading agreements. In its review of this Decision under what is now Article 230(4), the Court of Justice stated that:

> The applicants claim that at no time could they infer from this statement that the Commission intended to impose on them a condition such as that contained in the provision in issue, and one to which they would not be able, by reasons of its breadth, to adhere and which, without good reason, would harm their interests. If they had been in a position to realize the Commission's intentions they would not have failed to make known their objections on this matter so as to draw the Commission's attention to the inconvenience which would result from the obligation in issue and to the illegality by which it is vitiated. Since they were not given this opportunity, they allege that the Decision, insofar as the obligation in issue is concerned, must be annulled since it is vitiated by a procedural defect.

Where individual rights and interests are likely to be affected, Community law generally provides *express* procedural safeguards but in this case, natural justice and the right to a fair hearing were invoked. The Commission had not afforded the applicant the opportunity to make its views known and was therefore in breach of 'an essential procedural requirement' necessary as a safeguard for the protection of substantive rights.

The decision in the *Johnston* case above can be seen in the same light. The Secretary of State's certificate purported to deny Mrs Johnston access to the legal process and thus to effective judicial control as regards her employer's compliance with Community law in the form of the Equal Treatment Directive.

The balancing of interests also lies at the heart of the move towards 'transparency' and 'openness' in Community institutional procedures so as to make them more accessible to the public. In leading Case T-194/94 *Carvel v Council*, the CFI ruled that:

> It is clear both from the terms of Article 4 of Decision 93/731 and from the objective pursued by that Decision, namely, to allow the public wide access to Council documents, that the Council must, when exercising its discretion under Article 4(2), genuinely balance the interests of citizens in gaining access to its documents against any interest of its own in maintaining the confidentiality of its deliberations.

A later challenge to the Commission, Case T-105/95 *WWF UK v Commission*, concerned similar issues with respect to the Commission's refusal to allow access to documents following its Decision that a project in Ireland did not infringe Community environmental law. The challenge rested on (a) breach of the 'Code of Conduct on Public Access to Commission and Council Documents' (which speaks of 'the widest possible access'); (b) infringement of Commission Decision 94/90 which adopted the

Code; and (c) breach of Article 190 (now 253) regarding the Commission's requirement in this case to give reasons for its rejection of the WWF's complaint.

The CFI upheld this challenge to the contested Decision primarily on the basis of Article 190, but found the Commission had failed in its duty to undertake a genuine balancing of the interests involved as required by the Code. It examined both the obligatory 'public interest' exception to the general access rule (covering clear evidence of a danger to public security or court proceedings, etc) and the discretionary 'institutional interest' exception, which provides that the Commission (and the Council: see above) 'may also refuse access in order to protect the institution's interest in the confidentiality of its proceedings'.

Article 1 (formerly A) TEU now provides that 'decisions are [to be] taken as openly as possible and as closely as possible to the citizen'. Article 255 (formerly 191a) EC also now provides that:

> Any citizen of the Union, or any natural or legal person residing or having its registered office in a Member State, shall have a right of access to European Parliament, Council and Commission documents, subject to ... principles and limits on grounds of public or private interest ... determined by the Council ... within two years of the entry into force of the Treaty of Amsterdam.

(See also Article 41 on the 'Right to Good Administration' and Article 42 on the 'Right to Access to Documents' in the EU Charter of Fundamental Rights.)

In the wider context, and bearing in mind the almost invariable clash of interests in human rights cases, we have seen at the Community/national levels the need to balance, in Case C-260/89 *ERT v DEP and SK*, respect for the freedom of expression against (Greek) national interests claimed as grounds for derogation from the free movement of (radio and television) services, a fundamental principle of the Common Market. In a similar but reverse situation, in Case C-368/95 *Familiarpress v Heinrich Bauer*, the need arose to balance another aspect of freedom of expression, the diversity or plurality of the press, as pleaded *by* a Member State whose legislation clashed with another fundamental Common Market principle, the free movement of goods.

Finally, it is noteworthy that, at national level, the House of Lords in the *Factortame (No 2)* case was called upon, following a ruling by the Court of Justice to that effect, to grant an interim injunction against the Crown in order to protect the interests of a party, at least until a decision had been reached regarding directly effective rights to which that party laid claim. Their Lordships stated that as regards the balance of convenience (or interests), matters of considerable weight had to be put in the balance to outweigh the desirability of enforcing, in the *public* interest, what was on the face of it the law of the land (in this case, provisions of the Merchant Shipping Act 1988). It was enough, however, to swing the balance if the applicant could 'show that there was a serious case to be tried'. (This case is discussed in more detail in Chapter 20, where it will be seen that the Act's provisions were disapplied.)

Proportionality

Derived from German law concerning fundamental rights and freedoms (and possessing a clear relationship with the English law concept of reasonableness), the principle of proportionality has been explained by Hartley in the following terms:

According to the principle of proportionality, a public authority may not impose obligations on a citizen except to the extent to which they are strictly necessary in the public interest to attain the purpose of the measure. If the burdens imposed are clearly out of proportion to the object in view, the measure will be annulled. This requires that there exists a reasonable relationship between the end and the means ... the means must be reasonably likely to bring about the objective, and ... the detriment to those adversely affected must not be disproportionate to the benefit to the public ...

Proportionality is particularly important in the sphere of economic law, since this frequently involves imposing taxes, levies, charges or duties on businessmen in the hope of achieving economic objectives.

In Case C-131/93 *Commission v Germany*, the Court of Justice laid down the following test to establish whether or not a legislative measure adopted by the Community institutions (or by a national authority acting under powers conferred on it by Community law) was 'proportional':

(a) It must be an appropriate and effective way to achieve the legislative objective.

(b) It must be necessary, that is, there is no less restrictive alternative and the adverse effect (on the individual) is not excessive when weighed against the aim of the measure.

The principle of proportionality has been applied on numerous occasions by the Community Courts, and Article 5(3) EC, introduced at Maastricht, states that 'any action by the Community shall not go beyond what is necessary to achieve the objectives of this Treaty'.

In Case 11/70 *Internationale Handelsgesellschaft* (discussed above and in Chapter 4), the Court of Justice gave an Article 177(1)(b) (now 234(1)(b)) ruling on the validity of certain Community Regulations to the effect that a CAP system, whereby a West German exporter lost a deposit of DM 17,000 on failing to export cereals during the period of validity of an export licence granted to him by the National Cereals Intervention Agency, was 'appropriate' and did not violate the principle of proportionality. The 'end' was the proper regulation of the Community cereals market; the licence and deposit requirements were one of the means of bringing about that objective and were reasonably likely to bring it about. There was no unnecessary or undue detriment imposed on the cereals exporter who failed to fulfil his obligations. The penalty was not excessive in relation to the aim of the Regulations.

However, in Case 181/84 *R v Intervention Board for Agricultural Produce ex p Man (Sugar) Ltd*, MSL tendered for the export of 30,000 tons of sugar outside the Community. Under the relevant Community Regulation, MSL had to lodge a security and undertake to apply for a licence from the Board within four days if the tender was accepted, otherwise the security was forfeited. The tender was accepted, MSL put up a security of £1,670,000 and applied for a licence. Owing to difficulties in their offices, their application was four hours late and the Board forfeited the whole security. In this action for judicial review, Glidewell J referred questions to the Court of Justice under Article 177(1)(b) (now 234(1)(b)) regarding the alleged invalidity of the authorising Regulation because of its disproportionate effect. The Court of Justice ruled that:

... the automatic forfeiture of the entire security, in the event of an infringement significantly less serious than the failure to fulfil the primary obligation [to export the sugar] which the security itself is intended to guarantee, must be considered too drastic a penalty in relation to the export licence's function of ensuring the sound management of the market in question.

The forfeiture was a disproportionate act and Man (Sugar) recovered the entire sum with interest and costs.

In the *Bela-Mühle* case referred to above, and others which arose out of the Community's attempt to reduce the skimmed-milk powder 'mountain', Regulation 563/7 obliged animal feed producers to purchase expensive skimmed-milk powder in place of soya as the protein ingredient of their product. In this indirect Article 177(1)(b) (now 234(1)(b)) challenge, the Court held that the Regulation was invalid. It was contrary to the principle of equality in that it obliged feed producers to purchase skimmed-milk powder at such a *disproportionate* price (skimmed milk was three times more expensive than soya) and it was equivalent to a discriminatory distribution of the burden of costs between the various agricultural sectors.

Apart from its application in the context of challenges to Community legislation, the principle also operates in the context of substantive Treaty Articles. It has been seen that Member States may seek to justify derogations from the principle of free movement of goods on specified grounds under Article 36 (now 30) and as regards free movement of persons under Article 48(3) (now 39(3)). The case law of the Court of Justice clearly demonstrates that such restrictive *national* measures must hinder trade no more than is necessary to achieve the desired objective. For instance, in Case 178/84 *Commission v Germany (Re Purity Requirements for Beer)*, German legislation, originally enacted in the 16th century, required beer to be produced from a limited number of natural ingredients and banned the marketing of beer containing additives. These German rules, which applied to all beers, had the effect, amongst other things, of preventing beers from other Member States which contained domestically authorised additives from being sold in Germany. All the additives at issue were allowed under German law to be used in other foodstuffs. The total ban was found to be contrary to Article 30 (now 28) (as regards measures having an effect equivalent to a quantitative restriction) and could not be justified on public health grounds under Article 36 (now 30). That objective could be achieved by less restrictive means which took account of evidence to a threat to health regarding individual additives to beer. Not being 'necessary', the total ban was disproportionate to its objective. (For various other examples, see Chapter 12.)

Legal Certainty

It is customary to link the next general principle referred to by Mertens de Wilmars, the protection of legitimate expectations, to those relating to the non-retroactivity of new rules of law and the protection of vested rights under the general heading of *legal certainty*. This is how they will be treated here. As Brown and Kennedy put it: '... these principles shade into one another, and the same case may raise one or more of them.'

The significance of the general principle of legal certainty (together with its related or component principles) is at its most apparent within the relationship between Community undertakings (business entities) and Community or national administrative bodies in a highly regulated sector such as agriculture. Of course, economic agents must act within the law, but they may also legitimately operate on the basis of reasonable expectations or predictions as to the way they *will be* treated by an administrative body in the future application of Community law. Thus, Wyatt and Dashwood explain that:

The principle of legal certainty requires that those subject to the law should not be placed in a situation of uncertainty as to their rights and obligations. The related concept of legitimate expectation constitutes an important corollary to this principle: those who act in good faith on the basis of the law as it is or seems to be should not be frustrated in their expectations.

Thus, Community measures should not take effect without adequate notice to those concerned and should not as a general rule take effect retroactively from their date of publication. In Case 98/78 *Racke v HZA Mainz*, the Commission adopted a Regulation with financial implications for certain wine importers and then in two further Regulations altered the amounts of money involved. Each new Regulation was stated to apply 14 days *prior* to publication. The Court of Justice held, following an Article 177(1)(b) (now 234(1)(b)) reference on validity, that it was a fundamental principle of Community law that a measure adopted by public authorities shall not be applicable to those concerned before they have the opportunity to make themselves acquainted with it. However, in this case, the Commission had provided special notice to bring the changes to the attention of those concerned; the new amounts being necessary to stabilise the market. As regards retroactive measures, the Court stated that:

Although in general the principle of legal certainty precludes a Community measure from taking effect from a point in time before its publication, it may exceptionally be otherwise where the purpose to be achieved so demands [see also Case 108/81 *Amylum*, below] and where the legitimate expectations of those concerned are duly respected [see the *Kent Kirk* case, above].

A new Community measure should not apply to an act or transaction which has been completed before the measure came into effect. If it does so, in principle it offends against respect for *vested or acquired rights*, that is, those rights which have been acquired by an individual (or undertaking) within the then existing legal framework and according to due process. In Case 100/78 *Rossi*, the Court explained that:

The Community rules could not, *in the absence of an express exception consistent with the aims of the Treaty*, be applied in such a way as to deprive [individuals] of the benefit of a part of the legislation of a Member State [emphasis added].

Neither should a new Community measure apply to an act or transaction which has begun and is *in the process of completion*. Here, the offence is against the principle of the *protection of the legitimate expectations* of the individual concerned rather than against the principle of non-retroactivity.

For expectations to be legitimate, they must be held by a prudent person acting in accordance with the law. Such a person's reliance on the certainty of the law should be rewarded by the protection of his *confidence* in the system. It should not be disrupted by a sudden, unforeseeable change in the law to his detriment in the absence of an overriding matter of public, rather than individual, interest. As regards this final point, to put the situation in perspective and looking at it from the point of view of the legislator, Sharpston has explained that:

The background to all economic activity is that economic operators live in an uncertain world. Changes in the regulatory framework within which they operate are one further hazard. Indeed, one might say that, in the general economic interest (as distinct from the interest of any particular individual economic agent), there should probably be a presumption of legislative freedom: legislators should normally be left with their hands untied, free to modify the regulatory framework in order to implement desired policy in the face of changing economic circumstances. At the simplest level of argument, therefore, expectations should never be permitted to invalidate legislative change.

'Legislative freedom' overrode a plea for the protection of legitimate expectations in the following case which also involved the question of retroactivity.

Case 108/81 *Amylum v Council*

At a time of concern regarding the size of the Community 'sugar mountain' (that is, a huge surplus), a system of quotas and levies was imposed on sugar producers and also, under Regulation 1293/79, on producers of isoglucose, which competes with sugar for certain purposes. This Regulation was annulled by the Court, not on substantive grounds but because the Council had failed to consult the Parliament on the matter (a breach of an essential procedural requirement).

The Council therefore issued Regulation 387/81, having this time consulted the Parliament, reimposing the scheme with retrospective effect. This new Regulation was challenged by Amylum and other isoglucose manufacturers under Article 173(2) EEC (now 230(4) EC) – like its predecessor it was a 'disguised decision': see Chapter 4 – as being in breach of the principle that Community measures may not have retroactive effect. The Court of Justice ruled:

> *I – First submission: Breach of the principle that Community measures may not have retroactive effect*
>
> As the Court has already held ... although in general the principle of legal certainty, as the applicant states, precludes a Community measure from taking effect from a point in time before its publication, it may exceptionally be otherwise where the purpose to be achieved so demands and where the legitimate expectations of those concerned are fully respected.
>
> As regards the first of those two conditions, it is well to call to mind certain matters of fact or law which are moreover well known to the parties. During the period of application of the contested regulation sugar producers were, in particular, subject to quotas and production levies. Isoglucose is a product which may be substituted for sugar and is in direct competition with it. Any Community decision concerning one of those products necessarily has repercussions on the other. Having regard to that situation, although by judgments of 29 October 1980 the Court declared Regulation No 1293/79 void for infringement of an essential procedural requirement, namely the absence of the Parliament's opinion, the Court nevertheless considered that it was a matter for the Council, in view of the fact that isoglucose production was contributing to an increase in sugar surpluses and that it was open to it to impose restrictive measures on that production, to take such measures in the context of the agricultural policy as it judged to be useful, regard being had to the similarity and interdependence of the two markets and the specific nature of the isoglucose market.
>
> If, following the declaration of the nullity of Regulation No 1293/79, the Council had adopted no measure restrictive of isoglucose production – in the present case the reinstatement with effect from 1 July 1979 of the quotas allocated and the levies imposed on the producers – the objective, which it was pursuing, namely the stabilization, in the general interest, of the sugar market, could not have been achieved or could only have been achieved to the detriment of sugar producers, who alone would have had to finance the costs of Community surpluses, or even to the detriment of the Community as a whole, whilst isoglucose producers whose production competed with that of sugar undertakings would have escaped all restraints ...

Thus, the Council was lawfully entitled to consider that the objective to be achieved in the general interest, namely, the stabilization of the Community market in sweeteners without arbitrary discrimination between traders, required the contested provisions to be retroactive in nature and thus the first of the conditions which the Court lays down for the applicability *ratione temporis* of a Community measure to a date prior to the date of its publication may be regarded as satisfied.

To ascertain whether the second of the conditions set out above is satisfied, it is necessary to inquire whether the action of the Council in publishing on 17 February 1981 Regulation No 387/81 has frustrated a legitimate expectation on the part of the applicants to the effect that the production of isoglucose would not be regulated during the period from 1 July 1979 to 30 June 1980, the period to which that regulation makes applicable Article 9 relating to quotas and production levies on isoglucose which it inserted in Regulation No 1111/77.

It should first be pointed out that the contested provisions of Regulation No 387/81 do not include any new measures and merely reproduce the provisions of Council Regulation No 1293/79 declared void by the Court on 29 October 1980.

In view of the fact that Council Regulation No 1293/79 of 25 June 1979 retained its full effect within the Community legal order until it was declared void, so that the national authorities responsible for its implementation were required to subject the production of isoglucose to the restrictive system which it laid down, such a legitimate expectation could only be founded on the unforeseeability of the reinstatement with retroactive effect of the measures contained in Regulation No 1293/79 declared void by the Court.

In the present case, the applicant cannot claim any legitimate expectation worthy of protection.

In the first place, the traders concerned by the rules in question are limited in number and are reasonably well aware of the interdependence of the markets in liquid sugar and isoglucose, of the situation of the Community market in sweeteners and therefore of the consequences which, following the declaration that Regulation No 1293/79 was void, the imposition on the production of sugar in respect of the period from 1 July 1979 to 30 June 1980 of stabilization measures from which the production of isoglucose would have been entirely exempt might have had.

As this case shows, legitimate expectations must be reasonable expectations. Would a reasonably experienced and *prudent* isoglucose manufacturer have relied on the expectation? If not, the expectation does not merit protection.

The plaintiffs in the next case, a *damages claim* based on an alleged wrongful act by the Commission, were more successful.

Case 74/74 *CNTA v Commission*

CNTA, producers of colza oils, alleged, in support of a claim for damages against the Community under Article 215(2) (now 288(2)), the illegality of Regulation 189/72. This measure had, without warning, discontinued agricultural compensatory amounts (introduced earlier to compensate for losses following a devaluation of the French franc) in dealings in colza seeds. The company claimed that this sudden curtailment frustrated the legitimate expectations of the persons concerned that the compensatory amounts would be maintained for deliveries in progress, which had been severely disrupted by the curtailment; traders thereby suffering extensive losses.

It was argued that even a prudent trader might in such circumstances fail to cover himself by insurance, as he could legitimately expect that no unforeseeable change would be made such as unexpectedly to expose him to exchange risks and unavoidable loss.

The Court of Justice stated that the monetary compensatory amounts could not be seen as providing a guarantee to exporters that they would not suffer loss as a result of fluctuations in the exchange rate. Nevertheless, continued the Court:

> In these circumstances, a trader may legitimately expect that for transactions irrevocably undertaken by him because he has obtained, subject to a deposit, export licences fixing the amount of the export subsidy in advance, no unforeseeable alteration will occur which could have the effect of causing him inevitable loss, by re-exposing him to the exchange risk.

> The Community is therefore liable if, in the absence of an overriding matter of public interest, the Commission abolished with immediate effect and without warning the application of compensatory amounts in a specific sector without adopting transitional measures which would at least permit traders either to avoid the loss which would have been suffered in the performance of export contracts, the existence and irrevocability of which are established by the advance fixing of the export subsidies, or to be compensated for such loss.

> In the absence of an overriding matter of public interest, the Commission has violated a superior rule of law, thus rendering the Community liable, by failing to include in Regulation 189/72 transitional measures for the protection of the confidence which a trader might legitimately have had in the Community rules.

By its failure either to give reasonable notice to traders in the sector or to provide protective transitional measures for committed exporters, the Commission had violated the principle of the protection of legitimate expectations – *a superior rule of law* in terms of the *Schöppenstedt* formula as it operates in the context of claims for damages under Article 215(2) (now 288(2)): see Chapter 19.

Whereas Community acts may only have retroactive effect in those exceptional circumstances where individual rights must give way to Treaty based economic and social policy considerations, conversely Court of Justice rulings, as we have seen in the previous chapter with regard to preliminary rulings, are in normal circumstances retroactive. Its judgments are *declaratory*, stating the law as it always has been. Thus an interpretative ruling clarifies and defines the meaning of a rule of Community law, which should have been understood and applied since the time of its coming into force: see, for example, the meaning and effect of Article 12 (now 25) in *Van Gend en Loos*. The national court is required to apply the rule as so interpreted even to legal relationships established *before* the preliminary ruling was made, except again where, in exceptional circumstances, 'important considerations of legal certainty' have been called in aid by the Court to validate a finding that its ruling should only apply prospectively – as in *Defrenne (No 2)* and a handful of other cases (see the final section of Chapter 9).

REFERENCES AND FURTHER READING

Alston, E (ed), *The EU and Human Rights*, 1999.

Arnull, A, *The European Union and its Court of Justice*, 1999, Chapter 6.

Burrows, R, 'Question of Community accession to the European Convention determined' (1997) 2 EL Rev 58.

Coppel, J and O'Neil, A, 'The European Court of Justice: taking rights seriously?' (1992) 12 Legal Studies 227.

Craig, PP, 'Substantive legitimate expectations in domestic and Community law'(1996) 55(2) CLJ 289.

De Búrca, G, 'Fundamental human rights and the reach of EC law' (The abortion case) (1993) 13 OJLS 283.

De Búrca, G, 'The drafting of the European Union Charter of Fundamental Rights' (2001) 26 EL Rev 126.

Ellis, E (ed), *The Principle of Proportionality in the Laws of Europe*, 1999.

Jacobs, FG, 'Human rights in the European Union: the role of the Court of Justice' (2001) 26 EL Rev 331.

Koopmans, T, 'European public law: reality and prospects' (1991) PL 53.

Lamoureux, F, 'The retroactivity of Community acts in the case law of the Court of Justice' (1983) 20 CML Rev 269.

Lenaerts, K. 'Fundamental rights in the European Union' (2000) 25 EL Rev 575.

Lenaerts, K and De Smijter, E, 'A "Bill of Rights" for the European Union' (2001) 38 CML Rev 273.

Lenaerts, Van Nuffel and Bray (eds), *Constitutional Law of the European Union*, 1999.

Mertens de Wilmars, J, 'The case law of the Court of Justice in relation to the review of the legality of economic policy in mixed-economy systems' (1982) 1 LIEI 1.

O'Leary, S, 'The relationship between Community citizenship and the protection of fundamental rights in Community law' (1995) 32 CML Rev 519.

Phelan, D, 'Right to life of the unborn v promotion of trade in services ...' (1992) 55 MLR 670.

Schermers, H, 'The European Community bound by fundamental human rights' (1990) 27 CML Rev 249.

Sharpston, E, 'Legitimate expectations and economic reality' (1990) 15 EL Rev 103.

Shonfield, A, 'The politics of the mixed economy in the international system of the 1970s' (1980) International Affairs 1.

Usher, J, *General Principles of EC Law*, 1998.

Weiler, J, 'Eurocracy and distrust ...' (the Court of Justice and Human Rights) (1986) 61 Washington L Rev 1103.

Weiler, J and Lockhart, N, '"Taking rights seriously" seriously: the European Court and its fundamental rights jurisprudence – Parts I and II' (1995) 37 CML Rev 51, 74–78 and 579.

Wyatt and Dashwood, *European Community Law*, section on 'The general principles of Community law' in Chapter 4.

CHAPTER 11

COMMON MARKET AND INTERNAL MARKET: THE FOUR FREEDOMS

The Single [Internal] Market was not a panacea for all problems facing European firms, but rather it was about taking opportunities [Commission Report, March 1994].

COMMON MARKET

A clear relationship was established in Chapter 2 between the economic concept of *negative integration* (the removal of restrictions and discrimination) and the Community law concept of Common Market as found in Article 2 of the Treaty. There is no definition of 'Common Market' in the Treaty. It can be loosely described as a unitary market covering the entire territory of the Community and governed by a single set of Community rules. The basic legal principle underlying this market (and the Internal Market, see below) is that national measures which obstruct or hinder – have a negative effect on – the free movement of goods, persons, services and capital, the fundamental economic freedoms guaranteed by the Treaty, are in contravention of Community law unless they can be justified by overriding matters of public interest.

Of those Community 'activities' or objectives listed in Article 3 which were crucial for the establishment and functioning of the Common Market – objectives 3(a)–(f) and 3(h) in the original 1957 Treaty – it is apparent that they are to a considerable extent concerned with the question of free movement. We will initially introduce 'the cornerstone of the Common Market' – the *free movement of goods* (references, where we are discussing the earlier developments after 1957, are to the EEC Treaty. Subsequent developments and amendments to the Treaty are noted where appropriate):

Article 3 EEC

For the purposes set out in Article 2, the activities of the Community shall include ...

(a) the elimination, as between Member States, of customs duties and quantitative restrictions on the import and export of goods, and of all other measures having equivalent effect;

(b) the establishment of a common customs tariff and a common commercial policy towards third countries ...

The fundamental principle of the *free movement of goods within the Community*, that is, as regards inter-Member State trade, was embodied in Article 3(a) and remains basically unchanged: ('prohibition' has replaced 'elimination').

In part, Article 3(a) and (b) constituted the Treaty basis for the Community's *Customs Union*, by reference firstly to the elimination by Member States of customs duties on the import and export of goods in trade between themselves and of 'measures [that is, charges] having equivalent effect' to customs duties, and, secondly, to the establishment of a common (external) customs tariff, that is, system of duties, on goods *entering* the Community from the rest of the world: see also Article 9 (now 23), which provides a definition of the Community's Customs Union. (The Community's

Common Commercial Policy is linked to the Common Market but concerns external trade policy.)

However, as seen, Article 3(a) went further than financial tariff barriers by also requiring the elimination, as between Member States, of *quantitative* restrictions (bans or quotas) and, again, other 'measures' – having an equivalent effect to a quantitative restriction. The latter 'measures' do not amount to express prohibitions or quotas, but they similarly impede cross-border trade and must be eliminated. They include significantly differing national standards and technical requirements relating to goods and, together with quantitative restrictions proper make up what are known as *non-tariff barriers*.

The common customs (or external) tariff was established for the original six Member States primarily on the basis of an unweighted average of the import duties of the four customs territories (France, Germany, Italy and the Benelux Customs Union). It was completed by mid-1968 and has been progressively adopted by new Member States. (There is no reference to it in the new Article 3(b) of the EC Treaty.) As a result of Community participation in *international* tariff negotiations within the GATT (the General Agreement on Tariffs and Trade), now the WTO (World Trade Organization), the level of external duties has been reduced in subsequent years. Community agricultural products are, however, subject to a different legal regime from industrial products. Protection from fluctuations in world agricultural market prices, through a system of Community import levies and export refunds, lay at the heart of difficulties experienced in 1992–93 between the Community and the USA within the GATT Uruguay Round:

Article 3 EEC

   ...

(c) The abolition, as between Member States, of obstacles to freedom of movement
     for persons, services and capital ...

The Maastricht Treaty rephrased Article 3(c) EC in terms of the Internal Market to include goods. In any event, the Treaty therefore encompasses not only those *factors of production* which make up the mobile resources or input of economic enterprise: *labour and entrepreneurship* (in as much as the Treaty provisions on persons apply to workers, self-employed persons, and business undertakings on the basis of the *right or freedom of establishment*) and *capital*, but it also applies to the output or end products of such enterprise (*goods* and *services*).

The Court of Justice has on many occasions stated that the free movement of goods is a fundamental principle of Community law – and so too the other freedoms in Article 3. In Case 203/80 *Casati*, the Court explained that:

> The first question concerns the effects of Article 67 [now 56] and, more particularly, Article 67(1), after the expiry of the transitional period. That Article heads the chapter on capital which belongs to Title II, 'Free movement of persons, services and capital', incorporated in Part Two of the EEC Treaty, entitled 'Foundations of the Community'. The general scheme of those provisions is in keeping with the list, set out in Article 3 of the EEC Treaty, of the methods provided for the attainment of the Community's objectives. Those methods include, according to Article 3(c) 'the abolition, as between Member States, of obstacles to freedom of movement for persons, services and capital'. Thus the free movement of capital constitutes, alongside that of persons and services, one of the fundamental freedoms of the Community. Furthermore, freedom

to move certain types of capital is, in practice, a pre-condition for the effective exercise of other freedoms guaranteed by the Treaty, in particular the right of establishment.

However, capital movements are also closely connected with the economic and monetary policy of the Member States ...

What is of particular importance in this extract from the Court's judgment is its insistence on the *inter-relationship* between the freedoms, particularly here between capital movements and the right of undertakings to *establish* themselves in other Member States. Also, the Court makes a clear link between free movement of capital (an element of *negative* integration) and the convergence of the economic and monetary policies of the Member States (a key aspect of *positive* integration) in the movement towards economic and monetary union: see 'The Bonds between Negative and Positive Integration' in Chapter 2.

Effective functioning of the Common Market therefore entails effective functioning of the four freedoms. As regards free movement of goods, whereas the customs duties and quota restrictions of Article 3(a) have been very largely eliminated, in a Community of 15 Member States, other national barriers and discriminatory practices remain and are in practice still only in the process of being removed under the Internal Market legislative programme and by the Court of Justice. Therefore, in order to obtain a more comprehensive picture of what the establishment of a 'true' Common Market entails, it is necessary to draw attention to a wider range of protectionist and anti-competitive barriers than merely the 'measures' – particularly, differing national rules and standards applied to goods – in Article 3(a):

(a) *The anti-competitive practices* both of individual firms which dominate markets for goods (and services) and of firms which act together to, for example, fix prices and share markets. Such activities (of undertakings, not Member States) are contrary to the Common Market and they are subject to the Community's *competition policy* rules, which seek to establish and maintain fair and effective competition: Article 3(f) EEC (now 3(g) EC), as developed in Articles 85–90 EEC (now 81–86 EC) (see Chapters 15 to 17).

(b) Discriminatory and anti-competitive *State aids* to national industries, which are incompatible with the Common Market, subject to certain exceptions, under Articles 92–94 EEC (now 87–89 EC).

(c) Differences in national *indirect taxation*, particularly Value Added Tax (VAT) and excise duties, as regards scope and rates. Subject to *harmonisation* measures under Article 99 EEC (now 93 EC) (see Chapter 12).

(d) *Nationalistic public purchasing policies of Member State governments*, which exclude foreign undertakings from procurement contracts, and which are subject now to Community legislation designed to introduce effective competition on a Community wide basis, for example, Directive 93/37 on Public Works Tendering.

(e) Frontier checks and formalities which caused delays to the transport of goods and which increased costs to an estimated value of 80p of every £10 spent by consumers were subject to abolition or simplification under the Internal Market programme (see below and Chapter 12).

It should also be noted that a fifth freedom, *free movement of payments*, is to be found in Articles 56(2) and 105(2) EC. Such payments include payments for goods imported and dividends on capital invested in another Member State. The 'basic' freedoms would clearly be ineffective if financial benefits arising from the transactions involved could not be 'repatriated'. Remaining *exchange controls* in relation to capital and as affecting financial services have been removed either through Commission action or the Member States' own volition. The introduction of the Euro is beginning to facilitate the transactions involved.

COMMON MARKET AND INTERNAL MARKET

Article 8(1) of the 1957 Rome Treaty (Article 7(1) EC following the TEU and repealed by the ToA) laid down that:

> The Common Market shall be progressively established during a transitional period of 12 years.

Although considerable progress was made in the fields of trade liberalisation and the free movement of workers by the time of the expiry of the transitional period at the end of 1969, the objective expressed in Article 8(7) (now repealed) was not achieved:

> Save for the exceptions and derogations provided for in this Treaty, the expiry of the transitional period shall constitute the latest date by which all the rules laid down must enter into force and all the measures required for establishing the common market must be implemented.

It was not until the mid-1980s, and the initiative provided by the Commission White Paper on Completing the Internal Market (Com (85) 310), that renewed political will on the part of the Member States, as evidenced by the Single European Act of 1986, introduced not only a new programme but also a new Community law concept, the Internal or Single European Market.

Article 8a of the EEC Treaty (Article 7a EC following Maastricht and now Article 14) states in paragraph 2 that:

> The internal market shall comprise an area without frontiers in which the free movement of goods, persons, services and capital is ensured in accordance with the provisions of this Treaty.

The upshot of these Treaty renumberings and the repeal of Article 7 is that the *Common Market* Article, being now a matter of history, has disappeared from this particular part of the Treaty, although it is still a valid economic law concept and is still to be found elsewhere in the Treaty, for example, Article 2 and Article 32 on agriculture. The *Internal Market*, as defined now in Article 14, is also to be found as appropriate elsewhere in the Treaty, for example, in Article 4 and Article 95.

The concept of the Internal Market, focusing as it does on the four freedoms, is therefore narrower in scope than that of the Common Market as found in the original Treaty and the case law of the Court of Justice. However, the words 'without frontiers' have raised new questions in relation to border controls, immigration and the movement of, for example, drugs and terrorists. In essence, the completion of the Internal Market by the end of 1992 represented:

> ... a plan for a large scale onslaught on the 'omissions' in the *'acquis'* with respect to Treaty obligations crucial to market integration, and a simultaneous endeavour to make progress on issues where the Treaty provides a permissive legal basis but no

obligations [Pelkmans and Winters]. [The second part of this sentence relates to 'positive' measures.]

Following its acceptance of the Commission's White Paper, the European Council instructed the Council of Ministers to introduce an action programme, priority to be given to:

(a) the removal of *physical* barriers to the free movement of goods within the Community (the aim being not merely to simplify frontier controls, which cause expensive delays, but to remove frontiers in relation to the movement of goods – and persons);

(b) the removal of *technical* barriers to the free movement of goods within the Community (particularly differing national rules and standards which fragment the market);

(c) the creation of a free market in *financial services* (for example, banking and insurance) and in *transport* (so far as the market was still subject to national transport quotas limiting the number of journeys that could be made by foreign hauliers);

(d) the creation of full freedom of establishment for the *professions*;

(e) the liberalisation of *capital* movements.

The '1992' Internal Market programme involved some 300 legislative measures (virtually all Directives) to be adopted by the Community and implemented by the Member States in the time scale provided, and the Single European Act provided for legislative decisions in most of the areas involved to be taken by a qualified majority vote in the Council (acting in co-operation with the Parliament): Article 100a(1) (now Article 95(1) and the co-decision procedure in Article 251). Thus, the primary legal mechanism for the completion of the Internal Market was 'the approximation [harmonisation] of the provisions laid down by law, regulation or administrative action in Member States' and unanimity was only required as regards fiscal provisions and those relating to the free movement of persons and the rights and interests of employed persons: Article 100a(2) (now 95(2)).

As will be seen in the following chapter, of particular importance are those Directives concerning the harmonisation of the many differing national rules and standards which have continued to impede the free movement of goods. Also significant are the Directives relating to professional qualifications, the free movement of services and public procurement.

As Pelkmans and Winters have indicated, the Internal Market programme did not focus on all Common Market activities, only on 'omissions', those aspects of the original programme where progress was limited. However, developments in related fields continue: for example, the regulation of corporate mergers, the extension of competition policy further into the fields of air and sea transport, reform of the Common Agricultural Policy, and participation by the Community in the liberalisation of world trade in the GATT Uruguay Round.

In 1989, Owen and Dynes listed 10 actual or potential benefits of the Single (Internal) Market:

- EASIER TRAVEL. Frontier controls will be all but abolished at the EC's internal frontiers, although not at its external points of entry (if anything, external controls will be increased to ensure that non-EC citizens do not find 'soft' entry points and then go on to exploit the benefits of the single market.) Computer-read, single-format EC passports will cut down delays, and police and immigration forces will tackle crime more through behind-the-scenes co-ordination than through frontier controls. Duty free sales will disappear.

- A BUSINESS BOOM. 320 million customers await the efforts of EC business, from Britain to Denmark to Greece and Portugal, with all firms competing on equal terms in a huge open market. One of the key provisions obliges public authorities to give enterprises from any EC nation an equal opportunity to win high-value contracts.

- BORDER SAVINGS. Frontier delays for goods vehicles (many trucks and lorries now wait at borders for eight hours or more) cost an estimated £17 billion, according to the European Parliament. Restrictions on tendering for public contracts cost a further £60 billion. The simplified customs procedures of the Single Administrative Document – which Britain was one of the first EC countries to introduce – will save costs.

- JOB RECOGNITION. A teacher from Glasgow will be able to teach in Lyons or Copenhagen, and an accountant from Brighton could go and work in Naples or Frankfurt, all on the basis of mutually recognised qualifications and diplomas. Linguistic barriers will still cause problems – and will work against the British, since as a nation, our grasp of Continental languages is still poor.

- FINANCIAL SERVICES. Restrictions on capital movements are to be lifted in 1990. EC citizens will be able to open bank accounts in due course or take out mortgages anywhere in the Community, with some exceptions in Southern Europe. There is a long term plan (still under discussion) for a European Central Bank.

- CONSUMER PROTECTION. EC States will no longer be able to block imports of foodstuffs or toys because they do not meet national labelling, health or safety standards. Broad criteria and common standards are being devised.

- FREE COMPETITION. Protectionist practices preventing free competition – including competition in transport by road, sea and air – will become illegal. The first stages of liberalisation in aviation and road haulage are already in effect, preventing cartels and quotas and allowing smaller operators increased market access.

- VAT AND INDIRECT TAXES HARMONISED. This is a controversial area because of the government's electoral commitment not to allow the abolition of VAT zero rating on basic goods such as food and children's clothes. However, the basic principle of the 1992 programme is that, once border controls have gone, trade in the integrated market will be distorted if there are large differentials between VAT rates.

- TELEVISION AND BROADCASTING. Technical standards for television and satellite technology are to be harmonised in conjunction with the 1992 programme to ensure that the twelve EC nations do not have incompatible systems, obstructing sales and communication. To prevent European television being dominated by American or Australian soap operas, a 'majority' of programmes 'where practicable' will have to be of EC origin once the Commission's plans are approved.

- THE TELECOMMUNICATIONS MARKET. This is being opened up, under a plan (tabled by the Commission in June 1987) for ending the monopoly supply of customer terminal equipment and telecommunications services, including databases and electronic mailboxes. Eventually, electrical plugs and sockets may also be standardised so that travellers do not have to carry adaptors or change plugs – but at the moment this seems unlikely.

It must be remembered, however, as many commentators stressed and as the Single European Act and the Maastricht Treaty demonstrated, that:

> ... it is hard to see how a transnational unified common marketplace could be created and remain viable without adequate monetary and fiscal powers ... the achievement of the single market will necessitate far greater attention to the formation of common economic policies and major changes in the decisional processes of the Community. The need for such policies was, indeed, foreshadowed in the opening Articles of the [Rome] Treaty: the programme set out in Articles 2 and 3 EEC remains today, as it was in 1958 when the Treaty came into force, a truly inspired and radical blueprint for European integration [Bieber *et al*, 1988].

In particular, integrationists argued strongly that the lack of a common currency and a European Central Bank to manage it were major weaknesses of the Internal Market.

In June 1992, the status of the Internal Market legislative programme was as follows:

- 282 proposals comprised the programme
- 228 proposals had been finally adopted by the Council
- 5 proposals had been partially adopted by the Council
- 4 proposals had reached the stage of a Council Common Position
- 2 proposals had reached the stage of a Council Political Agreement

(Figures supplied by the DTI in June 1992.)

Transposition of these measures into national law proceeded, but in some cases not as speedily as was required to meet the non-binding deadline of 31 December 1992. (As regards these obligations of the Member States, see Chapter 8, concerning the direct effect of Directives and the *Francovich* decision and also the Maastricht based Article 171(2) (now 228(2)) which allows defaulting Member States to be financially penalised.)

In March 1994, the Commission published a survey of European businesses which highlighted the following effects of the Single Market:

> Companies had started to notice the effects of the Single Market, particularly in reducing transport and administrative costs and introducing greater export potential. Almost every firm said that intra-EC transactions were both faster and cheaper and that border delays were shorter. On the financial side, several companies welcomed the greater flexibility in the insurance market – some British firms reported taking out French insurance for a better deal. The most common complaint on the financial side concerned not the failure of the existing structure, but the lack of a single currency. Almost all companies said that competition had become fiercer. Many had been spurred into forming joint ventures, and numerous licensing and distribution agreements had sprung up across borders.

The Commission nevertheless conceded that in 1996, the Single Market remained incomplete. Apart from the immigration, security and drug-trafficking problems relating to the free movement of persons (discussed earlier in connection with the Schengen Agreement of 1985), the Commission reported that as regards the free movement of goods:

The biggest problems have arisen in the area of mutual recognition of national norms and standards in those sectors where there is no European legislation for harmonizing national rules. A number of Member States are still finding reasons or pretexts to refuse the import of goods from other EU countries on grounds linked to national regulations concerning norms or standards.

The European Commission has received hundreds of complaints about such illegal barriers. They concern such widely diverse items as caravans, pharmaceuticals, Greek ceramic tiles, Belgian bedding quilts and even Dutch radishes.

In response, the Council adopted a Decision to ensure that any exceptions to the free movement of goods are clarified. From 1 January 1997, Member States have had to justify any bans on products manufactured or sold legally elsewhere in the Union (see also Chapter 12).

FREE MOVEMENT OF PERSONS, SERVICES AND CAPITAL

The basis of free movement can be explained in terms of the economic concept of the *optimum division of labour*:

> ... the object of optimum division of labour within the Community can be inferred from the objectives of Article 2. This optimum division of labour not only implies ensuring a free outlet for the economically most favourable supply of certain goods or services throughout the common market. It also implies the requirement of optimum allocation of production factors within the Community. Besides the necessity of mobility of the principal production factors – capital, labour, technical and managerial know-how – this latter requirement also entails the requirement of equal possibilities of establishment and exercise of a trade or profession in the most favourable place of establishment which may be attractive either on account of its shorter distance from buyers ... or because the general socio-economic, fiscal and financial climate is more favourable [Gormley].

Freedom of movement of persons and services and the right of establishment are dealt with in separate chapters of the Treaty although from an economic standpoint they are closely related. Article 39 (formerly 48) provides for the free movement of workers and, via the expression 'nationals of a Member State', Articles 43 and 49 (formerly 52 and 59) provide for employers (including *companies and firms*: see Article 48 (formerly 58)) and the *self-employed, for example, professional persons*. Such 'nationals' may or may not be in business to provide services.

The obligations placed upon Member States to secure free movement of workers and services and the right of establishment are underpinned by the prohibition of discrimination on grounds of nationality to be found in Article 12 (formerly 6) and the main Treaty provisions (including Article 56 on Capital) are directly effective.

Article 39 (formerly 48) of the Treaty provides that freedom of movement for workers:

> 2   ... shall entail the abolition of any discrimination based on nationality between workers of the Member States as regards employment, remuneration and other conditions of work and employment ...

The term 'worker' extends not only to a person in employment in a Member State other than that of which he or she is a national but also, according to the case law of the Court of Justice, to others (whose Community rights are usually more limited) such as work-seekers and involuntarily unemployed workers. In addition, members of a migrant worker's *family* are covered, even if they are not workers, as regards rights of entry and residence.

Provision is made in Article 42 (formerly 51) and Community Regulations for the transferability and aggregation of the social security rights of migrant workers and their dependants. This *social*, rather than economic, aspect of free movement is also apparent with respect to Directives originally adopted in 1990 granting rights of free movement to persons who are not economically active: students, retired persons and persons of independent means.

The impact of recent decisions of the Court of Justice regarding the post-Maastricht rights of EU *citizens* (see particularly Articles 17 and 18 EC) with respect to non-discrimination on grounds of nationality (Article 12) and rights of free movement and residence, as introduced in Chapter 7 on the Court, are dealt with in Chapter 13.

Articles 43–48 (formerly 52–58) governing the *right of establishment* cover both self-employed persons and companies and firms. The rights which are granted cover both the right of an individual to become established as a self-employed person on a *permanent basis* in another Member State and the right of a company incorporated in one Member State to set up a subsidiary or branch in another Member State. Such a person or company may be established in order to provide services in that other Member State, but if such provision of services is merely on a *temporary* basis, the rules relating to the provision of cross-border services, and not those on the right of establishment, will apply. Thus, Article 43(2) provides that:

> Freedom of establishment shall include the right to take up and pursue activities as self-employed persons and set up and manage undertakings, in particular companies and firms ... under the conditions laid down for its own nationals by the law of the country where such establishment is effected ...

Thus, the basic principle of non-discrimination applies: X or X Ltd shall be treated in the same way as 'nationals' of the host Member State. The main problems which have arisen in this respect, and which have to some extent been solved on the basis of harmonisation measures, concern mutual recognition of professional qualifications (for example, doctors, architects and lawyers) and obstacles arising from differences in the laws of Member States relating to companies, not least those providing banking and insurance services.

Articles 49–55 (formerly 59–66) deal with the *provision of services* of an industrial, commercial or professional character. Under the Treaty regime, the provision of services is seen as an act, or series of acts, carried out from an establishment in one Member State, the services being provided for a person situated *in another Member State*. Under Article 49 (formerly 59), 'restrictions on freedom to provide services within the Community shall be prohibited' and Article 50 (formerly 60) provides that such services are those which are 'normally provided for remuneration'. Persons to whom these provisions would apply include consulting engineers, architects and advertising agents engaged on a *temporary or spasmodic* basis by a client in another Member State. Article 50(2) states that:

> ... the person providing a service may, in order to do so, temporarily pursue his activity in the State where the service is provided, under the same conditions as are imposed by that State on its own nationals.

Thus, a host State's binding professional rules 'justified by the general good' (and see above as regards harmonisation) may be applied to the cross-border provider of a service. Steiner has rightly stated that: 'The difference between the right of establishment and the right to provide services is one of degree rather than kind. Both apply to business or professional activity pursued for profit or remuneration.'

The Court of Justice has held that tourists, as *recipients* of services, are entitled to immigration rights and, more significantly, to equal treatment in the country visited: see Case 186/87 *Cowan*. Similarly, on the basis of, amongst other things, Article 12 (formerly 6) and the concept of vocational training, the Court has extended the principle of non-discrimination to most university students who are nationals of a Member State.

The basic provisions relating to the abolition of restrictions on the *free movement of capital* throughout the Community are now to be found in Article 56 (formerly 73(b)). We are concerned here primarily with the movement of funds for investment in industry and commerce from one Member State to another. Examples would include *direct* investment by a company establishing a subsidiary in another Member State (attainable under the right of establishment rules), the provision of long term loans for industry by a bank or building society, and the cross-border acquisition of bonds or shares.

Article 56 provides that:

1   Within the framework of the provisions set out in this Chapter, all restrictions on the movement of capital between Member States and between Member States and third countries shall be prohibited.

2   ... all restrictions on payments between Member States and between Member States and third countries shall be prohibited.

Liberalisation involves the removal of restrictions on the underlying transaction, for example, exchange control restrictions on the transfer of investment funds *into*, and profits such as dividends *out* of, the host Member State. Other obstacles, amenable to harmonisation measures, include differing national tax laws and stock exchange rules.

Capital movements have an immediate bearing on government short term economic and budgetary policy and therefore Community action in this area is, as seen, closely linked to the further progress of the process of positive integration towards full economic and monetary union, including the introduction of a single currency. The links between capital movements and the provision of financial services by banks and insurance companies are also close. Developments in all these fields leads to the concept of a European Financial Area.

Reference was made earlier to a fifth freedom, *the free movement of payments*, now found in Articles 56(2), above, and 105(2): see also Cases 286/82 and 26/83 *Luisi and Carbone* concerning payments for travel as a tourist and for medical treatment in another Member State. The EEC Treaty originally provided that:

Each Member State undertakes to authorise, in the currency of the Member State in which the creditor or the beneficiary resides, any payments connected with the movement of goods, services or capital, and any transfers of capital or earnings, to the extent that the movement of goods, services, capital and persons between Member States has been liberalised pursuant to this Treaty.

In the past, *exchange controls* operated by national governments proved a more effective instrument for maintaining protectionist policies than any other restrictive measure. Freedom of payments allows goods to be paid for (prior to the full operation of a single currency) in the seller's currency and similarly allows the migrant worker to transfer earnings home.

Finally, it is important to understand that Member States' obligations regarding free movement are *not absolute*. Derogations or escape clauses are to be found in the Treaty itself with respect to all aspects of free movement. Some of these will be examined in detail at the appropriate point. Examples include:

Article 30 (formerly 36)

The provisions of Articles 28 and 29 shall not preclude prohibitions or restrictions on imports, exports or goods in transit justified on grounds of public morality, public policy or public security; the protection of health and life of humans, animals or plants; the protection of national treasures possessing artistic, historic or archaeological value; or the protection of industrial and commercial property ...

and:

Article 39(3) (formerly 48(3))

[Freedom of movement for workers] shall entail the right, subject to limitations justified on grounds of public policy, public security or public health:

(a) to accept offers of employment actually made;

(b) to move freely within the territory of Member States for this purpose;

(c) to stay in a Member State for the purpose of employment ...

The case law of the Court of Justice shows that the effect of such provisions is, as seen at the beginning of this chapter, to allow national rules to override the Community's fundamental free movement principle on the basis of justified matters of general public concern in the area concerned. Such limitation on freedom of movement can nevertheless be removed by the adoption of Directives establishing Community-wide rules which restore free movement while dealing with the concern or risk, for example, to health, previously encountered.

REFERENCES AND FURTHER READING

Bieber, R *et al* (eds), *1992: One European Market?*, 1988.

Brearley, M and Quigley, C, *Completing the Internal Market of the European Community*, 1989.

EC Commission, 'Implementation of the legal acts required to build the Single Market', COM (90) 473 final, October 1990.

Forwood, N and Clough, M, 'The Single European Act and free movement' (1986) EL Rev 383.

Gormley, LW (ed), *Kapteyn and VerLoren van Themaat's Introduction to the Law of the European Communities*, 1998, Chapter 7(1), etc.

Legal Issues of European Integration, Special Issue on the Internal Market (Goods, Persons, Institutional Aspects, etc) 1989/1.

Lintner, V and Mazey, S, *The European Community: Economic and Political Aspects*, 1991, Chapters 3 and 4.

Owen, R and Dynes, M, *The Times Guide to 1992*, 1989.

Pelkmans, J and Winters, A, *Europe's Domestic Market*, 1988.

Pinder, J, 'The Single Market: a step towards European Union', in Lodge, J (ed), *The EC and the Challenge of the Future*, 1989 (now 1993).

Pinder, J, *European Community: The Building of a Union*, 1998, Chapter 4.

Taylor, P, 'The new dynamics of EC integration in the 1980s', in Lodge, J (ed), *The EC and the Challenge of the Future*, 1989 (now 1993).

Weatherill, S, *Cases and Materials on EC Law*, 2000, Chapter 5.

Weiler, J, 'The constitution of the common market place', in Craig and De Búrca, *The Evolution of EU Law*, 1999.

CHAPTER 12

FREE MOVEMENT OF GOODS

I have lost no opportunity in or out of Parliament of disputing the path of those who seek to reverse the free trade basis of our commercial system and to erect in one form or another, under one pretext or another, a preferential, retaliatory, or protective tariff [Winston Churchill, 1908].

A NOTE ON THE ECONOMICS OF INTERNATIONAL TRADE

It has been generally accepted by economists that an international free trade policy is desirable to optimise world output and income levels in the long run. Free trade is the condition in which the flow of goods (and services) in international exchange is neither restricted nor encouraged by direct government intervention.

In an ideal world, on the basis of the economic law of comparative advantage, it is economically beneficial for countries to specialise in producing and exporting goods in the production of which their resource endowments make them relatively more efficient, and to import from other countries the goods which they are relatively less efficient in producing. However, where governments are involved in regulating overseas trade, this picture is distorted. The most visible means of affecting the distribution and levels of international trade are import duties, import quotas, export subsidies and currency exchange controls.

The purpose of import restrictions is to divert expenditure away from foreign-produced goods in favour of domestic products. Such controls can correct a balance of international payments problem. They may also be imposed in order to protect the market of a domestic industry, which may be less efficient and therefore less competitive. Where, as with tariffs (customs duties) and taxes, the controls increase the price of imported goods, such restrictions also have a revenue-raising purpose.

In the 19th century, the prevailing concept of economic liberalism and the doctrine of *laissez-faire* promoted the strongest support for a free trade policy. However, the first major breaks in this policy came early in the 20th century:

There is much truth in the claim that war is the ultimate experience of, and justification for, protection; and the First World War left a heavy legacy of increased protection. Not only did protection of industrial products increase – even Britain made a major breach in its traditional policy of free trade, largely on the grounds of defence considerations – but the European countries took steps to protect their farmers against the competition of cheap grains from North and South America, Australia, and South Africa [Johnson, *The World Economy at the Crossroads*, 1965].

In the inter-war period, economic nationalism reached a peak and free trade was abandoned for protectionism. In line with its new 'isolationalist' policy, the US Congress enacted the Hawley-Smoot Tariff Act in 1930. Originally designed to help farmers suffering from declining agricultural prices, the scope of the Act was later widened to include industrial products. The Act led to massive resentment and retaliation throughout the world at a time following the Wall Street stock market crash of 1929: 'Italy objected to duties on hats and bonnets of straw, wool-felt hats, and olive oil; Spain reacted sharply to increases on cork and onions': Kindelberger.

Following the Great Crash – and the Great Depression – came a period of severe monetary disorganisation from which countries sought to rescue themselves at each other's expense by resorting to greatly increased protection, combined with preferential trading arrangements (for example, the British Imperial Preference and Sterling Bloc systems) and bilateral agreements. The result was an enormous contraction of the volume and a choking-up of the channels of international trade.

After the Second World War, the major economic powers, and the USA in particular, sought to establish a new world economic order. The International Monetary Fund was devised to deal with monetary matters. The General Agreement on Tariffs and Trade (GATT) was established in Geneva in 1947 and, through the medium of GATT negotiating 'Rounds', it remained the focal point of international trade bargaining until it became part of the World Trade Organization (WTO) in 1995.

As Swann explains:

> GATT gave rise to rules concerning international trade matters. Those required that tariff bargaining should be based on reciprocity and should not give rise to discrimination. The latter was particularly important in the context of EEC trade policy. It implied that if a country offered to cut its import duties on goods coming from country A, then it should also apply that treatment to all other countries – this is called most-favoured-nation treatment. The reader may wonder how the Community was able to form a customs union and still stay within GATT rules. Obviously, a customs union is discriminatory – import duties on partner goods are eliminated but are maintained on goods coming from third countries. The answer to that question is quite simple, GATT provided an exception in the case of customs unions (and free trade areas). Various rules were devised, including the requirement that in the case of a customs union the CET (Common External Tariff) should on the whole be no higher than the general incidence of duties which the parties had imposed prior to the union. The EEC drew attention to the fact that the CET was based on the arithmetic average of the previous national duties and that therefore it had not breached GATT rules.

It is important, therefore, that initially it is appreciated that the liberalisation of trade *within* the Common Market (that is, the establishment and maintenance of the free movement of goods on a *regional* basis) must be seen in the wider context of GATT efforts since the end of the Second World War to liberalise trade on a *global* basis. Article 18 of the original Treaty of Rome (in the section on the setting up of the customs union's common customs or external tariff wall vis à vis third countries' products) acknowledged this point and indicated that customs duties on goods entering the Community would be reduced as a result of the Community's participation in GATT negotiating Rounds. This Treaty Article has since been repealed by the ToA but remains of significance for historical reasons:

Article 18 EEC

> The Member States declare their readiness to contribute to the development of international trade and the lowering of barriers to trade by entering into agreements designed, on a basis of reciprocity and mutual advantage, to reduce customs duties below the general level of which they could avail themselves as a result of the establishment of a customs union between them.

In Title IX of the Treaty on Common Commercial Policy, Article 110 (now 131) remains:

Article 131 EC

By establishing a customs union between themselves, Member States aim to contribute, in the common interest, to the harmonious development of world trade, the progressive abolition of restrictions on international trade and the lowering of customs barriers ...

FREE MOVEMENT OF GOODS IN THE COMMON MARKET

Economic integration through competitive interpenetration of national markets depends in large part on the fundamental Community law principle of the free movement of goods. Trade liberalisation within the Community involves the removal of a variety of obstacles or barriers to inter-Member State trade. Although obstacles may be created by business undertakings (see, in particular, Chapters 15 and 16 on competition law), they are, as has already been seen, generally put in place by States themselves through the medium of *national law*.

The EEC Treaty recognised the following main obstacles to intra-Community trade:

(a) Customs duties (tariffs) on imports (and exports): Article 3(a) (now 3(1)(a)) and Articles 9 and 12 (now 23 and 25).

(b) Charges having an equivalent effect to customs duties: Article 3(a) (now 3(1)(a)) and Articles 9 and 12 (now 23 and 25).

(c) Discriminatory internal taxation of imports: Article 95 (now 90).

(d) Quantitative restrictions (bans and quotas) on imports (and exports): Article 3(a) (now 3(1)(a)) and Articles 30 and 34 (now 28 and 29).

(e) Measures having an equivalent effect to quantitative restrictions: Article 3(a) (now 3(1)(a)) and Articles 30, 34 and 100a (now 28, 29 and 95).

(f) State monopolies of a commercial character: Article 37 (now 31).

(g) State aids to national industries or undertakings: Articles 92–94 (now 87–89).

Note also Member States' public authorities' procurement policies which favour national suppliers: they are now covered by harmonisation Directives, the purpose of which is to open up the procedures for awards of public contracts (for example, for public works and public supply of goods) to competition from all undertakings situated in the Community.

None of the above Treaty provisions (other than Article 100a (now 95)) was significantly affected by the TEU or the ToA. We will concentrate on the first five of these obstacles to free movement.

In the period 1958 to 1986, considerable progress was made, particularly by the Commission and the Court of Justice, in removing, in whole or in part, customs duties (and charges), quantitative restrictions (QRs) and equivalent measures (MEEQRs, such as different national rules and standards relating to goods) that had hindered inter-Member State trade. This was so despite successive enlargements of the Community.

However, as a result of fears of renewed protectionism and the need for a new impetus, the Internal Market programme was launched by the Single European Act of

1986. A little earlier, the Commission's White Paper of 1985 on the *Completion of the Internal Market* identified three sets of barriers which still significantly hindered the free movement of goods (and, in certain respects, persons, services and capital also):

(a) physical barriers;

(b) fiscal barriers;

(c) technical barriers.

Although this categorisation of barriers might not immediately relate to that found in the Treaty (see above), the following extract explains the position:

> ... the categorisation by the EC of these three types of barrier is somewhat arbitrary. Physical barriers are concerned with frontier controls on the movement of goods and persons. Fiscal barriers consist of all impediments and substantial distortions among member states that emanate from differences in the commodity base as well as in the rates of VAT and the duties on excises ... All remaining impediments fall into the category of technical barriers. Therefore, this category comprises not only barriers arising from absence of technical harmonisation and public procurement procedures, but also institutional impediments on the free movement of people, capital and financial services, including transport and data transmission ... [El-Agraa (ed), *Economics of the European Community*].

As regards the free movement of goods, therefore, the Commission's Internal Market programme focused on the continuing need to remove costly frontier controls (physical barriers), to harmonise VAT and other forms of indirect taxes on goods (fiscal barriers), and to eliminate or harmonise those differing national rules and standards relating to goods (MEEQRs) that still proliferated in inter-Member State trade (technical barriers). Discriminatory public procurement procedures and problems relating to national patents and trade marks were also targeted.

However, before examining those aspects of the post-1986 programme of Community legislation which were designed to complete the Internal Market in relation to the free movement of goods, it is clearly necessary to look at problems posed and progress made in the earlier period. It will be seen that the attack on trade barriers is essentially two-pronged: *elimination* as a result of litigation in the Court of Justice or national courts and *harmonisation* of Member States' differing rules by means of Community legislation (Council Directives). An important link between the two attacks is to be found in the *Cassis de Dijon* decision, which will be examined in due course.

A number of further introductory points must be made. First, subject to certain exceptions, the rules laid down for the establishment of the Common Market, and hence the rules relating to the free movement of goods, apply to agricultural products as well as industrial goods: Article 38 (now 32).

Secondly, the free movement rules apply both to goods which originate in a Member State and to those which come from a third country and are in free circulation in a Member State. Such goods are in free circulation when they have crossed the Common Customs Tariff wall with all import formalities complied with and duties or charges paid: Article 24 (formerly10).

Thirdly, although the free movement provisions of the Treaty are addressed to the Member States, the more important Articles are *directly effective* and may be invoked by individuals (and undertakings) in their national courts, for example, Article 12 (now 25) in *Van Gend en Loos* (see also the list in Collins, *European Community Law in the United Kingdom*, Chapter 2).

Finally, the case law of the Court of Justice clearly demonstrates that the Court's primary aim is to establish the *effect* (not the purpose) of a national rule on the fundamental concept of the unity of the market. If it is in breach of the free movement rules, the national measure will be struck down, unless it comes within one of the restrictively interpreted derogations or exceptions provided for in the Treaty. For example, Article 30 (formerly 36) allows Member States to prohibit imports on grounds of the protection of the life and health of humans. However, even where derogation has been allowed on this or other meritorious grounds, the creation of a single market demands that to the extent that they differ from Member State to Member State, such national rules (regarding, for example, foodstuffs) be *harmonised* at Community level to ensure that, whilst the *objective* of the national rules is maintained, so is the principle of free movement.

The creation of a single market encompassing the 15 (soon 25) Member States and, under the Agreement on the European Economic Area, a further four EFTA countries, results in the formation of a regional trading bloc capable of competing on world markets with the USA and Japan.

INTERNAL FISCAL BARRIERS: CUSTOMS DUTIES AND CHARGES

Article 9(1) (now 23(1)) of the Treaty established the Community's customs union (an integral part of the Common Market):

> The Community shall be based upon a customs union which shall cover all trade in goods and which shall involve the prohibition between Member States of customs duties on imports and exports and of all charges having equivalent effect, and the adoption of a common customs tariff in their relations with third countries.

When in 1958 the Treaty came into effect for 'the Six', Article 12 (now re-worded in Article 25) operated as a 'standstill' provision regarding all customs duties and charges (see Case 26/62 *Van Gend en Loos* in Chapter 4) and Articles 13–17 (now repealed) provided either specific timetables for their progressive elimination or powers whereby the Commission could establish such a timetable. As regards duties, Member States were allowed to 'accelerate' their abolition and it was announced in mid-1968 that all duties had been abolished – 18 months ahead of schedule (the end of a 12 year transitional period):

> The customs union continued to fulfil high expectations through the 1960s. Trade among the Community's Member States grew twice as fast as trade in the wider international economy, quadrupling in the first decade after the Community was established in 1958 ... There was no way of knowing how much of this growth was due to the creation of the customs union ... but the Community had evidently provided a framework in which it had been possible [Pinder, *European Community: The Building of a Union*].

When the UK, Ireland and Denmark joined the Community in 1973, they were allowed a five year period in which to dismantle their various forms of protection so as to comply with the free movement rules. Greece, joining in 1981, was given a similar period to adapt and Spain and Portugal, which became full members in 1986, were allowed seven years. Subject to certain specific derogations and transitional measures (for example, as regards agricultural products), Sweden, Finland and Austria (EEA members and former EFTA States) were fully integrated into the Community's customs union and Internal Market from the 1995 date of accession.

Inter-Member State trade can now be said to be largely free, at least of customs duties (cases still arise), and it is more than possible that some of the less visible charges (see below) remain.

The nature and purpose of the Treaty provisions on the elimination (now 'prohibition': see Article 3(1)(a)) of customs duties and charges were explained by the Court of Justice in Cases 2 and 3/69 *Social Fund for Diamond Workers*:

> It was submitted that a small levy imposed under Belgian law on imported diamonds could not be in breach of Articles 9 and 12 (now 23 and 25) because (a) it had no protectionist purpose as Belgium did not produce diamonds; and (b) the levy's purpose was to provide social security benefits for Belgian diamond workers. The Court explained that:

>> In prohibiting the imposition of customs duties, the Treaty does not distinguish between goods according to whether or not they enter into competition with the products of the importing country. Thus, the purpose of the abolition of customs barriers is not merely to eliminate their protective nature, as the Treaty sought on the contrary to give general scope and effect to the rule on elimination of customs duties and charges having equivalent effect in order to ensure the free movement of goods. It follows from the system as a whole and from the general and absolute nature of the prohibition of any customs duty applicable to goods moving between Member States that customs duties are prohibited independently of any consideration of the purpose for which they were introduced and the destination of the revenue obtained therefrom. The justification for this prohibition is based on the fact that any pecuniary charge – however small – imposed on goods by reason of the fact that they cross a frontier constitutes an obstacle to the movement of such goods.

In Cases 2 and 3/62 *Commission v Luxembourg and Belgium (Gingerbread)*, charges were defined by the Court of Justice as:

> ... duties whatever their description or technique, imposed unilaterally, which apply specifically to a product imported by a Member State but not to a similar national product and which by altering the price, have the same effect upon the free movement of goods as a customs duty.

In this case, the Court disallowed a 'tax' levied by the two Member States on imported gingerbread, the object of which was to offset the competitive disadvantage of domestic gingerbread, the price of which was higher due to the incidence of a national tax on rye, an ingredient of gingerbread.

The nature of a charge having equivalent effect to a customs duty was further elaborated by the Court in Case 24/68 *Commission v Italy (Re Statistical Levy)*, a case in which a levy was imposed on goods *exported* to other Member States in order to fund the compilation of statistical data relating to trade patterns:

... any pecuniary charge, however small and whatever its designation and mode of application, which is imposed unilaterally on domestic or foreign goods by reason of the fact that they cross a frontier and which is not a customs duty in the strict sense ... even if it is not imposed for the benefit of the State, is not discriminatory or protective in effect and if the product on which the charge is imposed is not in competition with any domestic product.

The charge in this case was found to be in breach of Article 16 relating to exports (see now Article 25). The Italian government had argued that the disputed charge constituted the 'consideration for a service rendered' for the benefit of traders. It was, it was claimed, part of a commercial transaction and could not be designated as a charge having equivalent effect to a customs duty. The Court accepted that a fee might be levied as consideration for a *specific benefit* actually conferred on the importer. However, whatever advantages traders gained from the statistics, they were so general and so difficult to assess (applying to the economy as a whole) that, in the Court's view, the argument failed.

It is an argument which has similarly failed in respect of charges or fees imposed for compulsory national veterinary and public health inspections carried out on imported products at frontiers: Case 87/75 *Bresciani* (raw cowhides) and Case 39/73 *Rewe-Zentralfinanz* (plant health inspection on imported apples). In these cases, the Court held that the inspections were not for the specific benefit of the traders themselves but were rendered for the benefit of the public as a whole. Thus, in *Bresciani*, the Court stated that the cost of such inspections (if still allowable) must be met by the general public (that is, the importing State) which, as a whole, benefits from the free movement of goods.

It should therefore also be appreciated that such inspections may themselves be contrary to the free movement rules. If, by means of a harmonisation Directive, a common system of health controls and standards to be applied *away from* frontiers (usually in the exporting State) has been established, then further unilateral requirements imposed by the importing State may amount to a discriminatory *technical* barrier to trade in the form of a measure having an equivalent effect to a quantitative restriction (MEEQR): see Case 4/75 *Rewe-Zentralfinanz (San José Scale)*, a companion to the charges case above. In this case, however, no comprehensive Community system of inspections existed and the national inspections were *justified* on public health grounds under Article 36 (now 30). A charge cannot be justified in this way: the *customs union* Treaty rules allow for no derogation.

In the context of the 'fee for services' argument, the Court has held that 'a charge may escape prohibition as a charge having equivalent effect if the charge in question is the consideration for a service actually rendered to the importer and is of an amount commensurate with that service', for example, temporary storage facilities requested by a trader: see Case 132/82 *Commission v Belgium*.

Importing Member States are also permitted to recoup from traders the cost of compliance with mandatory *Community* measures, such as a harmonised system of health inspections of live animals, as required by a Commission Directive in Case 18/87 *Commission v Germany (Re Animals Inspection Service)*. Such a fee is not considered by the Court to be a charge having equivalent effect to a customs duty so long as it does not exceed the actual cost of the inspection. Arguably, such costs should not be borne by the trader (and in all probability therefore the consumer) but by the Community itself.

DISCRIMINATORY INTERNAL TAXATION (ARTICLE 90 (FORMERLY 95))

Article 90

No Member State shall impose, directly or indirectly, on the products of other Member States any internal taxation of any kind in excess of that imposed directly or indirectly on similar domestic products ...

Furthermore, no Member State shall impose on the products of other Member States any internal taxation of such a nature as to afford indirect protection to other products.

A Member State's 'internal taxation' comprises financial charges levied within a general system applying systematically to both domestic and imported products according to the same objective criteria. Such taxation must not discriminate against imported products where those products are 'similar' to domestic products, that is, the level of tax on imports must not exceed that on directly comparable domestic products: Article 90(1). Neither must internal taxation be applied to imported products in order to protect the market position of a domestic product which, while not the same or similar, nevertheless competes in the same market: Article 90(2). In Case 170/78 *Commission v UK (Re Excise Duties on Wine)*, a competitive relationship was established between beer and more highly taxed imported wines of the cheaper variety. A case of *indirect* protection was established by the Court and as a result the relative tax burden on wine was reduced by the UK by increasing the tax rates on beer and reducing those on wine.

The purpose of Article 90 (formerly 95) (which is directly effective) was explained by the Court of Justice in Case 171/78 *Commission v Denmark*:

The above mentioned provisions supplement, within the system of the Treaty, the provisions on the abolition of customs duties and charges having equivalent effect. Their aim is to ensure free movement of goods between the Member States in normal conditions of competition by the elimination of all forms of protection which result from the application of internal taxation which discriminates against products from other Member States. As the Commission has correctly stated, Article 95 must guarantee the complete neutrality of internal taxation as regards competition between domestic products and imported products.

It follows that a charge on imported goods falls *either* under Articles 23–25 (formerly 9–17) or Article 90 (formerly 95). The two regimes are mutually exclusive and cannot be applied at the same time to the same situation. Articles 23–25 prohibit charges having equivalent effect to a customs duty which are imposed specifically on imported products by reason of their crossing a frontier (domestic products bearing no such charge), whereas Article 90 permits the taxation of imported products provided similar, or otherwise competing, domestic products bear the same taxes. The tax system must have what is called 'origin neutrality'. The purpose of Article 90 is to prevent the Member States from circumventing the customs union rules by the imposition of discriminatory internal taxation.

Under Article 90(1) covering 'similar' domestic and imported products, it is possible to make direct comparisons (but see *Humblot* below) and the relevant rates of tax may at first sight appear non-discriminatory. However, discrimination may be revealed (to the detriment of imported goods) because the *basis of imposition* of the taxes differs. The same rate must be applied to both products, be imposed at the same *marketing* stage and the chargeable event giving rise to the tax must be the same. The rules for levying and collecting the tax must be non-discriminatory and clear proof of a *specific link* between the tax and a refund to *domestic* producers can lead to a breach of Article 90.

In Case 132/78 *Denkavit v France*, it was argued that a charge on imported meat products (lard, etc) was equivalent to a similar charge on meat slaughtered in France. The Court held that the charge was of equivalent effect to a customs duty because (a) it was charged on imported goods by virtue of their crossing a frontier; (b) it was charged at a different stage of production and on the basis of a different chargeable event; and (c) no account had been taken of fiscal charges imposed on the imported products in the Member State of origin.

Much of the case law focuses on the question of whether the domestic and imported products are sufficiently similar or compete with each other so as to bring Article 95(1) or (2) (now 90(1) or (2)) into play. All Member States tax the various types of alcoholic drinks (frequently in a complicated way) for both social and revenue-raising purposes. There is an obvious tendency to favour domestic products. A higher tax on the imported products is usually defended on the basis that they are not 'similar' to the domestically produced drinks. Case 168/78 *Commission v France (Re Taxation of Spirits)* involved French legislation which imposed a higher tax on grain based spirits (imported whisky and gin, etc) than on wine or fruit based spirits (home-produced brandy, armagnac and calvados). The Court held that 'similar' must be interpreted widely from the point of view of the consumer. The home-produced and imported products were 'in at least partial competition', the French legislation was discriminatory and protectionist, and it was contrary to Article 95 'taken as a whole'. In the *UK Excise Duty on Wine* case above, the issue, as seen, centred not on similarity but on competitiveness and Article 95(2).

The issue was one of indirect discrimination under Article 95(1) in Case 112/84 *Humblot v Directeur des Services Fiscaux*, in which the French government, using 'objective' criteria, taxed cars over a certain power rating more heavily than those below it. Below a 16 CV power rating, annual car tax increased in a graduated way in proportion to the car's power up to a maximum of 1,100 francs. For cars rated above 16 CV, a flat rate of 5,000 francs was imposed. H was charged this amount on his imported 36 CV car but, on discovering that no French-produced car was rated above 16 CV, he claimed the tax was in breach of Article 95. Following an Article 177 (now 234) reference, the Court stated that:

> Article 95 of the EEC Treaty prohibits the charging on cars exceeding a given power rating for tax purposes of a special fixed tax the amount of which is several times the highest amount of the progressive tax payable on cars of less than the said power rating for tax purposes, where the only cars subject to the special tax are imported, in particular from other Member States.

The basis of this ruling, in which the Court ignored the argument that 'standard and luxury models were dissimilar', was that: '... the special tax reduces the amount of competition to which cars of domestic manufacture are subject and hence is contrary to the principle of neutrality with which domestic taxation must comply.' However, as Weatherill and Beaumont (*EC Law*) have pointed out:

If a state is able to show that it taxes particular types of cars at punitively high rates in order to encourage the use of more environmentally friendly models, which are given substantial tax concessions, then the Court would be prepared to hear submissions that the State's system is lawful even if it were shown that most of the models subjected to higher rates were imported ... it is not unlawful to discriminate according to the capacity to pollute.

In this connection, see Case C-132/88 *Commission v Greece* on the permitted use of tax policy to achieve social ends.

Harmonisation of Indirect Taxation

Of particular significance among the internal taxation systems of the Member States, at least as regards *indirect* taxation applied to goods and services, is value added tax (VAT). The essential feature of this tax is that a supplier of goods or services is liable for tax assessed on the value of the product when he disposes of it, and he may set off against this liability the tax paid on the value of the product when he acquired it, in other words the net liability is to pay tax on the added value.

On the basis of Article 99 (now 93) of the Treaty, much work has been done over the years to harmonise various aspects of indirect taxation and, in particular, to develop a Community system of VAT. This involves harmonisation of the base or scope of the tax (some countries allow zero rating for some goods), harmonisation of the number of rates and harmonisation of the *actual rates*. It would now appear to be agreed that identical rates throughout the Member States are not necessary, and that if they are brought sufficiently close together, this will prevent any significant distortion of trade and competition.

Council Decisions on the adoption of provisions for the harmonisation (in practice, approximation or standardisation) of VAT require unanimity: see Articles 93 and 95(2) (formerly 100a(2)). Since 1993, a standard rate not lower than 15 per cent has been agreed: a form of what is known as 'minimum harmonisation'. The standard rate in the UK is 17.5 per cent (France 20.6 per cent, Germany 15 per cent, etc) with allowable zero rating for certain goods including books, passenger transport and children's clothing.

This was a result which, politically, in the absence of a single currency, was as far as the Community could apparently go towards the elimination, through the harmonisation process, of a fiscal barrier to the free movement of goods (and services) between Member States, which reduces or eliminates elaborate and costly bureaucratic procedures at frontiers regarding the collection of VAT (physical barriers). Similar work is proceeding in relation to *excise duties* and in 1991, the Member States accepted the principle of binding minimum excise rates on petrol, tobacco and alcohol.

INTERNAL TECHNICAL BARRIERS: QUANTITATIVE RESTRICTIONS AND MEASURES HAVING EQUIVALENT EFFECT

The creation of an integrated Community Common (or Internal) Market for goods in which free movement has been secured would be impossible purely on the basis of the customs union rules on the elimination and prohibition of *tariff barriers*, that is, nationally imposed duties and charges. The drafters of the Treaty therefore had to launch a similar attack on those other *non-tariff barriers* to inter-Member State trade, often of a discriminatory nature, which fragment markets for goods along national lines. These barriers or restrictions can take the form of outright prohibitions or quota limitations on imports or exports (quantitative restrictions or QRs) or measures which are not QRs *per se* but which have the same or equivalent effect (MEEQRs).

As seen, the latter are usually of a *technical* nature, such as national requirements regarding the composition of goods, the use of additives, etc, or they may have a *physical* element in that the need for inspections of imported goods at the border can create undue or expensive delays. As will be seen, these measures may be discriminatory or non-discriminatory (in the latter case, home-produced goods having to comply with the same requirements) but, as Court of Justice case law demonstrates, any such measure is to be struck down if it has a *restrictive effect* on inter-Member State trade and cannot be justified on grounds of general public interest.

As with customs duties and charges, the Treaty basis for the Community's attack on these non-tariff barriers is Article 3(1)(a). The more detailed rules are to be found in Articles 28–30 (formerly 30–36):

Article 28 (formerly 30)

Quantitative restrictions on imports and all measures having equivalent effect shall be prohibited between Member States.

Article 29 (formerly 34) makes similar provision as regards exports. The scheme laid down by the EEC Treaty broadly corresponded to that applied to customs duties and charges: 'standstill' provisions and gradual elimination by the end of the 12 year transitional period at the latest (that is, by the end of 1969 – a target, certainly as regards measures having equivalent effect, which was not achieved). However, as seen in Chapter 11, Article 30 (formerly 36) allows Member States to *derogate* from the free movement rules in Articles 28 and 29 within strictly defined limits for the purpose of protecting certain listed interests of general public importance, for example, public health. However, the history of the Court's case law in this area and of Community harmonisation legislation shows that those national rules that were justified under Article 36 were nevertheless not to be allowed to remain as obstacles to the free movement of goods between Member States. By the process of harmonisation, the interests they protected were to be secured – but on the basis of *common* Community standards which the goods in question of all Member States must meet. Clearly, as the scope of harmonisation increased to cover more and more products, the less Member States were able to rely on Article 36 (and now on Article 30): see, for example, Case C-5/94 *Hedley Lomas* in Chapter 20.

There is no definition of a quantitative restriction (QR) in the form of a quota in the Treaty, but it was defined by Ehlermann in 1972 as follows:

Any governmental measure adopted in a general form and directed to individuals [normally undertakings] which provides that a certain amount of goods, defined either by quantity or value, may be imported or exported during a specific period of time.

The prohibition on QRs covers measures which amount to a partial or total (zero quota) restraint on imports or exports: see Case 34/79 *R v Henn and Darby*, below.

Quantitative restrictions on imports (total or partial) can clearly prove more effective as protectionist measures than customs duties. Partial restraints reduce the supply of imported goods, raise their price, and so reduce or eliminate any competitive advantage they may have over domestic products. However, in terms of free movement within the Community, national quota systems dating from the years before or during the Second World War had ceased to be a major problem by the time the Community was established in 1958, due to measures of liberalisation achieved in the more immediate post-war years within the framework of GATT and the Organisation for European Economic Co-operation (OEEC).

Nevertheless, cases do still arise involving specific import bans which Member States seek to justify under Article 36 (now 30). For example, in Case 40/82 *Commission v UK (Re Imports of Poultry Meat)*, a UK policy adopted in 1981 imposed a prohibition on imports of poultry and eggs from all other Member States except Denmark and Ireland. This policy was allegedly designed to prevent the spread of 'Newcastle disease' (a contagious disease affecting poultry) and was defended on the basis of the public health grounds for derogation under Article 36 (now 30), below. In Article 169 (now 226) proceedings, the Court of Justice found that the UK measure did not form part of a *seriously considered health policy*; it operated as a disguised restriction on trade and was contrary to Article 30 (now 28).

Similarly, at the height of concern in the UK in late 1989 about 'mad cow disease' (BSE), West Germany banned UK beef products on the grounds that they were a danger to human health and life on the basis of Article 36 (now 30). The ban was eventually lifted and no legal action was taken. Arguments against such a ban included the existence at Community level of a comprehensive, harmonised health safety system operating within exporting States.

National measures which are contrary to Article 28 (formerly 30), in that they amount to measures having an equivalent effect to quantitative restrictions (MEEQRs), are many and various. They frequently operate in a subtle and disguised way with the purpose of protecting home produced products from competing imports. They operate to isolate national markets, contrary to the concept of a single market, and such fragmentation has the effect of increasing the costs (and prices) of producers, who are required to meet the differing requirements of the various Member States.

As stated, such measures may or may not discriminate against imported goods but, for the Court of Justice, the prime mark of an MEEQR is its *restrictive effect* on inter-Member State trade.

Article 2 of the Commission's explanatory Directive 70/50 on the abolition of MEEQRs on imports states that:

1   This Directive covers measures, *other than those applicable equally to domestic or imported products*, which hinder imports which could otherwise take place, including measures which make importation more difficult or costly than the disposal of domestic products [emphasis added].

2   In particular, it covers measures which make imports or the disposal, at any marketing stage, of imported products subject to a condition – other than a formality – which is required in respect of imported products only, or a condition differing from that required for domestic products and more difficult to satisfy. Equally, it covers, in particular, measures which favour domestic products or grant them a preference, other than an aid ...

FREE MOVEMENT OF GOODS
with special reference to Articles 28–30*

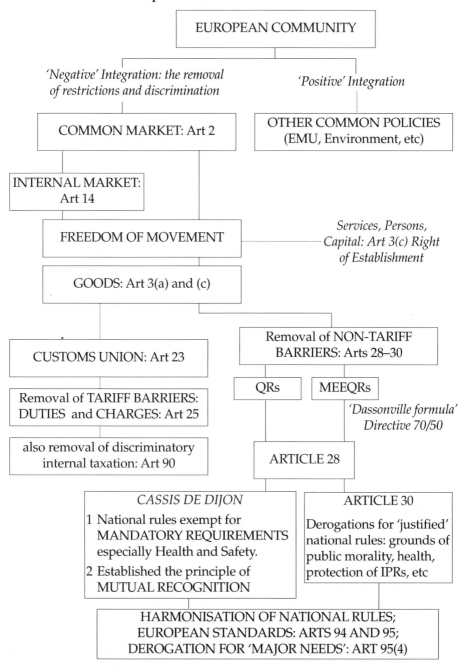

EUROPEAN COMMUNITY

'Negative' Integration: the removal of restrictions and discrimination

'Positive' Integration

COMMON MARKET: Art 2

OTHER COMMON POLICIES (EMU, Environment, etc)

INTERNAL MARKET: Art 14

FREEDOM OF MOVEMENT

Services, Persons, Capital: Art 3(c) Right of Establishment

GOODS: Art 3(a) and (c)

CUSTOMS UNION: Art 23

Removal of NON-TARIFF BARRIERS: Arts 28–30

QRs

MEEQRs

'Dassonville formula' Directive 70/50

Removal of TARIFF BARRIERS: DUTIES and CHARGES: Art 25

also removal of discriminatory internal taxation: Art 90

ARTICLE 28

CASSIS DE DIJON

1 National rules exempt for MANDATORY REQUIREMENTS especially Health and Safety.

2 Established the principle of MUTUAL RECOGNITION

ARTICLE 30

Derogations for 'justified' national rules: grounds of public morality, health, protection of IPRs, etc

HARMONISATION OF NATIONAL RULES; EUROPEAN STANDARDS: ARTS 94 AND 95; DEROGATION FOR 'MAJOR NEEDS': ART 95(4)

---

*   Post-Amsterdam EC Treaty numbers.

Article 2(3)(a)–(s) contains a long, non-exhaustive list of such measures, which it is not necessary to refer to here.

The Directive provides clear indications of the Commission's view of Article 28 (formerly 30) as applied to MEEQRs. Article 2 covers national measures which apply only to imports in the sense that a *distinction* is made between home-produced and imported goods to the detriment of the latter. MEEQRs are therefore measures which discriminate against imports and are on the face of it overtly protectionist. They are referred to as '*distinctly applicable*' measures. In respect of such a measure (as with a QR), a derogation from Article 28 under Article 30 (formerly 36) will only be allowed if it can be justified under one of the six heads in Article 30 and it does not constitute a means of *arbitrary* discrimination or a disguised restriction on trade between Member States.

As seen, expressly omitted from Article 2(1) of the Directive are national measures which are 'applicable equally to domestic or imported products' ('*indistinctly applicable*' or '*equally applicable*' measures). These are to be found in Article 3:

> This Directive also covers measures governing the marketing of products which deal, in particular, with shape, size, weight, composition, presentation, identification or putting up and which are *equally applicable to domestic and imported products*, where the restrictive effect of such measures on the free movement of goods exceeds the effects intrinsic to trade rules [emphasis added].
>
> This is the case, in particular, where:
>
> – the restrictive effects on the free movement of goods are out of proportion to their purpose;
> – the same objective can be attained by other means which are less of a hindrance to trade.

The national technical rules and standards in Article 3 which do not draw a distinction between home-produced and imported goods (which are 'equally applicable' to them) relate, as stated, to the *marketing* of goods. Again, *they may have a justifiable purpose* regarding, for example, the protection of public health or environmental protection. If such is the case, measures of this kind will, according to the Directive, only breach Article 28 (30) where their 'restrictive effects on the free movement of goods are out of proportion to their purpose' or where the same objective can be achieved by alternative means less restrictive of trade.

As we have already seen in the case of allowable Article 30 *derogations* from the free movement rules in Article 28 for *distinctly* applicable national measures, where, as here, equally applicable national rules reflecting the public interest (in what are termed 'mandatory requirements' by the Court of Justice) override Article 28, obstacles to free movement will again remain. In both cases, the national rules embodying such obstacles must be harmonised so that common 'European' standards can be set as the criteria for goods from all the Member States, so enabling free movement to prevail.

'Equally applicable' measures, although not discriminatory, are frequently restrictive of trade in their effect. In practice, whereas *domestic* products will meet the technical rules and minimum standards laid down by the national authorities, goods from other Member States, which meet their own national requirements, may well not do so and hence may be excluded from the market of the importing State – subject, as above, to the measure being justifiable and complying with the principle of proportionality. Alternatively, where an equally applicable national measure serves no purpose of public interest but merely acts as a ban on imports, it will be struck down as being in its effect a disguised restriction on inter-Member State trade which partitions the market: see, in particular, the decision of the Court of Justice in Case 120/28 *Cassis de Dijon*, below.

Although, on occasion, the Court has referred to Directive 70/50 (the main purpose of which was to provide guidance on MEEQRs to the Member States), it has laid down its own definition of MEEQRs. In Case 8/74 *Dassonville*, it defined them as:

> All trading rules enacted by Member States which are capable of hindering, directly or indirectly, actually or potentially, intra-Community trade are to be considered as measures having an effect equivalent to quantitative restrictions.

This '*Dassonville* formula' does not make discrimination a condition of prohibition and the phrase 'rules enacted by Member States' excludes the activities of undertakings and private individuals acting independently without backing from the State: see Case 249/81 *Commission v Ireland*, below. It should also be recalled that, although Article 28 is addressed to Member States, it is directly effective. Thus, the cases which follow cover both Article 169 (now 226) enforcement actions brought by the Commission against Member States and Article 177 (now 234) references arising out of actions brought by traders against a variety of public authorities in national courts. They are merely a sample of the several hundred that have already been decided.

DISTINCTLY APPLICABLE MEASURES (AS IN ARTICLE 2(1) AND (2) OF DIRECTIVE 70/50)

(1) *Conditions imposed on imports but not on similar domestic products and differing conditions which hinder imports*

Case 4/75 *Rewe-Zentralfinanz (San José Scale)*

Stringent plant health inspections (obstacles of a physical and technical nature) of the kind applied by regional West German authorities only to imported apples were caught by Article 30 (now 28). However, being designed to control a pest called San José Scale, which was not to be found in domestic apples, the inspections were found to be justified on health grounds under Article 36 (now 30). There was a genuine risk of the harmful organism spreading if no such inspections were held on importation. The discrimination against imports was therefore not arbitrary.

The Court stressed the fact that frontier inspections make imports more difficult or costly (although any charges made, as we have seen, are contrary to the customs union rules). Common rules for the control of the pest in exporting States under Directive 69/446 did not disallow protective measures taken by importing States.

A further condition 'differing from that required for domestic products and more difficult to satisfy' (Article 2(2) of the Directive) is illustrated by the following case.

Case 42/82 *Commission v France (Re Italian Table Wines)*

Italian wine imported into France was first tested by the Italian authorities. At French customs, it was delayed for an excessive period of time pending analysis to ensure that it complied with French quality standards. Although the Court conceded that random checks might be made, it found that the French measures, involving systematic testing greatly in excess of that required for domestically produced wine, were discriminatory. A defence plea for derogation on public health grounds under Article 36 (now 30) failed as the French tests did not comply with the principle of proportionality.

(2) *Measures which make imports more difficult by, for example, discriminating between channels of trade*

The following case concerned a measure affecting imports only – Belgian rules concerning certificates of origin for imported Scotch whisky.

Case 8/74 *Procureur du Roi v Dassonville*

D, a Belgian importer of Scotch whisky, was unable to obtain, as required by Belgian law, a British certificate of origin made out in his name from his French suppliers. No such certificate was required under French law. He therefore produced one of his own making and was charged with forgery. He pleaded that the national rule was contrary to Article 30 (now 28).

The Court of Justice held that the Belgian legislation favoured direct importers as distinct from traders importing the authentic product from other Member States where it was already in free circulation.

(3) *Measures which favour domestic products or grant them a preference*

Case 152/78 *Commission v France (Re Advertising of Alcoholic Beverages)*

The French government adopted measures which placed restrictions on the advertising of grain spirits (whisky, gin, vodka, etc) which were almost entirely imported. Restrictions were not placed on the advertising of fruit based spirits such as cognac.

The Court held that national rules on advertising may amount to MEEQRs if there is a possibility that they may affect the marketing prospects of goods imported from other Member States. The advertising restrictions did not directly affect the entry of the imported spirits but their effect on marketing opportunities brought them within the scope of Article 30 (now 28).

Case 249/81 *Commission v Ireland (Re 'Buy Irish' Campaign)*

In 1978, the Irish government introduced a three year 'Buy Irish' campaign to help promote Irish products. The campaign was conducted by a company known as the Irish Goods Council. The aims of the campaign were decided by the Ministry of Industry, which also provided financial support particularly for a massive advertising campaign.

The Court held that the activities in question were in breach of Article 30 (now 28). In the Court's view:

> Such a practice cannot escape the prohibition laid down by Article 30 of the Treaty solely because it is not based on decisions which are binding upon undertakings. Even measures adopted by the government of a Member State which do not have binding effect may be capable of influencing the conduct of traders and consumers in that State and thus of frustrating the aims of the Community as set out in Article 2 and enlarged upon in Article 3 of the Treaty.

A distinction was made by the Court in a case with similar facts. In Case 222/82 *Apple and Pear Development Council v Lewis*, the Court stated that:

> ... a body such as the Development Council, which is set up by the government of a Member State and is financed by a charge imposed on growers, cannot under

Community law enjoy the same freedom as regards the methods of advertising used as that enjoyed by producers themselves or producers' associations of a voluntary character.

In particular, such a body is under a duty not to engage in any advertising intended to discourage the purchase of products of other Member States or to disparage those products in the eyes of consumers. Nor must it advise consumers to purchase domestic products solely by reason of their national origin.

On the other hand, Article 30 [now 28] does not prevent such a body from drawing attention, in its publicity, to the specific qualities of fruit growing in the Member State in question or from organizing campaigns to promote the sale of certain varieties, mentioning their particular properties, even if those varieties are typical of national production.

The use of national measures to favour domestic products is clearly at the heart of the Community's drive to eliminate discrimination within the field of public authorities' procurement policies at national, regional and local level. Competition must be based on quality, not national origin.

Case 43/87 *Commission v Ireland (Re Dundalk Water Supply)*

The contract specification for tender for a public works contract for the Dundalk water supply augmentation scheme included a clause stipulating that pressure pipes must be certified as complying with Irish Standard 188 of 1975 as drafted by the Irish Institute for Industrial Research and Standards. An Irish company, in response to an invitation to tender, submitted a tender providing for the use of pipes manufactured by a Spanish firm. These pipes had not been approved and certified by the IIRS, but they complied with internationally recognised standards and were suitable for the Dundalk scheme.

The absence of IIRS approval was given as the ground for the local authority proceeding no further with the Irish/Spanish bid. The Commission acted on a complaint and the matter came before the Court of Justice.

It was held that Ireland was in breach of Article 30 (now 28) by restricting the contract only to tenderers proposing to use Irish materials, thereby excluding suitable products lawfully made in other Member States complying with different recognised standards. Any pipes might be rejected on quality grounds but the use of Irish Standards alone was in breach of Community law by impeding the importation of pipes into Ireland.

See also Case 72/83 *Campus Oil v Minister for Industry and Energy,* in which a requirement that importers into Ireland purchase a proportion of their oil supplies from a national supplier was held to fall within Article 30 (now 28). This case is discussed in more detail below.

(4) *Failure to apply national measures so making importation difficult*

Article 28 (formerly 30) is addressed to Member States and the measures adopted by them which prohibit or restrict inter-Member State trade. It does not, it would appear, apply to action taken by private parties, although the *'Buy Irish'* case above might seem close to the borderline. The following case presents a new angle on this distinction.

Case C-265/95 *Commission v France (Re Private Protests)*

In this Article 169 (now 226) direct action, the Commission stated that for more than a decade it had received complaints concerning the passivity of the French authorities in the face of violent acts committed by private individuals and by protest movements of French farmers directed against agricultural products from other Member States. Apart from incidents referred to by the Commission involving agricultural products from Belgium, Italy and Denmark, a campaign against Spanish strawberries in the mid-1990s had involved threats against shopping centres and the destruction of goods and their means of transport. This was despite frequent reminders by the Commission to the French government of their obligation under the Treaty with respect to the free movement of goods.

In May 1995, the Commission, in compliance with the terms of Article 169, delivered a reasoned opinion on the matter stating that, by failing to take all necessary and proportionate measures in order to prevent the free movement of fruit and vegetables from being obstructed by the actions of private individuals, France had failed to fulfil its obligations under the common organisations of the markets in agricultural products and Article 30 (now 28), in conjunction with Article 5 (now 10).

In June and July 1995, further acts of violence were committed against consignments of Spanish and Italian fruit and vegetables without the intervention of the French police. The Commission therefore brought the present action before the Court of Justice.

Reasoning from its *Dassonville* formula, the Court stated that as an indispensable instrument for the realisation of a market without internal frontiers, Article 30 does not solely prohibit measures emanating from the State which, in themselves, create restrictions on inter-Member State trade. It also applies where a Member State abstains from adopting the measures required in order to deal with obstacles to the free movement of goods which are not caused by the State. Article 30, when read in conjunction with Article 5, therefore requires the Member States to take all necessary and appropriate measures to ensure that the fundamental freedom is respected on their territory.

It was clear to the Court that, when the incidents complained of occurred, the French police were either not present at the scene, despite warnings of the imminence of demonstrations in certain cases, or did not intervene although in a position to do so.

The conclusion reached was that the French government had manifestly and persistently failed 'to adopt all necessary and proportionate measures in order to prevent the free movement of fruit and vegetables from being obstructed by actions by private individuals'. France had therefore failed to fulfil its obligations under Article 30, in conjunction with Article 5, and under the common organisation of the markets in agricultural products.

See also disturbances by private individuals jeopardising the export of goods in *R v Chief Constable of Sussex ex p International Trader's Ferry Ltd* [1999] 1 All ER 129, HL.

DEROGATION FROM ARTICLES 28 AND 29 (FORMERLY 30 AND 34) UNDER ARTICLE 30 (FORMERLY 36)

Article 30

The provisions of Articles 28 and 29 shall not preclude prohibitions or restrictions on imports, exports or goods in transit justified on grounds of public morality, public policy or public security; the protection of health and life of humans, animals or plants; the protection of national treasures possessing artistic, historic or archaeological value; or the protection of industrial and commercial property. Such prohibitions or restrictions shall not, however, constitute a means of arbitrary discrimination or a disguised restriction on trade between Member States.

Although Article 30 (formerly 36) applies to 'prohibitions or restrictions on imports' *generally* (both QRs and MEEQRs), since the Court of Justice in Case 120/78 *Cassis de Dijon* established, as regards *indistinctly* applicable MEEQRs, that, although they fall within the scope of the *Dassonville* formula, where they are necessary for the protection of mandatory requirements (as noted above), they do not breach Article 28 (formerly 30), *derogation from* Article 28 under Article 30 normally only applies to *distinctly* applicable national measures (and QRs).

Article 30 can be broken down into three overlapping parts:

(a) *An exhaustive list of possible grounds for derogation.* A Member State seeking to defend its restrictive rules must show that they fall within one of these grounds. Thus, in Case 95/81 *Commission v Italy (Re Advance Payments for Imports)* and other cases, the Court held that Article 36 (now 30) did not justify derogation from Article 30 (now 28) on the ground of the protection of consumers (but see *Cassis de Dijon*, below).

(b) *A stipulation that any prohibition or restriction must be justified.* A national trading rule is justified if it can be proved to be necessary, and no more than necessary, to achieve its particular objective, for example, the protection of health and life of humans. Derogation therefore involves compliance with the principle of *proportionality.* The burden of proof here rests on the national authorities, who must show (i) a protectable interest; and (ii) that the prohibition or restriction is appropriate and stands in proportion to the risk allegedly created by the imported product; and (iii) that no alternative means of protection against such risk, which are less restrictive of inter-Member State trade, are available.

(c) *The proviso in the second sentence that national prohibitions or restrictions must not constitute a means of arbitrary discrimination or a disguised restriction on trade.* These requirements must be considered in conjunction with the question of justification, and any purported justification must be examined very carefully to ascertain *whether it is genuine.* Arbitrary discrimination is not capable of justification on objective grounds: in the *San José Scale* case discussed earlier, the discrimination against the imported apples was justifiable in terms of the necessity of inspecting the apples in the face of the risk of the insect disease spreading. Similarly, a failure to stay within the bounds of the proportionality principle can result in a measure being struck down as a disguised restriction on trade, for example, the excessive testing of Italian wine at the French frontier in Case 42/82 *Commission v France*, also discussed earlier.

What all this amounts to is that Article 30 (formerly 36), although allowing derogation from the fundamental principle of the free movement of goods, must, for that reason, be interpreted strictly. Obstacles to free movement will delay the establishment of a genuine Internal Market at least until the national rules which remain to create such obstacles are harmonised.

Turning to the six grounds in Article 30 (formerly 36) upon which prohibitions or restrictions may be justified, the case law on the protection of industrial and commercial property (for example, patent and trade mark rights established under national law) is closely related to certain aspects of competition policy and is therefore dealt with separately in Chapter 18. It will be seen that the grounds for derogation are essentially of a non-economic nature. As Oliver states: 'It follows that such objects as the promotion of employment or investment, curbing inflation and controlling the balance of payments fall outside Article 36 [now 30].'

Protection of the Health and Life of Humans, Animals and Plants

Much of the case law on Article 36 (now 30) (some of which has already been referred to, for example, the inspections of imported apples in the *San José Scale* case and Italian wine in Case 42/82 *Commission v France*) concerns the protection of health. To be capable of justification, a measure must form part of a 'seriously considered health policy'. This, as seen, was not demonstrated in Case 40/82 *Commission v UK (Re Imports of Poultry Meat)* in which, shortly before Christmas 1981, the Ministry of Agriculture, Fisheries and Food suddenly imposed what amounted to a ban (a QR) on imports of French turkeys. It sought to justify this measure on the basis that it was necessary to control Newcastle disease (which affects poultry) and that the measures taken to do this in France were insufficient. There had been no outbreak of Newcastle disease in France for five years. The Court held that the ban was excessive and constituted a disguised restriction on trade. (See as a sequel to this case, *Bourgoin v MAFF* (1986) in Chapter 20.)

Similarly, the French authorities' attempt to justify their restrictions on the advertising of (largely imported) grain spirits on the ground of the protection of health, when no such restrictions were imposed on home-produced cognac and armagnac, was not accepted by the Court of Justice: Case 152/78 *Commission v France* (see also above).

In Case 104/75 *De Peijper*, the Court stated that:

Health and the life of humans rank first among the property or interests protected by Article 36 [now 30] and it is for the Member States, within the limits imposed by the Treaty, to decide what degree of protection they intend to assure and in particular how strict the checks to be carried out are to be.

Nevertheless, it emerges from Article 36 that national rules or practices which do restrict imports of pharmaceutical products or are capable of doing so are only compatible with the Treaty to the extent to which they are necessary for the effective protection of health and life of humans.

National rules or practices do not fall within the exception in Article 36 if the health and life of humans can be as effectively protected by measures which do not restrict intra-Community trade so much.

Difficult scientific and dietary questions can arise in relation to national rules regarding the composition of foodstuffs, in particular the presence of additives. An added *legal* complication is that although such rules are normally neutral, that is, they amount to non-discriminatory *indistinctly applicable* MEEQRs applying to both imported and domestic products, where the issue is that of the protection of health, the Court of Justice has at times chosen to deal with it on the basis of Article 36 (as in the case below) rather than under the *Cassis de Dijon* 'mandatory requirements' of which the protection of health is one. (Clearly, Article 36 would be pleaded in cases prior to the *Cassis de Dijon* decision in 1979.)

Case 174/82 *Sandoz BV*

Muesli bars to which vitamins had been added were not subjected to marketing restrictions in West Germany and Belgium. In the Netherlands, where it was considered that the vitamins could be a danger to public health, prior authorisation was required from the Dutch health authorities. S imported such bars into the Netherlands but was refused permission to market them.

Following a reference to the Court of Justice under Article 177 (now 234), the Court held that the Dutch rules were in breach of Article 30 (now 28). On the question of derogation under Article 36 (now 30), the Court stated that:

> It appears from the file that vitamins are not in themselves harmful substances but on the contrary are recognized by modern science as necessary for the human organism. Nevertheless excessive consumption of them over a prolonged period may have harmful effects, the extent of which varies according to the type of vitamin: there is generally a greater risk with vitamins soluble in fat than with those soluble in water. According to the observations submitted to the Court, however, scientific research does not appear to be sufficiently advanced to be able to determine with certainty the critical quantities and the precise effects.

> It is not disputed by the parties who have submitted observations that the concentration of vitamins contained in the foodstuffs of the kind in issue is far from attaining the critical threshold of harmfulness so that even excessive consumption thereof cannot in itself involve a risk to public health. Nevertheless such a risk cannot be excluded in so far as the consumer absorbs with other foods further quantities of vitamins which it is impossible to monitor or foresee.

> ... in so far as there are uncertainties at the present state of scientific research it is for the Member States, in the absence of harmonization, to decide what degree of protection of the health and life of humans they intend to assure, having regard however for the requirements of the free movement of goods within the Community.

> Those principles also apply to substances such as vitamins which are not as a general rule harmful in themselves but may have special harmful effects solely if taken to excess as part of the general nutrition, the composition of which is unforeseeable and cannot be monitored. In view of the uncertainties inherent in the scientific assessment, national rules prohibiting, without prior authorization, the marketing of foodstuffs to which vitamins have been added are justified on principle within the meaning of Article 36 [now 30] of the Treaty on grounds of the protection of human health.

> Nevertheless, the principle of proportionality which underlies the last sentence of Article 36 of the Treaty requires that the power of the Member States to prohibit imports of the products in question from other Member States should be restricted to what is necessary to attain the legitimate aim of protecting health. Accordingly, national rules providing for such a prohibition are justified only if authorizations to market are granted when they are compatible with the need to protect health.

> Such an assessment is, however, difficult to make in relation to additives such as vitamins the above mentioned characteristics of which exclude the possibility of foreseeing or monitoring the quantities consumed as part of the general nutrition and the degree of harmfulness of which cannot be determined with sufficient certainty. Nevertheless, although in view of the present stage of harmonization of

national laws at the Community level a wide discretion must be left to the Member States, they must, in order to observe the principle of proportionality, authorize marketing when the addition of vitamins to foodstuffs meets a real need, especially a technical or nutritional one.

The first question must therefore be answered to the effect that Community law permits national rules prohibiting without prior authorization the marketing of foodstuffs lawfully marketed in another Member State to which vitamins have been added, provided that the marketing is authorized when the addition of vitamins meets a real need, especially a technical or nutritional one.

Similar questions arose regarding (equally applicable) German rules, which in practice constituted an absolute ban on the marketing of beers containing additives, in Case 178/84 *Commission v Germany (Re Beer Purity Laws)*. The German legislation dated back to the 16th century. The ban being in breach of Article 30 (now 28), on the question of derogation on the ground of the protection of health under Article 36 (now 30) – the German government pointing out the high consumption of beer by German drinkers – the Court ruled that:

It must be observed that the German rules on additives applicable to beer result in the exclusion of all the additives authorised in the other Member States and not the exclusion of just some of them for which there is concrete justification by reason of the risks which they involve in view of the eating habits of the German population; moreover those rules do not lay down any procedure whereby traders can obtain authorisation for the use of a specific additive in the manufacture of beer by means of a measure of general application.

... Consequently, in so far as the German rules on additives in beer entail a general ban on additives, their application to beers imported from other Member States is contrary to the requirements of Community law as laid down in the case law of the Court, since that prohibition is contrary to the principle of proportionality and is therefore not covered by the exception provided for in Article 36 [now 30] of the EEC Treaty.

(For further treatment of this case, which also involves a designation issue, see below and Chapter 20.)

Public Morality

Case 34/79 *R v Henn and Darby* involved a criminal prosecution following a seizure (a QR) of pornographic literature imported by the defendants from the Netherlands into the UK. Their defence was that the legislation on the basis of which the customs authorities had impounded the goods was contrary to the free movement rules in Article 30 (now 28). This was met by the argument that the seizure was justified on the grounds of public morality under Article 36 (now 30). Following a reference from the House of Lords under Article 177 (now 234), the Court of Justice held that it was for each Member State to determine the standards of morality within its territory and that a prohibition on the importation of obscene publications and articles may be justifiable on public morality grounds. However, a ban would probably amount to arbitrary discrimination if there existed in the importing Member State a lawful trade in the goods denied access. The Court took the view that, subject to certain exceptions of limited scope, there was no lawful trade in the goods in question in the UK.

The House of Lords, on the basis that the UK operated an internal ban on the type of material seized (internal restrictions on manufacture and trade varied from region to region), held that the prohibition on importation did not amount to arbitrary discrimination. The defendants' convictions therefore stood. (There must be some doubt about the key findings of fact and their implications in this case.)

Similar questions arose later, but led to a different outcome in the following case.

Case 121/85 *Conegate Ltd v Customs and Excise Commissioners*

C imported a consignment of inflatable rubber 'love dolls' from West Germany. The customs authorities seized the goods on the ground that they were 'indecent or obscene' and therefore subject to a prohibition on importation under the Customs Consolidation Act 1876. When C claimed that the seizure was in breach of Article 30 (now 28), the customs authorities relied on the 'public morality' justification in Article 36 (now 30).

There was no ban on the manufacture of such goods in the UK although their marketing was subject to certain restrictions. Following a reference to the Court of Justice under Article 177 (now 234), the Court stated that:

> [This] question raises, in the first place, the general problem of whether a prohibition on the importation of certain goods may be justified on grounds of public morality where the legislation of the Member State concerned contains no prohibition on the manufacture or marketing of the same products within the national territory.

> So far as that problem is concerned, it must be borne in mind that according to Article 36 of the EEC Treaty the provisions relating to the free movement of goods within the Community do not preclude prohibitions on imports justified 'on grounds of public morality'. As the Court held in its judgment [in *Henn and Darby*], in principle, it is for each Member State to determine in accordance with its own scale of values and in the form selected by it the requirements of public morality in its territory.

> However, although Community law leaves the Member States free to make their own assessments of the indecent or obscene character of certain articles, it must be pointed out that the fact that goods cause offence cannot be regarded as sufficiently serious to justify restrictions on the free movement of goods where the Member State concerned does not adopt, with respect to the same goods manufactured or marketed within its territory, penal measures or other serious and effective measures intended to prevent the distribution of such goods in its territory.

Although certain restrictions on the sale of the products in question existed in the UK, they did not amount to a prohibition on manufacturing and marketing. The UK was unable to rely on Article 36 and the High Court quashed the forfeiture order.

Public Policy and Public Security

Very few cases have raised these issues of general interest. However, public policy and public security were both argued by the Irish government in the *Campus Oil* case, noted above with reference to public procurement.

Case 72/83 *Campus Oil v Minister for Industry and Energy*

Irish legislation required importers of petroleum products to purchase up to 35 per cent of their requirements from Ireland's only (State owned) refinery at prices fixed by the Minister. The measure was clearly discriminatory and protective and contrary to Article 30 (now 28). It was argued, however, that the measure was necessary on the grounds that the importance of oil for the maintenance of the life of the country made it indispensable to maintain refining capacity on the national territory and the system under question was the only means of ensuring that the refinery's output could be marketed.

The Court accepted that an interruption of supplies of petroleum products could be regarded as a matter of public security (even though the measure also achieved purely economic objectives). The Court held that:

(a) The purchasing obligation could only be continued if no less restrictive measure was capable of achieving the same objective.

(b) The quantities covered by the scheme must not exceed the minimum supply requirements without which the public security of the State would be affected or the level of production necessary to keep the refinery's production capacity available.

INDISTINCTLY (OR EQUALLY) APPLICABLE MEASURES (ARTICLE 3 OF DIRECTIVE 70/50)

It will be recalled that Article 3 of Directive 70/50 covers measures governing the marketing of products which deal with such 'technical' matters as their shape, size, composition or identification. Unlike the measures covered in Article 2, they apply to both domestic and imported goods. Such national rules are, as we have seen, 'origin neutral' and non-discriminatory, but they may nevertheless impede imports where the rules in the Member State of importation differ from those in the exporting Member State. On the basis of Article 3, such measures will be in breach of Article 28 (formerly 30), in particular, where:

– the restrictive effects on the free movement of goods are out of proportion to the purpose;

   [or]

– the same objective can be attained by other means which are less a hindrance to trade.

Thus, for example, in Case 261/81 *Walter Rau*, Belgian rules required all margarine to be packed in cube-shaped boxes. The alleged purpose of the national rules was to enable consumers to distinguish margarine from butter. Evidence showed that Belgian margarine prices were higher than those found in other Member States, and that no foreign producers marketed their product on the Belgian market. The Court of Justice accepted protection of the consumer as a legitimate objective (a 'mandatory requirement') but made it clear that the national rules must conform to the tests of proportionality and alternative means. The Belgian legislation did not satisfy those tests. It was held that the rules were in breach of Article 30 (now 28); the same objective could be achieved by clear labelling.

The Belgian rules were not discriminatory; they did not expressly treat similar products (domestic and imported margarine) in different ways. However, in so far as they were different from similar rules in other Member States, they had the effect of treating different situations in the same way. In practice, an apparently neutral criterion (cube-shaped), which would obviously be met by domestic producers, would probably not be met by producers in other Member States, unless they went to the expense of putting another costly production line into operation in order to meet

FREE MOVEMENT OF GOODS: QRs and MEEQRs

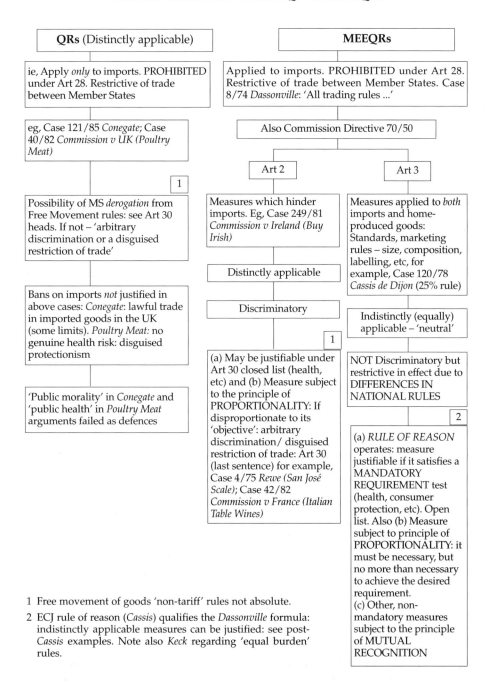

QRs (Distinctly applicable)

ie, Apply *only* to imports. PROHIBITED under Art 28. Restrictive of trade between Member States

eg, Case 121/85 *Conegate*; Case 40/82 *Commission v UK (Poultry Meat)*

1

Possibility of MS *derogation* from Free Movement rules: see Art 30 heads. If not – 'arbitrary discrimination or a disguised restriction of trade'

Bans on imports *not* justified in above cases: *Conegate*: lawful trade in imported goods in the UK (some limits). *Poultry Meat*: no genuine health risk: disguised protectionism

'Public morality' in *Conegate* and 'public health' in *Poultry Meat* arguments failed as defences

MEEQRs

Applied to imports. PROHIBITED under Art 28. Restrictive of trade between Member States. Case 8/74 *Dassonville*: 'All trading rules ...'

Also Commission Directive 70/50

Art 2

Measures which hinder imports. Eg, Case 249/81 *Commission v Ireland (Buy Irish)*

Distinctly applicable

Discriminatory

1

(a) May be justifiable under Art 30 closed list (health, etc) and (b) Measure subject to the principle of PROPORTIONALITY: If disproportionate to its 'objective': arbitrary discrimination/ disguised restriction of trade: Art 30 (last sentence) for example, Case 4/75 *Rewe (San José Scale)*; Case 42/82 *Commission v France (Italian Table Wines)*

Art 3

Measures applied to *both* imports and home-produced goods: Standards, marketing rules – size, composition, labelling, etc, for example, Case 120/78 *Cassis de Dijon* (25% rule)

Indistinctly (equally) applicable – 'neutral'

NOT Discriminatory but restrictive in effect due to DIFFERENCES IN NATIONAL RULES

2

(a) *RULE OF REASON* operates: measure justifiable if it satisfies a MANDATORY REQUIREMENT test (health, consumer protection, etc). Open list. Also (b) Measure subject to principle of PROPORTIONALITY: it must be necessary, but no more than necessary to achieve the desired requirement.
(c) Other, non-mandatory measures subject to the principle of MUTUAL RECOGNITION

1 Free movement of goods 'non-tariff' rules not absolute.

2 ECJ rule of reason (*Cassis*) qualifies the *Dassonville* formula: indistinctly applicable measures can be justified: see post-*Cassis* examples. Note also *Keck* regarding 'equal burden' rules.

the Belgian requirement. The real intention behind the rules was protection of domestic producers.

In the most important case on measures of this kind, the Court concentrated on the *exclusionary effects* of such rules.

Case 120/78 *Rewe (Cassis de Dijon)*

German legislation laid down that certain fruit liqueurs (such as Cassis) could only be marketed if they contained a minimum alcohol content of 25 per cent. German products met this requirement but it made it impossible for Rewe lawfully to import and sell French 'Cassis de Dijon', which had an alcohol content of between 15 and 20 per cent.

Rewe brought an action against the German alcohol monopoly, and the national court asked the Court of Justice if the German rules were consistent with Article 30 (now 28).

The Court concentrated first on the exclusionary nature of the German rule and examined whether there might exist grounds for its justification:

> The plaintiff takes the view that the fixing by the German rules of a minimum alcohol content leads to the result that well known spirits products from other Member States of the Community cannot be sold in the Federal Republic of Germany and that the said provision therefore constitutes a restriction on the free movement of goods between Member States which exceeds the bounds of the trade rules reserved to the latter.

> In its view, it is a measure having an effect equivalent to a quantitative restriction on imports contrary to Article 30 of the EEC Treaty.

> In the absence of common rules relating to the production and marketing of alcohol – a proposal for a regulation submitted to the Council by the Commission on 7 December 1976 (Official Journal, C309, p 2) not yet having received the Council's approval – it is for the Member States to regulate all matters relating to the production and marketing of alcohol and alcoholic beverages on their own territory.

> Obstacles to movement within the Community resulting from disparities between the national laws relating to the marketing of the products in question must be accepted in so far as those provisions may be recognised as being necessary in order to satisfy mandatory requirements relating in particular to the effectiveness of fiscal supervision, the protection of public health, the fairness of commercial transactions and the defence of the consumer.

Having introduced the concept of *mandatory requirements* in relation to obstacles to free movement arising from disparities between national marketing rules, the Court rejected claims by the German authorities that the minimum alcohol rule was necessary for the protection of public health (based on a dubious 'tolerance' argument) and for the protection of the consumer against unfair commercial practices (based on the argument that Cassis, with a lower alcohol content, gained an unfair competitive advantage, tax on alcohol being the most expensive cost item). As a result:

> It is clear from the foregoing that the requirements relating to the minimum alcohol content of alcoholic beverages do not serve a purpose which is in the general interest and such as to take precedence over the requirements of the free movement of goods, which constitutes one of the fundamental rules of the Community.

The actual effect of such a rule was explained by the Court of Justice in the following terms:

> In practice, the principal effect of requirements of this nature is to promote alcoholic beverages having a high alcohol content by excluding from the national market products of other Member States which do not answer that description.
>
> It therefore appears that the unilateral requirement imposed by the rules of a Member State of a minimum alcohol content for the purposes of the sale of alcoholic beverages constitutes an obstacle to trade which is incompatible with the provisions of Article 30 of the Treaty.
>
> *There is therefore no valid reason why, provided that they have been lawfully produced and marketed in one of the Member States, alcoholic beverages should not be introduced into any other Member State*; the sale of such products may not be subject to a legal prohibition on the marketing of beverages with an alcohol content lower than the limit set by the national rules [emphasis added].

In the first part of the final paragraph, the Court introduced the principle of *mutual recognition* (or *equivalence*), which has *general* effect in such cases as a *presumption*. It applies, in the pursuit of free movement, unless national rules can be justified on the basis of mandatory requirements. The relationship between (a) mutual recognition; (b) what is termed the *mandatory requirements* 'rule of reason', which takes a national rule *outside* Article 30 (now 28); and (c) the Commission's drive to harmonise national rules has been explained by Swann:

> In the process of delivering its judgment, the Court of Justice also made the point that any product legally made and sold in one member state must in principle be admitted to the markets of the others. National rules and standards can only create barriers where they are necessary to satisfy 'mandatory' requirements such as public health, consumer protection, etc. Moreover, and this is the key point, any rule must be the 'essential guarantee' of the interest, the protection of which is regarded as being justified. It will be remembered that, in the *Cassis* case, the German Government defended its minimum alcoholic content rule on grounds of consumer protection. But the Court noted that that objective could have been achieved by merely requiring the label to show the actual alcoholic content. The rule was not essential to guarantee the protection of the consumer. It does not follow that in the light of *Cassis* the need to harmonize no longer exists. There will be some situations where the need to have rules is essential and goods not conforming to them will be excluded. In such cases, the only way forward is to harmonize. But there will be many cases where the differences of standards as between States are really relatively trivial and are not essential to protect the public. In such cases, harmonization will no longer be required.

Where differences between standards are 'relatively trivial', mutual recognition will apply; where mandatory requirements or 'essential guarantees' must be preserved, the rules which embody them (like the rules embodying justifiable Article 36 (now 30) derogations) must be harmonised to ensure the free movement of goods.

As Weatherill and Beaumont have stressed:

> The decision in *Cassis* reinvigorated Article 30 [now 28] in an area where it had previously had minimal impact and where it had been widely assumed legislative harmonization of divergent national rules was required to eliminate obstacles to interstate trade.

The decision serves to eliminate protectionist measures of this kind and by enhancing opportunities for exporters makes consumer choice the determining factor.

In *Cassis de Dijon*, the Court of Justice *in effect* provided new grounds for derogation from Article 30 (now 28) where obstacles to free movement arise from disparities in national marketing rules (*indistinctly or equally* applicable MEEQRs), although strictly speaking in the cases involving the mandatory requirement argument, national rules are examined in the context of Article 30 (now 28) to establish if they are in breach of that Article at all.

Article 36 (now 30), with its *closed* list of justifiable derogations, remains to be applied in cases involving QRs and *distinctly* applicable and discriminatory equivalent measures, although, as we have seen, the protection of public health features in both lists, leading the Court on occasion to apply Article 36 (now 30) to equally applicable, albeit clearly restrictive rules: see, for example, Case 124/81 *Commission v UK (Re UHT Milk)*, in which the Court held that there was no genuine health risk because exporting States maintained standards and controls equivalent to those in the UK and there was little chance of the hermetically sealed milk being tampered with in transit.

Since *Cassis de Dijon*, the Court of Justice has added to the list of mandatory requirements. Apart from the protection of public health, the original list included, 'in particular', three further issues of public interest: 'the effectiveness of fiscal supervision' (for example, national rules applied to goods and designed to prevent and detect tax evasion), 'the fairness of commercial transactions' (for example, passing off rules) and 'the defence of the consumer' (for example, bans on false or misleading labelling of products: see Case 788/79 *Gilli and Andres*).

In Case 240/83 *Brûleurs d'Huiles Usagées*, environmental protection was added – and argued successfully in part in Case 302/86 *Commission v Denmark (Re Disposable Beer Cans)*. In Case 155/80 *Oebel*, the Court accepted that the improvement of working conditions (in bakeries) could constitute a mandatory requirement, although the national rules in question were held not to fall within Article 30 (now 28) in any event. There was therefore no need for such a justification. In Cases 60 and 61/84 *Cinéthèque*, national rules were apparently justified on cultural grounds – protection of the film industry (see below). A further mandatory requirement (and fundamental right), the plurality of the press, was introduced by the Court of Justice in Case C-368/95 *Familiapress* (see also below).

Of the many cases where national marketing rules have failed the mandatory requirements test, the following are taken as illustrations, in addition to those discussed above.

In Case 178/84 *Commission v Germany (Beer Purity)*, discussed earlier with respect to the additives ban, Germany had argued that its ban on the use of the term 'Bier' for any beers other than those brewed in accordance with the beer purity law was essential to protect German consumers, who linked the term only with beers brewed using natural products, malted barley, hops, yeast and water. Whilst imported beer could be sold, it could not be marketed with the designation 'Bier'. The Court held that:

> It is admittedly legitimate to seek to enable consumers who attribute specific qualities to beers manufactured from particular raw materials to make their choice in the light of that consideration. However ... that possibility may be ensured by means which do not prevent the importation of products which have been lawfully manufactured and marketed in other Member States and, in particular, by the compulsory affixing of suitable labels giving the nature of the product sold.

By indicating the raw materials utilised in the manufacture of beer, such a course would enable the consumer to make his choice in the full knowledge of the facts and would guarantee transparency in trading and in offers to the public. The Court held the ban to be disproportionate and thus contrary to Article 30 (now 28).

In Case 207/83 *Commission v UK (Re Origin Marking of Retail Goods)*, a UK regulation required certain textile and electrical goods to be marked with their country of origin when offered for retail sale. All such goods, not merely imports, were subject to this requirement. Rejecting justification arguments based on consumer protection grounds, the Court spoke of covert discrimination which enabled British consumers to assert any prejudice they might have against foreign goods. Manufacturers remained free to indicate their own national origin if they wished, but it was not necessary to compel them to do so.

In Case 286/86 *Deserbais*, national rules restricted the name 'Edam' to cheese having a minimum fat content of 40 per cent. French legislation excluded from the domestic market Edam cheese made in other Member States according to different preferences as regards fat content. The rules could not be supported by any objective justification. Similarly, in Case C-196/89 *Italy v Nespoli*, in a similar situation, consumer protection and public health arguments failed to impress the Court.

In Case 16/83 *Prantl*, German rules were designed to protect the 'Bocksbeutel' (a distinctive bulbous-shaped bottle) and its contents, a quality wine from the Franconia region, from unfair competition. The Court did not allow the rules to restrict the importation of Italian wine traditionally produced in similar bottles. The principle of mutual recognition overrode the rules' restrictive and protective effects.

In Case 407/85 *Drei Glocken GmbH v Centro-Sud*, Italian rules restricted the marketing of pasta to products made from durum wheat. The Court held that the rules were not necessary to satisfy mandatory requirements, so opening the Italian market to importers of pasta made from common wheat flour and other varieties.

In Case 113/80 *Commission v Ireland (Re Restrictions on Importation of Souvenirs)*, the Court held that Irish Orders requiring that imported souvenirs either be marked 'Foreign' or with their country of origin were:

> ... not measures which are applicable to domestic products and to imported products without distinction but rather a set of rules which apply only to imported products and are therefore discriminatory in nature, with the result that the measures in issue are not covered by the decisions cited above which relate exclusively to provisions that regulate in a uniform manner the marketing of domestic products and imported products.

'The decisions cited above' included *Cassis de Dijon* and *Gilli and Andres*. Therefore, the Irish government's attempt to justify the Orders on the ground that it was necessary to prevent the consumer from suffering confusion failed – and also failed under Article 36 (now 30) as consumer protection does not feature in that Article as a ground for derogation.

Nevertheless, there is an important link between Article 36 (now 30) and mandatory requirements. Just as a distinctly applicable measure must comply with the principle of proportionality in order to qualify for derogation from Article 30 (now 28) under Article 36 (now 30), the same principle also applies to claims that equally applicable national marketing rules are 'necessary' in order to meet mandatory requirements. In *Walter Rau*, the Court stated that:

It is also necessary for such rules to be proportionate to the aim in view. If a Member
State has a choice between various measures to attain the same objective it should
choose the means which least restrict the free movement of goods.

Thus, in *Cassis de Dijon* itself, even if the protection of public health and fairness of
commercial transactions defence claims were genuine, the minimum alcohol content
rule was not necessary to achieve those aims. Clear labelling and pricing were all that
was necessary and the consumer could exercise his right to choose. (Remember the
last two sentences of Article 3 of Directive 70/50.)

Indistinctly Applicable Measures: the Limits of Article 28 (formerly 30)

As we have seen, the Court's definition of MEEQRs in *Dassonville*, with its reference to
'all trading rules', is very broad. *Cassis de Dijon* applies to indistinctly applicable
national rules relating to the *marketing* of products, in particular, in terms of Article 3
of Directive 70/50, to rules relating to their 'shape, size, weight, composition,
presentation, identification or putting up'. These 'technical' rules, which apply to the
characteristics of goods, have been termed *dual-burden* rules: goods 'lawfully produced
and marketed in one Member State', that is, complying with the relevant trading rules
of the exporting Member State, are faced with significantly differing rules concerning
the characteristics of the goods in the importing Member State. These latter rules, as
seen, are incompatible with Article 28 (formerly 30) unless justified on a mandatory
requirements basis.

Although most of the case law based on *Cassis de Dijon* has concerned dual-
burden, 'characteristics' rules, rules of a rather different nature have also called for
examination under Article 30 (now 28). These rules, for example, UK trading laws
which prohibited certain retail outlets from selling on Sundays, have been termed
equal-burden rules. A national measure of this kind is, to quote Advocate General Slynn
in *Cinéthèque* (see below), 'not specifically directed at imports, does not discriminate
against imports, does not make it any more difficult for an importer to sell his
products than it is for a domestic producer, and gives no protection to domestic
producers ...'. However, a trader may well be able to show that a restriction on sales of
this type has a considerable impact on his or her overall volume of trade including
trade in imported goods. Are such restrictions caught by Article 28 (formerly 30),
subject to justification, or do they fall outside Article 28 (formerly 30) altogether?

The Court's approach in the cases concerning equal-burden rules relating to
selling conditions has been less than consistent. In *Oebel*, the Court of Justice held that
the Belgian rules, which prohibited the delivery of bakery products to consumers and
retailers, but not to wholesalers, at night, did not fall within Article 30 (now 28). The
rules against delivery applied to all producers, whichever side of the border they were
established, trade between Member States remained possible at all times, and the rules
only operated to the disadvantage of Belgian bakers who were prevented from
benefiting from early morning sales in adjacent Member States. In Case C-23/89
Quietlynn and Richards Ltd v Southend Borough Council, the Court held that a
prohibition on the sale of lawful sex aids on licensed premises did not contravene
Article 30 (now 28). The UK rules merely regulated the distribution (selling
conditions) of the goods without discrimination against imported products.

However, in other equal-burden cases, the Court had held that Article 30 (now 28) did apply to the national rules in question and that they were only allowable if capable of justification. Although the Court has since had 'second thoughts' on this question (see Cases C-267 and 268/91 *Keck and Mithouard* below), it is necessary to examine this development, albeit briefly.

Cases 60 and 61/84 *Cinéthèque*

French rules prohibited the sale or hire of videos of films within a year of their first showing at a cinema. The basic purpose of the rules was to protect the film industry and they applied in the same manner to both domestic and imported videos. Advocate General Slynn in effect presented to the Court two possibilities: (a) that the rules did not fall within Article 30 (now 28), at all; or (b) that, although falling within Article 30, they might be justified on cultural grounds. He stated his preference for the first of these approaches. Nevertheless, the Court took the second route and held that the national rules, although caught by Article 30's prohibition of MEEQRs, were justified on *Cassis de Dijon* principles.

In a series of cases in the late 1980s and early 1990s, a number of multiple retail outlets in the UK (B & Q, Payless, Wickes Building Supplies, etc) were prosecuted by local authorities for breach of the Sunday trading rules laid down by the Shops Act 1950. The companies involved raised the defence that the Act's provisions prohibiting them from trading on Sundays amounted to an MEEQR within the meaning of Article 30 (now 28) and could not be justified. (The effect of the prohibition was of course to reduce the companies' sales of goods in absolute terms, including goods imported from other Member States.)

In Case 145/88 *Torfaen Borough Council v B & Q plc*, the Court of Justice held that the Sunday trading rules were capable of justification in order to achieve the objective of ensuring that 'working and non-working hours are so arranged as to accord with national or regional socio-cultural characteristics'. The Court further stated that it was for national courts to establish whether the effects of the Sunday trading rules were proportionate, that is, that they were not excessive in relation to the objective they sought to achieve. The Court's approach was essentially the same as in *Cinéthèque*.

When it came to the application of this ruling at national level in the various cases pending, confusion ensued and conflicting conclusions were reached. For example, some courts which determined that the purpose of the Sunday trading rules was the regulation of workers' hours concluded that the rules were disproportionate; others saw the purpose of the rules to be to 'preserve the traditional character of the British Sunday' and found them to be necessary but no more than necessary to achieve that end.

In two later references from French and Belgian courts, Case C-312/89 *Conforama* and C-332/89 *Marchandise*, regarding national rules which in France prohibited and in Belgium restricted the employment of staff on Sundays, the Court shifted its position. It accepted that these were equal-burden rules, applied the *Torfaen* test but *itself* stated that the rules did not appear to create restrictive effects on cross-border trade which were excessive in relation to the aim pursued.

Following a further reference by the House of Lords in Case C-169/91 *Stoke City Council and Norwich City Council v B & Q plc*, the Court similarly held that the Sunday trading rules were justified as regards their objective (although in truth it is difficult to know what the policy objective of the bizarre assortment of rules regarding what could or could not be sold on Sundays really was; the rules have since been relaxed) and that they were not disproportionate.

Despite these shifts, the Court's basic approach (in *Cinéthèque, Torfaen* and the later cases) remained the same (but note *Quietlynn*, above, decided in 1990): the rules in question, although of an equal-burden nature, were *prima facie* caught by Article 30 (now 28) but could be taken out, beyond that Article's scope, as justifiable and proportionate. However, if, as Gormley has stated, 'the key to understanding these cases is that the Court is concerned that Article 30 [now 28] should not become simply a busybody's charter for attacking national measures in purely national situations with scarcely the most tenuous link with intra-Community trade', then the Court should have followed Advocate General Slynn's alternative advice in *Cinéthèque* in the first place, that is, that such equal-burden rules do not fall within Article 30 (now 28) at all.

In 1993, in a French case concerning 'selling arrangements', this is the position that the Court has now adopted, while bringing itself in line with its own previous decision in, for example, *Quietlynn* above. It is a case which, like the Sunday trading cases, has been described as having a fact pattern 'with negligible integrationist merit'.

Joined Cases C-267 and C-268/91 *Keck and Mithouard*

K and M were prosecuted for reselling goods in an unaltered state at prices lower than cost contrary to French law on unfair competition. The defendants contended that a general prohibition on resale at a loss (that is, using certain goods as 'loss-leaders' to attract customers, a tactic that can work to the advantage of supermarkets and the like which carry a wide range of goods – as opposed to small retailers who do not) was incompatible with Article 30 (now 28). The Strasbourg national court submitted a question on the interpretation of Article 30 to the Court of Justice pursuant to Article 177 (now 234).

The Court ruled as follows:

It was not the purpose of the French legislation at issue to regulate the trade in goods between Member States.

Although the legislation might restrict the volume of sales, and hence the volume of sales of imports from other Member States, it remained to be determined whether this possibility brought the legislation within the terms of Article 30 (that is, could it be said to be a measure having equivalent effect to a quantitative restriction on imports?).

The application to products from other Member States of national provisions restricting or prohibiting certain selling arrangements was not such as to hinder trade between Member States within the meaning of the *Dassonville* formula provided that those provisions applied to all affected traders operating within the national territory and affected in the same manner, in law and in fact, the marketing of both domestic products and those from other Member States.

Where those conditions were fulfilled, the application of such rules to the sale of products from another Member State which complied with the manufacturing and marketing requirements of that Member State [see the mutual recognition principle in *Cassis de Dijon*] was not by nature such as to prevent their access to the market or to impede their access any more than it impeded the access of domestic products.

Article 30 was to be interpreted as not applying to national rules which imposed a general prohibition on resale at a loss.

In the course of its judgment, the Court stated that in view of the increasing tendency of traders to invoke Article 30 (now 28) in order to challenge any national rules the effect of which was to limit their commercial freedom (as in the Sunday trading cases) even where such rules were not aimed at products from other Member States, it was necessary 'to re-examine and clarify its case law' on this matter. Therefore, 'contrary to what had previously been decided', national *equal-burden* rules regarding selling arrangements now fall *outside* the scope of Article 30 (now 28), so obviating the need to justify them on the grounds that they have a legitimate objective and satisfy the principle of proportionality, so long as they meet the 'equal burden' proviso in the *Keck* judgment.

The dubious 'Euro-defence' based on Article 30 (now 28) will no longer be available to traders where the conditions laid down by the Court in *Keck* are applicable. In Joined Cases C-401 and 402/92 *Tankstation 't Heukske vof* and *Boermans*, concerning Dutch rules on opening hours and periods of compulsory closure as applied to shops forming part of petrol stations owned by the two defendants, the Court applied its ruling in *Keck* and held that the national rules fell outside the scope of Article 30 (now 28).

The scope of the expression 'selling arrangements' in the *Keck* judgment may well prove difficult to define. It covers national rules concerning retail opening hours and hours of work (as in the Sunday trading and similar cases), the number of allowed, licensed outlets (Case C-387/93 *Banchero*) and forms of sales promotion (as in *Keck* itself) including bans on advertising (Case C-292/92 *Hunermund*). However, a line between 'selling arrangements' rules (equal burden) and rules applying to the product characteristics (dual burden) may prove difficult to draw.

Case C-368/95 *Familiapress v Heinrich Bauer*

F, an Austrian newspaper publisher, brought proceedings in Vienna against HB, a German publisher, for an order that HB should cease selling in Austria publications which offered readers the chance to participate in games with prizes, contrary to the Austrian Law on Unfair Competition 1991.

In the intervening Austrian government's view, the national prohibition fell outside Article 30 (now 28). The government argued that the possibility of offering readers of a periodical the chance to take part in games for prizes was merely a form of sales promotion and therefore a selling arrangement according to the ruling in *Keck*.

The Commercial Court referred a question on the interpretation of Article 30 to the Court of Justice.

The Court ruled that:

(a) The Austrian legislation applied to the actual content of the product; the games to which it referred being an integral part of the publications in which they appeared. Therefore, application of the national rules did not concern selling arrangements within the meaning of the ruling in *Keck*.

(b) As it required publishers in other Member States to *alter the contents* of their publications, the Austrian prohibition jeopardised access of the product concerned into the market of the Member State of importation and consequently hindered the free movement of goods.

(c) The national rules therefore constituted in principle an MEEQR within the meaning of Article 30.

(d) Maintenance of the pluralism of the press (a fundamental right guaranteed by the Community legal order as derived from the freedom of expression requirement of Article 10 of the Council of Europe's Convention for the Protection of Human Rights and Fundamental Freedoms of 1950, and see and now the EU Charter of Fundamental Rights) might constitute an overriding requirement justifying a restriction on free movement of goods, providing that the national rules were proportionate to the objective pursued and that the objective could not be achieved by measures less restrictive of intra-Community trade and freedom of expression.

In this final point, the Court of Justice accepted that the Austrian legislation was intended to protect 'small press publishers which were assumed to be unable to offer comparable prizes'. To reach a decision on this point, it was necessary for the court in Vienna to define the Austrian press market and consider the market share of each publisher or press group over a period of time. The crucial question was whether or not the publications offering the chance of winning prizes were competing with the smaller market participants.

If the pluralism of the press was endangered, alterations in demand causing the removal of small press publishers from the market, the national court had to ask whether the national rules, although creating an obstacle to inter-Community trade, were objectively justifiable and necessary but no more than necessary to safeguard the pluralism of the press, and that no less restrictive measures (of trade and expression) were appropriate to secure this objective.

In subsequent cases on selling arrangements, the Court of Justice, while maintaining its basic position in *Keck* – that the restrictive national measures at issue must 'affect in the same manner, in law and in fact, the marketing of domestic products and of those from other Member States' – has made an adjustment to that position in line with an approach adopted earlier by Advocate General Jacobs in Case C-412/93 *Leclerc-Siplec v TFI Publicité*.

This involves consideration of a possible *differential impact*, in law or in fact, for domestic traders and importers of non-discriminatory national measures on selling arrangements. It may be the case that such measures create a *substantial hindrance to market access* for importers, bearing in mind, as the cases show, such factors as the nature of the restriction, the availability or otherwise of alternative arrangements, the range of goods affected and whether the impact is direct or indirect.

Cases 34–36/95 *KO v De Agostini and TV-Shop*

A Swedish ban prohibited TV advertising directed at children under 12. It was contended that the ban was in breach of Article 30 (now 28), and could not be applied with respect to advertising broadcast from another Member State.

The Court ruled that the Swedish ban concerned selling arrangements which applied to all traders within the national territory. However, it felt that it was possible that such a ban of a type of promotion for a product lawfully sold in the Member State in question might have a greater impact on products from other Member States.

Noting that DA had stated that TV advertising was the only effective form of promotion enabling it to penetrate the Swedish market, the Court concluded that the ban was not covered by Article 30 unless it failed the *Keck* test by way of differential impact. If this were found to be the case by the national court, the ban could only be saved if found to be 'necessary to satisfy overriding requirements of general public importance or one of the aims listed in Article 36 [now 30] of the Treaty'. It would also need to satisfy the requirement of proportionality with no less restrictive measure being available to the Swedish authorities.

A further action brought by the Swedish Consumer Ombudsman concerned a ban on alcohol advertising. In Case C-405/98 *KO v Gourmet International Products*, GIP argued that the ban had a greater effect on imported goods than those produced in Sweden. After citing its findings in *Keck* and *De Agostini*, the Court continued:

> It is apparent that a prohibition on advertising ... not only prohibits a form of marketing a product but in reality prohibits producers and importers from directing any advertising messages at consumers, with a few insignificant exceptions.

> ... the Court is able to conclude that, in the case of products like alcoholic beverages, the consumption of which is linked to traditional social practices and to local habits and customs, a prohibition of all advertisements in the press, on the radio and television, the direct mailing of unsolicited matter or the placing of posters on the public highway is liable to impede access to the market by products from other Member States more than it impedes access by domestic products, with which consumers are instantly more familiar.

> A prohibition on advertising such as that in issue ... must therefore be regarded as affecting the marketing of products from other Member States more heavily than the marketing of domestic products and as therefore constituting an obstacle to trade caught by Article 30 [now 28] of the Treaty.

Austrian selling arrangements legislation in Case C-254/98 *Heimdienst* applied to bakers, butchers and grocers who make sales on rounds. It created a differential impact in that it required such traders also to have a local, permanent outlet selling the same goods. This requirement disadvantaged non-domestic traders in the goods, who would need to set up such an establishment at additional cost. In the Court's view:

> It follows that the application to all operators trading in the national territory of national legislation such as that in point ... in fact impedes access to the market of the Member State of importation for products from other Member States more than it impedes access for domestic products ...

Not being equal in its operation, the legislation was caught by Article 30 (now 28) and required justification if it was to be allowed to stand.

On the academic front, Weatherill (1996), drawing on recent case law not only from the field of free movement of goods, has summed up the position as follows:

> In *Keck*, *Leclerc-Siplec* and other similar cases, the limit on commercial freedom could not be directly connected to any cross-border aspect of the activity. In *Alpine Investments*, by contrast, the cross-border aspect was of direct significance; so too in *Bosman*, whose access to employment in another state was directly affected by the rules.

> ... The injection of an adequate cross-border element enables a claim not simply to an equality right, but instead to the dynamic protection of Community law on free movement, subject only to the capacity of the regulator to show justification for the restrictions.

Such 'cross-freedom' analysis is indicative of a current debate regarding the free movement rules. It will be briefly discussed at the end of the next chapter.

HARMONISATION MEASURES, THE FREE MOVEMENT OF GOODS AND THE INTERNAL MARKET

It will be recalled that, under Article 14 (formerly 7a) EC, the Internal Market 'shall comprise an area without internal frontiers in which the free movement of goods [amongst other things] is ensured'. We have seen how, to this end, the Commission's White Paper of 1985 on the completion of the Internal Market by the end of 1992 initiated a massive legislative programme to eliminate, in particular, remaining physical, fiscal and technical barriers to the free movement of goods. The main legal instrument for putting this programme into effect was the harmonisation Directive, which, while maintaining common 'European' standards, eliminates obstacles to free movement: see Article 95(1) (formerly 100a(1)).

In the course of discussing the Court's case law on free movement from the early 1960s, we have already seen how, for example, expensive delays (physical barriers) could arise from frontier controls applied to goods as a result of the need to subject them to import VAT at every internal Community frontier (a fiscal barrier), or from the perceived need to examine, test and certify imported food products at frontiers in accordance with national criteria in the interests of public health (physical and technical barriers). We have also seen how differing national rules and standards fragment the market, increase production costs and hinder free movement.

In many of the free movement cases already considered, the Court's decision has been given in the light of 'the present stage of Community law' in which there were 'no common rules', that is, in the absence of Community legislation which had established a common (or complete) regime of control. Where Directives have been in place, we have seen the onus for, say, inspections and certification move from the frontier and the authorities of the importing State to the production centres of the exporting State.

Although the categorisation of barriers into the physical, fiscal and technical is somewhat arbitrary and overlapping, the problems concerning frontier controls have been graphically illustrated by Pelkmans and Winter (1988):

Box 2.1 The cost of selling in Europe – transport

One man in a laden lorry travelling from London to Glasgow and back can cover 750 miles in 36 hours without violating government regulations. If, instead, he transported the same goods in the same lorry from London to Milan, which is a similar distance, he would take at least 58 hours (excluding the time necessary to cross the Channel). Much of the difference is accounted for by compulsory rest periods, but the need for these arises from the 6 to 10 extra 'working hours' entailed in inter-member trade. These extra hours are lost to Customs and commercial port formalities, which include:

- passport and health controls;
- transport quota checks – indeed, if permits for direct shipments of some goods between two EC countries have been used up, then the shipments must be rerouted via other EC countries whose quotas have not been used up;
- checks on cargoes carried by the lorry, since within the EC it was (until 1 January 1988) necessary to have one Community transit document for each country passed through en route to the destination, while for exporting outside the EC all that has been necessary is one TIR document;

- safety checks confirming that vehicles meet all weight and dimension regulations and that drivers' hours are not excessive;

- the requirement that lorry drivers purchase fuel from particular service stations at ports; and

- the non-coordination of border-post closing times on the two sides of certain frontiers. Some major (that is, busy) border posts are not even open 24 hours a day.

All these formalities require significant amounts of queuing and waiting. Of course, the 58 hours could be drastically reduced by having three drivers to a lorry, but this hardly constitutes a solution [source: Information from SITPRO].

It was estimated that barriers such as these cost the Community around £5.5 billion a year, and the White Paper stated that the Commission's aim was 'not merely to simplify the existing system but to do away with the internal frontier controls in their entirety'.

In 1993, in the Commission's opinion, the Internal Market programme had come to fruition – albeit as yet more in a legislative than a practical sense. In terms of the free movement of goods, the following developments were of particular significance. First, with regard to *physical* barriers:

(a) The Commission stated that all checks on goods (and on lorries) at border crossings between Member States had been eliminated.

(b) It was reported that work was progressing towards the elimination of national transport quotas.

(c) An estimated 60 million customs clearance documents a year (at a cost to industry of an average ECU 70/£50 per consignment) had been replaced by a Single Administrative Document, a single customs and entry and transit document, itself replaced by CADDIA (Co-operation in the Automation of Data and Documentation for Imports, Exports and Agriculture).

In the field of *fiscal* barriers:

(a) Until 1993, all goods traded between Member States were subject to import VAT at frontiers and exempt from VAT in the exporting Member State. Frontier formalities in connection with the collection of VAT had disappeared and VAT was to be levied in the country of destination via normal VAT returns. A computerised information system, VIES (VAT Information Exchange System) had been set up at Community level to check that VAT payments and exemptions were in order and to prevent tax evasion.

(b) The Member States had agreed on the approximation of VAT rates. The lower limit for the standard rate of VAT was fixed at 15 per cent (UK 17.5 per cent, France 18.6 per cent, Germany 15 per cent, etc). Agreement on reduced rates or exemptions for goods and services of particular social or cultural significance had been agreed (see the discussion of Article 99 (now 93) in the sections on internal taxation earlier in this chapter).

With regard to *technical* barriers (taking us back to the MEEQRs of Article 28 (formerly 30), including not only Member States' differing health, safety and packaging standards, etc but also their various inspection and certification procedures), the harmonisation process of Article 95 (formerly 100a) played a major role and it has been an enormous undertaking. In 1988, the Cecchini Report on the Internal Market found, for example, 200 such cost-increasing non-tariff barriers in 10 food and drink products alone in the five largest Member States.

It is now (and for some years has been) the case that a Member State may no longer unilaterally seek either to derogate from Article 28 (formerly 30) on the grounds listed in Article 30 (formerly 36), or plead that Article 28 (formerly 30) does not apply to its trade restrictions on the grounds of protection of mandatory requirements as established in *Cassis de Dijon* and later cases, where Community legislation (normally a harmonisation Directive) provides for the protection of the interests in question. (This will *not* be the case, for example, in cases involving public morality.) These developments have been referred to several times in the earlier parts of this chapter and were explained by the Court of Justice in Case 25/88 *Wurmser*:

> ... the justification ... of a unilateral measure impeding intra-Community trade presupposes that the sphere in question is not the subject of Community rules. In that regard, it should be noted that there are no general rules at Community level concerning verification of the conformity of products with the rules in force on the relevant [exporter's] market. Although there are harmonising directives in regard to misleading advertisements and the designation of certain products, their provisions do not govern the question at issue in the main proceedings. It follows that, as Community law stands at present, the question is still subject to national law within the limits laid down in Articles 30 and 36 [now 28 and 30] of the Treaty.

Alternatively, in a later case, the Court of Justice ruled that:

> It is contrary to Article 30 [now 28] of the EC Treaty for national rules to prohibit, for reasons of consumer protection, the marketing of foodstuffs lawfully manufactured and marketed in another Member State, where consumers are protected by means of labelling in accordance with the provisions of Council Directive 79/112/EEC of 18 December 1978 on the approximation of the laws of the Member States relating to the labelling, presentation and advertising of foodstuffs, in particular those concerning the description of products and the list of ingredients.

Since *Cassis de Dijon*, and as outlined in the White Paper of 1985, the Commission has been in the position of being able to concentrate its efforts regarding the adoption of harmonisation measures designed to secure the free movement of goods whilst at the same time protecting interests of general public concern because it can rely on the *Cassis de Dijon* principle of mutual recognition to operate towards the elimination of the restrictive effect of what Swann called 'trivial' differences between national marketing rules. In such cases, it will be recalled that the *presumption* is that goods lawfully produced and marketed in one Member State (that is, in accordance with the Member State's rules) are to be freely admitted into other Member States.

The Commission's new freedom to concentrate on the provision of 'essential guarantees' in the fields of health and safety and environmental and consumer protection was enhanced by the further change brought about by the Single European Act whereby, in the context of the completion of the Internal Market, the unanimity voting requirement of Article 100 (now 94) was replaced by majority voting in the Council under Article 100a(1) (now the amended Article 95: see below and also Chapter 6 on Treaty Basis):

Article 100a EEC

1   By way of derogation from Article 100 and save where otherwise provided in this Treaty, the following provisions shall apply for the achievement of the objectives

set out in Article 8a [regarding the Internal Market, now Article 14]. The Council shall, acting by a qualified majority on a proposal from the Commission in co-operation with the European Parliament and after consulting the Economic and Social Committee, adopt the measures for the approximation [or harmonisation] of the provisions laid down by law, regulation or administrative action in Member States which have as their object the establishment and functioning of the internal market.

2   Paragraph 1 shall not apply to fiscal provisions, to those relating to the free movement of persons nor to those relating to the rights and interests of employed persons.

3   The Commission, in its proposals envisaged in paragraph 1 concerning health, safety, environmental protection and consumer protection, will take as a base a high level of protection.

....

Harmonisation was frequently a slow, laborious process prior to Article 100a, but nevertheless Community legislation was adopted which by its *comprehensive* regulation of the issue in question therefore *excluded* the application of national rules. The following case provides a good example.

Case 28/84 *Commission v Germany (Re Compound Feedingstuffs)*

The Commission contended that Council Directives adopted in 1970, 1974 and 1979 constituted a complete and exhaustive set of rules covering the whole field of production and marketing of compound animal feedingstuffs, including questions of public health raised by the use of certain ingredients.

The Court held that the Directives did establish a comprehensive system as regards the composition and preparation of animal foodstuffs with the effect that German rules on the minimum and maximum levels of certain ingredients could not apply.

(In Case 73/84 *Denkavit Futtermittel*, it was held that the same Directives did not, however, regulate health inspections of animal foodstuffs and so did not preclude (at that time) national health inspections justifiable under Article 36 (now 30).)

Putting the main point here another way: once a Directive which lays down a comprehensive system for the marketing of goods, including such matters as health controls, is law within the Member States, goods which comply with its provisions are in a position to be marketed anywhere within the Community: see, for example, Case 148/78 *Ratti* (dealing with the packaging and labelling of solvents and varnishes) in Chapter 8 and Case 60/86 *Commission v UK (Re Dim-Dip Headlights)* in which the Court said:

It follows that the Member States cannot unilaterally require manufacturers who have complied with the harmonized technical requirements set out in Directive 76/756/EEC to comply with a requirement which is not imposed by that directive, since motor vehicles complying with the technical requirements laid down therein must be able to move freely within the common market.

It must therefore be declared that, by prohibiting, in breach of Council Directive 76/756/EEC of 27 July 1976, the use of motor vehicles manufactured after 1 October 1986 and put into service after 1 April 1987 which are not equipped with a dim-dip device, the United Kingdom has failed to fulfil its obligations under Community law.

Weatherill, identifying this method of harmonisation as 'the uniform rule', puts forward two arguments against its use:

(a) Harmonisation of this nature is conservative. The standard is fixed until such time as the legislator is able to alter it – a laborious process, especially at Community level. The inflexible, rigid standard hinders innovation (for example, in respect of cheaper or safer lighting devices), and is consequently inefficient.

(b) Harmonisation of this nature suppresses national tradition. Why should one single Community rule replace national preference? Is free trade a goal which overrides the capacity of individual States to retain higher standards of, say, environmental and consumer protection?

These criticisms can be, and increasingly are being met by methods of *differentiated flexible integration*. As Weatherill notes:

It is deceptively simple to declare that in principle the passage of Community harmonisation legislation precludes an individual State's reliance on Article 36 [now 30]; and that interest can be protected in a Community measure which also facilitates free trade. The reality is that in a heterogeneous Community of 15 Member States a single Community rule cannot encompass all the diffuse interests at work in the structure. So, in practice, national derogations and differing standards may be judged necessary. [See Case 4/75 *Rewe (San José Scale)*, above, and Case 190/87 *Moormann*, in which the Court ruled that although a Directive on health problems affecting trade in poultry meat had legislated for full inspections in the exporting State, replacing inspections in the importing State, the Court allowed such inspections so long as they were conducted on an occasional basis and proportionate to any perceived risk to health.] The harmonisation legislation may itself allow for particular national concerns by providing for derogations.

The technique of *minimum harmonisation* is another form of differentiated integration which sets a basic Community level of regulation – a level below which protection of interests against risk must not fall – but which permits States to set rules at a stricter level if it wishes. For example, Article 153 (formerly 129a) on consumer protection provides that:

Action adopted [by the Council] pursuant to paragraph 2 shall not prevent any Member State from maintaining or introducing more stringent protective measures. Such measures must be compatible with this Treaty. The Commission shall be notified of them.

See also Case C-128/94 *Hönig v Stadt Stockach*, in which the relevant Directive laid down minimum standards for the protection of laying hens kept in battery cages. The cages had to 'at least comply' with $450cm^2$ of cage area for each hen.

The 'New Approach' to Harmonisation

Back in 1987, Pelkmans drew attention to the disadvantages and shortcomings of the 'traditional' approach to technical harmonisation and standardisation. They included time consuming and cumbersome procedures, excessive uniformity, the need for unanimity in the Council under Article 100 (now 94), and neglect of the problems of differing national requirements regarding the testing and certification of goods. By the time a Directive was adopted, it might be technically obsolete.

Already, in 1980, the Commission had announced that, following *Cassis de Dijon*, it would concentrate on steps for the harmonisation of national laws which could still hinder inter-Member State trade (that is, Article 36 (now 30) derogations and mandatory requirements exceptions). Council Resolution of 7 May 1985 set out a 'new approach to technical harmonisation and standards' which was essential for the improvement of the competitiveness of Community industry.

In an annex, the Council laid down the four fundamental principles on which the new approach was to be based:

(i)   legislative harmonization is limited to the adoption, by means of Directives based on Article 100 of the EEC Treaty, of the essential safety requirements (or other requirements in the general interest) with which products put on the market must conform, and which would therefore enjoy free movement throughout the Community;

(ii) the task of drawing up the technical specifications needed for the production and placing on the market of products conforming to the essential requirements established by the Directives, while taking into account the current stage of technology, is entrusted to organizations competent in the standardization area;

(iii) these technical specifications are not mandatory and maintain their status of voluntary standards;

(iv) but at the same time national authorities are obliged to recognize that products manufactured in conformity with harmonized standards (or, provisionally, with national standards) are presumed to conform to the 'essential requirements' established by the Directive. [This signifies that the producer has the choice of not manufacturing in conformity with the standards but that in this event he has an obligation to prove that his products conform to the essential requirements of the Directive.]

In order that this system may operate, it is necessary:

(i)   on the one hand, that the standards offer a guarantee of quality with regard to the 'essential requirements' established by the Directives;

(ii) on the other hand, that the public authorities keep intact their responsibility for the protection of safety (or other requirements envisaged) on their territory.

The Council further explained that, in following this system of legislative harmonisation in each area in which it was feasible, the Commission intended to halt the proliferation of excessively technical separate Directives for each product. The scope of Directives according to the 'general reference to standards' formula would encompass 'wide product categories and types of risk'. On this basis, the Commission proceeded to establish codes of essential requirements incorporating 'European' standards in both existing product markets and in newly emerging fields where rapid technological change was taking place.

Additionally, in 1983, in the proactive Council Directive 83/189, the Community established an 'early warning' system requiring prior notification to the Commission of draft technical standards and regulations introduced in the Member States. The Commission may require the adoption of any such national measure to be delayed for three months, in which it will be examined both by the Commission and the other Member States. There are several possible outcomes: for example, the measure may be given the 'all clear', it may be amended on an informal consultative basis, a formal legal challenge to it may otherwise ensue, or the Commission may decide to put the matter on a Community basis and proceed to the adoption of a harmonisation Directive. (Note that this is the Directive at the centre of Case C-194/94 *CIA Security*

International in Chapter 8, in which Belgian failure to notify regulations led to their unenforceability.)

Codes of Essential Requirements

By this method, any product lawfully manufactured and marketed in one Member State will enjoy free circulation throughout the Community *provided* certain minimum standards are met. To this end, the Council need now only agree on a majority basis under the new Article 95 (formerly 100a), using the co-decision procedure, 'codes of essential requirements' for broad, sufficiently homogeneous product areas or types of risk, thus leaving manufacturers greater flexibility in deciding how to meet such requirements.

Under the terms of Article 95, Article 95(3) lays down that these framework harmonisation codes will focus on essential health and safety requirements and environment and consumer protection. The Commission is to '*take as a base* a high level of protection taking account in particular of any new development based on scientific facts' (emphasis added). Measures have been adopted relating to health (for example, food additives), safety (for example, toys and construction products), the environment (for example, air pollution by gaseous emissions from motor vehicles) and consumer protection (for example, product liability: Directive 85/374).

These Directives have a common format covering such matters as definitions, rules about placing the product on the market, essential safety requirements, the obligation on Member States to respect the principle of free movement of goods, proof of and means of attestation to conformity, etc: see, for example, Council Directive 88/378 on the safety of toys, below.

It has been said in this regard that the idea that harmonisation leads to less variety is erroneous. At one time, fears arose as to the emergence of a single 'Euro-beer'. Although products may be standardised in certain essential respects, they can still exhibit wide variations of styling and performance. For example, so this argument runs, the car in the EC has been subject to considerable harmonisation, but the range of choice is still wide.

Goods complying with the 'essential requirements' of a framework Directive must be given free circulation, so ensuring that mutual recognition is made of Member States' individual product composition rules and quality standards. As the Council Resolution of 1985 indicated, this will involve close co-operation between the Commission, European standardisation organisations (see below) and national bodies such as the British Standards Institute (BSI):

> The quality of harmonized standards must be ensured by standardization mandates, conferred by the Commission, the execution of which must conform to the general guidelines which have been the subject of agreement between the Commission and the European standardization organizations. In so far as national standards are concerned, their quality must be verified by a procedure at Community level managed by the Commission, assisted by a standing committee composed of officials from national administrations.

In addition, and again in line with the Council Resolution, the Commission is charged with developing common criteria for the evaluation of testing laboratories and certification agencies in order to achieve mutual recognition of testing throughout the Community:

> At the same time, safeguard procedures must be provided for, under the management of the Commission assisted by the same committee, in order to allow the competent public authorities the possibility of contesting the conformity of a product, the validity of a certificate or the quality of a standard.

European Standards

The second principle in the Council Resolution states that 'the task of drawing up the technical specification [regarding design and composition, etc]' for products which will be deemed to conform to the 'essential requirements' established by the Directives, 'while taking into account the current state of technology, is entrusted to organisations competent in the standardisation area'. Such bodies are the *Comité Européen de la Normalisation (CEN)*, the *Comité Européen de la Normalisation Electronique* (CENELEC) and the European Telecommunications Standards Institute: see, for example, the Preamble to the Toy Safety Directive. The British Standards Institute (BSI) serves British interests on these bodies. Over 800 European standards were adopted between 1984 and 1990, three times as many as in the previous 20 years. The Community standardisation bodies operate on the basis of qualified majority voting.

As an illustrative indication of how the 'new approach' works, the Preamble to Council Directive 88/378 on the safety of toys states, in part:

> ... the laws, regulations and administrative provisions in force in the various Member States relating to the safety characteristics of toys differ in scope and content ... such disparities are liable to create barriers to trade and unequal conditions of competition within the internal market without necessarily affording consumers in the common market, especially children, effective protection against the hazards arising from the products in question;

> ... these obstacles to the attainment of an internal market in which only sufficiently safe products would be sold should be removed ... for this purpose, the marketing and free movement of toys should be made subject to uniform rules based on the objectives regarding protection of consumer health and safety as set out in the Council resolution of 23 June 1986 concerning the future orientation of the policy of the European Economic Community for the protection and promotion of consumer interests;

> ... to facilitate proof of conformity with the essential requirements, it is necessary to have harmonized standards at European level which concern, in particular, the design and composition of toys so that products complying with them may be assumed to conform to the essential requirements ... these standards harmonized at European level are drawn up by private bodies and must remain non-mandatory texts ... for that purpose the European Committee for Standardization (CEN) and the European Committee for Electrotechnical Standardization (CENELEC) are recognized as the competent bodies for the adoption of harmonized standards ...

> ... in accordance with the Council resolution of 7 May 1985 on a new approach to technical harmonization and standards, the harmonization to be achieved should consist in establishing the essential safety requirements to be satisfied by all toys if they are to be placed on the market.

... toys placed on the market should not jeopardize the safety and/or health either of users or of third parties .

... compliance with the essential requirements is likely to guarantee consumer health and safety ... all toys placed on the market must comply with these requirements and, if they do, no obstacle must be put in the way of their free movement;

... toys may be presumed to comply with these essential requirements where they are in conformity with the harmonized standards, reference numbers of which have been published in the *Official Journal of the European Communities* ...

... cases might arise where a toy does not satisfy the essential safety requirements ... in such cases, the Member State which ascertains this fact must take all appropriate measures to withdraw the products from the market or to prohibit their being placed on the market ... a reason must be given for this decision and, where the reason is a shortcoming in the harmonized standards, these, or a part thereof, must be withdrawn from the list published by the Commission;

... the Commission is to ensure that the harmonized European standards in all the areas covered by the essential requirements listed in Annex II are drawn up in sufficient time to enable Member States to adopt and publish the necessary provisions by 1 July 1989 ... the national provisions adopted on the basis of this Directive should consequently become effective on 1 January 1990 ...

In Annex II 'Essential Safety Requirements for Toys', particular risks are listed under the headings physical and mechanical properties, flammability, chemical properties, electrical properties, hygiene and radioactivity.

The 'new approach' is nevertheless not without its critics (see, for example, materials in Weatherill, Chapter 16 under the heading 'Harmonisation policy') and problems have arisen and will continue to arise:

For example, a cellular phone may enjoy free circulation, but for technical reasons (that is, it is only compatible with its own domestic network), it cannot be used in another Member State. Therefore, where necessary, the Commission aims to develop specific European standards, so that not only can the product in question enjoy free circulation to other Member States, but can actually be used there. This will also entail some harmonisation of testing procedures, so that each country accepts certificates awarded in other Member States [*Deloitte's 1992 Guide*].

Similarly, an article by James Erlichman (Consumer Affairs Correspondent) in *The Guardian* in February 1991 under the heading 'EC reopens door to foam fire hazard' reported that:

Highly flammable furniture foam, banned in Britain two years ago, will go back on sale unless fire chiefs and consumer groups can force changes to new European Community law.

The old style foam was removed from new bedding and furniture after fire chiefs blamed its noxious smoke for the death of 24 people in house fires during the Christmas period in 1988. Their campaign won public sympathy and forced the Government to require manufacturers to use only safer 'combustion modified foam' after February 1989.

Deaths from house fires have fallen since the introduction of the new foam, which is harder to ignite and gives off much less toxic smoke.

But an EC draft directive requires furniture foam to pass only a simple ignition test. It does not limit the amount and speed of toxic smoke from ignited foam. 'This omission will allow the old-style conventional foam back on the market', said Bob Graham, assistant chief fire officer for Greater Manchester, who led the fight to have the lethal foam banned. 'The standard is being determined by businessmen, not by scientists and consumers.'

Critics say the draft directive is weak because it is being written by DG3, the European Commission department concerned only with creating a single market. The regulations would also lower British standards for foam furniture in cinemas, discos and other public buildings ...

Article 95(4)–(10): 'Major Needs' and 'New Scientific Evidence'

Article 95

4 If, after the adoption by the Council or by the Commission of a harmonization measure, a Member State deems it necessary to maintain national provisions on grounds of major needs referred to in Article 36, or relating to protection of the environment or the working environment, it shall notify the Commission of these provisions as well as the grounds for maintaining them.

5 Moreover, without prejudice to paragraph 4, if, after the adoption by the Council or by the Commission of a harmonization measure, a Member State deems it necessary to introduce national provisions based on new scientific evidence relating to the protection of the environment or the working environment on grounds of a problem specific to that Member State arising after the adoption of the harmonization measure, it shall notify the Commission of the envisaged provisions as well as the grounds for introducing them.

Article 95(4) is a modification of Article 100a(4) and Article 95(5) is a new provision introduced by the ToA.

Under Article 95(4), a Member State may seek to maintain national provisions only on grounds of 'major needs' as listed in Article 30 (formerly 36), for example, protection of health and life of humans, animals or plants, together with the environment and working environment, where it considers that European standards do not constitute a sufficient guarantee of the particular public interest objective in question.

Within its terms, Article 95(5) concerns the introduction (not maintenance as in 95(4)) of national provisions, based on new scientific evidence and problems specific to the Member State in question. Article 95(8) covers specific problems relating to public health, which must be notified and dealt with by the Commission immediately.

Article 95(6)–(8) deals generally with Commission procedure following notification. Bearing in mind danger for public health, it shall approve or reject national provisions notified under Article 95(4) and (5) within six months (or complex matters within 12 months). If the national provisions are verified as a means of arbitrary discrimination or disguised restriction on inter-Member State trade or as obstacles to the functioning of the Internal Market, they will be rejected. Approval may well follow a negotiated settlement.

A special direct enforcement action is provided for in Article 95(9) whereby 'the Commission and any Member State may bring the matter directly before the Court of Justice if it considers that another Member State is making improper use' of the derogations provided for in Article 95. A harmonisation measure may itself contain a 'safeguard clause' authorising Member States to take temporary measures, subject to a

Community control procedure, in the event of sudden and unforeseen dangers to health, etc: Article 95(10).

At the time of its introduction, there were fears that Member States would regularly turn to Article 100a(4) (now 95(4)) – the so called 'price paid for majority voting' – and so undermine the 'new approach' to harmonisation. This has not proved to be the case: in only one instance, concerning Council Directive 91/173 on the marketing and use of dangerous substances, has the Commission had cause formally to confirm the national (German) provisions in question. These provisions related to a substance known as pentachlorophenol (PCP) which is dangerous to both health and the environment. However, in Case C-41/93 *France v Commission (Re PCP Rules)*, the Commission's Decision based on Article 100a(4) confirming German rules, which virtually prohibited the commercial or industrial use of PCP (in derogation from the less restrictive provisions of Directive 91/173) was challenged by France on the basis of the third paragraph of Article 100a(4) (see now 95(4)). The Court held that the Commission's Decision, which merely stated that the objective of the German measures was the protection of health and the environment, was insufficiently reasoned in terms of fact and law as required by Article 190 (now 253). The Decision was therefore annulled.

1992 AND AFTER

The concept of an internal or single market, not only for goods but also services, persons and capital, rests on an acceptance by the Member States, in political and economic terms, of the culture of the 'market'. This implies trust in the effectiveness of a high degree of free enterprise and 'effective competition', within a regulatory framework, in order to bring about the anticipated benefits not only for 'players' such as the business entities with the capacity to operate successfully in such a vast market but also to consumers and workers. It is also a market in which both economically powerful and economically weaker Member States must necessarily participate. These are matters which remain fertile ground for disagreements and tensions within the Community.

The 'completion' of the Internal Market in 1992 was as much a matter of theory as of reality. The legislation was mostly in place but it had not necessarily been implemented by the Member States. The principle of mutual recognition established by the Court in *Cassis de Dijon* and the cornerstone of the harmonisation programme was not necessarily being respected. A great many equivalent measures remained and may still remain to hinder inter-Member State trade. The Member States are still notifying a great many new draft technical regulations which could undermine the Single Market.

Since 1992, the Commission has turned increasingly towards the task of ensuring efficient management of the Single Market particularly as regards monitoring Member States' compliance with the legal framework. In 1997, it published an 'Action Plan for the Single Market' which, as endorsed by the European Council at Amsterdam, contained the basis for the removal of remaining obstacles to free movement. The Plan established four 'Strategic Targets':

(a) *Making the Rules More Effective*, involving proper enforcement of the common rules and simplification of the rules at both Community and national level:

The primary responsibility for enforcing Single Market rules rests with the Member States. The Single Market will not operate effectively unless they ensure that the rules are fully respected by all concerned. Those who breach the rules should be subject to penalties under national law that are effective and proportionate and that act as a deterrent. Problems need to be sorted out quickly in today's Single Market to avoid undermining the confidence of businesses and consumers.

(b) *Dealing with Key Market Distortions* on the basis of general agreement that tax barriers and anti-competitive behaviour constitute distortions that need to be tackled.

(c) *Removing Sectoral Obstacles to Market Integration* which may require legislative action to fill gaps in the Single Market framework and a change in national administrations' attitudes towards the Single Market.

(d) *Delivering a Single Market for all Citizens* on the understanding that the Single Market generates employment, increases personal freedom and benefits consumers, while ensuring high levels of both health and safety and environmental protection. Further steps are required to enhance the social dimension of the Single Market; citizens must be aware of their Single Market rights and be able to obtain speedy redress.

REFERENCES AND FURTHER READING

International Trade

Buckley, PJ and Brooke, MZ, *International Business Studies*, 1992, Part 2.5, 'Barriers to world trade'.

Hine, RC, *The Political Economy of European Trade*, 1986.

Kindelberger, CP, 'Commercial policy between the wars', in *The Cambridge Economic History of Europe*, Vol XIII.

Swann, D, *The Economics of the Common Market*, 1995, Chapters 4 and 5.

Charges and Taxation

Danusso, M and Denton, R, 'Does the European Court of Justice look for a protectionist motive under Article 95?' (1990) 1 LIEI 67.

Easson, AJ, 'Fiscal discrimination: new perspectives on Article 95' (1981) 18 CML Rev 521.

Lonbay, J, 'A review of recent tax cases' (1989) 14 EL Rev 48.

Van der Zanden, JB and Terra, BJM, 'The removal of tax barriers' (1989) 1 LIEI 137 (Harmonisation).

Non-Tariff Barriers

Alter, KJ and Meunier-Aitsahalia, S, 'Judicial politics in the European Community: European integration and the pathbreaking *Cassis de Dijon* decision' (1994) 26 Comparative Political Studies 535.

Arnull, A, 'What shall we do on Sunday?' (1991) 16 EL Rev 112.

Barnard, C, 'Fitting the remaining pieces into the goods and persons jigsaw' (2001) 26 EL Rev 35.

Chalmers, D, 'Repackaging the Internal Market – the ramifications of the *Keck* judgment' (1994) 19 EL Rev 385.

Koutrakos, P, 'On groceries, alcohol and olive oil: more on free movement of goods after *Keck*' (2001) 26 EL Rev 391.

Oliver, P, 'Measures of equivalent effect: a reappraisal' (1982) 19 CML Rev 217.

Oliver, P, 'Some further reflections on the scope of Articles 28–30 (ex 30–36) EC' (1999) 36 CML Rev 783.

Steiner, J, 'Drawing the line: uses and abuses of Article 30 EEC' (1992) 29 CML Rev 749 (Sunday trading).

Weatherill, S, 'After *Keck*: Some thoughts on how to clarify the clarification' (1996) 33 CML Rev 885.

Weatherill, S, 'Recent case law concerning the free movement of goods: mapping the frontiers of market deregulation' (1999) 36 CML Rev 51.

Wils, WPJ, 'The search for the rule in Article 30 EEC: much ado about nothing?' (1993) 18 EL Rev 415.

See also case notes, particularly in the Common Market Law Review and the European Law Review and surveys of cases on the free movement of goods in those journals.

Internal Market and Harmonisation

Bieber, R *et al* (eds), 1992: *One European Market?*, 1988.

Brearley, M and Quigley, C, *Completing the Internal Market of the European Community*, 1989, sections on 'Control of goods' and 'Free movement of goods'.

Dougan, M, 'Minimum harmonisation and the Internal Market' (2000) 37 CML Rev 853.

Gormley, LW, 'Some reflections on the Internal Market and free movement of goods' (1989) 1 LIEI 9.

McGee, A and Weatherill, S, 'The evolution of the Single Market – harmonisation or liberalisation?' (1990) 53 MLR 578.

Pelkmans, J and Winter, A, *Europe's Domestic Market*, 1988.

Slot, PJ, 'Harmonisation' (1996) 21 EL Rev 378.

Sun, J-M and Pelkmans, J, 'Regulatory competition and the Single Market' (1995) 33 JCMS 67.

Van Empel, M, 'The 1992 programme: interaction between legislation and judiciary' (1982) 2 LIEI 1.

Vignes, D, 'The harmonisation of national legislation and the EEC' (1990) 15 EL Rev 358.

Weatherill, S, *Cases and Materials on EC Law*, 2000, Chapter 16, '(B) Harmonisation policy'; '(C) Methods of harmonisation'.

Weatherill, S, 'New Strategies for managing the EC's Internal Market' (2000) 53 CLP 595.

CHAPTER 13

THE FREE MOVEMENT OF PERSONS
AND CITIZENSHIP

INTRODUCTION

The European Community legal regime originally provided rights of free movement for nationals of the Member States only on the narrow ground of taking up, either as an employee or as a self-employed person, an economic activity in the host State:

> The founding Treaties do not purport to establish an absolute freedom of migration in a general sense. They confine themselves to the movement of persons as an economic factor of production of the commodities envisaged by each Treaty [Lasok, *The Law of the Economy in the European Communities*, 1980].

Since then, both primary and secondary legislative provisions and judicial developments have extended the range of persons who may claim rights to move and reside in a host Member State and the range of rights available to them. From 1968, it has been the case that members of the family of the person qualified to exercise the rights of free movement are not similarly restricted to being nationals of the Member States. Furthermore, the focus now has moved on to consider both general rights of movement, even of those who are not economically active, and the meaning and rights stemming from the concept of European Union Citizenship contained in Articles 17 and 18 (formerly 8 and 8a) of the EC Treaty, although this consideration is far from new, as can be witnessed by early articles on the topic as listed in 'References and Further Reading' at the end of the chapter. Additionally, the status and rights of nationals from third countries (TCNs) who are lawfully resident in one Member State are also receiving the attention of the Court of Justice, the Commission and academic authors.

This chapter will consider in turn: the Treaty and secondary legislation and case law arising from and interpreting the provisions on workers and the self-employed, the rights of those and their family exercising free movement, the derogations allowed to the Member States, general free movement developments, citizenship and the rights of TCNs.

First of all, what were the reasons for the inclusion of persons in the original Treaty? Free movement of persons is one of the four fundamental freedoms outlined in Article 14 (formerly 7a), but was their inclusion to help the economic development of the Communities and the Member States or was it a concern for individual rights of freedom? The arguments are finely balanced and not all academic opinion has been in agreement. In the view of Hartley, who has written extensively on the free movement of persons and immigration in the Community:

> ... the EEC does not give the right of free movement to everyone, but only to certain categories of persons – workers, self-employed persons and providers of services. The absence of a general right of free movement, and the consequent categorization of the persons who benefit from it, is one of the basic features of the Community law on this subject ... If we just look at the EEC Treaty, especially if we concern ourselves only with the Treaty in its original form, the economic viewpoint predominates.... One can conclude, therefore, that the authors of the EEC Treaty regarded the Community as predominantly an economic organisation.

However, Hartley later observed that:

> ... though the Community law on the free movement of persons was originally adopted for the purpose of attaining economic objectives, in particular the establishment of the common market, its nature has changed, together with that of the Community itself: freedom of movement for the citizens of the Community is now regarded as an objective in its own right [in Green *et al*, *The Legal Foundations of the Single European Market*, 1991].

In other words, the individual right was merely a by-product of the legal economic construction of the Common Market:

> ... most importantly of all, and most revealingly, when an alleged social right has been even remotely perceived as threatening an economic objective, then the latter has consistently been supported. In *Gebroeders Beentjes* (Case 31/87 [1988] ECR 4635) the Court allowed a contractor to evade Community provisions designed to aid the long-term unemployed, in order to protect freedom of contract in the public procurement field ... Free movement is only free so long as it does not cost money [Ward, 1996].

On the other hand, Wyatt and Dashwood, even in their first edition, noted that:

> It is significant that the macroeconomic objectives of the Community are placed second to the personal rights of the Community worker to improve his standard of life by the exercise of rights by Art 48 [now 39] [Wyatt and Dashwood, *The Substantive Law of the EC*, 1980].

The Commission's view was that:

> The right to go from one country to another is important on several levels. On the human level first of all. A citizen of one Member State of the Community who goes to live and work in a second Member State, enjoying the same economic rights as its nationals, is exercising a new freedom, a new personal right. [European Documentation Series – 3/1982 'Freedom of movement for persons in the European Community', European Commission, Office for Official Publications of the European Communities, 1982].

So, was the inclusion of such rights a reflection of the economic conclusion? In the past, it may have been easier for labour to move to capital than to move capital to set up productive forces where labour surpluses existed. Evidence of the former was shown in the 1950s and 1960s by the vast number of workers imported by France, West Germany and the UK from third world and southern Mediterranean countries in order to feed the growing industrial capacity. Cheap labour and, at the time, workers from North Africa, Turkey and the West Indies (and when these countries were not in the EU, from Greece, Ireland, Portugal and Spain) were very welcome. These workers still represent a sizeable proportion of the EU working population: 4% of EU nationals are non-EU citizens, which is almost 13 million throughout the EU; other estimates put this figure lower at 10 million (EC COM (1994) 23, Annex I, 22). Northern Europeans, however, did not respond to this situation to migrate in large numbers, even from the worst black spots of unemployment in the EU. Nor have they done so subsequently, regardless or despite the aims and provisions of the Treaty:

> Some studies have been undertaken of the trend and pattern of migration within the Community. One study (Yannopoulos, 1969), based on the years 1958 to 1965 inclusive, reveals the following facts. The number of work permits granted for the first time to foreign workers (intra-Community migration) rose from 156,000 in 1958 to 305,000 in 1965. In 1965 80 per cent of all permits issued in respect of intra-

Community migration were for movement to West Germany. Italy was the main provider of migrant labour – between 1958 and 1965 the Italian percentage of total Community workers migrating ranged from 75 per cent to 83 per cent [Swann, *The Economics of the Common Market*, 1981].

And, as can be observed from another commentator a year later:

Even within the Community the view was that capital should move to labour rather than the other way round. In a Recommendation and Opinion of July 1962 (JO 1962, 2118), the Commission argued that this freedom was not concerned with traditional notions of emigration and immigration. These notions assumed that individuals migrated because they were unable to secure satisfactory living standards in their own countries. The Community, however, sought to ensure uniformly high living standards throughout its territory. The problems of depressed areas of high unemployment should be remedied through investments in those areas rather than though emigration. In effect capital should be moved to the unemployed rather than vice versa ... Consequently, in the context of the Community the traditional motive for migration would cease to exist ... Therefore, the freedom of movement in Community law represented a considerable expansion of personal freedom [Evans].

Hence then, even from the 1960s, there has been and is limited advantage for workers within Europe to migration because of the disincentives of culture and linguistics which exist and because of the limited economic gain to be achieved. Also, it is hardly contestable now that capital is easier to move than labour and that, rather than a large scale of migration from areas of higher unemployment to areas of lower unemployment, companies, especially multinationals, can far more easily set up productive capacity or, even more simply, enter into joint ventures or even franchise production in lower cost third world countries. The examples of manufacturing in China and call centres in India could not be more obvious. And, in order to gain a place in the Internal Market, Asian capital and capital from other non-EU countries is transferring to Europe.

What are the conclusions to be drawn here? That the EU globally is doing little to encourage movement! Certainly, the provisions of the Treaty have had limited success in promoting wholesale development of economic activity or encouraging mass movement of workers, but in individual circumstances, it clearly brings great benefits. But, even if the original aims were only economic, it is fair to say that other objectives in the realms of social policy do now have a greater significance in the Community as can be observed from the content of legislation and policy outlines of the Community: see Articles 17 and 18 EC, the Directives on general rights of residence not based on economic activities, and the EU Charter of Fundamental Rights. Furthermore, the rights that have been established are of concrete benefit to those EU workers who do take advantage of them. The rights themselves are valuable and enforceable, as will be seen from the examples which follow.

The Scope of Legal Protection

The scope of protection of EC law is determined initially by reference to the two main concepts of territorial and personal scope (*ratione materiae* and *ratione personae*). The territorial scope is, for the most part, clear, but see Case C-214/94 *Boukhalfa v Germany*, in which Article 39 (formerly 48) was applied to a Belgium national resident in a non-

Member State (Algeria) because she was employed in the German embassy there but had not been employed or even been to the other Member State (Germany).

Personal scope is defined by the possession of nationality of a Member State. More will be said about this under the citizenship section below. Then it is necessary to come within the material scope envisaged by a particular Treaty Article. Article 39, for example, provides for the free movement of workers. Whilst the cases below, in the section on citizenship, do show now that some fundamental rights may stem from EU citizenship *alone*, being classified as a worker or self-employed for the purposes of Community law is very important, because many other rights and benefits flow from this for the worker and his or her family. Note that it is not necessary for the members of a worker's family to be Member State nationals in order to obtain benefits, as will be seen when considering the secondary legislation and case law below. However, the development of citizenship and case law relating to wholly internal situations and TCNs means that status as an economically active Member State national may not be as important today as previously: see the sections at the end of the chapter.

EC Treaty Provisions

Free movement for the self-employed is broadly outlined in Articles 3(1)(c) and 14(2) EC:

Article 3

1   For the purposes set out in Article 2, the activities of the Community shall include, as provided in this Treaty and in accordance with the timetable set out therein:

    ...

    (c) an internal market characterised by the abolition, as between Member States, of obstacles to the free movement of goods, persons, services and capital;

Article 14 (formerly 7a)

...

2   The internal market shall comprise an area without internal frontiers in which the free movement of goods, persons, services and capital is ensured in accordance with the provisions of this Treaty.

Article 12 (formerly 6) EC has also been very important in the development of this area of law in outlawing various discriminatory rules and practices by Member States and organisations which do not easily fit directly within the provisions on workers, establishment or services:

Article 12 (formerly 6)

Within the scope of application of this Treaty, and without prejudice to any special provisions contained therein, any discrimination on grounds of nationality shall be prohibited.

Specifically, free movement is provided for by Article 39 (formerly 48) for workers, by Articles 43–48 (formerly 52–58) for freedom of establishment and Articles 49–55 (formerly 59–66) for the freedom to provide services.

WORKERS

Article 39 (formerly 48)

1   Freedom of movement for workers shall be secured within the Community.

2   Such freedom of movement shall entail the abolition of any discrimination based on nationality between workers of the Member States as regards employment, remuneration and other conditions of work and employment.

Article 39 has been held to be directly effective, first in Case 167/73 *Commission v France (Re French Merchant Seamen)*, in which a requirement that bridge crew should be French nationals was held to be a breach of Article 39. This position was confirmed in Case 41/74 *Van Duyn v Home Office*. Its horizontal direct effects were implied in Case 36/74 *Walrave and Koch v Association Union Cycliste Internationale* because this was a sporting association set up under public law. However, horizontal direct effects were definitively established in Case C-281/98 *Angonese* in which Article 39(2) was upheld in a case brought by an individual against a private bank.

The Court of Justice has adopted a very liberal approach to the interpretation of the free movement of workers provisions, both the Treaty principles and the further extensions of these principles in the secondary legislation, whereas the exceptions to the rights granted to the Member States are interpreted strictly. The provisions of the Treaty have been subject to considerable expansion and interpretation, for example, the concept of 'worker', considered below.

The Definition of 'Worker'

In order for a person to benefit personally, or for his or her family to benefit from derived rights arising under Articles 39–42 (formerly 48–51) and law made thereunder, that person must be classified as a worker. Although there is no definition of the term 'worker' in the EC Treaty, the Court of Justice has held that the term must have a Community meaning, and cannot be the subject of differing interpretations by the Member States. This means that it is for the Court and not the national courts to define the scope of the term. The Court is progressively defining the scope of 'worker' in a Community context. In the *Hoekstra* case, it declared the reason for this view:

If the definition of this term were a matter for the competence of the national courts, it would be possible for every Member State to modify the term worker and so to eliminate at will the protection afforded by the EEC Treaty to certain categories of person.

Then, in a series of cases, the Court has steadily defined those coming within the status of worker as understood by Community law.

Case 53/81 *Levin v The Minister of State for Justice*

This case concerned the level of work that a person needs to do before he or she can be classed as a worker. The female plaintiff was a British citizen married to a South African and working in Holland as a chambermaid for 20 hours per week at £30.00 per week. These earnings were well below the subsistence level in the Netherlands. The Dutch government argued that because she was a part time worker earning below the subsistence level, she was not a 'favoured EEC citizen' and could not benefit from the provisions of EEC law guaranteeing freedom of movement of workers.

The Court of Justice held that these considerations were irrelevant to her status as a worker, and declared that whether she was a full or part time worker, she was entitled to the status of worker provided that the work was genuine and effective and not so infinitesimal as to be disregarded. The Court ruled, however, that the 'rules cover only the pursuit of effective and genuine activities, to the exclusion of activities on such a small scale as to be regarded as purely marginal and ancillary', and that 'those rules guarantee only the free movement of persons who pursue or are desirous of pursuing a genuine economic activity'.

Hence, the essential defining characteristic of work is that it is activity of an economic nature.

Case 139/85 *Kempf v Minister of Justice*

A German national worked as a part time flute teacher giving only 12 lessons per week. His limited income was topped up to the Dutch minimum income level with supplementary benefit under the Unemployment Benefit Act. He was refused a residence permit on the grounds that he was not a 'favoured EEC citizen'.

The Court ruled that if a person is in effective and genuine part time employment, he may not be excluded from the sphere of application of the rules on freedom of movement of workers merely because the remuneration he derives from it is below the minimum level of subsistence set by national law. It was 'irrelevant whether those supplementary means of subsistence are derived from property or from the employment of a member of his family, as was the case in *Levin*, or whether, as in this instance, they are obtained from financial assistance drawn from the public funds of the Member State in which he resides'.

The Dutch court had found that the work was genuine and effective.

Case 66/85 *Lawrie-Blum v Land Baden-Würtemberg*

The Court of Justice considered the compatibility of German rules restricting access to a preparatory service stage which was necessary to become a teacher. They laid down three essential characteristics to establish an employment relationship.

The Court stated that:

> The essential feature of an employment relationship, however, is that for a certain period of time a person performs services for and under the direction of another person in return for which he receives remuneration.

A generous application of these criteria occurred in the following case.

Case 196/87 *Steymann v Staatssecretaris van Justitie*

S was a German national living in the Netherlands. His work as a plumber in the Bhagwan Religious Community's activities for which remuneration was paid in the form of pocket money and the meeting of material needs was considered by the Court to satisfy the criteria laid down previously in *Lawrie-Blum*:

> In a case such as the one before the national court it is impossible to rule out *a priori* the possibility that work carried out by members of the community in question constitutes an economic activity within the meaning of Article 2 of the Treaty. In so far as the work, which aims to ensure a measure of self-sufficiency for the Bhagwan Community, constitutes an essential part of participation in that community, the services which the latter provides to its members may be regarded as being an indirect *quid pro quo* for their work.

The actual length and type of employment was considered in the following case.

Case 357/89 *Raulin v Netherlands Ministry of Education and Science*

Raulin had worked for 60 hours in total over eight months under an on-call contract. The Court of Justice held that:

> The national court may, however, when assessing the effective and genuine nature of the activity in question, take account of the irregular nature and limited duration of the services actually performed under a contract for occasional employment. The fact that the person concerned worked only a very limited number of hours in a labour relationship may be an indication that the activities exercised are purely marginal and ancillary. The national court may also take account, if appropriate, of the fact that the person must remain available to work if called upon to do so by the employer.

This would appear to hand the discretion to the Member States to decide who is a worker where there is most room for argument. Some limits to the definition appear to have been found in Case 344/87 *Bettray v Staatssecretaris van Justitie*. The Court of Justice held that work under the Social Employment Law cannot be regarded as an effective and genuine economic activity if it constitutes merely a means of rehabilitation or reintegration for the persons concerned and the purpose of the paid employment, which is adapted to the physical and mental possibilities of each person, is to enable those persons sooner or later to recover their capacity to take up ordinary employment or to lead as normal as possible a life.

Hence, persons on these schemes cannot be regarded as workers for the purposes of Community law, as the activities could not be carried out as real and genuine economic activities. Here the position was artificially created with government money and was not therefore genuine. So, although Bettray carried out work under supervision and was remunerated, the Court (in contrast to its position in *Levin*) looked at purpose and found that he was not a worker. This probably has the effect that all State sponsored training schemes are taken out of the scope of Article 39 (formerly 48) and there will neither be access to them nor unlawful discrimination as a result even if other EU citizens are refused entry to them.

Work Seekers

The term 'worker' is, however, wider than just referring to those in employment, and in certain circumstances also applies to those who are seeking work and those who, having lost one job involuntarily, are capable of taking another. This was confirmed in Article 7(1) of Directive 68/360, which provides that the right of residence is not lost through involuntary unemployment. However, although they may retain the status of worker they do not acquire all the additional advantages 'true' workers enjoy. Also, there is the question of how long that status is retained. When Directive 68/360 was discussed in Council, three months was the period of time suggested as the acceptable time a person could remain unemployed yet still enjoy the favoured status of EC worker. Increasingly, these discussions were pleaded before the Court of Justice as the actual time a Member State should allow a national of another Member State to remain in the country looking for work and thus be classed as a worker.

Two leading cases address these points.

Case 316/85 *Marie-Christine Lebon*

The Court of Justice held that those in search of work are not entitled to receive workers' benefits (in this case a social security support payment). Miss Lebon no longer lived with her parents, who were ex-workers, and therefore she did not qualify for benefits as a dependant of a worker. She then asked if she qualified for workers' benefits if she was looking, or intended to look, for work. The Court held that the benefits provided by legislation on free movement were only for those in actual employment and not for those who migrate in search of work and have not found it. She could temporarily be classified as a worker but not for the purposes of benefits.

Then is it just a question of how long the temporary status entitles a person to look for work?

Case C-292/89 *R v Immigration Appeal Tribunal ex p Antonissen*

The UK wished to deport Antonissen, who had been convicted of drugs offences, possession and intent to supply cocaine and was in the country for over three years without work before his imprisonment. UK legislation gave EC citizens six months in which to find employment.

The Court of Justice held:

> Article 48(3) must be interpreted as enumerating, in a non-exhaustive way, certain rights benefiting nationals of Member States in the context of the free movement of workers and that that freedom also entails the right for nationals of Member States to move freely within the territory of the other Member States and to stay there for the purposes of seeking employment.

The Court also held that statements recorded in Council minutes regarding the acceptable time for the pursuit of work before deportation would not be allowable, had no legal significance and could not be used to interpret the relevant legislative provisions. A Member State may deport an EC migrant worker subject to an appeal if he has not found employment after six months, unless evidence shows he or she is continuing to seek employment and that there are genuine chances of his or her being engaged. Therefore, after the expiry of a reasonable period, depending on the circumstances, persons may no longer be afforded the status and benefits of a worker under Community law and may lawfully be deported by a Member State.

Whether, following the case law discussed under citizenship below, the Member States retain this right to deport persons who have lawfully been resident without recourse to the public policy or security proviso remains to be seen.

Worker Training and Education

There have been occasions when the status of worker has been retained by EU nationals when they are, in fact, undergoing vocational training or in education. Previously, Community competence in this matter was limited to vocational training for work; now, however, it has been expanded by recent Treaty changes (see Articles 3(1)(q) and 149(2)), which in turn have been noted by the Court of Justice: see Case C-224/98 *Marie-Nathalie D'Hoop*).

Rights to education and training will also be considered below in respect of the right of family members to receive education, and in respect of the right to receive educational services.

Case 39/86 *Lair v Universität Hannover*

A French national employed in West Germany was refused a grant by the university for a maintenance award because she had not worked in the country continuously for at least five years. She could not be assisted under Article 7 (now 12) EC because the Court held that Article 7 only concerned access to vocational training which was within the Community sphere, whereas grants were a part of the Member States' sphere. However, the refusal was also considered under Regulation 1612/68 which prohibits discrimination in relation to social benefits for workers. The problem was, of course, that Mrs Lair, whilst at university, was not a worker. It was stated in the case that the period at university would lead to a professional qualification and was only a break in employment.

The Court of Justice held that, since there was no fixed legislative definition of worker, there was nothing to say that the definition must always depend on a continuing employment relationship. Certain rights have been guaranteed to workers after employment has finished, for example, the right to stay and social security rights. This could also apply to university training providing there was a link or continuity between work and university, in which case the university award could be considered a right under Regulation 1612/68.

Therefore, the status of worker was retained if a link exists between the previous occupation and the studies in question.

Returning to the case of *Raulin*, considered above, the Court of Justice held that the 60 hours' work had enabled Raulin to claim the protection of Article 39 (formerly 48) EC, despite the temporary nature of the work. However, a migrant worker who then left that employment to begin a course of full time study unconnected with the previous occupational activities did not retain the status as a worker for the purposes of Article 39. Such persons did, however, have a right of residence in the host State for the duration of the course of study, regardless of whether or not the host State had issued a residence permit.

Finally, in Case 197/86 *Brown*, the Scottish education department refused Brown (a dual national) a maintenance grant for university. He had worked for eight months in the UK prior to and as a precursor to university. The Court of Justice held that, whilst university training is to be regarded as mainly vocational, it is not part of the EC worker rights, but is only covered by Article 12 (formerly 7) EC generally outlawing discrimination. This covers tuition fees but not the maintenance grant, so a person who enters employment for eight months and who does so for the purposes of attending university is not a worker for the purposes of Article 39 (formerly 48) EC and Regulation 1612/68.

Given the generosity of more recent rulings on citizens' rights, below, *Brown* has probably now been overruled by Case C-184/99 *Grzelczyk*.

Thus, definitions of what constitutes vocational training and the link to work are therefore crucial for the determination of the status of a worker and the consequent benefits and rights, as is the number of weeks or hours worked. Citizens' rights, however, may have extended general rights to such an extent that it is no longer necessary to prove a link between past work and studies in order to avoid being discriminated against or indeed deported (see below).

The Prohibition of Discrimination

Having determined who is a worker, the next matter is to determine the rights that he or she has as a worker. The first and most fundamental right is not to be discriminated against, hence the need to determine the scope of discrimination. The concept of discrimination in EC law has been held by the Court of Justice to apply to both direct and indirect discrimination and applies to Articles 39, 43 and 49 (formerly 48, 52 and 59) equally. Clearly, where different rules apply to nationals and non-nationals, the discrimination will be struck down unless it comes within the exceptions provided in Articles 39(3) or (4) and 45 (formerly 55): see Case 167/73 *Commission v France (Re French Merchant Seamen)*, above. Covert or indirect discrimination which leads to the prejudicial treatment of non-nationals or rules which seem to apply fairly to both but which have an indirect discriminatory effect on non-nationals may also offend Community law, unless such rules or measures can be objectively justified.

Case 33/88 *Allué and Coonan v Università degli Studi di Venezia*

This case specifically concerned discrimination under Article 39(2) (formerly 48(2)) EC. The applicants, after five years of employment as foreign language lecturers, were informed that they could not be retained under a 1980 Italian Decree which limited the duration of employment of foreign language lecturers. Not all the foreign language lecturers were non-nationals (some 25 per cent were nationals) and, therefore, there was no dissimilar treatment, that is, no overt discrimination. Although the rule applied regardless of nationality, it nevertheless mainly affected the nationals of other Member States who made up 75 per cent of such language teachers, and it was held to be indirectly discriminatory where such limitations do not exist in respect of other workers.

It may be the case in future that the statutory definitions of direct and indirect discrimination now contained in Directives issued under Article 13 (formerly 6a), will be used by the Court of Justice: see, for example, Directive 2002/73. Furthermore, non-discriminatory obstacles to free movement can also be held contrary to the Treaty. Such obstacles may, however, be objectively justified. Hence, in this area of law, the prohibition of harmful rules goes beyond discrimination to cover rules which impede market access. The developing similarities to rules relating to goods are considered in Chapter 11.

Case 415/93 *Union Royal Belge des Sociétés de Football Association v Bosman*

This case concerned national football transfer rules which limited transfers and applied to all players and both national and cross border transfers; hence there was no discrimination on the grounds of nationality. The Court held that the rules were an obstacle to free movement by preventing or deterring players from leaving clubs. Such rules may be objectively justified if there is a legitimate aim compatible with the Treaty for pressing reasons of public interest and the measure is proportionate. The rules in this case were not so justified.

As Castro Oliviera has explained:

It seems clear that the case law on obstacles to the free movement of workers deals with two different types of cases. On the one hand, there are those cases in which the Court has found that a migrant worker, because he exercised his right to free movement, is at a disadvantage when his situation is compared to that of a non-migrant worker. However, this disadvantage does not result from a measure that is discriminatory on the grounds of nationality. On the other hand, in other cases, such a disadvantage does not appear to exist, but the possibility of moving to work in another Member State is, nonetheless, clearly restricted ... In both types of cases the Court has found that an obstacle to free movement exists and considered that the national measure was contrary to Art 39.

Workers' Rights

In addition to the right not to be discriminated against, workers enjoy a number of other rights. Article 39(3) outlines rights to enter, move freely, reside, seek and take up employment in another Member State. These rights are enumerated and supplemented by secondary legislation, notably Directive 68/360, Regulation 1612/68 and Regulation 1251/70, but note that virtually all the existing secondary legislation on the free movement of persons is due to be replaced by a consolidating Directive on free movement and residence of EU citizens: COM (2001) 257; [2001] OJ C270/150 in its latest draft and considered below:

Article 39(3) (formerly 48(3))

It [freedom of movement] shall entail the right, subject to limitations justified on grounds of public policy, public security or public health:

(a) to accept offers of employment actually made;

(b) to move freely within the territory of Member States for this purpose;

(c) to stay in a Member State for the purpose of employment in accordance with the provisions governing the employment of nationals of that State laid down by law, regulation or administrative action;

(d) to remain in the territory of a Member State after having been employed in that State, subject to conditions which shall be embodied in implementing regulations to be drawn up by the Commission.

Directive 68/360 provides for workers to leave one Member State and enter the territory of another and prescribes the entry formalities which it is permissible for Member States to impose, in particular the rules regarding the issue and withdrawal of residence permits. It applies to workers only and not to the self-employed, to whom Directive 73/148 applies.

Article 1 of Directive 68/360 abolishes restrictions on the movement and residence of nationals of Member States and family members who enter under the provisions of Regulation 1612/68, considered below.

Article 2 provides that exit States are obliged to allow nationals to leave and to grant passports. In the UK, this provision conflicts with the fact that the issue of passports is a royal prerogative which is discretionary on the part of the Home Secretary (see *R v Secretary of State for Foreign and Commonwealth Affairs ex p Everett* (1989)), although in practice this does not cause problems and the public policy proviso would probably provide the same right on the part of the UK to refuse to issue a passport in appropriate circumstances.

Article 3 provides that entrance States cannot demand an entry visa or equivalent documents from EU nationals. They can, however, require a passport or valid identity card from Member State nationals and visas from non-Union members of the family.

Case 68/89 *Commission v Netherlands (Re Entry Requirements)*

The Court held that the requirements for documentation under Directive 68/360 do not give a Member State the right to further questioning regarding the purpose and duration of stay, once the correct papers have been shown.

Whilst this sounds fine in legal theory, it does not always relate to the practice experienced by most travellers and, especially post-September 11 2001, it is not so sustainable. Arguably, questioning might be justified under the public policy or public security provisos.

Case C-344/95 *Commission v Belgium*

In this case, a delay in issuing documents, the limited duration of residence permits and payments demanded in excess of that comparable for national identity cards were all measures held by the Court to breach Directive 68/360.

Case C-378/97 *Criminal Proceedings v Florus Wijsenbeek*

In what was a test case for the rights under the European citizenship provisions, a Dutch MEP refused to show his passport and state his nationality on entering Holland. He was prosecuted for that failure. He claimed that the rights under Articles 7a and 8a (now 14 and 18) EC had direct effect and that he could rely on them. The Court held that even if they gave a right of free movement, Member States still had the right to carry out border checks, but that any penalty must be in line with similar national penalties.

Article 4 requires that a residence permit be granted to any worker who produces a passport and certificate of proof of employment. The latter is not a nationally produced or sanctioned work permit; it can merely be a letter of an offer of employment or job confirmation. Members of the worker's family must also be afforded a residence permit on production of a passport and proof of relationship or dependence. These rights must not be weakened by disproportionate penalties which hinder free movement when the worker has failed to comply with national legal requirements demanded of them.

Case 157/79 *R v Pieck*

In this case, a Dutch national re-entered the UK after his original six month entry permit had expired and he had failed to renew it. The authorities sought to deport him. The Court of Justice held that Article 4 means that a failure to obtain a permit could only result in penalties for minor offences. It was also held that the residence permit is not a precondition for residence, but merely evidence of the entitlement to enter and reside.

So the documents do not constitute the right itself but merely the proof of it. Administrative rules regulating the paperwork needed are acceptable, as is an appropriate sanction or penalty for their breach, but this would not usually justify deportation under normal circumstances, as this would be regarded as disproportionate.

Case C-24/97 *Commission v Germany*

In this case, it was held by the Court of Justice that it was a breach of Articles 39, 43 and 49 EC and Articles 4 of Directives 68/360 and 73/148 where non-EU nationals were fined more than nationals for a failure to carry a valid ID and strict liability was imposed on EU non-nationals, whereas actual intention (and not mere negligence) had to be proved on the part of nationals.

Article 5 provides that delays in furnishing a residence permit must not hinder taking up employment.

Article 6 provides that the permits must be valid for the whole territory of the Member State and valid for at least five years with automatic renewal.

Article 8(2) states that Member States may require EU nationals to report their presence in the host State. Any penalty, however, for a breach of the national rules must be proportionate.

Case 118/75 *Italy v Watson and Belmann*

In this case, Miss Watson, a UK national, was acting as an 'au pair' whilst staying with Mr Belmann. Both had failed to report this to the national authorities as required and faced imprisonment and fines under national law. In addition, Miss Watson was to be deported. The Italian Magistrate asked the Court of Justice if the punishments were compatible with EC law. The Court ruled that the use of internal rules, that is, the requirement to report, was acceptable but the penalty must be in proportion to the offence or damage caused, that is, a small fine. Therefore, any decision to deport would be contrary to the Treaty.

Regulation 1612/68 provides more substantive rights as an expansion of those in Article 39(2) and (3). Article 1 provides a right to take up employment in the host State under the same conditions as nationals. In particular, Article 7 is very far reaching and has been subject to considerable judicial elucidation. Notably, the Regulation provides significant rights for the family of a worker which are not provided under the primary Treaty provisions:

Regulation 1612/68

Article 1

1   Any national of a Member State, shall, irrespective of his place of residence, have the right to take up an activity as an employed person, and to pursue such activity, within the territory of another Member State in accordance with the provisions laid down by law, regulation or administrative action governing the employment of nationals of that State.

2   He shall, in particular, have the right to take up available employment in the territory of another Member State with the same priority as nationals of that State.

Article 2

Any national of a Member State and any employer pursuing an activity in the territory of a Member State may exchange their applications for and offers of employment, and may conclude and perform contracts of employment in accordance with the provisions in force laid down by law, regulation or administrative action, without any discrimination resulting therefrom.

Article 3(1) exempts the requirement of non-discrimination in terms of linguistic ability:

Article 3

1   Under this Regulation, provisions laid down by law, regulation or administrative action or administrative practices of a Member State shall not apply:

- where they limit application for and offers of employment, or the right of foreign nationals to take up and pursue employment or subject these to conditions not applicable in respect of their own nationals; or
- where, though applicable irrespective of nationality, their exclusive or principal aim or effect is to keep nationals of other Member States away from the employment offered. This provision shall not apply to conditions relating to linguistic knowledge required by reason of the nature of the post to be filled.

Case 379/87 *Groener v Minister for Education*

In this case, a language requirement for permanent positions in Irish schools was upheld by the Court of Justice even though it was not needed for the particular post applied for. The Court held that the requirement represented a clear policy of national law to promote and protect the Gaelic language, providing the level of language and testing was not disproportionate. The Court also held that a State cannot demand that the required linguistic knowledge be acquired within the national territory only. (For example, in Case C-281/98 *Angonese*, the requirement that a certification of bilingualism, required as a part of public policy, could only be accepted if issued by the local authorities, was held to be disproportionate.)

Article 7 has proved to provide a highly significant right for workers and their family:

1   A worker who is a national of a Member State may not, in the territory of another Member State, be treated differently from national workers by reason of his nationality in respect of any conditions of employment and work, in particular as regards remuneration, dismissal, and should he become unemployed, reinstatement or re-employment;

This provision has been applied to work experience gained in the home State prior to moving. This should be taken into account by a new employer in the host State to which a EU worker moves. To ignore this is to discriminate contrary to Article 7(1).

Case C-187/96 *Commission v Greece*

The Court of Justice held that a Greek administrative regulation and practice which did not take into account periods of employment in the public service of another Member State when determining seniority increments and salary grading breached Article 39 (formerly 48) EC and Article 7(1) of Regulation 1612/68. The Greek argument that in practice it was difficult to make the comparison was not accepted by the Court.

Similarly, in Case C-195/98 *Österreichischer Gewerkschaftsbund v Austria*, Austrian rules taking into account previous employment for the determination of teachers' pay was applied disadvantageously to periods spent in other Member States and held to infringe Article 39 and Article 7(1) of the Regulation.

Article 7(2) of the Regulation, in spite of its brevity, has proved to be a broad, flexible and far reaching right for workers:

Article 7(2) of Regulation 1612/68, which provides that the migrant worker shall enjoy the same social and tax advantages as national workers, has emerged as an increasingly important feature in the legal protection of the migrant and his family. It has been applied to areas as diverse as entitlement to social security benefits and the right to use a particular language before a national court. Its personal and territorial scope has also been developed and it has been held to apply to nationals of third countries who are family members of EEC migrant workers, and to cover the case of an EEC national working outside the Community in relation to social advantages with the Community [O'Keefe, 1986].

In Case C-279/93 *Schumacker*, S, a Belgian national, worked in Germany but continued to live in Belgium. He was taxed as a non-resident which meant he was denied certain allowances enjoyed by national workers. The Court held that the right to be taxed on the same basis as nationals where he worked was a tax advantage within Article 7(2).

In Case 137/84 *Mutsch*, a Luxembourg national living in a German speaking commune in Belgium was denied the use of German before a court, a right granted to the Belgian German minority. The Court held that right was a social advantage under Article 7(2), despite there being no link to a contract of employment.

Article 7(2) has even been interpreted to include a grant to cover funeral expenses in Case C-237/94 *O'Flynn* and the right to companionship of a co-habitee in Case 59/85 *Netherlands v Reed*, considered below.

In Case 207/78 *Ministère Public v Even*, the Court of Justice held that the advantages referred to in Regulation 1612/68 extended to:

[advantages] which whether or not linked to a contract of employment, are generally granted to national workers primarily because of their objective status as workers or by virtue of the mere fact of their residence on the national territory and the extension of which to workers who are nationals of other Member States therefore seems suitable to facilitate their mobility within the Community.

In the case, 'advantage' was not held to extend to a war pension benefit.

As will be seen below, Article 7(2) has also been extensively employed to provide rights for members of the worker's family.

Article 7(3) states: 'He shall also, by virtue of the same right and under the same conditions as national workers, have access to training in vocational schools and retraining centres.' This right has been employed to provide workers with the right to go to university and nevertheless retain their status as a worker providing there was a link between the genuine economic activity and the vocational studies pursued, as was seen in the *Lair* case above.

Article 9 provides that workers shall enjoy all the rights and benefits accorded to national workers in matters of housing including ownership and access to local authority housing lists. The Court of Justice held, in Case 305/87 *Commission v Greece*, that the Greek ban on foreigners owning property in Greece was in breach of that provision.

Rights of the Family of Workers

Regulation 1612/68

Article 10

1   The following shall, irrespective of their nationality, have the right to install themselves with a worker who is a national of one Member State and who is employed in the territory of another Member State:

(a) his spouse and their descendants who are under the age of 21 years or are dependants;

(b) dependent relatives in the ascending line of the worker and his spouse.

Other members of the family not covered by Article 10(1) are subject to Article 10(2):

> 2 Member States shall facilitate the admission of any member of the family not coming within the provisions of paragraph 1 if dependent on the worker referred to above or living under his roof in the country whence he comes.

Thus far, there has been no judicial help on this provision, so it is open as to just how far it might be interpreted by the Court of Justice. The proposed consolidation Directive, if passed in its present form, would, under the proposed Article 2, extend the right to join a worker in the host State to unmarried partners and children over 21 who are not necessarily dependent on their worker parent and to any direct member of the family as there seems to be no logic in denying them the right to join their family in the host State. Under the existing law, Article 10(1) refers to 'spouse' and this has been given its literal meaning by the Court.

Case 59/85 *Netherlands v Reed*

The Court of Justice was required to consider whether the term 'spouse' includes co-habitees. Miss Reed applied for a residence permit in Holland, claiming that her right to remain was based on her co-habitation with a UK national working in the Netherlands. The Dutch government refused to recognise this. The Court of Justice was aware that provisions of national laws regarding co-habitees' legal rights could be quite varied but it was unable to overcome the clear intention of Article 10 which referred to a relationship based on marriage. The Court referred instead to the 'social advantages' guaranteed under Article 7 of the Regulation as being capable of including the companionship of a co-habitee which could contribute to integration in the host country. Where such relationships amongst nationals were accorded the legal advantages under national law, these could not be denied to nationals of other Member States without being discriminatory and thus breaching Articles 7 and 48 (now 12 and 39) of the Treaty.

This is a somewhat convoluted decision, but it does provide a just result in the case. The co-habitee does not have independent rights, but the companionship of a co-habitee is regarded as one of the advantages to which workers are entitled.

Case 267/83 *Diatta v Land Berlin*

The Court of Justice considered the effect of separation and living apart on the rights of a third country national to remain in a Member State. Mrs Diatta, a Senegalese citizen, was married to a Frenchman living and working in Berlin. She obtained work in Berlin shortly after which the couple separated to live apart. Upon application to extend her residence permit, the German authorities refused on the ground that she was no longer a member of the family for the purposes of Regulation 1612/68.

The Court of Justice ruled that the rights under 1612/68 were not dependent on the requirements as to how or where members of the family lived, and a permanent common family dwelling could not be implied as a condition of the rights granted under Regulation 1612/68.

Thus, under a separation, providing that the marriage persists, the right to stay and work of a third country national also persists and, as was demonstrated in Case 370/90 *Singh* involving an impending divorce, only a formal divorce would seem to remove this right.

In Case 316/85 *Marie-Christine Lebon*, the Court of Justice defined dependency as a factual situation of support being supplied by the worker to the family member.

However, as in this case, as soon as a family member becomes independent, the derived rights via the worker under Article 7(2) cease.

Once it is established that a family member has the right to stay in the host State, he or she is also provided with statutory rights to work and receive education and training under Articles 11 and 12 of the Regulation, which have been subject to extensive interpretations by the Court of Justice to the effect that Article 7(2) has been interpreted to apply not just to workers, but also to the family of a worker, as seen in the cases featured below:

Regulation 1612/68

Article 11

Where a national of a Member State is pursuing an activity as an employed or self-employed person in the territory of another Member State, his spouse and those of the children who are under the age of 21 years or dependent on him shall have the right to take up any activity as an employed person throughout the territory of that same State, even if they are not nationals of any Member State.

The right to take up any activity under Article 11 is to be interpreted widely, to include any activity or profession providing the appropriate qualifications and formalities are observed:

Article 12

The children of a national of a Member State who is or has been employed in the territory of another Member State shall be admitted to that State's general educational, apprenticeship and vocational training courses under the same conditions as the nationals of that State, if such children are residing in its territory.

Member States shall encourage all efforts to enable such children to attend these courses under the best possible conditions.

In Case 32/75 *Fiorini aka Christini v SNCF*, a reduced fare entitlement was claimed by the Italian widow of an Italian SNCF Worker. Widows of French workers were allowed such a family entitlement but it was denied to the Italian. The SNCF claimed that since it was not expressly granted under the contract of employment, the entitlement was not available to foreign workers. The Court was asked if this was the kind of social advantage envisaged by Article 7(2) and it held that Article 7(2) applies to all advantages, not just those limited to the contract of employment and it applies to the family of workers in the same way as to nationals.

In Case 261/83 *Castelli v ONPTS*, the Italian mother of a retired Italian worker in Belgium claimed an old age pension. Mrs Castelli had never worked herself in Belgium, therefore, her claim was based on her status as a member of her son's family. The Belgian authorities refused to pay on the grounds that she was not Belgian and they did not have a reciprocal agreement with Italy. The Court of Justice held that Mrs Castelli was entitled to install herself with her son under Article 10 of Regulation 1612/68, and had rights to remain after the son's retirement and claim a pension under Article 7(2).

In Case 94/84 *ONE v Deak*, an unemployed Hungarian national living with his mother, an Italian national working in Belgium, was refused special unemployment benefits for non-nationals on the basis that no agreement for such benefits existed between Belgium and Hungary. The Court of Justice held that special unemployment benefits were a social advantage within the meaning of Article 7 and that Deak, regardless of nationality, could derive rights as the descendant of a worker, otherwise a worker might be hindered from moving if descendants were discriminated against thus causing financial difficulty.

Article 12 has been interpreted more widely than Article 10 and its case law would seem to allow. It applies not just to access to education but also to general measures intended to facilitate educational attendance including a maintenance grant in Case 9/74 Casagrande.

Cases 389 and 390/87 *Echternach and Moritz*

The Court of Justice held that the right under Article 12 persists even when the worker parent has returned home. This is to ensure that the children of the former Community worker can complete their education in the host State.

Case 7/94 *Gaal*

In this case the Court of Justice extended the right under Article 12 to an independent and over 21 year old child of a migrant worker who had been employed in another Member State. Gaal was the Belgian son of an EC worker in Germany who had since died. He was attending university and applied for a grant to undertake an eight month course in the UK but this was refused on the grounds that he was over 21 and was not dependent, hence, he could not obtain rights any longer as a descendant of an EC worker.

The Court held that he still fell within the personal scope of Article 12 of the Regulation as the definition of a child was not subject to the same definition as in Articles 10 and 11. Article 12 extends to all forms of education including university education and must include older children no longer dependent on their parents. The case was, however, decided on the basis that the child must have lived at some time with his parent whilst the latter was an EC worker.

A proposed Directive (COM (2001) 257 final) aims to consolidate the existing secondary legislation on the right of entry, the right to reside and the right to remain, including all the procedural rights for workers and the self-employed and their families, as well as to incorporate the existing case law. It is progressing steadily through the institutions and on 11 February 2003 the European Parliament sent its opinion to the Commission. When it enters into force, Directives 64/221/EEC, 68/360/EEC, 72/194/EEC, 73/148/EEC, 75/34/EEC, 75/35/EEC, 90/364/EEC, 90/365/EEC and 93/96/EEC will be repealed in their entirety, Articles 10 and 11 of Regulation (EEC) 1612/68 will be omitted and Regulation 1251/70 will be replaced and repealed at a later date.

The Public Service Proviso

Article 39(4) (formerly 48(4)) EC

The provisions of this Article shall not apply to employment in the public service.

There is no Treaty definition of public service, the scope of which can vary considerably from State to State, but both the Court of Justice and the Commission have offered their views in the face of Member State views reflecting both the narrow and wider interpretations of what constitutes employment in the public sector. The Court has constantly stressed the need for strict interpretation of the exemption in

Article 39(4), which applies to entry only and not to conditions of employment once engaged.

Case 152/73 *Sotgui v Deutsche Bundespost*

In this case, Mr Sotgui, an Italian national employed by the German Post Office was not paid the same allowance as German nationals. The Court of Justice had stressed the necessity for a Community definition of what constituted the public service and held that the difference in allowances, in what amounted to pay, could not be justified by Article 48(4) (now 39(4)) which applies to admission and not conditions of work.

The Commission has tried to obtain from the Court of Justice a strict definition of public service in a number of cases against Member States. For example, in Case 149/79 *Commission v Belgium (Re Public Employees)*, the Court of Justice held that public service only applies to typical public service posts which exercise power conferred by public law and safeguard interests of State, regardless of the status in Member States. As such, the exception was similar to the narrower exercise of official authority derogation contained in Article 45 (now 55), considered below.

The Court of Justice has on this basis excluded from the scope of Article 39(4):

- Case 307/84 *Commission v French Republic* – nurses;
- Case 66/85 *Lawrie-Blum v Land Baden-Würtemberg* – trainee secondary school teachers;
- Case C-4/91 *Bleis v Ministry of Education* – secondary school teachers;
- Case 33/88 *Allué and Coonan v Università degli Studi di Venezia* – foreign language lecturers.

In order to try and restrict the number of posts the Member States claim to come within Article 39(4), the Commission has issued a notice, OJ 1988 C72/2, listing those sectors in which it considers that positions would rarely be covered by the public service proviso. These include public health care, teaching in State educational establishments, non-military public research and public administration of commercial activities.

The Right to Remain

Article 39(3)(d) EC and Article 2 of Regulation 1251/70 provide the right to remain in the host State after retirement or incapacity and applies also to the family even if the worker dies, and to those to whom Article 7(2) of Regulation 1612/68 will continue to apply.

FREEDOM OF ESTABLISHMENT AND FREEDOM TO PROVIDE SERVICES

Introduction

The self-employed are granted rights under the Treaty to move to another Member State to establish themselves either permanently or on a long term basis (Articles 43–48 (formerly 52–58)) or to provide services temporarily (Articles 49–55 (formerly

59–66)). These provisions, like those applying to workers, are in favour of nationals of a Members State who are already established in that home State (Articles 43 and 49 (formerly 52 and 59)). Family members do not have to be nationals of a Member State. Article 12 (formerly 6) provides the general legislative base to ensure there is no discrimination, thus securing equal treatment on the grounds of nationality for those establishing or providing services, rather than relying on secondary legislation such as Regulation 1612/68 in the case of workers: see Case C-221/89 *R v Secretary of State for Transport ex p Factortame Ltd*.

Whilst the legislation appears to be concerned with achieving equality of treatment between nationals and the Community self-employed by the removal of restrictions (Articles 43 and 49) and therefore discrimination, there has also been an attack on national rules which, although applying to both home professionals and those establishing in the host country, are regarded as inappropriate for host professionals including, under the latest case law, also those establishing. The Court has ruled that non-discriminatory rules which hinder market access and thus the movement of the self-employed are also contrary to the Treaty. It will be seen that some rules can survive, but are only applicable to national citizens, introducing therefore a form of reverse discrimination considered further below. Hence, as with goods and workers, prohibited rules applying to the self-employed also include those which hinder market access, as seen in Chapter 11.

Scope and Definitions

Article 43 (formerly 52) EC

Freedom of establishment shall include the right to take up and pursue activities as self-employed persons and to set up and manage undertakings, in particular companies or firms.

[A definition has been given in Case C-221/89 *Factortame*: 'the actual pursuit of an economic activity through a fixed establishment in another member state for an indefinite period.']

Services, on the other hand, envisage a temporary state of affairs. Appearance, if at all, in the host State would only be for a limited period to provide specific services and there would be no permanent personal or professional presence in the host State or a necessity to reside:

Article 50 (formerly 60) EC

Services shall be considered to be 'services' within the meaning of this Treaty where they are normally provided for remuneration, insofar as they are not governed by the provisions relating to freedom of movement for goods, capital and persons.

'Services' shall in particular include:

(a) activities of an industrial character;

(b) activities of a commercial character;

(c) activities of craftsmen;

(d) activities of the professions.

The provision of services is traditionally associated with the areas of banking, finance, insurance and legal service. Now, with modern technology, telephone, broadcasting and Internet services have become big services areas, notably without even the need to move physically from the host State in order to provide services in other Member States: see, for example, Case C-384/93 *Alpine Investments*. Establishment certainly seemed to be based on achieving complete equality of treatment, whereas the provision of services under Article 50, whilst allowing for the same conditions to be imposed by the host State, was developed on the basis that not all home rules were found by the Court of Justice to be suitable or acceptable to those providing services. The distinction therefore between establishment and services is important, but where do you draw the line if services are provided over a longer period so that the position starts to look like establishment? The Court of Justice has advised that the provision of services may even justify the setting up of infrastructure in the host State. The leading case on this and how to distinguish establishment from services is *Gebhard*.

Case C-55/94 *Gebhard v Milan Bar Council*

The Court of Justice characterised 'establishment' as the right of a Community national to participate on a stable and continuous basis in the economic life of a Member State other than his or her own and 'services' by the temporary, precarious and discontinuous nature of the services:

> The temporary nature of the activities in question has to be determined in the light, not only of the duration of the provision of the service, but also of its regularity, periodicity or continuity. The fact that the provision of services is temporary does not mean that the provider of services within the meaning of the Treaty may not equip himself with some form of infrastructure in the host Member State (including an office, chambers or consulting rooms) in so far as such infrastructure is necessary for the purposes of performing the services in question.

In this case, the setting up of chambers in Italy by a German lawyer on a long term basis, although still practising in Stuttgart, was held to be establishment. The case also confirms that establishment in more than one State is possible.

It is a matter for the national courts to decide on the facts whether a person has overstepped the mark between providing services on a temporary basis or establishing. However, in the light of further considerations below on the convergence of rules in these two areas, the actual distinction may not now be so important.

Rights of Entry, Residence and Secondary Legislation

Under old Treaty Articles 53 (now repealed), 57 and 63 (now 47 and 52), the Commission was charged with the issue of Directives to obtain the general objectives set out in the Treaty. A General Programme was set up and Directives 73/148 and 75/34 were enacted to facilitate free movement, to regulate the rules on exit and entry and to provide the right to remain after the economic activity has finished. As these are the equivalent of Directive 68/360 and Regulation 1251/70 considered above in respect of workers, no further details will be provided here. Whilst Regulation 1612/68 does not apply formally to the self-employed, Article 1 of Directive 73/148 provides that the Directives also apply to the same family members as listed in Regulation 1612/68. As noted above, these enactments may soon be replaced by a consolidating Directive covering all aspects of free movement of persons, but in any event, the Court of Justice has taken a common approach in the application of secondary legislation rights to the freedom of persons generally.

Derogations

As with workers, Member State derogations are allowable on the grounds of public policy, public security and public health under Articles 45 and 55 (formerly 55 and 66), which are considered in detail below. There is also the equivalent of the public service exception in Article 39(4) (formerly 48(4)), but on the more tightly defined ground only of 'positions concerned with the exercise of official authority'.

Case 2/74 *Reyners v Belgian State*

The Court held that the derogation was limited to those activities which, taken on their own, constitute a direct and specific connection with the exercise of official authority profession but not where an occupation's activities connected with the exercise of official authority are separable from the professional activity in question taken as a whole. 'Professional activities involving contacts, even regular and organic, with the courts, including even compulsory cooperation in their functioning, do not constitute, as such, connection with the exercise of official authority.'

The Realisation of the Treaty Rights

Articles 43 and 50 (formerly 52 and 60) EC subject both freedoms to national rules including rules, regulations and conditions of the various professional organisations and bodies. These have very often proved to be the biggest impediments to free movement. The initial approach of the Commission in fleshing out the bare bones of the Treaty Articles was to harmonise the rules. It adopted a general programme of Directives to abolish the restrictions on free movement and to provide for the mutual recognition of qualifications in all sorts of trades and professions on a occupation by occupation basis, covering both establishment and the provision of services. However, the attempt to harmonise the conditions of the various professions proved extremely difficult and time consuming. For example, it took 18 years to enact a harmonisation Directive for architects. This approach also encouraged the view throughout the Community that the only way in which these rights could be achieved was through Directives and not directly under the Treaty. Thus, little progress was made and, even prior to the issue of Directives, case law had developed the law considerably.

Case Law and Direct Effects

Two leading cases, in which Articles 52 and 59 (now 43 and 49) were held by the Court of Justice to create direct effects, radically changed the approach of the Commission in taking steps to achieve free movement. The Court was able to decide in favour of the applicants, in the absence of secondary legislation, largely on the basis of the general prohibition of discrimination in Article 12 EC.

Case 2/74 *Reyners v Belgian State*

This case involved the attempt by a suitably qualified Dutchman to establish and obtain access to the Belgian Bar. The Belgian government had refused access on the grounds of nationality and had also argued that Article 52 (now 43) was not directly effective because it was incomplete without the issue of Directives as required by Article 52. The Court of Justice held that the clear prohibition of discrimination under Article 52 did not need additional law to realise the right. It was directly effective and determined that nationality could be no barrier to appropriately qualified lawyers entering a country to practise. The Directives were simply to facilitate free movement and not to establish it, which had already been done by the Treaty by the end of the initial transition period of the Communities in 1969.

Case 33/74 *Van Binsbergen v BBM*

The problem here was not nationality but the imposition of a residence requirement on a professionally qualified Dutchman, resident in Belgium, who was refused audience rights before the Dutch courts. The Court of Justice held that Article 59 (now 49) was directly effective and was not conditional on the issue of a subsequent Directive in respect of the specific professions, nor on a residence requirement in Holland, which would effectively defeat the freedom of a person to provide services who did not want to establish in the host State.

Following these and other cases, the Commission realised that the initial approach was not the best solution and commenced work on a new approach involving the provision of rules for many professions across the board, as considered below.

Establishment

Article 43 (formerly 52) provides that restrictions on the freedom of establishment of nationals of a Member State in the territory of another Member State shall be prohibited and subjects establishment to the conditions laid down for nationals by the law of the country where such establishment takes place. In other words, there should be no discrimination and home and host establishments should be treated equally. Even whilst the Commission was struggling to reach agreement from the Member States and professional bodies in harmonising professional qualifications and educational requirements and certainly before the more general approach was embarked upon, a number of cases had already allowed the Court of Justice to attack what it regarded as unreasonable demands and rules, in particular with regard to adequate qualifications.

Case 71/76 *Thieffry v Paris Bar Council*

The Belgian applicant was refused access to the Paris Bar despite having obtained a Belgian diploma in law, recognised by the University of Paris as the equivalent of a French diploma, and having sat and passed the French Certificate for the Profession of Advocate. The Court of Justice held that the relevant national authorities should apply any laws or practices which allow for the securing of freedom of establishment in accordance with the EEC policy although no Directives may have been enacted in that particular area. Therefore where the competent authorities have recognised a foreign diploma as equivalent to a domestic qualification, recognition of that diploma may not be refused in an individual case solely because it is not a diploma of the host State.

This position was taken further where the national authorities had simply refused to consider a particular diploma which was held by an applicant.

Case C-340/89 *Vlassopoulou*

A Greek national, who possessed a Greek law degree but had studied for a doctorate in law and practised in Germany for a number of years, was refused admittance to the German bar because she did not possess the German State law examinations.

The Court of Justice held:

> A Member State which receives a request to admit a person to a profession to which access, under national law, depends upon the possession of a diploma or a professional qualification must take into consideration the diplomas, certificates and other evidence of qualifications which the person concerned has acquired in order to exercise the same profession in another Member State by making a comparison between the specialized knowledge and abilities certified by those diplomas and the knowledge and qualifications required by the national rules.

Even though this judgment predated and to some extent predicted the general mutual recognition Directives (89/48 and 92/51), it has not been made redundant by them as it may be of importance to catch some diplomas omitted by the Diplomas Directive, that is, where they are not of long enough duration or are only a part way to a full qualification but nevertheless have some merit in themselves and should not be dismissed out of hand. For example, the many exchange students taking one year courses abroad who obtain a diploma on examined performance spring to mind as deserving some consideration.

The New Approach: Legislative Intervention

Whilst the Court of Justice was moving things on, a change of tactic was undertaken by the Commission to try to overcome the problems of tackling one profession at a time. The new approach involved the enactment of the Mutual Recognition Directives to apply to many professions. It proceeded along the lines of the new free movement of goods harmonisation measures, with a comprehensive or umbrella approach to mutual recognition, rather than trying to achieve a harmonisation of rules and regulations. There were three main reasons for the new approach:

(a) Slow progress on specific professions.

(b) After case law developments, especially in *Reyners* and *van Binsbergen*, the Commission decided that it was not necessary to issue Directives for each individual trade and profession, especially in the case of establishment.

(c) It was observed by the Court that progress in many professions not subject to specific Directives was minimal and uncertain.

The Directives that had already been enacted, mainly in the area of the medical professions, and those in the pipeline, were not rendered redundant and were, according to the Court of Justice, amplifications or guidelines to the requirements of the Treaty Articles, although work on a number was abandoned.

The Mutual Recognition of Diplomas Directive (89/48)

With the exception of those professions subject to specific Community Directives, Directive 89/48 applies to professionals who have completed a minimum period of three years of post secondary education and professional training for professions which are regulated under national law or subject to the requirement of a diploma, or other similar professional qualifications equivalent to a diploma. It applies, amongst others, to surveyors, chemists, town planners, chartered colourists, shipbrokers, foresters, accountants and biologists – to professionally qualified persons as opposed to those who have only completed the University or college element of instruction, and it includes workers, not just the self-employed.

The basic principle contained in Article 3 of the Directive denies the right of Member State authorities to refuse the right of entry and practice of a profession on the grounds that the holder does not possess the appropriate national qualifications, but where qualifications are insufficient or different, a period of adaptation or an aptitude test may be required. The Member States remain free under the terms of the Directive to regulate the conduct and organisation of the professions as they see fit and such regulation will continue to apply to nationals of all the Member States. However, following the *Gebhard* and *Säger* cases, discussed below, not all rules may be suitable for those establishing or providing services. The host Member State may require (under Article 4(1)) the would-be applicant to provide evidence of experience and complete either a period of supervised training in the host State – an adaptation period – or an examination of his knowledge appropriate to that required; referred to as an aptitude test in Article 4(1)(a) and (b). Once the applicant has satisfied Article 4 and becomes established in the Member State, he or she is then entitled under Article 7(1) to use the professional title of the host State.

It is to be noted that a clear distinction between the legal and other professions is made. The Directive requires that, other than with regard to lawyers, the Member States should offer the entrant a choice of either the adaptation period or the test, but Article 4(1)(b) provides:

> For professions whose practice requires precise knowledge of national law and in respect of which the provision of advice and/or assistance concerning national law is an essential and constant aspect of the professional activity, the host Member State may stipulate either an adaptation period or an aptitude test.

Thus, the Directive inherently recognises the necessarily distinct role played by lawyers as compared to other professions; law, like language, is often nationally distinct in concept.

Directive 92/51 on mutual recognition concerns a lower level of training, not at degree or necessarily diploma level. Both Directives have been subject to Directive 2001/19, which requires Member States to take account of any other qualifications a person possesses to see whether they bridge any gaps over the lack of formal qualifications, and thus takes account of the case law noted above.

Unlike the medical professions and architects, there was never an attempt to produce for lawyers an all-encompassing directive covering both establishment and services and it was some time after the Lawyers Services Directive (77/249) that a lawyers establishment Directive (98/5) was finally enacted, considered below. Before this, lawyers had made use of Directive 89/48, but only to a limited extent.

The *Gebhard* case is an important case for the free movement of persons. It establishes that Article 43 (formerly 52) is also applicable to non-discriminatory situations.

Case C-55/94 *Gebhard v Milan Bar Council*

A German lawyer who had set up a second chamber in Milan was prevented from using the title Avvocato under disciplinary proceedings by the Milan Bar Council for not having the necessary Italian qualifications and for not registering with the Milan Bar. No Community secondary law was held to apply to the situation, therefore in principle and according to the general Treaty provision Article 43 (formerly 52), he was required to comply with national rules.

The Court of Justice held:

> National measures liable to hinder or make less attractive the exercise of
> fundamental freedoms guaranteed by the Treaty must fulfil four conditions: they
> must be applied in a non-discriminatory manner; they must be justified by
> imperative requirements in the general interest; they must be suitable for securing
> the attainment of the objective which they pursue; and they must not go beyond
> what is necessary in order to attain it.

Perhaps this extension of Community considerations to establishment is a fair result,
that is, regardless of where or how one practises, one should be accepted without
hindrance, either on a temporary or permanent basis, provided that qualifications are
roughly equivalent. Rules which seek to prevent this must satisfy the criteria or be
struck out, at least as regards non-national EU citizens. Eventually, this might also
lead to internal pressure in Member States and thus to the rules being abolished in
respect of nationals also: see the comments on reverse discrimination below.

Practice Under Home Title Directive (98/5) (Lawyers' Establishment)

Directive 98/5 provides, under Article 2, that any lawyer shall be entitled to practise
on a permanent basis, in any other Member State under his or her home country
professional title, as an independent or salaried lawyer. To practise, lawyers need only
register with the competent authority in the host State on the basis of their registration
in the home Member State (Article 3). Article 5 provides that the host lawyer may give
advice on the law of his or her home Member State, on Community law, on
international law and on the law of the host Member State. He or she must comply
with the rules of procedure applicable in the national courts. Article 5(3) provides that
activities relating to the representation or defence of a client in legal proceedings may
be reserved to lawyers practising under the professional title of that State, where the
host State law provides for this. The State may require lawyers practising under their
home country professional titles to work in conjunction with a lawyer who practises
before the judicial authority in question and who would, where necessary, be
answerable to that authority. In addition, access to supreme courts may be reserved to
specialist lawyers.

Article 6 provides that in addition to the professional rules of the home State, a
lawyer practising under his or her home country professional title shall be subject to
the same rules of professional conduct as practising lawyers of the host State in
respect of all the activities he or she pursues in its territory. However, as we saw in the
Gebhard case, the facts of which arose before this Directive was enacted, it may be that
not all rules, which even though applicable to both home and established lawyers,
will be suitable for established lawyers.

Article 10 provides that a lawyer practising under his or her home country
professional title, who has effectively and regularly pursued for a period of at least
three years an activity in the host Member State in the law of that State including
Community law, shall, with a view to gaining admission to the profession of lawyer in
the host Member State, be exempted from the conditions set out in Article 4(1)(b) of
Directive 89/48. This so called third approach provides an easier way of acquiring the
professional title of the host Member State and circumvents the necessity under the
Directive 89/48 to undertake the aptitude test to establish in another Member State.
The reason given for providing this is that it was primarily directed at experienced
professionals, for whom an aptitude test would constitute an obstacle on account of

the time that would have elapsed since they obtained their qualifications. It is hard to see how it would not be used by all lawyers of over three years length of service.

The Provision of Services

Article 49 (formerly Article 59) EC

Within the framework of the provisions set out below, restrictions on freedom to provide services within the Community shall be prohibited in respect of nationals of Member States who are established in a State of the Community other than that of the person for whom the services are intended.

Article 50 (formerly Article 60) EC

...

Without prejudice to the provisions of the Chapter relating to the right of establishment, the person providing a service may, in order to do so, temporarily pursue his activity in the State where the service is provided, under the same conditions as are imposed by that State on its own nationals.

We have noted above in *Van Binsbergen* that Article 49 has been held to have direct effect. Services, as indicated in Article 50, is a residual category covering that free movement not catered for by workers or establishment. As we have seen, the dividing line between establishment and services which is important because not all rules may be relevant to the temporary provision of services, especially some of the professional rules.

Case 205/84 *Commission v Germany (Re Insurance Services)*

Although the Court had held that a permanent presence in the host State such as the setting up and staffing of an office would equate more with establishment than services, the requirement to establish a residence in the host State to provide insurance services was held not to be compatible with Article 59 (now 49). The Court of Justice held that Member States were under a duty not only to eliminate all discrimination based on nationality but also all restrictions based on the free provision of services on the grounds that the provider is established in another Member State.

We know now from *Gebhard*, above, that providing infrastructure in a host State to assist in providing services does not necessarily amount to establishment.

'Services' has been interpreted widely to include lottery services in Case C-275/92 *Schindler* and financial services offered by telephone in Case C-384/93 *Alpine Investments*, as in both cases, a cross-border element was established for remuneration. Remuneration is a criterion required by Article 50. The law on services has also been extended to cover the receipt of services. Services are also subject to the public policy, security and health derogations of Article 46 (formerly 55) by Article 55 (formerly 66) considered below.

The main aim of the Community legal regime for services is not just to ensure that there is no direct discrimination but also to remove restrictions, so that any indirectly discriminatory rules will also breach Article 49 unless justified. Furthermore, non-discriminatory rules which prevent or hinder the provision of services in some way may also fall foul of Article 49 unless coming within the criteria laid down by the Court in case law.

In *Van Binsbergen*, the Court held that the residence requirement ran contrary to the basic aim of Article 49, but allowed for the objective justification of the rule providing it was proportionate and there were no alternative lesser means which would have the same result. Hence, therefore, the Court introduced into the concept of services criteria very much along the lines of those introduced later in Case 120/78 *Cassis de Dijon* and later to be seen in the Lawyers' Services Directive (77/249), considered in brief below.

In *Commission v Germany*, above, the providers of insurance were also required to be authorised. The Court had emphasised that not all of those national rules which apply to firms permanently established in a Member State will necessarily automatically apply to those 'activities of a temporary character which are carried out by enterprises established in other Member States'. Furthermore, in keeping with its previous case law, specific requirements can be imposed which are objectively justified by the general good and applied without discrimination in view of the restriction imposed also in the home State. In this case, authorisation was regarded as a restriction, but the Court considered that the need for consumer protection in the insurance sector justified the particular German requirement. There was not existing adequate protection at either the Community level or within the home Member State.

Therefore, particular national rules for the protection of consumers, amongst other reasons, can survive providing they meet the criteria of the Court, applied and refined in later case law.

Cases C-154, C-180 and C-198/89 *Commission v France, Italy and Greece (Tourist Guides)*

The Court of Justice held that national provisions requiring persons who provide services as tourist guides accompanying groups of tourists from another Member State to hold a licence which is only awarded on the passing of an examination were disproportionate to the objective sought: the dissemination of knowledge concerning a country's artistic and cultural heritage and the protection of consumers.

The Court of Justice has moved further in the development of a rule which prevents the restriction of services from other Member States but may still persist to limit activities of the home providers of services.

Case C-76/90 *Säger v Dennemeyer*

Dennemeyer, an English company, wished to provide patent services in Germany, a service requiring a licence whose issue was restricted. It claimed a breach of Article 59 (now 49) because the requirement was hindering its access to the German market. The national rule was non-discriminatory in that it applied to all patent agents regardless of residence.

The Court held that it is not just discriminatory rules that are prohibited, but any rules which are liable to prohibit or otherwise impede persons providing a service which they already lawfully carry out in the State of their establishment. Such rules only be allowed provided:

(a) they are justified by an imperative reason relating to the public interest; and

(b) the public interest is not already protected by the rules of the State of establishment; and

(c) the same result cannot be obtained by less restrictive means.

In *Säger*, the licensing requirement was disproportionate and contravened Article 59 (now 49).

In *Alpine Investments*, the telephone sales system of cold-calling customers to sell financial investments was prohibited under Dutch law. Whilst the national rule applied to all calls originating from the Netherlands and regardless to where they were made, the Court of Justice was not prepared to treat it analogously with the *Keck* case and declare it as not coming within the Treaty. It held the rule to be a restriction on cross-border services which could however, be justified, which it was in the case itself.

The Lawyers' Services Directive was enacted because, at the time, getting the agreement for an all-encompassing Directive on lawyers could not be achieved. It combines the principle of mutual recognition with the recognition of some national restrictions.

Lawyers' Services Directive (77/249)

In essence, Directive 77/249 provides that practising lawyers from Member States must be accepted on the basis that the training of lawyers in other Member States is as strict as that in the host State. The Directive was not intended to interfere with the rules applicable to home or established Community lawyers.

Article 4(1) dispenses with residence and registration requirements for 'the representation of a client in legal proceedings'.

Article 4(4) states that where justifiable, the same rules apply to those providing services as to nationals.

Article 4(2) provides that lawyers providing services in judicial proceedings are required to observe both sets of rules of professional conduct, which means that lawyers must observe both those of the home and host States.

Article 5 provides that, for 'the pursuit of activities relating to the representation of a client in legal proceedings, a Member-State may require lawyers ... to work in conjunction with a lawyer who practises before the judicial authority in question and who would, where necessary, be answerable to that authority ...'.

The requirements of Directive 77/249 have been specifically considered in the following case.

Case 427/85 *Commission v Germany (Re Lawyers' Services)*

The Court of Justice held that local rules were acceptable but could not go beyond the strict requirements of Community law as to become a hindrance to free movement. The requirement to have local lawyers alongside at all times and the requirement to live locally when only providing services was far too restrictive and therefore a breach of the Treaty. The rule that lawyers could only operate in strictly defined areas was not justified by Article 5 of the Directive and could not be applied to activities of a temporary nature carried out by lawyers established in another Member State, although they may still apply to national lawyers. This case is another example of reverse discrimination.

The Freedom to Receive Services

Whilst the Treaty does not refer to the right to receive services (although Article 1 of Directive 64/221 does), the Court of Justice has upheld the right to receive services in a number of cases.

Case 286/82 and 26/83 *Luisi and Carbone*

This leading case concerned a prosecution under Italian currency regulations for taking money out of the country to pay for tourist and medical provisions abroad. The Court of Justice held that:

> The freedom to provide services includes the freedom, for the recipients of services, to go to another Member State in order to receive a service there, without being obstructed by restrictions, even in relation to payments, and that tourists, persons receiving medical treatment and persons travelling for the purposes of education or business are to be regarded as recipients of services.

The right to receive services has often been considered in relation to the right to receive general educational services by non-workers, who had their own rights to vocational educational training, or by those who could obtain derived rights from EC workers. The cases were considered before Directive 93/36.

After avoiding a direct answer in Case 293/83 *Gravier*, the Court of Justice held in Case 263/86 *Humbel* that courses provided under the general State system of education do not fall within the concept of services for the purposes of Article 60 (now 50). However, if concerned with vocational training, as was the position in Case 24/86 *Blaizot*, it was held that Community rules meant that a Member State could not discriminate in favour of nationals in the payment of fees for vocational courses, which included university education. At the time, it was stressed that the same would not apply in favour of maintenance grants; however, see now the comments below on the case of *Grzelczyk*.

Finally, in Case C-109/92 *Wirth*, a German court questioned whether courses available in an institute of higher education had to be classified as services under Article 50 (formerly 60). A German national was attempting to obtain a grant from German authorities to study in Holland. The Court held that courses given in a university or institute of higher education which is financed essentially out of public funds do not constitute services within the meaning of Article 50 of the EC Treaty, although courses in private educational establishments could.

Subject to the comments on *Grzelczyk* below, Member States remain able to determine their own system of grants and so discriminate against non-nationals. In conclusion, the right to receive educational services covers access to institutions for vocational training and tuition fees, but not grants. Note now that Directive 93/96 (OJ 1993 L317/59) provides that financially self-sufficient students can get access to vocational training, if not obtained in any other way.

The Derogations from the Freedoms

Treaty Articles 39(3), 46 and 55 (formerly 48(3), 56 and 66) and secondary legislation (Directive 68/360, Article 10) provide that the Member States may restrict entry and residence in the grounds of public policy, public security and public health. As regards the free movement of workers:

Article 39 (formerly Article 48)

...

3   It shall entail the right, subject to limitations justified on grounds of public policy, public security or public health ...

Whilst these, as with all derogations, will be interpreted strictly by the Court, the Member States do retain some discretion in their application, as will be seen in some of the cases below. Directive 64/221 (Free Movement Derogations) seeks to clarify the extent of the discretion given to the Member States under the Treaty and further provides various procedural rights to prevent premature and arbitrary deportation. The scope of the Directive is provided in Article 2(1) and includes all measures taken by the Member States to exclude EC nationals on the basis of public health, public policy and public security. The latter two overlap to such an extent that they can be regarded in practice as a single category. The grounds of public health which justify exclusion are given in Article 4(1) and an Annex, and are relatively straightforward, although drug addiction can also be covered by the proviso of public policy. Article 2(2) provides that the grounds for derogation 'shall not be invoked to service economic ends'.

Article 3 of the Directive then outlines the criteria that must and must not be considered when reaching a decision not to allow entry or to deport a person under the derogations:

3(1) Measures taken on grounds of public policy or of public security shall be based exclusively on the personal conduct of the individual concerned.

This latter point has been confirmed by case law to the effect that general categories of persons are excluded but it has allowed the Member States some leeway in the definition of personal conduct.

Case 67/74 *Bonsignore*

An Italian national faced deportation as a general preventative measure after conviction for fatally shooting his brother in a firearms accident.

The Court of Justice held:

Measures adopted on grounds of public policy and for the maintenance of public security against the nationals of Member States of the Community cannot be justified on grounds extraneous to the individual case ... 'only' the 'personal conduct' of those affected by the measures is to be regarded as determinative. As departures from the rules concerning the free movement of persons constitute exceptions which must be strictly construed, the concept of 'personal conduct' expresses the requirement that a deportation order may only be made for breaches of the peace and public security which might be committed by the individual affected'.

A second opportunity to interpret Article 3(1) the Directive was taken in *Van Duyn v Home Office*, as seen also in Chapter 8.

Case 41/74 *Van Duyn v Home Office*

A Dutch woman obtained a position as secretary with the Church of Scientology in the UK but was refused entry by the Home Office on the grounds that public policy declared the Church to be socially harmful. Miss Van Duyn claimed that the refusal was not made on personal conduct but on the conduct of the group.

The Court of Justice held that personal conduct must be an act or omission to act on the part of the person concerned and must be voluntary. It need not, however, be illegal or criminal to offend public policy. The Court stated that:

Although a person's past association cannot, in general, justify a decision refusing him the right to move freely within the Community, it is nevertheless the case that present association, which reflects participation in the activities of the body or of the organization as well as identification with its aims or designs, may be considered a voluntary act of the person concerned and, consequently, as part of his personal conduct within the meaning of the provision cited.

In the particular case then, the inevitable consequence was that of a disparity of treatment between nationals and non-nationals in the UK because nationals could work for the Church without sanction. A different view was taken in the next case.

Cases 115 and 116/81 *Adoui and Cornuaille*

Two French women euphemistically described by the Court of Justice as waitresses had their residence permits withdrawn by the Belgian authorities on the grounds that their personal conduct justified the invocation of the public policy proviso. Belgium was trying to clamp down on the number of French prostitutes settling in Belgium. A reference was made to the Court, which held that the public policy proviso does not allow expulsion where similar conduct by nationals does not incur a penalty or repressive measures. It does not require illegality. The Belgian prostitutes were tolerated and not prosecuted.

In Case 36/75 *Rutili*, an order taken out to restrict R's activities and movement to certain French Departments, was considered under 'personal conduct'. The Court held that:

Right of entry into the territory of Member States and the right to stay there and to move freely within it is defined in the Treaty by reference to the whole territory of those States and not by reference to its internal subdivisions.

If R's activities were considered serious enough, he could be excluded from the whole of France but not part of it. However, see the next case.

Case C-100/01 *Aitor Oteiza Olazabal*

This case concerned criminal measures, as opposed to administrative measures in *Rutili*, preventing movement in certain parts of France. The Court of Justice held:

Neither Article 48 of the EC Treaty [now, after amendment, Article 39 EC] nor the provisions of secondary legislation which implement the freedom of movement for workers preclude a Member State from imposing, in relation to a migrant worker who is a national of another Member State, administrative police measures limiting that worker's right of residence to a part of the national territory, provided:
- that such action is justified by reasons of public order or public security based on his individual conduct;
- that, by reason of their seriousness, those reasons could otherwise give rise only to a measure prohibiting him from residing in, or banishing him from, the whole of the national territory; and
- that the conduct which the Member State concerned wishes to prevent gives rise, in the case of its own nationals, to punitive measures or other genuine and effective measures designed to combat it.

Under Article 3(2) of the Directive, previous criminal convictions shall not in themselves constitute grounds for the taking of such measures.

Case 30/77 *R v Bouchereau*

A Frenchman had been convicted in the UK on a number of occasions for drug possession. The UK magistrate asked the Court of Justice whether he could be deported to stop him committing acts in the future. The Court held it was not possible to look at the past record to decide future conduct unless it constituted a present threat and 'a sufficiently serious threat to the fundamental interests of society'.

Article 3(3) provides that the expiry of an identity card or passport is no justification for expulsion: see *R v Pieck*, considered above.

Hence then, in the light of these cases, the Member States do still seem to retain a sufficient measure of discretion to exclude persons they regard as threatening.

Procedural Safeguards

Directive 64/221 also provides a number of procedural rights in Articles 5–9 for Member State nationals facing measures taken against them under the provisos.

Article 5 provides the right to remain in the Member State pending a decision either to grant or refuse a residence permit, which itself should be taken no longer than six months after an application.

Article 6 provides that the person concerned shall be informed of the grounds of public policy, public security or public health upon which the decision taken in his case is based, unless this is contrary to the interests of security of the State involved.

Article 7 provides the right to be notified of any decision to expel or the refusal of a residence permit and should also state the minimum period given to leave the country. This cannot be less than 15 days for refusal in the first place and one month for expulsion for those already in residence.

Article 8 requires that the same legal remedies as for nationals questioning administrative decisions shall be available.

Article 9(1) provides that where there is no right of appeal to a court of law, or where such an appeal may only be on validity, not merits, or where appeal cannot have suspensory effect, a decision to expel can only be taken, save in cases of urgency, after an opinion has been obtained from a competent authority before which the person concerned enjoys such rights of assistance and representation as are provided for by the domestic law.

Article 9(2) provides that any decision refusing the issue of a first residence permit or ordering expulsion before the issue of the permit shall be referred to the authority whose opinion is required under Article 9(1) above. The person shall be entitled to submit his defence in person, save where this would be contrary to the interests of national security.

The appeal body must be independent of the immigration service who refused entry in the first place. In the UK it is the Immigration Appeal Tribunal.

The above rights are comprehensively summed up in the cases of *Adoui and Cornuaille*, above, and the following case.

Case 98/79 *Pecastaing v Belgium State*

A French prostitute was ordered by the Belgium authorities to leave on grounds of personal conduct. She claimed under Articles 8 and 9 of Directive 64/221 that she should be able to stay in the country whilst the decision was being reviewed, which could be up to three years during the course of an Article 177 (now 234) reference.

The Court of Justice held that the grounds for the deportation must be precisely and comprehensively stated and that the concerned person has a right to be informed of the grounds of refusal or deportation unless security is at stake. The Court further held that the reasons must be sufficiently detailed to allow a migrant to defend his or her interests, and drafted in such a way and language as to enable the person to comprehend the content or effect. However, the Court also held that even under Article 177, the right of appeal is not to be diluted and only in cases of emergency should automatic expulsion take place. However, the urgency could only finally be determined by the Member States and Articles 8 and 9 do not grant rights to remain in the host State pending hearing, which could be two to three years under an Article 177 reference, provided the person concerned can get a fair hearing and full facilities even whilst out of the country.

Case C-175/94 *R v Secretary of State for the Home Department ex p Gallagher*

G had been convicted of the possession of rifles for unlawful purposes in Ireland and had been deported from the UK. In questioning this decision, he was interviewed in Ireland before the case was heard by the Home Secretary. He challenged those authorities as not being independent within the meaning of Directive 64/221, Article 9.

The Court held that it was a matter for the national courts to decide whether the body hearing an appeal was independent but that the Directive did not specify how it should be appointed. It should, however, be genuinely independent and not subject to any control by the authority empowered to take deportation measures.

As noted elsewhere in this chapter, a new Directive is in the final stages of enactment which will consolidate much of the above case law and more, providing, amongst other matters, more protection and revision of deportation orders against persons who have been established for more than a few years in a Member State: see Commission Document Com (2001) 257 final.

THE WHOLLY INTERNAL RULE AND REVERSE DISCRIMINATION

It has been recognised that EC law sometimes engenders reverse discrimination internally against nationals of Member States in relation to other EU nationals who have moved there and benefit from EC law – see *Commission v Germany (Lawyers' Services)*, above:

... the resultant existence of 'reverse' discrimination – where a (static) home national may be treated less favourably than someone from another Member State who could invoke EC law in similar factual circumstances – is usually conceived as an unusual but inevitable, and acceptable, corollary on non-interference by the Community in the internal affairs of the Member States [Shuibine].

It is certainly the case in the earlier references that the Court of Justice would not interfere in what was perceived as being a wholly internal matter, and it could be argued that the Court should refuse to accept references from national courts when dealing with wholly internal matters, because under Article 234 (formerly 177) no question of Community law arises.

In Case 175/78 *R v Saunders*, a criminal sanction imposed a mobility restriction on Saunders, which was applicable within the UK only and was claimed by Saunders to be contrary to Article 48 (now 39). The Court held that there was no factor connecting the situation with Community law. Hence, the provisions on free movement of workers cannot be applied to situations which are wholly internal to a Member State.

The next cases illustrate clearly how the wholly internal rule appears to give rise to reverse discrimination because nationals are denied rights which EU nationals from other Member States can uphold.

Cases 35 and 36/82 *Morson and Jhanjan v Netherlands*

The applicants, both Surinamese nationals, claimed the right to stay in Holland with their Dutch national son and daughter working there. It was held by the Court that there was no application of Community law to the wholly internal situation where national workers had not worked in any other Member State, and because where there was no movement from one Member State to another, Community law did not apply. Movement from a third country did not qualify.

This was confirmed in Cases 64 and 65/96 *Land Nordrhein-Westfalen v Uecker and Jacquet* concerning two third country nationals trying to rely on Community law as spouses of German nationals in Germany. The case was deemed to be wholly internal and thus not within the scope of application of EC law.

If in both cases, the applicants were, for example, Spanish nationals moving to those countries, they would be allowed to take TCN spouses or relatives with them. Of late, however, there appears to be some softening of the wholly internal rule. Some cases look wholly internal but because some increasingly slight prior movement is involved, Community law rights can be triggered against the home State.

Case C-370/90 *R v Immigration Appeal Tribunal and Surinder Singh ex p Secretary of State for the Home Department*

An Indian spouse of a British national was able to use EC law to derive a right of residence in the UK on the basis that the spouse had previously exercised the right of free movement but then re-established herself in the UK. (In Case 419/92 *Scholz*, it was held that a frontier worker who lives in his or her home State and is just employed in another State triggers Community rights which can be claimed against the home State.)

Case C-60/00 *Carpenter v Secretary of State for the Home Department*

A Philippine national claimed a right of residence in the UK with her British spouse on the grounds that he provided services from time to time in other Member States. The case is similar to the *Singh* case, except that Mrs Carpenter had not left UK soil whilst services were being provided by her husband both from the UK and travelling to other Member States. The argument put forward by the applicants was that if Mrs Carpenter had also gone to another Member State, both would have rights of residence and the right to work in the other host EU States. However, she chose to stay put to look after the children and thus assist her husband in providing services in other Member States. Because of her lack of movement, the EC Commission regarded the case as a wholly internal matter for the Member State and thus just subject to its law.

The Court referred to EC secondary legislation, including Regulation 1612/68 which, strictly, does not apply to the provision of services, but provides rules protecting the family life of nationals of the Member States in order to eliminate obstacles to the exercise of the fundamental freedoms guaranteed by the Treaty. The Court stated:

> It is clear that the separation of Mr and Mrs Carpenter would be detrimental to their family life and, therefore, to the conditions under which Mr Carpenter exercises a fundamental freedom. That freedom could not be fully effective if Mr Carpenter were to be deterred from exercising it by obstacles raised in his country of origin to the entry and residence of his spouse.

Here, the Court of Justice showed itself to be in the lead again on the development of rights, and the case highlights the use by the Court of provisions of the European Convention on Human Rights in the area of free movement and citizenship where it had only infrequently previously employed such provisions in this field. The Court considered the rights could be subjected to objective restrictions, but that they must comply with fundamental rights:

> The decision to deport Mrs Carpenter constitutes an interference with the exercise by Mr Carpenter of his right to respect for his family life within the meaning of Article 8 of the Convention for the Protection of Human Rights and Fundamental Freedoms and does not strike a fair balance between the competing interests, that is, on the one hand, the right of Mr Carpenter to respect for his family life, and, on the other hand, the maintenance of public order and public safety.

> The Court noted that the marriage appeared genuine; there were no official complaints against Mrs Carpenter and she genuinely looked after the children while he was providing services.

> The Court held that Article 49 EC, read in the light of the fundamental right to respect for family life, is to be interpreted as precluding a refusal, by the Member State of origin, to a provider of services established in that Member State who provides services to recipients established in other Member States, of the right to reside in its territory to that provider's spouse, who is a national of a third country.

Case C-281/98 *Angonese*

> An Italian citizen applied for a job in Italy but was refused entry to the selection process as he did not have the appropriate local authority certificate of bilingualism, despite being accepted by the local court as perfectly bilingual and possessing certificates of language study from the University of Vienna where he had studied. The Italian government and defendant bank argued that the matter was wholly internal and had no connection with Community law. The Advocate General agreed with them.

> The Court did not address this issue in its ruling that the 'requirement to provide evidence of his linguistic knowledge exclusively by means of one particular diploma, such as the Certificate, issued only in one particular province of a Member State, constitutes discrimination on grounds of nationality contrary to Article 48 [now 39] of the EC Treaty'.

Whilst there was movement in this case, in that Mr Angonese had studied in Austria, the only economic activity was the receiving of educational services. However, these points were simply not discussed by the Court. The Advocate General, on the other hand, was of the clear opinion that the studies, which were the factor triggering Community law rights, were too remote from the post and the requirements of the post advertised.

Therefore, provided there has been some previous movement to another Member State or if services have been provided to another Member State with no physical movement, the situation ceases to be wholly internal. Also, the movement can be to receive services rather than to provide services or engage in an economic activity personally. Whilst receiving services has been held to be a right under EC law, is it necessary for these rights to fall within the concept of engaging in an economic activity? If not, then simply receiving services will trigger the application of Community law rights. For example, if an author in the UK advertises advisory services over the Internet to the world including, of course, the EU, will he or she have the right to have his or her third country national (TCN) relation enter the UK, despite the refusal of the UK authorities? Or, would undertaking a couple of weeks' work in another Member State provide the same right? Or, if a UK national obtains professional advice over the Internet or telephone from another Member State, thus receiving services, does this give him or her the right to have his or her TCN relation enter the UK? No doubt, the Court of Justice will find many similar questions being posed over the next few years.

GENERAL RIGHTS OF FREE MOVEMENT, CITIZENSHIP AND INDEPENDENT NATIONALS OF THIRD COUNTRIES

General rights of free movement and citizenship are those rights which can now be regarded as being detached from economic activity, although the original reason for an EU citizen's lawful presence in the host State may have been as a worker, as a self-employed person or as a student. Also considered here is the position of how TCNs are treated who do not obtain derived rights from EU nationals, that is, they are not or are no longer family members. The rights of TCNs who are family members have been dealt with in the section on workers and family rights above.

The concept of citizenship was introduced into the EC Treaty legal order by the Maastricht Treaty on European Union (TEU), which came into force in 1993, but prior to that, general Directives concerning rights of residence had been enacted. Council Directive 90/364 gave a general right to nationals of the Member States and their families to reside in a host Member State. They were designed to provide a right of residence to nationals of Member States who do not enjoy this right under other provisions of Community law, and to members of their families. Such persons must, however, be covered by adequate all risks health insurance and have sufficient resources to avoid becoming a burden on the social security system of the host Member State (Article 1) – although this provision has been interpreted slightly differently in one of the cases considered below. It has been termed the 'playboy Directive' to suggest that only the financially self-sufficient would be able to take advantage of it. In a similar manner, Directive 90/365 grants the right of residence for employees and self-employed persons who have ceased their occupational activity, and Directive 93/96 provides similar rights for students to attend an educational establishment to obtain vocational training if not obtained in any other way, that is, through derived rights as a member of the family of a worker who has moved to the host State. For a few years, these Directives seemed to have little impact in providing a general right of free movement for all and, as formulated, do not provide an unconditional right to move and reside in another Member State.

The TEU introduced into the EC Treaty new Articles 17–22 (formerly 8–8e) on 'Citizenship of the Union', the key provisions being Articles 17 and 18:

Article 17

1   Citizenship of the Union is hereby established. Every person holding the
    nationality of a Member State shall be a citizen of the Union. Citizenship of the
    Union shall complement and not replace national citizenship.

2   Citizens of the Union shall enjoy the rights conferred by this Treaty and shall be
    subject to the duties imposed thereby.

Article 18

1   Every citizen of the Union shall have the right to move and reside freely within
    the territory of the Member States, subject to the limitations and conditions laid
    down in this Treaty and by the measures adopted to give it effect.

It has to be stressed that these are broad aims, but rights arising from these Articles
may be formally restricted by Community law limitations already in existence and
future implementing measures.

So, what is meant by European Union citizenship? Firstly, any definition of Union
citizenship inevitably must depend on the present 15 Member States' definitions of
nationality. Declaration No 2 on Nationality attached to the TEU provides that
nationality shall be settled solely by reference to the national law of the Member State
concerned. This was upheld in the Case C-192/99 *R v Secretary of State for the Home
Department ex p Manjit Kaur*, in which the Court of Justice held that it is for each
Member State to lay down the conditions for the acquisition and loss of nationality
and that the UK could exclude a UK overseas citizen from its territory without
infringing Community law. The case also confirms the wholly internal rule.

If a person is a national of a Member State, then Articles 17 and 18 can apply to
them, but it has been noted by Jacqueson that 'a deprival of nationality will
undoubtedly be in breach of Article 17(2) as it will at the same time deprive the person
of her/his Union Citizenship and the rights attached thereto'.

By reference to the case law, we have to determine what the citizenship rights
provide according to how they have been interpreted by the Court. We know from
Article 18 that free movement is subject to restrictions which must include the three
provisos of public health, public policy and public security, but does this also include
the public service derogation?

Case C-193/94 *Skanavi and Chyssanthakopoulos*

The Court, whilst considering Article 18, would not grant it primary status with other
Articles granting free movement and residence in host States. Later, in Case C-274/96
Criminal Proceedings v Bickel & Franz, the status of Article 18 appeared to be raised,
although not to an overriding Community law right but to one which could be
pleaded in support of other rights – in this case to support the view that the refusal to
allow Germans the use of German in Italian South Tyrol courts would be contrary to
Article 12 (prohibition of discrimination on the grounds of nationality), where Italian
citizens of Austrian extract in South Tyrol were allowed to use German. The Germans
in question had entered the South Tyrol according to their rights under Article 49
(formerly 59) EC.

Case C-85/96 *Maria Martinez Sala*

A Spanish national who had worked in Germany for many years lost her job but
remained in Germany and had received social assistance from 1989. Her residence
permit had expired, but the German authorities supplied her with certificates stating
she had applied for an extension to her permit. The authorities refused her a child

allowance because she did not have a valid residence permit. She claimed that this was contrary to Article 12 as German nationals were not subject to the same condition. Although in this case her actual status as a worker was not determined, the Court held that she was lawfully resident in Germany and thus came within the personal scope of Treaty citizenship. What is now Article 17(2) therefore acted to attach other rights to her, such as the right to be protected against discrimination under Article 12.

Case C-184/99 *Grzelczyk v CPAS*

A French national, who had studied and worked for three years in Belgium, at the beginning of his fourth and final year of study applied to the CPAS for payment of the minimex, a non-contributory minimum subsistence allowance. The CPAS granted Mr Grzelczyk the minimex, but later denied it on the basis that he was not Belgian: clear discrimination on the grounds of nationality.

The Court of Justice did not determine G's possible status as a worker, but nevertheless held that the citizenship rights enable Union citizens to be treated equally. Previously, students who worked just for the purpose of their studies would not be entitled to any non-contributory benefits (see the *Brown* case above). The Court distinguished this by emphasising the new citizenship provisions and new competences, albeit limited, in education which allowed it to hold that Articles 12 and 17 preclude discrimination as regards the grant of a non-contributory social benefit to Union citizens where they are lawfully resident, even though not economically active. The Court considered Directive 93/96 under which G entered Belgium and which required him not to be a burden on Member State finances, but using the preamble interpreted this to read not to be an 'unreasonable burden', which he appeared not to be.

So, instead of accepting a blanket exclusion or restriction on the citizenship rights of anyone who is a burden, it is now only those who are an unreasonable burden, which is a quite different matter and category. It remains to be answered who defines reasonableness here: the Court of Justice or the Member States?

Case C-224/98 *Marie-Nathalie D'Hoop v Office National de l'Emploi*

Miss D'Hoop was a Belgian national who had studied in France. She was refused a tideover allowance between study and work granted to nationals by the Belgian authorities on her return to Belgium on the ground that she had studied in another Member State. The Court of Justice had previously held the tideover allowance was a social advantage under Article 7(2) of Regulation 1612/68, but to take advantage of it the person must have participated in the employment market or have derived a right. Her parents had remained in Belgium, therefore, she had no rights in her own right nor derived rights from her parents.

The Court referred to the new contribution to education by the EC in encouraging mobility of students and teachers (Articles 3(1)(q) and 149(2) EC) and, citing *Grzelczyk*, paragraph 31, held that it would be incompatible with the right of freedom of movement if a citizen who had taken advantage of free movement then suffered discrimination as a consequence. The Court held:

> Such inequality of treatment is contrary to the principles which underpin the status of citizen of the Union, that is, the guarantee of the same treatment in law in the exercise of the citizen's freedom to move. The condition at issue could be justified only if it were based on objective considerations independent of the nationality of the persons concerned and were proportionate to the legitimate aim of the national provisions.

Belgium offered no such considerations; thus limiting the places of education which qualified for the tideover allowance went beyond what was necessary to attain the objective pursued.

In a case involving an American woman and her children, a Colombian woman and her two daughters, and a German man, the only person argued not to be protected by Community law and thus facing expulsion from the UK was Mr Baumbast, the German, because the other parties to the action had been given, during the course of the proceedings, indefinite leave to remain in the UK by the authorities before the case reached the Court of Justice. Therefore, on the face of it, and recognised as such by the full Court, no real dispute remained in respect of them. The Court nevertheless held that the question of the rights conferred under Community law on the persons concerned had not been resolved definitively, and that the questions raised by the national tribunal were admissible. It would appear that the Court is keen to extend the law on free movement and Union residence.

Case C-413/99 *Baumbast*

Mr Baumbast was self-employed in the UK, where he resided with his Colombian wife and two children, who were being educated in the UK. He was later employed by a German company and worked outside the EU, but the family remained in the UK. Their residence permits were not renewed, however, and Mrs Baumbast and the children faced deportation.

In considering the various claims and counter-claims, the Court interpreted Regulation 1612/68 in the light of Article 8 of the European Convention on Human Rights, which concerns respect for family life, and confirmed it as one of the fundamental rights recognised by Community law. The Court emphasised the right of children of EU nationals under Regulation 1612/68 to continue their education even if the worker, from whom their rights derived, was no longer working. The Court further stated that the text of the Treaty does not permit the conclusion that citizens of the Union who have lawfully established themselves in another Member State as employed persons are deprived, where that activity comes to an end, of the rights which are conferred on them by virtue of that citizenship.

In the most important statement of the judgment, the Court held that Mr Baumbast's right to stay under Article 18(1) was conferred directly on every citizen of the Union by a clear and precise provision of the EC Treaty. Purely as a national of a Member State, and consequently a citizen of the Union, Mr Baumbast therefore had the right to rely on Article 18(1) EC. The Court then considered Directive 90/364 and the fact that Mr Baumbast and his family were not a burden on the UK social security system and had German insurance cover. The Court stated:

> The answer to the first part of the third question must therefore be that a citizen of the European Union who no longer enjoys a right of residence as a migrant worker in the host Member State can, as a citizen of the Union, enjoy there a right of residence by direct application of Article 18(1) EC.

Once citizenship rights are established, then the political rights under Article 19 of the Treaty are acquired:

Article 19

1   Every citizen of the Union residing in a Member State of which he is not a national shall have the right to vote and to stand as a candidate at municipal elections in the Member State in which he resides, under the same conditions as nationals of that State. This right shall be exercised subject to detailed

arrangements adopted by the Council, acting unanimously on a proposal from the Commission and after consulting the European Parliament; these arrangements may provide for derogations where warranted by problems specific to a Member State.

2   Without prejudice to Article 190(4) and to the provisions adopted for its implementation, every citizen of the Union residing in a Member State of which he is not a national shall have the right to vote and to stand as a candidate in elections to the European Parliament in the Member State in which he resides, under the same conditions as nationals of that State. This right shall be exercised subject to detailed arrangements adopted by the Council, acting unanimously on a proposal from the Commission and after consulting the European Parliament; these arrangements may provide for derogations where warranted by problems specific to a Member State.

What is the overall view following these developments? One view of the importance of the new law and cases on it is as follows:

> The citizenship provisions do not introduce any new rights when compared with the situation before Maastricht ... and only [deal] with the codification of existing rights with the proviso that non-economically active persons are granted a right to move and reside directly by provisions of primary law and not by secondary law as was the case before 1993.
>
> ...
>
> Thus the application of Community law still involves some kind of migration. Such migration in turn can still be limited to non-economically active persons insofar as they shall be able to support themselves in order to acquire a right to reside. In this respect the protection of the principle of equal treatment is still limited to persons possessing sufficient financial means. Nevertheless, the Court enlarged the scope of this protection to persons not in possession of such means under certain circumstances as laid down in *Grzelcyzk*. Moreover, purely internal situations are still excluded from the scope of Community law [Jacqueson].

In summary, Article 18(1) is directly effective. It can be activated in favour of EU citizens in a variety of ways:

(a) Where the citizen is a worker or self-employed or a student under the previous Community law.

(b) Through exhausted free movement rights, that is, those once enjoyed but not any longer (*Baumbast*).

(c) By movement to another Member State to receive services (*D'Hoop*).

Articles 17 and 18 then trigger other rights, the most notable is the right under Article 12 not to be discriminated against on the grounds of nationality. According to the Court, whilst the right of residence under Article 18 continues to be restricted by the Directives previously issued, Articles 17 and 18 now seem to provide that where Union citizens are lawfully resident in a host State, they cannot be discriminated against in social benefits including non-contributory benefits. Hence the status of the person, that is, whether a worker or self-employed, is no longer an important factor in determining a right to move and reside in a host State and, once lawfully residing there, citizens will be entitled to be treated without discrimination compared to nationals in all matters.

Just how far will the Court go? Arguably, an unemployed tourist on holiday in another Member State receives services. In which case, does this activate Article 18 citizenship, which in turn then triggers a general right of equal treatment, including the right to non-contributory benefits including social security benefit? It will be necessary to watch new case law very carefully:

> The concept of Union citizenship embodied by the Treaty on European Union has formalized or constitutionalized certain already existing rights within the Community ambit; it has introduced certain new rights and, above all, it has provided a solid basis for further enlargement of the catalogue of rights attached to citizenship. From this point of view, it represents an advance on the situation under the Rome Treaty and the SEA [Single European Act]. The institutional role for the development of the dynamic character of citizenship will be the determinant factor to produce a qualitative leap forward. However, citizenship of the Union has not superseded nationality of the Member States, in much the same way as the European Union has not abolished the sovereign existence of the Member States [Closa, 'The concept of citizenship in the Treaty of European Union' (1992) 29 CML Rev 1168].

The Treatment of Third Country Nationals (TCNs)

This short section is only concerned with independent TCNs and not those seeking rights as family members of EU citizens, who have been dealt with in the sections above. Basically and originally, nationals from third countries lawfully or unlawfully resident in a Member State were not a concern for EC law unless specifically catered for in some way and TCNs obtained no rights under Community law to reside in the EU or to move from country to country. Their rights were entirely a matter for national law regulation. The first of the exceptions to this position is where TCNs have been provided with rights under the various association and co-operation agreements with countries such as Turkey, Algeria and Morocco.

Secondly, TCNs may form part of the workforce of a company established in the EU, which, for example, sends workers abroad to complete a contract in another Member State. In Case C-43/93 *Vander Elst*, the Court confirmed that nationals of third countries also have the right of free movement within the context of the right of free movement of companies which are established within the EU, providing that the non-EU nationals are part of the legal labour force of the company established in the home Member State and where the employer provides services in another Member State.

There are, according to estimates, approximately 13 million TCNs (4 per cent of the EU population) lawfully or unlawfully resident in the EU, a figure that will no doubt rise dramatically when the EU increases to 25 Member States. Whilst it might have been the case in the past that the treatment of TCNs was regarded as being below the standards of treatment to be expected from the European Community, as observed in some comments, more recently, the Court of Justice has been addressing the rights of TCNs in the latest case law:

> If the Community is to have an area without internal frontiers, it becomes progressively absurd that non-Community nationals established in the Community should not be afforded the protection of Community law. If third country nationals work and reside in the Community, as they will in increasing numbers, thereby contributing to the achievement of the aims of the EEC Treaty, the Community has a duty to come to terms with the phenomenon. To entrust competence in this area to the

Member States at this stage of European Integration only recalls and reinforces a statist view of Community law which is inappropriate in this area [O'Keefe].

More notorious still is the continued refusal to extend the right of free movement to non-EC migrants. Indeed, the whole issue of non-EC migration reveals a very familiar and very regrettable underside to the supposedly new Europe [Ward, *A Critical Introduction to European Law*, 1996].

Whilst a lot of attention has been directed to the immigration policies and the Schengen Agreement regarding of the entry and visa regulation of TCNs, less attention has been paid to the free movement rights of those already in the EU. The Court held in Case 238/83 *Mr and Mrs Richard Meade* that the Treaty Articles on free movement of workers apply solely to EU nationals and not therefore to TCNs. Since then, there has been legislative intervention in the form of Regulation 1091/2001, which provides limited rights of free movement for those TCNs in the EU on a long stay visa. The *Baumbast* case, considered above, has, however, provided a right of residence obtained under Community law in the face of an attempt to deport a TCN.

Case C-413/99 *Baumbast*

This case also involved an American woman, R, who moved to the UK with her then French husband, who had obtained work in the UK. R was later divorced and lost her strict legal right to remain in the host State under Regulation 1612/68, Article 10 (which simply confirms the *Diatta* and *Reed* cases). R and the children remained in the UK. Whilst the children were granted indefinite leave to remain, she was not. The UK authorities wanted to deport her and by necessity her children who, however, remained the children of a EU national, who was no longer working in the UK.

The Court of Justice held that Regulation 1612/68:

> ... must be interpreted as entitling the parent who is the primary carer of those children, irrespective of nationality, to reside with them in order to facilitate the exercise of that right notwithstanding the fact that the parents have meanwhile divorced. The fact that only one parent is a citizen of the Union and that parent has ceased to be a migrant worker in the host Member State and that the children are not themselves citizens of the Union are irrelevant in this regard.

There is therefore an implied right within Article 12 of the Regulation that the child of a migrant worker can pursue his education in the host Member State and that that child has the right to be accompanied by the person who is his primary carer. Furthermore, that person is able to reside with him in that Member State during his studies. To refuse to grant permission to remain to a parent who is the primary carer of the child exercising his right to pursue his studies in the host Member State infringes that right.

That is the state of the law so far, but note the proposals in this area which are, however, highly unlikely to become law in the short term. The new Directive 2000/34 is designed to prohibit discrimination based on race, but Article 3(2) states that it is without prejudice to the provisions and conditions relating to the entry and residence of third country nationals and to any treatment which arises from the legal status of third country nationals. So, whilst it may prevent unequal treatment in the country of residence, it is unlikely to provide a right of free movement.

Article 49(2) (formerly 59(2)) EC has, since amendment by the Single European Act, permitted the Community to extend freedom of services to TCNs:

> The Council may, acting by a qualified majority on a proposal from the Commission, extend the provisions of the Chapter to nationals of a third country who provide services and who are established within the Community.

After over 40 years of lying dormant, a proposal has finally been made: see COM (2000) 271 final ([2000] OJ C311/197). However, there has been no further action since May 2000 when an amended proposal was sent to the European Parliament. This proposal, which does not extend to allowing TCNs to establish in another Member State, restricts the freedom to provide services, apart from transport services, and does not cover the freedom to receive services in other Member States. TCNs are required to be lawfully resident in the State, where they must have been established and providing services for at least 12 months (see proposed Article 1) before being able to provide cross-border services subject to an 'EC service provision card' system.

As in other areas of free movement law, the case law of the Court is likely to take matters as far, if not further, whilst we are waiting for the Member States to enact the new legislation.

Convergence of the Free Movement Rules?

As briefly referred to at the end of Chapter 12, some academic commentators are of the view that an overall strategy is being developed by the Court of Justice across the freedoms – that there is a convergence of the Community rules, and that these rules, albeit appearing under different Treaty Chapters, are nevertheless so similar that an all-encompassing approach is being developed. Others regard the scope for convergence as being limited:

> A trend towards convergence is apparent in the Court's analysis, both as to the reasoning used and the results achieved. However, it is somewhat limited ... quite rightly the Court seems willing to go further in the protection of workers than in that of other economic factors [Castro Oliviera].

All the rules which have developed from what are now Treaty Articles 28, 39, 43 and 49 serve one purpose: to determine whether a particular rule or regulation of a Member State (or in certain circumstances, private parties) infringes or complies with Community rules on cross-border economic freedoms. The national rules can be categorised as those which discriminate directly; those which formally apply equally but nevertheless discriminate covertly; those involving no discrimination but which may prevent market access; and those which are truly equal in law and in fact in their application.

Direct discrimination in all areas can only be saved by the derogations contained in the appropriate Treaty Articles, for example, Articles 30 and 39(3). Other national rules regarding goods are 'beyond discrimination'; they apply equally to both home-produced products and imports but in practice, they nevertheless obstruct imports: see Cases 120/78 *Cassis de Dijon* and 178/84 *Commission v Germany (Beer Purity)*. They will breach Article 28 unless justified, normally under the Court's mandatory requirements exception.

As regards the free movement of persons, indirect discrimination can be objectively justified: see Cases 33/74 *Binsbergen* and 205/84 *Commission v Germany (Insurance Services)*.

Taking a lead from *Cassis de Dijon* with respect to goods, in a series of cases culminating in Case C-415/93 *Bosman* for workers, Case C-55/94 *Gebhard*, concerning freedom of establishment, and Case C-76/90 *Säger* for the provision of services, the Court has established that Community provisions can also be applied to non-discriminatory rules which hinder market access. It looked as if a common position was possible. However, as regards goods, the Court had decided in Case C-267/91 *Keck* to attempt to stop the use of Community law to challenge all manner of national rules, including those concerning many 'selling arrangements', which did not hinder free movement. These were held to fall outside the scope of what is now Article 28.

Would the Court follow suit in the free movement of persons field? A negative answer was given in Case C-384/93 *Alpine Investments*, in which it was stated that the *Keck* ruling did not apply. The Court stated that the national measure 'directly affects access to the market in services in other Member States and is therefore capable of hindering intra-Community trade in services'. Indeed, subsequently, as seen, Case C-254/98 *Heimdienst* and other goods cases show that 'selling arrangements' do not escape the prohibition in Article 28 where they have a greater adverse effect on imports.

It is therefore the case that a wholly common approach does not exist in the present state of Community law. It is perhaps neither advisable nor achievable. In Catherine Bernard's opinion:

> There is an argument against a global approach which treats goods and persons in a similar manner because they concern very different technological, economic and social situations. There is even ... an argument against treating workers, establishment and services in the same way since they concern different situations (the provisions on workers and establishment preclude discrimination on the grounds of nationality; services, as [Case C-288/89] *Gouda* made clear, precludes discrimination on the grounds of nationality and place of establishment). They also concern different regulatory patterns – in the context of workers and establishment the host state is the prime regulator whereas in services the home state is the principal regulator. From this perspective the cross-border provision of services has more in common with the cross-frontier provisions of goods, both of which might have to satisfy a double regulatory burden.

REFERENCES AND FURTHER READING

Andenas, M and Wulf-Henning, R (eds), *Services and Free Movement in EU Law*, 2002 (various contributions).

Barnard, C, *EC Employment Law*, 2000.

Barnard, C, 'Fitting the remaining pieces into the goods and persons jigsaw' (2001) 26 EL Rev 35.

Biondi, A, 'In and out of the Internal Market: recent developments on the principle of free movement' (1999/2000) 19 YEL 469.

Castro Oliviera, A, 'Workers and other persons: step by step from movement to citizenship' (2002) 39 CML Rev 77.

Davies, G, *European Union Internal Market Law*, 2002.

Davis, R, 'Citizenship of the Union ... rights for all?' (2002) 27 EL Rev 121.

Doogan, M, 'Minimum harmonisation and the Internal Market' (2000) 37 CML Rev 853.

Durand, A, 'European citizenship' (1979) 4 EL Rev 3.

Evans, A, 'European citizenship' (1982) 45 MLR 497.

Green, N, Hartley, T and Usher, J, *The Legal Foundations of the Single European Market*, 1991.

Hansen, J, 'Full circle: is there a difference between the freedom of establishment and the freedom to provide services?', in Andenas and Wulf-Henning (eds), *Services and Free Movement in EU Law*, 2002.

Hartley, T, *EEC Immigration Law*, 1978.

Hartley, T, 'The internal personal scope of the EEC immigration provisions' (1978) 3 EL Rev 191.

Hatzopoulos, V, 'Recent developments in the case law of the ECJ in the field of services' (2000) 37 CML Rev 43.

Hilson, C, 'Discrimination in Community free movement law' (1999) 24 EL Rev 445.

Jacqueson, C, 'Union citizenship and the Court of Justice: something new under the sun? Towards social citizenship' (2002) 27 EL Rev 260.

Johnson, E and O'Keefe, D, 'From discrimination to obstacles to free movement: recent developments concerning the free movement of workers 1989–1994' (1994) 31 CML Rev 1313.

La Torre, M (ed), *European Citizenship*, 1998.

O'Keefe, D, 'Equal rights for migrants: the concept of social advantages in Article 7(2), Regulation 1612/68' (1986) 5 YEL 93.

O'Keefe, D, 'The free movement of persons and the Single Market' (1992) 17 EL Rev 3.

Mortelmans, K, 'The Common Market, the Internal Market and the Single Market, what's in a Market?' (1998) 35 CML Rev 101.

Shuibine, N, 'Free movement of persons and the wholly internal rule: time to move on?' (2002) 39 CML Rev 731.

Swann, D, *The Economics of the Common Market*, 4th edn, 1981 (now The *Economics of Europe*, 9th edn, 2000).

Szyszczak, E, *EC Labour Law*, 2000.

CHAPTER 14

SOCIAL POLICY: EQUAL TREATMENT
FOR MEN AND WOMEN

INTRODUCTION

In a document heavily loaded towards economic policy, Article 119 of the EEC Treaty of 1957 laid down, within its brief, undeveloped social policy provisions, that the Member States should bring into effect national rules to ensure 'the application of the principle that men and women should receive equal pay for equal work'. For many years, however, some Member States failed to implement this principle and it required action by the Court of Justice in the mid-1970s to put teeth into Article 119 (now 141).

Since that time, a combination of Treaty amendments and legislative and judicial action at both Community and Member State level has led to a strengthening and widening of the gender equality principle in the field of employment and beyond. Article 119 (now 141) has been widened and modern thinking on gender has been recognised. Community harmonisation measures have since the late 1970s covered equality of treatment beyond pay to access to employment, training and promotion, and working conditions including dismissal. 'Positive Action' initiatives taken at national level to remove inequality may be permitted. Special provisions relate to pregnancy. Other Directives cover social security schemes and benefits.

These developments have increasingly to be seen within the widening scope of anti-discrimination law generally within the Union. Gender equality as an element of the general principle of equality is a fundamental right. As we have seen, Article 3(2) EC, added at Amsterdam, states that in all its policy areas 'the Community shall aim to eliminate inequalities, and to promote equality, between men and women'. The EU Charter of Fundamental Rights declares in Article 23 that: 'Equality between men and women must be ensured in all areas, including employment, work and pay [without preventing] the maintenance or adoption of measures providing for specific advantages in favour of the under-represented sex.' Article 21(1) states that discrimination based on a wide range of grounds, including sex and sexual orientation, shall be prohibited.

Nevertheless, this is not to deny that despite this impressive array of political and legal developments, in terms of practical reality, inequality is still to be found in many cases.

In this chapter, we will concentrate on the basic 'employment equality' principles of *equal* pay (Article 141 (formerly 119) and Directive 75/117) and *equal treatment* as regards access to employment including promotion, vocational training, and working conditions including dismissal (Article 141, as amended, and Directive 76/207, as amended by Directive 2002/73, together with Directive 92/85 on pregnancy and Directive 96/34 on parental leave). In addition, account must be taken of the main 'welfare equality' measures on the *progressive* implementation of equal treatment in *statutory* (that is, State) *retirement pensions* (Directive 79/7) and equal treatment in *occupational* (for example, company) *pension schemes* (Directive 86/378, as amended by Directive 96/97).

EQUAL PAY

Prior to the ToA, Article 119, paragraph 1 provided that:

> Each Member State shall during the first stage ensure and subsequently maintain the application of the principle that men and women should receive equal pay for equal work.

Although Article 119 spoke only of 'equal pay for equal work' and not of 'remuneration for work of equal value', the wider concept adopted by the International Labour Organisation Convention No 100 of 1951, the subsequent adoption by the Community of the Equal Pay Directive in 1975 meant that Community law was brought into line with ILO concepts and principles: see Case 149/77 *Defrenne (No 3)*.

Following the ToA, paragraph 1, and the rest of Article 141 (formerly 119), provides that:

1 Each Member State shall ensure that the principle of equal pay for male and female workers for equal work or work of equal value is applied.

2 For the purpose of this Article, 'pay' means the ordinary basic or minimum wage or salary and other consideration, whether in cash or in kind, which the worker receives directly or indirectly in respect of his employment from his employer.

Equal pay without discrimination based on sex means:

(a) that pay for the same work at piece rates shall be calculated on the basis of the same unit of measurement;

(b) that pay for work at time rates shall be the same for the same job.

3 The Council, acting in accordance with the procedure referred to in Article 251, and after consulting the Economic and Social Committee, shall adopt measures to ensure the application of the principle of equal opportunities and equal treatment of men and women in matters of employment and occupation, including the principle of equal pay for equal work or work of equal value.

4 With a view to ensuring full equality in practice between men and women in working life, the principle of equal treatment shall not prevent any Member State from maintaining or adopting measures providing for specific advantages in order to make it easier for the under-represented sex to pursue a vocational activity or to prevent or compensate for disadvantages in professional careers.

In the late 1950s, it was generally thought that it was necessary for 'the Six' to implement Article 119 by means of national measures in order to make the equal pay principle effective. Some of them had failed to do this, but the Commission took no enforcement actions against them. (Article 119 stated that the principle should be brought into effect 'during the first stage', that is, during the period 1958–62.) It was not until the *Defrenne* litigation of the 1970s that a breakthrough was made – by Belgian activists and the Court of Justice.

Case 43/75 *Defrenne v Sabena (No 2)*

Miss Defrenne was employed by the Belgian airline, Sabena, as an air hostess. In the Belgian courts she claimed compensation for discrimination in terms of the pay she received as compared with cabin stewards doing the same work. Her action was based on Article 119 and the *Court de Travail* asked the Court of Justice if Article 119 could be relied upon before national courts, independently of national legislation. The Court ruled:

(a) Article 119 pursued a double aim: (i) *economic*, by the removal of the competitive disadvantage suffered by undertakings in Member States which had implemented the equal pay principle as compared to those in States which had not, and (ii) *social*, by the improvement by common action of living and working conditions for workers throughout the Community. As such, the principle of equal pay formed one of the foundations of the Community.

(b) In interpreting Article 119, it was not possible to base any argument on the dilatoriness and resistance which had delayed the implementation of the basic principle.

With reference to the actual provisions of Article 119, the Court held that:

(c) Article 119 was directly effective and gave rise to individual rights which national courts must protect in cases of discrimination which could be identified by the court solely with the aid of the criteria based on equal work and equal pay in Article 119 itself.

(d) Such cases included those which had their origins in legislative provisions or in collective labour agreements and which might be detected on the basis of a purely legal analysis of the situation. There was certainly no difficulty in applying Article 119 where the facts clearly showed that a woman worker was receiving lower pay than a male worker performing the same task in the same establishment or service – whether *public or private*: '... the prohibition on discrimination between men and women applies not only to the action of public authorities, but also extends to all agreements which are intended to regulate paid labour collectively, as well as to contracts between individuals.' (As seen in Chapter 8, Article 119 (now 141) is therefore both vertically *and* horizontally directly effective; an equal pay policy cannot operate merely in some sectors of the economy.)

(e) For cases of discrimination which could only be identified by reference to more explicit implementing provisions of a Community or national character, the Court stated that:

> It is impossible not to recognise that the complete implementation of the aim pursued by Article 119, by means of the elimination of all discrimination between men and women workers, not only as regards individual undertakings but also entire branches of industry and even of the economic system as a whole, may in certain cases involve the elaboration of criteria whose implementation necessitates the taking of appropriate measures at Community and national level.

Therefore, in cases such as these, Article 119 was seen as not sufficient on its own to secure the equal pay objective – further Community or national measures would be required, as we will see below.

The Court's ruling that in essence its decision should only have prospective (not retrospective) effect was noted at the end of Chapter 9. This is what the Court said:

> The Governments of Ireland and the United Kingdom have drawn the Court's attention to the possible economic consequences of attributing direct effect to the provisions of Article 119, on the ground that such a decision might, in many branches of economic life, result in the introduction of claims dating back to the time at which such effect came into existence [the end of the first stage].

> In view of the large number of people concerned such claims, which undertakings could not have foreseen, might seriously affect the financial situation of such undertakings and even drive some of them to bankruptcy.

Although the practical consequences of any judicial decision must be carefully taken into account, it would be impossible to go so far as to diminish the objectivity of the law and compromise its future application on the ground of the possible repercussions which might result, as regards the past, from such a judicial decision.

However, in the light of the conduct of several of the Member States and the views adopted by the Commission and repeatedly brought to the notice of the circles concerned, it is appropriate to take exceptionally into account the fact that, over a prolonged period, the parties concerned have been led to continue with practices which were contrary to Article 119, although not yet prohibited under their national law.

The fact that, in spite of the warnings given, the Commission did not initiate proceedings under Article 169 against the Member States concerned, on grounds of failure to fulfil an obligation was likely to consolidate the incorrect impression as to the effects of Article 119.

Therefore, the direct effect of Article 119 cannot be relied on in order to support claims concerning pay periods prior to the date of this judgment, except as regards those workers who have already brought legal proceedings or made an equivalent claim.

In these circumstances, it is appropriate to determine that, as the general level at which pay would have been fixed cannot be known, important considerations of legal certainty affecting all the interests involved, both public and private, make it impossible in principle to reopen the question as regards the past.

The first UK equal pay case to be referred to the Court of Justice raised a slightly different question from that in *Defrenne (No 2)*.

Case 129/79 *Macarthys Ltd v Smith*

S brought an equal pay claim on the basis that she was paid £10 per week less than the man who had held the same position four months previously. In the Court of Appeal, a majority found that the wording of section 1(2)(a) and (b) of the Equal Pay Act ('where the woman is employed') limited the right to equal pay to situations of contemporaneous (and not sequential) employment. Following a reference to the Court of Justice on the interpretation of Article 119, the Court ruled that:

> As the Court indicated in the Defrenne judgment of 8 April 1976, that provision applies directly, and without the need for more detailed implementing measures on the part of the Community or the Member States, to all forms of direct and overt discrimination which may be identified solely with the aid of the criteria of equal work and equal pay referred to by the Article in question. Among the forms of discrimination which may be thus judicially identified, the Court mentioned in particular cases where men and women receive unequal pay for equal work carried out in the same establishment or service.

> In such a situation, the decisive test lies in establishing whether there is a difference in treatment between a man and a woman performing 'equal work' within the meaning of Article 119. The scope of that concept, which is entirely qualitative in character in that it is exclusively concerned with the nature of the services in question, may not be restricted by the introduction of a requirement of contemporaneity.

> It must be acknowledged, however, that, as the Employment Appeal Tribunal properly recognised, it cannot be ruled out that a difference in pay between two workers occupying the same post but at different periods in time may be explained by the operation of factors which are unconnected with any

discrimination on grounds of sex. That is a question of fact which it is for the court or tribunal to decide.

Thus, the answer to the ... question should be that the principle that men and women should receive equal pay for equal work, enshrined in Article 119 of the EEC Treaty, is not confined to situations in which men and women are contemporaneously doing equal work for the same employer.

On the question of pay differences (arising in this case following a lapse of time), which can be shown to have a basis in factors unconnected with sex, see the *Bilka Kaufhaus* case and others, below.

It would seem that the Court of Justice has left open the question whether the comparison between pay and work based on Article 141 (formerly 119) is to be confined to the same employer or whether it can be extended to the situation prevailing at other undertakings operating in the same field: see Case 143/83 *Commission v Denmark (Re Equal Pay Concepts)*, below.

With reference to the Court's observations in *Defrenne (No 2)* regarding Article 119's economic and social aims, it is significant that in 2000, in Joined Cases C-234 and 235/96 *Deutsche Telekom v Vick*, the Court declared that the social aim of what is now Article 141 prevailed over the economic. The right not to be discriminated against on grounds of sex was one of the fundamental human rights whose observance the Court had a duty to protect. See also 'Widening the Scope of Discrimination', below.

DISCRIMINATION: THE SCOPE OF ARTICLE 141 (FORMERLY 119)

The following case shows that Article 141 (formerly 119) does extend to what is termed 'indirect discrimination', such as a 'gender neutral' distinction made between full time and part time workers.

Case 96/80 *Jenkins v Kingsgate (Clothing Productions) Ltd*

Mrs J worked part time for K Ltd. She received an hourly rate of pay lower than that of her male (and female) colleagues employed full time on the same work. All the part time workers except one were women. The Employment Appeal Tribunal referred several questions to the Court of Justice under Article 177 (now 234). The Court ruled as follows:

It appears from the first three questions and the reasons stated in the order making the reference that the national court is principally concerned to know whether a difference in the level of pay for work carried out part time and the same work carried out full time may amount to discrimination of a kind prohibited by Article 119 of the Treaty when the category of part time workers is exclusively or predominantly comprised of women.

The answer to the questions thus understood is that the purpose of Article 119 is to ensure the application of the principle of equal pay for men and women for the same work. The differences in pay prohibited by that provision are therefore exclusively those based on the difference of the sex of the workers. Consequently the fact that part time work is paid at an hourly rate lower than pay for full time work does not amount *per se* to discrimination prohibited by Article 119 provided that the hourly rates are applied to workers belonging to either category without distinction based on sex.

If there is no such distinction, therefore, the fact that work paid at time rates is remunerated at an hourly rate which varies according to the number of hours worked per week does not offend against the principle of equal pay laid down in Article 119 of the Treaty in so far as the difference in pay between part time work and full time work is attributable to factors which are objectively justified and are in no way related to any discrimination based on sex.

Such may be the case, in particular, when by giving hourly rates of pay which are lower for part time work than those for full time work the employer is endeavouring, on economic grounds which may be objectively justified, to encourage full time work irrespective of the sex of the worker.

By contrast, if it is established that a considerably smaller percentage of women than of men perform the minimum number of weekly working hours required in order to be able to claim the full time hourly rate of pay, the inequality in pay will be contrary to Article 119 of the Treaty where, regard being had to the difficulties encountered by women in arranging to work that minimum number of hours per week, the pay policy of the undertaking in question cannot be explained by factors other than discrimination based on sex.

Where the hourly rate of pay differs according to whether the work is part time or full time it is for the national courts to decide in each individual case whether, regard being had to the facts of the case, its history and the employer's intention, a pay policy such as that which is at issue in the main proceedings although represented as a difference based on weekly working hours is or is not in reality discrimination based on the sex of the worker.

The reply to the first three questions must therefore be that a difference in pay between full time workers and part time workers does not amount to discrimination prohibited by Article 119 of the Treaty unless it is in reality merely an indirect way of reducing the level of pay of part time workers on the ground that that group of workers is composed exclusively or predominantly of women.

Approximately 90 per cent of part time workers in the EU are women, many of them women with other responsibilities of a family nature.

In Case 170/84 *Bilka-Kaufhaus*, which again involved a claim by a part time worker, the Court made it clear that it was for *the employer*, in his defence, to prove to the satisfaction of the national court an *objective justification* for the wage differential in question. The plaintiff's complaint was that, as a part time worker, she was excluded from the benefits of the employer's *occupational pension scheme*, at least until she had worked for the firm for at least 15 out of a total of 20 years. The scheme, which supplemented the State pension scheme, originated in a collective agreement; it was incorporated into contracts of employment and was financed solely by employer contributions (it has been seen that Article 119 (now 141) in defining pay speaks of 'indirect' consideration received by a worker from his employer in respect of his employment).

Case 170/84 *Bilka-Kaufhaus*

Karin Weber, a female part time worker, challenged BK's pension scheme as being indirectly discriminatory on the basis that the long service requirement applied only to part time workers (not full timers) and the majority of part timers were women. Men comprised 28 per cent of the total work force, but male part time workers comprised only 2.8 per cent of the total work force. The long service requirement therefore disproportionately disadvantaged women.

In Article 177 (now 234) proceedings, the Court of Justice was asked if the exclusion of part time workers from the scheme could be in breach of Article 119 (now 141). The Court referred to its decision in *Jenkins* (above) and held that if it was found that a considerably smaller percentage of men than of women worked part time, and if the difference in treatment could not be explained by any other factor than sex, the exclusion of part time workers from the occupational pension scheme would be contrary to Article 119.

The difference in treatment would however be permissible if the employer could explain it by *objectively justified factors* unrelated to discrimination based on sex. To do this, the employer must prove that the measures giving rise to the difference in treatment:

(a) 'correspond to a real need on the part of an undertaking';

(b) 'are appropriate with a view to achieving the objectives pursued'; and

(c) 'are necessary to that end'.

This 'economic objectives' test (which is similar to that applied to 'mandatory requirements' in *Cassis de Dijon*: see Chapter 12) was met by the employer in *Bilka-Kaufhaus* with the argument that part timers were less economic (in terms, for example, of high overhead and training costs), less willing to work evening and Saturday shifts, and that there was a need to provide incentives to full time employment. As a defence, these claims would have to be proved to the satisfaction of the *national* court and shown to satisfy the principle of proportionality, that is, that they were necessary, but no more than necessary. Where the employer has a choice as to how he may achieve a legitimate economic objective, he must choose the least discriminatory method.

The Court of Justice has consistently held that the issue of objective justification of indirect discrimination is a question of fact for the national court. Initially, the employee must show that the workers in receipt of lower pay are predominantly or disproportionately women (but see *Danfoss* below, where the employer's system of payment made this impossible). The onus then shifts to the employer to justify such indirect discrimination: see also Directive 97/80 (Burden of Proof). The case law of the Court has indicated various matters which will not constitute justification, for example, the exclusion (by statute) from entitlement to sick pay of part time workers could not be justified (by the German government, not the employer) on the basis of their alleged lack of 'integration' into the undertaking: Case 171/88 *Rinner-Kühn*. In Case 109/88 *Danfoss*, a general desire on the employer's part to have a 'flexible' workforce did not amount to justification. However, in Case C-400/93 *Royal Copenhagen*, the Court indicated that different rates of work in piece-rate work and differences in the type of work, working conditions, or the organisation of working time may all justify indirect discrimination.

Justification based on labour market factors was one of the issues in the following 'work of equal value' case.

Case C-127/92 *Enderby v Frenchay Health Authority (No 1)*

E was employed as a speech therapist by FHA. She considered that she was a victim of sex discrimination on the basis that, at her level of seniority (Chief III) within the National Health Service, members of her profession, which was overwhelmingly a female profession, were significantly less well paid than members of comparable professions in which, at an equivalent level, there were more men than women.

She brought proceedings against her employer in 1986 claiming that her annual pay was only £10,106 while the salaries of a principal clinical psychologist and of a Grade III principal pharmacist, jobs which were of equal value to hers, were £12,527 and £14,106 respectively. E's discrimination claim failed in the industrial tribunal and the Employment Appeal Tribunal. It was considered that there was no direct (intentional) discrimination and that the pay differences could be explained by the different collective bargaining processes (between management and trade union) specific to the three professions, together with the impact of market forces, that is, the need to attract pharmacists into the NHS by offering them higher salaries.

E appealed to the Court of Appeal, which felt that the crucial issues were whether the employer was under an obligation to demonstrate that the pay differences were justified and, if so, on what grounds. Three questions on the interpretation of Article 119 were referred to the Court of Justice for a preliminary ruling. They focused on the burden of proof, the separate (discrimination-free) collective bargaining processes and the effect of a shortage of entrants to a particular type of work.

The Court of Justice ruled as follows:

(a) Where significant statistics disclose an appreciable difference in pay between two jobs of equal value, one of which is carried out almost exclusively by women and the other predominantly by men, Article 119 requires the employer to show that the difference is based on objectively justified factors unrelated to any discrimination on grounds of sex.

(b) The fact that the respective rates of pay of two jobs of equal value, one carried out almost exclusively by women and the other predominantly by men, were negotiated by collective bargaining processes which, although carried out by the same parties, are distinct, and, taken separately, have in themselves no discriminatory effect, is not sufficient objective justification for the difference in pay between those two jobs. Otherwise, the employer could 'easily circumvent the principle of equal pay by using separate bargaining processes.'

(c) It is for the national court to determine, if necessary by applying the principle of proportionality, whether and to what extent the shortage of candidates for a job and the need to attract them by higher pay constitutes an objectively justified economic ground for the difference in pay between the jobs in question (speech therapists and pharmacists).

The 'equal value' aspect of the claim was assumed to be correct in *Enderby (No 1)* and was established in *Enderby (No 2)* before the Court of Appeal, in which it was held that an applicant for equal pay, who had established that she was employed on work of equal value with her chosen male comparator, was entitled to have her conditions of pay amended so as to receive a level of pay equal to that received by the comparator at the date of her claim (and thereafter the same entitlement to annual increments). She was not entitled to be placed on the comparator's pay scale at a point commensurate with her own years of service in her work.

In the following case, as similarly in *Rinner-Kühn* above, it was the task of the government to defend and justify allegedly indirectly discriminatory provisions of primary legislation.

Equal Opportunities Commission v Secretary of State for Employment (1994)

The Employment Protection (Consolidation) Act 1978 provided that full time workers (16 or more hours per week) had to be in continuous employment for two years to qualify for unfair dismissal and redundancy payments, while part time workers (8–16 hours per week) had to be in continuous employment for five years to qualify for these statutory rights. Employees working less than eight hours per week had no such rights.

The great majority of full time workers in the UK are men while the great majority of part time workers are women. The EOC claimed that the unfair dismissal and redundancy provisions of the Act resulted in indirect discrimination against women contrary to Article 119 of the Treaty (equal pay) and Council Directives 75/117 (equal pay) and 76/207 (equal treatment). Having been unsuccessful in the Divisional Court and the Court of Appeal, the EOC appealed to the House of Lords.

Their Lordships held that:

(a) The EOC had 'sufficient interest' for the purposes of RSC Ord 53, r 3(7) to bring judicial review proceedings and hence the necessary *locus standi* to seek a declaration that the provisions of the 1978 Act were incompatible with Community law: *Factortame* applied.

(b) The differing threshold provisions in the Act for full time and part time workers to qualify for unfair dismissal and redundancy payments were incompatible with Article 119 and the Equal Pay and Equal Treatment Directives. The Secretary of State had not provided sufficient evidence to show that they were objectively justified: Case 170/84 *Bilka-Kaufhaus* and Case 171/88 *Rinner-Kühn* considered.

The appeal was allowed.

This decision of the House of Lords, which did not refer the matter to the Court of Justice under Article 177 (now 234), is of significance on at least three counts.

First, in approving the use of High Court judicial review, the House of Lords has given parties with 'sufficient interest', such as the EOC (which has a statutory duty to work towards the elimination of discrimination), the opportunity of mounting a direct attack on primary national legislation in the context of EC law. As seen, and explained earlier in Chapter 8, the attack was successful – new direct powers of legislative review were granted, and the national court made a declaration that the relevant provisions of the 1978 Act were incompatible with Community law and inapplicable (that is, an implied repeal). (The EOC might otherwise have supported a claim by a part timer in an industrial tribunal, a course which might well have involved an Article 177 detour to Luxembourg.)

Secondly, this decision opened the way for retrospective claims by female part timers who had been excluded from unfair dismissal and redundancy rights but could show that they had worked at least eight hours per week for two years or more. Depending on the circumstances of each case, claims might be made against public employers on the basis of the vertical direct effect of Article 5 of the Equal Treatment Directive concerning equality of treatment as regards dismissal (Case 152/84 *Marshall (No 1)*, below). Claims might also be made against any employer on the basis of Article 141 (formerly 119) of the Treaty which is directly effective both vertically and horizontally (Case 43/75 *Defrenne (No 2)*). Redundancy pay is certainly 'pay' within the terms of Article 141 (formerly 119) (Case C-262/88 *Barber*). An inability to rely on any directly effective provisions of Community law could lead to a State liability claim for compensation against the Department of Employment on the basis of Case C-6/90 *Francovich*.

Finally, employers might succeed where the Secretary of State failed, that is, they may be able to show objective justification for the indirect discrimination against female part timers. The government, on whom the onus rested, had not shown that the differing thresholds were objectively justified. Although the reason given by the Secretary of State for the differing thresholds, namely that they would bring about an increase in the availability of part time work by reducing the costs to employers of employing part time workers, was properly to be regarded as a beneficial social policy aim and could be said to be a necessary aim of the provisions, the Secretary of State had not produced evidence to show that the provisions had actually been proved to result in a greater availability of part time work than would have been the case without them. The defence amounted to a mere assertion of belief. (See also Case C-127/92 *Enderby*, point (c), above.)

While the 'analytical rigour' applied to the question of objective justification by the House of Lords in this case has been welcomed, complaints have been voiced regarding 'the relative ease with which the commercial objectives of the undertaking or employer – such as the need to alleviate constraints on "small or medium-sized enterprises" – can defeat the claim of indirect discrimination [and undermine] its usefulness in remedying the considerable disadvantages suffered by women in the labour market': Craig and De Búrca. This issue is clearly seen in the following equal treatment case.

Case C-189/91 *Kirshammer-Hack v Sidal*

Mrs K-H worked as a dental assistant in the surgery of Mrs S who employed two full time employees, two part time employees (including Mrs K-H) working more than 10 hours per week and four employees working less than 10 hours per week. Mrs K-H was dismissed in 1991 as being an unsatisfactory worker. She claimed unfair dismissal under the relevant German national law which, however, exempts small businesses from its provisions. [The position is similar in the UK and France.] In Germany, a 'small business' for these purposes is one with five or less employees – not taking into account employees working less than 10 hours per week. The dental practice was therefore a 'small business'.

The Court of Justice was asked whether the legislative advantages conferred on small businesses constituted indirect discrimination against female employees contrary to the Equal Treatment Directive.

The German government argued that its legislation was 'intended to alleviate the constraints on small businesses, which play an essential role in economic development and job-creation within the Community'.

The Court doubted that a *prima facie* case of indirect discrimination was to be found in this case: the national rules did not discriminate against part time workers as such (about 90 per cent of part timers in Germany were women); they distinguished between businesses which employed more than five employees and those which employed five or less. It would only be possible to establish indirect discrimination if it were shown, as was not the case, that small businesses employed significantly more women than men.

The Court added that, even if the exclusion from protection were found to indirectly discriminate against women, the grounds put forward in defence of the legislation were potentially legitimate. Article 118a EC (now 138), which qualified the power to adopt Directives in the area of health and safety by reference to the need to avoid 'imposing administrative, financial and legal constraints in a way which would hold back the creation and development of small and medium-sized undertakings', meant that under EC law 'these undertakings, can be the object of special economic measures'.

However, in Case C-281/97 *Krüger*, part time workers were excluded by the terms of a collective agreement from an annual bonus because they were classified as being in 'minor employment'. The hospital employer sought to justify this on the basis that such workers (K was a nurse) did not pay social security contributions and that this exclusion, in accordance with German government policy aimed to encourage part time work, justified the workers' exclusion from the collective agreement. The Court of Justice did not agree, declaring that the margin of discretion accorded to Member States was not to be accorded to employers:

> In this case, it is not a question of either a measure adopted by the national legislature in the context of its discretionary power or a basic principle of the German social security system, but of the exclusion of persons in minor employment from the benefit of a collective agreement which provides for the grant of a special annual bonus, the result of this being that, in respect of pay, those persons are treated differently from those governed by the collective agreement.

On this basis, therefore, the Court ruled that the exclusion 'constitutes indirect discrimination based on sex, where that exclusion applies independently of the sex of the worker but actually affects a considerably higher percentage of women than men'.

Turning to a different although related question, recent Court of Justice case law has thrown up the question as to whether direct (not indirect) pay discrimination can be objectively justified. Put another way, where men and women appear to receive different pay for equal work or work of equal value, can it be determined that no pay discrimination exists because they are, in the Court's words, 'differently situated'. What the Court has held in these cases is that where the respective situations of the male and female workers is not comparable, then the inequality in pay does not amount to discrimination:

> ... it is settled case law that, for the purpose of applying the principle of equal pay, the situation of a male worker is not comparable to that of a female worker where the advantage granted to the female worker alone is designed to offset the occupational disadvantages, inherent in maternity leave, which arise for female workers as a result of being away from work [Case C-218/98 *Abdoulaye and Others* – maternity leave granted to a woman on expiry of the statutory protective period falls within the special derogation provisions of Article 2(3) of the Equal Treatment Directive: see below].

Conversely, national rules may be based on the presumption that the situation of male and female workers is not comparable and the rules have granted a pay advantage to the apparently occupationally disadvantaged sex on that basis. However, if cases arise where this presumption is found to be rebutted, then it may well be that factual comparability demands that the inequality in pay be redressed.

Case C-366/99 *Griesmar v Ministre de l'Economie*

G, a father of three children, was granted a retirement pension based on years of service under the Civil Military Retirement Pensions Code to which Article 119 (now 141) applied. No account was taken of a linked yearly 'service credit' provided under Article L.12(b) of the Code to which female civil servants were entitled on retirement in respect of each of their children.

G claimed that Article L.12(b) was contrary to Article 119. Following a reference, the Court of Justice held:

(a) The purpose of the 'service credit' (which dated back to 1924) was to assist female civil servants in the bringing up of their children.

(b) Article L.12(b) of the Code did not prevent a male civil servant who could prove that he had the task of bringing up his children from receiving the yearly credit.

(c) Article L.12(b) of the Code created a difference in treatment on grounds of sex as regards male civil servants who had assumed the task of bringing up their children. The principle of equal pay was infringed.

(d) The Court did not accede to the French claim that the ruling should only apply prospectively.

These cases can be explained in terms of the scope of the concept of pay within EC law. There is in them no question that the male and female employees involved were not doing equal work or work of equal value. The differences in pay arose through the receipt of supplementary social welfare benefits from the employer which came within the scope of Article 119 according to the jurisprudence of the Court of Justice, hence the 'different situations' finding, rather than one based on justification.

THE CONCEPT OF PAY

As some of the cases already discussed show, Article 141 (formerly 119) is not confined to wages and salaries alone. It also covers in paragraph 2:

... any other consideration, whether in cash or in kind, which the worker receives, directly or indirectly, in respect of his employment from his employer.

As regards *benefits in kind*, see the following case.

Case 12/81 *Garland v British Rail Engineering Ltd*

BRE employees and their families were entitled to special rail travel concessions. On retirement, however, families of female ex-employees lost these concessions while those of male ex-employees continued to enjoy them.

The Court ruled that such benefits constituted 'pay' within the meaning of Article 119, even though employment had ceased, providing they were granted as a result of the employment relationship. It was immaterial that: (a) the entitlement was not part of any contractual obligation; and (b) the discrimination related to the worker's family and not to the benefits accruing to the ex-employee herself.

The case of *Kowalska* shows that, in respect of *benefits arising from a collective wage agreement*, the terms of such an agreement may be contrary to Article 141 (formerly 119) if they indirectly discriminate against women and cannot be objectively justified by factors unrelated to sex.

Case C-33/89 *Kowalska*

Under a German 'white collar', public services collective agreement, employees normally working less than 38 hours per week were excluded from its severance payments provisions. The purpose of such severance grants was to help employees who involuntarily left employment (for example, on retirement or through disability) to adjust to their new situation.

The Court of Justice ruled that severance pay constituted pay within the terms of Article 119, and, since a higher proportion of part time workers were women, the agreement was contrary to Article 119 unless it could be shown that the exclusion was justified by objective factors unrelated to sex. If not, both full and part timers were to receive severance payments on a proportionate basis.

In Case C-184/89 *Nimz*, which involved a challenge not to pay rates in themselves but to the rules governing the system of salary classification into grades, the Court of Justice stated that:

> Where there is indirect discrimination in a provision in a collective agreement, the national court is required to disapply that provision, without requesting or awaiting its prior removal by collective negotiation or any other procedure, and to apply to members of the group which is disadvantaged by that discrimination the same arrangements which are applied to other employees, arrangements which, failing the correct application of Article 119 of the EEC Treaty in national law, remain the only valid system of reference.

It would appear therefore that those indirectly discriminated against in such circumstances can look to the application of an equality clause where the discriminatory term has been incorporated into their contracts of employment or at least to a declaration that they are to enjoy comparable rights.

From the standpoint of *part time workers*, such cases as *Kowalska* and *Nimz* and Case 171/88 *Rinner-Kühn*, in which a part time office cleaner had been excluded by her employer from sick pay entitlement (*prima facie* a statutory social security benefit; 80 per cent of such payments made to employees who qualified for them being reimbursed by the State) indicate that national legislation which allows certain categories of workers (for example, part timers) to be treated differently by employers, that is, discriminated against, is in breach of Article 141 (formerly 119). As Steiner pointed out at the time, these cases 'have profound implications for employers of part time workers in the UK, since the majority of statutory employment rights allow for derogation in the case of part time workers' – and see the House of Lords' decision in the 1994 *Equal Opportunities Commission* case, above. National 'welfare' legislation which currently *requires* certain groups to be treated differently, for example, State social security schemes providing, say, for different 'pensionable' ages for men and women for the purposes of granting State retirement pensions, still remains outside Article 141 (formerly 119).

It is in relation to the Court's extension of the concept of 'pay' under Article 119 (now 141) to cover *employers' contributions to employees' pension schemes* that considerable complications have arisen. Only the main issues will be considered here.

In Case 12/81 *Garland* (see above), the Court stated that pay covered any consideration '... whether immediate or future, provided that the worker receives it, albeit indirectly, in respect of his employment from his employer'. However, earlier, in Case 80/70 *Defrenne (No 1)*, in which D challenged Belgian Royal Decrees laying down rules governing retirement and pensions in the civil aviation industry, the Court had said that:

> A retirement pension established within the framework of a social security scheme laid down by legislation does not constitute consideration which the worker receives indirectly in respect of his employment from his employer within the meaning of the second paragraph of Article 119 of the EEC Treaty.

This ruling appeared to exclude from Article 119 (now 141) all social security benefits directly governed by legislation and available to workers generally or to certain categories of workers. In *Defrenne (No 1)*, the employer made different contributions to the scheme in respect of male and female employees, but the Court stated that the benefits arising from such a statutory social security scheme were 'no more emoluments paid directly by the employer than are roads, canals or water drains'. What were not considered in this case were *employers' occupational pension schemes*.

The nature of one such scheme was outlined by the Court in Case 69/80 *Worringham and Humphreys v Lloyds Bank Ltd*:

> Lloyds applies to its staff two retirement schemes, one for men and one for women. Under these retirement benefits schemes, which are the result of collective bargaining between the trade unions and Lloyds and which have been approved by the national authorities under the Finance Act 1970 and certified under the Social Security Pensions Act 1975, the member contracts out of the earnings-related part of the State pension scheme and this is replaced by a contractual scheme.

In 1986, the Court of Justice held that occupational pension benefits fall within the scope of 'pay' in Article 119 (now 141) notwithstanding that they are fitted into a statutory framework.

Case 170/84 *Bilka-Kaufhaus*

A pension scheme, adopted in accordance with German legislation, originated, however, in a collective agreement and was incorporated into contracts of employment. This occupational pension supplemented the State pension scheme and was financed solely by employer contributions.

The Court ruled that the scheme fell within Article 119 and that (as seen above) a long service requirement for part time workers could amount to indirect discrimination. The Court stressed that:

> The contractual, and not the statutory, origin of the disputed scheme is confirmed by the fact that the scheme and its rules are considered ... to form an integral part of the contracts of employment between Bilka and its employees.

The supplementary nature of the pension and its relationship to the employment involved were factors which overrode the social security and social policy aspects of the scheme. The benefit constituted consideration paid by the employer indirectly (via the pension fund) to the employee in respect of his employment.

In this next case, the Court held that Article 119 (now 141) applied to UK employers' contracted-out occupational pension schemes (see the *Worringham* reference above) in a situation where benefit was subject to an *age requirement* which was discriminatory, the difference in age resulting in a difference in 'pay'. In addition, Article 119 was applied to all redundancy payments. Thus, only statutory social security schemes still remain outside the ambit of Article 119.

Case C-262/88 *Barber v Guardian Royal Exchange Assurance Group*

B was a member of GRE's contracted-out occupational pension scheme, that is, the scheme was contracted out of the State earnings related pension scheme (SERPS) and was a substitute for it. The scheme had been established by B's employer and was wholly financed by GRE. The pensionable age for employees in his category was 62 for men and 57 for women. However, contracts of employment further provided that, under severance terms, employees made redundant were entitled to an immediate pension if they were aged 55 for men and 50 for women.

B was made redundant at 52 and he claimed an immediate pension – which he would have received if he had been a woman. (The five year age difference reflected the different *State* pensionable ages for men and women.) He also claimed entitlement to redundancy benefit.

The Court of Appeal referred various questions to the Court of Justice under Article 177 (now 234), particularly as regards whether contracted-out pensions and statutory redundancy payments came within Article 119.

The Court held:

(a) Benefits paid to an employee by his employer in connection with his *redundancy* fell in principle within the concept of pay for the purposes of Article 119. This was so whether such benefits were paid under a contract of employment, under statute (*prima facie*, a social security payment), or on a voluntary basis: see also *Garland* [1982] 1 CMLR 696, paragraph 5. The 'employment relationship' was paramount.

(b) Unlike the benefits (for example, pensions) awarded by national statutory social security schemes, a pension paid under a contracted-out scheme constituted consideration paid by the employer to the worker in respect of his employment and so fell under Article 119: see *Bilka-Kaufhaus*. (Note also that the payment is made indirectly, via the pension fund.)

(c) It was contrary to Article 119 to impose an *age condition* which differed according to sex in respect of pensions paid under a contracted-out scheme. It was therefore discriminatory for a man made compulsorily redundant to be entitled to claim only a deferred pension, when a woman in the same position was entitled to an immediate pension as the result of the application of an age condition that varied according to sex in the same way as was provided for by the national statutory pension scheme: cf *Marshall* as regards equality in *retirement*, as opposed to pension ages.

(d) Each *element* of the consideration must comply with Article 119 to ensure transparency of the pay system.

(e) The direct effect of Article 119 to the situation in issue was confirmed: if a woman was entitled to an immediate retirement pension when she was made compulsorily redundant and a man of the same age was only entitled to a deferred pension, then the result was unequal pay within Article 119, identifiable by a national court.

(f) The judgment was limited to entitlement to pensions with effect from the date of the judgment (17 May 1990), except for cases already pending before the national courts: cf the Court's ruling in the *Defrenne (No 2)* equal pay case. The justification for this was that in the light of the *exemption* from the equal treatment principle in Article 9 of the Occupational Social Security Directive 86/378 of the 'determination of pensionable age for the purposes of granting old-age or retirement pensions, and the possible implications for other benefits', Member States and the parties concerned were reasonably entitled to consider that Article 119 did not apply to pensions paid under contracted-out schemes and that, accordingly, it was permissible to discriminate. [Article 9 of the Directive has virtually been construed out of existence by the Court's equal pay decision in *Barber*.]

Concern regarding the precise meaning of the Court's temporal limitation on its judgment and its effect on pensions and pension funds was so great as to lead to the addition of a Protocol to Article 119 at the Maastricht Summit conference. The Protocol makes it clear that, subject to the Court's proviso in (f) above, *benefits* under occupational social security schemes are not to be considered as pay – and so do not attract the equality principle in the directly effective Article 119 (now 141) – in so far as they are attributable to *periods of employment prior* to 17 May 1990. In other words, companies would not be required to provide equal pension benefits for men and women for any period of service prior to that date. As the Court itself had stated:

> ... overriding considerations of legal certainty preclude legal situations which have exhausted all their effects in the past from being called in question where that might upset retroactively the financial balance of many contracted-out pension schemes.

The effect of this temporal limitation was to save the British economy an estimated £35–45 billion.

The Court of Justice confirmed that the Protocol expresses the correct interpretation of its ruling in *Barber* in Case C-109/91 *Ten Oever*, in which it was held that a survivor's pension provided for by an occupational pension scheme of the type in question was within the equality principle of Article 119 (now 141). The applicant was the widower of a former employee and at the time of her death the company's scheme only provided for widows' pensions.

However, the *Barber* ruling left the position regarding the requirements of Community law concerning sex equality in occupational pension schemes distinctly confused. It was not surprising that several further references to the Court of Justice on related questions were made by national courts. In September 1994, the Court gave rulings in six of these references: Case C-200/91 *Coloroll Pension Trustees Ltd*, Case C-408/92 *Smith v Advel Systems Ltd*, Case C-7/93 *ABP v Beune*, Case C-28/93 *Van den Akker v SSP*, Case C-57/93 *Vroege* and Case C-128/93 *Fisscher*. These rulings clarified various matters, for instance, in the last two cases, the scope of Article 119 (now 141) with respect to the right of part time workers to be members of pension schemes:

> The only possible decisive criterion is whether the pension is paid to the worker by reason of the employment relationship between him and his former employer, that is to say the criterion of employment based on the wording of Article 119 itself [*ABP v Beune*].

In *Coloroll*, the Court held that as regards claims related to benefits under occupational pension schemes, the equal pay principle can be relied upon against pension fund trustees as well as employers. In *Fisscher*, it was established that where such a scheme excludes married women from membership, discrimination directly based on sex has occurred contrary to Article 119 (now 141).

It is now also the case that equality in occupational pension schemes may lawfully be achieved *for the future* by providing that both men and women receive pensions at the age of 65, even where women previously received a pension at 60 under the scheme.

For example, Deakin and Morris see the result in a case such as *Smith v Advel Systems* as follows:

> ... first, that no rights accruing prior to 17 May 1990 are affected by *Barber*, so that women retain a right to a pension at 60 in respect of service up to that point; secondly, that men and women alike may claim a pension at the age of 60 in respect of service from 17 May 1990 to the point at which the common pensionable age of 65 is introduced [by the employer or the State as the case may be], which in Advel Systems itself was 1 July 1991; but finally, that service from that date will only earn a pension at 65 for men and women alike.

A transitional period of 'levelling up can be followed by levelling down'.

In Case C-152/91 *Neath v Hugh Steeper Ltd*, the Court held that the use of different actuarial factors to take into account women's (average) longer lives is permissible in calculating *employers'* contributions to defined benefit pension schemes. Thus, Article 119 (now 141) 'does not necessarily have to do with the funding arrangements chosen to secure the periodic payment of the pension', which thus remain outside the scope of application of Article 119 (now 141).

However, there are still problems in this area and Curtin's (1990) assessment that *'legislative* guidance, taking full account of the terms of Article 119, is urgently required' still holds true. The effect of further post-*Barber* rulings by the Court of Justice (see, for example, Case C-132/92 *Birds Eye Walls v Roberts*) and the amendments to Directive 86/378 by Directive 96/97 has been to attract criticism in this now extremely complex area of pay and pensions.

One of the most important recent cases on the scope of the term 'pay' (and indirect discrimination) concerned not occupational pension scheme benefits but whether compensation for unfair dismissal (rather than redundancy payments as in *Barber*) constitutes pay within the meaning of Article 119 (now 141).

Case C-167/97 *R v Secretary of State for Employment ex p Seymour-Smith*

S (and another) were dismissed from their jobs in 1991 after 15 months' service. Their claim for unfair dismissal was blocked as they lacked a two years' service requirement under a 1985 Order varying the Employment Protection (Consolidation) Act 1978. They therefore sought (a) judicial review of the 1985 Order on the basis that it affected more women than men and was indirectly discriminatory; and (b) a ruling that an award of compensation for unfair dismissal was 'pay'.

In answer to questions referred to the Court of Justice by the House of Lords, the Court ruled that:

(a) The basic element of a judicial award of compensation for unfair dismissal referred directly to the remuneration the employee would have received but for the dismissal. Such compensation was paid to the employee by reason of his or her employment and therefore fell within the definition of pay for the purposes of Article 119. The fact that it was a judicial award based on the applicable legislation did not invalidate the conclusion reached. It was irrelevant that the right to such compensation, rather than deriving from the contract of employment, was a statutory right.

(b) The right of access to such 'pay' following unfair dismissal fell within Article 119, but the right to reinstatement or re-engagement (the primary national remedy) fell within Directive 76/207 on equal treatment.

(c) It was for the national court, taking into account all the material legal and factual circumstances, to determine the point in time (time of adoption or application) at which the legality of a rule of the kind in issue (an allegedly discriminatory rule) was to be assessed.

(d) In order to determine whether the disputed rule had disparate effect as between men and women to such a degree as to amount to indirect discrimination for the purposes of Article 119, the national court must verify whether the statistics available indicated that a considerably smaller percentage of women than men are able to satisfy the condition of two years' employment required by the disputed rule. That situation would be evidence of apparent sex discrimination unless the disputed rule was justified by objective factors unrelated to any discrimination based on sex. If a considerably smaller percentage of women than men was capable of fulfilling the requirement, it was for the Member State, as the author of the allegedly discriminatory rule, to show that the rule reflected a legitimate aim of its social policy, that that aim was unrelated to any discrimination based on sex, and that it could reasonably consider that the means chosen were suitable for attaining that aim.

Students are urged to read the article by Barnard and Hepple on this case, 'Indirect discrimination: interpreting *Seymour-Smith*'. It reveals problems and differing approaches to the questions raised by this case, which were not, in the authors' view, satisfactorily met by the Court of Justice. Among their conclusions, they write:

> In *Seymour-Smith*, the reference was made by the highest court, yet the opportunity was missed to give clear guidance to national courts. The problem is more deep-seated than the overloading of the Court.

> The real problem is that while the Court of Justice is capable of pronouncing on questions of formal equality, it lacks access to the statistical and social science advice which is needed to assess arguments about disparate impact and objective justification. This is inherent in the Article 177 procedure which rests upon providing generalised answers to abstract questions. Most national courts in Europe also lack the capacity to undertake the kind of sociological and statistical analysis found in major US litigation, nor have they developed class actions which nurtured disparate impact litigation in the USA. But, at least, the national courts are closer to the real situation and more likely to be able to evaluate differences in impact and justifications for apparently neutral practices. The one virtue of the ECJ's judgment is that it leaves the House of Lords and other courts and tribunals in the UK virtually free to step boldly back into the domain of indirect discrimination, and to make their own assessments rather than hang on to the many nuances of nebulous words from Luxembourg.

When the case returned to the House of Lords, it was held that the complaint should be dismissed. The introduction of the two year period in the 1985 Order did *not* amount to indirect discrimination according to two Law Lords because, although there was a 'persistent and constant' smaller percentage of women than men able to fulfil the requirement over the period 1985–93, the figures were not sufficiently significant to establish discrimination. Three Law Lords felt that the statistics *did* show a 'persistent and constant' disparity – for every 10 men who were qualified to pursue unfair dismissal claims, only nine women were eligible – and this was significant. However, the adverse effect on women had been justified by the government, the aim of the order being to encourage recruitment by employers, a legitimate aim: *R v Secretary of State for Employment ex p Seymour-Smith* (2000) (HL).

ARTICLE 141 (FORMERLY 119) AND THE EQUAL PAY DIRECTIVE: WORK OF EQUAL VALUE

Under Article 1 of Council Directive 75/117 on the approximation of the laws of the Member States relating to the application of the principle of equal pay for men and women (adopted under Article 100 (now 94)):

> The principle of equal pay for men and women outlined in Article 119 of the Treaty, hereinafter called 'principle of equal pay', means, for the same work or for work to which equal value is attributed, the elimination of all discrimination on grounds of sex with regard to all aspects and conditions of remuneration.

In particular, where a job classification system is used for determining pay, it must be based on the same criteria for both men and women and so drawn up as to exclude any discrimination on grounds of sex.

Although this Article appeared to introduce the concept of 'work of equal value' (different work but of equivalent value) into Community law, the Court of Justice has held that the Directive merely restated the equal pay principle in Article 119 (now 141). Therefore, even before the ToA amendment, Article 119 applied to both 'same work' and 'work of equal value'. It applies to discrimination which is found in national legislative provisions (social security provisions excluded), in collective bargaining agreements between management and unions (see *Enderby*, above), in wage scales, in job evaluation schemes affecting undertakings or industries at national level and in individual contracts of employment.

The Directive (see Article 1, paragraph 2 and Article 6) does not make job evaluation schemes compulsory, but Member States must establish some effective machinery whereby it can be decided whether work is of equal value:

Article 6

Member States shall, in accordance with their national circumstances and legal systems, take the measures necessary to ensure that the principle of equal pay is applied. They shall see that effective means are available to take care that this principle is observed.

Where this is not the case, an employee will be deprived of her or his enforceable rights under Article 2:

Article 2

Member States shall introduce into their national legal systems such measures as are necessary to enable all employees who consider themselves wronged by failure to apply the principle of equal pay to pursue their claims by judicial process after possible recourse to other competent authorities.

In Case 61/81 *Commission v UK (Re Equal Pay for Equal Work)*, under UK legislation (the Equal Pay Act 1970, as amended by the Sex Discrimination Act 1975), equal pay was required in cases where a man and a woman were employed in work 'rated as equivalent' on the basis of a job evaluation scheme. Such schemes could, however, only be implemented with the consent of the employer. The Court held that the UK was in breach of its Community obligations. UK law was purportedly brought into line in 1983 by the Equal Pay (Amendment) Regulations under which machinery was provided whereby independent experts were required to report to an industrial tribunal on 'equal value' claims in the absence of a job evaluation scheme. (However, these are the regulations castigated by the Court of Appeal in *Pickstone v Freemans plc* as being of 'outstanding obscurity' and which, on further appeal, were given a very 'purposive' interpretation by the House of Lords: see Chapter 8.)

As early as the mid-1970s, in *Defrenne (No 2)*, the Court of Justice had, as seen, been prepared to speculate on the full implications of the equal pay principle:

It is impossible not to recognise that the complete implementation of the aim pursued by Article 119 EEC, by means of the elimination of all discrimination, direct or indirect, between men and women workers, not only as regards individual undertakings but also entire branches of industry and even the economic system as a whole, may in certain cases involve the elaboration of criteria whose implementation necessitates the taking of appropriate measures at Community or national level.

The scope of the comparisons which may be necessary in order fully to implement Directive 75/117 was indicated by Advocate General VerLoren van Themaat in Case 143/83 *Commission v Denmark (Re Equal Pay Concepts)*:

> As appears from the second sentence of Article 1 of the Directive, however, a comparison of duties within the same fixed establishment of an undertaking or even within a single undertaking will not always be sufficient. In certain circumstances, comparison with work of equal value in other undertakings covered by the collective agreement in question will be necessary ... in sectors with a traditionally female workforce comparison with other sectors may even be necessary. In certain circumstances, the additional criterion of 'the same place of work' for work of equal value may therefore place a restriction on the principle of equal pay laid down in Article 119 of the EEC Treaty and amplified in the Directive in question. The mere fact that such a supplementary condition for equal pay which has no foundation in Article 119 or the Directive has been added must in any event be regarded as an infringement of the Treaty. That supplementary condition limits the scope, governed by the Treaty, of the extension of the principle of equal pay for men and women to equal value ... which is recognised in Denmark.

The establishment of agreed methods for making the wider equal value comparisons indicated here on a uniform basis throughout the Member State clearly presents enormous difficulties, not the least of which is the resistance of employers (and national governments) in the face of the cost burdens involved. Uniformity can only be achieved on the basis of further clarification and harmonisation at Community level. Some guidance has been forthcoming from the Court of Justice.

Case 143/83 *Commission v Denmark (Re Equal Pay Concepts)*

In this case, the Court of Justice ruled that where collective bargaining was the dominant basis for wage structures, a Member State was nevertheless under a duty to provide effective protection for all workers, particularly non-union members and those in sectors where collective bargaining did not cover or fully guarantee the equal pay principle. Relying on general principles of law (the principle of legal certainty and the protection of the individual) and Article 7 of the Directive, the Court ruled that all workers required an unequivocal statement of the rights flowing from Directive 75/117 so that national courts were in a position to ensure that its obligations were being observed.

Case 237/85 *Rummler v Dato-Druck*

R challenged the classifications used in the framework wage-rate agreement for the German printing industry. She claimed that her work should have been placed in a higher category since her job as a packer involved lifting parcels weighing more than 20 kilograms, which, for a woman, represented heavy physical work.

On a reference for a preliminary ruling, the Court of Justice held that a job classification scheme based on such factors as the strength and physical effort required to perform the work was not contrary to the provisions of Directive 75/117 as long as:

(a) the system as a whole precluded discrimination on grounds of sex; and

(b) the criteria employed were objectively justified, that is, they must:

    (i) be appropriate to the tasks to be carried out; and

    (ii) correspond to a genuine need of the undertaking.

The scheme must also take into account the criteria for which each sex has a particular aptitude. Criteria based exclusively on the attributes of one sex contained 'a risk of discrimination'.

Case 108/88 *Danfoss*

A trade union-backed claim was brought on behalf of a group of women workers who earned on average 7 per cent less than male workers covered by the relevant collective agreement. Although the same basic wage was applied to all workers, the employer was able to supplement this on the basis of various neutral criteria including 'flexibility', professional training and 'seniority'. There was no clarification of how and when the criteria were being used and the applicants alleged that the criteria must be discriminatory.

The Court ruled that where a pay system showed a 'total lack of transparency' (that is, where the criteria for determining pay increments were not clear to those affected) and where the system operated to the patent disadvantage of women, there must be a reversal of the burden of proof such that the employer must prove that the criteria employed were justified, and that the non-transparent pay policy was therefore not discriminatory.

By reference to Article 6 of Directive 75/117, without knowledge of how the criteria applied, the complainants would be denied access to an effective remedy.

Council Directive 97/80 on the burden of proof in cases of discrimination based on sex, as discussed in the context of *Bilka-Kaufhaus* (above), reflects the position adopted by the Court in this case. Whether many of the Member States have in fact intervened in order to establish if sex discrimination is checked within their existing job classification and payment systems is doubtful.

DIRECTIVE 76/207: THE PRINCIPLE OF EQUAL TREATMENT

Council Directive 76/207 governs the implementation within the Member States of the principle of equal treatment for men and women as regards access to employment including promotion, vocational training, and working conditions (including those governing dismissal): see Article 1(1).

Equal treatment in matters of social security, referred to in Article 1(1) and (2), covering *national statutory schemes* providing protection against sickness, incapacity, old age, accidents at work or occupational diseases, and unemployment, was implemented by means of Directive 79/7 (effective 1984). The principle of equal treatment in *occupational* (as opposed to statutory) *pension schemes* was implemented by Directive 86/378, which was not fully effective until 1 January 1993. However, as *Barber*, which was decided in 1990, demonstrates, discrimination claims in respect of occupational pension benefits may be decided on the basis of 'pay' under the directly effective terms of Article 119 (now 141) (as may also sick pay claims: see *Rinner-Kühn*, above), and as noted earlier Directive 86/378 was amended by Directive 96/97 to take account of *Barber* and related decisions. As no Treaty Article specifically provides for the application of the equal treatment principle, except in relation to pay, Directive 76/207 was based on the residual legislative powers embodied in Article 235 (now 308). The addition by the ToA of new paragraphs 3 and 4 to Article 141 (119) does not make the equal treatment principle directly effective on the basis of that Article, although the paragraphs are phrased in terms of that principle. The Directive should be seen in the light of Article 136 (formerly 117) of the Treaty, which states that:

> The Community and the Member States, having in mind fundamental social rights such as those set out in the European Social Charter signed at Turin on 18 October 1961 and in the 1989 Community Charter of the Fundamental Social Rights of Workers, shall have as their objectives the promotion of employment, improved living and working conditions, so as to make possible their harmonization while the improvement is being maintained ...

In September 2002, the Equal Treatment Directive was amended by Directive 2002/73, which can be found at [2002] OJ L269/15. The preamble reaffirms equality between men and women as a fundamental principle under Articles 2 and 3(2) of the EC Treaty and within the Court's case law. Such equality is an 'aim' of the Community which imposes a positive obligation to 'promote' it in all its activities.

The main aims of the amendments are: (a) to define in legislative terms the concepts of direct and indirect discrimination within the field of operation of Directive 76/207 consistent with definitions found within Directive 2000/43 on the principle of equal treatment between persons irrespective of racial or ethnic origin and Directive 2000/78 establishing a general framework for equal treatment in employment and occupation; and (b) to bring within the scope of the Directive definitions of harassment related to the sex of a person and sexual harassment, which are contrary to the equal treatment principle and therefore prohibited.

The new Directive takes cognisance of the existing case law of the Court of Justice particularly that relating to discrimination generally (for example, Case C-394/96 *Brown v Rentokil Ltd*), occupational activities that Member States may exclude from the scope of the Directive (for example, Case C-222/84 *Johnston v CC of the RUC*), effective judicial protection for those discriminated against (for example, Case C-185/97 *Coote v Granada Hospitality Ltd*), and effective and adequate compensation (for example, Case C-271/91 *Marshall (No 2)*). (These cases are discussed below.)

The Member States are prevented from taking action contrary to the terms of the Directive, as amended, from its date of publication (23 September 2002) and must have legislation in conformity with its objectives in place by 5 October 2005. It is not unlikely that the Court of Justice will draw upon its new terms before that date. In the nature of things, however, gender equality case law will rest basically on the original Directive 76/207 Articles for some time.

Turning to the precise terms of the Directive, its scope, as laid down in Article 1(1) above, remains unchanged, but a new Article 1a promotes the concept of the *mainstreaming* of gender equality into decision making in this field:

> Member States shall actively take into account the objective of equality between men and women when formulating and implementing laws, regulations, administrative provisions, policies and activities in the areas referred to in paragraph 1.

Article 2(1) states that 'the principle of equal treatment shall mean that there shall be no discrimination whatsoever on grounds of sex either directly or indirectly ...'. A new Article 2(2) and (3) provides the statutory definitions of direct and indirect discrimination and of harassment for the purposes of the Directive:

> –   direct discrimination: where one person is treated less favourably on grounds of sex than another is, has been or would be treated in a comparable situation,

- indirect discrimination: where an apparently neutral provision, criterion or practice would put persons of one sex at a particular disadvantage compared with persons of the other sex, unless that provision, criterion or practice is objectively justified by a legitimate aim, and the means of achieving that aim are appropriate and necessary,

- harassment: where an unwanted conduct related to the sex of a person occurs with the purpose or effect of violating the dignity of a person, and of creating an intimidating, hostile, degrading, humiliating or offensive environment,

- sexual harassment: where any form of unwanted verbal, non-verbal or physical conduct of a sexual nature occurs, with the purpose or effect of violating the dignity of a person, in particular when creating an intimidating, hostile, degrading, humiliating or offensive environment.

(3) Harassment and sexual harassment within the meaning of this Directive shall be deemed to be discrimination on the grounds of sex and therefore prohibited.

A person's rejection of, or submission to, such conduct may not be used as a basis for a decision affecting that person.

Allowable derogations from the general prohibition, originally found in Articles 2(2)–(4) and relating to special occupational requirements, pregnancy and maternity, and positive action, are retained in amended form in a new Article 2(6)–(8) and are discussed below.

The original Articles 3, 4 and 5 of the Directive are consolidated into a new Article 3, which provides that as regards access to employment including promotion, vocational training, employment itself and working conditions including dismissals, Member States shall ensure that:

(a) any laws, regulations and administrative provisions contrary to the principle of equal treatment are abolished;

(b) any provisions contrary to the principle of equal treatment which are included in contracts or collective agreements, internal rules of undertakings or rules governing the independent occupations and professions and workers' and employers' organisations shall be, or may be, declared null and void or are amended.

Litigation in the UK regarding Directive 76/207 has been largely concerned with the original Article 5 (now 3) and challenges by employees to different (male and female) retirement ages, that is, dismissals.

As previously indicated, in this country, the ages at which men and women retire from employment have been linked to the differing ages at which they qualify for State pensions: 65 for men and 60 for women (65 for both by 2020; the age for women being gradually increased from 2010). Thus, as seen in Case 152/84 *Marshall (No 1)* in Chapter 8, section 6(4) of the Sex Discrimination Act 1975 *excluded* from the prohibition of discrimination by an employer on the ground of sex 'provision in relation to ... retirement'. Article 5 (now 3) of the Directive applies the equal treatment principle to 'the conditions governing dismissal'. However, Article 7(1)(a) of Directive 79/7 on equal treatment in matters of social security does still allow 'Member States to exclude from its scope ... the determination of pensionable age for the purposes of granting old-age and retirement pensions and the possible consequences thereof for other benefits'. (In Case C-9/91 *R v Secretary of State for Social Security ex p Equal Opportunities Commission*, the Court of Justice stated that the exceptions to the principle of equal treatment for men and women provided for in Directive 79/7 were 'intended to allow Member States to maintain temporarily the advantages accorded to women with respect to retirement in order to permit them progressively to adapt their pension systems in this respect without disrupting the complex financial equilibrium of those systems'.)

Although the decision of the Court of Justice in the first case to be discussed has been undermined (impliedly overruled) in subsequent decisions, it represents an important step in understanding the development of the law in this area.

Case 19/81 *Burton v British Railways Board*

Under the BRB scheme, women were entitled to apply for voluntary early retirement, and the receipt of appropriate redundancy payments and pension benefits, at 55 and men at 60. Mr B, aged 58, alleged that the scheme was discriminatory. A claim in national law being blocked by section 6(4) of the Sex Discrimination Act 1975, B sought to rely on Directive 76/207.

Following a reference under Article 177, relating to Article 119, Directive 75/117 and Directive 76/207, the Court of Justice held that:

(a) The claim, relating as it did to *conditions* of access to BRB's redundancy scheme, could only be covered, if at all, by Directive 76/207 on equal treatment. [Note the effect of later developments referred to below.]

(b) The word 'dismissal' in Article 5 (now 3) of the Directive was to be widely construed to cover termination of employment even under a voluntary redundancy scheme.

(c) However, it was not contrary to Directive 76/207 to provide unequal access to such payments and benefits since the ages of retirement under the BRB scheme were calculated by reference to, and tied to, the *minimum statutory retirement ages*, and Directive 79/7 explicitly allowed Member States to exclude from the scope of the equal treatment principle the determination of minimum pensionable age 'and the possible consequences thereof for other benefits'.

In the next case, a female employee made redundant at the age of 53 attempted to justify her claim of discrimination as regards access to early retirement occupational pension benefits by tying her dismissal, as in *Burton*, to the differing qualifying ages for pensions under the State pension scheme.

Case 151/84 *Roberts v Tate and Lyle Industries Ltd*

TLI agreed with the unions that all employees made compulsorily redundant aged 55 and over would be entitled to immediate accelerated pension rights under the company's occupational pension scheme. (This replaced a previous agreement, linked to State pension ages, whereby immediate pensions were payable to women at 60 and men at 65.)

R claimed that the revised scheme was discriminatory since women were not entitled to a pension until five years before their normal retirement age, whereas men received an immediate pension up to 10 years before their normal retirement age. A 10 year rule for both men and women, tied to State pension ages, would have brought R within the scope of the entitlement.

The Court ruled that the case was concerned exclusively with dismissal and was therefore covered by Article 5 (now 3) of Directive 76/207, and not by Article 7 of Directive 79/7, which related to the consequences which *pensionable age has for social security benefits.* As the retirement age was fixed at 55 for both men and women, the scheme was not discriminatory.

Here then, redundancy again being classed as dismissal, the receipt of an occupational pension on redundancy was a condition of dismissal under the Equal Treatment Directive. There was no breach by TLI of Article 5 (now 3) of Directive 76/207 because the age conditions for men and women were the same. The differing pensionable ages allowed under Directive 79/7 did not apply as they only concerned 'social security benefits', that is, 'old age and retirement pensions and the possible consequences thereof for other benefits falling within the statutory social security schemes'.

It should also be noted that at this time, before the rulings in *Bilka* and *Barber*, occupational pension benefits and redundancy payments (see *Burton*) were not thought to be pay within the terms of Article 119 (now 141).

Marshall, the next in this line of cases, involved a claim under the Equal Treatment Directive 76/207, her action, as seen in Chapter 8, concerning an allegation of discriminatory compulsory *retirement*. As with *Burton*, she was faced by section 6(4) of the 1975 Act plus the view of the UK government that the Equal Treatment Directive permitted discrimination in compulsory retirement ages.

Case 152/84 *Marshall v Southampton and SW Hampshire AHA (No 1)*

The Area Health Authority's normal retirement policy was linked to the State pension age: 60 for women, 65 for men. Miss M, who had been allowed to stay on after the normal age, was compulsorily retired at 62. As she wished to continue working, she challenged the defendant's policy as being discriminatory. Following a reference from the Employment Appeal Tribunal, the Court of Justice held that:

(a) The retirement scheme was a 'condition governing dismissal' within Article 5 (now 3) of Directive 76/207.

(b) Article 7 of Directive 79/7 only allowed differing pensionable ages in the context of 'granting old-age and retirement pensions and the possible consequences thereof for other benefits'. Where differing pensionable ages were being used for other purposes, as here, for the purpose of retirement, discrimination was not allowed. (The question of dismissal was therefore again separated from the issue of the exclusion of State pension ages from the equal treatment principle.)

(c) Directive 76/207 could be invoked against the Area Health Authority ('an emanation of the State') in its capacity as employer (see Chapter 8).

It is important to note that, following the decision in *Marshall*, the Sex Discrimination Act 1986 was passed and discriminatory *retirement* (not pensionable) ages were made unlawful, thereby amending section 6(4) of the 1975 Act. (The amendment did not have retrospective effect: see *Duke v GEC Reliance* in Chapter 8.) Again at the national level, under the Employment Act 1989, men and women enjoy an equal right to receive redundancy benefits up to the age of 65, or the normal retirement age for their occupation, if that is less than 65. However, neither this Act nor that of 1986 was in force *at the time Mr Barber's claim arose.*

At Community level, the key to Barber's success with respect to occupational pension benefits, resting on the decision by the Court of Justice that they fall within the concept of pay under the directly effective Article 119 (now 141) and not the non-horizontally effective Equal Treatment Directive, was the Court's earlier decision in Case 170/84 *Bilka-Kaufhaus* (see above). There, the German employer's contractual occupational pension scheme, albeit negotiated within a statutory framework laying down minimum requirements, was differentiated from the statutory State scheme which it supplemented. In *Barber*, the British employer's occupational pension scheme was similar, being at least in part a *substitute* for the statutory scheme (the State earnings related pension scheme (SERPS)). As regards the finding in *Barber* that, again, redundancy payments fell within the equal pay principle in Article 119 (now 141), the Court, it will be recalled, stressed that where the benefit is received by the worker from his employer as a result of the employment relationship, the employment nexus is decisive (see *Defrenne (No 2)*) and overrides the social policy aspect of statutory redundancy payments – and this was so even though the discrimination arose directly from legislative provisions. The payment was the employer's responsibility – but only as a result of a statutory obligation.

As Fitzpatrick explained:

> Until recently, it had been presumed that payments made under statutory obligation were outside the scope of employment equality measures. However, the ECJ in *Rinner-Kühn* [see above] concluded that sick pay paid directly to the employee was still 'pay' within Article 119/EEC, even if dictated by legislation. The more reasoned re-affirmation of this position in *Barber*, in relation to both statutory redundancy pay and also the minimum statutory obligations applicable to contracted-out OP schemes, is not, in itself, surprising.

Derogations from the Equal Treatment Principle within Article 2 of Directive 76/207

Article 2 (prior to amendment)

....

2   This Directive shall be without prejudice to the right of Member States to exclude from its field of application those occupational activities and, where appropriate the training leading thereto, for which, by reason of their nature or the context in which they are carried out, the sex of the worker constitutes a determining factor.

3   This Directive shall be without prejudice to provisions concerning the protection of women as regards pregnancy and maternity.

4   This Directive shall be without prejudice to measures to promote equal opportunity for men and women, in particular by removing existing inequalities which affect women's opportunities in the areas referred to in Article 1(1). [Access to employment, including promotion, and to vocational training, and as regards working conditions.]

Sex of the Worker a Determining Factor: Article 2(2) (now 2(6) as amended)

This exemption from the principle was allowed in Case 165/82 *Commission v UK (Re Equal Treatment for Men and Women)*. The UK's refusal to allow men full access to training for midwifery, on the basis of section 41 of the Sex Discrimination Act, was held to fall under the original Article 2(2) as the profession was one 'in which respect for the patient's sensitivities is of particular importance'.

In Case 248/83 *Commission v Germany (Re Sex Discrimination Laws)*, in relation to the scope of the derogations in Article 2(2), the Court stated that it was for the Member States 'to complete a verifiable list, in whatever form, of the occupations and activities excluded from the application of the principle of equal treatment and to notify the results to the Commission'. Otherwise, in the Court's opinion, the Commission would be prevented from exercising effective supervision, and individuals would have difficulty in defending their rights.

The following case involving Article 2(2), and the ones which follow, raised significant constitutional issues and similar questions of 'gender stereotyping':

Case 222/84 *Johnston v Chief Constable of the RUC*

In view of the deteriorating situation in Northern Ireland at the time, the Chief Constable decided that: (a) men in the RUC and RUC Reserve would in future carry firearms in the normal course of duties; (b) women would not be equipped with firearms nor be trained in their use; (c) policewomen should no longer be asked to perform general duties (which might involve the use of firearms); and (d) women in the RUC Reserve would only be required to perform duties which were assigned to women officers only.

Mrs Johnston had been an unarmed member of the RUC Reserve performing general duties for several years. In 1980, her three year contract came up for renewal but the Chief Constable refused to renew it on the basis of the new policy towards female officers.

Mrs J challenged this refusal and her exclusion from firearms training arguing that they amounted to unlawful sex discrimination.

In the face of a certificate issued by the Secretary of State which, under Article 53 of the Sex Discrimination (Northern Ireland) Order 1976, amounted to 'conclusive evidence' that the Chief Constable's refusal was 'for the purpose of safeguarding national security or of protecting public safety or public order', Mrs J sought to rely on the Equal Treatment Directive 76/207. Following an Article 177 reference regarding the interpretation of various provisions of the Directive, in particular the scope for derogation from the equal treatment principle, the Court of Justice ruled as follows:

(a) *Article 53 of the Order and Article 6 of the Directive.* The obligation imposed upon Member States under Article 6 was for them to introduce into their national legal systems the measures necessary to enable alleged victims of sex discrimination 'to pursue their claims by judicial process'. Article 53 of the Order was 'contrary to the principle of effective judicial control laid down in Article 6' because it enabled the individual to be deprived of the 'possibility of asserting by judicial process' the right that the Directive conferred.

The principle of effective judicial control was, said the Court, 'a general principle of law which underlies the constitutional traditions common to the Member States. That principle was also laid down in Articles 6 and 13 of the European Convention for the Protection of Human Rights and Fundamental Freedoms' (see Chapter 10). Member States must ensure that the rights conferred by the Directive 'may be effectively relied upon before the national courts by the persons concerned'.

(b) *The protection of public safety.* Derogations on the grounds of national security, public safety or public order such as those found in Articles 36, 48, 56, 66, 223 and 224 of the Treaty (pre-ToA numbering) were concerned with 'exceptional and clearly defined cases': the question of derogations from the equal treatment principle was to be dealt with in the light of the specific provisions of the Directive.

(c) *The derogations in the Directive.* In terms of the permitted derogation in Article 2(2) relating to 'occupational activities' and 'training' for them, the crucial question was whether, in view of the 'context' in which police work in Northern Ireland was carried out, the sex of police officers could amount to being 'a determining factor'.

The Court reviewed the reasons underlying the Chief Constable's change of policy: (i) if women were armed, they might more frequently become targets for assassination attempts and their firearms could fall into the hands of their attackers; (ii) the carrying of firearms by women conflicted too much with the ideal of an unarmed police force; (iii) policewomen would be hindered in carrying out their valuable social work if they were armed.

In considering whether these reasons were covered by Article 2(2), the Court stressed that that provision, as a derogation from the fundamental principle of equal treatment, must be interpreted strictly. However, the Court did accept that:

> ... the possibility cannot be excluded that in a situation characterised by serious internal disturbances the carrying of firearms by policewomen might create additional risks of their being assassinated and might therefore be contrary to the requirements of public safety.

> In such circumstances, the context of certain policing activities may be such that the sex of police officers constitutes a determining factor for carrying them out. If that is so, Member States may therefore restrict such tasks, and the training leading thereto, to men.

It was for *the national court* (i) to assess whether the Chief Constable's reasons were well founded and thus justified his refusal to renew Mrs J's contract; and (ii) to ensure that the principle of proportionality was respected and so determine 'whether the refusal ... could not be avoided by allocating to women duties which, without jeopardising the aims pursued, can be performed without firearms' (that is, if there was a less discriminatory way of ensuring that the demands of public safety were met, the principle of proportionality was not satisfied).

The Court dismissed Article 2(3) of the Directive 'concerning the protection of women, particularly as regards pregnancy and maternity' as irrelevant and it would appear that the provision only permits derogations from equal treatment where they relate to 'a woman's biological condition and the special relationship which exists between a woman and her child'. The Court stated that:

> ... the Directive does not therefore allow women to be excluded from a certain type of employment on the ground that public opinion demands that women be given greater protection than men against risks which affect men and women in the same way and which are distinct from women's specific needs for protection, such as those expressly mentioned.

(d) *The question of the Directive's direct effect.* The crucial issue was whether an individual could rely on the Directive as against a derogation laid down by the national authorities (in the Northern Ireland Order) which was found to have exceeded what was permitted by the Directive. The answer, in so far as it was held that a public authority responsible for the direction of the police was an 'emanation of the State', was in the affirmative:

> 'Whatever its relations may be with other organs of the State, such a public authority, charged by the State with the maintenance of public order and safety, does not act as a private individual. It may not take advantage of the failure of the State, of which it is an emanation, to comply with Community law [see also *Marshall* and the guidelines as to what constitutes 'the State' in the later case of *Foster* in Chapter 8].

The Court held that *Article 6 of the Directive had direct effect* as regards *access to the judicial process* and the obligation to provide an effective judicial remedy in the national court. (This finding is to be contrasted with that in *Von Colson,* where the Court stated that Article 6 was not directly effective as regards the provision of specific sanctions, not being unconditional or sufficiently precise in that respect.)

In a perceptive comment on this case, Arnull states that:

The *Johnston* decision represents an attempt by the European Court to reconcile the need to promote the *effet utile* of the Directive with a reluctance to interfere with the discretion of the Chief Constable in a situation of serious internal disorder. That attempt seems to have been largely successful, although the Court perhaps gives the impression of accepting a little too readily the justifications advanced by the Chief Constable for refusing to allow women to be trained in the use of firearms. The idea that armed policewomen would more frequently be subject to assassination attempts than male officers and that their guns might fall into the hands of their attackers seems somewhat fanciful. In addition, while it is probably true that the public would not relish the sight of armed policewomen, it must be doubtful whether the carrying of guns by male officers is particularly welcome. Arming women does not conflict with the ideal of an unarmed police force any more than arming men: to treat it as if it does is simply discriminatory. Moreover, even if women police officers were to be armed on some occasions, there would be no necessity for them to carry guns while performing duties of a social nature. It is therefore to be hoped that the Industrial Tribunal takes seriously the duty imposed on it by the European Court to examine whether these reasons were in fact well founded and justified the specific measure taken in Mrs Johnston's case.

Finally, with regard to the question of restrictive interpretation of a derogation from a fundamental principle and the operation of the principle of proportionality, Docksey concluded that: 'As a result, it is difficult to imagine how to argue that public safety in Northern Ireland could only be effectively protected by restricting general policing to men equipped with firearms.'

This case was eventually settled, the Chief Constable agreeing to pay 30 former policewomen a total of £250,000. He also agreed to provide equal access for men and women to all forms of employment opportunities and to consider possible reinstatements. It was later reported that RUC policewomen were carrying firearms: nevertheless, the security context can change (see Articles 3(2)(c) and 5(2)(c)).

Two further cases have raised similar questions to those in *Johnston* regarding derogation by a Member State under Article 2(2).

C-285/98 *Kreil v Germany*

K applied for voluntary service in the German army with the intention of working on weapon electronic maintenance. She was rejected on the basis of German law which laid down that female volunteers could only be engaged in the medical and military-music services and were excluded in any event from armed service.

Following a reference by the Hanover court, the German government argued that matters of defence did not come within the scope of EC law at all, and, alternatively, that the limitations on the access of women to the *Bundeswehr* was justified by Article 2(2).

Following its decision in Case C-273/97 *Sirdar v Army Board,* the Court stated that Article 2(2) applied in principle to the situation but that, in determining the scope of derogations from the equal treatment right, the principle of proportionality had to be observed.

The national authorities could not, without contravening the proportionality principle, adopt the *general position* that the composition of all armed units in the *Bundeswehr* had to remain exclusively male.

In *Sirdar*, in seeking to justify the refusal to employ a woman with seven years' service as a chef in another branch of the forces as a chef in the Royal Marines, Article 224 (now 297), which concerns national measures which may have to be taken in the event of war or for the purpose of maintaining peace and international security, etc, was invoked together with the interests of national defence. The basis for this claim was the UK Royal Marines' special policy that all members, including chefs, are required to serve as front-line commandos. This is known as the principle of 'interoperability'.

The Court of Justice ruled that:

The exclusion of women from service in special combat units such as the Royal Marines may be justified under Article 2(2) by reason of the nature of the activities in question and the context in which they are carried out. The principle of proportionality applies and the Member States must periodically assess the activities involved in order to decide whether the derogation, if allowed, may be maintained. It is the task of the tribunal to which the case has returned to decide the issue.

The Court's somewhat imprecise use of the proportionality principle with respect to public security was therefore the key factor in these cases. On the basis that there was no general exception from Community law covering all measures stated as being taken for public security reasons, the Court rejected the German and UK governments' competence arguments regarding national defence and decisions on the internal organisation of the armed forces. The *Kreil* decision has led to changes in the German constitution; the Basic Law now permitting women to apply voluntarily for any type of military service employment, including service in the armed forces.

German federal law which lays down that *compulsory* military service (or alternative civilian service) applies only to men was challenged as being a form of unlawful discrimination against men in the following case.

Case C-186/01 *Alexander Dory v Germany*

D was refused exemption from call-up by the army. The defendant argued that no provision of the EC Treaty allowed compulsory military service to be regarded as an activity falling under Community law; the organisation of that service being within the competence of each Member State and a matter of national defence and public security.

Following an Article 234 reference, the Court of Justice, referring to *Johnston, Sirdar* and *Kreil*, stated that the Treaty contains no inherent general exception excluding all measures taken for reasons of public security from the scope of Community law, and it was clear that Directive 76/207 applied to employment in the public service including access to posts in the armed forces: *Sirdar* and *Kreil*. However, as stated in those cases, it did not follow that Community law governed the Member States' choices of military organisation for the defence of their territory or of their essential interests.

Therefore, it was for the Member States, which have to adopt appropriate measures to ensure their internal and external security, to take decisions on the organisation of their armed forces. The decision of the Federal Republic to ensure its defence in part by compulsory military service was the expression of such a choice of military organisation to which Community law was consequently not applicable.

Note now the amended Article 2(6):

> Member States may provide, as regards access to employment including the training leading thereto, that a difference of treatment which is based on a characteristic related to sex shall not constitute discrimination where, by reason of the nature of the particular occupational activities concerned or of the context in which they are carried out, such a characteristic constitutes a genuine and determining occupational requirement, provided that the objective is legitimate and the requirement is proportionate.

Equal Treatment, Pregnancy and Maternity: Article 2(3) (now amended as 2(7)) and Directive 92/85

As seen, the original Article 2(3) of Directive 76/207 allows for special protection for women in relation to pregnancy and maternity. In particular, it is aimed to protect two kinds of female need:

(a) the biological condition of women during and after pregnancy; and

(b) the relationship between mother and child during and after pregnancy and birth: Case 184/83 *Hofmann v Barmer Ersatzkasse*.

Is a *refusal to employ* a woman because she is pregnant a breach of the equal treatment principle? Similarly, is the *dismissal* of a woman for reasons connected with pregnancy or childbirth a breach of this principle? The first question was addressed by the Court of Justice in Case C-177/88 *Dekker v VJV-Centrum*, in which it was held that an employer's refusal to employ a woman on the grounds of pregnancy was a form of direct discrimination contrary to Articles 1(1), 2(1) and 5(1) of the Equal Treatment Directive. The Court stated that 'as employment can only be refused because of pregnancy to a woman, such a refusal is direct discrimination on the grounds of sex'. The employer had attempted to justify his refusal on financial grounds, but the Court rejected this argument in the following terms:

> ... a refusal to employ because of the financial consequences of absence connected with pregnancy must be deemed to be based principally on the fact of the pregnancy. Such discrimination cannot be justified by the financial detriment in the case of recruitment of a pregnant woman suffered by the employer during her maternity leave.

Case C-179/88 *Hertz* concerned dismissal, but the discrimination claim failed. The female employee was absent from work for a considerable period of time as a result of illness which, although connected with pregnancy or childbirth, was suffered some time after the end of the period of maternity leave allowed her under national law. The Court held that dismissal on the grounds of absence arising from illness resulting from pregnancy and maternity after the maternity leave period could not be distinguished from illness such as that which might be suffered by a man and which *could* justify dismissal. It could be said that in this case the causal link between pregnancy and absence was too tenuous. As Ellis has explained: '... at one level of abstraction, a "pregnancy-related illness" can be said to be something from which a person cannot suffer *but for* her sex; at another level of abstraction, it can be said that "illness" can be suffered alike by either sex.' The Court chose the latter route. This decision means that women are only guaranteed protection from dismissal relating to their pregnancy during the period of national statutory maternity leave and it leaves women suffering abnormal pregnancies such as in this case without protection.

In Case C-421/92 *Habermann-Beltermann*, the question was whether it was compatible with the Equal Treatment Directive for an employee, who had chosen to work 'nights only' as an attendant in a residential home, to be dismissed on becoming pregnant, on the basis of a statutory prohibition upon women working at night while pregnant. The Court of Justice held that a *prohibition* on night work by pregnant women was compatible with Directive 76/207 but 'the termination of a contract without a fixed term [see also *Webb*, below] on account of the woman's pregnancy ... cannot be justified on the ground that a statutory prohibition, imposed because of pregnancy, temporarily prevents the employee from performing night time work'. The Court drew particular attention to Article 2(3) of the Directive as it relates not only to the particular position of women with regard to pregnancy and maternity but also to the disadvantages which women may suffer as a result within the employment situation.

In the following case, the Court of Appeal was concerned to strike the 'proper balance' between employer and employee and the claim, which was not dissimilar from that in *Dekker*, appeared likely to fail on the basis of arguments similar to those in *Hertz*. However, on appeal to the House of Lords, a reference was made to the Court of Justice.

Case C-32/93 *Webb v EMO Air Cargo (UK) Ltd*

Mrs Webb was recruited by EMO in 1987 to replace Mrs S who found she was pregnant. It was envisaged that W would continue to work for the defendant company following S's return. Three weeks after starting work and whilst being trained by S, W discovered that she too was pregnant. The company dismissed her on the grounds of her pregnancy.

W brought proceedings against EMO under the Sex Discrimination Act 1975 as her short period of service did not entitle her to claim unfair dismissal. The industrial tribunal dismissed her action and her appeals to the Employment Appeal Tribunal and then to the Court of Appeal were also unsuccessful. In the House of Lords, their Lordships again felt that this was not a case of discrimination: they were of the view that a hypothetical man unavailable for work in similar circumstances could be justifiably dismissed. In the Court of Appeal, Glidewell LJ had given the example of a man with an arthritic hip who found, shortly after taking up employment, that he required a hip replacement operation necessitating a lengthy absence from work. Their Lordships indicated that W's dismissal was not on account of her pregnancy but because she was unavailable for work.

Nevertheless, the House of Lords stayed proceedings and referred questions to the Court of Justice for a preliminary ruling regarding the required interpretation of Directive 76/207 in the light of the Court's (allegedly conflicting) pregnancy decisions: *Dekker* and *Hertz*.

On the basis of Article 2(1) read with Article 5(1) of the Directive, the Court of Justice held that dismissal of a pregnant woman, who had been recruited for an indefinite period, could not be justified by the fact that she was prevented, on a purely temporary basis, from performing the work for which she was engaged.

As seen earlier, Article 2(1) of the Directive lays down the basic principle of equal treatment ('... there shall be no discrimination whatsoever on grounds of sex ...') and original Article 2(3) by way of derogation allows *special* protection to be afforded to women in relation to pregnancy and maternity. The original Article 5(1) applies the equal treatment principle to working conditions including the employee's dismissal.

The Court was careful to stress that W's contract was for an indefinite period. There was here the suggestion that the outcome might well have been different if the contract had been for a fixed term or until S's return to work. This point was settled by the Court in 2001 in two similar cases decided on the same day. In one of them, Case C-438/99 *Melgar v ALB*, on the basis of both Article 5(1) of the Equal Treatment Directive and Article 10 of the Pregnancy Directive 92/85, the Court held that where non-renewal of a fixed term contract of employment is motivated by the worker's state of pregnancy, such a dismissal constitutes direct discrimination based on sex. In the other, Case C-109/00 *Tele Danmark v HK*, the women appointed to a six month job requiring two months' training did not inform the employer at the time of the interview that she was pregnant. She was only able to perform two months' work following the training period. The Court held that the dismissal was contrary to both Directives and that the fixed term was irrelevant: 'Had the Community legislature wished to exclude fixed-term contracts, which represent a substantial proportion of the employment relationships, from the scope of those directives, it would have done so expressly.'

The Court was in no doubt in *Webb* that it was incorrect to compare the situation of a woman who, very shortly after commencing work, found herself incapable as a result of pregnancy of performing the work for which she had been recruited with that of a man similarly incapable for health or other reasons. The Court stated that pregnancy was not comparable with a pathological condition and even less so with unavailability for work on non-medical grounds, both of which were situations that might justify the dismissal of a woman without discriminating on the grounds of sex.

The Court stated that Article 2(3) of the Directive recognised the legitimacy of Member States' provision of special protection for women during pregnancy and after childbirth and drew particular attention to the post-*Webb* provisions of Directive 92/85, which prohibit dismissal from the start of the pregnancy to the end of maternity leave. In the light of 'that general context', the Court stated that 'such protection could not be dependent on whether her presence at work during maternity is essential to the proper functioning of the undertaking in which she is employed. Any contrary interpretation would render ineffective the provisions of the Directive'.

Contrary to judicial sentiments expressed earlier in the national proceedings, when *Webb* was returned to the House of Lords, their Lordships found little difficulty in construing the relevant provisions of the Sex Discrimination Act in accordance with the Court's ruling. (Mrs Webb could not rely on the direct effect of the Directive as against her private sector employer.)

Case C-400/95 *Larsson v Føtex Supermarket* saw the Court of Justice reaffirm its ruling in *Hertz* and take it further. It held (a) that the Equal Treatment Directive did not preclude dismissals which were the result of absence from work due to an illness attributable to pregnancy or confinement even where that illness arose during pregnancy and continued during and after maternity leave; and (b) that the Directive did not prevent account being taken of absences during both the pregnancy and maternity leave when computing the period providing grounds for dismissal. This ruling, which has been described as a 'step backward', was re-examined in the course of the following case.

Case C-394/96 *Brown v Rentokil Ltd*

In August 1990, B informed her employer, R Ltd, that she was pregnant. Shortly thereafter, she suffered a series of pregnancy related disorders and did not work again after mid-August. In February 1991, B was dismissed under a clause in her contract of employment whereby, if an employee was absent through illness for more than 26 weeks continuously, he or she would be dismissed. B's child was born in March 1991.

Her action under the Sex Discrimination Act 1975 failed in the industrial tribunal, the Employment Appeal Tribunal and the Scottish Court of Session, which considered that, since, in Case C-179/88 *Hertz,* the Court of Justice had drawn a distinction between pregnancy and illness attributable to pregnancy, B, whose absence was due to illness, and who had been dismissed for that reason, could not succeed. (In *Hertz*, as seen, dismissal followed a pregnancy related illness suffered some time after the end of maternity leave.)

On appeal to the House of Lords, their Lordships referred questions to the Court of Justice, regarding the application of Directive 76/207.

The Court of Justice ruled that:

(a) Articles 2(1) and 5(1) of the Directive precluded dismissal of a female worker at any time during her pregnancy for absences due to incapacity for work caused by illness resulting from that pregnancy; and

(b) the fact that a female worker had been dismissed during her pregnancy on the basis of a contractual term providing that the employer could dismiss employees of either sex after a stipulated number of weeks of continuous absence did not affect that answer. Such a term was itself directly discriminatory.

The Court stressed the point it had made in *Webb* that although pregnancy is not in any way comparable to a pathological condition, it is a period in which disorders and complications may arise which, while they may cause incapacity for work, form part of the risks inherent in the condition of pregnancy and are therefore a specific feature of that condition. The principle of non-discrimination required protection against dismissal in the circumstances of B's claim: 'Such a dismissal can affect only women and therefore constitutes direct discrimination on grounds of sex.'

The Court also, while reaffirming its ruling in *Hertz* regarding post-maternity leave pregnancy related illness, retracted that part of its ruling in *Larsson* concerning the taking into account of absences during pregnancy and maternity leave when calculating the period justifying dismissal: 'As to ... absence after maternity leave, this may be taken into account under the same conditions as a man's absence, of the same duration, through incapacity for work.'

Following *Brown*, as Barnard has pointed out:

... dismissed for a reason resulting from pregnancy must now be regarded as automatically unfair and automatically sex discriminatory. It also does not matter if the employer's decision is based on pregnancy as such, or on the consequences of pregnancy, such as absence. Thus, the entire period from the beginning of the pregnancy to the end of the maternity leave must now be regarded as a protected period, during which any pregnancy related absence must be discounted [All ER Annual Review 1998].

In *Brown, Webb,* and other pregnancy cases at the time, the Court drew attention to the Pregnancy Directive 92/85, which is a health and safety rather than an equal treatment measure, but which provides for a 'protected period' such as Barnard describes. It also requires Member States to provide a minimum period of 14 weeks' maternity leave.

Two further cases have involved the question of the pay to be received by a woman on maternity leave. In Case C-342/93 *Gillespie v DHSS*, in a ruling on facts arising before the Pregnancy Directive was applicable, the Court ruled that, although maternity pay was a form of pay and covered by Article 119 (now 141) EC, an employer was not required to continue to pay full pay. However, the amount paid could not be so low as to undermine the purpose of maternity leave. (The Directive speaks of entitlement to an adequate allowance not less than the amount of statutory sick pay.) The Court was of the view that the position of 'special protection' was 'not comparable either with that of a man or with that of a woman actually at work'. In Case C-411/96 *Boyle v Equal Opportunities Commission,* to which the Pregnancy Directive did apply, the Court held that Article 119 (now 141) and Article 11 of the Directive did not forbid a clause in a contract of employment which made the payment of maternity pay higher than the statutory benefits regarding maternity leave conditional on the worker's promise to return to work after the birth of the child for at least one month.

It was reported at the time that some 4,000 claims based on *Dekker* had been registered by women dismissed from the armed forces for being pregnant between 1978 and 1990. The Ministry of Defence had reportedly paid £31 million in settlements, but industrial tribunal awards of up to £350,000 had also been made, and it was estimated that, on the then current basis for awarding compensation, 2,500 outstanding claims could cost the taxpayer £100 million. In *Ministry of Defence v Cannock and Others* (1994), Mr Justice Morison, President of the Employment Appeal Tribunal, stated that there was a need for industrial tribunals to keep a sense of proportion when assessing compensation. He stated that the policy of the law was to treat absence due to pregnancy as an event which involved only a relatively short absence from employment. A tribunal should not make an award of a size which was more appropriate to compensate a person who had a long term disability. New guidelines were laid down by the Appeal Tribunal.

In late 1998, another report stated that 'an astonishing £58 million has been paid out to pregnant servicewomen who have had to leave the forces' by the Ministry of Defence. 'The rules have since been changed to allow maternity leave.' The report then turned to another recent development within sex discrimination law:

> Homosexual campaigners now believe they could win even more money for around 1,000 men and women drummed out under the traditional rule banning gay soldiers, sailors and airmen.

> If they are successful, the MoD report estimates that they would win an average £100,000 each ...

> The challenge came as a complete surprise to the Defence Ministry yesterday. It believed that a European Court ruling in July had ended any threat of it being sued for sexual discrimination against gays – on the grounds that it treated gay men and gay women with equal severity.

> But now gay campaigners will attempt a different approach, arguing that they were victims of sexual harassment because of the treatment they received when accused, detained, interrogated and finally dismissed from the Services.

The new Article 2(7) reads as follows:

7   This Directive shall be without prejudice to provisions concerning the protection
     of women, particularly as regards pregnancy and maternity.

     A woman on maternity leave shall be entitled, after the end of her period of
     maternity leave, to return to her job or to an equivalent post on terms and
     conditions which are no less favourable to her and to benefit from any
     improvement in working conditions to which she would be entitled during her
     absence.

     Less favourable treatment of a woman related to pregnancy or maternity leave
     within the meaning of Directive 92/85/EEC shall constitute discrimination within
     the meaning of this Directive.

     This Directive shall also be without prejudice to the provisions of Council
     Directive 96/34/EC of 3 June 1996 on the framework agreement on parental leave
     ... and of Council Directive 92/85/EEC of 19 October 1992 on the introduction of
     measures to encourage improvements in the safety and health at work of
     pregnant workers and workers who have recently given birth or are breastfeeding
     ... It is also without prejudice to the right of Member States to recognise distinct
     rights to paternity and/or adoption leave. Those Member States which recognise
     such rights shall take the necessary measures to protect working men and women
     against dismissal due to exercising those rights and ensure that, at the end of such
     leave, they shall be entitled to return to their jobs or to equivalent posts on terms
     and conditions which are no less favourable to them, and to benefit from any
     improvement in working conditions to which they would have been entitled
     during their absence.

Positive Action: Article 2(4) (now amended as 2(8))

This basis for derogation from the principle of equality relates to what have been
called measures of *positive action* taken by Member States to 'promote equal
opportunity for men and women, in particular by removing existing inequalities
which affect women's opportunities' in the areas covered by the Directive. The
original Article 2(4) (see above) was considered in the following case.

Case C-450/93 *Kalanke v Freie Hansestadt Bremen*

Two candidates were shortlisted for a managerial post in the Bremen parks
department. Both of them, Mr Kalanke and Miss Glissmann, were already employed
by the department. They were equally qualified for the post.

The Bremen Law on Equal Treatment for Men and Women in the Public Service 1990
provided that women who had the same qualifications as men applying for
promotion to the same post were to be given priority if they were under-represented.
This was the case if women did not make up at least half the staff in the individual
pay brackets and function levels in the relevant personnel group in the department.

Kalanke was recommended for the promotion but was rejected on the ground that the
relevant provisions of the 1990 Law applied; women being under-represented at
management level in the parks department. It was necessary therefore to appoint
Miss Glissmann.

In the course of proceedings brought by Kalanke, the Federal Labour Court referred
to the Court of Justice the question whether Article 2(1) and (4) of Directive 76/207
precluded the Bremen promotion rules.

The Court ruled that: 'National rules which *guarantee* women absolute and unconditional priority for appointment or promotion go *beyond promoting* equal opportunities and overstep the limits of the exception in Article 2(4) of the Directive.' They involved discrimination on the grounds of sex and were therefore precluded by the Directive.

The Court of Justice recognised the prejudicial effects on women in employment which arise from social attitudes, behaviour and structures. However, Article 2(4), as a derogation from the basic right to equal treatment, had to be interpreted strictly. Although it permitted national measures relating to promotion which gave a specific advantage to women with a view to improving their ability to compete on the labour market, it did not permit a quota system such as the one in issue. Such a system, in the Court's view, 'substituted for equality of opportunity as envisaged in Article 2(4) the result which was only to be arrived at by providing such equality of opportunity'.

As might be expected, this ruling received a mixed reception. It appeared to clash with the European Commission's own programme for promoting women among its 19,000 staff, but was welcomed by the Equal Opportunities Commission in Britain as being in line with the Sex Discrimination Act 1975, which outlaws quotas or positive discrimination but allows special single sex training programmes. An EOC representative said that the ruling 'made clear that it was unlawful to appoint someone on grounds of sex – even if they were equally good candidates in other respects – to redress any imbalance'.

The Bremen rules involved what is known as a 'soft' as opposed to a 'rigid' quota, and in the following case, the Court of Justice shifted its position, coming in line with a proposed Commission amendment by stating that while national measures guaranteeing 'absolute and unconditional priority' for women were not permissible, a 'softer' quota which allowed for individual consideration of circumstances would fall within Article 2(4).

Case C-409/95 *Marschall v Land Nordrhein-Westfalen*

M, employed as a teacher by the defendant German provincial region, applied for promotion to a higher grade at the Schwerte comprehensive school. The Arnsberg District Authority informed him that it intended to appoint a female candidate to the post.

M lodged an objection which the Authority rejected, relying on paragraph 25(5) of the Law on Civil Servants of the Land which provides that:

> Where, in the sector of the authority responsible for promotion, there are fewer women than men in the particular higher grade post in the career bracket, women are to be given priority for promotion in the event of equal suitability, competence and professional performance, unless reasons specific to an individual candidate tilt the balance in his favour.

M brought proceedings contesting the legality of the national provision under Community law before the Gelsenkirchen Administrative Court. The court found that M and the female candidate selected were, according to their official performance assessments, equally qualified but at the time the higher grade post was advertised, there were fewer women than men in the relevant career bracket. Having determined that the outcome of the proceedings depended on the compatibility of the national provision with Article 2(1) and (4) of Directive 76/207 and being unsure of the scope of the ruling of the Court in *Kalanke*, the court referred a question to the Court of Justice regarding the interpretation of Article 2(1) and (4).

The Court of Justice ruled that:

> A national rule which, in a case where there are fewer women than men at the level of the relevant post in a sector of the public service and both female and male candidates for the post are equally qualified in terms of their suitability, competence and professional performance, requires that priority be given to the promotion of female candidates unless reasons specific to an individual male candidate tilt the balance in his favour is not precluded by Article 2(1) and (4) of Directive 76/207 provided that:
>
> (a) in each individual case the rule provides for male candidates who are equally as qualified as the female candidates a guarantee that the candidatures will be the subject of an objective assessment which will take account of all criteria specific to the candidates and will override the priority accorded to female candidates where one or more of those criteria tilts the balance in favour of the male candidate; and
>
> (b) such criteria are not such as to discriminate against the female candidates.

The crucial difference for the Court which distinguished this case from *Kalanke* was that the national provisions contained a 'saving clause' to the effect that women were not to be given a priority if reasons specific to an individual male tilted the balance in his favour. The Court pointed out that Article 2(4) was specifically and exclusively designed to authorise measures which, although discriminatory in appearance, are in fact intended to eliminate or reduce actual instances of inequality which may exist in the reality of social life.

The Court went on to say that even where male and female candidates are equally qualified, male candidates tend to be promoted in preference to female candidates particularly because of prejudices and stereotypes concerning the role and capacities of women in working life and the fear, for example, that women will interrupt their careers more frequently, that owing to household and family duties they will be less flexible in their working hours, or that they will be absent from work more frequently because of pregnancy, childbirth and breastfeeding.

It was for these reasons, in the Court's view, that the mere fact that a male candidate and a female candidate were equally qualified did not mean that they had the same chances. It therefore followed that a national rule in terms of which, subject to the application of the saving clause, female candidates for promotion who are equally as qualified as the male candidates are to be treated preferentially in sectors where they are under-represented may fall within the scope of Article 2(4) if such a rule may counteract the prejudicial effects on female candidates of the attitudes and behaviour described above and thus reduce actual instances of inequality which may exist in the real world.

This decision should be considered in the light of the new, Amsterdam Treaty based, Article 141(4) EC, which provides that:

> ... with a view to ensuring full equality in practice between men and women in working life, the principle of equal treatment shall not prevent any Member State from maintaining or adopting measures providing for specific advantages in order to make it easier for the under-represented sex to pursue a vocational activity or to prevent or compensate for disadvantages in professional careers.

The Court of Justice reaffirmed its position in *Marschall* in a later ruling in Case C-158/97 *Application by Badeck and Others* regarding a challenge to provisions of a German national law the aim of which was equal access of men and women to posts in the public services by the adoption of 'advancement plans' in sectors where women were under-represented. The applicants maintained that the law in question was contrary to the constitutional principle of 'choosing the best'. The Court held that national measures giving priority to women for promotion in sectors of the public service in which they were under-represented were not contrary to Community equal treatment principles, if women were not given 'automatic and unconditional' priority when women and men were equally qualified and candidatures were assessed with the specific personal situations of all candidates being taken into account.

The way lies open for positive action along the lines indicated but it may be no easy task for policy and decision makers successfully to juggle with the finer points of equality, priority and objectivity. Indeed, Swedish positive action legislation failed to meet the approval of the Court of Justice in Case C-407/98 *Abrahamsson v Fogelqvist*. Here, the Court prefaced its ruling by speaking of legitimate assessment and selection of candidates in terms of:

> ... positive and negative criteria to be taken into account which, although formulated in terms which are neutral as regards sex and thus capable of benefiting men too, in general favour women. Thus, it may be decided that seniority, age and date of last promotion are to be taken into account only in so far as they are of importance for the suitability, qualifications and professional capability of candidates.

Such criteria, in the Court's view, should have the clear aim of preventing or compensating for disadvantages in the professional career of persons belonging to the under-represented sex. The application of the appropriate criteria 'must be transparent and amenable to review in order to obviate any arbitrary assessment of the qualifications of candidates'.

The Swedish legislation, as regards the selection procedure, was not based on such clear and unambiguous criteria:

> On the contrary, under that legislation, a candidate for a public post belonging to the under-represented sex and possessing sufficient qualifications for that post must be chosen in preference to a candidate of the opposite sex who would otherwise have been appointed, where that measure is necessary for a candidate belonging to the under-represented sex to be appointed.

> It follows that the legislation at issue in the main proceedings automatically grants preference to candidates belonging to the under-represented sex, provided that they are sufficiently qualified, subject only to the proviso that the difference between the merits of the candidates of each sex is not so great as to result in a breach of the requirement of objectivity in making appointments.

> The scope and effect of that condition cannot be precisely determined, with the result that the selection of a candidate from among those who are sufficiently qualified is ultimately based on the mere fact of belonging to the under-represented sex, and that this is so even if the merits of the candidate so selected are inferior to those of a candidate of the opposite sex. Moreover, candidatures are not subjected to an objective assessment taking account of the specific personal situations of all the candidates. It follows that such a method of selection is not such as to be permitted by Article 2(4) of the Directive.

Nor was the Swedish selection procedure justifiable under Article 141(4) of the Treaty (see opening pages of this chapter) as it was totally 'disproportionate to the aim pursued'.

In the *Dory* case above, D submitted that, for men, compulsory military service has the effect of prohibiting the exercise of an occupation during the period of service and of delaying access to employment, thereby constituting discrimination prohibited by the Directive. The Court's reasoning and its ruling made this question irrelevant but it had been the issue in the earlier Case C-79/99 *Julia Schnorbus v Land Hessen*.

Hessen rules in respect of entry to the second stage of German practical legal training gave priority to men by deferring acceptance of applications by females by up to 12 months in comparison with males who applied at the same time. When challenged by a female applicant, the defendant argued that the rule was fair and designed to counterbalance the disadvantage suffered by men.

The Court of Justice held (a) that the priority given to men amounted to indirect discrimination arising from their statutory obligation; and (b) that with respect to Article 2(4) of the Directive and the automatic preferential admission of men under the *Hessen* rule, the provisions at issue were justified by objective reasons and prompted solely by a desire to counterbalance to some extent the delay resulting from the completion of military or civilian service.

Note the new Article 2(8) which now backs up Article 141(4) EC rather than the reverse and puts the emphasis on securing equality in practice rather than removing inequalities:

> 8 Member States may maintain or adopt measures within the meaning of Article 141(4) of the Treaty with a view to ensuring full equality in practice between men and women.

It remains to be seen how this will be interpreted by the Court of Justice.

Questions concerning remedies for persons discriminated against, as regards both pay and treatment – case law and relevant changes to Directive 76/207 – are examined in Chapter 20.

WIDENING THE SCOPE OF DISCRIMINATION

Issues raised in a number of the more recent sex discrimination cases have moved beyond differential treatment of male and female employees and issues of economic and social law to questions of the dignity of the individual, equality as a fundamental right, and the protection of minorities. These cases are to be understood against a backdrop of changes in social and moral attitudes and more specifically the introduction by the ToA of new Council powers, when acting unanimously, to take 'appropriate action to combat discrimination based on sex ... or sexual orientation': Article 13 EC.

P v S, a case decided in 1996, concerned gender reassignment and fell to be decided under the Equal Treatment Directive.

Case C-13/94 *P v S and Cornwall County Council*

P, who was employed by the county council, informed S, the chief executive, of his intention to undergo gender reassignment. This involved a period during which P dressed and behaved as a woman. It was followed by surgery to give P the physical attributes of a woman. P was later dismissed because of her transsexuality and claimed discrimination on grounds of her sex. Questions were referred to the Court of Justice as to whether the Equal Treatment Directive applied to transsexuality.

The Court of Justice ruled that:

(a) 'The Directive is simply the expression, in the relevant field, of the principle of equality, which is one of the fundamental principles of Community law.'

(b) Since the right not to be discriminated against on grounds of sex was one of the fundamental human rights whose observance the Court has a duty to ensure (see Case 149/77 *Defrenne v Sabena (No 3)*), the scope of the Directive could not be confined to discrimination based on the fact that a person is one sex or the other.

(c) The Equal Treatment Directive therefore applied to discrimination based on the gender reassignment of the person in question 'since such discrimination is based, essentially if not conclusively, on the sex of the person concerned'. P had been treated unfavourably by comparison with a person of the sex P was deemed to belong to (male) prior to the gender reassignment.

The basis of this ruling is the principle of equality, and the Court's justification for its decision comes in its statement that:

To tolerate such discrimination [against a transsexual] would be tantamount, as regards such a person, to a failure to respect the dignity and freedom to which he or she is entitled, and which the court has a duty to safeguard.

At a more matter of fact level, Barnard has offered the view that 'it would seem in reality the basis of the judgment is not discrimination on the grounds of sex ... but discrimination on the grounds of having a sex change'. In any event, the decision has rightly been described as 'dramatic', 'remarkable' and 'courageous'. The next case raised the question of whether sexual orientation came within the scope of the Community's sex equality provisions relating to pay.

Case C-249/96 *Grant v South West Trains*

SWT granted free and reduced-rate travel concessions to employees and also 'for one legal spouse' and 'for one common law opposite sex spouse ... subject to a statutory declaration being made that a meaningful relationship has existed for a period of two years or more'.

G, an SWT employee, applied for concessions for her female partner. She provided a 'meaningful relationship' declaration but was refused the concessions on the ground that her partner was not of the opposite sex.

The Southampton industrial tribunal referred questions under Article 177 (now 234) as to whether the refusal constituted discrimination prohibited by Article 119 (now 141) EC and Council Directive 75/117 on equal pay for men and women.

The Court of Justice ruled that an employer's refusal to grant travel concessions to an employee's partner of the same sex, where they were allowed to the spouse or partner of the opposite sex of an employee, did not constitute discrimination contrary to Community law.

As a preliminary point, it will be recalled that Article 141 (formerly 119) is not confined to wages and salaries but also covers 'any consideration, whether in cash or in kind which the worker receives ... in respect of his employment from his employer': see Case 12/81 *Garland*, in which travel concessions were held to constitute pay.

In *Grant*, the Court proceeded by way of answers to three questions:

(a) *Did a condition such as that in issue constitute discrimination based directly on the sex of the worker?*

   In that the concessions were refused to a male person living with a male just as they were to a female worker living with a female, the condition did not constitute discrimination directly based on sex. The Court by taking a homosexual male as the comparator found no discrimination. G had argued that the correct comparator was a heterosexual male.

(b) *Did Community law now require stable relationships between two persons of the same sex to be regarded by all employers as equivalent to marriages or stable relationships outside marriage between two persons of the opposite sex?*

   On this point, the Court held that, in the present state of law within the Community, the two situations were not regarded as equivalent, so that employers were not required to treat them as such.

   This finding was based on a survey of the legal position in the various Member States (which did not, however, take account of the number of Member States which prohibit discrimination on grounds of sexual orientation) and the position adopted by the European Commission on Human Rights to the effect that stable homosexual relationships did not fall within the scope of the right to respect for family life under Article 8 of the European Convention on Human Rights. The Court further noted that the Commission did not regard national provisions which, for the purpose of protecting the family, accorded more favourable treatment to married persons and persons of opposite sex living together as man and wife than to persons of the same sex in a stable relationship as contrary to Article 14 of the Convention, which prohibited discrimination on the ground of sex.

(c) *Did discrimination based on sexual orientation constitute discrimination based on the sex of the worker?*

   Here, the Court distinguished *P v S*, in which the Court's conclusion that there was discrimination was limited to the case of a worker's gender reassignment and did not apply to differences of treatment based on sexual orientation.

Having rejected further submissions on behalf of G, the Court stated that the scope of Article 119 (now 141) was to be determined having regard only to its wording and purpose, its place in the scheme of the Treaty and its legal context. It was not for the Court to extend the scope of Community law beyond that provided for in the Treaty. However, it did refer to the new Article 6a (now 13) of the Treaty which, as seen, allows the Council to take action on the sexual orientation issue.

The Court reached the same conclusion in Case C-122 and 125/99P *D v Council*, another unequal benefits case involving an EU official whose same sex relationship, although legally recognised in Sweden, was not recognised under the married allowances provisions of the Staff Regulations.

At national level in 1996, in *R v Ministry of Defence ex p Smith*, the Court of Appeal declined to intervene regarding the Ministry of Defence (MoD) policy which required the dismissal of any serviceman or woman found to be of a homosexual orientation. It was held that the Equal Treatment Directive applied only to discrimination on grounds of gender. In *R v Secretary of State for Defence ex p Perkins (No 2)* in 1998, P claimed that the Royal Navy's decision to discharge him in pursuance of the MoD policy contravened the Directive. A reference was made to the Court of Justice asking whether the Directive was to be interpreted as including discrimination based on a person's sexual orientation. However, following the ruling in *Grant*, the Court's senior administrator asked the referring judge if he wished to withdraw the reference. In July 1998, Lightman J withdrew the reference on the basis that *Grant* left no reasonable doubt that Community law did not cover or render unlawful discrimination based on sexual orientation. There was 'no realistic possibility that the European Court would change its mind' and the matter could accordingly be resolved at the national level. In his conclusions, the judge did add that:

> It is uncertain what degree of orientation attracts the draconian response of dismissal and how this degree is to be measured. I set out my concerns about the policy in my previous judgment, but I cannot allow these considerations to affect my decision on the narrow question now before me. Albeit reluctantly, I consider that I am bound to withdraw the reference in this case. I may however add that even if there is no change in the policy, its future must in any event be uncertain. The Council acting under powers conferred by the Treaty of Amsterdam and the European Court of Human Rights on references to the [European] Commission [of Human Rights] currently before the Commission (but stayed pending the determination of these proceedings) may bring it to an end, and a challenge may be possible in judicial review proceedings once the Human Rights Bill becomes law ...

Similarly, in the same year, in *Smith v Gardner Merchant Ltd*, in the light of *Grant*, it was conceded in the Court of Appeal that harassment of a homosexual because of their sexual orientation was not sex discrimination. Harassment was also claimed as a feature of investigations by the armed forces of service personnel in pursuance of the MoD policy on homosexuality.

This line of cases next moves to Strasbourg. In September 1999, in *Lustig-Prean and Beckett v UK* and *Smith and Grady v UK*, the European Court of Human Rights dealt with the applications of persons dismissed from the armed services following very intrusive investigations into their homosexuality. The Court considered that the policy within the UK armed services of banning the employment of homosexuals and of conducting investigations of the kind in question were in violation of the applicants' right to respect for their private lives under Article 8 of the European Convention on Human Rights. The Court also held that there had also been a breach of Article 13, which lays down a right to an effective remedy in the event of violation of rights.

Contrary to the House of Lords' decision in 2000 in *Fitzpatrick v Sterling Housing Association Ltd* (a 3:2 majority decision), the European Court of Human Rights did not extend the concept of family life (to be found in Article 8 of the European Convention) to homosexuals. This decision of the House of Lords also clearly contrasts with that of the European Court of Justice in *Grant*.

The pressure for change, for the adoption of more liberal attitudes, is clear and change is underway. As a result of the *P v S* decision, the Sex Discrimination Act 1975 was amended in 1999 to extend protection in employment and training to anyone who 'intends to undergo, is undergoing or who has undergone gender reassignment'. The *Grant* decision moved the UK Association of Train Operators, of which South West Trains is a member, to extend concessionary travel benefits to same sex partners.

At Community level, Council Directive 2000/78, based on Article 13 EC, which establishes a general framework for equal treatment in employment, states that discrimination based on sexual orientation should be prohibited throughout the Community, and that harassment shall be deemed a form of discrimination. In the European Court of Human Rights in 2002, in *Goodwin v UK*, the UK was found to have breached the human rights of transsexuals. It was held that there had been violations of the right to respect for private and family life and the right to marry and to found a family as guaranteed by Articles 8 and 12 of the European Convention on Human Rights. G's complaints and those of another applicant were concerned in particular about their treatment in relation to employment, social security and pensions and their inability to marry.

This last case serves as well as any to highlight the considerable complexity but also the importance of a maturing gender equality law in Europe as viewed against a background of long standing stereotyped ideas concerning gender and gender rules in society. Reactions to the continuing contribution of the Court of Justice and other courts have inevitably been mixed as progressives push for more radical changes in the legal structure. Equality between men and women and non-discrimination are fundamental principles of Community law; they find their place in the EU Charter and now have a 'mainstream' position within the strategy which covers all Community policies.

REFERENCES AND FURTHER READING

Arnull, A, 'The beat goes on' (Case note on Case 222/84 *Johnston*) (1987) 12 EL Rev 56.

Barnard, C, 'The principle of equality in the Community context: *P, Grant, Kalanke* and *Marschall*: four uneasy bedfellows' (1998) 57(2) CLJ 352.

Barnard, C and Hepple, B, 'Indirect discrimination: interpreting *Seymour-Smith*' (1999) 58 CLJ 399.

Bell, M, *Anti-Discrimination Law and the EU*, 2002.

Curtin, D, 'Scalping the Community legislator: occupational pensions and *Barber*' (1990) 27 CML Rev 475.

Davies, P, 'Market integration and social policy' (1995) 24 ILJ 49.

Deakin, S and Morris, G, *Labour Law*, 2001, Chapter 6, 'Equality of treatment'.

Docksey, C, 'The principle of equality between women and men as a fundamental right under Community law' (1991) 20 ILJ 258.

Ellis, E, 'The recent jurisprudence of the Court of Justice in the field of sex equality' (2000) 37 CML Rev 1403.

Fitzpatrick, B, 'Equality in occupational pensions – the new frontiers after *Barber*' (1991) 54 MLR 271.

Fitzpatrick, B, 'Equality in occupational pension schemes' (1994) 23 ILJ 155.

Fredman, S, 'European Community discrimination law: a critique' (1992) 21 ILJ 119.

Honeyball, S and Shaw, J, 'Sex, law and the retiring man' (Case note on Case 262/88 *Barber*) (1991) 16 EL Rev 47.

Koutrakos, P, 'EC law and equal treatment in the armed forces' (2000) 25 EL Rev 433.

Mancini, GF and O'Leary, S, 'The new frontiers of sex equality law in the European Union' (1999) 24 EL Rev 331.

Nielsen, R and Szyszczak, E, *The Social Dimension of the European Community*, 1997.

Shaw, J, 'European Community judicial method: its application to sex discrimination law' (1990) 19 ILJ 228.

Stott, D, 'What price certainty?' (Case note and commentary on the *Melgar* and *Tele Danmark* cases) (2002) 27 EL Rev 351.

Schiek, D, 'A new framework on equal treatment of persons in EC law?' (2002) 8 ELJ 290.

Wynn, M, 'Pregnancy discrimination: equality, protection or reconciliation?' (1999) 62 MLR 435.

See also regular contributions to the Journal of Social Welfare and Family Law.

CHAPTER 15

COMPETITION LAW: RULES APPLYING TO UNDERTAKINGS – ARTICLE 81 (FORMERLY 85)

At one moment, they would be battling fiercely for markets, cutting prices, trying to undersell one another; at the next, they would be courting one another, trying to make an arrangement to apportion the world's markets among themselves; at still the next, they would be exploring mergers and acquisitions. On many occasions, they would be doing all three at the same time in an atmosphere of great suspicion and mistrust, no matter how great the cordiality at any given moment [Yergin, *The Prize: the Epic Quest for Oil, Money and Power*].

INTRODUCTION TO COMMUNITY COMPETITION POLICY

As we have seen, Article 3 of the EC Treaty sets out the activities to be carried on by the Community in order to achieve fulfilment of the two related aims of Article 2: the establishment of a Common Market and an Economic and Monetary Union. Within the context of the first aim, Article 3(g) requires the institution of:

> ... a system ensuring that competition in the internal market is not distorted.

Article 3(g) is implemented by the 'Rules on Competition' comprising Articles 81–86 (formerly 85–90) of the Treaty. Articles 81–86 contain the rules applying to undertakings (private and public sector). Only these rules will be discussed here – to the exclusion of Articles 87–89 (formerly 92–94) on illegal *State aids* which distort competition by favouring national undertakings.

In its Fifth General Report on the Activities of the EEC (1971), the Commission drew attention to the close relationship between the free movement of goods principle and Community competition policy, whilst highlighting the two main targets of the latter:

> The creation and development of this unified market would be difficult if not impossible if while conventional trade barriers among the Six were being speedily reduced, other obstacles, less visible but equally restrictive, were allowed to persist. These may arise from Member States applying different economic and fiscal regulations, or systems of State aid, or *from the abuse of dominant positions on the part of private firms or from agreements to restrict competition among them* [emphasis added].

Community competition policy (as distinct from the national competition policies of Member States) is therefore mainly directed towards the following anti-competitive activity:

(a) Restrictive trading agreements between otherwise independent firms (undertakings) which *may affect trade between Member States and which distort competition within the Common Market*: Article 81 (formerly 85). Restrictive agreements may be designed, for example, to fix prices or otherwise control markets for goods or services.

(b) Abusive (anti-competitive and exploitative) practices of undertakings (which dominate markets for goods or services) which, *again, may affect trade between Member States*: Article 82 (formerly 86). Dominant firms may, for example, have the power to charge excessive and unfair prices to their customers.

(c) In that they can lead to or strengthen conditions of market dominance, major cross-border mergers (concentrations) between undertakings are subject to control under Council Regulation 4064/89.

Although the Community has thus established a regulatory framework – a system of law within which competition between undertakings is encouraged – the Treaty does not define competition. The following extract from a late 1980s American anti-trust (competition policy) case provides valuable insights:

> Competition is the driving force behind our free enterprise system. Unlike centrally planned economies, where decisions about production and allocation are made by government bureaucrats who ostensibly see the big picture and know to do the right thing, capitalism relies on decentralized planning – millions of producers and consumers making hundreds of millions of individual decisions each year – to determine what and how much will be produced. Competition plays the key role in this process: it imposes an essential discipline on producers and sellers of goods to provide the consumer with a better product at a lower cost; it drives out inefficient and marginal producers, releasing resources to higher-valued uses; it promotes diversity, giving consumers choices to fit a wide array of personal preferences; it avoids permanent concentrations of economic power, as even the largest firm can lose market share to a feistier and hungrier rival. If, as the metaphor goes, a market economy is governed by an invisible hand, competition is surely the brass knuckles by which it enforces its decisions.

> When competition is impaired, producers may be able to reap monopoly profits, denying consumers many of the benefits of a free market. It is a simple but important truth, therefore, that our anti-trust laws are designed to protect the integrity of the market system by assuring that competition reigns freely. While much has been said and written about the anti-trust laws during the last century of their existence, ultimately the court must resolve a practical question in every monopolization case: is this the type of situation where market forces are likely to cure the perceived problem within a reasonable period of time? Or, have barriers been erected to constrain the normal operation of the market, so that the problem is not likely to be self-correcting? In the latter situation, it might well be necessary for a court to correct the market imbalance; in the former, a court ought to exercise extreme caution because judicial intervention in a competitive situation can itself upset the balance of market forces, bringing about the very ills the anti-trust laws were meant to prevent.

The opinions – of economists, politicians and lawyers – vary over time, from one country or political system to another, regarding the degree of regulation or intervention through law to which markets should be subjected by public authorities. The shift by the former Soviet Union and the countries of Central and Eastern Europe from centrally planned economies to free market economies, in which the forces of demand and supply will largely determine prices, is a clear illustration of this point.

Competition policy (and law) must therefore be dynamic, changing in terms of direction and objectives as political and economic situations change and develop. In its First Report on Competition Policy in 1972, the Commission stated that:

> Competition is the best stimulant of economic activity since it guarantees the widest possible freedom of action to all. An active competition policy pursued in accordance with the provisions of the Treaties establishing the Communities makes it easier for the supply and demand structures continually to adjust to technological development. Through the interplay of decentralised decision making machinery, competition enables enterprises continuously to improve their efficiency, which is the

sine qua non for a steady improvement in living standards and employment prospects within the countries of the Community. From this point of view, competition policy is an essential means for satisfying to a great extent the individual and collective needs of our society.

This statement focuses upon freedom of action for undertakings (and hence wide choice for their customers), upon the pressure on firms to invest in research and to innovate in line with changes in technology and consumer preferences, and thus upon the improved efficiency of firms in free market conditions. Human and material resources will be allocated effectively to meet demand for goods and services when and where it exists. Above all, competition keeps suppliers under pressure to keep costs and prices as low as possible in order not to lose sales to more efficient undertakings.

This somewhat idealised picture of the attractions of competition becomes obscured in the real world, not least in times of continued inflation. Although competition and free markets reflect the basic tenets of capitalism and western democracy, all the Member States operate what are called 'mixed' economies. On the basis of nationalisation measures, many governments moved undertakings, or whole sectors of their economies, out of private into public ownership. In this way, government-sanctioned legal monopolies were created. This applied particularly to public services and utilities such as gas (as in *Foster v British Gas plc* in Chapter 8), electricity, telecommunications, health services and rail transport. In such cases, competition, and the profit motive, were not necessarily eliminated (gas can compete with electricity) but were subordinated to social welfare principles. In recent years, throughout Europe, right-wing, free market policies have encouraged privatisation in such sectors to varying degrees, allowing more undertakings to operate and market forces to become stronger.

Within the private sector itself, there is a natural tendency for concentrations of economic power to develop in markets for goods and services. The forces of competition themselves tend to throw up large and dominant, often multinational, corporations. Alternatively, firms may agree to act in concert in order to obtain a greater degree of market power. Market structures within the Community may therefore be viewed according to the degree of *concentration* they exhibit, that is, according to the extent to which market power is concentrated in the hands of one or a few suppliers (or buyers).

It is against this background that it has been said that Community competition law and policy must aim to achieve *'workable competition'*, that is, competition which is *effective* and secures the most efficient allocation of available resources, against a background in which a variety of economic and social factors (for example, market integration, the environment, regional economic imbalances, equal pay policy, consumer protection) must be weighed and kept in balance:

> What is needed is to ensure access to the markets in question, for changes in supply and demand to be reflected in prices, for production and sales not to be artificially restricted and for the freedom of action and choice of suppliers, buyers and consumers not to be compromised [Commissioner von der Groeben in 1969].

Later, the Court of Justice in Case 26/76 *Metro (No 1)* spoke of workable competition in terms of market structures and Treaty objectives, particularly the creation of a single market:

The requirement contained in Articles 3 and 85 [now 81] of the EEC Treaty that competition shall not be distorted implies the existence on the market of workable competition, that is to say, the degree of competition necessary to ensure the observance of the basic requirements and the attainment of the objectives of the Treaty, in particular the creation of a single market achieving conditions similar to those of a domestic market.

In accordance with this requirement, the nature and intensiveness of competition may vary to an extent dictated by the products or services in question and the economic structure of the relevant market sectors.

Workable competition will ensure that all markets, whether there are many participants, few participants, or even where there is only one market player, are exposed to the competitive action of existing, or potential, competitors. Markets of this type fall somewhere between the two polar market models of economic theory:

(a) *The perfectly competitive market*, in which many small firms compete in the supply of a single product, and no single firm (seller or buyer) has sufficient power to have an impact on market price.

(b) The *monopolistic market*, in which a single firm, responsible for the supply of the total output of the product, is able, *in the absence of substitutes*, to control its price. Such a monopolist will maximise its profits at some point where its output is less than it would be under perfect competition, that is, where demand exceeds supply, so ensuring the firm a high monopoly price.

A monopolistic market can be broken down if new firms are able to enter the market. This will probably involve overcoming considerable *entry barriers*. These may be exceptionally high investment costs, control by the monopolist of production methods covered by patents granted under national law, or even, as we have seen, the granting of monopoly power to an undertaking by the State, for example, British Telecom before privatisation.

BASIC OBJECTIVES OF COMMUNITY COMPETITION POLICY

Article 2 of the EC Treaty speaks of the need for 'a high degree of competitiveness within the Union' and Article 4 (formerly 3a) of 'close co-ordination of Member States' economic policies ... conducted in accordance with the principle of an open market economy with free competition'.

In its Ninth Report on Competition Policy (1980), the Commission stated that undistorted competition was 'a prerequisite for the proper functioning of the Common Market, which is the rock on which economic integration is to be founded'.

The introduction to the Ninth Report outlined four basic objectives of the Community's policy:

(a) An open and unified market – not partitioned by restrictive, anti-competitive agreements between undertakings.

(b) The right amount of effective competition in markets not subject to over-concentration or the abuses of dominant firms.

(c) Fairness in the market place – hence support for small and medium-sized businesses, consumer protection measures and the attack on illegal State aids.

(d) Maintenance of the Community's competitive position vis à vis its main rivals (the USA and Japan) within the world economy.

The conclusion reached (at a time of severe economic difficulties arising in large part from big increases in oil prices) was that:

> The sheer scale of the common market and its inextricable enmeshment in world trade dictate that the need for a universal regulator of economic activity throughout the Community can only be answered by a Community competition policy. To yield to the persuasions of those who would respond to the crisis by a retreat into self-sufficient isolation would simply aggravate the situation beyond redemption by deepening the trauma of the structural changes thrust upon Europe by the shifting patterns of world trade. If we delude ourselves that we can dispense with the forces of competition and a decentralized economy and can steer through the necessary restructuring by purely legislative means, we run the irremediable risk of cutting our Community off from the economic reality of its surroundings.

In several respects, Community competition policy involves the Commission in a delicate balancing act. The market integration function of competition policy did not stop with the establishment of the Internal Market – not with a number of Central European countries waiting to join the Community. The encouragement of small and medium-sized firms must not be at the expense of the need for some firms to achieve optimum size in order to operate effectively not only throughout the Common Market but in competition with large scale undertakings in the USA and the Far East. The attack on agreements which restrict competition must not stifle efficiency:

> Competition policy fosters market integration in a positive way as well. Subject to the maintenance of an adequate level of competition, it allows scope for cooperation between firms likely to further technical and economic progress, especially in research and development and the transfer of technology. Hence the Commission can take favourable decisions on inter-company cooperation or government intervention that is in the wider Community interest and not just the interest of the firms or countries concerned. This is especially evident in the case of measures which stimulate R & D and innovation, as well as boosting dynamic growth, or which help realize the growth potential of underdeveloped areas.

> These two sides of the Commission's competition policy, control of the action of governments and of firms, thus pursue the same aim of ensuring open, efficient markets in which firms determine their prices and output independently according to market conditions. It is this type of environment in which firms can best develop and can take on world competition [Sixteenth Commission Competition Report].

THE ENFORCEMENT OF COMMUNITY COMPETITION LAW (PRIOR TO 'MODERNISATION')

Community competition law comprises common rules for a Common Market. It is the 'effect on trade between Member States' requirement of both Articles 85 and 86 (now 81 and 82) which constitutes the natural dividing line between the enforcement of the Treaty's rules and national competition laws – which increasingly approximate to those of the Treaty – that operate both within the Union and elsewhere in Europe.

On the basis of Article 87 (now 83), Council Regulation 17 of 1962 (subject now to the introduction of a new 'modernised' Regulation) was the original instrument providing for the 'balanced application of Articles 85 and 86 [now 81 and 82] in a uniform manner in the Member States'. The administration and enforcement of the competition rules applying to undertakings was entrusted to the Commission (in particular Directorate General IV (now DG Competition), the Legal Service and later the Merger Task Force), 'acting in close and constant liaison with the competent authorities of the Member States'. Such competent authorities include the Director General of Fair Trading in the UK and the German *Bundeskartellamt* (Federal Cartel Office).

Under Regulation 17, the Commission was empowered, amongst other things, for the purpose of bringing to an end infringements of Articles 85 and 86 (now 81 and 82), to address quasi-judicial Decisions to undertakings, enforceable by means of fines and periodic penalty payments. In addition, the Commission had sole power under Article 9(1) of the Regulation to grant exemption under Article 85(3) (now 81(3)) of a notified agreement caught by Article 85(1) (now 81(1)) which nevertheless produced economic or other benefits which outweighed its anti-competitive effects. Block exemptions could also be granted under Article 85(3) (now 81(3)) to 'categories of agreements' by way of Commission Regulations.

Decisions made by the Commission under the Treaty's competition rules have, since 1989, been subject to review by the Court of First Instance (previously by the Court of Justice) under Article 230(4) (formerly 173(4) and previously Article 173(2)) in challenges brought (usually) by undertakings on the various grounds stipulated in that Article. Article 229 (formerly 172) also applies to the CFI, giving it unlimited jurisdiction as regards penalties imposed on undertakings by the Commission. Fines or penalty payments may be cancelled, reduced or increased. As seen in Chapter 7, decisions of the CFI are subject to a right of appeal to the Court of Justice on points of law.

The role of national courts in the enforcement of Articles 81 and 82 (formerly 85 and 86) has its basis in the ruling of the Court of Justice in Case 127/73 *BRT v SABAM*, in which it stated that:

> ... as the prohibitions of Article 85(1) and 86 tend by their very nature to produce direct effects in relations between individuals, these Articles create direct rights in respect of the individuals concerned which the national courts must safeguard.

This means that a breach of Article 81 or 82 (formerly 85 or 86) may give rise to a private action in a national court. The power of such a court to apply Article 81(1) necessarily includes the power to apply paragraph 2 of that Article and thus declare void any agreement prohibited under paragraph 1 (See also the 'prohibition' in Article 82.) The question of damages or interim relief is one of national law. However, until the new Regulation comes into force, national courts have no power to apply Article 81(3), the Commission until then having the monopoly on the power to grant exemptions under that paragraph to agreements, etc which offend Article 81(1). This monopoly will soon be brought to an end. It is one of several issues that have been debated at an official level over the last few years and which are now the subject of EC legislation or proposed legislation regarding Articles 81 and 82 and their enforcement. These issues will be covered later in this chapter and in Chapter 17.

ARTICLE 81 (FORMERLY 85): RESTRICTIVE AGREEMENTS, DECISIONS AND CONCERTED PRACTICES

Article 81

1   The following shall be prohibited as incompatible with the Common Market: all agreements between undertakings, decisions by associations of undertakings and concerted practices which may affect trade between Member States and which have as their object or effect the prevention, restriction or distortion of competition within the Common Market, and in particular those which:

    (a) directly or indirectly fix purchase or selling prices or any other trading conditions;

    (b) limit or control production, markets, technical development, or investment;

    (c) share markets or sources of supply;

    (d) apply dissimilar conditions to equivalent transactions with other trading parties, thereby placing them at a competitive disadvantage;

    (e) make the conclusion of contracts subject to acceptance by the other parties of supplementary obligations which, by their nature or according to commercial use, have no connection with the subject of such contracts.

2   Any agreements or decisions prohibited pursuant to this Article shall be automatically void.

3   The provisions of paragraph 1 may, however, be declared inapplicable in the case of:

    –   any agreement or category of agreements between undertakings;

    –   any decision or category of decisions by associations of undertakings;

    –   any concerted practice or category of concerted practices,

which contributes to improving the production or distribution of goods or to promoting technical or economic progress, while allowing consumers a fair share of the resulting benefit, and which does not:

    (a) impose on the undertakings concerned restrictions which are not indispensable to the attainment of these objectives;

    (b) afford such undertakings the possibility of eliminating competition in respect of a substantial part of the products in question.

In broad terms, Article 81 (formerly 85) is directed against forms of co-operation between firms which are anti-competitive. The Article formulates (1) a prohibition (followed by a non-exhaustive list of anti-competitive practices); (2) the consequences attached to breach of that prohibition; and (3) a qualification concerning the Commission's power to grant an exemption from the prohibition to agreements, etc, which achieve beneficial ends which outweigh the harm to competition. There are two positive conditions and two negative conditions.

Commenting on Article 85 (now 81), Sharpston explains that:

We are dealing with heavily economic law: what is being assessed and approved or condemned is the effect of certain types of behaviour on markets, prices and product availability.

Article 85(3) is essentially an economic balancing act: will the benefits from a particular arrangement (in terms of enhanced product choice or better quality service, or similar) be deemed to outweigh the costs (in terms of the associated reduction in competition)? If so, the agreement may be exempted; if not, it will continue to be caught by the general prohibition contained in Art 85(1).

'Assessment' implies an assessor – in this case, Directorate General IV of the Commission of the European Communities: the Commission's view of the likely effects of a proposed or implemented arrangement does not necessarily coincide with the client company's.

The power to exempt under Art 85(3) is a discretionary power: the Commission is not obliged to grant an exemption in a particular case.

The very first decision of the Court of Justice on Article 85 (now 81) illustrates, amongst other things: (a) the close relationship between competition policy and the free movement of goods; and (b) the need to establish a Common Market based on the competitive interpenetration of existing national markets for goods and services.

Cases 56 and 58/64 *Consten and Grundig v Commission*

In 1957, as part of its international distribution network, the German company Grundig appointed Consten as its sole distributor in France. G agreed to supply only C in France and to ensure that its distributors outside France did not deliver G's radio, television and recording equipment into France. In return, C undertook not to sell competing products and not to sell G's products to other countries.

By means of the *export bans* included in these exclusive distributorship agreements, C, and G's other dealers, were granted a position of *'absolute territorial protection'* within their contract areas. In addition, C was granted exclusive rights in France to G's GINT (Grundig International) trade mark.

UNEF, a French firm, bought G's products in Germany and, as a result of price differentials in the German and French markets, was able to sell them in France below the prices charged by C.

C sued the *parallel importer* UNEF in the French courts for infringement of its GINT trade mark. On an application by UNEF to the Commission that the Grundig-Consten agreement was in breach of Article 85(1), the Commission issued a Decision to that effect. G and C sought to annul that Decision under Article 173(2) EEC (now 230(4) EC). The Court of Justice struck down those clauses of the agreement, relating to the export bans and the supplementary use of the trade mark, which sought to partition the market and so prevent the creation of a Common Market. This was so despite strong economic arguments which sought to justify the arrangements in question.

The Court ruled, in part, as follows:

> *The complaints relating to the concept of 'agreements ... which may affect trade between Member States'*
>
> The applicants and the German Government maintain that the Commission has relied on a mistaken interpretation of the concept of an agreement which may affect trade between Member States and has not shown that such trade would have been greater without the agreement in dispute.
>
> The defendant replies that this requirement in Article 85(1) is fulfilled once trade between Member States develops, as a result of the agreement, differently from the way in which it would have done without the restriction resulting from the agreement, and once the influence of the agreement on market conditions reaches a certain degree. Such is the case here, according to the defendant, particularly in view of the impediments resulting within the Common Market from the disputed agreement as regards the exporting and importing of Grundig products to and from France.
>
> The concept of an agreement 'which may affect trade between Member States' is intended to define, in the law governing cartels, the boundary between the areas

respectively covered by Community law and national law. It is only to the extent to which the agreement may affect trade between Member States that the deterioration in competition caused by the agreement falls under the prohibition of Community law contained in Article 85; otherwise it escapes the prohibition.

In this connection, what is particularly important is whether the agreement is capable of constituting a threat, either direct or indirect, actual or potential, to freedom of trade between Member States in a manner which might harm the attainment of the objectives of a single market between States. Thus, the fact that an agreement encourages an increase, even a large one, in the volume of trade between States is not sufficient to exclude the possibility that the agreement may 'affect' such trade in the above mentioned manner. In the present case, the contract between Grundig and Consten, on the one hand by preventing undertakings other than Consten from importing Grundig products into France, and on the other hand by prohibiting Consten from re-exporting those products to other countries of the Common Market, indisputably affects trade between Member States. These limitations on the freedom of trade, as well as those which might ensue for third parties from the registration in France by Consten of the GINT trade mark, which Grundig places on all its products, are enough to satisfy the requirement in question.

Consequently, the complaints raised in this respect must be dismissed.

The complaints concerning the criterion of restriction on competition

The applicants and the German Government maintain that since the Commission restricted its examination solely to Grundig products the decision was based upon a false concept of competition and of the rules on prohibition contained in Article 85(1), since this concept applies particularly to competition between similar products of different makes; the Commission, before declaring Article 85(1) to be applicable, should, by basing itself upon the 'rule of reason', have considered the economic effects of the disputed contract upon competition between the different makes. There is a presumption that vertical sole distributorship agreements are not harmful to competition and in the present case there is nothing to invalidate that presumption. On the contrary, the contract in question has increased the competition between similar products of different makes.

The principle of freedom of competition concerns the various stages and manifestations of competition. Although competition between producers is generally more noticeable than that between distributors of products of the same make, it does not thereby follow that an agreement tending to restrict the latter kind of competition should escape the prohibition of Article 85(1) merely because it might increase the former.

Besides, for the purpose of applying Article 85(1), there is no need to take account of the concrete effects of an agreement once it appears that it has as its object the prevention, restriction or distortion of competition.

Therefore, the absence in the contested decision of any analysis of the effects of the agreement on competition between similar products of different makes does not, of itself, constitute a defect in the decision.

It thus remains to consider whether the contested decision was right in founding the prohibition of the disputed agreement under Article 85(1) on the restriction on competition created by the agreement in the sphere of the distribution of Grundig products alone. The infringement which was found to exist by the contested decision results from the absolute territorial protection created by the said contract in favour of Consten on the basis of French law. The applicants thus wished to eliminate any possibility of competition at the wholesale level in Grundig products in the territory specified in the contract essentially by two methods.

First, Grundig undertook not to deliver even indirectly to third parties products intended for the area covered by the contract. The restrictive nature of that undertaking is obvious if it is considered in the light of the prohibition on exporting which was imposed not only on Consten but also on all the other sole concessionaires of Grundig, as well as the German wholesalers. Secondly, the registration in France by Consten of the GINT trade mark, which Grundig affixes to all its products, is intended to increase the protection inherent in the disputed agreement, against the risk of parallel imports into France of Grundig products, by adding the protection deriving from the law on industrial property rights. Thus, no third party could import Grundig products from other Member States of the Community for resale in France without running serious risks.

The defendant properly took into account the whole distribution system thus set up by Grundig. In order to arrive at a true representation of the contractual position the contract must be placed in the economic and legal context in the light of which it was concluded by the parties. Such a procedure is not to be regarded as an unwarrantable interference in legal transactions or circumstances which were not the subject of the proceedings before the Commission.

The situation as ascertained above results in the isolation of the French market and makes it possible to charge for the products in question prices which are sheltered from all effective competition. In addition, the more producers succeed in their efforts to render their own makes of product individually distinct in the eyes of the consumer, the more the effectiveness of competition between producers tends to diminish. Because of the considerable impact of distribution costs on the aggregate cost price, it seems important that competition between dealers should also be stimulated. The efforts of the dealer are stimulated by competition between distributors of products of the same make. Since the agreement thus aims at isolating the French market for Grundig products and maintaining artificially, for products of a very well known brand, separate national markets within the Community, it is therefore such as to distort competition in the Common Market.

It was therefore proper for the contested decision to hold that the agreement constitutes an infringement of Article 85(1). No further considerations, whether of economic data (price differences between France and Germany, representative character of the type of appliance considered, level of overheads borne by Consten) or of the corrections of the criteria upon which the Commission relied in its comparisons between the situations of the French and German markets, and no possible favourable effects of the agreement in other respects, can in any way lead, in the face of above mentioned restrictions, to a different solution under Article 85(1).

As seen, the Court confined its decision to the export bans imposed on the distributors and the related agreement regarding the use of the 'GINT' trade mark. It also annulled for lack of reasoning (see Article 253 (formerly 190)) that part of the Commission's Decision condemning the obligation on Grundig not to make direct deliveries in France except to Consten (and see also Case 56/65 *Société-Technique Minière*, below).

As a result of this decision, it is clear that:

(a) Article 81 (formerly 85) applies not only to *horizontal* agreements between competing firms operating at the same level of the market, but also to *vertical* agreements between non-competing firms operating at different levels of the market which seek to exclude others from the distributor's market.

(b) An agreement may be caught by Article 81(1) (formerly 85(1)), even though it encourages trade between Member States, if, as a result of (i) export bans, and (ii) the use of national industrial property rights (the GINT trade mark), the agreement nevertheless has an adverse effect on competition and the free movement of goods.

(c) Article 81 (formerly 85) covers not only agreements which restrict competition between competing manufacturers, that is, *inter-brand competition*, but also agreements which restrict competition between distributors of a single manufacturer's products; intra-brand competition.

(d) The consumer interest in choice and fair prices is a constituent element in the concept of workable or effective competition.

Critics of this decision point out that market power (inter-brand competition) and not regulation would ensure that Grundig's products could not continue to be sold at unreasonably high prices. In the USA, the Supreme Court, in *Continental TV Inc v GTE Sylvania Inc* (1977), stated that:

> Inter-brand competition ... is the primary purpose of anti-trust law ... When inter-brand competition exists ... it provides a significant check on the exploitation of intra-brand market power because of the ability of consumers to substitute a different brand of the same product.

It may be argued that, unlike the Court of Justice in 1964 (and later), the Supreme Court in 1977 was not concerned with the establishment of a single market.

Further developments, regarding both the case law and subsequent legislative measures in relation to distribution agreements and vertical restraints generally, are considered later in this chapter: see particularly 'Block Exemption of Exclusive Distribution Agreements' and 'Reform of the Law on Vertical Restraints'.

INTERPRETATION OF ARTICLE 81 (FORMERLY 85): ITS CONSTITUENT ELEMENTS: 'AGREEMENTS ... DECISIONS ... AND CONCERTED PRACTICES'

For Article 81(1) (formerly 85(1)) to apply, there must be an *agreement between undertakings, or a decision by an association of undertakings or a concerted practice*. The case law shows that these concepts may overlap and, for example, an informal agreement may also be a concerted practice.

Agreements and Concerted Practices

In *Consten and Grundig*, the German government submitted, in effect, that a vertical agreement (in that case, between supplier and distributor) did not constitute an 'agreement between undertakings' within the meaning of Article 85 (now 81), since the parties were not on 'an equal footing according to the level in the economy at which they operated'. This argument, which the Court had no difficulty in rejecting (see above), attempted to confine Article 85 to horizontal arrangements between firms of the type typical of the traditional economic concept of the cartel. On this basis, a cartel is defined as an association of manufacturers/suppliers with the purpose of maintaining prices at a high level and/or controlling production or markets.

While anti-competitive arrangements (including agreements) between suppliers of goods or services – operating at the same level of the economy – are caught by Article 81 (formerly 85), so too, as seen in *Consten and Grundig*, are agreements between parties operating at different levels.

However, just as significantly, Article 81 does not confine itself to agreements, that is, binding contracts. Firms, otherwise independent, who are operating together – in concert – in an anti-competitive way, in defiance of a regulatory system which can impose very large fines on them, are unlikely to advertise the fact. Therefore, Article 81 applies not only to agreements but also, with its focus on intent rather than form, on arrangements which fall short of being binding contracts and which operate on a covert basis. This is typical of horizontal 'concerted practices' between suppliers in, as the case law shows, product markets such as cement, sugar or steel. In addition, tacit supplementary understandings between parties to formal agreements of a vertical nature, for example, exclusive distribution agreements, may also be caught by Article 81 on a similar basis.

'Horizontal' Cases

Cases 41/69, etc, *ACF Chemiefarma v Commission (Quinine Cartel)*

A number of suppliers operating on the quinine market put into effect arrangements to fix prices and divide the market. An export agreement operated as regards trade with non-Member States and a similar 'gentleman's agreement' guaranteed protection of each national market for the producers in the various Member States.

In this judicial review of the Commission's Decision, the Court of Justice ruled that the so called 'gentleman's agreement' fell within Article 85 (now 81):

> It is not necessary, in order for a restriction [of competition] to constitute an agreement within the meaning of Article 85(1) for the agreement to be intended as legally binding on the parties. An agreement exists if the parties reach a consensus on a plan which limits or is likely to limit their commercial freedom by determining the lines of their mutual action or abstention from action in the market ... Nor is it necessary for such an agreement to be made in writing.

Concerted practices amount to 'a form of co-ordination between undertakings which, without having reached the stage where an agreement properly so-called has been concluded, knowingly substitutes practical co-operation between them for the risks of competition': the Court of Justice in *Dyestuffs*.

Case 48/69 *ICI v Commission (Dyestuffs)*

Three uniform price increases were introduced by the leading producers of aniline dyes in Benelux and Italy in 1964, 1965 and 1967. The Commission found that the parties were guilty of concerted practices and it imposed heavy fines. The Commission's Decision was based, among other things, upon (a) the uniform identity of the rates of increase; (b) the similarity of the dates upon which the increases were announced or applied; (c) the simultaneous despatch of instructions to subsidiaries; and (d) the fact and nature of informal contact between the undertakings in question.

Following a challenge to the Decisions under Article 173(2) (now 230(4)), the Court upheld the Commission's Decision.

In the *Dyestuffs* case (in 1969, ICI was a non-EEC undertaking, controlling an EEC subsidiary), it was argued that the price increases were parallel increases made without collusion and were a natural feature of what is known as an *oligopolistic* market. This is a market in a relatively homogeneous product with high barriers to entry, dominated by a small number of suppliers, for example, petrol. Price is thus a crucial determinant of demand and if one company reduces prices, the others will follow *independently* in order to retain their market share. If costs increase, all are affected and prices rise – not as a result of collusion but on the basis of what is known as mutual interdependence or conscious parallelism of action.

In *Dyestuffs*, the Court held that the defendants must prove that parallel prices were not collusive and thus that the absence of effective competition arose from the oligopolistic nature of the market:

> Although parallel behaviour may not by itself be identified with a concerted practice, it may however amount to strong evidence of such a practice if it leads to conditions of competition which do not correspond to the normal conditions of the market, having regard to the nature of the products, the size and number of the undertakings, and the volume of the said market.

The Court went on to say that:

> Although every producer is free to change his prices, taking into account in so doing the present or foreseeable conduct of his competitors, nevertheless it is contrary to the rules on competition contained in the Treaty for a producer to co-operate with his competitors, in any way whatsoever, in order to determine a coordinated course of action relating to a price increase and to ensure its success by prior elimination of all uncertainty as to each other's conduct regarding the essential elements of that action, such as the amount, subject matter, date and place of the increases.

The oligopoly argument was rejected by the Court, which was of the view that the more powerful of the producers might indeed have been in a position to refrain from following an increase by a price leader, and have attempted to increase their market share by maintaining existing price levels. On the facts, however, the price collusion found by the Court had, in practice, the effect of dividing the Common Market into five national markets with different price levels and structures.

In Cases C-89/85, etc, *Ahlström and Others v Commission (Wood Pulp)*, the Commission found sufficient evidence of concerted practices between a large number of wood pulp producers, who charged similar prices and made simultaneous and uniform alterations to them. However, having heard expert economic evidence on the matter, the Court of Justice did not agree with the Commission regarding *proof* of concertation:

> It must be stated that, in this case, concertation is not the only plausible explanation for the parallel conduct. To begin with, the system of price announcements may be regarded as constituting a rational response to the fact that the pulp market constituted a long term market and to the need felt by both buyers and sellers to limit commercial risks. Further, the similarity in the dates of price announcements may be regarded as a direct result of the high degree of market transparency ... Finally, the parallelism of prices and the price trends may be satisfactorily explained by the oligopolistic tendencies of the market and by the specific circumstances prevailing in

certain periods. Accordingly, the parallel conduct established by the Commission does not constitute evidence of concertation.

In the absence of a firm, precise and consistent body of evidence, it must be held that concertation regarding announced prices has not been established by the Commission. [For further aspects of this case, see below.]

In the *Polypropylene* cases, the Commission held that a concerted practice may be found where, 'in a complex cartel, some producers at one time or another might not express their definite assent to a particular course of action agreed by the others but nevertheless indicate their general support for the scheme in question and conduct themselves accordingly'.

Cases T-1/89, etc, *Rhone Poulenc and Others v Commission (Polypropylene)*

At meetings of competing polypropylene (thermoplastic materials used for films, fibres, etc) suppliers, RP disclosed company price and production figures. The Commission's finding that the meetings had the purpose of influencing market conduct within the industry was confirmed by the CFI. In the Court's view, mere attendance at the meetings (passive contact) would amount to participation in a concerted practice.

The point was made that an undertaking:

... by its participation in a meeting with an anti-competitive purpose, not only pursued the aim of eliminating in advance uncertainty abut the future conduct of its competitors but could not fail to take into account, directly or indirectly, the information obtained in the course of those meetings in order to determine the policy which it intended to pursue on the market.

Bearing in mind that effective competition may be curtailed both by collusion, caught by Article 81 (formerly 85), or oligopolistic conscious parallelism falling short of collusion, it is perhaps surprising that it was not until the mid-1980s that the Commission moved against oligopolies, primarily on the basis of the words of Article 86 (now 82) – 'one or more undertakings' – and the concept of collective dominance of the relevant market. In 1989, in *Italian Flat Glass*, the Commission stated that three Italian glass manufacturers:

... as participants in a tight oligopoly, enjoy a degree of independence from competitive pressures that enables them to impede the maintenance of effective competition, notably by not having to take account of the behaviour of other market participants.

The Commission concluded that the three firms 'present themselves on the market as a single entity and not as individuals'. Although the CFI to a large extent annulled this Decision on the basis of serious procedural irregularities by the Commission, it did not rule out the idea of collective dominance: see Chapter 16.

'Vertical' Cases

In the following 'vertical' case, it was held that an apparently unilateral act by one party amounted to a tacit understanding between that party and others sufficient to bring it within the terms of Article 85(1) (now 81(1)). The supplier's restrictive sales policy was regarded as implicitly accepted by its distributors so as to give rise to an agreement under Article 85(1).

Cases 25 and 26/84 *Ford Werke AG v Commission*

The Court upheld the Commission's refusal to grant exemption under Article 85(3) for Ford Werke's apparently acceptable standard distribution agreement. Ford Werke was refusing to supply its distributors in Germany with right hand-drive cars likely to be exported to the UK, where prices were high. This action was taken following complaints from Ford's UK dealers who were being undercut by these parallel imports. It was seen by the Court as a tactic designed to partition the market and to maintain different price levels in different Member States.

Although there was no evidence of an express agreement or of concerted action, the Court ruled that the refusal to supply had been impliedly accepted by the distributors, so forming a sufficient basis for an agreement between Ford Werke and its distributors.

The Court stated that:

> Such a decision [the refusal to supply] on the part of the manufacturer does not constitute, on the part of the undertaking, a unilateral act which, as the applicants claim, would be exempt from the prohibition contained in Article 85(1) of the Treaty. On the contrary, it forms part of the contractual relations between the undertaking and its dealers.

Similarly, in *Bayer/Adalat*, the Commission found the German chemicals group B to have limited supplies of certain pharmaceutical products from its *wholly owned subsidiaries* (see the section 'Undertakings', below) in other Member States to wholesalers there in order to stop them parallel exporting the goods to the UK market, where prices were higher. Although the wholesalers did not agree to the export ban and resisted B's attempts to limit supplies, the Commission was of the view that there was an agreement between B's distributors and the wholesalers on the basis of the latter's continuing to deal. B was fined 3 million Euros.

In Case T-41/96 *Bayer v Commission*, the President of the CFI having at an interlocutory stage suspended the operative part of the Commission's Decision on the basis that B had established a *prima facie* case that the refusal to supply did not constitute an agreement, the CFI held that the absence of a 'concurrence of wills' between B and its wholesalers took the case outside the ambit of Article 85(1). The Commission had failed to produce sufficient evidence to prove tacit acquiescence.

Konica UK Ltd and Konica Europe GmbH

Konica UK, a distributor of photographic goods and equipment, imposed a ban on dealers within its territory aimed at preventing the export of Konica colour film from the UK to other Member States where prices were considerably higher. Konica Europe, established in West Germany, entered into a linked commitment towards German dealers to prevent the resale of parallel imported colour film on the German market by buying up the film.

As regards Konica UK, the Commission held that:

> Where a distribution company issues a circular establishing the conditions under which it will supply wholesalers, and the latter continue to order the goods in question and do not contradict those conditions in their dealings, that circular cannot be deemed to be a unilateral measure but the offer of an agreement accepted by the dealers. In any event, such circumstances at least point to a concerted practice between the distributor and the dealers within the meaning of Article 85(1).

As regards Konica Europe, it was held that:

> A commitment given by a distribution company, at the wish of and in the interests of its specialist dealers in one Member State, to buy up contract goods parallel imported into that State, and offering to refund dealers who do the same, is to be regarded as a term of the supply contract between the distributor and its dealers and constitutes an agreement within the meaning of Article 85(1) or at least points to a concerted practice between them. An agreement pursuant to Article 85(1) does not require the written assent of the other party but can consist in the continuing business relationship between the parties.

Decisions by Associations of Undertakings

Article 81 (formerly 85) applies here when undertakings act in concert through the intermediary of an association to which they belong.

Such 'decisions' typically cover the rules, decisions and recommendations of trade associations which apply to their members and produce results prohibited under Article 81(1) (formerly 85(1)): see, for example, Cases 96/82, etc, *NV IAZ International Belgium* as regards a non-binding recommendation from a trade association, which was normally complied with by its members and was held to be capable of falling within Article 85(1).

In Case T-66/89 *Publishers Association v Commission (Net Book Agreement)*, the CFI held that the Association's non-binding Code of Conduct, which laid down uniform conditions for the sale of books at fixed, 'net book' prices, was in breach of Article 85(1) and not eligible for exemption under Article 85(3) despite strong arguments that this system of collective price maintenance was necessary to protect the small, specialist bookseller. Although, as the CFI conceded, the net book agreement might produce beneficial results within the UK market, as it applied not only to that market but also to exports of books (mainly to Ireland), it was held to restrict competition within the Common Market.

On appeal in Case C-360/92 P, the Court of Justice held that the CFI's judgment was vitiated by errors of law and inadequate reasoning (for example, as regards previous UK decisions concerning the benefits of the agreement in both the UK and Ireland) and its decision was annulled in respect of that part which rejected exemption under Article 85(3). (Developments in the publishing industry and the breakaway from the agreement by a large scale book retailer contributed to the collapse of the agreement in 1997.)

In Case C-309/99 *Wouters v Netherlands Bar*, the Court held that:

> ... a professional organisation such as the Bar of the Netherlands must be regarded as an association of undertakings within the meaning of Article 85 of the Treaty where it adopts a regulation [which] constitutes the expression of the intention of the delegates of a profession that they should act in a particular manner in carrying on the economic activity.

The case concerned the regulation's prohibition of multi-disciplinary partnerships between members of the Bar and accountants.

'UNDERTAKINGS'

Although not defined in the Treaty, it has been held by the Commission that the term 'undertaking' is not restricted to those business entities which possess legal personality (for example, limited companies) but any such entity which is engaged in commercial activity. Similarly, the Court has held that it covers any entity engaged in economic activity regardless of its legal status (for example, companies, partnerships, individuals and State owned corporations) and the way in which it is financed.

Such undertakings may be concerned with the supply of goods or the provision of services: see, for example, Case 155/73 *Sacchi* (television broadcasts), *UNITEL* (1978) (opera singers). In a number of cases, the Court has focused attention on the corporate group rather than the separate legal units which comprise it. A parent company and its subsidiaries are not considered as separate undertakings for the purpose of Article 81 (formerly 85) where the subsidiaries are not economically independent of the parent.

In practice, it is unlikely that an agreement between parent and subsidiary will be found to fall within Article 81(1) (formerly 85(1)); financial and/or directorial control by the former being readily assumed. For example, in Case 15/74 *Centrafarm*, the Court stated that:

> Article 85, however, is not concerned with agreements or concerted practices between undertakings belonging to the same concern and having the status of parent company and subsidiary, if the undertakings form an economic unit within which the subsidiary has no real freedom to determine its course of action on the market, and if the agreements or practices are concerned merely with the internal allocation of tasks as between the undertakings.

Case 22/71 *Béguelin Import Co v GL Import-Export*

B was appointed exclusive distributor for Belgium and France for WIN gas pocket lighters by Oshawa, the Japanese manufacturers.

B later transferred the exclusive concession for France to its wholly dependent subsidiary in that country. The French company concluded an agreement to that effect with Oshawa.

B and its subsidiary brought actions against a parallel importer of the lighters in the French courts in circumstances similar to those in the *Consten and Grundig* case.

In this Article 177 (now 234) preliminary ruling, the Court of Justice held, *inter alia*, that:

(a) The agreement between B and its French subsidiary could not affect competition between the parties but it could do so between one of the parties and third parties such as the defendants.

(b) The fact that one of the undertakings which are parties to an agreement is situated outside the Community does not prevent the application of Article 85 when the agreement is operative within the Common Market. (Oshawa had established an exclusive distribution network that, like Grundig's, operated to partition the Common Market along national lines.)

Case C-73/95P *Viho Europe v Commission*

Parker Pen had four subsidiaries in Belgium, France, Germany and the Netherlands which it fully owned. The subsidiaries' marketing and sales arrangements were controlled by a regional team appointed by Parker Pen. Thus, the Parker group formed a single economic unit in which the subsidiaries could not independently decide their own actions.

The subsidiaries followed a policy not to sell to customers established in the territory of another subsidiary. Viho complained against a Commission Decision which stated that the subsidiaries were covered by the single economic unit principle, arguing that the arrangement went beyond an allocation of tasks.

The CFI and the Court of Justice rejected this argument and held that despite the fact that they were separate legal entities, the unity of conduct prevailed over formal separation as long as the arrangement between subsidiaries and parent concerned an allocation of tasks within the group.

Further implications of (a) the 'integrated undertaking' or 'single economic unit' principle; and (b) the extra-territorial reach of Community competition law will be examined in due course.

'WHICH MAY AFFECT TRADE BETWEEN MEMBER STATES'

As noted earlier, these words determine the jurisdiction of the Community in that if an agreement, etc, has no such effect, EC rules will not apply – although national competition rules may do so.

Nevertheless, an agreement between two undertakings situated within the same Member State may be examined under Article 81 (formerly 85) in order to establish whether, within the context of a network of similar national agreements, they are capable *in aggregate* of affecting inter-Member State trade. Case 23/67 *Brasserie de Haecht* concerned a typical 'tied-house' or beer supply agreement between a Belgian cafe proprietor and Belgian brewery. In this Article 177 (now 234) reference, the Court's concern was whether such national agreements might (in aggregate) significantly foreclose outlets in Belgium to breweries situated in other Member States and so partition the Common Market. Clearly, in terms of our next section, it was not the 'object' of this particular agreement to restrict competition such as to effect trade between Member States, but the Court was anxious to establish the practical 'effect' of Belgian 'tied-house' agreements in general: see also Case C-234/89 *Delimitis v Henninger Brau*, in which the tenant/purchaser was, however, allowed to obtain supplies from other Member States. There is no decision that a brewery tie does infringe Article 81 (formerly 85) and the position was covered by block exemption Regulation 1984/83 on exclusive purchasing agreements until it was replaced by the new Block Exemption for Vertical Restraints 2790/99 (see below).

The question (amongst others) also arose in the following case.

Case C-393/92 *Municipality of Almelo v IJM*

The electricity system in the Netherlands was based on a network of contractual relationships between generators, between generators and regional distributors and on to end-users. The exclusive purchasing clause in issue before the national court was contained in the general conditions for supply by a regional distributor to local distributors.

By prohibiting local distributors from obtaining electricity from other suppliers, this clause was found to have a restrictive effect on competition. Whether it had an *appreciable effect on competition as required by Article 85 (see below on the de minimis rule),* it was necessary to assess it in its economic and legal context and to take into account any cumulative effect resulting from the existence of other exclusivity agreements.

The Court itself held that, as the conditions governing the relationship between the parties to the main proceedings followed the model General Terms and Conditions for the supply of electricity in the Netherlands:

> Those contractual relationships have the cumulative effect of compartmentalising the national market, in as much as they have the effect of prohibiting local distributors established in the Netherlands from obtaining supplies of electricity from distributors or producers in other Member States.

(See also the section on 'Collective Dominance' in the next chapter.)

Similar questions also arise in relation to horizontal agreements which extend throughout a Member State. In Case 8/72 *Cementhandelaren*, a price-fixing cement cartel sought to argue that their agreement could not affect trade between Member States because it was limited to the Netherlands and did not apply to imports or exports. The Court of Justice held that the agreement by its very nature had the effect of reinforcing the compartmentalisation of markets on a national basis and of impeding the establishment of a Common Market.

For an agreement, etc, to affect trade between Member States, a very wide test was laid down by the Court in Case 56/65 *Société Technique Minière v Maschinenbau Ulm*:

> ... it must be possible to foresee with a sufficient degree of probability on the basis of a set of objective factors of law or fact that it may have an influence, direct or indirect, actual or potential, on the pattern of trade between Member States, such as might prejudice the aim of a single market ....

This test operates in a similar way to the Court's *Dassonville* formula under Article 28 (formerly 30). It is not necessary that an agreement is seen to have affected inter-State trade, merely that it is possible that it might do so. In Joined Cases T-66 and 77/92 *Herlitz* and *Parker Pen v Commission* (and see the *Viho* case, above), an export ban in the exclusive distribution agreement between PP and its German subsidiary/distributor had never been applied. Stating that such clauses restrict competition 'by their very nature', the CFI held that the non-application issue was irrelevant and that, in the light of PP's share of the German and Community markets and the aggregate turnover of the firms, the export ban *could have* an appreciable effect on trade between the Member States.

The question of direct or indirect effect on the pattern of trade is also significant. To give an example: if an agreement ties up the distribution of a particular product within a defined territory wholly within one Member State, the agreement itself will not affect the inter-State trade of the parties. But, the indirect effect of the agreement may be to make it more difficult for a distributor in another Member State to sell its goods within the territory covered by the agreement. Thus, the agreement would indirectly affect trade between Member States as in *Brasserie de Haecht*, above.

The case law shows that this requirement is easily met and it is sufficient that the goods or services are traded, or likely to be traded, between Member States. As the *Consten and Grundig* case shows, it is irrelevant that the agreement produces an increase in trade since the prime aim of the Treaty is to create a system of undistorted competition. The Grundig agreement infringed Article 85 (now 81) mainly because it partitioned the market, its export bans being designed to prevent parallel imports and the competitive interpenetration of markets which the Treaty is designed to bring about. This question also arose in the *Société Technique Minière* case, which is discussed below, and is relevant to the present debate regarding the 'modernisation' of the Community's competition rules on vertical restraints.

Horizontal market-sharing agreements between otherwise competing producers (see Article 81(1)(c)), can readily be seen as serious infringements of Article 81 (formerly 85). In Cases 40/73, etc, *Suiker Unie (Sugar)*, the parties agreed to keep out of each other's territory. In Case 41/69, etc, *ACF Chemiefarma (Quinine)*, the parties also jointly fixed the prices at which they would sell their products in the various national markets of 'the Six'. Such perpetuation of national markets was held to deny consumers the benefits of competition: see also Article 85(1)(a).

'OBJECT OR EFFECT THE PREVENTION, RESTRICTION OR DISTORTION OF COMPETITION'

In Case 172/80 *Zückner (Bank Charges)*, which concerned uniform service charges imposed by banks with respect to transfers of money by cheque from one Member State to another, the Court of Justice made the following statement of principle:

> A basic principle of the EEC competition rules is that each trader must determine independently the policy which he intends to adopt on the common market and the conditions which he intends to offer to his customers. This does not prevent the traders adapting themselves intelligently to the existing or anticipated conduct of their competitors; it does, however, strictly preclude any direct or indirect contact between such traders the object or effect of which is to create conditions of competition which do not correspond to the normal conditions of the relevant market, in the light of the nature of the products or services offered, the size and number of the undertakings and the size of the market.

Horizontal price-fixing and market-sharing agreements of the cartel type clearly have the *object* of preventing, restricting or distorting competition. However, in many other situations, where the agreement is not *designed* to restrict competition within the Common Market, for example, *Brasserie de Haecht* above, an examination of its *effect* will often require a detailed analysis of the surrounding economic and legal circumstances. Virtually all the cases involved with such analysis are of the 'vertical' agreement variety.

Case 56/65 *Société Technique Minière v Maschinenbau Ulm*

A German manufacturer of heavy earth-moving equipment, MBU, granted exclusive distribution rights in France to STM. MBU agreed not to compete with STM in France and STM agreed not to sell competing machines. However, as no exports bans were imposed on STM (nor it would appear on other distributors of MBU's products), distributors were not given 'absolute territorial protection' and there were no impediments to parallel imports.

A dispute between the parties led STM to argue that the contract with MBU was invalid under Article 85. A reference was made to the Court of Justice.

The Commission claimed that the restriction accepted by MBU not to compete with STM necessarily brought the agreement within Article 85(1). The Court disagreed and held that exclusive distribution agreements did not in themselves ('of their very nature') restrict competition within the meaning of Article 85(1).

The conclusions reached by the Court distinguished this case from *Consten and Grundig* and (following the analysis by Bellamy and Child) yield the following propositions:

(a) In deciding whether Article 81(1) (formerly 85(1)) applies, it is first necessary to consider 'the object' of the agreement. The export bans in *Consten and Grundig* were 'of their nature' restrictive of competition irrespective of their actual effects. Thus, the object of the agreement in that case was to restrict competition and it was not necessary to examine the effects. The agreement in *Consten and Grundig* was therefore of a type (like horizontal price-fixing agreements) which clearly restrict competition without the need for further analysis. They may only be exempt, if at all, under Article 81(3) (formerly 85(3)). There were no export bans in the agreement between STM and MBU, which was not part of a large network and concerned companies of only modest importance. The agreement was therefore not necessarily restrictive of competition. Whether or not this was the case depended on the '*effects*' of the agreement, taking into account the economic context in which it operated.

(b) In judging the effect of an agreement, regard must be had to the competition which would occur in the absence of the agreement in question. The effect on competition must be appreciable: the introduction of a *de minimis* rule (see below).

Taking into account in particular (i) the market shares of the parties in the relevant market; (ii) whether the agreement stood alone or as part of a network; and (iii) whether the agreement precluded the possibility of parallel imports, the Court stated that 'it may be doubted whether there is an interference with competition if the said agreement [between MBU and STM] seems really necessary for the penetration of a new area by an undertaking'.

The conclusions reached by the Court in *STM* (for the benefit of the referring national court) are said by some commentators (but see Whish and Sufrin in 'References and Further Reading' at the end of the chapter) to be based on a US anti-trust '*rule of reason*', which carries disputed agreements outside the scope of Article 81(1) (formerly 85(1)) altogether. Such agreements contain 'ancillary' restrictions on competition (for example, MBU's acceptance that it would not compete with STM within its contract territory), but so long as they do not have the 'object' of restricting competition, their anti-competitive 'effect' will be weighed against any pro-competitive advantages (in *STM/MBU*, the need to penetrate a new territory through the medium of a national distributor in touch with the market in question). Where the latter outweigh the former, the restrictions will be seen as 'necessary' for the agreement, which is pro-competitive overall, to go ahead and the analysis adopted by the Court will mean that no breach of Article 81(1) (85(1)) has taken place. The agreement poses no real threat to competition or the functioning of a single market. (Compare the operation of a 'rule of reason' here to that in *Cassis de Dijon* in Chapter 12.)

This 'rule of reason' approach (not expressly acknowledged as such by the Community Courts – and see also *Metropole*, below) can arguably also be seen applied to 'necessary' or 'essential' ancillary restrictions in agreements in the following examples.

Case 26/76 *Metro (No 1)*: *selective* distribution systems do not infringe Article 81(1) (85(1)) where dealers are chosen on the basis of *objective* criteria of a qualitative nature (relating to such matters as specialist expertise, adequacy of premises, qualified staff and after-sales service) and the conditions for the application of such criteria are laid down uniformly for all potential resellers. Such 'restrictions' as those above (which generally exclude discount stores and the like) may be objectively justified on the basis of a business policy consideration such as the need to ensure the proper distribution of high quality and technically advanced products, for example, top range motor cars, electronic goods and luxury perfumes.

Case 258/78 *Nungesser*: a case involving the justification of restrictive but 'necessary' clauses in licences of plant breeders' rights in order to encourage the licensee to take the business risk of adopting a new and untried technology: see also Chapter 18.

Case 42/84 *Remia*: another case involving justification of a non-competition clause imposed on the seller of a business, 'necessary' for the protection of the goodwill taken over by the buyer. (The 10 year restriction was, however, excessive; compare with the English common law restraint of trade approach.)

Case 161/84 *Pronuptia*: a case involving the application of Article 85(1) to a franchise agreement. Such agreements have as their object the establishment of a special distribution system whereby the franchisor provides for the franchisee, in addition to goods (in this case wedding dresses and accessories), certain trade names, trade marks, merchandising material and services. The Court of Justice, in response to an Article 177 (now 234) reference, stated that:

> The compatibility of franchise agreements for the distribution of goods with Article 85(1) depends on the provisions contained therein and on their economic context.

> Provisions which are strictly necessary in order to ensure that the know-how and assistance provided by the franchisor do not benefit competitors do not constitute restrictions of competition for the purposes of Article 85(1).

> Provisions which establish the control strictly necessary for maintaining the identity and reputation of the network identified by the common name or symbol do not constitute restrictions of competition for the purposes of Article 85(1).

> Provisions which share markets between the franchisor and the franchisee or between franchisees constitute restrictions of competition for the purposes of Article 85(1).

> The fact that the franchisor makes price recommendations to the franchisee does not constitute a restriction of competition, so long as there is no concerted practice between the franchisor and the franchisees or between the franchisees themselves for the actual application of such prices.

> Franchise agreements for the distribution of goods which contain provisions sharing markets between the franchisor and the franchisees or between franchisees are capable of affecting trade between Member States.

Thus, the Court's (unacknowledged) 'rule of reason' approach, which clearly narrows the scope of Article 81(1) (formerly 85(1)) itself, only operates to take provisions of an agreement outside Article 81(1) where they are economically justifiable ('necessary') in terms of the agreement's purpose and where their restrictive effect poses no danger to the Common Market.

Provisions which do not meet these requirements may however still escape Article 81(1) by means of exemption under Article 81(3). There are, therefore, in effect two filters at work: one at Article 81(1), adopted where appropriate by the Court of Justice, another at Article 81(3) in the sole hands of the Commission, subject to possible review on appeal. This has not been helpful in terms of coherence in the application of Article 85 (now 81).

The Commission's favoured approach has been to give paragraph 1 a wide interpretation, which, as seen in *Société-Technique Minière*, can catch provisions which the Court has nevertheless ultimately excluded under the 'rule of reason'. On the Commission's 'wide' view, restrictions on competition are only allowed if the Commission (the Court of Justice, the CFI and national courts possess no such power) grants an individual or block exemption under paragraph 3. A national court which finds that an agreement falls *within* paragraph 1 only has *at present* the option of declaring the agreement void or adjourning its proceedings until the Commission reaches a decision taking paragraph 3 into account (but see also the later section in this chapter on 'Reform of the Law on Vertical Restraints' and the Commission's 1993 'Notice on Co-operation between National Courts and the Commission in Applying Articles 85 and 86', discussed in Chapter 17).

The structure of Article 81 clearly indicates an intention on the draftsman's part that the Commission alone should weigh the pro- and anti-competitive effects of an agreement – and weigh them under paragraph 3. Coherence and uniformity of interpretation would in this way be forthcoming. What the draftsman apparently did not envisage was the massive pressure on the Commission brought about in the 1960s by the receipt of many thousands of notified distribution agreements containing applications for individual exemption. The delay and uncertainty which resulted, and which has continued, could not be relieved by the national courts. Advocates of the 'rule of reason' therefore pointed to the effect it has on reducing the Commission's burden and proposed that national courts should have it at their disposal: that is, in a decentralisation of the system.

In practice, one of the most important developments, which went some way to solving these problems, was for the Commission, acting under delegated authority from the Council, increasingly to use its powers to issue block exemption Regulations: exemption of *categories* of agreements (see Article 81(3)). Business parties whose agreements fall within such a category (for example, exclusive distribution agreements, franchising agreements or research and development agreements) merely have to ensure that the terms of their agreement comply with the exemption rules to be found in the appropriate Regulation (see below).

In 2001, in Case T-112/99 *Metropole Television and Others v Commission*, the applicants based their annulment action under Article 230(4) against a Commission Decision on the 'rule of reason', so giving the CFI an opportunity to clarify the previous case law and also provide guidelines for national courts and tribunals when, as indicated, they will have jurisdiction over Article 81 as a whole:

> M and other French TV companies entered into a partnership agreement establishing 'Television par Satellite' (TPS) to provide a range of digital satellite programmes for payment. Their aim was to break into a market dominated by the rival Canal+ organisation.
>
> The agreement contained certain exclusivity clauses to which, it was argued, the application of a 'rule of reason' would carry them outside the scope of Article 81(1).

The Commission had instead found these clauses caught by Article 81(1), but had granted them individual exemption under Article 81(3).

The CFI ruled that:

(a) The existence of a 'rule of reason' in EC competition law was 'doubtful'. Earlier decisions could not be interpreted as establishing its existence, although some of them (*STM, Nungesser*, etc) had favoured a flexible approach to prohibition in Article 81(1). These cases showed that it was not necessary (in contrast to the Commission's usual approach) to hold that any agreement restricting the freedom of action of one or more of the parties was necessarily caught by the Article 81(1) prohibition.

(b) The approach taken by the Community Courts in the above cases entailed an analysis of the *economic and juridical context* of a practice, aimed at verifying the existence of anti-competitive effects when considering market structure and conduct as a whole.

(c) It was nevertheless the case that it was only within the precise framework of Article 81(3) that the pro- and anti-competitive effects of a restriction could be weighed. Article 81(3) would lose much of its effectiveness if such an examination had already been carried out under Article 81(1).

Thus, the first and third paragraphs of Article 81 must work in conjunction and in the manner outlined; each with its particular but related function. When considering the pro- and anti-competitive effects part of the exercise, the CFI made no reference to the 'rule of reason'.

A final point on the existence or otherwise of a 'rule of reason' takes us back to the *de minimis* rule mentioned in the *Société-Technique Minière* case analysis.

In Case 5/69 *Völk*, the Court established that an agreement falls outside Article 85 (now 81) if it is unlikely to have an appreciable effect on competition and inter-Member State trade, even if its object is plainly restrictive of competition. The exclusive distribution agreement in this case sought to establish absolute territorial protection for the Dutch distributor of a small-scale German washing machine manufacturer. On the basis that the manufacturer's share of the relevant market was less than 1 per cent, it was decided that the *de minimis* principle applied and no breach of Article 85(1) had occurred. In Case 19/77 *Miller International*, the Court held that a 5 per cent share in the product market did not come within the *de minimis* principle.

The Commission's Notice on Agreements of Minor Importance 1986 stated that an agreement would not fall within Article 85(1) if it covered no more than 5 per cent of the total market and the aggregate turnover of the participating undertakings did not exceed ECU 200 million (raised to ECU 300 million in 1994). The ECU is now the Euro.

The Notice has been amended several times since 1986, thresholds being raised each time. Under the current 2001 Notice, an agreement will not fall within Article 81(1):

(a) where the aggregate market share held by the parties to it does not exceed 10 per cent on markets where the parties are actual or potential competitors (normally 'horizontal' agreements);

(b) where the aggregate market share does not exceed 15 per cent where the parties are not competitors on the relevant markets (normally 'vertical' agreements). A network of agreements will reduce the threshold to 5 per cent;

(c) where it is difficult to classify the agreement, a 10 per cent threshold applies.

The Commission will not, as a general rule, open proceedings against undertakings covered by the Notice (which itself has no legal effect) unless the agreements contain hardcore restrictions on prices, output or markets, etc.

'WITHIN THE COMMON MARKET'

As seen, *Béguelin* and the *ICI (Dyestuffs)* cases (and others) show that a non-EC undertaking may be liable under Article 81 (formerly 85) where the effects of its agreements or participation in concerted practices are felt within the Common Market. Three of the companies fined for price-fixing in *Dyestuffs*, including at that time ICI, were situated outside the Community. The Court ruled on the basis of the 'integrated undertaking' principle that the fact that a parent (for example, ICI) had the ability to control the activities of its subsidiary within the Common Market was sufficient to justify the application of Article 85 against the parent: see also the *Commercial Solvents* case and others in the next chapter on Article 82 (formerly 86) and dominant positions.

In a more recent case, the 'integrated undertaking' principle did not apply and the Court had to consider the *effects doctrine* of jurisdiction under international law, that is, that jurisdiction under the Community's competition rules could be founded on proof of an appreciable effect on competition within the Common Market of activities outside the Community by non-EC undertakings.

> **Case C-89/85, etc, C-125–29/85 *Ahlström and Others v Commission (Wood Pulp)***
>
> Forty-three forestry undertakings in Finland, Sweden and Canada were held by the Commission to have infringed Article 85(1) with respect to agreements and concerted practices relating to prices of wood pulp supplied to the paper industry in the Community. Considerable fines were imposed.
>
> Although the Commission had based its decision on the 'effects doctrine', that is, jurisdiction existed because the producers' agreements and practices exerted effects within the Community, the Court, by stating that the determining factor was the place where an agreement, decision or concerted practice was *implemented*, avoided explicit adoption of the 'effects doctrine' in favour of a territorial nexus. The Court explained that:
>
>> The applicants have submitted that the [Commission's] decision is incompatible with public international law on the grounds that the application of the competition rules in this case was founded exclusively on the economic repercussions within the Common Market of conduct restricting competition which was adopted outside the Community.
>>
>> It should be observed that an infringement of Article 85, such as the conclusion of an agreement which has had the effect of restricting competition within the Common Market, consists of conduct made up of two elements: the formation of the agreement, decision or concerted practice and the implementation thereof. If the applicability of prohibitions laid down under competition law were made to depend on the place where the agreement, decision or concerted practice was formed, the result would obviously be to give undertakings an easy means of evading these prohibitions. The decisive factor is therefore the place where it is implemented.
>>
>> The producers in this case implemented their pricing agreement within the Common Market. It is immaterial in that respect whether or not they had recourse

> to subsidiaries, agents, sub-agents, or branches within the Community in order to
> make their contacts with purchasers within the Community.

Thus, although the Commission had held that the effects doctrine applied, the Court preferred to develop what may be called the implementation doctrine. As seen earlier, the Commission was found not to have provided sufficient proof of concerted practices, but the producers' periodic agreements to fix prices and to notify proposed changes in those prices was held to restrict competition within the terms of Article 85(1).

ARTICLE 81(2) (FORMERLY 85(2))

Agreements or decisions prohibited by Article 81(1) (formerly 85(1)) are 'automatically void' under Article 81(2) (formerly 85(2)). However, as established by the Court of Justice in Cases 56 and 58/64 *Consten and Grundig*, only the offending clauses in an agreement are void. The effect of the nullity of the prohibited parts on the rest of the agreement is a matter to be decided by reference to the law applicable to the agreement. Thus, under English law, the contract rules of severance will apply. It may be possible to cut out offending clauses (for example, export bans) and uphold the remainder of the agreement.

Thus, in Case 56/65 *Société Technique Minière v Maschinenbau Ulm* (see above), the Court of Justice held that:

> The automatic nullity in question applies to only those elements of the agreement
> which are subject to the prohibition or to the agreement as a whole if those elements
> do not appear severable from the agreement itself. Consequently all other contractual
> provisions which are not affected by the prohibition, since they do not involve the
> application of the Treaty, fall outside the Community law.

The question of the availability of damages arising out of a breach of Article 81 (or Article 82) will be examined later in Chapter 17, as will the matter of fines.

ARTICLE 81(3) (FORMERLY 85(3))

Even when the prohibition in Article 81(1) (formerly 85(1)) does apply, it is, as we have seen, nevertheless possible that an exemption from Article 81(1) may be obtained under Article 81(3) (formerly 85(3)).

Article 81(3) provides that the provisions of Article 81(1) may be declared inapplicable in the case of:

> ... any agreement or category of agreements between undertakings, any decision or
> category of decisions of associations of undertakings and any concerted practice or
> category of concerted practices which fulfils all the following four conditions:
>
> (a) it contributes to improving the production or distribution of goods or to
>   promoting technical or economic progress; and
>
> (b) allows consumers a fair share of the resulting benefit; and
>
> (c) it imposes on the parties only restrictions which are indispensable to the
>   attainment of these objectives; and

(d) does not afford such undertakings the possibility of eliminating competition in respect of a substantial part of the products in question.

In essence, therefore, exemption may be granted in cases where the anti-competitive effects of an agreement, etc are outweighed by its economic benefits. (In a few cases, other factors such as environmental protection and regional policy appear to have played a part in the Commission's reasoning.)

It is also clear that an agreement, although caught by Article 81(1), can be exempted from prohibition either by an individual Decision to that effect or on the basis of a block ('category') exemption. The Commission's powers regarding exemption are based on delegated authority from the Council under Article 83(b) with particular reference to effective supervision and good administration.

The law in this field has recently changed, or is in the process of changing, in two main ways: (a) through the introduction in 1999 of a new block exemption Regulation covering virtually all *vertical restraints* (replacing a number of separate 'category' Regulations); and (b) through the introduction of a new, decentralised approach to enforcement of the competition rules, which (when it comes into force) will abolish the Commission's exclusive power over Article 81(3). Nevertheless, it is necessary to examine the operation of Article 81(3) (formerly 85(3)) from the outset in order to appreciate the reasons for the changes and their possible effect.

Individual Exemption

The Commission did not begin to adopt block exemption Regulations until the mid-1960s; therefore, in the earlier days of the Community, undertakings wishing to secure exemption under Article 85(3) and so ensure that the operation of their agreements did not fall foul of Article 85(1) were wise to *notify* their agreements to the Commission, as required under Regulation 17 of 1962, on the individual basis. Later, and until the abolition of the Commission's sole power to grant exemptions, this remained the safest procedure to follow if it appeared that an agreement did not conform to the terms of a block exemption – although adjustment following an informal discussion with DG IV in Brussels might well have been the way to clarify the position.

The Commission's response to an application (often long delayed) was to grant or refuse it; its Decision being subject to review by the Court of Justice, and later the CFI. The Decision might be to grant *negative* clearance, meaning that Article 85(1) did not apply at all, or to grant exemption where the four conditions laid down in Article 85(3) were felt to be fulfilled – or where the *'de minimis'* principle applied to the agreement.

The Commission might grant exemption for a specified period only, other conditions might be attached, and the exemption could be renewed or revoked in the light of changed circumstances. It also had a duty to consider all the relevant features of an application and to have due regard for the applicant's rights within the administrative procedure laid down in Regulation 17: see Case 17/74 *Transocean Marine Paint v Commission* in Chapter 10.

At a time when delays in responding to notifications had reached two to three years, an under-resourced Commission was obliged to undertake full investigations of an agreement and the issue of a formal Decision only in 'priority cases'. Otherwise, perhaps after informal meetings, an administrative communication, known as a 'comfort letter', might be sent to the parties concerned. The letter stated that, in the Commission's opinion, the agreement either did not infringe Article 85(1) or was of the type to qualify for exemption. Unless material legal or factual circumstances changed, the parties had a legitimate expectation that the Commission would take no further action. Being a non-binding measure, a 'comfort letter' could not be challenged under what is now Article 230(4), for example, by a third party directly and individually concerned by the parties' agreement, although the case law on this point is not consistent: see, for example, Case 99/79 *Lancôme v Etos BV*.

The modernised and decentralised approach to enforcement of the competition rules, referred to above, which has removed the Commission's monopoly regarding exemption has, by abolishing the need for notification, also removed the comfort letter's *raison d'être*.

Regarding the Commission's policy under Article 85(3) before these changes came into effect, Bellamy and Child stated that:

> Although not always clearly stated, the Commission's policy is to encourage those agreements which it considers to be, on balance, pro-competitive. Broadly speaking, in respect of production, and the introduction of new technology, the Commission's policy is to permit agreements to co-operate in manufacture, or in joint research and development, that seem genuinely likely to lead to better use of resources, such as rationalisation of production, the achievement of economies of scale, or the faster, or more effective, development of new products, particularly where the firms concerned are likely to be better able to compete with third parties. Article 85(3) may also be used to assist the process of change in older industries, particularly through restructuring agreements to remove excess capacity. At the distribution level, in broad terms the Commission's policy is to permit certain restrictions in exclusive dealing, exclusive purchase or selective distribution agreements if they enable new markets to be developed, or if they ensure better regularity of supply, or a genuinely better service to the consumer, but only on condition that there is no absolute impediment to the free flow of the goods throughout the common market.

Horizontal agreements, which almost certainly would not be exempted under Article 85(3) included price-fixing agreements, agreements limiting production or controlling markets, and those seeking to protect a particular national market. Such agreements were unlikely to be notified in the first place. Also, as seen above and already discussed, export bans in vertical agreements, and other measures to inhibit parallel imports, were not granted individual exemptions (and see the 'black' list in Regulation 1983/83, below).

The following illustration of the Commission operating in the form of a cost/benefit analysis required in Article 85(3) (now 81(3)) applications for exemption is just one of the hundreds of Decisions issued by the Commission on the question. It deals with a *horizontal* co-operation agreement involving research and development, manufacture and sale between two manufacturers, and it is an example of an agreement meeting, as it must, all four (positive and negative) conditions for exemption (see above).

Vacuum Interrupters (No 1) (1977)

Two UK undertakings, AEI and Reyrolle Parsons, who were important competing manufacturers of heavy electrical equipment, including switchgears, entered into a joint venture. Previously, they had independently tried to develop vacuum interrupters as a commercially viable alternative form of circuit breaker in switchgears. (In the event of a fault, a circuit breaker cuts off the flow of electric current in a fraction of a second.) The research being difficult and expensive, AEI and RP agreed to pool resources to develop, manufacture and sell vacuum interrupters through Vacuum Interrupters Ltd (VIL), a jointly owned subsidiary.

The 10 year agreement stipulated that VIL would only manufacture vacuum interrupters and not the switchgear into which they would be installed; that AEI and RP would not compete with VIL, and would obtain all their requirements of vacuum interrupters from VIL except if a customer stipulated otherwise.

At the time of the Commission's Decision in 1977, VIL's products were first coming on to the market and VIL, the only EEC manufacturer of vacuum interrupters, faced strong competition from non-EEC manufacturers.

The Commission decided that Article 85(1) applied as, at the time of the joint venture agreement, AEI and RP were potential competitors in the vacuum interrupter field within the Common Market and the agreement brought the possibility of such competition to an end.

However, the Commission granted an exemption under Article 85(3). The sharing of risks and technical skills facilitated the development, manufacture and sale of an efficient product at a reasonable cost, quicker than otherwise possible, and to the benefit of consumers. VIL were able to sell their interrupters independently to switchgear manufacturers other than AEI and RP, and continued research would promote technical progress to allow VIL to compete with American and Japanese manufacturers.

The Commission was also satisfied that the agreement contained only 'indispensable' restrictions. It therefore accepted the provisions whereby the parties agreed not to compete with VIL and to buy their requirements from VIL unless the customer specified otherwise. [A change in circumstances led the Commission to issue a new Decision in *Vacuum Interrupters (No 2)* (1981).]

Block Exemption

The law based on Article 81(3) (formerly 85(3)) regarding the Commission's block exemption of certain forms of collaboration between undertakings is extensive and highly technical. Its basis lies within the field of welfare economics (see below) and in the question of exemptions, although economists' opinions vary, critics of the Commission have strongly attacked the Commission for applying Article 81(1) (formerly 85(1)) too broadly in the first place – as already referred to above – to catch agreements having no appreciable effect on competition.

The law regarding the block exemption of 'vertical restraints' was dramatically changed in 1999 and the law regarding block exemptions in other respects is at present in the process of changing.

The result is that the legal position is not only highly complex but also fluid. Although obviously of great importance – to undertakings and their advisers – it is beyond the scope of this book to present more than a broad survey of the origins and development of the law in this area. Specialist works on competition law, some of which are listed in the 'References and Further Reading' at the end of the chapter, should be consulted for full details.

As already mentioned, as a result of the administrative burdens placed on the Commission's limited resources in following the procedure laid down in Regulation

17 for granting individual exemptions, and the delay and resulting uncertainty for undertakings, the Commission (using the experience gained from the Court's case law and its own granting of individual exemptions in the early years) increasingly relied on its power to adopt block exemption Regulations from the mid-1960s. Undertakings were therefore in a position to examine whether their agreements had been drafted in compliance with the terms of an applicable exemption Regulation – perhaps after informal talks with the Commission's DG IV. An alternative would be an application for individual exemption. Agreements found to benefit from block exemptions were no longer required to be notified to the Commission. They were automatically valid and enforceable despite containing restrictive but 'indispensable' clauses. This meant that Article 85(1) (now 81(1)) was disapplied. Policing of the system could come about through Commission investigations or on receipt of complaints from third parties.

The main block exemptions in force in early 2000, *prior* to the coming into force of Regulation 2790/99 on Vertical Restraints on 1 June of that year, together with the definition of the agreements covered by each Regulation, are as follows.

Regulation 1983/83 Exclusive Distribution Agreements (expired 31 May 2000). Article 1: '... agreements to which only two undertakings are party and whereby one party agrees with the other to supply certain goods within the whole or a defined area of the common market only to that other.'

Regulation 1984/83 Exclusive Purchasing Agreements (expired 31 May 2000). Article 1: 'agreements to which only two undertakings are party and whereby one party, the reseller, agrees with the other, the supplier, to purchase certain goods specified in the agreement for resale only from the supplier.' The purchaser is not allocated a contract area as with exclusive distribution (see, for example, Case T-7/93 *Langnese-Iglo v Commission*). Special provision was made for 'brewery ties' (see Case 23/67 *Brasserie de Haecht (No 1)*, above).

Regulation 417/85 Specialisation Agreements (now Regulation 2658/2000). Article 1: '... agreements on specialisation whereby, for the duration of the agreement, undertakings accept reciprocal obligations: (a) not to manufacture certain products or to have them manufactured, but to leave it to other parties to manufacture the products or have them manufactured; or (b) to manufacture certain products or to have them manufactured only jointly'. See, for example, the Commission's Decision in *Bayer/Gist-Brocades* (1976).

Regulation 418/85 Research and Development Agreements (now Regulation 2659/2000). Article 1: '... agreements entered into between undertakings for the purpose of (a) joint research and development of products or processes and joint exploitation of the results of that research and development ...'. See *Vacuum Interrupters (No 1)* (1977) above.

Regulation 4078/88 Franchise Agreements (expired 31 May 2000). Article 3: '... "franchise" means a package of industrial or intellectual property rights relating to trade marks, trade names, shop signs, utility models, designs, copyrights, know-how or patents, to be exploited by the resale of goods or the provision of services to end users. A franchise agreement involves the grant by one undertaking to another of the right to exploit a franchise for the marketing of specified goods or services'. See, for example, Case 161/84 *Pronuptia*.

Regulation 240/96 Technology Transfer Agreements. Article 1: '... pure patent licensing or know-how licensing agreements and ... mixed patent and know-how licensing agreements, including those agreements containing ancillary provisions relating to intellectual property rights other than patents ...' See also Chapter 18.

In broad terms, a similar pattern followed throughout these Regulations which, in their preamble, stated the reasons why exemption could be granted on this basis in the co-operative activity in question. As seen, they laid down a definition of the category of agreements to which they applied, followed by restrictions of competition which were acceptable as essential to the achievement of economic advantages within the terms of Article 81(3) (formerly 85(3)). This was (or remains) the 'white list'. The 'black list' contained restrictions which were forbidden and took the agreement outside the Regulation, as being incompatible with the Common Market. A procedure in some Regulations providing for 'opposition' to 'grey' restrictions (those not clearly falling into the 'black' or 'white' categories) does not appear to have been of practical significance.

Block Exemption of Exclusive Distribution Agreements

In order to provide a degree of continuity through the changing law on Article 85(3) (now 81(3)) exemption, exclusive distribution agreements provide perhaps the best example. The route begins with the earliest case law of the Court of Justice on Article 85, examined above, moves to the specific block exemption Regulation, and ends with the Vertical Restraint Regulation which is examined next.

The Court's decision in *Consten and Grundig, Société Technique Minière* and *Béguelin* decisions over 30 years ago clearly showed that the export ban was the principal sign of an exclusive distribution agreement that would not be accepted:

> The Commission had become fully aware that it is the removal of export bans which enables the parallel movement of goods through unofficial channels of distribution, whose availability keeps downward pressure on price levels that otherwise ... might tend to rise [Goyder].

Exclusive distribution agreements made up the largest proportion of the huge number of agreements notified to the Commission and which required detailed examination. In so far as these agreements contained many pro-competitive features, and restrictions which fell within the letter and spirit of Article 85(3), it was felt that the way forward was to proceed by way of block exemption ('exemption by category').

The Commission first proceeded (on the basis of Council Regulation 19/65) by means of Regulation 67/67 for specified forms of exclusive distribution and exclusive purchasing. Many of the advantages of exclusive dealing were outlined in the preamble to Regulation 67/67:

> ... exclusive distribution agreements lead in general to an improvement in distribution because the undertaking is able to concentrate its sales activities, does not need to maintain numerous business relations with a larger number of dealers and is able, by dealing with only one dealer, to overcome more easily distribution difficulties in international trade resulting from linguistic, legal and other differences;

> ... exclusive distribution agreements facilitate the promotion of sales of a product and lead to intensive marketing and to continuity of supplies while at the same time rationalising distribution ... they stimulate competition between the products of

different manufacturers ... the appointment of an exclusive distributor who will take over sales promotion, customer services and carrying of stocks is often the most effective way, and sometimes indeed the only way, for the manufacturer to enter a market and compete with other manufacturers already present ... this is particularly so in the case of small and medium-sized undertakings ...

... as a rule, such exclusive distribution agreements also allow consumers a fair share of the resulting benefit as they gain directly from the improvement in distribution, and their economic and supply position is improved as they can obtain products manufactured in particular in other countries more quickly and more easily ...

Regulation 67/67 was replaced by Regulation 1983/83 as regards exclusive distribution but its basic pattern was retained. It is important to understand its provisions and the part it played in the evolution of DG IV's thinking with respect to these agreements. The Regulation became the standard model for such agreements within the Community.

The main provisions of Regulation 1983/83 were as follows:

(a) *The exemption applied to agreements to which only two undertakings – the supplier (S) and the distributor (D) – were party*: Article 1. Distribution networks did not offend this requirement but it did strike at horizontal arrangements or collusion either between suppliers or dealers.

(b) *The goods were to be for resale and not for use*: Article 1.

(c) *It was acceptable for S to agree to supply only D within the whole or a specified part of the Common Market*: Article 1. In addition, S could also agree that he himself would not sell the contract goods to users in D's territory: Article 2(1).

The Regulation did not permit S to accept any other restrictions which might affect competition.

The only acceptable restrictions on competition which might be imposed on D were contained in Article 2(2):

No restriction on competition shall be imposed on the exclusive distributor other than:

(a) the obligation not to manufacture or distribute goods which compete with the contract goods;

(b) the obligation to obtain the contract goods for resale only from the other party;

(c) the obligation to refrain, outside the contract territory and in relation to the contract goods, from seeking customers, from establishing any branch and from maintaining any distribution depot. [D was therefore only free to sell outside his territory as a passive recipient of orders.]

Article 2(3) listed further obligations that D might undertake which were acceptable, for example, not to manufacture or distribute competing goods, to advertise the goods, and to provide after sales services. D remained free to determine his prices and terms of resale and S could not impose restrictions upon D as to the persons to whom he might resell if, in the circumstances, such provisions were restrictive of competition.

Article 3(d) provided that Regulation 1983/83 would not apply where:

... one or both of the parties makes it difficult for intermediaries or users to obtain the contract goods from other dealers inside the common market or, in so far as no alternative source of supply is available there, from outside the common market, in particular where one or both of them:

1   exercises industrial property rights so as to prevent dealers or users from obtaining outside, or from selling in, the contract territory properly marked or otherwise properly marketed contract goods;

2   exercises other rights or takes other measures so as to prevent dealers or users from obtaining outside, or from selling in, the contract territory contract goods.

Clearly, those provisions were aimed at measures which the parties might have adopted to protect D against parallel imports, such as the improper use of trade mark rights (*Consten and Grundig*) and differential pricing according to the territory into which the goods were to be delivered (*Distillers* (1978) – low prices for 'home trade' which did not apply if the goods were to be exported).

As also seen above, another strategy designed by a supplier to protect national distributors from parallel imports was exposed in the Commission Decision in *Konica* (1988), in which Konica film was being parallel imported into Germany, where prices were high, from the UK, where prices were considerably lower. Following complaints from its German distributors, Konica bought up the cheap imported film itself. This action was condemned in terms of the elimination of intra-brand competition and the isolation of national markets.

REFORM OF THE LAW ON VERTICAL RESTRAINTS

For many years, the European business community, legal practitioners and competition lawyers have criticised what they have regarded as the Commission's over-zealous operation of Article 85 (now 81) as a *brake* on economic efficiency in pursuit of the cause of 'economic freedom'. Apart from the use of the *de minimis* principle, the argument runs, agreed restraints on competition, in the sense of curtailment of the business activity of other market participants, have too often been denied exemption under Article 85(3) (now 81(3)), although producing economic benefits outweighing less than appreciable restrictive effects.

The Commission, although recognising the problems this balancing act entails, as seen in the preamble to the Exclusive Distribution Agreements Block Exemption, has, however, not until recently managed to assuage its critics. They remained constant in their complaints – directed at what they saw as a legalistic, 'straitjacket' system of sectoral exemptions which not only led to legal uncertainty and huge expense for undertakings but which was at odds with current economic analysis on the economic *effects* of distribution systems, a form of highly regarded co-ordinated vertical integration through contract between producers and their resellers. The critics also argued that the Commission in large part ignored the impact of inter-brand competition and questions of structure and power in the markets in which such agreements operated – that is, the presence or otherwise of market concentration.

In 1995, Barry Hawk a leading specialist on competition policy, discussed these issues in a highly influential article in terms which should be familiar to readers of this chapter:

> The most fundamental, and the most trenchant, criticism is that the Commission too broadly applies Article 85(1) to agreements having little or no anticompetitive effects. This criticism rests on three pillars: 1) an inadequate economic analysis under Article 85(1); 2) an unpersuasive rationale for this overbroad application of 85(1), notably the 'economic freedom' notion; and 3) the Commission's historical and continuing

resistance to Court judgments evidencing a more nuanced economics-based interpretation of 85(1).

Inadequate economic analysis under 85(1)
The majority of Commission decisions fail adequately to consider whether the restraint at issue harms competition in the welfare sense of economics, ie, effect on price or output. Concomitantly, market power, which should be the threshold issue, frequently is hardly examined (let alone given a central role) or is simply found to exist in a conclusory fashion under the rubric of 'appreciability'.

...

The Commission's rationale under 85(1) is unpersuasive
The ... explanation for the inadequate economic analysis under 85(1) lies in the Commission's stubborn (in the face of Court judgments) adherence to the definition of a restriction on competition as a restriction on the 'economic freedom' of operators in the marketplace. The principal weaknesses of the Freiburg School notion of restriction on economic freedom are (1) its failure to generate precise operable legal rules, (ie its failure to provide an analytical framework); (2) its distance from and tension with (micro) economics which does provide an analytical framework; (3) its tendency to favour traders/competitors over consumers and consumer welfare (efficiency); and (4) its capture under Article 85(1) of totally innocuous contract provisions having no anti-competitive effects in an economic sense.

...

Commission refusal to follow Community Courts
The Court of Justice and the Court of First Instance have taken a more nuanced approach toward vertical arrangements under Article 85(1). The Courts have increasingly required an analysis of economic effects, particularly the possibility of foreclosure. This approach has been largely ignored or distinguished by the Commission, which adheres to its non-economics based application of Article 85(1), ie restriction on economic freedom.

A response came in 1997 with a Commission Green Paper on Vertical Restraints in EC Competition Policy, which promoted a lengthy consultation period with business and other interested parties at both Community and national level on a number of proposed options for meeting current concerns. Several important points emerged:

(a) The Commission accepted that it had not normally followed a policy of applying serious economic analysis to Article 85(1) (now 81(1)) – the first filter – leaving this to its examination of restraints under Article 85(3) (now 81(3)) – the second filter. As we have seen, this has been at variance with the 'rule of reason' approach taken by the Court of Justice and the CFI. These Courts have, as seen above, where necessary required an analysis of economic effects in order to decide whether or not to condemn an agreement under Article 85(1). This approach has focused on *market power* factors such as market share, concentration within the market, barriers to entry and product differentiation. Evidence of this approach has been seen, for example, in the exclusive distribution case, *Société Technique Minière* discussed above, in Case C-234/89 *Delimitis v Henninger Brau*, in which the Court held that exclusive purchasing agreements did not appreciably restrict competition within the terms of Article 85(1), unless in aggregate they foreclosed the market to competitors (see also *Brasserie de Haecht*, above), in Case T-7/93 *Langnese-Iglo v Commission*, where the

CFI took a similar approach. Market power at the production level was limited in these cases and barriers to entry were not excessive.

(b) The Commission agreed that market structure is a key factor and that the pressure of *inter-brand* competition (market self-regulation), as discussed with reference to the *US Sylvania* case (1977) and *Consten and Grundig* above, could take an agreement out of the ambit of Article 85(1)'s form of legal regulation. (Also, one should recall the pro-competitive and economic efficiency aspects of exclusive distribution agreements as found in the preambles to Regulations 67/67 and 1983/83.)

(c) The Commission nevertheless emphasised that the Internal Market could not be established and maintained in the face of vertical restraints which operated to partition that market by affording absolute territorial protection to distributors: see again *Consten and Grundig* and also Case 258/78 *Nungesser v Commission (Maize Seeds)* in Chapter 18.

The Commission's approach to the application of Article 85(1) with its history of a broad interpretation of what constitutes a restriction on competition, based on the vague 'economic freedom' approach, was generally regarded as the main flaw in the system. The Commission has in fact now agreed that analysis should concentrate on the *impact on the market* of a vertical agreement containing restrictive provisions, rather than the form of the agreement.

An additional problem, of an administrative nature, was also highlighted. The Commission's DG IV (now DG Competition) has only limited resources, as we have seen, and at the end of 1997, it had a backlog of 1,262 notified agreements to examine. At the same time, not only were many innocent agreements being caught by Article 85(1), but seriously anti-competitive agreements between parties with high market shares were falling within one of the block exemptions.

In September 1998, a Commission Communication, a 'Follow up to the Green Paper', put forward proposals for reform based on the following main points:

(a) The adoption of a wider *Single Block Exemption Regulation* which would cover exclusive distribution, exclusive purchasing, franchising and selective distribution; the latter not previously subject to block exemption. It would apply not only to finished goods, as under the existing system, but extend to intermediate goods (that is, those not yet in their finished state) and to services. Multi-party agreements as well as bilateral agreements would be covered. The new Regulation would operate on the basis of a market share threshold, below which agreements would have a 'safe harbour', and also on a 'black list' only approach.

(b) The Commission would issue guidelines on the policy to be applied to agreements above the threshold and to possible withdrawal of the block exemption.

(c) A modification of Regulation 17 would be undertaken to reduce the need for notification of agreements to the Commission.

(d) Further efforts would be made to increase the participation of national courts and competition authorities in the application of Article 85(1) above the market share thresholds and the withdrawal of exemption below the threshold.

The Commission's aims in moving to these changes were stated to be:

(a) To provide undertakings with greater legal certainty by removing the 'straitjacket' of the existing sectoral block exemptions.

(b) To reduce compliance costs to industry by removing the need to notify agreements in order to obtain exemption.

(c) To reduce the administrative burden on DG Competition prior to enlargement of the Union into Central and Eastern Europe.

A 'black list' only approach means that agreements are assessed only as regards what cannot be exempted, rather than what can be exempted by means of identified 'white list' clauses. This clearly makes it easier for undertakings to draft agreements which fit their practical business requirements. 'Black list' hard-core restrictions automatically disqualify an agreement from exemption.

Further consultations with the Member States and other interested parties were followed by the publication in May 1999 of a Commission White Paper on the Modernisation of the Rules Implementing Articles 85 and 86 of the EC Treaty. It became evident that a 30 per cent market share threshold criterion would be adopted as the restriction on the benefit of general exemption under the new Regulation.

However, more significantly, the White Paper contained a new Commission proposal to abolish the authorisation (notification and exemption) system that has been the sole preserve of the Commission since Regulation 17 was adopted in 1962. On the basis that the conditions for exemption have, over the past nearly 40 years, 'been largely clarified by case law and decision making practice and are known to undertakings', and that the centralised system of Regulation 17 has become 'cumbersome, inefficient and impose[s] excessive burdens on undertakings', the White Paper proposed, in paragraph 72 that:

> Adopting a directly applicable (that is, effective) exception system and *ex post* control could help to meet the challenges facing competition policy in the coming decades. Under such a system, any administrative authority or court endowed with the necessary powers could carry out a full assessment of restrictive practices referred to it, examining both their restrictive effects under Article 85(1) and any economic benefits under Article 85(3). Adopting a directly applicable exception system would thus mean removing the sole power conferred on the Commission by Article 9(1) of Regulation No 17 as regards the application of Article 85(3). This would facilitate decentralised application of the competition rules. A directly applicable exception system would also remove the bureaucratic constraint of notification for undertakings, since authorisation would no longer be required to make restrictive practices that meet the tests of Article 85(3) legally enforceable. Freed from the burden of having to process notifications, the Commission for its part could concentrate on taking action against the most serious infringements.

This means that national courts and competition authorities (such as the Director General of Fair Trading in the UK and the *Bundeskartellamt* in Germany) before which Article 81(1) was an issue would also be able to apply Article 81(3). Private parties would be in a position to *rely directly* on Article 81(3). Restraints prohibited by Article 81(1) which, however, met the conditions in Article 81(3) would be valid and enforceable from the point at which they were entered into without the need of a prior decision to that effect. In addition, restraints which met the conditions of Article 81(3) – so being valid from the time of agreement – would cease to be valid once those conditions were no longer fulfilled.

Ex post control of restrictive practices of which undertakings have made their own assessment of their compatibility with EC law would necessitate a strengthening and intensification of the Commission's powers to act effectively against undisclosed restrictions. Such control is based on complaints and own initiative investigations and inquiries.

Reaction to this proposal was, as usual, mixed. Bearing in mind the introduction of the new wide ranging Block Exemption which would cover the vast majority of vertical restraints, it was wondered whether the then *existing* Article 81(3) authorisation system would remain a burden either to undertakings or the Commission. If the proposal was adopted, Wesserling, while conceding that 'it would not seem impossible for national [competition] authorities to apply Article 81(3). They are administrative bodies accustomed to balancing interests and policy concerns', was less confident about national courts:

> Conversely, it is very difficult to foresee how national courts will apply the administrative discretion implied in the application of Article 81(3). Given that the ECJ considers itself incompetent to assess the complex economic facts involved [?], it follows that national courts are even less well placed to balance the various interests which arise in the context of a request for an exemption from the Community rules.

Only eight Member States had competent competition authorities in 2000, and there obviously exists the general question of a lack of uniform application of the Community rules even if anti-competitive conduct is vigorously pursued at national level. The White Paper did put forward a variety of safeguards, such as exchanges of information and files and the possibility of Commission intervention before national courts as an *amicus curiae*, that is, a friend of the court, as measures to regulate the relationship between the Commission, national competition authorities and national courts.

Implementing legislation later took the place of consultation and debate. Amendment of Council Regulation 19/65 enabled the Commission to adopt Commission Regulation 2790/99 on the Application of Article 81(3) of the Treaty to Categories of Vertical Agreements and Concerted Practices (the Vertical Restraints Block Exemption Regulation) along the lines of the 1998 Communication and the White Paper.

Block Exemption Regulation 2790/99 on Vertical Restraints

This 'new style', economics-directed block exemption Regulation giving effect to Article 81(3) applies to all vertical restraints (except motor vehicle distribution agreements, covered by their own separate new regulatory regime) and it replaces the previous sectoral block exemptions on exclusive distribution, exclusive purchasing and franchising.

Article 2(1) of the Regulation provides that (within prescribed criteria):

> ... Article 81(1) shall not apply to agreements or concerted practices entered into between two *or more* undertakings each of which operates, for the purposes of the agreement, at a different level of the production or distribution chain, and relating to the conditions under which the parties may purchase, sell, or resell certain goods *or services* ('vertical agreements') [emphasis added].

This exemption shall apply to the extent to which such agreements contain restrictions of competition falling within the scope of Article 81(1) ('vertical restraints').

It is claimed for the Regulation that it creates a 'safe harbour' for vertical agreements, particularly for small and medium-sized undertakings; that it removes the 'straight-jacket' effect of previous block exemptions (it contains no 'white list' of clauses); and that, on a basis of legal certainty, by facilitating co-ordination and reducing distribution costs, economic efficiency will be enhanced.

As regards the prescribed criteria referred to above, Article 3 of the Regulation shows that assessment of an agreement under Article 81(1) is to take account of the *market share* of an undertaking on the supply side or, where necessary, on the purchasing side. Generally, where the share of the relevant market (a concept examined in the following chapter) does *not* exceed 30 per cent, vertical agreements which do not contain severely anti-competitive 'black list' restraints (for example, the imposition on the buyer of fixed or minimum resale prices or export bans aimed to achieve absolute territorial protection for the buyer) fall within the Block Exemption. Restrictions indispensable for the attainment of the positive, efficiency enhancing effects in Article 81(3) are regarded as outweighing their anti-competitive effects in such cases.

Above the 30 per cent market share threshold, there is no presumption that Article 81(1) vertical agreements give rise to positive effects sufficient to outweigh their anti-competitive disadvantages.

Article 4 contains a list of hard-core black-listed clauses which take the *entire* agreement out of the benefit afforded by exemption and Article 5 contains a further list of terms which again have that effect unless they can be severed from the agreement.

The benefit of the Regulation may be withdrawn under Articles 6–8 where an agreement falling within the Regulation is nevertheless found to have effects incompatible with Article 81(3). This action may be taken either by the Commission or by the competent authorities of Member States where such effects are felt in their territory, which has the characteristics of a distinct geographical market.

The Commission issued 'Guidelines on Vertical Restraints' in May 2000 containing the rationale underlying the Regulation and an analysis of how it plans to enforce Article 81 for vertical agreements which do not qualify for exemption (see [2000] OJ C 291/1).

Two further points should be noted. New block exemptions on (horizontal) specialisation agreements (Regulation 2658/2000) and research and development agreements (Regulation 2659/2000) were adopted in late 2000, which take a similar approach to that in the Vertical Restraints Regulation. Guidelines on the applicability of Article 81 to horizontal cooperation agreements were also published (see [2001] OJ C 3/1).

Finally, further details regarding the progress of the Commission's 1999 White Paper on 'Modernisation of the Rules Implementing Articles 85 and 86 of the EC Treaty', which proposed the abolition of notification and the Commission's exclusive powers over Article 81(3) and the establishment of a decentralised system of enforcement involving national competition authorities and national courts, will be found in Chapter 17.

REFERENCES AND FURTHER READING

Antunes, L, 'Agreements and concerted practices under EEC competition law' (1991) 11 YEL 57.

Bellamy, C and Child, G, *European Community Law of Competition*, 2001.

Bishop, S and Ridyard, D, 'EC vertical restraints guidelines: effect-based or *per se* policy? [2002] ECLR 35.

Bright, C, 'EU competition policy: rules, objectives and deregulation' (1996) 16 OJLS 535.

Ehlermann, C-D, 'The contribution of EC competition policy to the Single Market' (1992) 29 CML Rev 257.

Forrester, I and Norall, C, 'The laicisation of Community law: self-help and the rule of reason' (1984) 21 CML Rev 11.

Hawk, B, 'System failure: vertical restraints and EC competition law' (1995) 32 CML Rev 973.

Jones, A and Sufrin, B, *EC Competition Law: Text, Cases and Materials*, 2001.

Korah, V, *Cases and Materials on EC Competition Law*, 2001.

Manzini, P, 'The European rule of reason – crossing the sea of doubt' (2002) ECLR 392.

Sharpston, E, 'When is an agreement anti-competitive?' (1991) Sol Jo 1186.

Van Gerven, G and Varona, EN, 'The *Wood Pulp* case and the future of concerted practices' (1994) 31 CML Rev 575.

Van Gerven, W, 'Twelve years of EEC competition law (1962–73) revisited' (1974) 11 CML Rev 38.

Walker-Smith, A, 'Collusion: its detection and investigation' (1991) 12 EL Rev 71.

Wesseling, R, 'The Commission White Paper on Modernisation of EC Anti-trust Law' (1999) ECLR 420.

Whish, R, *Competition Law*, 2001.

Whish, R, 'Regulation 2790/99, The Commission's "New Style" block exemption for vertical agreements' (2000) 37 CML Rev 887.

CHAPTER 16

COMPETITION LAW: ABUSE OF A DOMINANT POSITION – ARTICLE 82 (FORMERLY 86)

While Article 81 (formerly 85) primarily concerns anti-competitive horizontal and vertical agreements between undertakings, Article 82 (formerly 86), which is similarly based on Article 3(g) EC, is primarily aimed at an abusive use of market power by a single undertaking which dominates a market for goods or services. A market which is dominated by such an economically powerful undertaking is characterised by a high degree of concentration (see the Introduction to Chapter 15).

Such concentration of power clearly weakens the structure of competition in the market in question. The case law shows that the degree of concentration may, albeit rarely, amount to a pure monopolist's 100 per cent control: see, for example, Case 226/84 *British Leyland* (a State created monopoly indulging in excessive pricing of a service), but more usually it amounts to a lesser degree of dominance in the hands of a single undertaking, a corporate group (an integrated undertaking) or, in the light of recent developments, two or more independent undertakings operating on the market as a single entity in a position of joint or collective dominance.

Dominance is not in itself contrary to Article 82. The optimum size needed to be able to compete effectively in large, perhaps global, markets frequently means that undertakings must acquire massive financial and other resources. What is incompatible with the Common Market is an abuse of that dominant position. According to the Court of Justice in Case 85/76 *Hoffman-La Roche*, this involves conduct on the part of an undertaking which '... has the effect of hindering the maintenance of the degree of competition still existing on the market or the growth of that competition'.

The opening paragraph of Article 82 is therefore directed to ensuring that market conduct on the part of a dominant undertaking (or undertakings) – no matter how that dominance was achieved – does not impair the maintenance of effective competition in the Common Market. It should also be borne in mind that where an abuse is proved, heavy fines may be imposed by the Commission:

Article 82

Any abuse by one or more undertakings of a dominant position within the Common Market or in a substantial part of it shall be prohibited as incompatible with the Common Market in so far as it may affect trade between Member States. Such abuse may, in particular, consist in:

(a) directly or indirectly imposing unfair purchase or selling prices or unfair trading conditions;

(b) limiting production, markets or technical development to the prejudice of consumers;

(c) applying dissimilar conditions to equivalent transactions with other trading parties, thereby placing them at a competitive disadvantage;

(d) making the conclusion of contracts subject to acceptance by the other parties of supplementary obligations which, by their nature or according to commercial usage, have no connection with the subject of such contracts.

Article 82(a)–(d) indicates various types of abusive conduct and covers unfair behaviour (Article 82(a)), prejudicial behaviour (Article 82(b)), and discriminatory behaviour (Article 82(c)). Taking just two examples from the list, which itself is not exhaustive, an abuse of a dominant position can come about through the charging of discriminatory prices or through a refusal to supply an existing customer. The dominant firm is able to act in this way, to the detriment of customers, who may be driven out of the market (to the detriment of consumers), because there is insufficient competitive pressure on the firm to prevent it from using such tactics.

Article 82 therefore has the same broad aim as Article 81: the maintenance of effective competition within the Common Market. In deciding whether any particular action falls within Article 82, the three most important questions are:

(a) whether there exists a *dominant position* held by one or more undertakings in the Common Market or a substantial part of it;

(b) whether there has been an *abuse* of that dominant position;

(c) whether *trade between Member States* may thereby be affected.

DOMINANT POSITION AND RELEVANT MARKET

The Court of Justice defined a dominant position under Article 86 (now 82) in Case 27/76 *United Brands* as:

> ... a position of economic strength enjoyed by an undertaking which enables it to hinder the maintenance of effective competition on the relevant market by allowing it to behave to an appreciable extent independently of its competitors and customers and ultimately of consumers.

In *AKZO Chemie* (1986), the Commission stated that:

> The power to exclude effective competition is not ... in all cases coterminous with independence from competitive factors but may also involve the ability to eliminate or seriously weaken existing competitors or prevent potential competitors from entering the market.

In order for the Commission to establish dominance, it is clearly first necessary to determine what it is that is allegedly being dominated. The extract from the decision in *United Brands* shows that this is the '*relevant market*'. Secondly, it is necessary, by means of various criteria, to assess whether the *market strength* of the undertaking amounts to the dominant position required by Article 82.

Swann has explained that:

> ... it may be that a firm is deemed to be in a position of absolute dominance because it controls the whole supply of a particular product. But it may be that there are close substitutes to which consumers can turn if the price of the product in question is raised. In other words, to be absolutely dominant at any moment in time, a firm must have total control over all the products which are substantially interchangeable.

From this, it is apparent that at the heart of a definition of the relevant market lie questions relating to the *product* involved – and possible substitutes for it. Questions must also be answered as regards the *territorial scope* of the relevant market; interchangeable products may only be available in a specific geographical area. Article 82 speaks of a 'dominant position within the Common Market or in a substantial part of it'. Swann also indicates a *temporal* dimension concerning the durability of a dominant position. We will see that dominance must have a considerable degree of permanence. Dominance is thus a dynamic, not a static concept. An inquiry into the relevant market may show a real likelihood of actual or potential rivals eroding the dominant firm's position.

Dominance: the Relevant Product Market

In economic theory, the relevant product market is one in which products are substantially interchangeable as regards their end uses: see Swann, above. On the basis of this test of *demand* substitutability, it is necessary to determine which products are sufficiently similar in terms of function, price and other attributes to be regarded by *users* as reasonable substitutes for each other. Such products will determine the nature and size of the relevant product market, and it is implied that there can be effective competition between them. To take some examples: bananas and other fresh fruit; one brand of soap powder as opposed to another; tyres for heavy goods vehicles and tyres for motor cars.

The case law of the Court of Justice shows that in practice, identification of the relevant product market is often very difficult indeed. Tests of interchangeability may only provide the basis for the necessary analysis. Whish has explained that identification of the relevant product market, using tests of substitutability:

> ... should be simply the beginning of the inquiry: having identified it, it is then necessary to consider the extent of the competitive pressures upon the firms in that market. At this stage, it is perfectly possible that a firm faces competition both from within and from outside the relevant market.

And later:

> The mistake is to suppose that in the commercial world there is a whole series of independent, discrete relevant product markets which exert no influence on one another. In fact in business there exists a complex web of interlocking markets and sub-markets which may have an influence on one another in a more or less tangential way. Once that has been recognised, the danger of identifying the market too narrowly ceases to be a problem, because the identification of the market is seen to be only a staging post on the way to the really important question which is whether a firm is in a position to behave independently of its competitors [within the defined product market and from those other markets outside it].

Fortunately, in some cases, the problem of identifying the relevant product market presents no difficulty, for example, there may be no interchangeable goods or services. In Case 226/84 *British Leyland*, BL held a State created monopoly to issue national type approval certificates to dealers and individuals who wished to import left-hand drive BL cars. The Court stated that an abuse had occurred 'where [a company] has an administrative monopoly and charges for its services fees which are disproportionate to the economic value of the service provided'.

In *United Brands*, a case in which the US undertaking was found guilty of various breaches of Article 86 (now 82) (see below), full blown investigations of demand substitutability were carried out. The preliminary question was whether bananas made up the relevant product market (as claimed by the Commission), or whether it consisted of fresh fruit as a whole (as claimed by United Brands). Clearly, the narrower the relevant product market is defined on the basis of substitutability, the easier it is for the Commission to establish dominance. The Court of Justice agreed with the Commission that bananas formed a separate market, and a market on which United Brands was dominant. The analysis involved the use of the economic concept of cross-elasticity (of demand). Thus, for example, where a fall in the price of product A has little or no effect on the demand for product B, cross-elasticity is not significant and the products are not to be regarded as substitutes. If they were substitutable, consumers would have switched from using B to using A following its fall in price: limited interchangeability is not enough. The Court ruled as follows on this point:

> The applicant submits in support of its argument that bananas compete with other fresh fruit in the same shops, on the same shelves, at prices which can be compared, satisfying the same needs: consumption as a dessert or between meals ...

> The applicant concludes ... that bananas and other fresh fruit form only one market and that UBC's operations should have been examined in this context for the purpose of any application of Article 86 of the Treaty.

> The Commission maintains that there is a demand for bananas which is distinct from the demand for other fresh fruit especially as the banana is a very important part of the diet of certain sections of the community.

> The specific qualities of the banana influence customer preference and induce him not to readily accept other fruits as a substitute.

> The Commission draws the conclusion from the studies quoted by the applicant that the influence of the prices and availabilities of other types of fruit on the prices and availabilities of bananas on the relevant market is very ineffective and that these effects are too brief and too spasmodic for such other fruit to be regarded as forming part of the same market as bananas or as a substitute therefor.

> For the banana to be regarded as forming a market which is sufficiently differentiated from other fruit markets, it must be possible for it to be singled out by such special features distinguishing it from other fruits that it is only to a limited extent interchangeable with them and is only exposed to their competition in a way that is hardly perceptible ...

> Since the banana is a fruit which is always available in sufficient quantities the question whether it can be replaced by other fruits must be determined over the whole of the year for the purpose of ascertaining the degree of competition between it and other fresh fruit.

> The studies of the banana market on the Court's file show that on the latter market there is no significant long term cross-elasticity any more than – as has been mentioned – there is any seasonal substitutability in general between the banana and all the seasonal fruits, as this only exists between the banana and two fruits (peaches and table grapes) in one of the countries (West Germany) of the relevant geographic market.

> As far as concerns the two fruits available throughout the year (oranges and apples), the first are not interchangeable and, in the case of the second, there is only a relative degree of substitutability.

> This small degree of substitutability is accounted for by the specific features of the banana and all the factors which influence consumer choice.

> The banana has certain characteristics, appearance, taste, softness, seedlessness, easy handling, a constant level of production which enable it to satisfy the constant needs

of an important section of the population consisting of the very young, the old and the sick.

As far as prices are concerned, two FAO studies show that the banana is only affected by the prices – falling prices – of other fruits (and only of peaches and table grapes) during the summer months and mainly in July and then by an amount not exceeding 20% ...

It follows from all these considerations that a very large number of consumers having a constant need for bananas are not noticeably or even appreciably enticed away from the consumption of this product by the arrival of other fresh fruit on the market and that even the personal peak periods only affect it for a limited period of time and to a very limited extent from the point of view of substitutability.

Consequently, the banana market is a market which is sufficiently distinct from the other fresh fruit markets.

In Case 6/72 *Europemballage Corp and Continental Can*, the Commission's finding that the American company CC, through its subsidiary SLW, held a dominant position in the German market for light metal containers for meat products, light metal containers for fish products, and metal closures for glass containers was rejected by the Court of Justice. As regards demand substitutability, the Court was of the view that the Commission, when defining the market, should have considered whether purchasers of the cans for these purposes could readily have switched their production lines so as to be able to use different cans. The Court also considered the question of *production substitution* on the supply side:

... a dominant position on the market for light metal containers for meat and fish cannot be decisive, as long as it has not been proved that competitors from other sectors of the market for light metal containers are not in a position to enter this market, by a simple adaptation, with sufficient strength to create a serious counterweight.

The argument here is as follows: if the allegedly dominant firm raises its prices quite considerably, are other suppliers, not currently in the market as identified, in a position to move into that market with substitutes for the product in question? If so, such potential competition must be taken into account. A sufficiently high cross-elasticity of supply, where other manufacturers could begin to produce an interchangeable product without the need for considerable time and expense changing production lines, will draw these competitors into the market and weaken the position of the allegedly dominant firm.

In the following case, demand side substitutability was relevant in order to answer the question whether a business *purchaser* could readily switch from the product in question to another to satisfy his particular purpose. If not, that product made up the relevant product market.

Cases 6 and 7/73 *Istituto Chemicoterapico Italiano SpA* and *Commercial Solvents Corporation v Commission*

CSC (an American company) and its Italian subsidiary ICI cut off supplies to another Italian company, Zoja, of a chemical, aminobutanol, an effective and cheap raw material used in the production of ethambutol, a drug for treating tuberculosis. CSC, which had (allegedly) almost a worldwide monopoly in aminobutanol, was considering manufacturing ethambutol itself in Italy through ICI. Substitutable end products existed in the form of other drugs based on different but less effective raw materials.

The Commission having decided that CSC and ICI had abused a dominant position on the raw material (aminobutanol) market, the applicants (an integrated undertaking) argued that, amongst other things, the relevant product market was that of the end product, anti-tuberculosis drugs, a market in which there was effective competition and on which they were not dominant.

The Court rejected this argument as irrelevant where the complaint concerned the refusal to supply aminobutanol, the raw material.

The desired effect of CSC's refusal to supply Zoja was to eliminate one of the main manufacturers of ethambutol in the Common Market and a potential competitor of ICI. The Court was not prepared to accept that Zoja could readily adapt its production facilities to other raw materials for the manufacture of ethambutol. Only if other raw materials could be substituted without difficulty could they be regarded as acceptable substitutes.

This was not the case and the Court upheld the Commission's Decision that the relevant product market was aminobutanol and that CSC and ICI had abused their dominant position on that market. [The case is therefore illustrative of the need to protect competition at the manufacturing level, that is, on the supply side.] Apart from the fine imposed, CSC was ordered to resume supplies to Zoja.

The elusive search for the relevant product market is essentially one for applied economists. Questions of interchangeability and barriers to entry require research into the economic facts in each case. According to the eminent American economist George Stigler, writing in 1982, this search has not been particularly successful:

My lament is that this battle on market definition ... has received virtually no attention from us economists. Except for a casual flirtation with cross-elasticities of demand and supply, the determination of markets has remained an undeveloped area of economic research at either the theoretical or empirical level.

Nothing daunted, the Commission, which is not of course the final arbiter on the question, in a recent Notice, which is not legally binding, announced its intention to adopt the SSNIP test, first proposed by the US Department of Justice at the time of Stigler's comments. SSNIP stands for 'small but significant non-transitory [that is, lasting] increase in prices' and is a test for assessing demand-side substitution. In its Notice on the Definition of the Relevant Market for the Purpose of Community Competition Law of 1997, the Commission states that if a sufficient number of customers (of the allegedly dominant firm) were to switch to readily available substitutes or to suppliers located elsewhere in response to a hypothetical small (in the range of 5–10 per cent) price increase to such an extent that the increase would be unprofitable, due to the resulting loss of sales, the relevant market will include the substitutes and other areas.

Empirical evidence to support this approach can be obtained, according to the Commission, from what is called 'shock analysis', which involves the analysis of market disturbances which offer concrete examples of product substitution. Elsewhere in the Notice, the Commission downplays 'product characteristics and intended use [as being] insufficient to show whether two products are demand substitutes'.

What the effect of this change in approach will be is awaited with interest and it is hoped that it produces a higher degree of clarity on the question. For present purposes, it should be understood that relevant market analysis is important not just for Article 82 purposes but for Article 81 as well (for example, see the discussion of the Vertical Restraints Block Exemption Regulation).

The Geographic Market: Dominance 'Within the Common Market or a Substantial Part of It'

Sir Leon Brittan, a former head of DG IV has explained that:

> ... market power makes no sense whatsoever as a concept unless a market is first defined, both in product or service terms and in geographical terms. Geography here is not political, it is economic. For some products or services, there is a Community market; for others, there are still markets covering one or more Member States. There are even world markets for some products or services ...

Where necessary, therefore, the 'substantial part' requirement of Article 82 is not to be assessed on a simple geographic basis, but in terms of an area which is important enough in an economic sense (in product or service terms) to fulfil the requirement.

In Cases 40/73, etc, *Suiker Unie (Sugar)*, which involved market sharing, it was established that there was a significant volume of business in sugar in Belgium and Luxembourg, the area in which wrongful economic pressure had been brought to bear (by the undertaking RT) on Belgian dealers. On this point, the Court ruled as follows:

> The Commission takes the view that RT brought economic pressure to bear on the Belgian dealers Export and Hottlet, hereinafter called 'the dealers', with the object of compelling them only to resell the sugar supplied to them to specific customers or destinations and to impose these restrictions on their own customers ...
>
> II   *Examination of the Submission*
>
> RT's main submission is that the Belgo-Luxembourg market is not a substantial part of the Common Market, that it does not occupy a dominant position on this market and has not abused its position, so that the Commission infringed Article 86 of the Treaty when it applied this provision to its conduct.
>
> 1   *The question whether the Belgo-Luxembourg market is a substantial part of the Common Market*
>
> RT considers that, in view of the relatively small volume of Belgian production and the number of consumers in Belgium and Luxembourg this question must be answered in the negative.
>
> For the purpose of determining whether a specific territory is large enough to amount to a 'substantial part of the Common Market' within the meaning of Article 86 of the Treaty, the pattern and volume of the production and consumption of the said product as well as the habits and economic opportunities of vendors and purchasers must be considered.
>
> So far as sugar in particular is concerned, it is advisable to take into consideration in addition to the high freight rates in relation to the price of the product and the habits of the processing industries and consumers the fact that Community rules have consolidated most of the special features of the former national markets.
>
> From 1968/69 to 1971/72, Belgian production and total Community production increased respectively from 530,000 to 770,000 metric tons and from 6,800,000 to 8,100,000 metric tons ...

During these marketing years, Belgium consumption was approximately 350,000 metric tons whereas Community consumption increased from 5,900,000 to 6,500,000 metric tons ...

If the other criteria mentioned above are taken into account, these market shares are sufficiently large for the area covered by Belgium and Luxembourg to be considered, so far as sugar is concerned, as a substantial part of the Common Market in this product.

Some very small geographic markets (dominated by an undertaking which operates merely on a localised basis) are capable of being considered as 'a substantial part of the Common Market' due to their economic importance. This has been seen in the Commission's Decision in *Sealink/B and I* (1992), where the port of Holyhead and the ferry service to Ireland were considered to fulfil the requirement. The Commission emphasised that it was one of the main links between the UK and Ireland; indeed it was the most popular route for both passengers and vehicles. A similar Decision was reached regarding the Heathrow to Dublin air route in *British Midland v Aer Lingus* (1992).

In some instances, defining the geographic market may be an easy matter, as in the case of a national State monopoly (see, for example, *British Leyland* (above) or *British Telecom*, a Commission decision of 1983). Similarly, in *ICI (Soda Ash)* (1990), the Commission established that the UK was the relevant geographic market as follows:

For the purpose of assessing ICI's market power, the EEC can be divided into two broad zones or 'spheres of influence', one dominated by SOLVAY, the other by ICI.

Conditions in the United Kingdom are, for reasons set out earlier, both relatively homogeneous and separate from those prevailing in other EEC Member States. ICI is the sole national producer and neither SOLVAY nor the other West European producers market their product in its 'home' territory. ICI's important customers in the EEC are all located in the United Kingdom.

The second paragraph indicates that the geographic market of which the dominant firm is a part forms an area in which the conditions of competition applying to the product are the same or sufficiently similar for all participants. In Article 9(7) of Merger Regulation 4064/89, where the question of a 'distinct' market is addressed, it is stated that:

7   The geographical reference market shall consist of the area in which the undertakings concerned are involved in the supply and demand of products or services, in which the conditions of competition are sufficiently homogeneous and which can be distinguished from neighbouring areas because, in particular, conditions of competition are appreciably different in those areas. This assessment should take into account in particular the nature and characteristics of the products or services concerned, of the existence of entry barriers or of consumer preferences, of appreciable differences of the undertaking's market shares between the area concerned and neighbouring areas or of substantial price differences.

The main sales area of the dominant firm may be coterminous with the relevant geographic market as defined above and as in *ICI (Soda Ash)*, but within the total sales area there may be factors at play which distinguish certain sectors and mark them off as displaying different patterns of demand and supply.

In *United Brands*, the Court stated that the opportunities for competition under Article 86 (now 82) must be considered:

> ... with reference to a clearly defined geographic area in which [the product] is marketed and where the conditions are sufficiently homogeneous for the effect of the economic power of the undertaking concerned to be able to be evaluated.

United Brand's bananas were sold throughout the Community, via its European subsidiary, but the Commission excluded the UK, France and Italy from the geographic market because each of these countries applied a different preferential system for banana imports. The UK, for example, gave preferential treatment to bananas from the Commonwealth.

The Court agreed that in the remaining six Member States, taking into account differing transport costs and other charges, the conditions of competition were sufficiently similar for all traders. There were no factors of sufficient weight to disturb the unity of that geographic market.

A total of six Member States, in terms of the economic importance of the market situated there, would certainly amount to a 'substantial part' of the Common Market. The same would apply to any one of the larger Member States.

Dominance: the Temporal Dimension

Markets change over time, particularly in terms of technological innovation and refinement (for example, the markets for fountain pens, coal or computers), and market power must be sustained in the face of such possible changes over a considerable period of time for a position of dominance to be established under Article 82. It has been suggested that a period of less than three years would be too short a period for a high market share to be an indicator of dominance. See also the extract from the Court's decision in *Hoffman-La Roche*, below.

In general terms, a dominant firm in a stable market, which possesses massive technical and financial resources and a high market share, can feel reasonably secure in as much as its position cannot be undermined by those already in the market or, owing to entry barriers, those who might wish to do so.

Market Power and Dominance

In *United Brands*, the Commission (as later confirmed by the Court of Justice) stated that:

> Undertakings are in a dominant position when they have the power to behave independently without taking into account, to any substantial extent, their competitors, purchasers and suppliers. Such is the case where an undertaking's market share, either in itself or when combined with its know-how, access to raw materials, capital or other major advantage such as trade-mark ownership, enables it to determine the prices or to control the production or distribution of a significant part of the relevant goods. It is not necessary for the undertaking to have total dominance such as would deprive all other market participants of their commercial freedom, as long as it is strong enough in general terms to devise its own strategy as it wishes, even if there are differences in the extent to which it dominates individual submarkets.

Of the various factors which may indicate a position of dominance, a highly important one is the existence of a large market share. As the Court explained in Case 85/76 *Hoffman-La Roche*:

> An undertaking which has a very large market share and holds it for some time by means of the volume of production and the scale of the supply which it stands for – without those having much smaller market shares being able to meet rapidly the demand from those who would like to break away from the undertaking which has the largest market share – is by virtue of that share in a position of strength which makes it an unavoidable trading partner and which, already because of this secures for it, at the very least during relatively long periods, that freedom of action which is the special feature of a dominant position.

Market Share: Absolute and Relative Values

In *Hoffman-La Roche*, market shares over a three-year period of 75 per cent to 87 per cent in various vitamins markets were held to be 'so large that they are in themselves evidence of a dominant position'. However, in *United Brands*, a market share of between 40 per cent and 45 per cent did not 'permit the conclusion that UBC automatically controls the market. It must be determined having regard to the strength and number of the competitors'. UBC's best placed competitor, Castle and Cooke, had a 16 per cent share of the market, the other competitors coming far behind. Together with other factors, this was 'evidence of UBC's preponderant strength'.

Overall, the cases indicate that once market share reaches 30–35 per cent, dominance becomes an issue.

Financial and Technical Resources

Ownership of, or ready access to, massive financial resources will clearly greatly assist an undertaking in the pursuit or maintenance of market power. A firm's ability to establish and maintain a lead in product development or technical services may well be a contributory factor to a dominant position. This will be more likely in newer, high technology markets and will only be possible if the firm also possesses very considerable financial resources.

Financial power (relative to its competitors) can assist an undertaking in maintaining dominance through large scale advertising of its product, for example, United Brand's 'Chiquita' banana. Financial strength ('deep pockets') can allow an undertaking to remove a competitor, and so increase its dominance, by means of persistent price-cutting, which the smaller firm cannot match: see Case C-62/86 *AKZO Chemie*, below. Perhaps most important of all, such resources enable an undertaking to own or control its sources of supply and its distributive outlets. This strategy of backward and forward vertical integration is discussed next.

Scale of Activities: Vertical Integration

A significant feature of the *United Brands* case was that the US corporation controlled virtually all the various stages of its banana production and distribution. Its activities reached back to ownership of banana plantations and to specially designed refrigerated transport facilities used to move the perishable product both from the plantations and to the consumer via its distribution system. The scale of its capital investment at each stage of the production and distribution process enabled it to react more easily than its competitors to changes in demand, so giving it a strategic advantage and appreciable independence from its competitors, customers and consumers. United Brands possessed what are termed 'economies of scale' that were not available to other suppliers:

> The Commission bases its view that UBC has a dominant position on the relevant market on a series of factors which, when taken together, give UBC unchallengeable ascendency over all its competitors: its market share compared with that of its competitors, the diversity of its sources of supply, the homogeneous nature of its products, the organisation of its production and transport, its marketing system and publicity campaigns, the diversified nature of its operations and finally its vertical integration.
>
> ...
>
> In general, a dominant position derives from a combination of several factors which, taken separately, are not necessarily determinative.
>
> In order to find out whether UBC is an undertaking in a dominant position on the relevant market, it is necessary first of all to examine its structure and then the situation on the said market as far as competition is concerned.
>
> ...
>
> UBC is an undertaking vertically integrated to a high degree. This integration is evident at each of the stages from the plantation to the loading on wagons or lorries in the ports of delivery [in Europe] and after those stages, as far as ripening and sale prices are concerned, UBC even extends its control to ripener/distributors and wholesalers by setting up a complete network of agents.
>
> At the production stage, UBC owns large plantations in Central and South America.
>
> ...
>
> The effects of natural disasters which could jeopardise supplies are greatly reduced by the fact that the plantations are spread over a wide geographic area and by the selection of varieties not very susceptible to diseases.
>
> ...
>
> At the production stage, UBC therefore knows that it can comply with all the requests which it receives.
>
> At the stage of packaging and presentation on the premises, UBC has at its disposal factories, manpower, plant and material which enable it to handle the goods independently.
>
> The bananas are carried from the place of production to the port of shipment by its own means of transport including railways.
>
> At the carriage by sea stage, it has been acknowledged that UBC is the only undertaking of its kind which is capable of carrying two thirds of its exports by means of its own banana fleet.
>
> ...
>
> In the field of technical knowledge, and as a result of continual research, UBC keeps on improving the productivity and yield of its plantations by improving the draining system, making good soil deficiencies and combating effectively plant disease.

It has perfected new ripening methods in which its technicians instruct the distributor/ripeners of the Chiquita banana.

...

This general quality control of a homogeneous product makes the advertising of the brand name effective.

Since 1967, UBC has based its general policy in the relevant market on the quality of its Chiquita brand banana.

...

UBC has made this product distinctive by large scale repeated advertising and promotion campaigns which have induced the consumer to show a preference for it in spite of the difference between the price of labelled and unlabelled bananas (in the region of 30 to 40%) and also of Chiquita bananas and those which have been labelled with another brand name (in the region of 7 to 10%).

...

It has thus attained a privileged position by making Chiquita the premier banana brand name on the relevant market with the result that the distributor cannot afford not to offer it to the consumer.

Industrial Property Rights

The ownership of industrial property rights may contribute to establishing dominance. For example, the granting to an inventor of patent rights over an innovatory and highly efficient industrial process confers a *legal* 'monopoly' (under national law) upon the owner for a number of years. This may help the owner/undertaking to dominate the market through its ability to impede effective competition unless (or until) alternative patented processes and products can be developed by other participants in the market.

In its decision in *Tetra Pak II*, the CFI noted that Tetra Pak could protect its 90 per cent share in asceptic packaging through its patent rights.

Establishment of the brand name 'Chiquita' in the eyes of consumers was a factor in United Brand's position of dominance. (On industrial property rights, see Chapter 18.)

Barriers to Entry

The very fact that an undertaking with a dominant position is able to earn high monopoly profits is likely to attract new competition. However, the presence of barriers to entry into the market may hinder or prevent such competition from arising and so reduce or eliminate its threat to the dominant firm: see, for example, the legal State monopoly barrier in Case 41/83 *Italy v Commission (British Telecom)*, in a sector since privatised and therefore now open to competition if new entrants can achieve economies of scale.

Bellamy and Child have explained this factor as follows:

Many of the foregoing factors, whether technical resources, overall strength, economies of scale, intellectual property rights or other attributes possessed by the dominant firm may give rise to 'barriers to entry', a compendious phrase used to describe difficulties new undertakings face in entering the market. Barriers to entry may also arise for legal or financial reasons, or because of the structure of the market. The presence or absence of barriers to entry will be highly relevant to an assessment of dominance. Sometimes, the risks faced by new undertakings in attempting to enter the market to compete with established undertakings may of themselves indicate dominance.

The impact of barriers to entry in *United Brands* was similarly explained by the Court of Justice:

> UBC's economic strength has thus enabled it to adopt a flexible overall strategy directed against new competitors establishing themselves on the whole of the relevant market.
>
> The particular barriers to competitors entering the market are the exceptionally large capital investments required for the creation and running of banana plantations, the need to increase sources of supply in order to avoid the effects of fruit diseases and bad weather (hurricanes, floods), the introduction of an essential system of logistics which the distribution of a very perishable product makes necessary, economies of scale from which newcomers to the market cannot derive any immediate benefit and the actual cost of entry made up *inter alia* of all the general expenses incurred in penetrating the market such as the setting up of an adequate commercial network, the mounting of very large scale advertising campaigns, all those financial risks, the costs of which are irrecoverable if the attempt fails.
>
> Thus, although, as UBC has pointed out, it is true that competitors are able to use the same methods of production and distribution as the applicant, they come up against almost insuperable practical and financial obstacles.

ABUSE OF A DOMINANT POSITION

The illustrative list of abuses in Article 82(a)–(d) focuses attention on behaviour in its business relations by the dominant firm which *exploits* (takes advantage of for its own ends) other trading parties (buyers and sellers) and consumers. Such conduct may be unfair, prejudicial or discriminatory. Thus, a monopolist's market power may allow it to charge unfair high prices, conduct which for a firm operating under normal competitive conditions would spell disaster. Production may be limited so that, with demand exceeding supply, monopoly prices again prevail in the market to the prejudice of consumers. The practice of charging different prices in different parts of the Common Market for the same product means that the dominant firm is in a position to charge what the different national markets will bear, contrary to the integrative aims of the Treaty.

However, the case law of the Court of Justice shows that the scope of Article 82 is wider than exploitative abuse of market power. In *Continental Can*, the Court stated that Article 86 (now 82): '... is not only aimed at practices which may cause damage to consumers directly, but also at those which are detrimental to them through their impact on an effective competitive structure.' Thus, for example, where a dominant firm's below cost, predatory pricing policy (see *AKZO Chemie*) succeeds in driving the target firm out of a market, a competitor is eliminated and that market becomes more concentrated, probably to the detriment of the consumer (certainly as regards choice). It is true that such conduct could be called unfair or prejudicial but the dominant firm's primary objective is the elimination of a competitor. (Many abuses fall into both the exploitative and *anti-competitive* categories.)

The Court's classic, often quoted statement regarding abuse was made in Case 85/76 *Hoffman-La Roche*:

> The concept of abuse is an objective concept relating to the behaviour of an undertaking in a dominant position where, as a result of the very presence of the undertaking in question, the degree of competition is weakened and which, through recourse to methods different from those which condition normal competition in products and services on the basis of the transactions of commercial operators, has the effect of hindering the maintenance of the degree of competition still existing in the market or the growth of that competition.

Bellamy and Child have summed up the position by saying that:

> In general, the governing principle of Article 86 is that conduct by a dominant firm which seriously and unjustifiably distorts competition within a properly defined relevant market will be prohibited, in so far as it effects trade between Member States.

Illustrations

(1) Excessively High Selling Prices

There is not a great deal of case law in this area. In theory at least, monopoly profits will attract new entrants into the market, unless barriers to entry are insuperable. This would be the case with a statutory monopoly (for example, in electricity or gas supply), and even a private sector dominant firm in a high technology sector can justify, or purport to justify, the need to secure very high profits in order to finance research and development.

The following case concerns a statutory monopoly.

Case 26/75 *General Motors*

Under Belgian law, GM had an exclusive inspection service for imported second-hand Opel cars. The Commission decided that it had charged excessive prices for the legally required certificates of conformity.

The Court adopted a test of unfairness based on the relationship between the price and the 'economic value' of goods or services provided and held that GM's prices were excessive. (As GM had amended its charges and reimbursed excessive charges, the finding of an abuse was not sustained.) 'Economic value' is inferred by ascertaining the costs of the relevant goods or services or by examining the prices of comparable goods or services.

Cost/price analysis may present formidable problems and instead, in *United Brands*, the Commission operated mainly from the fact that United Brands' prices differed widely from one Member State to another. On the assumption that the prices charged in Ireland were sufficiently high to yield a profit (which UB denied), and considering that prices in other Member States were perhaps double the Irish price, the Commission reached the conclusion that such prices and profits were excessive. As the Commission had not examined UB's costs, a task which the Court thought did not present any insuperable problems, the Court decided that the unfair pricing charge had not been proved.

(2) Predatory Pricing

Heavy and persistent price cutting (even below cost) by a dominant firm aimed at a financially weaker, but not necessarily less efficient, rival with the aim of eliminating it from (or preventing it from entering) the market may well be contrary to Article 82 (formerly 86). Short term gains by consumers will probably become longer term losses when the dominant firm, having improved or consolidated its position, raises its prices again.

Case 62/86 *AKZO Chemie v Commission*

The Dutch firm AKZO held a dominant position within the Community in the market for benzole peroxide, used in the manufacture of plastics and for the blanching of flour. In order to prevent a British firm, Engineering and Chemical Supplies, a small-scale competitor of AKZO's in the flour additives market, from entering the market in organic peroxides for plastics, AKZO initiated a series of massive and prolonged price cuts aimed at ECS customers in the flour additives market. The prices offered by A were below average total costs but could be subsidised from profits in the plastics market. Following complaints to the Commission by ECS, AKZO was fined ECU 10 million. AKZO appealed under Article 173(2) (now 230(4)) against the Commission's Decision.

The Court of Justice reaffirmed its statement of principle made in *Hoffman-La Roche* regarding the concept of abuse, see above. In the Court's view, it therefore followed that Article 86 prohibited a dominant undertaking from eliminating a competitor and thereby reinforcing its position by having recourse to means other than those based upon competition on merit. In that context, not all competition based on price could be regarded as legitimate.

The only interest for a dominant undertaking in applying such prices was to eliminate competitors in order, subsequently, to raise its prices and thus profit by its monopoly situation, since every sale would result in its suffering a loss.

Such prices might remove from the market undertakings which might be just as efficient as the dominant undertaking but which, because of their lesser financial capacity, were unable to resist such competition against them.

The Court upheld the Commission's decision in large part, but reduced the fine to ECU 7,500,000.

The Court's formula in *AKZO* was applied by the Court of First Instance in Case T-83/91 *Tetra Pak II*, with regard to that firm's pricing policies in Italy and the UK.

In an interesting development, the question raised was whether the bringing of legal proceedings by a dominant firm (here against an undertaking operating in a related market) could be regarded as an infringement of Article 86 (now 82). In Case T-111/96 ITT *Promedia v Commission*, the CFI was of the view that in exceptional circumstances, the bringing of proceedings by a dominant firm could amount to an abuse. For this to be so, it would appear that the dominant firm's action must be predatory. On that basis, the action must be such that, on the evidence: (a) it could not reasonably be considered as a genuine attempt by the dominant firm to establish its rights and could therefore only serve to harass the other party; and (b) it was conceived and planned with the aim of eliminating competition. The circumstances must be exceptional because a finding of abuse (which was not made in this case) constituted 'an exception to the principle of access to the courts' which 'must be construed and applied strictly, in a manner which does not defeat the application of this general rule'.

(3) Discriminatory Prices

In *United Brands*, the Court held that UBC, selling one product, unloaded at one place (Rotterdam or Bremerhaven), should charge one quayside price for all customers, the ripener-distributors, whatever the ultimate destination of the bananas. Selling the bananas at the European port of unloading to customers from the various Member States at widely differing prices fell within Article 86(c) (now 82(c)): the application of dissimilar prices to equivalent transactions with other trading parties, thereby placing those charged higher prices at a competitive disadvantage.

It was certainly true, as UBC pointed out, that retail prices for ripened bananas did vary considerably from one Member State to another for a variety of reasons (for example, transportation charges and wage rates). However, the Court held that UBC was not entitled to take account of market pressures at the retail level as it did not operate directly at that level. UBC's aim was to obtain maximum profits by fixing its prices at the highest level that each of the national markets would bear. The national markets were isolated, preventing their ripener-distributors from any Member State who did have a price advantage via à vis their counterparts in other Member States from exerting competitive interpenetration of the latters' markets. This was achieved by means of, amongst other things, a *restriction on distribution* imposed by UBC under what was known as the 'green banana' clause in UBC's conditions of sale. Under this clause, ripener-distributors, who all required suitable storage facilities, were not allowed to resell bananas while they were still green. Cross-border trade was therefore generally unpracticable:

> ... by reason of its dominant position, UBC, fed with information by its local representatives, was in fact able to impose its selling price on the intermediate purchaser ... These discriminatory prices, which varied according to the circumstances of the Member States, were just so many obstacles to the free movement of goods and their effect was intensified by the clause forbidding the resale of bananas while still green and by reducing the deliveries of the quantities ordered. A rigid partitioning of national markets was thus created at price levels which were artificially different, placing certain distributor/ripeners at a competitive disadvantage, since compared with what it should have been competition had thereby been distorted.

(4) Exclusive Rights of Supply: Abusive Discounts

Discounts granted by a dominant supplier to a dealer in its products must be objectively justifiable, for example where bulk buying by the dealer enables the supplier to reduce costs. On the other hand, Article 82 catches 'loyalty' or 'fidelity' discounts granted by a dominant supplier on condition that the dealer enters into an obligation to purchase *all or a very high percentage* of its requirements from the dominant firm. Such discounts are regarded as both anti-competitive (they create a barrier to entry to potential suppliers) and discriminatory as between different customers.

In Case 85/76 *Hoffman-La Roche*, the Commission based its finding of abuse against HLR, the largest pharmaceutical company in the world, with a dominant position in seven separate vitamins markets, on the following grounds:

(a) The fact that customers were bound by an exclusive or preferential purchasing commitment in favour of Roche for all or for a very large proportion of their requirements either as a result of an express obligation of exclusivity, or fidelity rebates, or other means.

(b) The fact that the price advantages granted were based not on the differences in costs borne by Roche in relation to the quantities supplied, but on the supply of all or a very large proportion of a customer's requirements.

(c) The fact that in certain cases the rebate was based on all purchases, so that purchases of vitamins of one group were aggregated with purchases of vitamins of other groups ('across-the-board' rebates).

(d) The fact that the agreements generally contained a provision known as the 'English clause', the significance of which is as follows: purchasers were obliged to inform Roche of offers from other manufacturers more favourable than those of Roche; should Roche not match such offers, purchasers were free to purchase from such manufacturers without losing the rebate in respect of purchases made from Roche. In some agreements, Roche stipulated that the offers should emanate from 'reputable' manufacturers (thereby excluding dealers and brokers). Such a clause clearly enabled Roche to gain valuable information on competitors' prices.

(5) Refusal to Supply

A dominant firm's refusal to supply goods or services in the ordinary course of business, or a refusal to supply except on very unreasonable terms, may constitute a breach of Article 82: see particularly Article 82(b) and (c). A refusal must be capable of objective justification (for example, *force majeure*: see Case 77/77 *BP v Commission*), otherwise it will be regarded as unfair, anti-competitive and exclusionary in so far as a trading partner is denied its source of supply or at least its best source of supply.

In Cases 6 and 7/73 *Commercial Solvents* (discussed above with reference to the relevant product market), the refusal to supply the raw material was motivated by the wish to replace the customer, Zoja, in the market for the end product. The Court of Justice stated that:

When Zoja sought to obtain further supplies of aminobutanol, it received a negative reply. CSC had decided to limit, if not completely to cease, the supply of nitropropane and aminobutanol to certain parties in order to facilitate its own access to the market for the derivatives.

However, an undertaking being in a dominant position as regards the production of raw material and therefore able to control the supply to manufacturers of derivatives, cannot, just because it decides to start manufacturing these derivatives (in competition with its former customers) act in such a way as to eliminate their competition which, in the case in question, would amount to eliminating one of the principal manufacturers of ethambutol in the Common Market. Since such conduct is contrary to the objectives expressed in Article 3(f) of the Treaty and set out in greater detail in Articles 85 and 86, it follows that an undertaking which has a dominant position in the market in raw materials and which, with the object of reserving such raw material for manufacturing its own derivatives, refuses to supply a customer, which is itself a manufacturer of those derivatives, and therefore risks eliminating all competition on the part of this customer, is abusing its dominant position within the meaning of Article 86. In this context it does not matter that the undertaking ceased to supply in the spring of 1970 because of the cancellation of the purchases by Zoja, because it appears from the applicants' own statement that, when the supplies provided for in the contract had been completed, the sale of aminobutanol would have stopped in any case [that is, there was no objective justification for the refusal].

In Case 27/76 *United Brands*, the dominant supplier of bananas to most of the Member States was, as we have seen, guilty of several abuses, one of which was its decision to discontinue supplies of green bananas to Olesen, a Danish ripener-distributor. The Court stated that:

It is advisable to assert positively from the outset that an undertaking in a dominant position for the purpose of marketing a product – which cashes in on the reputation of a brand name known to and valued by the consumers – cannot stop supplying a long standing customer who abides by regular commercial practice, if the orders placed by that customer are in no way out of the ordinary.

Such conduct is inconsistent with the objectives laid down in Article 3(f) of the Treaty, which are set out in detail in Article 86, especially in paragraphs (b) and (c), since the refusal to sell would limit markets to the prejudice of consumers and would amount to discrimination which might in the end eliminate a trading party from the relevant market.

It is therefore necessary to ascertain whether the discontinuance of supplies by UBC in October 1973 was justified.

The reason given is in the applicant's letter of 11 October 1973 in which it upbraided Olesen in no uncertain manner for having participated in an advertising campaign for one of its competitors.

Later on, UBC added to this reason a number of complaints, for example, that Olesen was the exclusive representative of its main competitor on the Danish market.

This was not a new situation since it goes back to 1969 and was not in any case inconsistent with fair trade practices.

Finally, UBC has not put forward any relevant argument to justify the refusal of supplies.

Although it is true, as the applicant points out, that the fact that an undertaking is in a dominant position cannot disentitle it from protecting its own commercial interests if they are attacked, and that such an undertaking must be conceded the right to take such reasonable steps as it deems appropriate to protect its said interests, such behaviour cannot be countenanced if its actual purpose is to strengthen this dominant position and abuse it.

Even if the possibility of a counter-attack is acceptable, that attack must still be proportionate to the threat taking into account the economic strength of the undertakings confronting each other.

The sanction consisting of a refusal to supply by an undertaking in a dominant position was in excess of what might, if such a situation were to arise, reasonably be contemplated as a sanction for conduct similar to that for which UBC blamed Olesen.

In fact, UBC could not be unaware of the fact that by acting in this way it would discourage its other ripener/distributors from supporting the advertising of other brand names and that the deterrent effect of the sanction imposed upon one of them would make its position of strength on the relevant market that much more effective.

> Such a course of conduct amounts therefore to a serious interference with the independence of small and medium-sized firms in their commercial relations with the undertaking in a dominant position and this independence implies the right to give preference to competitors' goods.
>
> In this case, the adoption of such a course of conduct is designed to have a serious adverse effect on competition on the relevant banana market by only allowing firms dependent upon the dominant undertaking to stay in business.

Important features of this extract from the Court's decision include UBC's aim to *strengthen* its dominant position and the Court's use of the principle of proportionality.

A further, interesting refusal to supply case is *British Brass Band Instruments v Boosey and Hawkes* (1998), a Commission Decision regarding a discontinuance by B and H of supplies to BBBI to prevent its emergence as a competitor in the relevant product market (instruments for British style brass bands) in which B and H possessed a 90 per cent market share. BBBI obtained an interim order requiring B and H to resume supplies.

It is also worth noting at this point the Commission's Decision in *Napier Brown v British Sugar* (1990). The value of this case is that key aspects of Article 82 (formerly 86) are present and readily explicable: relevant product and geographic market, indicators of dominance, dominance on the raw material and derived product markets, and a range of abuses including refusal to supply (*Commercial Solvents* applied), loyalty rebates (*Hoffman-La Roche* applied) and elimination of competition on an ancillary market (*Télémarketing*, below, applied).

(6) Refusal to Supply and 'Essential Facilities'

In Case 311/84 *CBEM-Télémarketing v CLT*, a case in which a dominant firm had extended its monopoly from one market to a related market, the Court of Justice condemned the refusal by CLT, a Luxembourg television station dominant on the market in television advertising aimed at viewers in French-speaking Belgium, to sell television time to CBEM-Télémarketing, a Belgian telephone marketing company. CLT would only accept advertisements for telemarketing on the condition that its subsidiary IPB got the contract to answer calls from viewers.

Referring to its decision in *Commercial Solvents*, the Court gave a negative response to an Article 177 (now 234) question from a Brussels court asking whether an undertaking such as CLT had the right to reserve for itself, or for a subsidiary under its control – to the *exclusion* of any other undertaking – an auxiliary activity, the provision of TV telephone marketing services, which otherwise could be carried out by a third undertaking such as CBEM-TM. Stressing that telemarketing was a 'neighbouring but separate' market from that of the chosen advertising medium, the Court stated that:

> An abuse ... is committed where without any objective necessity [concerning such matters as the relationship between the parties and the market structure] an undertaking holding a dominant position on a particular market reserves to itself or to an undertaking belonging to the same group an auxiliary activity which might be carried out by another undertaking as part of its activities on a neighbouring but separate market, with the possibility of eliminating all competition from such undertaking.

Commercial Solvents, Télémarketing and other cases show that undertakings which have a dominant position in one market may not use their power in that particular market to hinder or eliminate competition in a related market.

Télémarketing is one of the Article 86 (now 82) cases which signalled a new approach by the Commission to a refusal to supply goods or services. It has sought to develop what has been described as an *'essential facilities'* theory. Whish has explained that this is the 'idea that the owner of a facility which is not replicable by the ordinary process of innovation and investment, and without access to which competition on a market is impossible or seriously impeded, has to share it with a rival'.

In *Sealink/B and I* (1992), a Commission Decision, Sealink owned and controlled the port of Holyhead, the UK terminal for the main UK–Dublin sea route, and organised the sailing schedules in a way which greatly favoured its own ferry operations. Following complaints, the Commission decided that it was an abuse of a dominant position for the owner of an *essential facility* (a concept not overtly recognised by the Community Courts) to use its power on one market to strengthen its position on another, related market, and that such strengthening would take place if it granted its competitors access to the related market on terms which were less favourable than those for its own services without any objective justification. The Commission put in place interim measures requiring the competing operators to be given access to the schedules on the same terms as Sealink.

Similar reasoning was used by the Commission, the CFI and the Court of Justice in the following case.

Joined Cases C-241 and 242/91 *Radio Telefis Eireann and Independent Television Publications Ltd v Commission (Magill TV Guide)*

The Irish magazine publisher, Magill, attempted to put on the Irish and Northern Ireland market a new weekly advance TV listing guide covering RTE, ITV and BBC programmes. At the time, no comprehensive weekly guide existed although each TV authority, which owned the copyright in the advance listings of its programmes, published its own weekly guide. Interim injunctions were obtained preventing publication of the Magill guide in breach of the authorities' copyrights. Magill complained to the Commission.

The Commission found that there had been a breach of Article 86 and ordered the three authorities to put an end to the breach. On appeal (in Cases T-69, 70 and 76/89 *RTE, BBC and ITP v Commission*), the CFI upheld the Commission's finding that the exercise of copyright in this matter exceeded the scope of the specific subject matter of that right (the ensuring of reward for creative effort and the right to oppose infringements). The companies had used their copyright to secure a monopoly in the derivative market of weekly TV guides and they had abused their dominant position by excluding competition from that market. The authorities were to supply the listings information under licence, for which Magill was to pay reasonable royalties. RTE and ITP appealed to the Court of Justice.

The Court ruled that:

(a) RTE, ITP and the BBC held a *de facto* monopoly over the information necessary to compile the listings for the TV programmes received in Ireland and Northern Ireland. They were therefore in a position to prevent effective competition on the market in weekly TV programmes.

(b) The exercise of an exclusive right by the proprietor could, in exceptional circumstances, involve abusive conduct under Article 86.

(c) The appellants' refusal to provide the listings information by relying on their national copyrights prevented the entry on the secondary market of a new product, which the appellants did not offer and for which there was consumer demand.

(d) This refusal constituted abuse of a dominant position under Article 86, that is, 'limiting production, markets or technical development to the prejudice of consumers'.

The appeals were to be dismissed.

This case is an extreme example of the tension that can exist between national intellectual (or industrial) property rights such as patents, copyright and trade marks and Community competition (and free movement of goods) rules. National IPRs protect the holders and afford a measure of protection from competition so encouraging research, investment and creativity (vital for a thriving economy). However, the holder's use of its rights can fall foul of the fundamental economic law principles of effective competition and the free movement of goods within the Internal Market (see Chapter 18).

The television authorities held a monopoly position on one market and their refusal to grant licences for the information which was subject to their rights barred the entry to a related market of a competitor and a product for which there was strong consumer demand. The compulsory licensing of the information created more competitive conditions on the weekly television guide market in the Member States in question.

The recent case of *Bronner v Mediaprint* has been seen by some commentators as a tightening up of the essential facilities concept. As Bergman has pointed out, 'too wide an application of the concept would jeopardise a firm's incentive to invest. If a firm cannot exclusively benefit from its own assets, there is a substantial risk that there will be too little investment, to the detriment of efficiency and the economy as a whole'.

The particular circumstances of *Bronner* do not fit what Bergman sees as the typical case for the application of the doctrine, which is 'when the exclusive control of critical assets is the result of a (previous) legal monopoly, geographical particularities or other circumstances that cannot be seen as any merit of the [dominant] firm itself'.

Case C-7/97 *Bronner GmbH v Mediaprint*

B published an Austrian daily newspaper with a national circulation of 3.6 per cent of the market. M published two rival papers which together had a market share of 46.8 per cent. M had also developed a unique nationwide home delivery service for the early morning distribution for newspapers from which B was excluded.

B argued (a) that the distribution system should be regarded as an essential facility as the company lacked the economic means to establish a competing system; and (b) that M's refusal to distribute B's paper was an abuse of a dominant position.

A reference was made to the Court of Justice which ruled:

(a) that it was for the national court to determine whether such a home delivery service constituted a distinct market for the distribution of newspapers (separate from distribution through shops or kiosks);

(b) that, if so, it was clear that M had a dominant position on that market, which constituted a substantial part of the Common Market; but

(c) that it was not indispensable (that is, essential) to B's operations and ability to
     compete on the newspaper market to have access to M's home-delivery service.

The Court stated that it did not follow that 'access to the existing system is ...
indispensable even if an alternative system would not be economically viable by
reason of the small circulation' of the other newspaper.

Writing in 2001, Doherty states that:

It is still not clear what, if anything, 'essential facilities' means in Community law. The
doctrine is disputed in the US, and the Court of Justice seems to share the Supreme
Court's reluctance to clarify the question .... The *Bronner* judgment does not state that
there is an 'essential facilities' rule in EC law ... and the label seems to add nothing
useful to traditional 'refusal to sell' doctrine. The whole difficulty in this area is
deciding whether competition is best served by requiring the dominant undertaking
to sell, or whether this will discourage investment in the future [cf Bergman, above].

... As a result, courts or competition authorities should be cautious in requiring
monopolists to sell ...

(7) Acquisition of Exclusive Access to Critical Technology

In Case T-51/89 *Tetra Pak I*, the company held a dominant position on the market for
aseptic cartons and the equipment used for their manufacture. TP acquired a small
undertaking in the same market which was the exclusive licensee of a patent for new
and important technology in the field of sterilisation of milk cartons. As a result, TP
effectively became the only company within the Community with access to this
technology. It was held that TP had reinforced its dominant position on the market for
liquid food packaging. The acquisition of the technology had the effect of preventing,
or at least considerably delaying, the entry of any new competitor into a market where
little if any competition remained. (The exclusive licence itself fell within block
exemption Regulation 2349/84 for the purposes of Article 85(3) (now 81(3)), but this
did not prevent the application of Article 86 (now 82) in the circumstances of this
case.)

EFFECT ON TRADE BETWEEN MEMBER STATES

Only very rarely has the expression 'which may affect trade between Member States'
as found in Article 82 precluded its application, in that the effects of abusive conduct
have been held to be confined to one Member State. The required effect may come
about through diversion of the flow of goods or services from normal channels or
through a modification of the structure of competition within the Common Market.
Thus, in *Commercial Solvents*, although Zoja exported the vast majority of its anti-TB
drug to the countries outside the Community, the Court held that its elimination from
the market, having an effect on the competitive structure of the Common Market,
would have the required effect on inter-Member State trade. Evidence that abusive
conduct *might* affect trade between Member States is also sufficient: Case 226/84
British Leyland.

However, in Case 22/78 *Hugin*, the Court of Justice held that H's refusal to supply
had no perceptible repercussions beyond the UK. The Swedish manufacturer of cash
registers (dominant in the market for its spare parts) had, following a disagreement,

refused to supply Liptons, an independent London-based company, with spare parts used by L to service and repair Hugin machines almost entirely within a 50 mile radius of London. The Court of Justice held that (a) the supply of spare parts from Sweden did not (at that time) involve trade between Member States; and (b) H's new policy of only supplying spares to its European subsidiaries did not entail the diversion of trade in them from channels they would otherwise have followed within the Community. A purchaser such as L, if unable to obtain spares from its local distributor, was very unlikely to approach a distributor in another Member State but instead, in normal circumstances, would purchase them directly from Hugin in Sweden.

JOINT OR COLLECTIVE DOMINANCE: ARTICLE 82 AND THE MERGER REGULATION

In the context of Article 82, where the 'integrated undertaking' principle applies (the subsidiary having no *economic* independence from its legally distinct parent company: see Chapter 15), the policies and conduct on the market of the subsidiary will be attributed to the parent. If a corporate group is regarded on this basis as an 'undertaking', this cannot amount to a case of joint dominance.

However, this is not to say that the 'integrated undertaking' principle has not played an important part in Article 86 (now 82) cases, not least when tying the activities of a subsidiary established within the Common Market to its parent established outside: in the USA (*Continental Can, Commercial Solvents, United Brands*) or elsewhere (for example *Hoffman-La Roche* in Switzerland). In *United Brands*, for example, the US parent and its Dutch subsidiary were fined 1 million units of account (now Euros), although the fine was subsequently reduced by the Court of Justice.

The reference in Article 82 to 'one or more undertakings' would therefore appear to apply to dominance held by two or more *independent* undertakings (or corporate groups). We have seen in the previous chapter that an *oligopolistic* market is one which is dominated by a small number of suppliers of a relatively homogeneous product. However, not only does the conscious parallelism of action between such suppliers (as regards 'follow my leader' pricing, etc) in itself fall short of collusion under Article 81 (now 85) (see *Dyestuffs*) but, in the late 1970s, in *Hoffman-La Roche*, the Court held that Article 86 did not apply either:

> A dominant position must also be distinguished from parallel courses of conduct which are peculiar to oligopolies in that in an oligopoly the courses of conduct interact, while in the case of an undertaking occupying a dominant position the conduct of the undertaking which derives profits from that position is to a great extent determined unilaterally. [Advocate General Lenz stated that there was a problem in knowing 'where a collective monopoly ends and an oligopoly begins'.]

In the mid-1980s, the Commission investigated the concept of 'shared dominance' (see Sixteenth Commission Competition Report, 1986) and developed an approach to oligopolies based on 'tacit collusion' between closely interdependent undertakings, each of which was aware of 'the probably unfavourable consequences of adopting a competitive attitude'.

If it proved difficult or impossible to provide evidence of such tacit collusion sufficient to show that a concerted practice existed under Article 85, it was thought that the 'awareness' of the undertakings concerned (none of which is dominant alone) might manifest itself in abusive conduct on the market sufficient to satisfy Article 86.

Italian Flat Glass (1990)

The Commission decided that three major Italian glass firms, FP, SIV and VP ('a tight oligopoly') were not only in breach of Article 85 as regards price-fixing and market-sharing, but that they also shared a position of collective dominance under Article 86 which they had abused by means of, amongst other things, identical pricing and discounts. They allegedly enjoyed a degree of independence from competitive pressures that enabled them to impede the maintenance of effective competition, notably by not having to take into account the behaviour of other market participants (the test in *United Brands*, etc).

The Commission noted (a) a joint market share of between 79 and 95 per cent for various types of glass; (b) significant insularity from competition; (c) high barriers to entry into the market (large scale investment was required at a time when demand for the products was unlikely to rise significantly over the next 10 years).

The Commission's analysis of collective dominance was, in part, as follows:

The undertakings present themselves on the market as a single entity and not as individuals.

...

The main producers jointly maintain special links with a group of wholesalers who are the main glass distributors in Italy; they instigate the meetings, and they do everything possible to get them to accept price list changes and to ensure that the changes are passed on downstream in a consistent manner, so as to prevent any individual decisions by the wholesalers from creating commercial pressures on each producer leading to changes in market equilibria.

The business decisions taken by the three producers display a marked degree of interdependence with regard to prices and terms of sale, relations with customers and business strategies.

The three undertakings have in addition established among themselves structural links relating to production through the systematic exchange of products ... The exchanges are, first, the result of some undertakings' structural lack of primary products or of certain processed products and, secondly, the expression and instrument of their desire to prevent this situation from resulting in changes in their relative positions on the market and in existing relations between them.

The glass producers appealed against the Commission's Decision and, in Cases T-68/89, etc, *SIV and Others v Commission (Italian Flat Glass)*, the Court of First Instance held that the Commission had only provided sufficient proof that two of the producers had infringed Article 85(1) by engaging in concerted practices.

The CFI did, however, confirm the *concept* of collective dominance in the following terms:

There is nothing, in principle, to prevent two or more independent economic entities from being, on a specific market, united by such economic links that, by virtue of that fact, together they hold a dominant position vis-à-vis the other operators on the same market. This could be the case, for example, where two or more independent undertakings jointly have, through agreements or licences, a technological lead affording them the power to behave to an appreciable extent independently of their competitors, their customers and ultimately of their consumers.

The CFI concluded that the Commission had not substantiated its assertion that the glass producers had acted 'as a single entity rather than as individuals'. It was insufficient to 'recycle' facts which constituted a breach of Article 85.

This test has subsequently been applied by the Commission in a number of cases in the maritime transport sector involving members of ships owners' committees or shipping conferences operating between certain Member States and certain African countries.

The Commission Decision in *Cewal and Others* (1993) concerned efforts by Cewal and other shipping conferences to restrict or eliminate 'outsider' competition from independent, non-member operators on routes between Northern and Western Europe and West Africa. (A shipping conference has been defined as 'a combination of shipping lines that has been formed to regulate and restrict competition in the carrying trade of a particular route'.) The Commission found that an agreement between Cewal and other conferences (a) was not a liner conference agreement as covered by block exemption Regulation 4056/86; and (b) that, being of a market-sharing nature, it was in breach of Article 85. However, no fines were imposed.

Further market conduct by the Cewal conference alone was treated by the Commission as an abuse of a collective dominant position on its routes between Northern Europe and Zaire (as 'protected' under the Article 85 agreement). A co-operation agreement between Cewal and the Zairian authorities whereby foreign currency was only issued by Zairian banks to shippers using Cewal's shipping services gave the conference, in the Commission's view, virtual monopoly rights on the trade routes in question. The Commission also stigmatised the conference's use of 'fighting ships', providing services at very low rates, with the aim of undercutting and eliminating its only competitor, and its imposition of 100 per cent loyalty rebates on shippers. Fines of between ECU 100,000 (Euros) and ECU 9.6 million (Euros) were imposed on Cewal members.

On appeal (judicial review), in Joined Cases T-24/93, etc, *Compagnie Maritime Belge Transports SA and Others v Commission*, the CFI rejected all the applicants' claims. As regards the collective dominance aspects of the case, the following pleas were raised:

(a) *That no effect on inter-Member State trade or on competition within the EC had occurred.* The CFI held that practices whereby a group of undertakings seek to eliminate from the market (in maritime services between Europe and Zaire) their main competitor in the EC (an Italian–Belgian shipping line) are inherently capable of affecting the structure of competition in that market and thereby of affecting trade between Member States.

(b) *That the members of the Cewal conference did not collectively hold a dominant position.* The CFI rejected this plea on the basis of (i) the close economic links between the conference members based on the conference agreement (and evidenced, for example, by the existence of a common scale of freight rates); and (ii) the pooling of the members' resources in order to present themselves on the market as a single entity in order to react unilaterally to any competitive challenge.

Dominance was evidenced by the difference between Cewal's market share (90 per cent dropping to 65 per cent) and that of its competitor (2 per cent rising to 25 per cent); agreements with the Zairian authorities under which Cewal sought to maintain exclusivity for shipments to and from Zaire (see below); and the preponderant capacity of the Cewal network including the frequency of its sailings.

(c) *That Cewal members did not abuse any dominant position.* The CFI found evidence of abuse regarding (i) the agreement with the Zairian authorities which, although allowing for new entrants to the market, Cewal had insisted on being complied with on an exclusive basis even after the Zairians had unilaterally admitted the independent shipping line (a situation similar to that in *Magill* above and the 'essential facilities' doctrine); (ii) the use of 'fighting ships' to drive the independent operator out of the market (a practice similar to predatory pricing) whether it was successful or not; and (iii) Cewal's practice of offering shippers only 100 per cent loyalty contracts according to which shippers could only obtain a rebate if they agreed to ship all their goods with Cewal.

It will be noted that in this case, as in *Italian Flat Glass*, the key feature of collective dominance is the presence of 'economic links' between undertakings, which operate such that they act on the market as a 'single entity'. In a preliminary ruling after *Flat Glass* and before *Cewal*, the Court of Justice had lent its weight to this requirement for a finding of collective dominance.

In Case C-393/92 *Municipality of Almelo v IJM* (see also previous chapter), the Court stated that 'the undertakings in the group [regional electricity distributors in the Netherlands] must be linked in such a way that they adopt the same conduct on the market'. The regional distributors had tied all local distributors by the same standard conditions of supply, including an exclusive purchasing clause, drawn up by the association of which they were all members: see *Hoffman-La Roche*. It was left 'for the national court to consider whether there exist between the regional electricity distributors in the Netherlands links which are sufficiently strong for there to be a collective dominant position in a substantial part of the Common Market'.

The next development was an appeal by the Cewal conference (see above) to the Court of Justice in Joined Cases C-395 and 396/96P *Comparative Maritime Belge Transport SA and Others v Commission*. The appeal was dismissed but the Court annulled the fines imposed as a result of a Commission failure to observe the essential procedural safeguards contained in the right to a fair hearing. The Court's most important finding was as follows:

> The existence of a collective dominant position may therefore flow from the nature and terms of an agreement, from the way in which it is implemented and, consequently from the links or factors which give rise to a connection between undertakings which result from it. Nevertheless, *the existence of an agreement or of other links in law is not indispensable to a finding of a collective dominant position; such a finding may be based on other connecting factors and would depend on an economic assessment and, in particular, on an assessment of the structure of the market in question* [emphasis added].

This concluding statement takes Community law a crucial step forward as regards its position on collective dominance – a step, like many others at this time, dependent upon applied industrial economics. The Court's statement is to the effect that in a specific case the structure of the market may be sufficient as a basis for a finding of collective market power providing that such economic factors enable the undertakings concerned to act as a collective entity in relation to competitors, trading partners and ultimately consumers.

This finding by the Court ties in with the slightly earlier view expressed by the CFI in Case T-102/96 *Gencor v Commission*, a case decided under the Merger Regulation (see below), in which it was stated that 'there is no reason in legal or economic terms to exclude from the notion of economic links the relationship of interdependence existing between the parties to a tight oligopoly'. No case as yet has been decided on this basis under Article 82.

However, before moving to the merger/collective dominance cases running parallel with the Article 86 (now 82) decisions, it is important to take account of a further CFI decision showing that collective dominance may be achieved not only, as above, on a horizontal, supplier's plane but also by means of vertical, supplier-distributor links.

Case T-228/97 *Irish Sugar v Commission*

IS, a dominant supplier, and its distributor SDL, through their close links, which gave them the power to adopt a common market policy, were found to hold a collective dominant position on the Irish retail and industrial purposes sugar markets. They were alleged to have committed abuses on both a joint and individual basis.

The CFI held that:

> The concept of a joint dominant position, whereby a number of undertakings were able in particular because of factors giving rise to a connection between them, to adopt a common market policy and act to a considerable extent independently of their competitors, customers, and ultimately consumers, was applicable to two or more undertakings in a vertical commercial relationship. It could not be accepted that undertakings in a vertical relationship, albeit not integrated to the extent of constituting one and the same undertaking, should be able to abusively exploit a joint dominant position. In the instant case, since the factors connecting IS and SDL showed that they had the power to adopt a common market policy, it followed that IS occupied a joint dominant position together with SDL.
>
> ....
>
> Whilst the existence of a joint dominant position may be deduced from the position which the economic entities concerned together hold on the market in question, *the abuse does not necessarily have to be the action of all the undertakings in question*. It only has to be capable of being identified as one of the manifestations of such a joint dominant position being held. Therefore, undertakings occupying a joint dominant position may engage in joint or individual abusive conduct. It is enough for that abusive conduct to relate to the exploitation of the joint dominant position which the undertakings hold in the market.

This decision was upheld on appeal in Case C-497/99P *Irish Sugar v Commission*.

Merger Control and Collective (Oligopolistic) Dominance

Mergers between undertakings (also known as acquisitions and takeovers) can take a variety of forms but generally involve the purchase by one company of another company's shares (particularly its equity or voting shares which give access to legal control) or of its assets. Where an offer or bid is successful and results in a complete merger (described as a *concentration* under the Community rules), the purchasing company taking control of the target company, the two undertakings become a new, single and larger, economic entity. Unless taking cash for their shares, the shareholders of the target company will now hold shares in the new, merged entity (for example, Cadbury Schweppes, Allied Lyons).

A *horizontal* merger, whereby one company takes control of a *competitor* in the same product (or services) market and at the same level of production or distribution, can have serious consequences for competition. As well as bringing about a *lasting* change in the *structure* of the undertakings involved, such a merger has brought about a change in the structure of the market in question. The number of independent operators has been reduced and the level of concentration in the market has been increased. Such a merger may lead to what is called, in terms of Article 82, a dominance situation. The market has become less competitive; competition may even have been eliminated.

Vertical mergers between an undertaking and its suppliers and/or distributors can lead to the scale of activity and control at various stages in the same market that characterised the *United Brands* case.

The combined economic strengths of fully merged undertakings can be viewed in terms of market control and the distortion or elimination of competition, but such mergers may also be defended on the basis of economies of scale, increased efficiency, and optimum size and strength in the struggle to compete effectively with economically powerful firms which are based both within and outside the Community. The legal control of mergers must therefore strike a balance. This was particularly the case in the context of the completion of the Internal Market:

> The dismantling of internal frontiers can be expected to result in major corporate reorganisations in the Community, particularly in the form of concentrations ... Such a development must be welcomed as being in line with the requirements of dynamic competition and liable to strengthen the competitiveness of European industry, to improve the conditions of growth and raise the standard of living in the Community ... It must be ensured that the process of reorganisation does not give rise to lasting damage to competition [and] the system of undistorted competition must therefore include provisions governing those concentrations which may impede effective competition in the common market [see recitals 3–5 of the 1989 Merger Control Regulation].

The Merger Control Regulation (MCR) was adopted in 1989 'to permit effective control of all concentrations from the point of view of their effect on the structure of competition in the Community and to be the only instrument applicable to such concentrations': recital 6 of the Preamble. It was amended in 1997 by Regulation 1301/97. The Regulation applies 'to all concentrations with a Community dimension': Article 1(1).

Concentrations (mergers) with a Community dimension are appraised by the Commission's DG Competition Merger Task Force as regards their compatibility with the Common Market under Article 2, paragraph 3 of which states that:

> A concentration which creates or strengthens a dominant position as a result of which effective competition would be significantly impeded in the Common Market or in a substantial part of it shall be declared incompatible with the Common Market.

The link to be made since 1989 between the assessment and possible prohibition of a merger under Article 2 of the MCR and the concept, as the cases will show, of joint or collective, oligopolistic dominance can be explained as follows. We have already seen (a) that, initially, Article 86 (now 82) did not, in the view of the Court of Justice, apply to parallel courses of action by two or more undertakings: see *Hoffman-La Roche* (1979), and (b) that the conscious parallelism in terms of pricing policy of a small number of suppliers within an oligopolistic market structure amounted to rational decision making falling short of illegal collusion under Article 85 (now 81): see *Italian Flat Glass* (1992).

Nevertheless, it was recognised that the lawful 'tacit co-ordination' of pricing policy exhibited by independent undertakings in a tight oligopolistic market (with its homogeneous product and high barriers to entry, etc) could be as damaging to competition – higher prices could well prevail than under conditions of effective competition – as collusion under Article 85, or abuse by a single dominant firm under Article 86. A gap existed in the competition rules; hence the need for serious economic analysis and investigation of oligopolies and the legal tools to ensure the maintenance of effective competition in such markets for goods and services.

The search for a solution proceeded under both the curative terms of Article 82 (formerly 86), with the need for acceptance of *collective* dominance and abuse, and also under the preventive terms of the MCR, whereby a merger could be blocked which would result in the creation or strengthening of a dominant position that would significantly impede effective competition in the Common Market contrary to the terms of Article 2(3) of the MCR (although the Regulation made no express reference to collective dominance).

The search under Article 82 has been traced above, with the focus on the nature of the *internal links* that enable undertakings in a highly concentrated market to present themselves (for example, as shipping conference members), vis à vis other market participants, as the dominant collective entity, and through the concerted (and abusive) way in which an agreement is implemented through 'other links in law', as held in the appeal decision in Joined Cases C-395 and 396/96P *Compagnie Maritime Belge*. However, in that case, it will be recalled that the Court of Justice added that a finding of collective dominance could be based on other connecting factors and would depend on an economic assessment and, in particular, on an assessment of the structure of the market in question.

This statement ties in with the CFI decision in Case T-102/96 *Gencor*, in which, as we have seen, 'other connecting [internal] factors' included 'the relationship of interdependence existing between the parties to a tight oligopoly'. *Gencor* was not the starting point of the Commission's move against oligopolies under the MCR, nor does it represent the complete position reached so far.

Following the disappointments for the Commission in the non-merger *Italian Flat Glass* case, in which the CFI did nevertheless accept the concept of collective dominance, the Commission shortly afterwards first raised the question of joint or collective dominance within the context of the new Merger Regulation in the *Nestlé/Perrier* case.

Nestlé/Perrier (Commission Decision of 27 July 1992)

N's acquisition of P would have led to N&P and BSN being jointly dominant on the French mineral water market with a combined market share of 82 per cent by value. The concentration was cleared by the Commission on the condition that N sold a number of brand names and water sources to a single, independent buyer approved by the Commission. This buyer would become a countervailing 'third force' on the market to prevent the joint dominance of N&P and BSN.

The Commission is required to be satisfied that this buyer would have sufficient financial resources and the relevant commercial expertise to exercise its role.

In this case, which was not subject to appeal, the Commission's view (although not essential to the decision) was that 'Article 2(3) [of the MCR] must be interpreted as covering both single firm and oligopolistic dominance ... as in all other major anti-trust systems with a merger control system'.

The next important step came with the decision of the Court of Justice in Joined Cases C-68/94 and 30/95 *France v Commission (Kali and Salz)*. These appeals, more correctly applications for judicial review of the Commission Decision, were brought by France and by companies affected by the Commission's Decision under Article 173(2) (now 230(2)):

> In 1993, the Commission declared the proposed merger between the German potash producers Kali and Salz AG and Mitteldeutsche Kali AG compatible with the Common Market subject to certain conditions. The Decision stated that, with respect to the Common Market (with the exception of Germany) as the relevant market, the proposed concentration would create a situation of oligopolistic dominance on the part of merged entity K and S/MdK together with the French owned company SCPA. The Commission therefore required K and S to eliminate its links with SCPA, comprising their common participation in an export joint venture and SCPA's position as the main distributor of K and S's supplies in France, before permitting the merger.

> The Court of Justice, while confirming that the Merger Regulation can be applied to mergers which give rise to positions of oligopolistic dominance, annulled the Commission's Decision on the grounds that it had not adequately established that such a position would be created or strengthened.

> The Commission's analysis was flawed in so far as the combination of the K and S/MdK and SCPA market shares of 23 and 37 per cent respectively could not in itself point conclusively to the creation of a dominant position. The Commission had also placed too much significance on the structural links between K and S and SCPA (there being, for example, insufficient evidence of a causal link between their co-operation in the export joint venture and the existence of anti-competitive behaviour), and it had not substantiated its claim that there was no effective competitive counterweight to the proposed grouping.

> In the Court's view, it was necessary for the Commission to analyse *prospectively* to see whether a concentration (merger):

>> ... leads to a situation in which effective competition in the relevant market is significantly impeded by the undertakings involved in the concentration and one or more other undertakings which together in particular because of factors giving rise to a connection between them are able to adopt a common policy on the market and act to a considerable extent independently of their competitors, their customers, and also of consumers.

This statement in context *appeared* to make 'structural links' between the companies concerned a *requisite* for a finding of oligopolistic dominance under the Merger Regulation. However, whether such links were necessary for oligopolistic dominance was doubted by several commentators on the case (see, for example, Bishop and Korah in 'References and Further Reading' at the end of the chapter). Bishop stated that 'such a finding would ... be at odds with the economic theory of co-ordinated effects' at the heart of oligopolistic markets.

As previously indicated, the importance of the later Case T-102/96 *Gencor v Commission*, decided by the CFI, lay in the fact that this Court did away with the idea that the existence of 'structural links' between the merged undertaking and another of the remaining undertakings in the market is a necessary or a sufficient condition for a finding of oligopolistic dominance. Factors giving rise to a connection between those undertakings (see the quote from the *Kali and Salz* case, above) may *include* 'structural links', however. Thus, in *Gencor*, the CFI stated (at paragraphs 273–79) that:

> ... the Court referred to links of a structural nature only by way of example and did not lay down that such links must exist in order for a finding of collective dominance to be made ...

> Nor can it be deduced from the same judgment that the Court has restricted the notion of economic links to the notion of structural links referred to by the applicant ...

> Furthermore, there is no reason whatsoever in legal or economic terms to exclude from the notion of economic links the relationship of interdependence existing between the parties to a tight oligopoly within which, in a market with the appropriate characteristics, in particular in terms of market concentration, transparency [of prices] and product homogeneity, those parties are in a position to anticipate one another's behaviour and are therefore strongly encouraged to align their conduct in the market, in particular in such a way as to maximise their joint profits by restricting production with a view to increasing prices. In such a context, each trader is aware that highly competitive action on its part designed to increase its market share (for example a price cut) would provoke identical action by the others, so that it would derive no benefit from its initiative. All the traders would thus be affected by the reduction in price levels.

> That conclusion is all the more pertinent with regard to the control of concentrations, whose objective is to prevent anti-competitive market structures from arising or being strengthened. Those structures may result from the existence of economic links in the strict sense argued by the applicant or from the market structures of an oligopolistic kind where each undertaking may become aware of common interests and, in particular, cause prices to increase without having to enter into an agreement or resort to a concerted practice.

> In the instant case, therefore, the applicant's ground of challenge alleging that the Commission failed to establish the existence of structural links is misplaced.

> The Commission was entitled to conclude, relying on the envisaged alteration in the structure of the market and on the similarity of the costs of Amplats and Implats/LPD, that the proposed transaction would create a collective dominant position and lead in actual fact to a duopoly constituted by those two undertakings.

Gencor involved a proposed merger between Impala Platinum, owned by G (a South African company) and Eastplats/Westplats owned by the Platinum Division of Lonrho (an English company). The merger was notified to the Commission for clearance by agreement of the parties, who made significant sales of platinum into the EU.

The Merger would have reduced from three to two the number of companies controlling platinum reserves in South Africa estimated at nearly 90 per cent of known world reserves. These companies would be the merged entity Implats/LPD and Amplats, which had a 6 per cent shareholding stake in Lonrho.

The Commission declared the proposed concentration incompatible with the Common Market as it would lead to the creation of a dominant duopoly in the world market, with the effect of significantly impeding competition in the Common Market.

In reaching its Decision, the Commission considered that, in output terms, Implats/LPD and Amplats would each have accounted for around 35 per cent of world platinum production, the merger having closed the gap between Amplats, the market leader, and Implats, the next largest. It also considered the fragmentation of marginal supplies from other sources (Russia, new entrants to the market, recycled metal, etc). As discussed above, these are factors likely to lead to co-ordinated market behaviour and joint dominance.

The Commission justified its extra-territorial jurisdiction over the proposed merger on the basis of the *effects* principle of international law, as applied by the Court of Justice in *Wood Pulp* (see Chapter 15), the necessary appreciable effects, in the Commission's view, being on the structure of competition within the Common Market through the significant volume of sales in that area. The CFI confirmed the Commission's Decision, stating that 'the concentration would have had the direct and immediate effect of creating the condition in which abuses were not only possible but economically rational, given ... the lasting alteration to the structure of the markets concerned'. The 'structure of the platinum market' and the fact that the 'two main producers would have had broadly similar cost structures' would have meant that 'anti-competitive parallel conduct would, economically, have constituted a more rational strategy than competing with each other, thereby adversely affecting the prospect of maximising combined profits'.

In the most recent merger case to reach the Community Courts, Case T-342/99 *Airtours v Commission*, the CFI has taken two important steps. It has brought its position clearly into line in substantive terms as regards the nature of collective dominance with that of the Court of Justice, as seen in *France v Commission (Kali and Salz)* and also insisted on 'convincing evidence' from the Commission (which was not forthcoming in *Airtours*) where that body takes the view that a concentration is to be prohibited under Article 2(3) of the MCR. With respect to collective dominance, the CFI stated that a collective dominant position:

> ... may arise as the result of a concentration where, in view of the actual characteristics of the relevant market and of the alteration in its structure that the transaction would entail, the latter would make each member of the dominant oligopoly, as it becomes aware of common interests, consider it possible, economically rational, and hence preferable, to adopt on a lasting basis a common policy on the market with the aim of selling at above competitive prices, without having to enter into an agreement or resort to a concerted practice within the meaning of Article 81 EC and without any actual or potential competitors, let alone customers or consumers, being able to react effectively.

The facts in *Airtours* displayed on the face of it a familiar pattern. A, a UK tour operator, announced its intention to acquire First Choice, a main competitor in the UK short-haul foreign package holiday market. The Commission, following notification, investigated the proposed merger and declared it contrary to Article 2(3) of the MCR on the grounds that it would create a collective dominant position in the market and significantly impede competition. It was contended that (a) the merger would remove competition between the three largest providers, A/FC, Thomson and Thomas Cook, together accountable for 79 per cent of the sales; and (b) that the degree of transparency and interdependence clearly evident in the market would be increased, giving the three large operators remaining after the merger every incentive to adopt parallel conduct – with the intention of reducing capacity (provision of package holidays) below demand so as to increase prices.

On appeal, the CFI found that the Commission had made errors of assessment in its analysis including an underestimate of the degree of competition in the market prior to the proposed merger, the volatility of the market, and the tendency towards setting capacity below demand. The analysis was not sufficiently dynamic particularly concerning the assessment of the future *internal* equilibrium or stability of an alleged dominant oligopoly (for example, with respect to 'cheating' by a member of it with respect to common policy) and also as to *external* factors such as the degree of possible countervailing competitive forces (other operators and consumers).

The Commission had failed to provide sufficient satisfactory evidence to substantiate its findings. This was a failure to prove to the requisite legal standard that the concentration would give rise to a significant impediment to effective competition in the relevant market. In his excellent review of the law in this area and this case in particular, Haupt concluded that:

> The judges thereby underlined the crucial feature of collective dominance, namely a future restriction of effective external and internal competition on a highly concentrated market as a result of long-term structural incentives for anti-competitive tacit co-operation.

The then Director General of DG Competition responded with the announcement of the establishment of a 'control commission for quality assurance' and the appointment of a 'Chief Economist', who would engage in systematic analysis of overall economic developments as well as the specific economic circumstances of single concentrations.

REFERENCES AND FURTHER READING

Baden Fuller, C, 'Economic analysis of the existence of a dominant position: Article 86 of the Treaty' (1979) 4 EL Rev 423.

Bellamy, C and Child, G, *European Community Law of Competition*, 2001, Chapters 10 and 6.6(c).

Bergman, MA, 'The *Bronner* case – a turning point for essential facilities doctrine?' (2000) ECLR 59.

Bishop, SB, 'Power and responsibility: the ECJ's *Kali-Salz* judgment' (1999) ECLR 37.

Caffara, C and Kühn, K-U, 'Joint dominance: the CFI judgment in *Gencor/Lonrho*' (1999) ECLR 355.

Dashwood, A, 'New light on Article 86 in the banana case' (1978) 3 EL Rev 314.

Doherty, B, 'Just what are essential facilities?' [2001] 38 CML Rev 397.

Fox, E, 'Monopolisation and dominance in the US and the EC: efficiency, opportunity and fairness' (*United Brands, Hugin,* etc) (1986) 61 Notre Dame L Rev 981.

Goyder, DG, *EC Competition Law*, 1998

Haupt, H, 'Collective dominance under Article 82 EC and EC merger control in the light of the *Airtours* judgment' (2002) ECLR 434.

Jones, A and Sufrin, B, *EC Competition Law: Text, Cases and Materials*, 2001.

Korah, V, 'The concept of a dominant position within the meaning of Article 86' (1980) 17 CML Rev 395.

Korah, V, '*Gencor v Commission*: collective dominance' (1999) ECLR 337.

Litvak, I and Maule, C, 'Transnational corporations and vertical integration: the banana case' (1977) Journal of World Trade Law 537.

Rodger, B, 'The oligopoly problem and the concept of collective dominance: EC developments' (1995/96) 2 Columbia Journal of European Law 25.

Tillotson, J and MacCulloch, A, 'EC competition rules, collective dominance and maritime transport' (1997) 21 World Competition (Geneva) (No 1) 51.

Treacy, P and Feaster, T, '*Compagnie Maritime Belge SA and Others v Commission*' (1997) ECLR 467.

Walker-Smith, A, 'Collusion: its detection and investigation' (1991) ECLR 71.

Whish, R, *Competition Law*, 2001.

Withers, C and Jephcott, M, 'Where to now for EC oligopoly control?' (2001) ECLR 295.

CHAPTER 17

ARTICLES 81 AND 82:
ENFORCEMENT AND PROCEDURE

The examination of the substantive law of Articles 81 (formerly 85) and 82 (formerly 86) in the preceding chapters inevitably made reference from time to time to the procedural framework for the application of the Treaty competition rules. The Council was originally given powers under Article 87 (now 83) to adopt appropriate measures to give effect to those rules, and Article 89 (now 85) stated that 'the Commission shall ensure the application of the principles set out in Articles 85 and 86' regarding anti-competitive agreements and abuses of a dominant position within the Common Market.

On the basis of the powers delegated to it by Council Regulation 17 of 1962, the Commission's executive role with respect to competition law and policy became very extensive indeed – investigations of undertakings, required notifications, powers of exemption, hearings of the parties and others, termination of infringements and the imposition of fines all came within the Commission's Regulation 17 portfolio. As seen, its powers regarding Article 81(3) exemptions were exclusive. Obviously, its quasi-judicial Decisions and penal powers were made subject to review by the Court of Justice, later the CFI, and Regulation 17 laid down strict procedural requirements to which it was bound to comply.

Although Articles 85 and 86 had direct effect and national courts could therefore apply Articles 85(1) and 86 but not Article 85(3), such application, at least in the UK, was very limited.

This centralised system came under strain, first regarding individual Article 81(3) exemptions, and despite efforts in the 1990s to encourage more enforcement at national level, it remained under strain, mainly owing to a lack of provision of the requisite resources necessary to deal with the vast workload.

The enforcement of EC competition law is now, however, in the process of change. In 1999, the Commission published a White Paper on the 'Modernisation of the Rules Implementing Articles 81 and 82 of the EC Treaty', in which a number of options for reform were considered. Following consultation, in 2000, the Commission put forward a 'Proposal for a Council Regulation on the implementation of the Rules laid down in Article 81 and 82 of the Treaty'.

The main features of this draft Regulation, which will replace Regulation 17 and implement a 'modernised' and 'decentralised' new structure for the implementation of the EC competition rules, are as follows:

(a) The abolition of notification of agreements to the Commission and of the Commission's exclusive powers over Article 81(3). National courts and National Competition Authorities (NCAs) may directly apply Article 81 in its entirety, leaving the Commission to deal with new issues and the more flagrant breaches.

(b) A self-assessment system to be operated by undertakings and their legal advisers, who will rely on the existing body of competition case law, decisional practice and Commission guidelines on such matters as the application of Article 81(3).

(c) Modification and reinforcement of the Commission's powers of investigation of suspected infringements of Articles 81 and 82 and of its powers to impose fines and penalty payments.

(d) A demarcation whereby national competition laws will only apply where a restrictive agreement, etc, or abuse of a dominant position can be shown to have no effect on trade between Member States. (Most national competition laws now operate on the same basis as that of the Community.)

(e) The establishment of a 'network' to enable NCAs and the Commission to inform each other of cases which arise under their respective jurisdictions and, where necessary, to allocate cases.

These proposals have received the usual mixed reception and many queries regarding its practical operation, particularly at the national level, have been raised. It is likely that changes will be found in the adopted measure. It is therefore appropriate that we focus only on the main features of the 'old' Regulation 17 regime and the new, 'modern' system of enforcement and procedure.

ENFORCEMENT AT COMMUNITY LEVEL

Commission Investigations and Inspections

The Commission's powers of investigation into suspected breaches of Articles 81 and 82 as originally found in Regulation 17 have been strengthened under the draft Regulation. The case law of the Court of Justice and CFI emphasises the need to obtain a balance in this area between effective enforcement and protection of the rights of the undertakings concerned.

The Commission's powers relate to *requests for information* – penalties, reviewable by the CFI, may be imposed for incorrect or delayed responses – and *inspections* of business premises and, under the new Regulation, the homes of directors and employees of suspected undertakings if judicial authorisation has been obtained. Statements may also be taken. Tight procedural rules apply and enforcement measures must not be arbitrary or excessive. Mandatory inspections must be based on a Decision to that effect, stating the purpose of the inspection and the possibility of financial penalties – no longer based on fixed limits (inflation has overtaken them) but on annual or daily turnover.

Investigative powers were considered in the following case.

Case 46/87 *Hoechst v Commission*

Suspecting that H was involved in illegal cartel operations, Commission officials, armed with the requisite authorisation Decision, arrived without warning at H's business premises (as they are entitled to do: see Case 136/79 *National Panasonic*) in order to carry out search and seizure operations.

H refused them entry until a search warrant had been obtained under national legal procedures. The Commission eventually gained admission in this way but imposed penalties on H for refusal to comply with the original Decision. In this challenge under Article 173(2) (now 230(4)), the Court held that the Commission had acted within it powers under Article 14 of Regulation 17. As the Court nevertheless stated:

... in all the legal systems of the Member States, any intervention by the public authorities in the sphere of private activities of any person, whether natural or legal, must have a legal basis and be justified on the grounds laid down by law, and, consequently, those systems provide, albeit in different forms, protection against arbitrary or disproportionate intervention. The need for such protection must be recognized as a general principle of Community law.

A further question which may arise out of a Commission investigation is that of *legal professional privilege* and confidentiality. In Case 155/79 *AM and S Europe Ltd v Commission*, the Court of Justice, in the absence of any express reference to the matter in Regulation 17, held that correspondence between an independent lawyer and his client undertaking was privileged, particularly as regards documents relating to the defence of the client after the initiation of proceedings by the Commission, but dealings with an in-house lawyer, as in this case, were not privileged. A Commission Decision ordering the handing over of documents which a party considers as privileged is open to challenge under Article 230(4) (formerly 173(4)).

Subject to the above, in Case 347/87 *Orkem v Commission*, which concerned *self-incrimination* and requests for information under Article 11 of Regulation 17, the Court of Justice ruled that, although the Commission could compel an undertaking to provide all factual information known to it and to disclose documentation relating to those facts in its possession, even if it could be used to establish a breach of the competition rules, the Commission could not compel an undertaking 'to provide it with answers [oral explanations] which might involve an admission on its part of the existence of an infringement which it is incumbent on the Commission to prove'.

In Case T-112/98 *Mannesmannröhren-Werke AG v Commission* in 2001, the CFI applied the *Orkem* ruling, in that an undertaking could confine itself to answering questions of a factual nature. The Commission was not entitled to ask for opinions or value judgments or to invite the applicant to make assumptions or draw conclusions.

MW was asked whether persons representing the firm attended certain trade association meetings of steel tube producers and, where they were unable to produce minutes of the meetings, to describe the purpose of the meetings and the decisions taken. MW refused to answer on the basis of the rules on self-incrimination. The Commission issued a Decision requiring a response and imposed a daily fine of 1,000 Euros per day of delay.

The CFI held that the applicant was not compelled to answer those particular questions which did not concern exclusively factual information but which were questions which might compel MW to admit its participation in an unlawful agreement contrary to Article 81(1). The applicant was entitled to refuse to answer. Attention was drawn by the CFI to Article 6 of the European Convention on Human Rights and the fundamental principles of the rights of the defence and the right to equitable proceedings. (The steel cartel was fined 99 million Euros.)

The question of *business secrets* can also arise in the course of Commission investigations and inspections. This issue, taken into account in Regulation 17, is also covered in the draft Regulation. The decision as to whether documents belonging to the suspected undertaking contain such secrets rests with the Commission, but if it intends to pass the documents to, for example, an undertaking intervening in an action which follows, it must issue a Decision to that effect informing the suspected undertaking who may challenge the Decision. The Court (now the CFI) must balance the applicant's legitimate interest in the non-disclosure of business secrets with the third party's legitimate concern to have the information to enable it to state its case before the Court. In Case 53/85 *AKZO Chemie v Commission*, it was decided that AKZO's business secrets should not be divulged.

Notification of Agreements

The significance of the Commission's notification requirement for the purposes of Article 85(3) (now 81(3)) exemption declined with the advent of the block exemption, particularly the Vertical Restraints Block Exemption Regulation of 1999. The requirement was based on Article 4 of Regulation 17, as amended by Regulation 1216/99. Notification is to be abolished under the draft Regulation's new approach and replaced by self-assessment.

Complaints to the Commission

Proceedings against undertakings suspected of infringement of the competition rules may be commenced by the Commission on its own initiative or following a complaint made by a Member State or a natural or legal person with a legitimate interest: Regulation 17, Article 3; draft Regulation, Article 7. Complainants are usually undertakings who become closely associated with proceedings begun by the Commission and usually claim loss as a result of the alleged breach. If proceedings are not commenced, the Commission must address a Decision (which is reviewable) to the complainant explaining the reasons.

Owing to the strain on its resources, the Commission changed its policy on complaints in the early 1990s. The change was a first step in the decentralisation process, which by the end of the decade saw the introduction of the Vertical Restraints Regulation, the White Paper on modernisation and the Draft Regulation. Judicial approval of this first step can be found in the following case.

Case T-24/90 *Automec v Commission*

Automec complained to the Commission that BMW had terminated its dealership in breach of Article 85(1). It sought an injunction ordering BMW to resume supply of its vehicles. The Commission rejected Automec's complaint. Automec challenged this refusal under Article 173(4) (now 230(4)). In its defence, the Commission argued that there was a need to prioritise in the light of its limited resources and that there was no sufficient Community interest to warrant proceeding with the complaint.

The 'Community interest' argument was accepted by the CFI, which advised the complainant to seek relief before the Italian court, which was already familiar with the facts of the case and was competent to deal with it.

In the slightly later Case T-114/92 *BENIM v Commission*, the Commission again declined to take up a complaint regarding restrictive practices basically confined to French territory. The CFI, while approving the Commission's refusal, drew attention to the need for confidence that the national legal system could adequately deal with the matter. Although confident enough in this instance, the Court stated:

... that the rights of a complainant could not be regarded as sufficiently protected before the national court if the court were not reasonably able, in view of the complexity of the case, to gather the factual information necessary in order to determine whether the practices criticised in the complaint constituted an infringement of the said Treaty provisions.

As regards 'Community interest', what the cases indicate is that the expression covers various elements, such as the exclusive competence of the Commission with respect to the discretion and formulation of Community policy, the need to ensure the uniform application of Community competition law, and questions relating both to the body best placed to establish that an infringement had occurred and to the extent and complexity of any investigation required. The case law shows that many Articles 81 and 82 cases are extremely complex and require extensive investigation and thus the application of detailed economic analysis.

Nevertheless, continuing the decentralising movement, the Commission published a 'Notice on Co-operation between National Courts and the Commission in Applying Articles 85 and 86': see [1993] OJ 39/5. Its aim was to encourage greater use of national courts in such cases, the Commission seeing its main role as responsibility for the direction and implementation of competition policy while concentrating on cases involving economic, legal or political significance for the Community. The role of the national courts was seen as the safeguarding of the rights of private parties affected by infringements of Community competition law. Companies and individuals were reminded that national courts, although having no jurisdiction to impose fines, had the power to award compensation for loss suffered as a result of infringements and to adopt interim measures (see below) more quickly than it could itself.

The Commission also proposed the introduction of a system whereby it could assist national courts by supplying opinions on points of law at the request of national courts and also provide them with statistics, market surveys and economic analyses.

At the time of the publication of the Commission's Notice – and since – serious doubts were expressed as to the competence of UK courts to deal with the more difficult economic law issues raised in many Article 81 and 82 cases. Riley has strongly argued that the Notice was 'aiming at the wrong target'. In his view: 'The most effective contribution that can be made to the enforcement of EC competition law ... is to give the NCAs [National Competition Authorities of the Member States] a greater role.' (Further developments concerning co-operation between the Commission and national courts and NCAs are considered below.)

Commission Enforcement

In addition to formal decisions on alleged infringements of Articles 81 and 82, we have already noted the availability in Brussels of *informal discussions* aimed at modification of agreements in order to secure their validity, and the use of *comfort letters* in lieu of formal individual exemption. As seen, the abolition of notification when the draft Regulation comes into force will mark the end of the use of this non-binding administrative device, formal decisions on individual exemptions playing no part in the 'modernised' system.

On the question of *interim measures*, Regulation 17 made no reference to the matter. A request for such measures may well arise where an undertaking suffers loss as a result of an alleged violation of the competition rules. It will be a considerable time before the case is finally decided and the loss may be of a continuing nature. The party suffering such loss therefore applies to the Commission for relief.

The Commission took the position that it had no power to issue interim orders. However, in the following case the Court of Justice decided that on a broad interpretation of Article 3(1) of the Regulation such a power was implied.

Case 792/79R *Camera Care Ltd v Commission*

The Court annulled a Commission Decision refusing to make an interim order requiring a camera manufacturer to supply CC with its cameras. It was of the view that a *prima facie* case of infringement had been made out and an order for termination should be made in the circumstances. The Court stated that it was essential that interim measures be taken 'only in cases proved to be urgent in order to avoid a situation likely to cause serious and irreparable damage to the party seeking their adoption, or which is intolerable for the public interest ... these measures [must] be of a temporary and conservatory nature and restricted to what is required in the given situation'.

Similarly, in the *AKZO Chemie* case, in Article 86 (now 82) predatory pricing litigation (see Chapter 16), ECS complained to the Commission regarding AKZO's price cutting policy, which they alleged was designed to drive ECS from the market. The Commission carried out an investigation at AKZO's premises in the Netherlands and the UK and later issued an interim Decision requiring AKZO's subsidiary in the UK to return to the price and profit levels applied before the alleged predatory pricing policy was implemented against ECS.

The new draft Regulation contains *express* powers for the Commission to award interim measures on the basis of the *Camera Care* decision.

Infringement Decisions and Procedural Safeguards

The existing power of the Commission under Article 3(1) of Regulation 17 to adopt prohibitive decisions declaring that an undertaking has infringed the competition rules and requiring the infringement to cease is retained in Article 7 of the draft Regulation. The existing powers are increased, in particular by powers to order structural remedies in oligopolistic situations, for example, divestiture of acquired undertakings in Article 86 proceedings.

It is not unusual for a Commission Decision to be annulled under Article 230(4) judicial review proceedings as a result of a breach of an essential procedural requirement by the Commission. Express procedural requirements or safeguards to which the Commission must conform are to be found in Regulation 17 and, in some regards in a modified or extended form, in the new draft Regulation. They refer to *hearing rights* for undertakings which are the subject of the proceedings (see Case 7/74 *Transocean Marine Paint* in Chapter 10) and for complainants and others who can show a sufficient interest. *Rights of defence* of the parties cover *access to the file*, subject to the rules concerning business secrets and confidential information. Since 1982, an independent Hearing Officer presides over the hearing to ensure that the rights of the defence are protected.

Fines and Periodic Penalty Payments

The Commission's power to impose these financial sanctions on undertakings are modified in the new draft Council Regulation. Fines are to be based on total turnover in the preceding business year for intentional or negligent breaches relating to, for example, the provision of information or a failure to co-operate in an investigation and to substantive breaches of Article 81(1) or 82 (up to 10 per cent of total turnover of each participating firm). A similar system, based on average daily turnover, will apply to periodic penalty payments regarding a failure to terminate an infringement of Article 81(1) or 82 or to compel submission to an inspection or to supply information.

As regards fines for substantive infringements of the competition rules, the Commission will first establish whether the infringement is intentional or negligent, and, in fixing the amount of the fine, it will have regard 'both to the gravity and to the duration of the infringement'. In Case 100/80 *Musique Diffusion Française (Pioneer)*, the Court of Justice said that:

> ... regard must be had to the duration of the infringements established and to all the factors capable of affecting the gravity of the infringements, such as the conduct of each of the undertakings, the role played by each of them in establishing the concerted practices, the profit which they were able to derive from those practices, their size, the value of the goods concerned and the threat that infringements of that type pose to the objectives of the Community.

The Court has also stated that the purpose of fines is to 'suppress illegal activities and to prevent any recurrences'. In addition, fines should have a general deterrent effect on other undertakings.

In 1998, the Commission published 'Guidelines on the Method of Setting Fines' with the purpose of increasing the transparency and coherence of the Commission's Decisions when fining companies. The Notice sets out the different steps involved in the setting of a fine. Depending on their *gravity*, infringements are classified as 'minor' (for example, vertical restraints with limited market impact), 'serious' or 'very serious' (for example, price or market-sharing cartels). As to *duration*, a distinction is drawn between 'short duration' (less than one year), 'medium duration' and 'long duration' (more than five years): see [1998] 4 CMLR 472.

In a further initiative concerning a renewed attack on secret or disguised cartels (Article 81 horizontal restraints based on collusion), the Commission in 2002 strengthened its 1996 Notice on Immunity from Fines and Reduction of Fines in Cartel Cases: see [2002] OJ C45/3. Following more closely the example of a successful US Leniency Programme, the Notice offers reduced fines or immunity from fines to a cartel member which 'blows the whistle' on its fellow members. Riley is of the view that by 'refocusing its operations away from the assessment of large numbers of vertical agreements and towards cartels [the Commission] is to bring about a virtual revolution in European antitrust enforcement'.

Judicial Review

Formal Commission Decisions, particularly concerning findings of infringement with fines, are subject to review, since 1989, by the CFI with a further right of appeal on points of law to the Court of Justice. Applications for annulment are brought under Article 230(4) (formerly 173(4)) and for failure to act under Article 232 (formerly 175): see Chapter 19.

The CFI contains several competition specialists, and it is very evident that the Court has in recent years subjected Commission Decisions under Article 230(4) to an intense degree of supervision where the case raises doubts concerning the Commission's assessment of, and reasoned application of the Community rules to, complex economic facts, and to its adherence to strict procedural safeguards. Not a few Commission Decisions have been annulled in whole or in part for this reason.

ENFORCEMENT OF ARTICLES 81 AND 82 AT NATIONAL LEVEL

National Competition Authorities

The Director General of Fair Trading (and his Office of Fair Trading) is the 'competent authority' in the UK, as is, for example, the Federal Cartel Office in Germany. As the Brussels-centred enforcement system presently stands, such authorities, on the basis of Article 84 (formerly 88) EC and under Article 9(3) of Regulation 17, are *competent* to apply Articles 81(1) and 82, but not Article 81(3) – so long as the Commission has not initiated any procedure as regards the issue in question.

In 1997, the Commission published a Notice on Co-operation between National Competition Authorities and the Commission in Handling Cases Falling Within the Scope of Articles 85 and 86 of the EC Treaty: see [1997] OJ C313/3. It is clear from the Notice that a National Competition Authority (NCA), although possessing the competence to apply Articles 81(1) and 82, also requires general enabling *national* provisions for them to do so. These the UK has not provided and at present, the national laws of only nine Member States confer express powers on their NCAs to directly apply the Community rules.

The Notice also contained guidelines on the allocation of cases between the Commission and NCAs. It was proposed that NCAs would deal with cases which (a) have mainly national effects; (b) are not likely to qualify for exemption under Article 81(3), and (c) do not display a particular 'Community interest'. NCAs, it was proposed, would deal with such cases either on their own initiative or at the Commission's request – as in the *Automec* ruling, above.

The Commission's 1999 White Paper on modernisation and the draft Regulation have, as already outlined, carried the proposals in the 1997 Notice much further for NCAs (and national courts) in terms of decentralisation and co-operation. Given the abolition of the system of notification and the Commission's exclusive powers of exemption under Article 81(3) as found in Regulation 17, the draft Regulation lays down a new system of control in Articles 1 and 2.

Article 81(3) is to be directly applicable not only by the Commission but also by NCAs (and national courts), that is, it will be capable of direct application by then. If an agreement comes under the prohibition in Article 81(1) but satisfies the conditions in 81(3), it will be declared valid. If it does not fulfil these conditions, it will be invalid *ab initio* and the 81(1) prohibition will apply. (However, these decisions, and those relating to Article 82, will bind only the NCA in question, not other NCAs or the Commission.) NCAs can act on their own initiative or on the basis of a complaint and the main bases for their decisions (including fines, etc) will be the Community case law, decisional practice and Commission Guidelines. The burden of proof that the conditions in Article 81(3) are satisfied will fall on the party invoking the benefit of that provision. The protection of a block exemption can also be withdrawn. All Member States must empower their NCAs to apply the new system.

The draft Regulation emphasises the need for uniformity of enforcement. The Commission and the NCAs will be required to apply the Community competition rules 'in close co-operation' (Article 11) and 'use every effort to avoid any decision that conflicts with decisions adopted by the Commission'. Information and documentation must be transmitted both ways between NCAs and the Commission and, in particular, if an NCA intends to adopt a prohibitive decision under Article 81 or 82, it must consult the Commission and send it a summary of the case. The Commission will have the power to take over such a case. The general principle to be applied to case allocation is that the national NCA best placed should deal with the case.

The Commission retains its overriding powers regarding regulatory policy, investigations, the adoption of block exemptions and cases with a 'Community interest'. If, as before, the Commission has initiated proceedings under Article 81 or 82, the NCAs will be 'relieved of their competence' to apply those provisions in the case in question.

In 1999, Zinsmeister *et al*, reviewing developments in both *national competition law* and EC competition law and moves towards decentralisation in the application of Articles 81 and 82, particularly by NCAs, wrote that:

> In practice, harmonisation of national competition law and EC competition law is taking place both through legislative changes which base national law on Articles 85 and 86 or by national competition authorities applying Community law directly. The competition law of 14 out of 15 EU Member States (the exception is Germany) is modelled on Articles 85 and 86, the most recent legislative changes in this direction having occurred in the Netherlands and the United Kingdom. In Member States where national competition law is closely modelled on Articles 85 and 86 and where the application of that national law is made in the light of the decisions of the Commission and the European courts, the ability also to apply Articles 85 and 86 will, in the view of the European Commission, contribute to the proper functioning of a decentralised system of effective competition. In Germany, where national law is not based on Articles 85 and 86, the German authorities are empowered to apply those Articles directly and take advantage of that power. The Commission may intervene where a particular case falls within the jurisdiction of more than one Member State. Finally, there are arguments for the proposition that all Member States enjoy the power to apply Articles 85(1) and 86 without the need for express power under national law. National laws modelled on Articles 85(1) and 86 provide a ready-made procedural framework for the application of those Articles by Member States.

> The Commission, in its White Paper of April 28, has given a clear indication of its intention to take advantage of that framework, to give Member States the power to apply Article 85(3) and to pass on to the national authorities in those Member States responsibility for the vast majority of cases falling within Articles 85 and 86.

It is extremely likely that the draft Regulation, which has come under criticism from both business and legal quarters (relating to points not necessarily covered in this brief summary) will require considerable changes, fine-tuning and elaboration before it is adopted.

The National Courts of the Member States

At the present time, the UK national courts, unlike the 'competent authority', do have jurisdiction, concurrent with that of the Commission, to apply Articles 81(1) and 82. This jurisdiction, and the availability of rights for private parties based on a breach of

Article 81(1) or 82, stem from the decision of the Court of Justice in Case 127/73 *BRT v SABAM*, where it ruled that:

> ... as the prohibitions of Articles 85(1) and 86 tend by their very nature to produce direct effects in relations between individuals, these Articles create direct effects in respect of the individuals concerned which national courts must safeguard.

The national courts may also apply the directly effective provisions of the block exemption Regulations: Case 63/75 *Fonderies Roubaix*. The complicating factor arose from the fact that these courts, prior to the modernisation reforms, did not have the authority to rule on an agreement's eligibility for individual exemption under Article 81(3). Guidelines to assist national courts in adjudicating on agreements falling within Article 81(1) were put forward by the Court of Justice in Case C-234/89 *Delimitis* and developed by the Commission in its 1993 'Notice on Co-operation between National Courts and the Commission in Applying Articles 85 and 86 of the EEC Treaty' (see above). In general terms, national courts would be on safe ground with cases where there was a clear infringement of Article 81(1), with no real possibility of an individual or block exemption. Where the possibility of an individual exemption did exist, the national court would be advised to stay its proceedings or adopt interim measures. Depending on the circumstances, there was also the possibility of seeking the Commission's advice or making a reference to the Court of Justice under Article 234 (formerly 177). The key concern of a national court is that it does not reach a decision which is in conflict with the position at Community level.

Despite encouragement from the Commission, there has been no evidence of private parties (usually undertakings) in the UK being keen to litigate Article 81 or 82 matters in the national courts, as opposed to making a complaint to the Commission. There are procedural and cost disadvantages and doubts regarding fact-finding powers and judicial experience in dealing with the economic and legal issues involved in the cases. Some of the problems which can arise if litigation is embarked upon at national level can be seen in the informative but, in enforcement terms, somewhat complicated circumstances of the following case.

Case C-344/98 *Masterfoods v HB Ice Cream*

M, a retailer, brought an action in the Irish courts on a contract containing a restrictive provision under which HB, a large-scale manufacturer, sold goods to M and others. M sought a declaration that the provision was void under Articles 81 and 82. HB in return sought an injunction to restrain M from inducing other retailers to act in breach of the provision. M's claim was dismissed and HB's injunction was granted. M appealed to the Irish Supreme Court.

M also lodged a complaint against HB with the Commission, who ruled that the contractual provision did infringe Articles 81 and 82. HB appealed to the CFI under Article 230(4) and applied for the Commission's Decision to be suspended until the CFI had given judgment in the main proceedings. The Decision was suspended.

In view of these developments, the Irish Supreme Court stayed the appeal at national level and referred questions to the Court of Justice under Article 234 for clarification of its position, bearing in mind (a) a possible further appeal from the CFI to the Court, and (b) HB's seeking to uphold the original Irish first instance decision in HB's favour in M's appeal to the Supreme Court.

The Court of Justice made it clear that (a) a national court cannot, where the issue is already subject to a Commission Decision, take a decision contrary to that of the

Commission, even though the latter's Decision conflicts with that of a national court of first instance. The suspension of the Commission's Decision was not relevant; and (b) the Supreme Court was correct to stay its proceedings pending a final judgment at the Community level.

The final outcome of this case is not yet known.

With the adoption of the draft Regulation, the position of the national courts under its terms will be largely the same as that of the NCAs. They will be able to apply Article 81 in its entirety and Article 82. They will be able to apply Article 81(3) and, if necessary, seek a preliminary ruling from the Court of Justice.

The draft Regulation contains provisions similar to those applying to NCAs regarding co-operation between the Commission and national courts, particularly with respect to Commission opinions concerning those courts' application of Community competition rules. The Commission may, for reasons of Community public interest (for example, the maintenance of the uniformity of competition law throughout the Member States), submit observations to national courts hearing Article 81 or 82 cases, and be represented at hearings in an intervener capacity.

The date for adoption of what will certainly be an amended draft Regulation is not presently known.

The question of *remedies* available to private parties seeking to enforce Community competition rules at national level is dealt with in Chapter 20.

REFERENCES AND FURTHER READING

Bourgeois, J and Humpe, C, 'The Commission's draft "New Regulation 17"' (2002) ECLR 43.

Ehlermann, C-D, 'The modernization of EC Antitrust Policy: a legal and cultural revolution' (2000) 37 CML Rev 537.

Gerber, D, 'Modernising European competition law: a developmental perspective' (2001) ECLR 122.

Jephcott, M, 'The European Commission's new Leniency Notice – whistling the right tune?' (2002) ECLR 378.

Joshua, JM, 'The element of surprise: EEC competition investigations under Article 14(3) of Regulation 17' (1983) 8 EL Rev 3.

Joshua, JM, 'Balancing the public interests: confidentiality, trade secrets and disclosure of evidence in EC competition procedures' (1994) ECLR 68.

Kerse, C, 'Enforcing Community competition policy under Articles 88 and 89 of the EC Treaty – new powers for UK competition authorities' (1997) ECLR 17.

Riley, AJ, 'More radicalism, please: the Notice on Co-operation between National Courts and the Commission in applying Articles 85 and 86 of the EEC Treaty' (1993) ECLR 91.

Shaw, J, 'Decentralisation and law enforcement in EC competition law' (1995) 15 Legal Studies 128.

Wesserling, R, 'The Commission White Paper on modernisation of EC Antitrust Law ...' (1999) ECLR 420.

Wesserling, R, 'The Draft Regulation modernising the Competition rules: the Commission is married to one idea' (2001) 26 EL Rev 357.

Zinsmeister, U, Rickers, E and Jones, T, 'The application of Articles 85 and 86 of the EC Treaty by National Competition Authorities' (1999) ECLR 275.

CHAPTER 18

INDUSTRIAL PROPERTY RIGHTS, FREE MOVEMENT OF GOODS AND COMPETITION

THE DELICATE BALANCE BETWEEN NATIONAL RIGHTS AND THE FREE MOVEMENT OF GOODS

The 'industrial and commercial property' which may be protected under Article 30 (formerly 36) in derogation from the free movement of goods principle (see Chapter 12) comprises certain valuable rights relating to the production and distribution of goods and services and which are to be found in patents, trade marks, copyrights and other analogous rights. (The expression 'intellectual property' is also generally used to describe these rights although it does not appear in the Treaty.) Key features of such rights are their *exclusive* and *national* character. As recognised by the various national legal systems of the Member States, special rights or protection are granted to the owner of such industrial property (the term which will be used here). A form of legal monopoly is acquired which may last indefinitely, as is the case with trade marks, or for a certain period of years: 20 years for patents, and the author's lifetime plus 70 years for copyrights.

The proprietary rights which are granted may serve to protect important and valuable technical information (as for a patented industrial process) or may protect the individuality and selling power of an established product (as is the case with trade marks). The justification for such protection may be expressed as a reward, in terms of monopoly profits, for innovation, industrial progress and efficiency or, more generally, for the effort, perhaps creative, and the expense involved. For example, a patentee (or, similarly, a person to whom the patent has been assigned or licensed) is the person – such rights are often held by undertakings – who alone is entitled to manufacture and distribute the patented product *for the first time* within the State granting the patent. A breach of these rights by a third party can attract infringement proceedings in national law: see, for example, the *Consten and Grundig* case in Chapter 15.

To the extent that varying national industrial property laws allowed a patentee (or, for example, a trade mark holder) absolute territorial protection of this kind, it appeared in the early days of the Community that, for goods that were protected by such rights, the Common Market could be partitioned on a national basis by private parties in a manner obviously contrary to the pursuit of single market integration. The difficulties posed by industrial property rights in this way were summed up at that time as follows:

> The potential uneasiness of the case of industrial property in the Common Market results from the basic contradiction between on the one hand, a Common Market which eliminates all economic barriers between the Member States and, on the other hand, the territorial monopolies resulting from the industrial property rights in the Member States [Jehoram].

At the root of the problem, as the case law of the Court of Justice demonstrates, is the fact that identical goods may be the subject of parallel industrial property rights registered in a *number* of Member States. For example, patent or other rights may have been registered in several Member States by the inventor and manufacturer itself, or licensed by it to undertakings in other Member States. Such undertakings may well be its own subsidiary companies. (Alternatively, similar and competing goods may be the subject of rights which have been established under the national laws of Member States in isolation from each other.)

To take one possibility: as we have seen, a patent holder, X (UK) Ltd, has in national law an exclusive right to put the patented product into circulation for the *first time* on the UK market. (After this first sale, the company's rights are *exhausted* so far as the goods sold are concerned; once on the market, they can be resold at will.) However, sales of the goods *elsewhere*, which are subject to parallel national rights, do not amount to the exercise of its rights by X (UK) Ltd. This can lead to a situation where X (UK) Ltd might, as a matter of *national* law, oppose the sale in the UK of the same (lower priced) goods imported by Y from Belgium where a parallel patent exists which is held by X (UK) Ltd's subsidiary, X (Belgium) Ltd, which itself first put these goods on the Belgian market.

Such a situation, and others similar, clearly present problems for the fundamental principle of the free movement of goods. In an early ruling on patents, Case 24/67 *Parke, Davis v Probel*, the Court stated that:

> The national rules relating to the protection of industrial property have not yet been unified within the Community. In the absence of such unification, the national character of the protection of industrial property and the variations between the different legislative systems on this subject are capable of creating obstacles both to the free movement of the patented products and to competition within the common market.

The Court of Justice has made it clear that the 'protection' afforded by Article 36 (now 30) leaves national industrial property rights intact in the sense that their existence cannot be incompatible with Articles 30–34 (now 28 and 29) on QRs and MEEQRs on imports and exports. In addition, Article 295 (formerly 222) of the Treaty lays down that:

> This Treaty shall in no way prejudice the rules in Member States governing the system of property ownership. [The Community may nevertheless seek by legislation to harmonise such rules or, more effectively, to place them on a unified Community-wide, as opposed to national, basis, see the statement by the Court, above.]

Thus, as Gormley has pointed out:

> The patentee or trade mark owner may be able to restrain importation of the product involved by an undertaking in another Member State which has made an imitation of the relevant product protected in the importing Member State by a patent, or which has illegally applied the mark protected in the importing Member State to its own products, without his consent.

It will also be recalled that, although Article 30 (formerly 36) allows for derogation from Articles 28 and 29 (formerly 30–34) in respect of 'the protection of industrial and commercial property', this is not the case where such rights 'constitute a means of arbitrary discrimination or a disguised restriction on trade between Member States'. It is therefore only restrictions on imports which are 'justified', that is, necessary (but no more than necessary), for the protection of industrial property which are allowable under Article 30 (formerly 36). What this means in practice rests on a distinction drawn by the Court of Justice between the '*existence*' of national rights and the '*exercise*' of those rights. To stay within Article 295 (formerly 222), the Court allows the derogation from free movement to operate but only in respect of those rights making up the *'specific subject matter'* (or essential core) of the property in question. These may be protected at the expense of free movement. The Court defined the specific subject matter of a patent in Case 15/74 *Centrafarm v Sterling Drug* as:

> ... the guarantee that the patentee, to reward the creative effort of the inventor, has the exclusive right to use an invention with a view to manufacturing industrial products and putting them into circulation for the first time, either directly or by the grant of licences to third parties as well as the right to oppose infringements.

In this way, a patent-holder's or his licensee's 'first time' monopoly profit is recognised and safeguarded against unauthorised manufacturing or marketing by others. However, the use of a patent (or other industrial property right) to obtain something further, or incidental, from the right will be in breach of Article 30 (formerly 36) (or Article 81 (formerly 85) if used in conjunction with a restrictive trading agreement: see the next section) if:

(a) the exercise is not made for the *bona fide* protection of the specific subject matter of the property; and

(b) its object is to frustrate the fundamental principle of free movement of goods (or the related objectives of the Community's competition policy).

The distinction drawn by the Court of Justice between the existence and exercise of rights has been criticised as being artificial. A patent, for example, is a bundle of rights under national law and if some of those rights cannot be exercised under Community law, then the value of the property is to that extent diminished. On the other hand, it has been said that: 'Metaphorically, the conception is that while the ownership of a motor car is allowed, its use may in certain circumstances be prevented, for example, when the alcohol content of the driver's blood exceeds a certain level': Barounos *et al*, *EEC Anti-Trust Law*.

Exhaustion of Rights: Consent

The Court's approach to trade marks is essentially the same as for patents and the following cases illustrate both this point and the operation of the *exhaustion of rights* principle in the context of the free movement of goods. Case 15/74 *Centrafarm v Sterling Drug* was concerned with patents and Case 16/74 *Centrafarm v Winthrop* with trade marks.

Case 15/74 *Centrafarm v Sterling Drug*; Case 16/74 *Centrafarm v Winthrop*

UK and Dutch patents relating to the process of manufacturing a medicament marketed under the trade name 'Negram' were owned by an American company, Sterling Drug, which had granted a patent licence to its marketing subsidiary in each of those Member States. Sterling Drug had also assigned the trade mark 'Negram' to those subsidiaries, Sterling Winthrop in the UK and Winthrop in the Netherlands.

Centrafarm, an independent Dutch company, bought 'Negram' on the open market in the UK and imported it for resale into the Netherlands. The price in the UK was around half that on the Dutch market as a result of UK government price control policies.

Sterling Drug and its subsidiaries invoked their patent and trade mark rights before the Dutch courts to prevent the parallel imports. The Dutch court referred a series of questions to the Court of Justice under Article 177 (234).

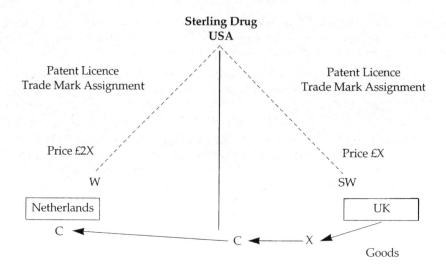

In the course of its ruling in the *Sterling Drug* patent case, the Court of Justice stated that:

> As a result of the provisions in the Treaty relating to the free movement of goods and in particular of Article 30 [now 28], quantitative restrictions on imports and all measures having equivalent effect are prohibited between Member States.

> By Article 36 [now 30], these provisions shall nevertheless not include prohibitions or restrictions justified on grounds of the protection of industrial or commercial property.

> Nevertheless, it is clear from the same Article, in particular its second sentence, as well as from the context, that whilst the Treaty does not affect the existence of rights recognised by the legislation of a Member State in matters of industrial and commercial property, yet the exercise of these rights may nevertheless, depending on the circumstances, be affected by the prohibitions in the Treaty.

> Inasmuch as it provides an exception to one of the fundamental principles of the Common Market, Article 36 [30] in fact only admits of derogations from the free movement of goods where such derogations are justified for the purpose of safeguarding rights which constitute the specific subject matter of this property.

> In relation to patents, the specific subject matter of the industrial property is the guarantee that the patentee, to reward the creative effort of the inventor, has the exclusive right to use an invention with a view to manufacturing industrial products and putting them into circulation for the first time, either directly or by the grant of licences to third parties, as well as the right to oppose infringements.

> An obstacle to the free movement of goods may arise out of the existence, within a national legislation concerning industrial and commercial property, of provisions laying down that the patentee's right is not exhausted when the product protected by the patent is marketed in another Member State, with the result that the patentee can prevent importation of the product into his own Member State when it has been marketed in another State.

> Whereas an obstacle to the free movement of goods of this kind may be justified on the ground of protection of industrial property where such protection is invoked against a product coming from a Member State where it is not patentable

and has been manufactured by third parties without the consent of the patentee and in cases where there exist patents, the original proprietors of which are legally and economically independent, a derogation from the principle of the free movement of goods is not, however, justified where the product has been put onto the market in a legal manner, by the patentee himself or with his consent, in the Member State from which it has been imported, in particular in the case of a proprietor of parallel patents.

In fact, if a patentee could prevent the import of protected products marketed by him or with his consent in another Member State, he would be able to partition off national markets and thereby restrict trade between Member States, in a situation where no such restriction was necessary to guarantee the essence of the exclusive rights flowing from the parallel patents ...

The question referred should therefore be answered to the effect that the exercise, by a patentee, of the right which he enjoys under the legislation of a Member State to prohibit the sale, in that State, of a product protected by the patent which has been marketed in another Member State by the patentee or with his consent is incompatible with the rules of the EEC Treaty concerning the free movement of goods within the Common Market.

Similarly, in the *Winthrop* trade mark case, the Court ruled that:

In relation to trade marks, the specific subject matter of the industrial property is the guarantee that the owner of the trade mark has the exclusive right to use that trade mark, for the purpose of putting products protected by the trade mark into circulation for the first time, and is therefore intended to protect him against competitors wishing to take advantage of the status and reputation of the trade mark by selling products illegally bearing that trade mark.

An obstacle to the free movement of goods may arise out of the existence, within a national legislation concerning industrial and commercial property, of provisions laying down that a trade mark owner's right is not exhausted when the product protected by the trade mark is marketed in another Member State, with the result that the trade mark owner can prevent importation of the product into his own Member State when it has been marketed in another Member State.

Such an obstacle is not justified when the product has been put onto the market in a legal manner in the Member State from which it has been imported, by the trade mark owner himself or with his consent, so that there can be no question of abuse or infringement of the trade mark.

In fact, if a trade mark owner could prevent the import of protected products marketed by him or with his consent in another Member State, he would be able to partition off national markets and thereby restrict trade between Member States, in a situation where no such restriction was necessary to guarantee the essence of the exclusive right flowing from the trade mark.

The question referred should therefore be answered to the effect that the exercise, by the owner of a trade mark, of the right which he enjoys under the legislation of a Member State to prohibit the sale, in that State, of a product which has been marketed under the trade mark in another Member State by the trade mark owner or with his consent is incompatible with the rules of the EEC Treaty concerning the free movement of goods within the Common Market.

Thus, having put the goods on the UK market for the first time through its licensed subsidiary, Sterling Drug's patent rights there were exhausted and it could not prevent the goods being purchased on the UK market by the Dutch firm Centrafarm and imported into the Netherlands to undercut Sterling Drug's subsidiary in that country. A similar analysis applies to the *Winthrop* trade mark case.

The exhaustion principle has been applied by the Court of Justice within the context of Article 36 (now 30) not only to patents and trade marks but also to copyrights and analogous rights such as industrial designs. In essence, in Community law, the owner's exclusive rights are exhausted by his putting the product in question into circulation anywhere within the Community. First time sale in such cases therefore has a Single or Common Market dimension, not a national dimension.

In Cases 55 and 57/80 *Musik-Vertrieb Membran v GEMA*, the Court held that the performing rights society GEMA could not rely on its German copyright in sound recordings to prevent parallel imports of records from the UK which had been put on the market there with its consent. Nor could GEMA collect the additional 2.25 per cent royalty rate reflecting the difference between the lower, statutorily-imposed rate in the UK and the rate applying in Germany. However, in Case 341/87 *EMI Electrola v Patricia*, records were exported to Germany from Denmark, but they had not been put on the Danish market with the consent of the German EMI company. These sales had arisen because the copyright protection in Denmark was for a shorter period than in Germany and had expired. The Court of Justice held that until such time as the rules were harmonised, it was for national law to determine the period of copyright protection and that EMI could rely on its German copyright to prevent the parallel imports: the right to do so was indissolubly linked to the exclusive right conferred under German copyright law.

The case law of the Court therefore reveals that the consent (or otherwise) of the owner of the rights in question to the first marketing elsewhere in the Common Market is the key factor in these decisions. Consent can arise where the owner markets the goods himself, where he does so through a subsidiary company, or where the owner and the undertaking responsible for the first marketing are under common control: see *Centrafarm v Sterling Drug*, above. In these instances, the owner who is seeking an injunction to prevent the lawfully marketed parallel imports cannot rely on national industrial property rights legislation, which will constitute a measure having equivalent effect to a quantitative restriction on imports under Article 28 (formerly 30). Such an exercise of the right in question is not justified within the terms of Article 30 (formerly 36). It amounts to a disguised restriction on trade and a means to partitioning the Common Market along national lines. The price of the parallel imports will in all probability be considerably less than that of the product on the home market, but it is immaterial whether the difference is due to government regulation in the exporting State or merely market forces.

Other patent cases similarly rest on the consent rule. In Case 187/80 *Merck v Stephar*, a Dutch patentee was unable to prevent the importation into the Netherlands of a pharmaceutical product previously marketed with its consent by its subsidiary in Italy. However, at that time, the drug was not patentable in Italy and therefore there was no possibility of earning a monopoly profit there. Although this is no longer the case, this decision was criticised as leading to products only being sold where patent protection was available; a division of the Common Market as serious as differential pricing. This decision was subject to challenge in the High Court in *Merck v Primecrown* (1995). M argued that the previous ruling should be changed or modified to hold that where there is a genuine ethical or legal obligation to sell a patented (pharmaceutical) product in a Member State where the party has no patent (Spain, where at the time of accession it was not possible and was only gradually becoming possible to obtain a patent), it should not be considered that companies have a 'free choice' to market the product in that Member State and, consequently, the goods sold should not be regarded as being put on the Single Market with the party's consent. Following a reference for a preliminary ruling, the Court of Justice, in Joined Cases C-267 and 268/95, refused to alter its position. No injunction in the UK could prevent the movement of the goods from Spain to the UK. This decision has been much criticised: M's consent reaped no monopoly profit in Spain, it was undercut by the parallel exports from Spain to the UK, and a decision not to market in Spain would leave consumers there without the product.

However, in Case 19/84 *Pharmon v Hoechst*, a Dutch patentee was able to invoke Article 36 (now 30) to prevent imports of products originally marketed in the UK by a licensee holding a *compulsory* licence granted under UK law. (This can occur where the patent would not otherwise be commercially exploited.) The element of consent was absent and the patent owner could assert his basic rights.

Other trade mark cases have addressed the situation where the proprietor of a trade mark in one Member State has marketed the same goods in another Member State under a different mark. For example, in Case 3/78 *Centrafarm v American Home Products*, AHP sold a tranquilliser as 'Serenid' in the UK and as 'Seresta' in the Netherlands. The two products were pharmaceutically identical but chemically different and tasted different. Centrafarm imported 'Serenid' into the Netherlands from the UK, having changed its name to 'Seresta'. Centrafarm was thus able to establish the identity of the goods in the Netherlands, was able to take advantage of AHP's promotion of 'Seresta', and was able to compete with, and undercut, AHP there. The Court of Justice was asked if AHP could rely on its Dutch rights to stop such imports. It ruled that, in principle, the trade mark proprietor was justified in opposing a sale by a third party in such circumstances even where the product had been marketed in the other Member State (under a different mark) by the same proprietor. Otherwise the essential guarantee for consumers of a product's origin would be compromised. The Court did, however, add, in the light of the second sentence of Article 36 (now 30), that whereas there might be good reasons for using different trade marks in respect of the same products in different Member States (for example, to avoid problems of similarity with existing marks causing confusion), such a strategy would amount to a disguised restriction on trade if it were used for anti-competitive and market-splitting purposes. This was a matter for the national court to decide.

In the later Case 1/81 *Pfizer v Eurim-Pharm*, the Court held that a trade mark owner may not oppose the parallel importation of goods (again pharmaceuticals) lawfully marketed by a subsidiary in another Member State where the importer has put properly labelled external packaging on the product without interfering with the internal packaging or obscuring the original trade mark.

The much publicised Case C-355/96 *Silhouette International v Hartlauer Handelsgesellschaft*, on reference from an Austrian Court, raised questions concerning the exhaustion of rights not within the EC (and by extension the wider European Economic Area) but on a worldwide basis. A thriving 'grey market' developed in the EEA in cut-price, branded designer goods available in outlets outside the normal selective distribution outlets favoured by the manufacturer/trade mark proprietor. Supermarkets and others bought the branded goods at prices much lower than those in the EEA from sources outside the EEA, and parallel imported them back into the

EEA for resale. The question in *Silhouette* was whether such importation and resale without the brand owner's consent constituted trade mark infringement.

Case C-355/96 *Silhouette International v Hartlauer Handelsgesellschaft*

S, which manufactures expensive spectacles in Austria, supplies them to approved outlets in Austria and throughout the world. The 'Silhouette' trade mark is registered in most countries. S sold 21,000 'out of fashion' frames to a company in Bulgaria on condition that they were only resold in that country or the former Soviet Union. The frames were, however, parallel imported back to Austria and put on the market by H, a cut-price company with no trading connections with S.

S brought an action in the Austrian courts to restrain H from selling these frames in Austria under its mark, where they had not been put on the market by S or by third parties with S's consent. The Austrian court asked the Court of Justice whether Article 7(1) of the 1989 Trade Mark Directive (a harmonisation measure) meant that a trade mark proprietor was entitled to prohibit a third party from using the mark for goods that had been put on the market under that mark in a State *outside* the EEA.

The Court of Justice ruled that a trade mark owner is entitled to prevent a retailer selling trade-marked goods imported into Austria from outside the EC/EEA without permission. Although Article 7 of the Directive states that, where goods are put on the market by the proprietor or with his consent, the exclusive rights conferred by the mark are exhausted, the Court ruled that such 'exhaustion occurs only where the products have been put on the market in the Community [or the EEA]'.

The outcome is that the 1989 Directive (see below) precludes the Member States from recognising the principle of worldwide exhaustion. The EC exhaustion of rights principle only applies to the free movement of goods between Member States in the EC/EEA. It does not apply to imports from outside those areas. On this basis, S was protected in any Member State in which he had registered his trade mark.

The Court also stated that Member States should not provide in their domestic law for international exhaustion of rights, as this would distort competition and affect the functioning of the Internal Market. In the press, the case was characterised as a battle between 'free trade' and 'Fortress Europe'. Certainly, the ruling does nothing to encourage parallel trading where third parties standing outside closed distribution networks seek to exploit price differentials in circumstances initiated by the trade mark proprietor.

Murphy (see 'References and Further Reading' at the end of the chapter) made a similar point and added that 'consumers benefit from lower prices and greater accessibility to brand name goods through grey marketing'. He examined *Silhouette*, and two subsequent decisions, Case C-173/98 *Sebago Inc v GB Unic SA* (1999) and the High Court ruling in *Zino Davidoff SA v A and G Imports Ltd* (1999), at the time when a reference had been made to the Court of Justice in the latter case, but no ruling had been made.

Murphy's (interim) conclusions were as follows:

These three cases are important to know the current boundaries of grey marketing. They are also compatible with each other. *Davidoff* follows from *Silhouette* and *Sebago*, but puts a further obligation upon the trade mark holder to take action to prevent the importation and sale of its products in the EEA. *Silhouette* and *Sebago* require the consent of the trade mark holder. *Davidoff* simply adds a further step. If the holder does not want to permit importation, positive steps must be taken to prevent this, otherwise there is a deemed consent to allow importation into the EEA.

In *Sebago*, the Court of Justice held that the required consent must cover the *individual items* (see also *Silhouette* note, paragraph 2, above) of goods which are traded in parallel: see also Article 7(2) of Directive 89/104 (Trade Marks). It is not enough for a finding of consent that anywhere in the world outside the Community, the proprietor of the mark sells good which are of an identical model to goods which it markets in the Community.

The limits of implied consent were explored further in *Davidoff* (joined with another case involving Levi jeans). Here the Court ruled that:

> ... the consent of a trade mark proprietor to the marketing within the European Economic Area of products bearing that mark which have previously been placed on the market outside the European Economic Area by that proprietor or with his consent may be implied, where it follows from facts and circumstances prior to, simultaneous with or subsequent to the placing of the goods on the market outside the European Economic Area which, in view of the national court, *unequivocally demonstrate* that the proprietor has renounced his right to oppose placing of the goods on the market within the European Economic Area [emphasis added].

In other words, the holder of the trade mark must take clear, positive steps to demonstrate that it *does not oppose* – it *consents* to – the placing of the goods on the EEA market; the reverse of the action put forward in Murphy's commentary following the UK Patents Court's pre-reference hearing of the case. The Court of Justice stressed that 'consent' was a 'Community concept' and as such must have the same meaning, irrespective of pre-existing definitions in the laws of the Member States, when determining whether the Article 28 prohibition on the free movement of goods applies or not.

Common Origin: the Trade Mark Cases

The delicate balance between national trade mark rights (as possible MEEQRs) and the free movement of goods has also been influenced in a different way by the concept of *common origin*.

Case 192/73 *Van Zuylen Frères v Hag AG*

H, a German company, owned trade marks for its decaffeinated coffee in several countries for many years. In the late 1930s and during the war its rights in Belgium and Luxembourg were held by its subsidiary Café Hag SA of Liege. Having been confiscated and sold off as enemy property in 1944, the Belgian company's trade mark eventually passed to VZF.

When H began exporting its coffee from Germany to Luxembourg, VZF brought infringement proceedings. The question of exhaustion of rights did not arise because the German company had not consented to the original transfer of its trade mark. H and VZF (between whom there were no legal or economic links) legitimately owned the same mark and H was exporting directly into VZF's 'territory'.

On an Article 177 (now 234) reference, the Court of Justice ruled that the free movement principle must prevail over the national trade mark rights: the right claimed by VZF could have the effect of partitioning the market indefinitely (on account of the indefinite duration of trade mark rights) and consumer interests could be safeguarded by appropriate labelling regarding the origin of the products. Thus: '... one cannot allow the holder of a trade mark to rely upon the exclusiveness of a trade mark right ... with a view to prohibiting the marketing in a Member State of goods legally produced in another Member State under an identical trade mark having the same origin.'

This decision did not meet with general approval and meant that neither holder of such a 'split' mark (of common origin) could prevent goods legitimately bearing the mark from being imported and sold either by the other holder or by purchasers from it in the Member State where it owned the mark. Hag had not consented to the use of the mark by VZF but, as we have seen in the *Pharmon* case decided in 1985, a patentee was able to invoke Article 36 (now 30) to protect its rights and prevent imports originally put on the market in another Member State by a *compulsory* licensee. This first *Hag* decision rendered the trade mark virtually valueless as a means of guaranteeing to the consumer the identity of the manufacturer responsible for the quality of the product and exaggerated the possibility of market-partitioning on any widespread basis.

In 1990, the Court of Justice considered it necessary to review its ruling in the *Hag I* decision 'in the light of the case law which had gradually developed'.

Case C-10/89 *CNL Sucal v Hag AG*

This case presented a reverse-fact situation to that in 1974. VZF had become a company, trading as Sucal (and owned by Suchard of Switzerland). VZF's trade mark rights, originally held by Hag (Belgium), having passed to Sucal, Hag was seeking an injunction in the German courts to restrain Sucal from supplying coffee under the 'Hag' mark to the German market.

Following a reference to the Court of Justice under Article 177 (now 234), the Court held that Articles 30 and 36 (now 28 and 30) did not prevent national legislation from allowing an undertaking, which was the proprietor of a trade mark in one Member State, from opposing the importation from another Member State of similar goods lawfully bearing an identical or confusingly similar trade mark to the protected mark, even though the mark under which the disputed product had been imported had initially belonged to a subsidiary of the undertaking which was opposing the importation and had been acquired by a third undertaking following the expropriation of that subsidiary.

In the course of its decision, the Court now stressed both the absence of consent between two undertakings with no legal or economic ties and also the possibility of confusion amongst consumers. The original *Hag* 'free movement' decision had led some commentators to fear that it would be applied to defeat attempts by trade mark owners in one Member State to prevent the use in that State of another trade mark originating from another Member State that might be confusingly similar, even where there was no question of common origin and there were no legal or economic ties between the parties.

However, the Court had quelled those fears in Case 119/75 *Terrapin (Overseas) Ltd v Terranova Industrie*, in which the German firm, Terranova, successfully invoked Article 36 (now 30) to prevent an English firm, Terrapin, from registering its trade mark in Germany. The marks had been acquired by different proprietors under different national laws; there were no links between the firms (and therefore presumably no question of the use of the different marks as a disguised restriction on trade), and the similarity between the names could give rise to confusion as both firms supplied building materials.

In Case C-9/93 *IHT v Ideal-Standard GmbH*, the Court of Justice answered a question left open in *Hag II*, which, as seen, concerned an involuntary assignment of a trade mark, an absence of legal or economic links between the relevant undertakings and a subordination of the free movement principle. Ideal Standard presented similar facts except that the assignment was voluntary.

Case C-9/93 *IHT v Ideal-Standard GmbH*

The 'Ideal Standard' trade mark was until 1984 held by a US company in both France and Germany and it marketed sanitary equipment and heating installations under that name through its subsidiaries in those Member States. In that year, however, the French subsidiary, facing financial difficulties, sold the trade mark covering heating equipment and it passed to an independent company outside the Ideal Standard group.

IHT, the German subsidiary of this company acquired 'Ideal Standard' heating installations on the French market and imported them into Germany. Ideal-Standard GmbH, the German subsidiary of the US parent and owner of the trade mark in Germany, sought to use its national rights to prevent the importation; that is, it sought a derogation from the free movement rules on the basis of Article 36 (now 30).

The Court reiterated and clarified the exhaustion of rights doctrine: goods placed on the Single Market by the trade mark owner or with his consent (first sale) can subsequently circulate freely within the Community. The doctrine applied where the owners of the right in the exporting and importing States were the same or, where they were separate, there was nevertheless an economic link between them. The doctrine therefore covered products placed into circulation by the same undertaking, by a licensee, by a parent company, by a subsidiary company within the same group, or by an exclusive distributor.

Turning to the essential functions of a trade mark of offering 'a guarantee that all goods bearing it have been produced under the control of a single undertaking which is accountable for their quality', the Court ruled that 'a contract of assignment by itself, that is, in the absence of an economic link, does not give the assignor any means of controlling the quality of the products which are marketed by the assignee and to which the latter has affixed the trade mark'. The consent implicit in the assignment was not the consent which was required for the purpose of invoking the exhaustion of rights doctrine.

Following its ruling in *Hag II*, the Court held that national property rights prevailed.

It has been said that 'this judgment therefore represents another of the Court's decisions of recent years [for example, *Keck*] where it pushes the margin somewhat further away from market integration, towards respect for national protection and thereby towards the need for legislative intervention'. The Court itself cited Article 100a (now 95) as the correct legal base for remedying the adverse effects to the Single Market created by this decision.

Unification of Industrial Property Law

Diverging or unco-ordinated national laws lay at the root of most of the problems faced by the Court of Justice in the above cases. Time and again the Court has explained that its ruling is set in the context of 'the present state of Community law' in the area and has drawn attention to 'the divergencies which remain in the absence of any unification of national rules concerning industrial property'. Goyder summed up the position as follows:

> If the founders of the Community were to be allowed today to redraw both the Treaty of Rome and Member State legislation in the way required to preserve the essential characteristics of the original Treaty, whilst providing a completely fresh basis for the framing of the rules relating to national rights of intellectual property, the experience of the last thirty years would mean that their objectives would clearly have to include the definition of such rights and their essential characteristics in a way which could be accepted as valid throughout the Community, rather than allowing the perpetuation by individual Member States of such national rights varying in both classification and content, and which through their very diversity raise major problems for the free movement of goods and commercial integration. While Article 36 [now 30] includes the 'protection of industrial and commercial property' as one of the exceptions to the basic principle of free movement of goods, there is no doubt that the attainment of an integrated market will remain difficult, if not impossible, so long as such varied exceptions to the basic rules are preserved. The harmonization, therefore, of the law relating to intellectual property within the Community, in particular that relating to patents and trade marks, as well as the gradual harmonization of the classification and definition of all the other various intellectual property rights found to exist within Member States covering rights as varied as copyright, registered design, and rights against unfair competition, remain an objective of great importance.

The tension between, on the one hand, national systems of industrial property rights and, on the other, the free movement of goods and fair and effective competition throughout the Common Market can only be satisfactorily removed by the adoption of Community legislation which will (a) achieve the harmonisation of national rules relating to industrial property; and (b) overlay the national territoriality principle with grants of industrial property rights covering the territory of the whole Community.

Progress along these lines has been very slow. The possibility of introducing a Community patent was first discussed in 1959. The *European Patent Convention* of 1973 (an international Convention involving a number of European countries including, since 1992, all the Member States of the Community; it is not a Community act) merely established a system whereby the European Patent Office in Munich can grant a 'batch' of national patents, so obviating the need for a patentee to take out individual patents in the required number of different European countries. The Convention brought about no change in the substantive national patent law of the contracting States.

The *Community Patent Convention*, signed in 1975, is not yet in force. Its purpose is to introduce a unitary patent for the Community as a whole as the only form of European patent available in the Member States. The rights of the owner of such a patent will be exhausted once he puts the protected product on the market anywhere within the Community. It will not be possible to partition the Common Market by granting patent licences limited to certain territories. National patents will still be available (but not for an invention covered by a Community patent) and the exhaustion of rights principle as developed by the Court of Justice will apply to such national patents. In 1988, the Council proposed an inter-governmental conference for the purpose of finalising the text of the Convention for entry into force on 1 January 1993. Although amendments to the Convention were agreed in 1989 and Member States were to ratify by the end of 1991, it is still not in force.

In 1980, the Commission put forward proposals for a Council Directive on the approximation of the laws of the Member States relating to trade marks and for a Council Regulation on a Community trade mark. The harmonisation measure was adopted in 1989 (Directive 89/104). The Directive applies the rules established by the Court of Justice, defines the rights relating to the ownership of national trade marks and the limitations on those rights within a Single Market. A common basis for the refusal of registration, for invalidity and for the loss or exhaustion of rights is provided.

A Community trade mark was established by Council Regulation 40/94. Article 2(1) states that:

> A Community trade mark shall have a unitary character. It shall have equal effect throughout the Community: it shall not be registered, transferred or surrendered ... save in respect of the whole Community.

While recognising that 'the barrier of territoriality of the rights conferred on proprietors of trade marks by the laws of the Member States cannot be removed by approximation of law', the Regulation does not replace Member State law on trade marks or require undertakings to apply for registration of their trade marks as Community trade marks.

As regards exhaustion of rights, Article 13(1) provides that:

> A Community trade mark shall not entitle the proprietor to prohibit its use in relation to goods which have been put on the market in the Community under that trade mark by the proprietor or with his consent.

The Community trade mark is to be seen as a necessary element of a Single Market in which barriers to the free movement of goods and services are removed and competition is not distorted. It is a legal instrument which enables undertakings to adapt their activities to the scale of the Community market in a more effective manner.

So far as they go, these latest developments stem from the Commission's view, expressed in its 1985 White Paper on the completion of the Internal Market that national industrial property laws still have: '... a direct and negative impact on intra-Community trade and on the ability of enterprises to treat the common market as a single environment for their economic activities.'

INDUSTRIAL PROPERTY RIGHTS AND THE COMPETITION RULES

In line with the decisions of the Court of Justice in connection with the free movement of goods, the mere *existence* of nationally protected industrial and commercial property rights does not infringe Articles 81 (formerly 85) or 82 (formerly 86). In Case 24/67 *Parke, Davis v Probel*, the Court stated that:

> The existence of rights granted by a Member State to the holder of a patent is not affected by the prohibitions contained in Article 85(1) and 86 of the Treaty.

> The exercise of such rights cannot of itself fall either under Article 85(1), in the absence of any agreement, decision or concerted practice prohibited by this provision, or under Article 86, in the absence of any abuse of a dominant position.

It follows, therefore, as we have seen with regard to the free movement rules, that the competition rules may be invoked to prevent the improper *exercise* of industrial property rights. In fact the distinction between the existence of such rights and their exercise was first brought out by the Court in Cases 56 and 58/64 *Consten and Grundig v Commission* (see Chapter 15). It will be recalled that, within the terms of G's exclusive distributorship agreement with C, its French dealer, the German company assigned to C exclusive use of its GINT trade mark in France. The Court ruled that G's purpose was not to protect the essential core or 'specific subject matter' of the trade mark (in order, for example, to prevent other goods being passed off as Grundig products) but to enable C to prevent parallel imports of Grundig products from other Member States, so reinforcing the absolute territorial protection for C, and in a similar manner for G's other dealers in other Member States, which the network of distribution agreements was designed to achieve. It was contrary to Article 85(1) for C to bring a trade mark infringement action in the French national courts pursuant to an agreement which had the object or effect of partitioning the Common Market. As stated by the Court:

> The injunction ... to refrain from using rights under national trade mark law in order to set an obstacle in the way of parallel imports does not affect the grant of those rights but only limits their exercise to the extent necessary to give effect to the prohibition under Article 85(1).

Similarly, the mere existence of a patent, trade mark or other industrial property right does not mean that the owner has a dominant position in terms of Article 82 (formerly 86). Nor is the exercise of such a right by an undertaking in a dominant position in itself abusive. However, an anti-competitive or exploitative exercise of industrial property rights by a dominant firm can infringe Article 82 (formerly 86).

Case 238/87 *Volvo v Erik Veng Ltd*

Volvo were the holders of registered design rights in the UK for spare parts for Volvo vehicles. The company brought an action to prevent Veng from acting in breach of its exclusive rights by copying the parts in question. Veng argued that this amounted to an abuse of Volvo's dominant position by excluding any competition in Volvo spare parts. To avoid this result, it was claimed, Volvo should be ordered to grant a licence of their rights.

Following a reference from the High Court under Article 177 (now 234) regarding the applicability of Article 86, the Court ruled that, in the present state of Community law, it was solely a matter for national law to determine what protection to grant to designs – even for such functional goods as motor vehicle spare parts.

Accordingly, the Court continued:

> ... the right of the proprietor of a protected design to prevent third parties from manufacturing and selling or importing, without its consent, products incorporating the design constitutes the very subject matter of his exclusive right. It follows that an obligation imposed upon the proprietor of a protected design to grant to third parties, even in return for a reasonable royalty, a licence for the supply of products incorporating the design would lead to the proprietor thereof being deprived of the substance of his exclusive right, and that a refusal to grant such a licence cannot in itself constitute an abuse of a dominant position.

> It must however be noted that the exercise of an exclusive right by the proprietor of a registered design in respect of car body panels may be prohibited by Article 86 if it involves, on the part of an undertaking holding a dominant position,

certain abusive conduct such as the arbitrary refusal to supply spare parts to independent repairers, the fixing of prices for spare parts at an unfair level or a decision no longer to produce spare parts for a particular model even though many cars of that model are still in circulation, provided that such conduct is liable to affect trade between Member States.

The Court of Justice did not, however, indicate whether the remedy for any of these abuses was an order for a compulsory licence or was merely a fine and/or an order to terminate the abuse.

Similarly, as seen in Chapter 16, in Cases C-241 and 242/91 *RTE and ITP v Commission (Magill TV Guide)*, the Court of Justice held that the exercise of an exclusive right by the proprietor could, in exceptional circumstances, amount to abusive conduct under Article 82 (formerly 86). It will be recalled that the appellants' refusal to provide the TV listings information by relying on their national copyrights prevented the entry on the secondary market (TV guides) of a new product (the comprehensive guide) which was not provided by the TV companies and for which there was a demand. In this case, a compulsory licence, opening the market to competition, and subject to the payment of reasonable royalties, was ordered.

It has also been seen, in Case T-51/89 *Tetra Pak I*, that, in line with the decision in *Continental Can*, a violation of Article 82 (formerly 86) can occur where an undertaking in a dominant position strengthens that position by taking over another company, thereby acquiring an exclusive licence to exploit industrial property rights.

Patent Licences and Similar Agreements

It is primarily in relation to the application of Article 81 (formerly 85) to patent licences and similar agreements that the competition rules have been invoked. Van Gerven has defined a licence agreement as:

> ... an agreement by which the proprietor of an industrial property right – usually a patent or trade mark, but also for example a plant breeder's right – or a (non-industrial) intellectual property right, particularly copyright or know-how rights, permits another party, the licensee, under certain limitations of time, space and scope defined in the agreement, to perform various production or distribution activities which fall within the legal or factual monopoly right ...

It has often been asked why the Commission is concerned to regulate patent licences at all. Such a licence may be said to 'open the door' on the patentee's monopoly, allowing the licensee to operate where he could not do so before. As in the Article 28 (formerly 30) free movement cases, the Community authorities must differentiate between the terms in a licence which relate to the *existence* of patent rights and those which relate to their *exercise*. The Commission has stated that Article 81(1) (formerly 85(1)) may only apply 'if a grant is accompanied by terms which go beyond the need to ensure the existence of an industrial property right'. As we have seen, the very opportunity to exploit a patent or other right through licences in return for royalties is recognised as an element of the 'specific subject matter' of a patent, as is a 'field of use' restriction in a patent licence which prevents the licensee from manufacturing a certain product which falls within the patent specification. However, Article 81(1) will, for example, be applied by the Commission, in its pursuit of economic integration within the Common Market, to terms similar to those in exclusive distribution agreements which seek to grant licensees 'absolute territorial protection' or which establish minimum prices at which protected products may be sold.

Article 81(1) applies to licence agreements on the same basis as other agreements, that is, where their terms adversely affect trade between Member States and prevent, restrict or distort competition within the Common Market to an appreciable extent. At present, although amendment along the lines of the Vertical Restraints Regulation is expected, exemption from Article 81(1) may be obtained under the terms of Regulation 240/96 (Technology Transfer Agreements). This Regulation provides a block exemption for certain bilateral patent licence agreements, know-how agreements and agreements which combine the licensing of a patent and the transfer of related know-how.

Article 1 exempts various obligations relating to exclusivity and territorial protection. Whish has put the question of exclusivity and the possibility that licensing agreements may isolate national markets into context as follows:

> A licensee may consider that the risk involved in the exploitation of the patented product or the high level of capital investment required are so great that it would not be worth taking a licence at all unless it can be offered some degree of immunity from intra-brand competition from the licensor, other licensees and their customers ...

> ... The licensor could agree to grant an exclusive right to manufacture the goods in a particular territory and to refrain from granting similar rights to anyone else there. In this situation the licensor retains the right to produce the goods in the territory itself, and such a licence is often called a 'sole' licence. It may be distinguished from an 'exclusive' manufacturing licence where the licensor also agrees not to produce the goods in the licensee's territory itself. This of course puts the licensee in a better position to exploit its licence. The licensor could go even further and grant the licensee sole or exclusive selling rights as well. In this situation, the licensee could prevent anyone who manufactured the goods outside its territory from selling them in it.

> The licensee's position may be further reinforced by the licensor agreeing to impose terms on its other licensees preventing them, or requiring them to prevent their customers, from invading the licensed territory. Apart from imposing export bans, there are indirect ways of achieving the same thing: for example a term fixing the maximum quantities of goods that a licensee may produce can be so calculated that it can produce only sufficient to satisfy the demand on its domestic market. In the absence of legal constraints, it would be possible for a licensor to give a licensee absolute territorial protection against any form of intra-brand competition. It would be foolish for the law to intervene and to prevent exclusivity if the result would be to deter firms from accepting licences to exploit new technology altogether. On the other hand, the conferment of geographical exclusivity is precisely the type of practice most likely to alert the EC competition authorities.

As with exclusive distribution agreements, the Community authorities have to strike a balance. There is a conflict and, as Bellamy and Child explain, whereas on the one hand a patent licence appears to be 'restrictive', on the other hand, 'the acceptance of the restrictions may well have led to the successful conclusion of the licence, with the prospect of the dissemination of new technology, increased innovation, and better exploitation of the patented invention'.

In the case which follows, concerning not a patent but the licence of plant breeders' rights, the Court of Justice followed a similar line to that in Case 56/65

Société Technique Minière (see Chapter 15), where it held that an agreement which merely granted exclusive distribution rights, but conferred no absolute territorial protection and contained no export ban, did not necessarily fall within the prohibition of Article 85(1) (now 81(1)), especially if the exclusivity was necessary for the penetration of a new market. In *Nungesser*, the Court was concerned that the licensee should not be deterred from accepting the commercial risks involved in dealing with a new product and should be encouraged to exploit new technology.

Case 258/78 *Nungesser v Commission (Maize Seeds)*

The French agricultural research institute INRA held plant breeders' rights for certain new varieties of maize seeds. INRA granted licences in France and it also granted an exclusive right to produce and sell the varieties in West Germany to Nungesser. INRA undertook to ensure that INRA seeds would not be exported to West Germany except via Nungesser.

In 1972, dealers in France acquired the certified seed and attempted to sell it in the Federal Republic. They were restrained from doing so by Nungesser although it would appear that any industrial property rights had been exhausted by the licensed French growers' sale of the seed to the dealers.

The Commission condemned the exclusive licence under Article 85(1) and refused to grant an exemption under Article 85(3). In Article 173(2) (now 230(4)) proceedings, the Court of Justice drew a distinction between (a) an 'open' exclusive licence, whereby the licensor merely undertakes not to compete himself nor to license anyone else for the same territory, and (b) a 'protected' exclusive licence, under which the parties propose to eliminate all competition from parallel importers purchasing from licensees in other territories; that is, to grant the licensee absolute territorial protection.

The Court was of the view that a licence of the first type was not incompatible with Article 85(1). However, a licence additionally containing obligations of the second type would usually fall under Article 85(1): see, for example, *Consten and Grundig*. The Court upheld that part of the Commission's refusal to grant an Article 85(3) exemption in respect of the absolute territorial protection conferred by the licence.

The Court referred to INRA's years of research and experimentation and to the considerable financial risk attached to the commercial exploitation of the new seeds to justify the exclusivity (which normally means higher royalties), but in trying to prevent the French licensees from exporting, INRA had gone beyond permissible bounds:

As it is a question of seeds intended to be used by a large number of farmers for the production of maize, which is an important product for human and animal foodstuffs, absolute territorial protection manifestly goes beyond what is indispensable for the improvement of production or distribution or the promotion of technical progress ...

It is noteworthy that Regulation 240/96 (and previously Regulation 2349/84) states in recital 10 that:

Exclusive licensing agreements, that is, agreements in which the licensor undertakes not to exploit the licensed technology in the licensed territory himself or to grant further licences there, may not be in themselves incompatible with Article 85(1) where they are concerned with the introduction and protection of a new technology in the licensed territory, by reason of the scale of the research which has been undertaken, of the increase in the level of competition, in particular inter-brand competition, and of the competitiveness of the undertakings concerned resulting from the dissemination of innovation within the Community. In so far as agreements of this kind fall, in other circumstances, within the scope of Article 85(1), it is appropriate to include them in Article 1 in order that they may also benefit from the exemption [see *Nungesser*, paragraphs 53–67].

Comparing the Court's approach in *Nungesser* with the Commission's later block exemption Regulations with regards patent licence agreements, and with the block exemption Regulation 1983/83 for exclusive distribution agreements, it can be seen that, in particular, Article 1 of Regulation 240/96 *exempts* the following obligations relating to exclusivity and territorial protection from the prohibition of Article 85(1) (now 81(1)), providing the bilateral licence agreement contains no other provisions that infringe Article 85(1):

(a) The licensor agrees not to license other undertakings in the licensee's territory: a 'sole' licence.

(b) The licensor agrees not to exploit the licensed invention itself in the licensed territory: a combination of obligations (a) and (b) amount to an 'exclusive' licence.

(c) The licensee agrees not to manufacture or use the licensed product or use the patented process in other licensees' territories, nor in the licensor's territory, within the Common Market.

(d) The licensee agrees not to pursue an active sales policy within other licensees' territories within the Common Market.

(e) The licensee agrees not to sell even passively in other licensees' territories (that is, in response to unsolicited orders) for a period of five years from when the product is first marketed in the Community by one of the licensees.

(f) The licensee agrees to use only the licensor's trade mark to distinguish the licensed product, provided that the licensee is not prevented from identifying itself as the manufacturer of the licensed product.

(g) The licensee agrees to limit production of the licensed product to quantities required in manufacturing its own products.

Among the items in the 'black list' of Article 3 of Regulation 240/96 are provisions which *forbid* requirements in the licence to the effect that the parties shall not meet orders from undertakings in their own territories which intend to resell them within other Member States, and attempts to impede parallel imports from elsewhere in the Community of products which have been lawfully put on the market by the patentee or with its consent (cf *Consten and Grundig*).

Finally, it is appropriate to examine a further patent licence decision of the Court of Justice concerning issues other than exclusivity and territorial protection. The case arose before Regulation 2349/84 came into effect but, as will be seen, it would still fall outside the exempting provisions.

Case 193/83 *Windsurfing International v Commission*

WI, an American company, obtained a patent in West Germany and other Member States for the rig (mast, sail and spars) attached to a sailboard. Boards and rigs are usually sold as a complete unit. The Court agreed with the Commission that all but one of the following restrictions in WI's patent licences with its German licensees were contrary to Article 85(1):

(a) An obligation on the licensee to sell only complete sailboards, that is, the patented rig and a board which had been approved by WI. The patent covered only the rig and WI's control over boards could not be seen as an allowable quality control, tying arrangement necessary for a technically satisfactory exploitation of the licensed products. The clause in question arbitrarily restricted the licensee's freedom and it fell outside the specific subject matter of the patent: see now Articles 2(5) and 4(2)(a) of Regulation 240/96.

(b) An obligation on the licensee to pay royalties on the net selling price of the complete sailboard rather than on the patented rig alone. Unlike the Commission, the Court found no objection to this provision because it was shown that this method of calculating royalties produced a sum no greater than that which would have been fair and acceptable in relation to the rig alone. According to the Commission, if this had not been so, and the licensee's competitive position had been disadvantaged by having to bear costs for which he was 'not compensated through the advantages conferred by the exploitation of the patent', the obligation would have fallen under Article 85(1): see now Article 2(7) of Regulation 240/96.

(c) A requirement that the licensee fix a notice on the board stating that it was 'licensed' by the licensor. This clause gave the erroneous impression that the boards were covered by WI's patent and it was not covered by the specific subject matter of the patent. It was likely to reduce consumer confidence in the licensees as being less technically competent than they in fact were and accordingly allow WI to gain a competitive advantage for itself: see also Article 2(11) of Regulation 240/96.

(d) Obligations on the licensee not to challenge the validity of WI's patent and trade mark. A licensee is obviously well placed to detect any possible flaws in the patentee's title but such a clause, which seeks to prevent a licensee from being released from a burdensome, and invalid, licence, is not within the specific subject matter of a patent and it is in the public interest that such an obstacle to economic activity be eliminated. The no-challenge clauses were contrary to Article 85(1): see also Articles 2(15) and 4(2)(b) of Regulation 240/96.

(e) A restriction on the licensee against manufacturing the sailboard except in certain factories in Germany. WI's argument that this was an essential quality control provision was rejected by the Court.

This case is important in particular (as seen throughout this chapter) for the light it throws on the distinction made between restrictions imposed by industrial property right holders which emanate from the inherent subject matter of the right and are allowable as forming part of the right itself, and those other restrictions which represent an attempt to extend the holder's rights further in a manner which tilts the balance into unjustifiable anti-competitive activity.

As a postscript, it is also important to appreciate with respect to industrial property rights, their existence and their exercise, that the prohibitions in Article 28 (formerly 30) and in Articles 81 and 82 (formerly 85 and 86) apply in a cumulative manner. In *Nungesser*, the Court stated that:

> ... one of the powers of the Commission is to ensure, pursuant to Article 85 of the Treaty and the regulations adopted in implementation thereof, that agreements and concerted practices between undertakings do not have the aspect or the effect of restricting or distorting competition, and that ... the power of the Commission is not affected by the fact that persons or undertakings subject to such restrictions [relating to absolute territorial protection] are in a position to rely upon the provisions of the Treaty relating to the free movement of goods in order to escape such restrictions [through the operation of the exhaustion of rights principle].

REFERENCES AND FURTHER READING

Alexander, W, 'Exhaustion of trade mark rights in the European Economic Area' (1999) EL Rev 56.

Groves, PJ, 'A European Community patent system?' (2000) 31 Student Law Review 58.

Hayes, T, 'Anti-competitive agreements and extra-market parallel importation' (2001) 26 EL Rev 468.

Jehoram, HC, 'The delicate balance between industrial property and European law: the law as it stands' (1976) 1 LIEI 71.

Marenco, G and Banks, K, 'Intellectual property and the Community rules on free movement: discrimination unearthed' (1990) 15 EL Rev 224.

Murphy, G, 'Who's wearing the sunglasses now?' (*Silhouette, Sebago and Davidoff*) (2000) ECLR 1.

Oliver, P, 'Of split trade marks and Common Markets' (1991) 54 MLR 587.

Shea, N, 'Parallel importers' use of trade marks: the ECJ confers rights but also imposes responsibilities' (1997) EIPR 43.

Stone, J, 'Some thoughts on the *Windsurfing* judgment' (1986) EIPR 242.

Vinje, T, 'Harmonising intellectual property laws in the European Union: past, present and future' (1995) EIPR 361.

Weatherill, S, 'Recent case law concerning the free movement of goods: mapping the frontiers of market deregulation' (1999) 36 CML Rev 51 (final section on IPRs, pp 70–85).

Whish, R, *Competition Law*, 2001, Chapter 19.

See generally the European Intellectual Property Review.

PART FOUR

REMEDIES AND THE ENFORCEMENT
OF COMMUNITY LAW AT
COMMUNITY AND NATIONAL LEVELS

JUDICIAL REVIEW AND SUPERVISION OF THE COMMUNITY INSTITUTIONS

INTRODUCTION: ARTICLE 230 (FORMERLY 173)

In Chapter 6, we examined the jurisdiction of the Court of Justice under Article 173(1) EEC (now 230(1) and (2) EC) regarding judicial review of acts of the Community's law makers in the context of Member State claims of defective Treaty basis and inter-institutional disputes. The first of the latter cases raised a question concerning the distribution of powers between the Commission (representing the Community interest) and the Council (representing the interests of the Member States): Case 22/70 *Commission v Council (European Road Transport Agreement)*.

We also saw how the Court extended the scope of its powers of review in Case 294/83 *Les Verts v European Parliament* to cover acts of the Parliament despite the Parliament not being a named defendant in Article 173. A further act of the Parliament was successfully challenged in Case 34/86 *Council v Parliament (Budget)*. In Case 70/88 *Parliament v Council (Chernobyl)*, it was seen that the Parliament was entitled to *challenge* Council or Commission acts where its prerogatives (for example, its right to participate in the legislative process as laid down by the Treaty) were directly affected under a *special right of action* devised by the Court akin to Article 173(1) EEC.

However, as pointed out when discussing these cases, questions of direct challenge to acts of the institutions, of supervision or judicial review of such acts and their possible annulment are not merely constitutional questions of institutional competence. It was argued in Case 70/88 that unless Parliament was entitled to challenge Commission or Council acts, it would stand in an unfavourable position as compared not only with the other institutions but also with the Member States under Article 173(1) and with private parties (natural and legal) under Article 173(2).

In this chapter, attention turns to challenges by private parties and their rights under Article 173(2) (now 230(4)) when seeking judicial review of Community acts. It will be seen that their rights are severely restricted with respect to their access to justice in these cases. This restrictive policy has in turn been severely criticised and is at present under considerable strain.

The history of Article 173 (now 230) is rather complicated. The original wording before the Court's decision regarding the Parliament's status as both defendant and applicant was as follows (it will be seen that private parties, the focus of this section, are covered by 173(2)):

Article 173 EEC

The Court of Justice shall review the legality of acts of the Council and the Commission other than recommendations or opinions. It shall for this purpose have jurisdiction in actions brought by a Member State, the Council or the Commission on grounds of lack of competence, infringement of an essential procedural requirement, infringement of this Treaty or of any rule of law relating to its application, or misuse of powers.

Any natural or legal person may, under the same conditions, institute proceedings against a decision addressed to that person or against a decision which, although in the form of a regulation or a decision addressed to another person, is of direct and individual concern to the former.

The proceedings provided for in this Article shall be instituted within two months of the publication of the measure, or of its notification to the plaintiff, or, in the absence thereof, of the day on which it came to the knowledge of the latter, as the case may be.

Following the Court's decisions regarding the Parliament's position under Article 173 and Treaty amendments at Maastricht, Amsterdam and Nice, the renumbered Article 173 became Article 230 and now takes the form which follows. Although the wording of the present paragraph 4 has not changed from what was paragraph 2, the Article can only be read properly as a whole:

Article 230 EC

The Court of Justice shall review the legality of acts adopted jointly by the European Parliament and the Council, of acts of the Council, of the Commission and of the ECB other than recommendations and opinions, and of acts of the European Parliament intended to produce legal effects vis à vis third parties.

It shall for this purpose have jurisdiction in actions brought by a Member State, the European Parliament, the Council or the Commission on grounds of lack of competence, infringement of an essential legal requirement, infringement of this Treaty or of any rule of law relating to its application, or misuse of powers.

The Court shall have jurisdiction under the same conditions in actions brought by the Court of Auditors and by the ECB for the purpose of protecting their prerogatives.

Any natural or legal person may, under the same conditions, institute proceedings against a decision addressed to that person or against a decision which, although in the form of a regulation or a decision addressed to another person, is of direct and individual concern to the former.

The proceedings provided for in this Article shall be instituted within two months of the publication of the measure, or of its notification to the plaintiff, or, in the absence thereof, of the day on which it came to the knowledge of the latter, as the case may be.

Annulment of a binding institutional act occupies a central place among the judicial sanctions provided for in the Treaty, and, although the procedure was modelled on that found in French administrative law, supervision of the legality of institutional acts is to be found, in one form or another, in the legal systems of all the Member States:

As in the Member States, so in the Communities, the administrative agencies have only limited powers of rule making and individual decision. The Treaties serve as constitutional documents to define those powers, including those of the Council when acting as a legislature. The Treaties also vest in the Court the necessary jurisdiction to control the lawful exercise of such power [Brown and Kennedy (and compare with Mertens de Wilmars in Chapter 10)].

Article 230 therefore now provides the basis for the Parliament, the Council, the Commission and the Member States, as 'privileged' applicants under paragraph 2 to challenge the validity of Community acts as listed in paragraph 1. Under paragraph 4, natural or legal persons (private parties or individuals) may, within the limits laid down, *apparently* only challenge Decisions. In all cases, the Court's function is to determine the validity or otherwise of an institutional act on the basis of the assumption that such an act is valid.

Actions under Article 230 are referred to as direct actions; they are at *Community level* and, for 'privileged' paragraph 2 applicants and other paragraph 3 applicants, are brought before the Court of Justice. Since 1989, applications for annulment made by 'non-privileged' paragraph 4 applicants (private parties) are brought before the Court of First Instance (see Chapter 7).

However, it is important to appreciate that, apart from their limited rights under Article 230(4), natural and legal persons may be able to challenge the validity of Community acts (not merely Decisions) by means of an *indirect action at national level*. This will arise where a national authority has, by way of implementation of Community legislation, brought into effect a measure which affects the rights of such natural or legal persons (usually an undertaking in the latter case). A challenge to the national measure will be based on the claim that its legal base, the relevant Community act, is invalid. This will fall to be determined by the Court of Justice under Article 234(1)(b) (formerly 177(1)(b)):

The Court of Justice shall have jurisdiction to give preliminary rulings concerning:

...

(b) the validity ... of acts of the institutions of the Community ...

Article 230 will now be examined more closely, together with the relationship between Article 230(4) and Article 234(1)(b). Later, it will be necessary to look briefly at Article 241 (formerly 184), which allows for *indirect* challenges at *Community level*, Article 232 (formerly 175), which allows actions to be brought against the Council, the Commission or, since Maastricht, the European Parliament for a *failure to act* (where there is a duty to act), and Articles 235 (formerly 178) and 288 (formerly 215), which enable *'non-contractual' claims* for damages to be brought against Community institutions for loss suffered as a result of unlawful action.

ARTICLE 230: DIRECT ACTIONS FOR ANNULMENT

Five questions arise from the provisions of Article 230:

(1) Which acts may be challenged, that is, are susceptible to judicial review?

(2) Who has the right to challenge? (This is a question of standing or *locus standi*.)

(3) What are the relevant time limits?

(4) On what grounds may the challenge be made?

(5) What are the effects of annulment?

(1)   Reviewable Acts

Measures which produce (or are intended to produce) legal effects are reviewable by the Court of Justice whatever their nature and form. The binding acts of Article 249 (formerly 189) (Regulations, Directives and Decisions) are therefore covered, and the Court itself has added a Council resolution (in Case 22/70 *ERTA*: see Chapter 6), a Commission Communication (withdrawing immunity from fines under the competition rules) which amounted to a Decision in Cases 8–11/66 *Re Noordwijk's Cement Accord* and a measure adopted by the Court of Auditors in Cases 193 and

194/87 *Maurissen and Others v Court of Auditors*. We have also seen in Chapter 6, as noted above, how the Court extended its jurisdiction under Article 173 to binding acts of the Parliament in the *Les Verts* case.

Another Commission Communication was reviewed (and annulled) by the Court of Justice in Case C-57/95 *France v Commission*. Two points are of particular significance. First, the Court confirmed (from previous case law) that all institutional measures 'whatever their nature or form, *which are intended to have* legal effects' (emphasis added) are subject to review. Secondly, the statement by the Advocate General that the Commission's 'operation of camouflaging the proposal for a directive as a communication had not – deliberately or through carelessness – been completely successful'. The Communication covered new important provisions on pension funds in an 'imperative' manner.

(2)   *Locus Standi* (the Standing of the Applicant)

As seen, 'privileged' applicants have an unlimited right to challenge and review under Article 230(2). The basis for this 'privileged' position is that every Community act is deemed to affect these parties (cf the position of the Crown in English administrative law) and they are considered to have a direct interest in any such act. As regards Member States, see also Case 166/78 *Italy v Council*.

The position is different for 'any natural or legal person' under Article 230(4). It is clear that a Decision, which is 'binding in its entirety upon those to whom it is addressed' under Article 249(4) and which is applied in specific cases, may be challenged by the person(s) to whom it is addressed. However, in exceptional circumstances, Regulations (normally of 'general application') and Decisions which are addressed to *others* may also be challenged.

The wording of Article 230(4) shows that a 'non-privileged' applicant may challenge:

(a) a Decision addressed to the applicant; or

(b) a Decision *in the form* of a Regulation which is of direct and individual concern to the applicant; or

(c) a Decision addressed *to another person* which is of direct and individual concern to the applicant.

A Decision Addressed to the Applicant

Little difficulty arises in the case of a Decision addressed to the applicant. For example, the Commission's quasi-judicial Decisions against specified undertakings under Articles 81 and 82 are frequently challenged (there being no *locus standi* problem) and subject to review under Article 230(4): see Chapters 15–17.

A Decision Addressed to Another Person: Individual Concern

Not being the addressee of the Decision, it would *appear* that the applicant will have difficulty in establishing 'direct and individual concern'. However, on the one hand, it will be seen that in the circumstances, there is usually no problem with the fact that the Decision is addressed to another person. In the cases in question, this is the normal, legitimate route whereby the Decision becomes effective – and binding on the applicant. On the other hand, on the basis of the case law as it presently stands, for the applicant to establish individual concern he will have to show that the decision affects him by reason of factors which distinguish him individually. He can only do this if he can show that he is a member of a closed group.

Case 25/62 *Plaumann v Commission*

Under the Common Customs Tariff, importers of clementines from non-EEC countries had to pay a customs duty of 13 per cent. Following requests from the importers, the German government asked the Commission for permission under the then Article 25(3) of the Treaty partially to suspend this duty. When the Commission issued a Decision refusing the government's request, P, one of 30 importers of clementines, challenged this refusal. The Commission claimed that P was not directly and individually concerned. On the question of admissibility, the Court ruled as follows:

> Under the second paragraph of Article 173 [now 230] of the EEC Treaty, 'any natural or legal person may ... institute proceedings against a decision ... which, although in the form of ... a decision addressed to another person, is of direct and individual concern to the former'. The defendant contends that the words 'other person' in this paragraph do not refer to Member States in their capacity as sovereign authorities and that individuals may not therefore bring an action for annulment against the decisions of the Commission or of the Council addressed to Member States.

> However, the second paragraph of Article 173 [now 230(4)] does allow an individual to bring an action against decisions addressed to 'another person' which are of direct and individual concern to the former, but this Article neither defines nor limits the scope of these words. The words and the natural meaning of this provision justify the broadest interpretation. Moreover, provisions of the Treaty regarding the right of interested parties to bring an action must not be interpreted restrictively. Therefore, the Treaty being silent on the point, a limitation in this respect may not be presumed.

> It follows that the defendant's argument cannot be regarded as well founded.

> The defendant further contends that the contested decision is by its very nature a regulation in the form of an individual decision and therefore action against it is no more available to individuals than in the case of legislative measures of general application.

> It follows however from Articles 189 and 191 [now 249 and 254] of the EEC Treaty that decisions are characterised by the limited number of persons to whom they are addressed. In order to determine whether or not a measure constitutes a decision, one must inquire whether that measure concerns specific persons. The contested Decision was addressed to the government of the Federal Republic of Germany and refuses to grant it authorization for the partial suspension of customs duties on certain products imported from third countries. Therefore, the contested measure must be regarded as a decision referring to a particular person and binding that person alone.

> Under the second paragraph of Article 173 of the Treaty, private individuals may institute proceedings for annulment against decisions which, although addressed to another person, are of direct and individual concern to them, but in the present case, the defendant denies that the contested decision is of direct and individual concern to the applicant.

It is appropriate in the first place to examine whether the second requirement of admissibility is fulfilled because, if the applicant is not individually concerned by the decision, it becomes unnecessary to enquire whether he is directly concerned.

Persons other than those to whom a decision is addressed may only claim to be individually concerned if that decision affects them by reason of certain attributes which are peculiar to them or by reason of circumstances in which they are differentiated from all other persons and by virtue of these factors distinguishes them individually just as in the case of the person addressed. In the present case the applicant is affected by the disputed Decision as an importer of clementines, that is to say, by reason of a commercial activity which may at any time be practised by any person and is not therefore such as to distinguish the applicant in relation to the contested Decision as in the case of the addressee.

For these reasons, the present action for annulment must be declared inadmissible.

Plaumann, therefore, being affected by the Decision (addressed to the German government) only as a member of a *general and open* class was not individually concerned and so lacked *locus standi*.

There is no doubt that this test as conceived and applied to the 30 clementine importers in *Plaumann* (and in similar circumstances in other cases) is extremely restrictive and makes it seemingly impossible for an applicant to secure *locus standi* except in retrospective cases (see below). The 'open class' element otherwise presents an apparently unsurmountable barrier. It is also economically unrealistic: Is importing clementines really a commercial activity which may at any time be practised by any person? Or manufacturing isoglucose?

Under Article 25(3) of the Treaty (now repealed), the Commission could suspend a duty on imports where 'serious disturbance of the market of the products concerned' would otherwise result. However, if the applicant lacks *locus standi*, the merits of the Decision are not open to question.

In the following case, the challenge was held to be admissible.

Cases 106 and 107/63 *Toepfer v Commission*

The relevant German authorities mistakenly set the levy on maize imported from France at zero. When T and others applied for import licences for a substantial amount of maize free of levy (so ensuring themselves large profits), the German intervention agency realised its error and refused to grant any licences. Three days later, the Commission confirmed the ban and authorised the German authorities to raise the levy on imports 'including those at present and duly pending'.

T brought an action under Article 173(2) EEC to annul the Commission's Decision addressed to the German authorities.

The Court held that T and the other importers who had applied for licences before the ban was imposed were individually concerned. Their number and identity had become fixed and ascertainable before the contested Decision was made. They were a 'closed group'; the Decision affected their interests and position in a significantly different way from other importers who might wish to apply for a licence after the Decision but during the remaining period of the ban. This Decision was therefore partly closed and partly open.

It will be seen that, as in *Plaumann*, 'another person' may (and in terms of how the Community decision making process often operates will) be a Member State and also that individual concern is established where the measure is of a retrospective nature, that is, at the time it was made, the Commission knew, or was in a position to know, exactly to whom it applied. However, it would appear that where such retrospective effect is missing, 'the possibility of determining more or less precisely the number or even the identity of the persons to whom a measure applies by no means implies that it must be regarded as being of individual concern to them': Case 123/77 *UNICME v Commission*. In such a case, the applicant is seen as being a member, at least theoretically, of an open class.

In *Toepfer*, the Decision addressed to Germany was annulled by the Court, the Commission only having the power to authorise a ban on imports if, as was not the case here, they threatened, as seen in *Plaumann*, to cause 'serious disturbance' of the market.

A Decision in the Form of a Regulation: Individual Concern

In the implementation of Community policy, the Commission frequently acts on the basis of Regulations. This is particularly the case concerning matters relating to the highly regulated common organisation of product markets under the Common Agricultural Policy. For example, production levies may be imposed, licences may be required, subsidies may be withdrawn or imports from third countries may be restricted.

It is arguable that many of these measures, which are frequently of a short term nature and only apply to a limited group of producers, importers or exporters, etc, are not, in a real sense, of a legislative, 'general application' character. It is arguable that they are not 'true' Regulations, but 'disguised Decisions', and that the Council and/or the Commission are using Regulations in order to avoid challenges by the individuals or, more likely, the undertakings involved. Nevertheless, in the main, the Court of Justice has adopted a restrictive approach in such cases. In Cases 789 and 790/79 *Calpak v Commission*, the Court stated that if a measure applies to 'objectively determined situations and produces legal effects with regard to categories of persons described in a generalised and abstract manner', then it is to be accepted as a 'true' Regulation and not susceptible to challenge by a private party. (This case concerned reductions of production aid for Community producers of William pears.)

In cases such as *Calpak*, the Court must have regard, on the one hand, to the often complex and difficult economic management role of the Community in agricultural and other markets and the discretionary powers accorded the institutions in the fulfilment of this role and, on the other hand, to the possibility of harm suffered by individuals as a result of the measures taken and their rights, if any: as discussed in Chapter 10. The adoption of a construction based, 'abstract terminology' test brings the scales down heavily in favour of the Community:

> A provision [in the *Calpak* Regulation] which limits the granting of production aid for all producers in respect of a particular product to a uniform percentage of the quantity produced by them during a uniform period is by nature a measure of general application within the meaning of Article 189 of the Treaty. In fact, the measure applies to objectively determined situations and produces legal effects with regard to persons described in a generalised and abstract manner. The nature of the measure as a regulation is not called in question by the mere fact that it is possible to determine

the number or even identity of the producers to be granted the aid which is limited thereby.

The same conclusion was reached in the following case.

Case 101/76 *KSH v Council and Commission*

At a time of over-production of sugar within the Community, the Council and the Commission introduced Regulations which the applicant alleged discriminated against it as one of only four large manufacturers of a new product, isoglucose, which in some respects competes with sugar. The challenge was inadmissible; the measures were true Regulations and KSH therefore had no *locus standi*.

Nevertheless, as seen in Chapter 4, although a Regulation is usually a Regulation both in form and substance, it may, at least in part, lose its general, objective character and, in deciding a specific issue, become in substance what the Court has called a 'disguised decision'. An individual or undertaking adversely affected by such a measure may be able to show 'direct and individual concern' as required by Article 230(4). A measure is of direct concern to an applicant if it is the direct cause of an effect on him (see below). We will first look in more detail at the rather difficult concept of 'individual concern' in the context of a disputed 'Regulation'.

In the case which follows, a Regulation was seen by the Court as a bundle of Decisions addressed to each applicant for an import licence.

Cases 41–44/70 *International Fruit Co v Commission*

Under Community rules, importers of dessert apples from non-EEC countries were required to apply in advance for import licences to the appropriate national authority. Applications were passed to the Commission on a weekly basis. The Commission then enacted a measure in the form of a Regulation laying down rules for deciding on the applications in question.

In this challenge to the Commission measure, IF argued that, in that it referred back to a *named group of applicant importers*, it concerned a *closed category* of which IF was a member. The measure, it was claimed, was therefore not a true Regulation.

The Court ruled as follows:

It is indisputable that Regulation No 983/70 was adopted [on 28 May 1970] with a view on the one hand to the state of the market and on the other to the quantities of dessert apples for which applications for import licences had been made in the week ending on 22 May 1970.

It follows that when the said regulation was adopted, the number of applications which could be affected by it was fixed. No new application could be added. To what extent, in percentage terms, the applications could be granted, depended on the total quantity in respect of which applications had been submitted.

Accordingly, by providing that the system introduced by Article 1 of Regulation No 565/70 should be maintained for the relevant period, the Commission decided, even though it took account only of the quantities requested, on the subsequent fate of each application which had been lodged.

Consequently, Article 1 of Regulation No 983/70 is not a provision of general application within the meaning of the second paragraph of Article 189 of the Treaty, but must be regarded as a conglomeration of individual decisions taken by the Commission under the guise of a regulation ... each of which decisions affects the legal position of each author of an application for a licence.

Thus, the decisions are of individual concern to the applicants.

In his analysis of the position, Hartley draws attention to two tests which are embodied in the *International Fruit* decision:

(a) Is *the act* a Regulation or a disguised Decision? This is a question of construction: if the act applies to abstractly defined categories of persons, it is a 'true' Regulation.

(b) Is *the applicant* a member of a closed category and therefore individually concerned? A closed category is one the membership of which is already fixed and determined when the measure comes into force (as opposed to a general class or open category, of which the membership is not fixed and determined when the measure comes into force).

Reviewing the cases concerning Regulations, in which the Commission is implementing policy and has a margin of discretion, Hartley has stated that, on the basis of its use of these tests, 'it is hard to avoid feeling that the Court decides first whether it wants the application to be admissible and then applies whichever test will produce the desired result'. A good example is one of the isoglucose cases, *KSH v Council and Commission*, discussed above. At the time, there were only four groups of companies operating in the high-investment isoglucose production field. They were in practical terms a closed category but, with sugar and wheat over-production in mind, the Court chose to deny the company's appeal against production levies by concentrating on the first test and finding the act to be a Regulation in both form and substance.

Although there are exceptions (*International Fruit*, above, decided in 1971 is one), the case law on Article 173(2) EEC, particularly since 1980, showed that where the act in question was in form a Regulation and the Commission was implementing Community policy thereby, the Court would not consider whether it was dealing with a situation where a closed category was involved, but would decide the matter on the basis of the wording of the Regulation. If it was expressed in general, abstract terms, the private applicant would not have *locus standi*. Other cases decided on this first ('true' Regulation) test as opposed to the second (closed category) test include Cases 103–09/78 *Beauport v Commission* (sugar refineries which had previously been allocated a sugar quota; challenge inadmissible) and Cases 789 and 790/79 *Calpak v Commission* (complaint, as seen above, regarding production aid to an identifiable class of producers of preserved pears inadmissible).

It is, however, worthy of note that, in several of these cases, the Advocate General was in favour of the admissibility of the challenge. A private party's challenge to a Regulation at this time which did succeed is to be found in Case C-152/88 *Sofrimport v Commission*, which concerned restrictions on the release into free circulation within the Community of apples imported from non-EEC countries. The Court of Justice concentrated on the question of individual concern rather than whether the measure was a 'true' Regulation. Applying the 'closed category' test, it held that importers (of whom S was one) whose goods were *in transit* when the Regulation was adopted were sufficiently well defined in relation to other importers to be individually concerned. This was particularly so because a further Regulation required that the Commission take special account of the position of such importers.

The Court's restrictive attitude to private applicants under Article 173(2) EEC was not free from criticism: see below, and note the approach taken by the Court in Case C-309/89 *Cordoniu v Council*, decided in 1994 and discussed shortly.

In another isoglucose case, decided in 1980, an undertaking within a closed category was allowed to challenge an act in the form of a Regulation, although it could be argued that the measure was, at least in part, a Decision and so met the requirements of the first test of construction.

Case 138/79 *Roquette Frères v Council*

The Council applied production quotas for isoglucose under Regulation 1293/79. This measure concerned a closed group of isoglucose producers who had previously been subjected to quota restrictions under an earlier Regulation which the Court had found to be discriminatory in an Article 177(1)(b) validity case: Cases 103 and 145/77 *RSH v Agricultural Intervention Board*.

In this case, in addition to the closed group argument, RF was able to point to an annex in the Regulation which listed the isoglucose producers by name and stated their precise quotas under the new rules. The Court ruled on admissibility that:

> It follows that Article 9(4) of Regulation No 1111/77 (as amended by Article 3 of Regulation No 1293/79) in conjunction with Annex II, itself applies the criteria laid down to each of the undertakings in question who are addressees and thus directly and individually concerned. Regulation No 1293/79 therefore is a measure against which the undertakings concerned manufacturing isoglucose may bring proceedings for a declaration that it is void pursuant to the second paragraph of Article 173 of the Treaty.

(The Court later held that, although the Regulation infringed neither the principle of equality of treatment nor that of proportionality, it was void on the procedural ground that the Council had not, as required, consulted the Parliament.)

Two further comments can be made regarding the 'true' Regulation or 'disguised decision' cases. First, in order to follow the case law one has to establish whether the Court has applied the 'general application' test or the 'individual concern' test. One can agree with Weatherill when he states (as regards the approach later taken by the Court) that:

> It is now the standard position of the Court that an applicant has to show that the measure entitled as a 'regulation' is not truly of a legislative nature as well as establish that the measure is of individual concern, in that it applies to a fixed and identifiable group of persons [*EC Law*, 1993].

Although this 'standard position' is, of course, very restrictive of a person's right to challenge, it may be defensible in cases where, as indicated earlier, the Commission and the Council, in pursuance of the Community interest, have acted, in terms of their management functions, in accordance with their wide discretionary powers when making economic policy decisions. This is particularly so in the context of agricultural policy (see the Court's statement in *Ludwigshafener* in Chapter 10), where the issue may be the appropriate means of disposing of a 'sugar mountain'. By denying *locus standi*, the Court thereby refuses to engage in second-guessing the policy decision taken.

Even so, the Court also created an expanding set of *special cases*, in which it may be possible for a challenger to show that a 'true' Regulation is of direct and individual concern to him.

Special Cases

Equality within the Electoral Process

A case with a number of unusual features, not least as regards Article 173(2) EEC, is Case 294/83 *Les Verts v European Parliament* (see also Chapter 6). The Decision in question was taken by the Parliament in 1982; it was addressed to itself and it involved the use of Community funds to subsidise the election expenses of the parties fighting the 1984 elections to the Parliament. The Greens, who did not exist at Community level at the time the Decision was made, challenged the Decision in that, by awarding the bulk of the money to parties already represented in the Parliament, it discriminated against them.

The Greens were clearly members of an open category (new parties who could contest the election), and the Decision applied generally to all political parties who decided to put up candidates. However, in what was clearly a policy decision, the Court held that *Les Verts* were individually concerned. They also held that the Parliament had no power to allocate funds for this purpose at all; the Decision was void. Hartley has put forward the following explanation:

> Thus, if a plainly illegal act were challenged by an applicant who had no alternative means of bringing the matter before the Court, and if the only persons with *locus standi* [parties already represented in the Parliament] would have no interest in bringing proceedings, the Court might well feel obliged to stretch a point in order to declare the application admissible.

Quasi-judicial Acts: Commission Competition and State Aid Decisions

Special considerations also apply, in respect of individual concern, when the Commission takes a Decision (not addressed to the applicant) which relates not to the implementation of Community policy (a function which contains a discretionary element) but which amounts to what has been called a 'quasi-judicial' determination. Such Decisions of fact and law apply in competition and State aid proceedings, and they are, of course, Decisions within the meaning of Article 249 (formerly 189).

The Court adopts a much less rigorous approach to *locus standi* in these cases. Thus, an undertaking which made the original *complaint of harm* (under Article 3 of Regulation 17) as a result of another company's alleged breach of Article 85 (now 81) was held to be individually concerned and so able to challenge the Commission's Decision, which was that no breach of the competition rules had taken place: Case 26/76 *Metro v Commission*. Application of the *Plaumann* test to M's application (M was a member of an 'open class') would have proved fatal.

Subject to certain exceptions, Article 87 (formerly 92) of the Treaty states that 'any aid granted by a Member State ... which distorts or threatens to distort competition by favouring certain undertakings or the production of certain goods shall, in so far as it affects trade between Member States, be incompatible with the Common Market'. If, following an investigation of an alleged violation of Article 87, the Commission finds that aid granted by a State is not compatible with the Common Market, it will address a Decision to that effect to the Member State concerned calling upon it to abolish or alter the aid: Article 88(2) (formerly 93(2)).

The Member State itself may challenge the Decision under Article 230(1) but of greater significance in the present context is the Court's decision in Case 169/84 *COFAZ v Commission*. COFAZ, a French fertiliser producer (a member of an open category), had been one of the original complainants to the Commission regarding Dutch government aid to the French undertaking's competitors. COFAZ and the other complainants also played a part in the Commission's Article 93(2) proceedings, which, however, were *terminated* by a Decision addressed to the Dutch government following alterations to the aid. This Decision was challenged by COFAZ under Article 173(2) EEC. The Court held that the Decision was of 'concern' to the undertaking; it had originated the complaint and played a part in the proceedings, and, providing it could adduce pertinent reasons to show that the Commission's Decision adversely affected its legitimate interests by seriously jeopardising its position on the market in question (this COFAZ could do), the application was admissible.

Quasi-judicial Acts: Community Anti-dumping Regulations

The dumping of goods on the Community market by a non-EC undertaking at unfairly low prices (generally at an export price lower than domestic market price) in order to achieve market penetration or for some other reason can be countered by the imposition of an anti-dumping duty on the goods. Where economic harm is caused, the Commission is empowered to impose a provisional anti-dumping Regulation and the Council a definitive Regulation.

Although such Regulations are of general application and apply to *any exporter* of the product in question, an exporter who is identified in the Regulation will have standing to challenge that part of the act which applies exclusively to him (for example, as regards the particular rate of duty payable on his goods): see Case 113/77 *NTN Toyo Bearing Co Ltd v Council* and compare it with the decision in Case 138/79 *Roquette Frères v Council*, discussed earlier in this chapter.

An *importer* of the product may be able to establish direct and individual concern on a similar basis. In Case 264/82 *Timex Corporation v Council*, the Court decided that a complaint on behalf of the leading Community watch manufacturer that the duty imposed on mechanical watches from the Soviet Union was too low was 'a decision which is of direct and individual concern to Timex'. The company's original complaint had led to the opening of the investigation procedure, its views were heard during that procedure, and the anti-dumping duty was fixed in the light of the effect of the dumping on Timex. The Court stated that 'the contested regulation is therefore based on the applicant's own situation'.

In the 'special situation' identified by the Court in Case C-358/89 *Extramet Industrie v Council*, the applicant importer was able to establish *locus standi* on the following grounds: (a) it was involved in the Commission's preliminary investigations; (b) it was the main importer and end-user of the product; (c) it was seriously affected by the duty imposed, it being very difficult to obtain alternative supplies.

Regulations, Policy and Individual Concern

In *Extramet*, the Court stressed that the anti-dumping Regulation was general in character although certain of its provisions were of direct and individual concern to the applicant importer. The Regulation was not a 'disguised decision'. The Court's decision in Case C-309/89 *Cordoniu v Council* moved this principle out of the field of quasi-judicial acts into the realm of general policy.

Case C-309/89 *Cordoniu v Council*

Council Regulation 2045/89 reserved the word 'crémant' (fizzy) for certain quality sparkling wines produced in specified areas of France and Luxembourg. The aim of the Regulation was to protect the traditional description used in those areas.

C produced quality sparkling wines in specified regions of Spain. One of the company's wines had been designated 'Gran Crémant de Cordoniu' since 1924 by means of a graphic trade mark of which the company was the holder. Other Spanish producers also used the term 'crément'. C sought annulment of the Regulation which prevented it using the term 'crémant' and thus from using its trade mark.

The Court stated that the relevant provision in the Regulation was 'by nature and by virtue of its sphere of application of a legislative nature' but that did not prevent it from being of individual concern to some of those who were affected. It was held that because of its ownership and use of the registered trade mark, C's situation was differentiated from all other persons (note the *Plaumann* test, above) and the Regulation was of direct and individual concern to the Spanish company.

It was further held that the Regulation's reservation of 'crémant' to France and Luxembourg could not be objectively justified and the position constituted discrimination contrary to Articles 7(1) and 40(3) EEC. 'Crémant' was also found to refer primarily to method of manufacture rather than origin.

In Usher's opinion at this time:

Cordoniu represents a considerable landmark. Not only does it confirm that genuinely general legislation may be of individual concern to a particular applicant, enabling that applicant to bring a direct action for annulment, but it would appear to be the first example of such a private direct action leading to the annulment of policy making legislation.

Strong Pressure on the Plaumann Test

For most of the 1990s, neither the case law of the CFI nor the appellate case law of the Court of Justice revealed any real sign that the sparsely reasoned *Cordoniu* judgment was to form the basis for a judicial change of policy with respect to Article 230(4) and a less restrictive approach to the claims of private parties. Perhaps that decision is to be explained by the singularly heavy losses that C would have suffered through the severe restriction of its national trade mark rights had its challenge not been found admissible and the Regulation not been annulled. C argued that the *Extramet* decision (see above) supported this contention and it was a factor taken into account by the Court in that case, the Court referring to Extramet being 'seriously affected' by the anti-dumping Regulation in question.

This approach, in which a finding of individual concern depends on a willingness by the Court to pursue a far deeper factual inquiry into the position of the applicant and the degree of injury suffered – or to be suffered – by him is of significance when considering later developments.

Of significance also is the following case in which, although their claim was declared inadmissible, the applicants made a direct attack on the *Plaumann* test and its related concept of the 'closed group or class' and put forward an alternative and much more general basis for admissibility. It also, as in the above cases, focused upon 'actual or threatened detriment' as the key factor in support of the claim for standing.

Case C-321/95P *Greenpeace International and Others v Commission*

G challenged a Commission Decision granting financial aid to Spain for the construction of two power stations in the Canary Islands by a company which had not carried out an environmental impact assessment. The applicants were environment groups and individuals concerned by the effect on both the environment and tourism.

The CFI declared the action inadmissible as it failed the 'closed category' test; G therefore not having *locus standi*. Before the Court of Justice, G argued, amongst other things, that:

(a) The 'closed category' test was inappropriate to environmental issues, where the interests are common and shared, and the rights related to such interests are normally held by a potentially large number of individuals.

(b) The CFI's approach was contrary to declarations of the Community institutions and the Member States on environmental matters.

(c) Their 'individual concern' was based on their individual rights conferred by Directive 85/337 on environmental impact assessment.

(d) A different approach to Article 173(4) (now 230(4)) should be adopted regarding individual concern with respect to Community acts violating environmental obligations. The applicant should be required to show that (i) he has personally suffered (or is likely personally to suffer) some actual or threatened detriment as a result of the allegedly illegal conduct of the Community institution concerned, such as a violation of his environmental rights or interference with his environmental interests; (ii) the detriment can be traced to the act challenged; and (iii) the detriment is capable of being redressed by a favourable judgment.

G claimed to meet all these requirements.

The Court rejected all these arguments. It stated that the contested Decision, regarding the financing of the power stations, could only affect the environmental rights arising out of Directive 85/337 *indirectly*. Rights under the Directive could be protected by a challenge to the Spanish administrative authorisations issued to the company involved in the construction of the power stations. The national court hearing that challenge could, if necessary, refer questions to the Court under Article 177 (now 234).

The *Greenpeace* decision gave no encouragement to those in support of a relaxation of the admissibility rules except, perhaps, by highlighting the applicants' alternative test. However, it is possible to say that two factors were at work in the late 1990s which gave heart to the reformers and suggested that a further push by them could bring about change. First, was it possible that in the existing case law there were now enough building blocks to construct a stronger, successful challenge to *Plaumann*? Secondly, and most importantly, did the presence of other, more general but related, factors serve to make up a more receptive political and legal climate into which the 'required' change would readily fit? In this latter regard, it was evident that, at both national and European level, pressure was at work, within the context of intensified debate and change in the field of fundamental human rights, concerning effective judicial protection for individuals, inevitably involving more liberal attitudes towards standing and access to justice. These were among the questions occupying the minds of drafters of the EU Charter of Fundamental Rights (and, by 2001, the Convention on the Future of Europe) and were issues which had already brought about relaxations in the rules at Member State level.

The first, more specific 'building block' factor could be seen in the following way. Extramet's successful challenge to the anti-dumping Regulation was, in part, based on factual findings including the degree of financial loss the company would incur as a result of its business activities being 'seriously affected'. If *Extramet* fell within a particular type of 'special case', the Regulation in *Cordoniu* fell within the general policy area of Internal Market regulation. Cordoniu was also in danger of suffering substantial loss. The *Greenpeace* challenge, to a Decision falling within the field of protection of the environment, although brushed aside by the 'closed category' test and by the availability of an alternative indirect challenge under Article 177 (now 234), witnessed, probably for the first time, a case presented by the applicants' legal representatives which was based on an expressly stated, more open approach to the individual concern requirement of Article 173(4) (now 230(4)). As seen, it too depended on actual or threatened detriment to the applicants. Additionally, argument in *Greenpeace* regarding the availability of the alternative route to the Court via Article 177 (now 234) had been subjected to strong criticism by Advocate General Jacobs in *Extramet*, particularly regarding the absence of such a route in situations where there was no national application of the Community measure to challenge – and, even if there was, the lack of expertise in national courts to deal, in *Extramet*, with anti-dumping issues.

It is perhaps not surprising that it was Advocate General Jacobs who returned to the fray in March 2002 in Case C-50/00P *Unión de Pequeños Agricultores v Council* (UPA), first heard by the CFI in late 1998.

Case C-40/00P *Unión de Pequeños Agricultores v Council (UPA)*

Facts and Decision at First Instance in UPA

The Spanish undertaking brought a direct action for partial annulment of a Regulation governing the system of financial aid for olive producers.

The CFI held that the action was inadmissible, UPA not being individually concerned within the terms of the *Plaumann* test. UPA appealed, arguing that they had no alternative cause of action under Article 234(1)(b) because there had been no national application of the Regulation which could be challenged in the Spanish courts. It considered itself denied the fundamental right of access to effective protection unless standing before the Court of Justice was permitted.

The Advocate General's Opinion in the UPA Appeal

Advocate General Jacobs delivered his reasoned submissions four years later in early 2002. It could not in his view be denied that the limited admissibility of actions by individuals was widely regarded as one of the least satisfactory aspects of the Community legal system. It was not merely the restriction on access which was being criticised; it was also the complexity and apparent inconsistency which had resulted from attempts by the Court to allow access where the traditional approach would lead to a manifest denial of justice. Access to the Court was one area above all where it was essential that the law itself should be clear, coherent and readily understandable.

The solution was for the Court to reconsider the case law and adopt a more satisfactory interpretation of the concept of individual concern. The Advocate General's reasons included:

(a) The Article 234(1)(b) indirect route to protection against general measures was open to serious objections: the applicant had no right to decide whether a validity reference was made; the national court could not grant the desired remedy; there might be no challengeable national implementing measures; there were lengthy delays and high costs involved.

(b) Granting standing by way of exception where the applicant had under national law no way of triggering a reference was no solution as it had no basis in the Treaty and would involve the Court in interpreting and applying rules of national law, a task for which it was neither well prepared nor competent.

(c) To create a legal obligation for Member States to ensure that references on the validity of general Community measures were available would not solve most of the above problems and would require interference with national procedural autonomy.

The answer was the need for a recognition that:

> ... an individual should be regarded as individually concerned within the meaning of the fourth paragraph of Article 230 EC by a Community measure where, by reason of his particular circumstances, the measure has, or is liable to have, a substantial adverse effect on his interests.

This would remove, he argued, all the problems set out above, 'and the simpler test would shift the emphasis in cases before the Community Courts away from purely formal questions of admissibility to questions of substance'.

As regards objections to his solution, the Advocate General stated that it was not precluded by the wording of Article 230; fears that the CFI would be overloaded were exaggerated; and the increasingly complex and unpredictable 40 year line of case law should be removed in the light of more liberal developments in the laws of the Member States, and the emphasis in recent years on effective judicial protection.

The Advocate General was of the opinion that the CFI's decision, being based on the restrictive interpretation of individual concern, should be annulled.

The next development was not the decision of the Court of Justice in *UPA*, but the CFI's decision in mid-2002 in Case T-177/01 *Jégo-Quéré v Commission*. It is a decision which marked a dramatic judicial reappraisal and relaxation of the procedural rules facing private parties under Article 230(4). It placed individual concern on a new footing, not dissimilar from that proposed by Advocate General Jacobs:

> ... a natural or legal person is to be regarded as individually concerned by a Community measure of general application that concerns him directly if the measure in question affects his legal position, in a manner which is both definite and immediate, by restricting his rights or by imposing obligations on him.

This statement of principle by a five judge chamber of the CFI arose in the course of a direct action brought by the applicant French company in a case concerning the Common Fisheries Policy and the conservation of fish stocks.

Case T-177/01 *Jégo-Quéré v Commission*

Commission Regulation 1162/2001 introduced urgent measures to reduce catches of young hake in waters off southern Ireland by imposing a general ban on the use of nets of less than a given mesh size on all operatives fishing in the area.

J-Q fished in the area using vessels with a net size smaller than that permitted by the Regulation. It maintained that it was the only company fishing for whiting, that over two-thirds of its average catch was whiting, and that its catches of hake were negligible. J-Q sought annulment of those provisions of the Regulation which would have a serious effect on its business as being unjustified and in breach of the general principles of proportionality and equality.

J-Q argued that the Regulation was not of general application but a bundle of individual Decisions (as in *International Fruit*), that the Commission's attention had been drawn to its sufficiently differentiated situation before the Regulation was adopted, and that a finding of inadmissibility would leave it without a remedy as no act had been implemented with regard to the Regulation at national level against which legal proceedings could be brought under Article 234(1)(b) regarding the validity of an institutional act.

The Commission denied the validity of the applicant's claims and maintained that the Regulation was of a general and abstract application, that it was not of individual concern to J-Q, and that J-Q therefore lacked the necessary standing to bring an action for annulment.

The carefully developed findings of the CFI were as follows:

(a) The contested provisions of the Regulation were addressed in abstract terms to undefined classes of persons and applied to objectively determined situations. Therefore, by their nature, they were of general application.

(b) The contested provisions might nevertheless be of direct and individual concern to the applicant as an economic operator affected by them: *Extramet* and *Cordoniu*.

(c) The contested provisions did not require the adoption of any additional measures at either Community or national level and were of *direct* concern to the applicant (see below).

(d) It was necessary to consider in the light of the *Plaumann* formula whether the applicant was individually concerned by the contested provisions.

(e) The provisions were of concern to the applicant only in its capacity as an entity which fished for whiting using a certain fishing technique in a specified area, in the same way as any other economic operator actually or potentially in the same situation. The applicant was therefore not sufficiently differentiated individually within the meaning of the existing case law. (The CFI was in effect saying that J-Q was in a *Plaumann* 'open category'.)

(f) Article 33 EC did not require the Commission, when adopting measures falling within the Common Agricultural Policy (of which fisheries is a part), to take account of the particular situation of individual undertakings.

(g) The applicant had produced no evidence to show that the contested provisions affected it by reason of a special factual or legal situation of the type found in the *Extramet* or *Cordoniu* cases. The meetings with the Commission prior to the Regulation's adoption did not distinguish the applicant individually in relation to its provisions.

(h) Consequently, the applicant could not be regarded as individually concerned on the basis of the criteria hitherto established by the case law.

(i) As regards the applicant's claim that a finding of inadmissibility would deny the company any remedy enabling it to challenge the legality of the contested provisions, the Court of Justice had confirmed that access to the courts was one of the essential elements of a Community based on the rule of law and was guaranteed in the legal order based on the EC Treaty: Case 249/83 *Les Verts v European Parliament*. The Court based the right to an effective remedy on the constitutional traditions common to the Member States and Articles 6 and 13 of the European Convention on Human Rights (ECHR): Case 222/84 *Johnston v Chief*

Constable of the RUC. This right to an effective remedy had been reaffirmed by Article 47 of the EU Charter of Fundamental Rights (not yet adopted as a legally binding instrument).

(j) In a case such as this, there were no acts of implementation capable of forming the basis of an action by the applicant before the national courts under Article 234(1)(b). The alternative restrictive procedural and substantive route of an action for damages under Articles 235 and 288(2) regarding the non-contractual liability of the Community did not provide a solution that satisfactorily protected the rights of the individual. Access to the right to an effective remedy could not be guaranteed by those alternative procedures in the light of the provisions in the ECHR and the EU Charter cited above.

(k) Although these matters were insufficient in themselves to change the system of remedies and procedures in Article 230(4), it was necessary to reconsider the strict interpretation of the notion of a person individually concerned as found in the earlier case law:

> In order to ensure effective judicial protection for individuals, a natural and legal person is to be regarded as individually concerned by a Community measure of general application that concerns him directly if the measure in question affects his legal position, in a manner which is both definite and immediate, by restricting his rights or by imposing obligations on him. The number and position of other persons who are likewise affected by the measure, or who may be so, are of no relevance in that regard.

(l) The facts showed that the contested provisions imposed detailed obligations (concerning mesh size of the nets to be used) on the applicant:

> It follows that the contested provisions are of individual concern to the applicant, that the inadmissibility objection raised by the Commission be dismissed, and that an order be made for the action to proceed in relation to the substance.

This was certainly a dramatic decision; the most significant since *Francovich* 10 years earlier. It is possible, however, to see it as a natural outcome of what might be called the previous 'liberalisation' cases. It goes to the heart of the difficulties created by the *Plaumann* formula as to the meaning of individual concern, but it does do damage to the wording of Article 230(4), which does not state that 'a measure of general application' can be challenged by an individual. On the other hand, the Court's interpretation of the meaning of individual concern in *Plaumann* is not necessarily written in stone and the Court of Justice itself, as seen, has been responsible for 'reinterpretations' of Article 230 (formerly 173) as in *Les Verts* and *Chernobyl*. The Regulation in *Cordoniu* was a 'true' Regulation. The stress laid by the CFI on the human rights aspect of the case – on access to the right to an effective remedy – reflects the prevailing political and, in large part, legal climate. The CFI was not apparently concerned about a 'floodgates' argument.

It is to be seen that the CFI's test, in terms of the required effect on the applicant's legal position, is that it must be 'both definite and immediate', a vague formulation not in line with previous judicial statements nor with that of Advocate General Jacobs in *UPA* where he speaks of 'a substantial adverse effect on his [the applicant's] interests'. The Court of Justice decision in that case had yet to be reached. Would the Court confirm the CFI's approach? Or, would it propose a reformulation of Article 230 by the Member States? In the circumstances, it could surely not merely stay wedded to the *Plaumann* test in the face of the twin thrusts of the CFI and the Advocate General. The *UPA* appeal was heard in July 2002.

Case C-50/00P *Unión de Pequeños Agricultores v Council*

The appeal against the CFI's inadmissibility decision went forward on the basis that the Regulation deprived the appellant of advantages previously enjoyed but, as it required no implementation at national level, it could not be indirectly challenged under Article 234(1)(b). It was argued that if not granted standing, the appellant would be denied access to effective judicial protection. The contention that no legal remedy was available at national level was disputed by the Commission.

The Court of Justice noted that UPA was not challenging the following findings of the CFI: (a) that the contested Regulation was of general application; (b) that the specific interests of the UPA association were not affected by the Regulation; and (c) that the members of UPA were not affected by the Regulation either by reason of certain attributes peculiar to them or by factual circumstances which differentiated them from all other persons. The Court therefore proceeded to examine the question whether standing could be accorded on the sole ground that, in the alleged absence of any legal remedy before the national courts, the right to effective judicial protection required it.

The Court rejected this contention as it would require the Community Court, in each individual case, to examine and interpret national procedural law. This would go beyond the jurisdiction of the Community Court. In such circumstances, therefore, the onus was on Member States to establish a system of legal remedies and procedures which ensured respect for the right to effective judicial protection. The reason for this being that the Treaty had established a complete system of legal remedies and procedures designed to ensure judicial review of the legality of acts of the institutions – a system, in the Court's view, which, on the basis of Article 234(1)(b), allowed a reference on validity to go forward from national courts to the Court of Justice, in the process bypassing the standing requirement of Article 230(4).

Thus:

> ... national courts are required, so far as possible, to interpret and apply national procedural rules governing the exercise of rights of action in a way that enables natural and legal persons to challenge before the courts the legality of any decision or other national measure relative to the application to them of a Community act of general application, by pleading the invalidity of such act.

Having confined itself strictly to UPA's single, Article 234 basis for its appeal, the Court next placed the onus on the Member States to ensure, so far as possible, that invalidity claims in the national courts reach the Court of Justice. This solution of course flies in the face of the three main points made by Advocate General Jacobs (see above) *against* change along these lines.

Declining any reappraisal of the existing case law, the major thrust of the Advocate General's Opinion was rendered virtually redundant although, immediately prior to suggesting a second way forward, the Court did state that any interpretation of the requirement of individual concern in an action challenging a Regulation cannot have the effect of setting aside the condition in question, expressly laid down in the Treaty, without going beyond the jurisdiction conferred by the Treaty on the Community Courts. This bold statement appears to sound the death knell for *Jégo-Quéré* and reform through the Community Courts.

The Court's second way forward was through an amendment of the Treaty. While this proposal is obviously sound, it requires the full support of all 15 (or 25) Member States – and the Council was opposed to the admissibility of UPA's claim. This proposal for change was also an admission by the Court, the only admission, that all is not well with the present state of Community law with respect to Article 230(4):

> While it is, admittedly, possible to envisage a system of judicial review of the legality of Community measures of general application different from that established by the founding Treaty and never amended as to its principles, it is for the Member States, if necessary, in accordance with Article 48 EU, to reform the system currently in force.

This decision will be a disappointment for those wishing to see the Court adopt an activist approach and follow the line taken by Advocate General Jacobs and the CFI. However, it was signposted in the Court's 1995 report on the application of the TEU prior to the 1996 Intergovernmental Conference. In that report, the Court asked:

> Whether the right to bring an action for annulment under Article 173 [now 230] of the EC Treaty ... which individuals enjoy only in regard to acts of direct and individual concern to them, is sufficient to guarantee for them effective judicial protection against possible infringements of their fundamental rights arising from the legislative activity of the institutions.

Providing the Community Courts feel they can deal with the workload (the CFI appeared to have no worries on this account in *Jégo-Quéré*), amendment of Article 230(4), enabling private parties to challenge any binding act which has a substantial adverse effect on their interests, would seem to be the solution. It would allow a fresh start to be made, drawing a line under the increasing disarray into which the present case law has fallen.

Direct Concern

Even after the necessarily lengthy discussion of individual concern, it should be recalled that, in order to establish *locus standi*, a 'non-privileged' applicant must establish both individual and *direct concern*. Direct concern is a matter of cause and effect: under Article 230(4) (formerly 173(4)) a natural or legal person will be directly concerned where there is a direct causal link between the challenged Community measure and its impact on the applicant. The question normally arises where the Commission issues a Decision to a Member State authorising or requiring it to act in a particular way. If the power granted to the Member State is merely discretionary, the fact that the power would, if exercised, affect the applicant does not mean that he has *locus standi* to challenge the Commission's original Decision. He is not directly concerned by it owing to the interposition of the autonomous will of the Member State between the Decision and its effect upon him.

However, if the Member State's power is *not* discretionary (as in the *International Fruit* case, concerning the implementation of the Commission's weekly Decisions regarding the availability of import licences for apples) or if a Member State exercises its power first and the Commission confirms it later (as in *Toepfer*, another import licence case), these are situations where no independent will stands between the Decision and its effect on the applicant, who will be directly concerned. The national measure is equated to the Community Decision, which accordingly directly affects (concerns) the private party.

It has, on occasion, been difficult to perceive a consistent line of approach by the Court regarding direct concern. In Case 69/69 *Alcan v Commission*, the Commission rejected (by a Decision) a request by the Belgian government which, if granted, would have authorised the government to act to the benefit of Alcan. As, theoretically at least, the Belgian government might have decided not so to act (but why did it make the request in the first place?), Alcan, who was individually concerned, was held not to be directly concerned and could not challenge the Commission's refusal. Conversely, in Case 11/82 *Piraiki-Patraiki v Commission*, a Commission Decision authorised the French government to impose a general quota system on imports of Greek yarn. Here the Court considered that the possibility that the government would not implement the Community Decision was 'purely theoretical'. France was not legally obliged to exercise the power granted but was in fact already exercising a restrictive system of licences for such imports from the new Member State. The Greek applicants were held to be directly concerned (and individually concerned so far as they had entered into export contracts, prior to the Decision, to be performed subsequently (This, however, was a point specially taken into account by a provision of the Greek Act of Accession.)

(3)　Time Limits

Article 230 (formerly 173) lays down a time limit of two months for bringing an action for annulment. Paragraph 5 states that 'proceedings ... shall be instituted within two months of the publication of the measure, or of its notification to the plaintiff, or, in the absence thereof, of the day on which it came to the knowledge of the latter, as the case may be'.

The two month limit does not apply to indirect challenges under Article 234 (formerly 177) although national limitation rules will apply.

(4)　Grounds for Annulment

Four grounds for annulment are set out in Article 230(1). An applicant may plead any one or more of these grounds. They are of an overlapping nature and the Court does not necessarily state upon which ground(s) it has decided a successful challenge.

(a) Lack of Competence

As we have seen, an institutional act must have a legal foundation in a Treaty provision – either directly or indirectly via another institutional act. If an institution adopts an act which has no sufficient legal base, that institution has acted, in English law terms, *ultra vires*. It has acted beyond its powers and the act will be annulled (declared void) for lack of competence.

The availability of residual legislative powers under Article 308 (formerly 235), the broad scope of Article 95 (formerly 100a) relating to Internal Market harmonisation measures, and the doctrine of implied powers (see Chapter 6) means that this ground is very rarely invoked. Nevertheless, in the *Tobacco Advertising Directive* case (see again Chapter 6) the Court of Justice ruled that the Directive could not be based on Article 100a.

(b) Infringement of an Essential Procedural Requirement

Similar to the English legal concept of procedural *ultra vires*, this ground has usually been invoked where there has been either an alleged failure to give adequate reasons for the act as required by Article 253 (formerly 190), or where it has been claimed that the Council has failed to consult the Parliament where the Treaty so prescribes.

In Case 24/62 *Germany v Commission (Brennwein)*, the Court struck down a Commission Decision because of the 'inadequacy, the vagueness and the inconsistency of the statement of reasons'. In Case 138/79 *Roquette Frères v Council* (yet another isoglucose case; see above and also Rudden in 'References and Further Reading' at the end of the chapter), a Council Regulation was annulled on the ground that the Council had not properly consulted the Parliament as required by what is now Article 37(2) of the Treaty.

We have also seen in Chapter 10 in Case 17/74 *Transocean Marine Paint Association* that the Commission's failure to grant TMPA a hearing when modifying its Article 85(3) individual exemption amounted to a breach of this requirement.

(c) Infringement of the Treaty or any Rule of Law relating to its Application

This ground, while encompassing the previous two, goes further and is pleaded in almost all cases. In particular, 'any rule of law' relating to the application of the Treaty brings into play those general principles of law developed by the Court (see Chapter 10) against which the validity of Community acts must be measured. Case law illustrations, which have been examined elsewhere (see, for example, Chapter 10) include *Transocean Marine Paint Association* (breach of the principle of natural justice, in particular the rule of *audi alterem partem*), Case 112/77 *August Töpfer v Commission* (Decision annulled for breach of the principle of legal certainty) and Case 4/73 *Nold v Commission* (an alleged breach of fundamental human rights).

(d) Misuse of Powers

The Court's case law defines misuse of powers as the adoption by a Community institution of a measure with the exclusive or main purpose of achieving an end other than that stated or evading a procedure specifically prescribed by the Treaty or other provision of Community law for dealing with the circumstances of the case.

A claim under this head therefore alleges the use of a legitimate power in an illegitimate way or for an illegitimate end. It is a ground which is very rarely invoked with success as it means that the applicant must establish the motive or intentions of the institution in question when exercising the power: see Cases 18 and 35/65 *Gutman v Commission*, in which a Community official purportedly transferred to Brussels 'in the interests of the service' had in fact been transferred for disciplinary reasons.

(5)   The Effect of Annulment

Article 231 (formerly 174)

If the action is well founded, the Court of Justice shall declare the act concerned to be void.

> In the case of a Regulation, however, the Court of Justice shall, if it considers this necessary, state which of the effects of the Regulation which it has declared void shall be considered as definitive.

Article 233 (formerly 176)

> The institution or institutions whose act has been declared void or whose failure to act has been declared contrary to this Treaty shall be required to take the necessary measures to comply with the judgment of the Court of Justice ...

If the Court declares an act to be void, such a declaration has a retroactive effect and, subject to Article 231(2), the act is therefore void *ab initio*.

The effect of Article 231(2) is that, where it is necessary in the interests of legal certainty and to avoid undue damage to the Community, which has based other measures upon it, or to others, who have relied upon it, an annulled Regulation may be kept in force, at least in part, until it is replaced. It will also be recalled that in Cases 56 and 58/64 *Consten and Grundig* and Case 27/76 *United Brands,* the Court held that the Commission's Decisions were only invalid in part.

The isoglucose cases illustrates in a graphic way successive attempts by the Council and Commission to adopt Regulations to control the sugar market in the face of a series of challenges to the Community measures by the manufacturers of isoglucose. As indicated above, a ruling by the Court that an act is void may lead to a further claim by the applicant for compensation in accordance with Article 235 (formerly 178) and Article 288(2) (formerly 215(2)) regarding the non-contractual liability of the Community.

ARTICLE 234(1)(b) (FORMERLY 177(1)(b)): INDIRECT ACTIONS FOR ANNULMENT AT NATIONAL LEVEL

Where a Community act requires and has achieved application by means of a national measure (this is particularly so in the agricultural field), provided a cause of action against such *national* measure can be established by an individual or an undertaking (probably judicial review proceedings), it is possible to claim before the national court or tribunal that the relevant Community act upon which the national measure is based is invalid. By means of a reference to the Court of Justice under Article 234(1)(b), this claim can then be determined. (However, the absence of any guarantee that the Article 234(1)(b) indirect route via a reference will be available to an applicant, as highlighted by Advocate General Jacobs in the *UPA* case, above, should be borne in mind.)

Where such indirect challenge is possible, the claimant avoids the difficult question of 'direct and individual concern' and the two month time limit in Article 230 (formerly 173). In addition, Article 234(1)(b) lays down no limitation as to the type of Community act which may be challenged; it does not limit the challenge to Decisions, disguised or otherwise. This Article therefore provides a significant, further form of protection for individuals under the Treaty. (It must be remembered that national courts themselves have no jurisdiction to declare that acts of the Community institutions are invalid: Case 314/85 *Foto Frost* – see Chapter 9.)

The isoglucose cases clearly illustrated the relationship between the 'old' Articles 173(2) and 177(1)(b) EEC. In Case 101/76 *KSH v Commission and Council,* the applicant isoglucose producer, as seen earlier, failed to establish *locus standi* in its challenge under Article 173(2) to a 'true' Regulation which it alleged discriminated against isoglucose in favour of sugar. When the Dutch Intervention Agency, in pursuance of the Regulation in question, claimed payment of a substantial levy from KSH, the company brought an action in the Dutch courts against the Agency's decision and again claimed that the Regulation was invalid: Case 125/77 *KSH v Netherlands Intervention Agency*. This case raised the same (previously inadmissible) claims regarding the Regulation as in the Article 173(2) challenge: its stated reasons were inadequate, it was discriminatory, the speed with which it had been adopted was a breach of the principle of legal certainty and it represented a misuse of power.

Following a reference to the Court of Justice on the basis of Article 177(1)(b), the Court ruled that 'consideration of the questions raised has disclosed no factor of such a kind as to affect the validity of Council Regulation (EEC) No 1862/76 and Commission Regulation (EEC) No 2158/77'.

A similar situation arose in connection with the Commission's Berlin butter scheme. In Case 97/85 *Union Deutsche Lebensmittelwerke v Commission*, a German margarine producer sought annulment of a Commission Decision addressed to the relevant German authorities authorising a scheme for selling cheap butter on the West Berlin market. The scheme was for only a short period of time and it had the object of researching into consumer demand for butter. UDL's challenge under Article 173(2) failed for lack of individual concern. The following case arose out of *the same set of facts*.

Case 133-136/85 *Walter Rau v BALM*

WR and other German margarine producers challenged the German measures which implemented the Commission's cheap butter scheme on the basis that the Commission Decision was invalid on several grounds including that of lack of proportionality. On the basis of a reference from the German national court under Article 177(1)(b), the Court of Justice ruled that:

> It must be emphasised that there is nothing in Community law to prevent an action from being brought before a national court against a measure implementing a Decision adopted by a Community institution where the conditions laid down by national law are satisfied. When such an action is brought, if the outcome of the dispute depends on the validity of that Decision the national court may submit questions to the Court of Justice by way of a reference for a preliminary ruling, without there being any need to ascertain whether or not the plaintiff in the main proceedings has the possibility of challenging the Decision directly before the Court.

> The answer to the first question must therefore be that the possibility of bringing a direct action under the second paragraph of Article 173 of the EEC Treaty against a Decision adopted by a Community institution does not preclude the possibility of bringing an action in a national court against a measure adopted by a national authority for the implementation of that Decision on the ground that the latter Decision is unlawful.

> ...

> Next, it must be emphasised that the operation constituted, as it was intended to, the basis of a scientific survey from which the Commission was able to derive useful information. Furthermore, the Commission chose the West Berlin market because of its isolated geographical location and the possibility of carrying out there, in view of its limited size, an operation at relatively low cost. In so doing,

> the Commission would not appear to have exceeded the discretion conferred upon it by the Council in Article 4 of Regulation No 1079/77.
>
> Accordingly, the answer to the eighth question must be that consideration of the Decision of 25 February 1985 has not disclosed any evidence of a breach of the principle of proportionality.

However, in its decision in Case C-188/92 *TWD Textilwerke v Germany*, the Court of Justice qualified the position it had adopted in *Walter Rau* with respect to the relationship between Article 173 and Article 177, at least as regards the rights of a plaintiff proceeding by way of Article 177 who has failed to mount a direct action under Article 173 when *clearly in a good position to do so*.

Case C-188/92 *TWD Textilwerke v Germany*

Commission Decision 86/509, which was addressed to the German government, declared State aid granted to 'a producer of synthetic yarns situated in Deggendorf' to be incompatible with the Common Market. The producer in question was obviously TWD. The German authorities were required to recover the aid. They informed TWD in writing of the Decision and indicated that it could be challenged under Article 173.

No Article 173 action was brought and a German ministerial decision was issued, revoking the aid and requiring TWD to repay it. TWD sought annulment of the Minister's decision in the national courts on the ground that it was based on an invalid prior Decision of the Commission. The Court of Justice was asked: (a) under Article 177(1)(a) whether a national court was bound by a Decision of the Commission which had not been challenged under Article 173 within the relevant time limit; and (b) under Article 177(1)(b) whether the Commission Decision was invalid.

The Court held that an indirect challenge was not possible in these circumstances. TWD had not instituted Article 173 proceedings previously (as was the case in *Walter Rau*), and it was settled law that, for the purpose of *locus standi*, the recipient of unlawfully paid State aid was directly and individually concerned by a Commission Decision to that effect. TWD had been notified of the Decision and of its right to challenge under Article 173.

TWD could clearly – 'without any doubt' – have challenged the Decision under Article 173 but the company had allowed the two month time limit to expire. It could not later challenge under Article 177 as this would enable it to overcome the definitive (that is, conclusive) nature the Decision assumed once the time limit expired. The national court was bound by the Decision at that time on the basis of the principle of legal certainty. Community acts cannot be called into question indefinitely.

It would seem to follow that, if it is not clear that a party has *locus standi* under Article 173 (now 230), the Court would be open to allowing an Article 177 (now 234) action – and even more so if a party had not been informed of the relevant measure in time to challenge under Article 173 (now 230). Perhaps the safest course is to commence a direct action just in case. Bearing in mind the case law in this area, it is rare that an applicant can know 'without any doubt' that he could have challenged directly. (Note, however, a recent case in which a company 'undoubtedly had a right of action before the Court of Justice': see the anti-dumping duty decision in Case C-239/99 *Nachi Europe v HZA Krefeld*.) What is clear from *TWD* and *Nachi Europe* is that State aid and dumping cases, which often raise difficult questions of economic fact, are better suited to a hearing before the Community Courts.

On the basis of the Court's decision in Case 66/80 *International Chemical Corporation*, the effect of a successful indirect challenge (see, for example, Case 181/84 *R v Intervention Board ex p Man (Sugar) Ltd* in Chapter 10) is that although the Court's ruling is only binding on the national court which made the reference, 'it is sufficient reason for any other national court to regard that act as void', although a further ruling may be requested by such a court.

Although the Treaty is silent on the matter, the grounds for annulment following an indirect challenge are the same as those following a direct challenge.

Indirect Challenges and Interim Relief in National Courts

Another Article 177 (now 234) validity case decided in 1991 is of considerable importance in two respects: (a) the Court's concern to develop effective remedies for individuals, here interim relief; and (b) its insistence on there being a coherent and inter-related system of remedies in this area at both Community and national level.

Cases C-143/88 and C-92/89 *Zuckerfabrik Süderdithmarschen v HZA Itzehoe*

Administrative decisions taken by the German customs authorities under a duty to implement Council Regulation 1914/87 relating to the sugar sector led to sugar producer ZS being required to pay over DM 3.5 million by way of a 'special elimination levy'. In the course of national proceedings, questions arose as to the validity of the Regulation and the power of a national court to suspend a national administrative act adopted on the basis of a disputed Regulation.

Questions were submitted to the Court of Justice under Article 177(1)(a) on the interpretation of the Treaty, in particular, under what conditions might a national court order stay of execution of a national measure based on a Community Regulation on the ground of doubts which it might have as to the validity of that Regulation? The Court was also asked on the basis of Article 177(1)(b) to consider the validity of Regulation 1914/87. On these questions, the Court ruled that:

(a) Suspension of such a national measure could be granted by a national court provided (i) that the court had serious doubts as to the validity of the Community act; and (ii) if the question of that act's validity had not already been referred, the national court *must* refer it; (iii) there must be urgency, the applicant being threatened by serious and irreparable harm (purely financial loss cannot be regarded as irreparable); (iv) the national court must give due consideration to the Community interest particularly where a stay of execution was likely to lead to a financial risk for the Community.

(b) No grounds had been revealed to affect the validity of Regulation 1914/87.

The significance of this decision is as follows. In the context of an application for annulment of a Community act under Article 230 (formerly 173), the Court may, under Article 242 (formerly 185), 'if it considers that the circumstances so require, order that application of the contested act be suspended' and under Article 243 (formerly 186), the Court 'may in any cases before it prescribe any necessary interim measures'. In the interests of coherence of the system of provisional protection, the Court felt that national courts should similarly possess the right to suspend a national measure based on a disputed Community Regulation or any other binding Community act.

Thus, in a case such as this, in national proceedings concerning an implementing measure, and where, as an ancillary matter, the validity of the originating Community

Regulation is seriously disputed, protection should be afforded a party in the context of an Article 234 (formerly 177) reference to the Court of Justice, which alone can decide on the Regulation's validity: Case 314/85 *Foto-Frost*.

The Court found additional support for this decision in its *Factortame* ruling where, for the protection of a party, similar suspensory rights had been afforded national courts regarding the application of disputed national legislation in the context of problems relating to its compatibility with Community law. (For a discussion of Case C-213/89 *R v Secretary of State for Transport ex p Factortame*, see the next chapter.)

In *Zuckerfabrik*, the Court of Justice indicated that it would allow national courts to suspend Community legislation on the same conditions. In the case which follows, the *Zuckerfabrik* ruling on suspension of a national measure was taken a step further. In similar circumstances, could a national court make a positive order provisionally disapplying the Regulation in issue?

Case C-465/93 *Atlanta v BEF*

Council Regulation 404/93 introduced a revised system of import quotas for bananas from non-ACP countries. Atlanta were assigned reduced quotas by BEF (the German Federal Food Office). The company sought interim relief in the form of an order that BEF grant additional import licences pending the decision of the Court of Justice regarding the Frankfurt court's reference on the validity of the Regulation.

The national court also referred two questions under Article 177(1)(a):

(a) Could a national court, having referred the question of validity, not only suspend the national measure based on the Regulation but also, by an interim order, provisionally settle or regulate the disputed legal positions or relationships until the Court gave its ruling?

(b) Under what conditions could such an order, if permissible, be granted and should any distinction be made between an interim order intended to preserve an existing legal position and one which was intended to create a new legal position?

The Court of Justice followed the reasoning it had adopted in *Zuckerfabrik* and drew attention to its authority under Article 185 (now 242) and its power under Article 186 (now 243) to prescribe any necessary interim measures. The conclusion reached was that:

The interim legal protection which the national courts must afford to individuals under Community law must be the same, whether they seek suspension of enforcement of a national administrative measure adopted on the basis of a Community regulation or the grant of interim measures settling or regulating the disputed legal positions or relationships for their benefit. [In the latter regard, the interim order effectively suspends the application of the contested Community act.]

In answering the second question, the Court 'refined' the conditions laid down in *Zuckerfabrik* and elaborated as follows:

(a) The national court must set out the reasons for which it considers the Court should find the Community measure invalid.

(b) The extent of the discretion allowed to the EC institutions by the Court's case law must be taken into account.

(c) The irreversible harm must be such as to materialise before the Court is able to rule on the validity question.

(d) In terms of the 'Community interest', the impact of suspension on the Community legal regime must be considered together with the appropriateness of financial guarantees or security.

(e) Due account must be taken of any previous Article 173 judgments concerning the legislation in question.

On this new final point, it is pertinent to note two earlier challenges to Regulation 404/93. Atlanta's own Article 173 action was dismissed by the CFI for lack of *locus standi*, and an action under Article 173(1) by Germany had also failed, the Court refusing to grant any interim relief. In the present case, the Frankfurt court *had already ordered* interim relief as it was empowered to do under national law (by ordering BEF to grant Atlanta additional licences) but, in the light of the Court's strict conditions concerning previous Article 173 rulings, it appears that it should not have done so.

The jurisdiction of national courts has been extended by this decision but the prospects for Atlanta did not appear good: later, a claim for damages also failed. In further 'bananas' litigation, Case C-68/95 *T Port GmbH v BLE*, a question was put to the Court of Justice concerning the powers of a national court to grant interim relief to importers pending a Commission Decision on requests for increased quotas. The question asked if the national court could make an interim order granting such an increase. This the Court held to be beyond the competence of the national court.

ARTICLE 241 (FORMERLY 184): INDIRECT CHALLENGE AT COMMUNITY LEVEL

Although the two month time limit on direct challenges under Article 230 (formerly 173) can be justified in the interest of legal certainty, and it has been argued that the *locus standi* restrictions for individuals under Article 230(4) prevent undue constraints being placed on the implementation of Community policy, this does mean that an illegal act, 'perfected' by lapse of time, may form the basis of further illegal acts.

The terms of Article 241 therefore provide, for example, for a situation where a Regulation, a general act, which has become immune from direct challenge by lapse of time, nevertheless forms the legal basis for a Decision of direct and individual concern to the applicant:

Article 241 (formerly 184)

Notwithstanding the expiry of the period laid down in the fifth paragraph of Article 230, any party may, in proceedings in which a regulation adopted jointly by the European Parliament and the Council, or a regulation of the Council, of the Commission or of the ECB is in issue, plead the grounds specified in the second paragraph of Article 230, in order to invoke before the Court of Justice the inapplicability of that regulation.

The Decision may be challenged by the person affected and set aside if the Court is satisfied that the Regulation upon which it is based is tainted with illegality on one or more of the grounds specified in Article 230. Where the Regulation is found to be 'inapplicable', the Decision becomes invalid, in that it has no legal foundation.

The operation of Article 184 was explained by the Court of Justice in Case 294/83 *Les Verts* in the following terms:

... Natural and legal persons are ... protected against the application to them of general measures which they cannot contest directly before the Court by reason of the special conditions of admissibility laid down in the second paragraph of Article 173 [now 230(4)] of the Treaty. Where the Community institutions are responsible for the administrative implementation of such measures, natural or legal persons may bring a direct action before the Court against implementing measures which are addressed to them or which are of direct and individual concern to them and, in support of such an action, plead the illegality of the general measure on which they are based ...

Thus, Article 241 does not give rise to a separate cause of action and in a leading case on the then Article 184, Case 92/78 *Simmenthal v Commission*, an Italian meat importer directly challenged a Commission Decision (under Article 173) on the basis that, in line with Article 184, several Regulations and notices on which the Decision was based (and which could not themselves be challenged for reasons of standing and time limits) were invalid. Although querying whether a notice of invitation to tender could be indirectly challenged in this way, the Court concluded that 'these notices are general acts which determine in advance and objectively, the rights and obligations of the traders who wish to participate' and went on to state that:

The field of application of the said Article must therefore include acts of the institutions which, although they are not in the form of a regulation, nevertheless produce similar effects and on those grounds may not be challenged under Article 173 by natural or legal persons other than Community institutions and Member States.

This wide interpretation of Article 184 derives from the need to provide those persons who are precluded by the second paragraph of Article 173 from instituting proceedings directly in respect of general acts with the benefit of a judicial review of them at the time when they are affected by implementing decisions which are of direct and individual concern to them.

The notices of invitations to tender of 13 January 1978 in respect of which the applicant was unable to initiate proceedings are a case in point, seeing that only the decision taken in consequence of the tender which it had submitted in answer to a specific invitation to tender could be of direct and individual concern to it.

There are therefore good grounds for declaring that the applicant's challenge during the proceedings under Article 184, which relates not only to the above-mentioned regulations but also to the notices of invitations to tender of 13 January 1978, is admissible, though the latter are not in the strict sense measures laid down by regulation.

Where an illegality plea is successful, the Regulation (or other act) in question is declared inapplicable. It will be withdrawn with the effect of removing the legal basis of any Decision adopted under it. Although seemingly providing a useful supplement to Article 230 for non-privileged applicants, the 'plea of illegality' under Article 241 is rarely brought before the Court of Justice. Nevertheless, it should be noted that in Joined Cases T-244 and 486/93 *TWD Deggendorf v Commission*, which followed the refusal of the Court of Justice to allow the German firm to resort to an Article 177 (now 234) indirect challenge to the Commission's State aid Decision when an available direct challenge under Article 173 (now 230) was available, the CFI limited access to Article 184 (now 241) as well. (This Article only refers to Regulations, although *Simmenthal*, above, offered some hope for success.)

ARTICLE 232 (FORMERLY 175):
DIRECT ACTIONS FOR FAILURE TO ACT

As we have seen, Article 230 (formerly 173) governs direct challenges to allegedly unlawful acts of the institutions; Article 232 (formerly 175) concerns challenges to omissions or failures to act where there is a duty to act:

Article 232 (formerly 175)

Should the European Parliament, the Council or the Commission, in infringement of this Treaty, fail to act, the Member States and the other institutions of the Community may bring an action before the Court of Justice to have the infringement established.

The action shall be admissible only if the institution concerned has first been called upon to act. If, within two months of being so called upon, the institution concerned has not defined its position, the action may be brought within a further period of two months.

Any natural or legal person may, under the conditions laid down in the preceding paragraphs, complain to the Court of Justice that an institution of the Community has failed to address to that person any act other than a recommendation or an opinion ...

Under the TEU, the Parliament was added to the named institutions in paragraph 1 *against whom* proceedings may be brought under Article 175 (now 232) for failure to act. In the *Transport* case in the early 1980s (see below), the Court of Justice held that the Parliament, as one of the 'other institutions of the Community' in what was then paragraph 1 had a right to *bring* proceedings under Article 175 (now 232). It is therefore now the case that the position of the European Parliament under both Articles 230 (formerly 173) and 232 (formerly 175) as an applicant and as a defendant institution is broadly in line with that of the other political institutions. This development, brought about initially by the Court of Justice in *Les Verts*, the *Budget* case and *Chernobyl* (Article 173) and the *Transport* case (Article 175), as traced in this chapter and the second part of Chapter 6, in large part reflects the increasingly enhanced powers of the Parliament in relation to the Community budget and the legislative process, as seen now in Article 251 (the 'co-decision' procedure) and Article 252 (the 'co-operation procedure').

Returning to Article 175 (now 232), inter-institutional disputes and the *Transport* case, see as follows.

Case 13/83 *Parliament v Council (Transport Policy)*

The Parliament called for a declaration that the Council had infringed the Treaty by failing to introduce a Common Transport Policy as required by Article 74 (now 70) and by failing to act on 16 Commission proposals relating to transport.

The Court held that:

(a) The Parliament had a right to bring an action under Article 175 (although it did not, at that time, have any such right under Article 173).

(b) The Council had been 'called upon to act' in the correct manner under Article 175(2) and the Council had failed to define its position: 'The reply neither denied nor confirmed the alleged failure to act nor gave any indication of the Council's views as to the measures which, according to the Parliament, remained to be taken.'

(c) ...o introduce a Common Transport Policy was insufficiently p... ...unt to an enforceable obligation. Although no complete nor consistent set o... ...egulations existed, the discretionary nature of the Council's policy role was such that its failure to act further was 'not necessarily a failure to act sufficiently specific in nature to fall within the purview of Article 175'.

(d) Other specific obligations should have been implemented by the Council before the end of the transitional period and to that extent the Council had failed to act.

Although 'privileged' applicants may challenge *any* failure to act (which therefore may include non-binding acts: as confirmed by the Court in the *Comitology* case: see Chapter 6), natural and legal persons have limited *locus standi* under Article 232(3). Such an applicant may only bring an action as regards a binding act that an institution has 'failed to address' to him. On the face of it, it therefore appears that such an action must relate to a legally binding measure (normally a Decision) which should have been adopted and of which the applicant *would have been the addressee*. In Case 15/71 *Mackprang v Commission*, the Court held that a measure of a *general* nature (a Decision addressed to the Member States) could not be described as an act which could be addressed to the applicant. Case 246/81 *Lord Bethell v Commission* lays down that the applicant must be seeking the adoption of an act which he was 'legally entitled to claim' and later case law shows that, in line with Article 230(4), a 'non-privileged' applicant has *locus standi* providing he is directly and individually concerned. The Court has taken a broad view of Article 232(3) and it is not necessary for the applicant to be the actual addressee of the act.

There are very few cases in which an applicant under Article 232(3) has succeeded. This has been because the institution has defined its position or because the applicant has lacked *locus standi*:

Case 246/81 *Lord Bethell v Commission*

Lord Bethell, an MEP and Chairman of the Freedom of the Skies Committee, attempted to force the Commission to act under Article 89 (now 85) of the Treaty against alleged anti-competitive practices of various European airlines regarding passenger fares. He wrote to the Commission to this effect and, not being satisfied with the reply, he brought proceedings under Article 175 (now 232) claiming that the Commission's reply was a failure to act and alternatively under Article 173 (now 230) claiming that the Commission's reply was an act which should be annulled.

The Court ruled as follows:

> In the words of the second paragraph of Article 173, any natural or legal person may, under the conditions laid down in that Article, institute proceedings 'against a decision addressed to that person or against a decision which, although in the form of a regulation or a decision addressed to another person, is of direct and individual concern to the former'.

> According to the third paragraph of Article 175, any natural or legal person may, under the conditions laid down in the Article, complain to the Court that an institution of the Community 'has failed to address to that person any act other than a recommendation or an opinion'.

> It appears from the provisions quoted that the applicant, for his application to be admissible, must be in a position to establish either that he is the addressee of a measure of the Commission having specific legal effects with regard to him, which is, as such, capable of being declared void, or that the Commission, having

being duly called upon to act in pursuance of the second paragraph of Article 175, has failed to adopt in relation to him a measure which he was legally entitled to claim by virtue of the rules of Community law.

In reply to a question from the Court, the applicant stated that the measure to which he believed himself to be entitled was 'a response, an adequate answer to his complaint saying either that the Commission was going to act upon it or saying that it was not and, if not, giving reasons'. Alternatively, the applicant took the view that the letter addressed to him on 17 July 1981 by the Director General for Competition was to be described as an act against which proceedings may be instituted under the second paragraph of Article 173.

The principal question to be resolved in this case is whether the Commission had, under the rules of Community law, the right and the duty to adopt in respect of the applicant a decision in the sense of the request made by the applicant to the Commission in his letter of 13 May 1981. It is apparent from the content of that letter and from the explanations given during the proceedings that the applicant is asking the Commission to undertake an investigation with regard to the airlines in the matter of the fixing of air fares with a view to a possible application to them of the provisions of the Treaty with regard to competition.

It is clear therefore that the applicant is asking the Commission not to take a decision in respect of him, but to open an enquiry with regard to third parties and to take decisions in respect of them. No doubt the applicant, in his double capacity as a user of the airlines and a leading member of an organisation of users of air passenger services, has an indirect interest, as other users may have, in such proceedings and their possible outcome, but he is nevertheless not in the precise legal position of the actual addressee of a decision which may be declared void under the second paragraph of Article 173 or in that of the potential addressee of a legal measure which the Commission has a duty to adopt with regard to him, as is the position under the third paragraph of Article 175.

It follows that the application is inadmissible from the point of view of both Article 175 and Article 173.

It is also clear that, having been called upon to act, once the institution has defined its position (that it will act in a certain way or will not act) within the prescribed time, a claim in relation to Article 232 (formerly 175) can go no further. However, a party to whom this definition of position has been addressed (or who is otherwise directly and individually concerned) may be in a position to attack it (it will normally be a Decision) under Article 230 (formerly 173).

However, where an application for the annulment of Commission Decisions (addressed to third parties) failed on the basis of a lack of direct and individual concern under Article 173, a further claim that the Commission's failure to revoke the Decisions was actionable under Article 175 was rejected by the Court. To provide an applicant 'with a method of recourse parallel to that of Article 173', which was not subject to that Article's conditions as to time limits, did not satisfy the requirements of Article 175: Cases 10 and 18/68 *Eridania v Commission*.

In its decision in Case T-95/96 *Gestevisión Telecino v Commission*, the CFI widened the right of access for the applicant in this State aid case to bring the company's position in line with that of applicant in a State aid case who is seeking to challenge a Commission Decision under Article 230 (formerly 173): see the *COFAZ* case, above.

The private Spanish television company had initiated the complaint concerning the proposed grant of aid to its competitors (regional television companies), and it was clear that the national authorities intended to implement their plan to grant the aid. The Commission did not define its position – nor did it adopt a Decision, having apparently agreed to investigate the position under the Treaty's State aid rules: Articles 92 and 93 (now 87 and 88).

The CFI held that GT was directly and individually concerned for the purposes of those rules, being an undertaking whose interests might be affected by the grant of the aid.

Under Article 233 (formerly 176), an institution whose failure to act (or whose act) has been declared contrary to the Treaty will be required by the Court to take remedial action so as to comply with the Court's judgment. This may not be the action required by the applicant. In the *Transport Policy* case (see above), the Court stated that 'it was for the Council to introduce the measures which it considered necessary ... and to decide in what order such measures should be adopted'.

ARTICLES 235 (FORMERLY 178) AND 288(2) (FORMERLY 215(2)): NON-CONTRACTUAL LIABILITY OF THE COMMUNITY – ACTIONS FOR DAMAGES

The Basis and Nature of Community Liability

Article 235 (formerly 178)

The Court of Justice shall have jurisdiction in disputes relating to the compensation for damage provided for in the second paragraph of Article 288.

Article 288 (formerly 215)

The contractual liability of the Community shall be governed by the law applicable to the contract in question.

In the case of non-contractual liability, the Community shall, in accordance with the general principles common to the laws of the Member States, make good any damage caused by its institutions or by its servants in the performance of their duties ...

Of particular importance is that, according to the Court's case law, these Treaty Articles vest in the Court of Justice *exclusive* jurisdiction over the 'non-contractual liability' of the *Community institutions themselves as public authorities*. In this respect, although no such requirement is expressed in the Treaty, the Court, drawing on 'the general principles common to the laws of the Member States' and Article 40 of the ECSC Treaty, has generally required proof of fault for an action for compensation to succeed.

It will be seen that Article 288(2) also covers wrongful acts performed by *Community servants* in the course of their duties, and for English lawyers, it might be thought that this category of acts embraces the whole field of Article 288(2). But, as Hartley has pointed out:

This is not entirely true, however, since there are certain acts which are more properly described as acts of the institution itself rather than of its officials. The best example consists of formal (official) acts, that is, those performed by the official organ of the institution, such as decisions of the Commission or Council, or resolutions of the Parliament. [Elsewhere, these have been called 'anonymous acts'.]

This liability of the Community itself has been generally classed in the UK as tort liability. However, the view taken by Lasok and Bridge is that:

> Regarding the principles governing the non-contractual liability of the Community it has to be borne in mind that the concept cannot be construed in the sense of 'tort' or unlawful act of private law giving rise to a civil remedy of damages and/or injunction but has to be seen in the context of the activities of the Community institutions.

> These activities include the exercise of administrative and legislative functions and, like any state system, may fall occasionally below the standard of sound and efficient administration ... Such malfunctioning would reveal a fault of the system (*faute de service*) for which the state should be responsible.

Elaborating on Community liability under Article 215(2) (now 288(2)), Lasok has explained that it must:

> ... be seen in the context of the activities of the Community institutions which are charged with various tasks (mainly administrative and legislative) falling in the domain of sound and efficient administration. Thus, the elements of damage and conduct of an institution or the persons who administer the system have to be balanced up, for it is unthinkable that every damage should be made good and every misconduct could lead to compensation. We have to think in terms of the 'fault of the system' in an objective sense rather than 'culpability' in a moral sense.

Faute de service (fault of the system) is to be distinguished from *faute personelle*, a purely personal wrongful act or omission by a particular Community employee acting in the course of his duties, that is, not on a 'frolic of his own'. Our discussion will concentrate on *faute de service*.

As stated in Article 288(2), the nature of such liability is to be based on 'the general principles common to the laws of the Member States'. In as much as there is no common body of legal principles regarding State non-contractual liability within the 15 Member States, it has been said that:

> The Court is not obliged to seek the highest common denominator in the Member States' laws on administrative liability, but should focus on tracking down the elements from which Community legal principles and rules can be construed which yield an appropriate, fair and viable solution to the problem of Community liability [Gormley].

In Case 4/69 *Lütticke v Commission*, the Court held that the 'general principles' in Article 215(2) required that the following conditions must be satisfied in order to establish liability against the Community:

(a) actual damage to the plaintiff;

(b) a causal link between the damage claimed and the conduct alleged against the institution;

(c) the illegality of this conduct (that is, a wrongful act or omission on the part of the institution, or its servants).

Cases 48/65 and 4/69) *Lütticke v Commission*

The German government imposed a levy on L's imports of powdered milk. L complained to the Commission that the rate of levy was in breach of Article 95 on discriminatory internal taxation (now Article 90) and urged the Commission to bring Article 169 (now 226) proceedings against the German government for breach of its Treaty obligations.

The Commission refused to bring such proceedings and L brought a claim against the Commission under Article 175 (now 232) for *failure to act*. The Commission responded by defining its position – again refusing to act; the decision as to whether or not to bring Article 169 proceedings being a matter within the Commission's discretion. The Court held that once the Commission had defined its position, the failure to act was at an end and the claim was inadmissible.

Having also failed in a claim under Article 173 (now 230) to annul the Commission's Decision not to act, L sued the Commission for damages in a separate action under Article 215(2) (now 288(2)): Case 4/69. (Actions under Article 215 (now 288) are subject to a limitation period of five years.)

L now argued that it had suffered loss as a result of the Commission's failure to address a Directive or Decision to Germany requiring it to modify the taxes it had been obliged to pay. The Court rejected the Commission's contention (which had been successful in an earlier case) that the claim was merely an attempt to circumvent the restrictions imposed by Article 175 regarding failure to act. The Court stated that:

> It would be contrary to the independent nature of this action as well as to the efficacy of the general system of forms of action created by the Treaty to regard as a ground of inadmissibility the fact that, in certain circumstances, an action for damages might lead to a result similar to that of an action for failure to act under Article 175.

Although admissible, the Court held that the action failed on the merits, there being no failure of duty on the Commission's part. It had conducted extensive negotiations with the German authorities (who had eventually withdrawn the levy) and no more could be expected of it.

Liability for Legislative Acts: the *Schöppenstedt* Formula

The Court has stated that the action for damages differs from an action for annulment 'in that its end is not the abolition of a particular measure but compensation for damage caused by an institution in the performance of its duties'. Nevertheless, a claim under Article 288(2) (formerly 215(2)) will be more likely to succeed if annulment of the act (or condemnation of the inaction) on which the claim is based has already taken place. Attention has been drawn to the extremely limited rights of private parties regarding challenges to the validity of Community acts of a legislative or administrative nature. However, where an act has been declared invalid by the Court on one or more of the grounds specified in Article 230 (formerly 173), this amounts to proof of *faute de service*. (A failure to act is treated in the same way.)

This means that the Community may, albeit exceptionally, be liable in damages in respect of its *legislative* functions. In Case 5/71 *Zuckerfabrik Schöppenstedt v Council*, ZS brought an action for damages under Article 215(2) against the Council on the basis of an allegedly invalid Regulation adopted in respect of pricing policy in the Community sugar market. The claim was held to be admissible on the basis of the reasoning in *Lütticke*, it being distinct from a clearly inadmissible application by an individual for the annulment of a genuine Regulation under the then Article 173(2). However, the Court went on to discuss in very restrictive terms the question of the Community's liability in damages in respect of 'legislative action involving measures of economic policy' (as discussed in Chapter 10):

> In the present case, the non-contractual liability of the Community presupposes at the very least the unlawful nature of the act alleged to be the cause of the damage. Where legislative action involving measures of economic policy is concerned, the Community does not incur non-contractual liability for damage suffered by individuals as a consequence of that action, by virtue of the provisions contained in Article 215, second paragraph, of the Treaty, unless a sufficiently flagrant violation of a superior rule of law for the protection of the individual has occurred. For that reason, the Court, in the present case, must first consider whether such a violation has occurred.

It is clear that the Court's '*Schöppenstedt* formula' refers to legislative measures which involve *choices* of economic policy and that they are therefore of a discretionary character. Considering the nature of the Community, a great deal of Community legislation is of this character. As the Court's statement shows, for liability to follow, three conditions must be met (in addition to the general rules stated above concerning damage and causation):

(1) There must be a breach of a superior rule of law.

(2) The breach must be sufficiently serious.

(3) The superior rule of law must be one for the protection of the individual.

The restrictive approach to liability taken by the Court over the years to claims requiring the Community to 'make good the damage caused' has centred mainly on just how 'sufficiently serious' the damage must be. However, as with claims under Article 230(4), there has been, as will be seen, some relaxation by the Court of its application of the conditions for liability. Not that this has satisfied all the critics. The question at the bottom of these decisions is usually that of whether the Community interest or the individual interest is to prevail. In the vast majority of the cases, it is the former.

(1) There must be a breach of a superior rule of law

The case law shows that the breach of such general principles as proportionality and non-discrimination: Case 83/76, etc, *Bayerische HNL v Council and Commission*, and legal certainty and the protection of legitimate expectations: Case 74/74 *CNTA v Commission* (see Chapter 10) are to be counted among such superior rules. In all probability, any rule of Community law which would normally be a ground for annulment of the measure in question will also amount to a superior rule for these purposes.

(2) The breach must be sufficiently serious

On the basis of the Court's decision in *Bayerische HNL*, where the institution is legislating in a complex economic field (such as agriculture) involving a wide discretion, the Community will not be liable unless the institution has 'manifestly [clearly] and gravely disregarded the limits of the exercise of its powers'. Even if the act complained of has been annulled, this does not mean that damages will automatically be awarded. The applicants in this case failed because this condition was not satisfied: the loss involved was spread over a wide category of persons (buyers of protein animal feed); the increase in price had only a limited effect on costs; the increase was not unusual when compared to increases caused by fluctuations on the world market; and the effect on profits of the market regulation in question was no greater than that brought about by the normal level of risk in the relevant agricultural sectors. (The Community interest in this case was the removal of a skimmed-milk 'mountain' caused by the over-production of milk.)

In the relevant isoglucose cases (Cases 116 and 124/77 *Amylum and Tunnel Refineries v Council and Commission* and Case 143/77 *KSH v Council and Commission*), the Court held that the Community would only be liable if its conduct was 'verging on the arbitrary'. Despite the producers succeeding in having Regulations imposing production levies annulled, and despite suffering enormous financial loss, no damages were recovered by them. In these cases, the Community interest prevailed over that of the individual producers. The 'sugar mountain' was a costly embarrassment to the Community and, although errors were made, the end pursued by the institutions, that of reducing capacity and stabilising the market, was a legitimate one.

Nevertheless, in the Quellmehl and Gritz cases (Case 90/78 *Granaria v Council and Commission*, Case 238/78 *Ireks-Arkady v Council and Commission*, etc), decided at virtually the same time as the isoglucose cases, the Court was more concerned with the seriousness of the *consequences of the breach* for the undertakings in question, stating that their loss 'went beyond that inherent in business' and was recoverable. As a result, it has been suggested that a complainant will only succeed in meeting this condition if *both* his scale of loss *and* the degree of the Community's breach of the rule of law are sufficiently serious.

More recent case law however suggests that the Court is willing to adopt a less restrictive approach to the question of 'manifest and grave' breach in Article 288(2) compensation actions. In Case C-220/91P *Stahlwerke Peine-Salzgitter v Commission*, the Court stated that conduct 'verging on the arbitrary' (see above) was not a necessary requirement. A breach that is *sufficiently serious* may therefore be rather less serious than hitherto. Also of significance is the Court's decision in *Mulder* in which, contrary to previous rulings, it is clear that the breach does not necessarily have to 'impact on a limited and identifiable number of economic agents'. In this case, damages were awarded in the knowledge that some 13,000 farmers could be entitled to claim, with a potential cost to the Community of £100 million.

Cases C-104/89 and C-37/90 *Mulder and Others v Council and Commission*

Mulder and other farmers brought an action against the Community under Article 215(2) for compensation for damage suffered as a result of the application of various Council and Commission Regulations concerning over-production and cut-backs in the dairy sector.

On the basis of the Regulations in question, the farmers were paid a premium for a period of five years for not marketing milk and milk products from their farms. At the end of the non-marketing period, they applied for but failed to be allocated 'special reference quantities' enabling them to resume production. Later, they were allocated quantities equal to 60 per cent of quantities sold prior to the non-marketing period. This reduction of 40 per cent was more than double the highest reduction applied to dairy producers who had not been party to the non-marketing rules.

The initial failures to allocate 'reference quantities' (by Dutch and West German national authorities acting on the basis of the Community Regulations) were successfully challenged following references to the Court of Justice under Article 177(1)(b) from the national courts in Cases 120/86 *Mulder* and 170/86 *Von Deetzen*. The Community rules on which these rejections were based were held to be invalid on the ground that they were in breach of the principle of the protection of legitimate expectations in so far as they failed to provide for the allocation of such quantities.

The later 60 per cent rule was also successfully challenged in Cases C-189/89 *Spagl* and C-217/89 *Pastätter*. The Court of Justice again made preliminary rulings of invalidity based on the legitimate expectations of the producers concerned.

In this action for damages, the Court of Justice reaffirmed that the Community did not incur liability on account of a legislative measure involving choices of economic policy unless a sufficiently serious breach of a superior rule of law for the protection of the individual had occurred (the *'Schöppenstedt* formula').

More specifically, the Court continued, 'in a legislative field such as the one in question, which was characterised by the exercise of a wide discretion essential for the implementation of the Common Agricultural Policy, the Community could not incur liability unless its institution had manifestly and gravely disregarded the limits on the exercise of its powers'.

Further, as the Court had previously held (in, for example, Case 90/78 *Granaria* and Case 238/78 *Ireks-Arkady*), for the Community to incur non-contractual liability, the damage alleged had to go beyond the bounds of normal economic risks inherent in the activities of the sector concerned.

On this basis, the Court concluded that the Community's initial total exclusion of the dairy farmers in question from the allocation of a 'reference quantity' once their non-marketing period expired met all the above requirements:

(a) The Regulation which brought their exclusion into effect was in breach of the principle of the protection of legitimate expectations, which was a general and superior principle of Community law for the protection of the individual.

(b) While failing to invoke any higher public interest (such as the need to reduce Community dairy stocks), the Regulation completely failed to take account of the specific situation of a clearly defined group of economic agents (producers who had marketed no milk in the reference year upon which 'reference quantities' were based). This manifest and grave disregard by the Community legislature of its discretionary limits led to an inevitable finding that there was in this case a sufficiently serious breach of a superior rule of law.

(c) From the applicants' viewpoint, their exclusion from a 'reference quantity' could not be regarded as foreseeable or as falling within the bounds of the normal economic risks inherent in milk production.

However, with respect to the later 60 per cent rule, the Community did not incur liability as regards the Regulation which brought it to effect. The Regulation was in breach of the legitimate expectations principle and was, therefore, invalid, but the breach was not sufficiently serious, within the meaning of the Court's case law on the non-contractual liability of the Community. The Community, while taking account of a higher public interest, had also stayed within the limits of its discretionary powers when trying to balance the need to avoid over-production with the interests of the farmers.

The Court ordered that the amount of compensation payable by the Community had to correspond to the damage it had caused the applicants. (Various complicating

**EC LEGISLATIVE MEASURES – ECONOMIC POLICY CHOICES –
INDIVIDUAL LOSS – JUDICIAL REVIEW – COMPENSATION**

(A) POLICY: Common Agricultural Policy – dairy products (for
                                 example, *Mulder* milk production based on allocation
                                 of supply quotas).

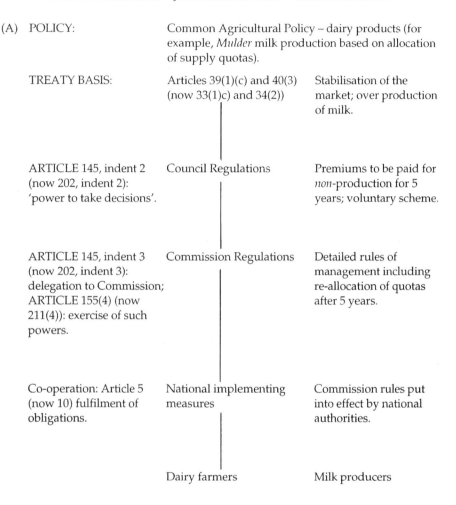

TREATY BASIS:	Articles 39(1)(c) and 40(3) (now 33(1)c) and 34(2))	Stabilisation of the market; over production of milk.
ARTICLE 145, indent 2 (now 202, indent 2): 'power to take decisions'.	Council Regulations	Premiums to be paid for *non*-production for 5 years; voluntary scheme.
ARTICLE 145, indent 3 (now 202, indent 3): delegation to Commission; ARTICLE 155(4) (now 211(4)): exercise of such powers.	Commission Regulations	Detailed rules of management including re-allocation of quotas after 5 years.
Co-operation: Article 5 (now 10) fulfilment of obligations.	National implementing measures	Commission rules put into effect by national authorities.
	Dairy farmers	Milk producers

(B) CHALLENGE TO COMMUNITY RULES: Commission error; milk producers not
re-allocated a quota on expiry of five year period.

1   Article 173(2) (now 230(4)) direct action for annulment of EC Regulations.

2   Article 177(1)(b) (now 234(1)(b)) indirect challenge in national court against
national implementation measures as being based on invalid EC law.

3   Article 215(2) (now 288(2)) actions for compensation against Council and
Commission.

factors made this a rather difficult quantification.) Interest was to be paid on the amounts of compensation from the date of judgment and the Court ordered the parties to inform the Court within 12 months of the amounts of damages arrived at by agreement.

(3) The superior rule of law must be one for the protection of the individual

As the case law shows, any of the general principles established by the Court of Justice, such as equality (non-discrimination), proportionality and the protection of legitimate expectations, constitutes a superior rule of law for the protection of the individual. In the *Ireks-Arkady* case, for example, the Court drew particular attention to the following points:

> In the first place, it is necessary to take into consideration that the principle of equality, embodied in particular in the second subparagraph of Article 40(3) [now 34(2)] of the EEC Treaty, which prohibits any discrimination in the common organisation of the agricultural markets, occupies a particularly important place among the rules of Community law intended to protect the interests of the individual. Secondly, the disregard of that principle in this case affected a limited and clearly defined group of commercial operators. It seems, in fact, that the number of quellmehl producers in the Community is very limited. Further, the damage alleged by the applicants goes beyond the bounds of the economic risks inherent in the activities in the sector concerned. Finally, equality of treatment with the producers of maize starch, which had been observed from the beginning of the common organisation of the market in cereals, was ended by the Council in 1974 without sufficient justification. [The Court's second point must now be read in the light of *Mulder*, above.]

Article 34(2) is but one of several Treaty expressions of the general principle of equality (see Chapter 10), while it is readily apparent that many Treaty Articles in themselves and Regulations (for example, Regulations upon which later Regulations are based) are also to be regarded as superior rules of law.

Recent Developments: Breach, Equivalence and Discretion

In Case C-352/98P *Laboratoires Pharmaceutiques Bergaderm and Goupil v Commission, a Community* liability damages claim under Article 288(2), the Court of Justice re-examined the concept of a 'sufficiently serious' or 'manifest and grave' breach in those cases in which the *Schöppenstedt* formula applies, that is, those involving wide institutional discretion in complex economic policy areas. The Court first drew attention to the *State* liability case of *Brasserie du Pêcheur*, decided in 1996 shortly after *Francovich*, in which it had stated that generally the conditions applying to State liability should correspond to those of Community liability in like circumstances. This was a particular application of the principle of *equivalence*. In *Brasserie du Pêcheur*, the Court had modified the conditions for liability as found in *Francovich* (see Chapters 8 and 20). It laid down that where a Member State acts in a field in which it has a wide discretion, an individual's Community law right to damages depends on the following conditions: (a) the rule of law infringed must be intended to confer rights on individuals; (b) *the breach must be sufficiently serious*; and (c) there must be a direct causal link between the breach by the State of its Community law obligations and the loss sustained by the injured party.

These conditions clearly correspond in substance to those found in the *Schöppenstedt* cases discussed earlier in this chapter. In *Bergaderm,* a full Court brought these two sets of conditions even closer together: it reviewed the assimilation process by redefining a 'sufficiently serious' Article 288(2) breach in terms of an application of the range of possible constituent elements of a *State's* 'sufficiently serious' breach as found in *Brasserie du Pêcheur.* These include the clarity and precision of the rule breached, the measure of discretion in the hands of the relevant authorities, whether the infringement and the damage caused was intentional or involuntary, and whether any error of the law was excusable or not. It was not that factors such as these have not been taken into account at Community level, but that the link has now been made explicit.

In like vein, the Court further stated that: 'Where the Member State *or the institution in question* has only considerably reduced, or even no discretion, the mere infringement of Community law may be sufficient to establish the existence of a sufficiently serious breach' (emphasis added).

As will be seen, this was a crucial finding by the Court in its State liability decision in Case C-5/94 *R v Ministry of Agriculture, Fisheries and Food ex p Hedley Lomas,* a case in which Community law had left no margin of discretion in the matter to the Ministry when it wrongfully refused to issue an export licence to HL. It was not a case involving the making of legislative choices but one in which the Ministry's decision, a 'mere infringement', was sufficient to establish State liability.

Returning to the *Bergaderm* Article 288(2) case, the Court continued by stating that the 'general or individual nature of a measure taken by an institution is not a decisive criterion for identifying the limits of the discretion enjoyed by the institution in question'. It therefore follows, through the assimilation process (or equivalence principle), that at both levels, Community or State, not only will the newly defined test or conditions brought about by the merging of the *Schöppenstedt* test and the *Brasserie du Pêcheur* conditions apply to wide general legislative choice situations but will also apply to individual administrative measures taken in difficult decision making situations, similarly involving complex questions of economic policy and a wide margin of discretion. In either case, at either level, the breach must be 'sufficiently serious' or 'manifest and grave'.

To complete the picture, conversely it also follows that if, at either level, the challenged act – general or individual – does *not* involve a wide discretion, a finding of liability does not fall to be made under the new, united test, but remains to be dealt with on the basis of the less strict general principles concerning illegal conduct, causation and actual loss: see *Hedley Lomas.*

This involves careful consideration by the courts of the margin of discretion, if any, and the meaning of illegal conduct. At Community level, the following case is instructive.

Case T-178/98 *Fresh Marine v Commission*

FM and other Norwegian companies were exempted from anti-dumping and countervailing duties imposed on imports into the Community of farmed Atlantic salmon originating in Norway by a Commission Decision in 1997. This followed FM and other exporters giving, and the Commission accepting, certain undertakings. However, by the adoption of a Regulation later the same year, the Commission reimposed the measures and duties with the effect of deleting the names of FM and others who had given undertakings from the earlier Decision.

FM charged that the Commission had committed a wrongful act in deleting its name and had thereby caused the company considerable loss.

In the action brought under Article 215(2) (now 288(2)), the CFI held that the key issue concerned the test to be applied when examining the non-contractual liability of the Community. It decided that the damage at issue arose not from a legislative act involving choices of economic policy but from 'an error which ... an administrative authority exercising ordinary care and diligence would not have committed ...'. The Commission had been at fault in such a way as to render it liable under Article 215(2) and FM did not have to prove a sufficiently serious breach since the Commission's error did not involve complex discretionary choices. A mere infringement of EC law was enough (see also the Ministry's 'error' in *Hedley Lomas*, and other State liability cases in Chapter 20). The *Bergaderm* decision was followed.

(Note that an appeal from the CFI's decision in *Fresh Marine* has been lodged by the Commission: Case C-472/00P.)

This case was therefore decided on the same basis as a negligence action under English law. Causation and actual loss were proved but contributory negligence by FM resulted in the damages being halved. (This decision can be seen as very similar to that in the much earlier Case 145/83 *Adams v Commission* concerning the defendant's breach of a duty of confidentiality to the applicant and the latter's own contributory negligence.)

In contrast to *Fresh Marine*, in Case C-390/95P *Antillean Rice Mills v Commission*, the Court of Justice confirmed a CFI finding that, although a contested measure was in the form of a Commission Decision, the key factor was that it was an act of a legislative character involving the exercise of a wide discretion. The Community therefore could not incur liability 'unless the institution concerned has manifestly and gravely disregarded the limits on the exercise of its powers ...'. The 'stricter criterion of liability' had to be applied, 'namely the requirements of a sufficiently serious breach of a superior rule of law for the protection of the individual'.

Causation and Damage

The damage suffered by the applicant under Article 288(2) must be a sufficiently direct consequence of the wrongful act (or omission) of the institution in question. Causality may often be 'direct, immediate and exclusive' but where the loss depends on the intervention of other causes, it will usually be regarded by the Court as being too remote: Case C-64/76, etc, *Dumortier Frères v Council*. Instances where both the Community and a Member State are responsible for the loss are discussed below.

The losses suffered are normally of an economic nature and such losses are recoverable, according to the Court's case law, so long as they are, in general, certain and specific; not speculative. In *Ireks-Arkady*, Advocate General Capotorti stated that damage 'covers both a material loss ... a reduction in a person's assets, and also the loss of an increase in those assets which would have occurred if the harmful act had not taken place ...'.

Cases 5/66, etc, *Kampffmeyer v Commission*

A number of German grain dealers applied for permits to import maize from France into Germany at a time when the German authorities had fixed the import levy at zero (see Cases 106 and 107/63 *Toepfer v Commission*, discussed earlier). When changed market conditions made it such that the German dealers would make substantial profits, the national authorities wrongfully refused to grant the permits. The Commission quickly raised the rate of levy and issued a Decision confirming the German ban.

The Court held that the Decision was unjustified and it was annulled. In this action for damages, the Court was only prepared to award damages to those importers who had signed contracts to buy French maize *before* the applications for import permits had been refused.

Those dealers who had gone through with their transactions and paid the levy were awarded a sum equal to the levy paid. Dealers who had cancelled their contracts as a result of the Decision were awarded cancellation costs incurred plus loss of profits. However, owing to the amount of risk involved in transactions of this nature, the sum awarded was equal to only 10 per cent of the profits which might have been made.

Dealers who had not concluded contracts before applying for import permits (a matter of normal business prudence?) were awarded no damages at all.

(Note that *Kampffmeyer* also raises questions of concurrent liability.)

The Court stated that compensation could be recovered 'for imminent damage foreseeable with sufficient certainty even if the damage cannot yet be precisely assessed'. However, the Court's restrictive approach should be contrasted with that in *Mulder*, where, nevertheless, the Court held that an award for lost profits must take into account income which could have been earned from alternative activities; that is, there is a duty to mitigate the loss sustained.

Concurrent Liability

As seen on numerous occasions, Community policies are normally implemented by agencies of the governments of the Member States. The individual therefore normally feels the impact of Community law (in this context he suffers loss) as a result of an act or failure to act on the part of such national authority (for example, a Ministry or an agricultural intervention board).

In some instances, it is not clear whether the action for compensation should lie against the national authority in the national courts under national law, or against a Community institution before the Court of Justice, or both. The position is clear if the harm suffered was caused solely by an act of the Community; similarly if it was caused by the national authorities acting independently. Concurrent liability arises where the national authorities are acting as agents of the Community or on the instructions of a Community institution.

The position as regards several of the issues that may arise is to be found in the following case.

Case 175/84 *Krohn Import-Export v Commission (No 1)*

K claimed under Article 215(2) (now 288(2)) for losses suffered as a result of the refusal of the national (German) intervention agency to grant the company licences to import manioc from Thailand. K's application was refused on the basis of mandatory instructions (a Decision) from the Commission given within the scope of the governing Regulation.

K brought an action in the German courts seeking annulment of the intervention board's decision and an injunction requiring it to issue the licences, and a further action before the Court of Justice for compensation for losses suffered as a result of the Commission's negative Decision.

The Commission raised three arguments against admissibility:

(a) The decision at issue was taken by a national agency within the framework of the CAP.

(b) A claim under Article 215(2) (288(2)) was only admissible if the applicant had exhausted his remedies in his national courts – and this was not the case.

(c) To admit liability would nullify the Commission's Decision, which K had not challenged within the required time limit under Article 173 (now 230).

The Court rejected all three arguments:

(a) The German authorities had not exercised a discretion when refusing to grant the licences. They were acting on the instructions of the Commission, which was the 'true author' of the Decision.

(b) There was nothing to suggest, after a lapse of several years, that the remedies claimed by K in the national courts would compensate for the losses suffered. Where national rights of action failed to afford an effective remedy, a claim under Article 215(2) remained – certainly where the Community was the sole wrongdoer.

(c) Article 215(2) was an autonomous form of action and the time limit in Article 173 could not operate as a bar to such an action for which the time limit was five years.

The Court of Justice went on in later proceedings (see [1987] ECR 97) to examine and reject K's claim on its merits.

On the basis of Article 10 (formerly 5) and the case law of the Court, Member State courts are duty bound to provide effective remedies for breach of Community law by their public authorities: see Case 99/74 *Société des Grands Moulins des Antilles v Commission*, and any doubts which arise can be resolved by means of a reference for a preliminary ruling under Article 234 (formerly 177).

Brown and Kennedy have suggested an alternative approach to the questions raised in this area:

The drastic alternative would be a revision of the Treaties so as to confer jurisdiction upon the Court of Justice [now the CFI] in respect of actions against Member States for non-contractual liability arising out of the administration of Community law by national authorities. The Communities and the Member States could then be sued jointly in the one Community Court, which could allocate liability between them as it thought fit. If the Communities alone were sued (and the plaintiff might often prefer to proceed thus) then the Communities would be able to join the Member State as a party and claim a contribution or even a complete indemnity from it, as appropriate.

REFERENCES AND FURTHER READING

Books

Brown, LN and Kennedy, T, *The Court of Justice of the European Communities*, 2000.

Heukels, T and McDonnell, A (eds), *The Action for Damages in Community Law*, 1997.

Hartley, TC, *The Foundations of the European Community*, 1998, Part IV.

Lasok, D, *Economic Law of the European Community*, 1980.

Lasok, D and Bridge, J, *Law and Institutions of the European Union*, 2000.

Rudden, B, *Basic Community Cases*, 1987, Part III, 'Community blunders: the *Isoglucose* story'.

Article 230 (formerly 173): *Locus Standi*

Arnull, A, 'Challenging EC anti-dumping Regulations: the problem of admissibility' (1992) ECLR 73.

Arnull, A, 'Private applicants and the action for annulment since *Cordoniu*' (2001) 38 CML Rev 7.

Barav, A, 'Direct and individual concern: an almost insurmountable barrier to the admissibility of individual appeal to the EEC Court' (1974) 11 CML Rev 191.

Berg, C and Bain, F, 'No room at the European Court' (2002) NLJ 1533 (11 October).

Craig, PP, 'Legality, standing and substantive review in Community law' (1994) 14 OJLS 507.

Harlow, C, 'Towards a theory of access for the European Court of Justice' (1992) 12 YEL 213.

Kirchner, E and Williams, K, 'The legal, political and institutional implications of the *Isoglucose* judgments 1980' (1983) 22 JCMS 173.

Neuwahl, N, 'Article 173 paragraph 4 EC: past, present and possible future' (1996) 21 EL Rev 17.

Rasmussen, H, 'Why is Article 173 interpreted against private plaintiffs?' (1980) 5 EL Rev 112.

Usher, J, 'Individual concern in general legislation – 10 years on' (Case note on *Cordoniu*) (1994) 19 EL Rev 636.

Article 234 (formerly 177): Validity References

Bebr, G, 'Preliminary rulings of the Court of Justice: their authority and temporal effect' (1981) 18 CML Rev 475.

Bebr, G, 'The reinforcement of the constitutional review of Community acts under Article 177 EEC' (1988) 25 CML Rev 667.

Harding, C, 'The impact of Article 177 of the EEC Treaty on the review of Community action' (1981) 1 YEL 93.

Interim Measures

Oliver, P, 'Interim measures: some recent developments' (1992) 29 CML Rev 7.

Non-contractual Liability

Oliver, P, 'Enforcing Community rights in the English courts' (1987) 50 MLR 881.

Tridimas, T, 'Liability for breach of Community law: growing up and mellowing down? (2001) 38 CML Rev 301.

Wakefield, J, Case note on *Fresh Marine* (2001) 38 CML Rev 1043.

Wils, W, 'Concurrent liability of the Community and a Member State' (1992) 17 EL Rev 191.

CHAPTER 20

MEMBER STATES AND THEIR COMMUNITY OBLIGATIONS: ACTIONS AGAINST MEMBER STATES AT COMMUNITY AND NATIONAL LEVEL

SUPERVISION AT COMMUNITY LEVEL: ENFORCEMENT ACTIONS

Direct Enforcement Actions against Member States: Article 226 (formerly 169)

Proceedings may be brought in the Court of Justice either by the Commission or by a Member State against a Member State which is alleged to be in breach of its Community obligations:

Article 226 (formerly 169)

If the Commission considers that a Member State has failed to fulfil an obligation under this Treaty, it shall deliver a reasoned opinion on the matter after giving the State concerned the opportunity to submit its observations.

If the State concerned does not comply with the opinion within the period laid down by the Commission, the latter may bring the matter before the Court of Justice.

Article 227 (formerly 170)

A Member State which considers that another Member State has failed to fulfil an obligation under this Treaty may bring the matter before the Court of Justice.

Before a Member State brings an action against another Member State for an alleged infringement of an obligation under this Treaty, it shall bring the matter before the Commission.

The Commission shall deliver a reasoned opinion after each of the States concerned has been given the opportunity to submit its own case and its observations on the other party's case both orally and in writing.

If the Commission has not delivered an opinion within three months of the date on which the matter was brought before it, the absence of such opinion shall not prevent the matter from being brought before the Court of Justice.

The procedure under Article 170 (now 227) has been rarely used. However, in Case 141/78 *France v UK*, France claimed that UK fishery conservation measures were contrary to Community law. The Commission's reasoned opinion supported the French claim, but the matter was pressed to the litigation stage, at which the Court gave judgment against the UK. Disputes of this nature between Member States are better resolved by political means rather than by such direct confrontation. In any event, if the matter is left to the Commission to initiate proceedings under Article 226 (formerly 169), the procedure laid down in that Article enables a satisfactory outcome to be reached on a non-contentious basis (prior to the litigation stage) in the majority of cases.

It will be recalled that, under Article 211 (formerly 155), it is the Commission's duty to 'ensure that the provisions of this Treaty and the measures taken by the institutions pursuant thereto are applied'. In addition, as we have also seen, Member States have a duty under Article 10 (formerly 5) to 'take all appropriate measures ... to ensure fulfilment of the obligations arising out of this Treaty or resulting from action taken by the institutions of the Community'.

Over the years, the increase both in the number of Member States and the extent of their obligations has inevitably lead to an increase in the number of violations. Although the principle of direct effect may be relied upon by individuals to secure the enforcement of Treaty obligations – in 1962, in *Van Gend en Loos*, the Court did not wish to restrict 'the guarantees against an infringement of Article 12 to the procedures under Article 169 and 170' – and the enforcement of Regulations, increased vigilance by the Commission as regards the full implementation of Directives was necessitated both by problems regarding the direct effect of those measures and by the need for the Commission to secure the establishment, by means of harmonisation Directives, of the Internal Market by the end of 1992. Indeed, in its Fifth Annual Report (1988) the Commission stated that:

> Article 169 of the EEC Treaty is now an instrument for the achievement of policy, and not solely an essential legal instrument. The objective of Article 8a of the Treaty [now Article 14], namely to achieve by 1992 an area without internal frontiers, is now the Commission's priority objective and requires a strict application of existing Community law. It is Article 169 which makes it possible to monitor this application and ensures its observance by the Member States.

Indeed, by 1990, it was clear that the Commission had adopted a new procedure, whereby it routinely issued letters of formal notice to Member States which had not notified to the Commission details of national measures transposing Directives due for implementation. The Commission's new policy was not designed to increase the number of enforcement actions but to secure compliance at the pre-contentious stage.

At Community level, the introduction by the Treaty on European Union of a power vested in the Court of Justice to impose financial sanctions upon a Member State which has not only failed to fulfil a Treaty obligation but has also failed to comply with a judgment of the Court to that effect (see Article 228(2) (formerly 171(2)), and, at national level, the *Francovich* decision, which enables an individual to bring an action for damages against the State as tortfeasor for loss suffered as a consequence of the State's failure to fulfil its Treaty obligations (for example, as regards the implementation of a Directive), have arguably increased the pressure on Member States to fulfil their Community obligations.

Alleged violations of Community law by a Member State usually reach the Commission as a result of complaints by undertakings or individuals, but they may also arise as a result of the Commission's own investigations. The procedure laid down in Article 226 (formerly 169) follows two distinct stages: the *administrative or pre-contentious stage* and the *judicial stage*. The administrative stage, the purpose of which is to enable the Member State to justify its position or make the necessary changes in its law to comply with Community law, falls into three parts:

(a) The Commission first advises the Member State of its alleged violation and asks the Member State to explain its position within a specified time. In many instances, the violation is acknowledged at this point and the matter is settled.

(b) If the matter is not informally resolved, a letter of *formal notice* is sent by the Commission to the Member State. According to the Court, this letter is intended to 'define the subject matter of the dispute and to indicate to the Member State, which is invited to submit its observations, the factors enabling it to prepare its defence ... the opportunity for the Member State concerned to submit its observations constitutes an essential guarantee required by the Treaty and ... observance of that guarantee [by the Commission] is an essential formal requirement of the procedure under Article 169': Case 51/83 *Commission v Italy*. The State is normally given two months to respond and at this point the issue may well be resolved.

(c) If it is not resolved, the Commission will deliver its *reasoned opinion*, setting out the legal arguments upon which it considers the alleged violation to rest. The Member State is given a period of time to comply so as to bring the alleged violation to an end.

If the Member State fails to comply, the Commission, as stated in Article 226(2), may bring the matter before the Court of Justice, that is, proceed to the *judicial stage*. It is to be noted that the Commission has a discretion (as, in practice, it has at each stage of the Article 226 procedure), whether or not to bring the Member State before the Court (see, for example, the *Lütticke* litigation in the previous chapter).

A Member State may even concede its failure to fulfil its obligations *after* the case has gone to the Court but before judgment, and the Commission in such circumstances will normally ask the Court to remove the case from the register: for example, Case 301/84 *Commission v UK* concerning 'Buy-British', preferential car purchase loan schemes applied by local authorities (see [1985] OJ C275/6). In any event, it is clear that the procedure under Article 226 (which is an improvement on the rules normally applying in public international law where a State fails to fulfil its Treaty obligations) is aimed primarily at avoiding rather than achieving a condemnation of a defaulting Member State. (Probably only around 10 per cent of recorded infringements reach the stage of judgment by the Court.)

Where a Member State has failed to remedy its alleged violation in compliance with the Commission's reasoned opinion within the stipulated time limit, and the Commission has exercised its power to move the matter to the judicial stage, the Court of Justice will examine the merits of the case and decide *de novo* whether a breach of Community law has occurred. The proceedings do not constitute a review of the Commission's reasoned opinion, although at this stage its legality may be questioned. In Case 293/85 *Commission v Belgium (Re University Fees)*, the action by the Commission against Belgium for its failure to implement the decision in Case 293/83 *Gravier* in a satisfactory manner was dismissed, as the Commission had not given the Belgian authorities sufficient time to respond to its complaints, either before or after the issue of its reasoned opinion.

In 1993, in the field of environmental policy alone, the Commission pursued successful Article 169 (now 226) actions against the UK for failure to implement Directives on the quality of drinking water and on bathing water standards. The Commission, however, dropped formal proceedings against the UK for infringing EC environment impact requirements at a BP industrial site in Scotland. The Commission had argued that BP had gained planning permission to increase its liquid gas installation without a prior environment impact assessment. Following BP's agreeing to put forward plans for public consultation, the Commission announced that the requirements of the Directive had been satisfied.

The 1985 Environment Assessment Directive was also at the heart of the dispute beginning in 1991 between the Commission and the UK concerning seven large scale construction and transport projects in the south of England, valued at £500 million and including the controversial construction of the M3 link through Twyford Down in Hampshire. The Commission's opening of formal proceedings was accompanied by a request from the Environment Commissioner, Signor Carlo Ripa di Meana, to the Secretary of State for Transport that work on the projects should stop. This request was branded in the UK as 'an unwarranted intrusion into Britain's national affairs' on the basis that the projects had no environmental effect on other Member States. In July 1992, the Commission abandoned proceedings regarding five of the seven projects, including that relating to the M3 motorway extension.

Article 226 cases that go to judgment usually go against the defendant Member State. In 1989, Dashwood and White reported how:

> In the small minority of cases that have run their full course, the Member State concerned has almost always taken the steps necessary to comply with the judgment, although sometimes after a considerable delay. Ireland, for example, took three years to amend the legislation on origin marking that gave rise to the *Irish Souvenirs* case (Case 113/80); while it was only in 1986 that France complied with judgments of 1980 and 1982 relating to discriminatory legislation on alcohol advertising (Cases 152/78, 83/82). In the *Mutton and Lamb* case (Case 232/78), an eventual solution was found through political negotiations.

> These cases suggest that the EEC system might benefit from the conferment on the European Court of a power to impose financial sanctions, as an incentive to timely compliance and to discourage opportunism. However, the ultimate guarantee of the effectiveness of infringement proceedings is Member States' recognition that respect for the rule of law in the Community is a condition of its survival. A Member State that adopted a policy of ignoring adverse judgments of the European Court would not be able to remain a member of the Community for very long.

As noted earlier, a power to impose financial sanctions was introduced by the TEU by means of a new second paragraph of Article 171 (now 228):

Article 228

1   If the Court of Justice finds that a Member State has failed to fulfil an obligation under this Treaty, the State shall be required to take the necessary measures to comply with the judgment of the Court of Justice.

2   If the Commission considers that the Member State concerned has not taken such measures it shall, after giving that State the opportunity to submit its observations, issue a reasoned opinion specifying the points on which the Member State concerned has not complied with the judgment of the Court of Justice.

If the Member State concerned fails to take the necessary measures to comply with the Court's judgment within the time limit laid down by the Commission, the latter may bring the case before the Court of Justice. In so doing, it shall specify the amount of the lump sum or penalty payment to be paid by the Member State concerned which it considers appropriate in the circumstances.

If the Court of Justice finds that the Member State concerned has not complied with its judgment it may impose a lump sum or penalty payment on it.

This procedure shall be without prejudice to Article 227.

Before the introduction of Article 171(2) (now 228(2)), the Commission's only legal weapon was a second Article 169 action against the Member State for breach of Article 171: see, for example, Cases 24 and 97/80R *Commission v France (Re Restrictions on Imports of Lamb)*. In June 1996, the Commission adopted criteria to be applied for deciding the amount of financial penalties it would ask the Court of Justice to impose on Member States which fail to comply with a judgment. The Commission's view was that the imposition of a periodic penalty payment (cf its powers under Regulation 17 to compel companies to terminate infringements of Articles 81(1) or 82) rather than a lump sum would be the most effective way of persuading a Member State to comply as quickly as possible. The size of the penalty would reflect the gravity and duration of the infringement and the need to ensure that the penalty acts as a deterrent: see [1996] OJ C242/6; [1997] OJ C63/2.

In July 2000, the Court of Justice exercised its jurisdiction under Article 228(2) for the first time. In April 1992, the Court held that Greece had failed to fulfil its obligations under various Directives regarding the disposal of toxic and dangerous waste in Crete. Having still failed to comply with this judgment, the Court ordered Greece to pay to the Commission a penalty payment of 20,000 Euros for each day of delay in implementing the measures necessary to comply with its earlier ruling, from the date of the present judgment until the 1992 judgment had been complied with: Case C-387/97 *Commission v Greece (Re Non-Compliance Penalties)*.

As regards the declaratory nature of a judgment of the Court against a defaulting Member State, it is clear that it is for the Member State to 'take the necessary measures to comply' with its Treaty obligations. The Commission's reasoned opinion will have spelt out the acts which have given rise to the breach and Member States are required to draw the necessary inferences from the Court's judgment. Thus, if, for example, the breach consists in the enactment of legislation contrary to Community law, the Court of Justice has no power to annul the offending national measure but, following its ruling that the measure conflicts with Community law, the Member State has a duty to amend its own law: see, in particular, the *Factortame* case discussed below.

In the majority of Article 226 (formerly 169) cases, the defendant Member State has failed to implement the obligations of a Directive, but in the case which follows (discussed also in Chapter 8), a Regulation stated that national measures were required in order to bring it fully into effect. The Court (as it almost invariably does) brushed aside the defences raised by the defendant Member State in the face of the principle of the equality of Member States before Community law and the duty of solidarity accepted by them on the basis of Article 10 (formerly 5).

Case 128/78 *Commission v UK (Re Tachographs)*

Regulation 1463/70 relating to the introduction of tachographs ('the spy in the cab') in commercial vehicles laid down that its use was to be compulsory from a specified date. In this action brought by the Commission against the UK for failure to comply, the Court ruled that:

It is not denied that provision for the installation and use of the recording equipment has been made by the British legislation only on an optional and voluntary basis as regards both vehicles engaged in intra-Community transport and those engaged in national transport. On the other hand, the British legislation has maintained in force the obligations relating to the keeping of an individual control book which were abolished by the said Regulation.

The defendant claims that this arrangement is sufficient to meet the objectives of promoting road safety, of social progress for workers and of the harmonization of conditions of competition. It maintains that the implementation of Regulation No 1463/70 on its territory is best achieved by the installation and use of the recording equipment on a voluntary basis, though this may be made compulsory at an appropriate time. It adds that implementation of the Regulation involving compulsory measures would meet with active resistance from the sectors concerned, in particular the trade unions, which would result in strikes in the transport sector and would therefore seriously damage the whole economy of the country.

It contends that since, in the case of the United Kingdom, the objectives of the Community policy in this field can be achieved just as satisfactorily by the maintenance of the system of the individual control book as by the compulsory introduction of recording equipment, the alleged failure to fulfil an obligation is of a purely technical nature and, in view of the difficulties referred to, should not be taken into account. Moreover the installation and use of recording equipment is in practice already guaranteed in respect of intra-Community transport by the fact that the other Member States have made it compulsory.

Article 189 of the Treaty provides that a Regulation shall be binding 'in its entirety' in the Member States. As the Court has already stated in its judgment of 7 February 1973 (Case 39/72 *Commission v Italian Republic* (1973) ECR 101), it cannot therefore be accepted that a Member State should apply in an incomplete or selective manner provisions of a Community Regulation so as to render abortive certain aspects of Community legislation which it has opposed or which it considers contrary to its national interests. In particular, as regards the putting into effect of a general rule intended to eliminate certain abuses to which workers are subject and which in addition involve a threat to road safety, a Member State which omits to take, within the requisite period and simultaneously with the other Member States, the measures which it ought to take, undermines Community solidarity by imposing, in particular as regards intra-Community transport, on the other Member States the necessity of remedying the effects of its own omissions, while at the same time taking an undue advantage to the detriment of its partners.

As the Court said in the same judgment, practical difficulties which appear at the stage when a Community measure is put into effect cannot permit a Member State unilaterally to opt out of fulfilling its obligations. The Community institutional system provides the Member State concerned with the necessary means to ensure that its difficulties be given due consideration, subject to compliance with the principles of the common market and the legitimate interests of the other Member States.

In these circumstances, the possible difficulties of implementation alleged by the defendant cannot be accepted as a justification.

Further, as the Court said in the case mentioned above, in permitting Member States to profit from the advantages of the Community, the Treaty imposes on them also the obligation to respect its rules. For a State unilaterally to break, according to its own conception of national interest, the equilibrium between the advantages and obligations flowing from its adherence to the Community brings into question the equality of Member States before Community law and creates discrimination at the expense of their nationals. This failure in the duty of solidarity accepted by Member States by the fact of their adherence to the Community strikes at the very root of the Community legal order.

> It appears therefore that, in deliberately refusing to give effect on its territory to the provisions of Regulation No 1463/70, the United Kingdom has markedly failed to fulfil the obligation which it has assumed by virtue of its membership of the European Economic Community.

The Commission does not have the resources to pursue every infringement of Community law by the Member States. (It should be recalled that the Commission has the power, but not a duty, to bring an enforcement action.) In any event, as Weiler has explained, other considerations may play a part:

> ... the decision of the Commission ... to bring an action against an alleged violation by [a] Member State will often be influenced by political considerations; the Commission, for example, might not wish to prejudice delicate negotiations with a Member State. Secondly, effective supervision will depend on the ability of the Commission to monitor the implementation of Community law. Given the vast range of Community measures, this becomes an impossible task ... Even if alleged violations were brought to the attention of the Commission, it is unrealistic to expect them to take up all but the most flagrant violations.

Other 'Commission-watchers' have been more critical of the Commission's discretionary administration of the Article 226 enforcement procedure. For example, Rawlings' view is summed up in the title of his recent article, 'Engaged elites: citizen action and institutional attitudes'. He charges the Commission with a tendency to be aloof, unresponsive and negative towards individuals who bring complaints to it regarding breaches of EC law. He sees, amongst other things, the need for some measure of control over the Commission's discretion, for a time limit for Commission decisions within the administrative procedure, for an improvement in the procedural position of complainants (along the lines seen in Article 230(4) State aid cases), and for better verification of Member State compliance with the Court's decisions.

Interim Measures

Article 242 (formerly 185)

> Actions brought before the Court of Justice shall not have suspensory effect. The Court of Justice may, however, if it considers that circumstances so require, order that application of the contested act be suspended.

Article 243 (formerly 186)

> The Court of Justice may in any cases before it prescribe any necessary interim measures.

Bearing in mind, therefore, that an action under Article 226 does not have any suspensory effect on the Member State law which is the subject of the enforcement action, and the merely declaratory nature of a decision of the Court to the effect that a violation of Community law has occurred, it may be that the Commission deems it necessary to seek interim measures in conjunction with its action under Article 226.

In Case 61/77R *Commission v Ireland (Re Fisheries Conservation Measures)*, the Court of Justice ruled that interim measures ordering a Member State to act in a certain way, for example, to suspend national rules considered by the Commission to be contrary to the Treaty, might be granted at the Commission's request within the ambit of Article 169 (now 226) proceedings. The availability of such a remedy, akin to an interlocutory injunction in English law, means therefore that, somewhat anomalously, the Court possesses wider powers in interim proceedings than at the final declaratory judgment stage.

However, as seen, interim relief will only be granted in exceptional circumstances. The Rules of Procedure of the Court of Justice state that interim measures may not be ordered 'unless there are circumstances giving rise to urgency and factual and legal grounds establishing a *prima facie* case for the measures applied for'.

The Court will therefore take into account the following considerations:

(a) As regards the main proceedings under Article 226, whether the Commission has established a *prima facie* case: one that 'does not appear to be without foundation'.

(b) The question of urgency, which must be assessed in relation to the prevention of serious and irreparable damage.

(c) That the interim measures requested are such as to prevent the damage which is alleged.

The second consideration will normally involve the weighing of a balance of interests. The Commission will be required to show that serious and irreparable damage to the Community interest will occur if the Court does not grant the order. However, the defendant Member State may well argue that such damage to its interests will result if the order is granted.

These considerations were examined by the Court of Justice in the following case, in which the Commission pursued its action against the UK under Articles 169 (now 226) and 186 (now 243).

Case 246/89R *Commission v UK (Re Merchant Shipping Rules)*

The UK government had taken steps to prevent Spanish business interests from 'quota-hopping', that is, fishing in vessels registered in Britain against UK fishing quotas as laid down under the Common Fisheries Policy, but landing their catch in Spain. These steps culminated in the passing of the Merchant Shipping Act 1988, which in essence required that vessels be under British ownership.

The Commission initiated an Article 169 procedure against the UK on the basis that the 1988 Act contravened Treaty rules prohibiting discrimination on grounds of nationality, in particular Article 7 (now 12) and Article 52 (now 43) (on the right of establishment). The Commission also asked the Court as a matter of urgency to make an interim order under Article 186 regarding suspension of the Act's nationality requirements.

Having considered the directly effective rights, particularly of establishment, *claimed* by the 'Anglo-Spanish' operators and UK national interests under the Common Fisheries Policy, the President of the Court ruled that the Commission had made out a *prima facie* case.

As regards the need for urgency, the President held that:

> ... for fishing vessels which until 31 March 1989 [the time when the new allegedly discriminatory UK rules came into operation] were flying the British flag and fishing under a British fishing licence, the loss of the flag and the cessation of their activities entail serious damage. There is no ground for believing that, pending delivery of the judgment in the main proceedings, these vessels can be operated in the pursuit of alternative fishing activities. The aforesaid damage must also,

should the application in the main proceedings be granted, be regarded as irreparable. [This last point refers to the absence, at that time, of a remedy in damages against the Crown.]

The President therefore ordered that:

Pending delivery of the judgment in the main proceedings, the United Kingdom shall suspend the application of the nationality requirements laid down in the Merchant Shipping Act 1988 as regards the nationals of other Member States and in respect of fishing vessels which, until 31 March 1989, were pursuing a fishing activity under the British flag and under a British fishing licence.

It is important to stress that this case clearly illustrates that at Community level the Court of Justice may grant interim relief against national measures which are the subject of an Article 226 (formerly 169) action and in relation to which a *prima facie* case that they are in breach of Community law has been established. (In the main proceedings, Case 246/89 *Commission v UK (Re Merchant Shipping Rules)*, the Court held that the stringent rules introduced by the 1988 Act, requiring British nationality for owners of British registered fishing vessels entitled to fish under the UK fishing quotas, infringed Articles 7 and 52 of the Treaty and the illegality of the national requirement was not affected by the EEC fishery quota system.) A challenge to the 1988 Act was also taken up at national level, marking the beginning of the long running *Factortame* litigation, as seen in the next section.

It is important to appreciate that the question of interim relief has now been examined in a number of different contexts: at Community level it may be granted by the Court of Justice against the application of a disputed *Community* act (see, for example, Case 113/77R *NTN Toyo Bearing v Council*, the main proceeding being referred to in the previous chapter), or against the application of national law alleged to be in violation of Community rules (*Re Merchant Shipping Rules*). Also, the Court has held that the Commission has powers to adopt interim measures in the context of the competition rules: see *Camera Care* in Chapter 17 and *La Cinq* below. In similar circumstances, at national level, an interim injunction has been granted: see *Cutsforth v Mansfield Inns Ltd* (1986), also discussed below.

At national level again, in Article 234(1)(b) (177(1)(b)) cases, a court may, as seen, grant interim relief against the application of a national measure based on a disputed Community act (*Zuckerfabrik Süderdithmarschen*) and, in similar circumstances and under the same conditions, grant interim relief which in effect suspends the disputed Community act itself (*Atlanta*): both cases were discussed in the previous chapter.

In the next section, it will be seen that a national court also has the power to grant interim relief against the application of national law alleged to be in violation of Community rules: Case C-213/89 *R v Secretary of State for Transport ex p Factortame*.

The overall aim of the Court of Justice is to achieve balance and coherence as regards enforcement and remedies.

SUPERVISION AT NATIONAL LEVEL: RIGHTS AND REMEDIES IN NATIONAL COURTS

The 'quota hopping' litigation (generally known as *Factortame*) not only involved the Commission's actions under Articles 169 and 186 (now 226 and 243) but claims at the

INTERIM MEASURES AT COMMUNITY AND NATIONAL LEVEL

EC LEVEL:

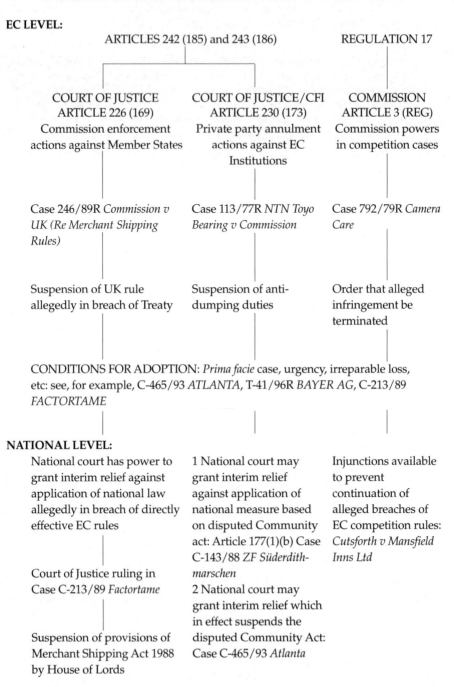

ARTICLES 242 (185) and 243 (186)   REGULATION 17

COURT OF JUSTICE ARTICLE 226 (169) Commission enforcement actions against Member States	COURT OF JUSTICE/CFI ARTICLE 230 (173) Private party annulment actions against EC Institutions	COMMISSION ARTICLE 3 (REG) Commission powers in competition cases
Case 246/89R *Commission v UK (Re Merchant Shipping Rules)*	Case 113/77R *NTN Toyo Bearing v Commission*	Case 792/79R *Camera Care*
Suspension of UK rule allegedly in breach of Treaty	Suspension of anti-dumping duties	Order that alleged infringement be terminated

CONDITIONS FOR ADOPTION: *Prima facie* case, urgency, irreparable loss, etc: see, for example, C-465/93 *ATLANTA*, T-41/96R *BAYER AG*, C-213/89 *FACTORTAME*

NATIONAL LEVEL:

National court has power to grant interim relief against application of national law allegedly in breach of directly effective EC rules	1 National court may grant interim relief against application of national measure based on disputed Community act: Article 177(1)(b) Case C-143/88 ZF *Süderdithmarschen*	Injunctions available to prevent continuation of alleged breaches of EC competition rules: *Cutsforth v Mansfield Inns Ltd*
Court of Justice ruling in Case C-213/89 *Factortame*	2 National court may grant interim relief which in effect suspends the disputed Community Act: Case C-465/93 *Atlanta*	
Suspension of provisions of Merchant Shipping Act 1988 by House of Lords		

national level as well: see diagram on page 578. The compatibility of the Merchant Shipping Act 1988 with Community law was the subject of challenge by Factortame Ltd and other members of the 'Anglo-Spanish' fishing fleet against the Secretary of State for Transport in the English courts. This challenge was similarly double edged.

Factortame claimed that the Act's new registration requirements were in violation of their directly enforceable Community right not to be discriminated against on grounds of nationality under Article 7 (now 12), in conjunction with their similar rights of establishment under Articles 52 and 58 (now 43 and 48) of the Treaty. These claims became the subject of an Article 177 reference from the Divisional Court of the QBD for an interpretative ruling. However, before examining this claim, or the second aspect of the case, Factortame's application for the relevant parts of the 1988 Act being suspended by the *national* court pending a determination of their compatibility with Community law by the Court of Justice, it is important to recall the relationship between the first, substantive issue (concerning directly effective rights) and the enforcement action brought by the Commission under Article 169 (now 226).

As we have seen on numerous occasions, on the basis of the twin principles of supremacy and the direct effect of Community law, an infringement of Community law by a Member State may be challenged by private parties at national level. Returning to the Court's landmark decision in Case 26/62 *Van Gend en Loos* regarding the standstill on customs duties in Article 12 (now 25), following a reference from the Dutch customs court under Article 177, the Court stated in clear terms that:

> A restriction of the guarantees against an infringement of Article 12 by Member States to the procedures under Article 169 and 170 would remove all direct legal protection of the individual rights of their nationals ... The vigilance of individuals concerned to protect their rights amounts to an effective supervision in addition to the supervision entrusted by Articles 169 and 170 to the diligence of the Commission and of the Member States.

It will be recalled that in this case, the importer successfully argued that he could resist the application of national law (and a higher rate of duty) as it conflicted with his rights under the Treaty (to pay a lower rate). In another important decision, in the case of *Defrenne v Sabena (No 2)*, the effect of the Court's ruling was that compensation must be paid by any employer who discriminates against his employees in terms of pay contrary to the equal pay principle of Article 119 (now 141). The equal treatment cases of *Marshall* and *Von Colson* each in their different way established the plaintiff's right to compensation where national law did not comply with Community rules. In the latter, we have seen how national law was interpreted so as to provide damages beyond the merely nominal.

All these Article 177 rulings of the Court of Justice (and many others of course) were returned to the originating national court or tribunal to be applied. An inquiry into the eventual outcome raises the important general question of the effectiveness of Community rights in national courts or tribunals in terms of the remedies available. For example, upon what terms did English law provide for compensation for Miss Marshall? What remedies were available for Factortame and the other members of the 'Anglo-Spanish' fishing fleet should their claims in the national courts succeed?

The general trend in the development of the law at Community level with respect to individual rights, through the operation of supremacy and Article 177 (now 234), is clear enough. Direct effect, indirect effect and State liability have increasingly strengthened the position of private parties.

Just as clearly, this strengthening has increased the pressure on national courts and tribunals to vindicate those rights in cases where the Court's preliminary rulings indicate such a final outcome. From the outset, in the continuing absence of Community rules in the area, and beyond guidance from the Court, the policy followed has been, despite inevitable variations in national law from Member State to Member State, to leave the question of remedies to the operation of national law. A division of function applies which, although not strictly defined, is based on the principle of national procedural autonomy.

When a preliminary ruling is applied (if one has been found to be necessary), the question as to the procedural rules which are to apply (for example, time limits for the initiation of proceedings, periods allowable for the back-dating of claims, limitations on recoverable loss) and even the question of the availability of an appropriate remedy to fit the particular case are matters which remain within the province of national law.

As stated, the Court of Justice has provided guidance for the national courts and tribunals – parameters within which they must operate when dealing with questions such as these – and above all, the Court has increasingly stressed the need for the provision of *effective* remedies. The extent of the Court's intervention, which blurs the functional division, has not been consistent with respect to procedural rules and has increased as regards remedies as the judiciaries endeavour to find their feet in this difficult field.

National Procedural Autonomy and the Court of Justice

Guidance concerning the impact of *national limitation rules* on claims in national courts in respect of directly effective Community rights was given by the Court of Justice in, amongst others, Case 33/76 *Rewe-Zentralfinanz v LS* and Case 45/76 *Comet v Produktschap*. In the latter case, a levy had been paid on exports which was found to be a charge equivalent to a customs duty contrary to Article 16 (see now Article 12) of the Treaty. C's claim for reimbursement was met by the argument that it had been lodged after the expiry of the limitation period for such claims under Dutch law. C in return argued that this was an independent right of action unaffected by limitations provided for under national law, which were liable to weaken the impact of directly effective Community law.

Following an Article 177 (now 234) reference, the Court of Justice endorsed the rights of Member States to apply national limitation periods in cases in national courts based on directly effective provisions of Community law, subject to two requirements which have been termed the principles of *equivalence or non-discrimination* and *practical possibility or effectiveness* within the general principle of *national procedural autonomy*:

> Thus, in the application of the principle of co-operation laid down in Article 5 [now 10] of the Treaty, the national courts are entrusted with ensuring the legal protection conferred on individuals by the direct effect of the provisions of Community law.

> Consequently, in the absence of any relevant Community rules, it is for the national legal order of each Member State to designate the competent courts and to lay down the procedural rules for proceedings designed to ensure the protection of the rights which individuals acquire through the direct effect of Community law, provided that such rules *are not less favourable than those governing the same right of action on an internal matter*.

Articles 100 to 102 and 235 [now 94–97 and 308] of the Treaty enable the appropriate steps to be taken as necessary, to eliminate differences between the provisions laid down in such matters by law, regulation or administrative action in Member States if these differences are found to be such as to cause distortion or to affect the functioning of the common market.

In default of such harmonisation measures, the rights conferred by Community law must be exercised before the national courts in accordance with the rules of procedure laid down by national law.

The position would be different *only if those rules and time limits made it impossible in practice to exercise rights which the national courts have a duty to protect.*

This does not apply to the fixing of a reasonable period of limitation within which an action must be brought.

The fixing, as regards fiscal proceedings, of such a period is in fact an application of a fundamental principle of legal certainty which protects both the authority concerned and the party from whom payment is claimed.

The answer must therefore be that, in the case of a litigant who is challenging before the national courts a decision of a national body for incompatibility with Community law, that law, in its present state, does not prevent the expiry of the period within which proceedings must be brought under national law from being raised against him, provided that the procedural rules applicable to his case are not less favourable than those governing the same right of action on an internal matter [emphasis added].

Thus, 'in the absence of any relevant Community rules' on the subject, national procedures applied – subject to the two requirements laid down by the Court. Further, until such national rules are harmonised, the availability of remedies for private parties may well vary from one Member State to another. However, it is clear that in no event may national rules exclude or discriminate against the exercise of directly effective rights. In *Comet*, the Dutch procedural rule imposing a limitation period of 30 days was upheld.

Case 199/82 *AFS v San Georgio*, another case concerning charges levied by national authorities contrary to the free movement rules, differed in that no right to repayment existed unless difficult conditions regarding proof were satisfied according to the Italian law, which applied to similar but purely *internal* situations. The Court of Justice was not impressed by a claim of equivalence as this would render repayment of the illegal charges in question 'virtually impossible or excessively difficult'. A right to repayment had to be made available in national law. This was so even though the Court had only two years earlier stated, in Case 158/80 *Rewe v HZA Kiel*, that 'it was not intended to create new remedies in the national courts to ensure the observance of Community law other than those laid down by national law'. This question of 'new remedies' was to develop dramatically and will be examined below.

A difficult question concerning time limits, within the context of Directives and the failure of Member States to implement them, arose in Case C-208/90 *Emmott v Minister for Social Welfare*. As regards the time limits within which proceedings must be brought before a national court by persons wishing to rely on a Directive against a defaulting Member State, the Court ruled that time begins to run not from the date of the expiry of the implementation period, but from the *later* date when national implementing legislation is correctly adopted.

Case C-208/90 *Emmott v Minister for Social Welfare*

Council Directive 79/7, which prohibits discrimination on grounds of sex in matters of social security, should have been implemented by the Irish authorities by 23 December 1984. Ireland did not implement it properly until 1986. In March 1987, E first learnt of her rights under the Directive following the ruling of the Court of Justice in Case 286/85 *McDermott and Cotter v Minister for Social Welfare*. She wrote to the Department of Social Welfare claiming that she was entitled to back payments from 23 December 1984 in respect of disability benefit, having received less benefit than a man would have done in equivalent circumstances.

The Department replied saying that the legal position was not yet clear, but that her application would be considered following the outcome of another relevant case. However, E heard no more from the Department and she commenced judicial review proceedings before the Irish courts in January 1988. The Ministry denied her claim and argued that in any event she was statute-barred from presenting it.

The Rules of the Superior Courts in Ireland provided that a claim for judicial review (for the purpose of recovering her benefits) must, except in exceptional circumstances, be brought within three months from the date when grounds for the application first arose – in Mrs Emmott's case, the date in December 1984 when the as then unimplemented Directive 79/7 came into force.

Under Article 177 (now 234), the High Court asked the Court of Justice whether it was 'contrary to the general principles of Community law for the relevant authorities of a Member State to rely upon national procedural rules, in particular rules relating to time limits', in order to refuse compensation for Mrs Emmott.

The Court ruled that:

> So long as a Directive has not been properly transposed into national law, individuals are unable to ascertain the full extent of their rights. That state of uncertainty for individuals subsists even after the Court has delivered a judgment finding that the Member State in question has not fulfilled its obligations under the Directive and even if the Court has held that a particular provision or provisions of the Directive are sufficiently precise and unconditional to be relied upon before a national court.

> Only the proper transposition of the Directive will bring that state of uncertainty to an end and it is only upon that transposition that the legal certainty which must exist if individuals are to be required to assert their rights is created.

> It follows that, until such time as a Directive has been properly transposed, a defaulting Member State may not rely on an individual's delay in initiating proceedings against it in order to protect rights conferred upon him by the provisions of the Directive and that a period laid down by national law within which proceedings must be initiated cannot begin to run before that time.

> The answer to the question referred to the Court must therefore be that Community law precludes the competent authorities of a Member State from relying, in proceedings brought against them by an individual before the national courts in order to protect rights directly conferred upon him by Article 4(1) of Directive 79/7/EEC, on national procedural rules relating to time limits for bringing proceedings so long as that Member State has not properly transposed that Directive into its domestic legal system.

In *Emmott*, the Court stated that the Irish time limits were reasonable and, in principle, did not have the effect of discriminating against or excluding the exercise of Community law rights. However, the State could not rely on its own default in failing to implement the Directive (a use of the concept of estoppel as previously seen in *Foster v British Gas*) and so benefit from the national time limit to bar the action. On this basis, Mrs Emmott gained access to an effective remedy. Nevertheless, this decision raised some difficult questions.

As Hoskins pointed out, 'the approach of the Court of Justice undermines the concept of direct effect. Directive 79/7 is directly effective and therefore could have been relied on in the national courts by Mrs Emmott as from 23 December 1984 to obtain equality of treatment'. Also, 'the combination of the judgment in *Emmott* with the principle of State liability for failure to implement directives established in ... *Francovich* ... is potentially explosive as it may expose a Member State to massive liability in damages which it will not be able to mitigate by reliance on national limitation periods, even if those limitations are wholly reasonable'.

This decision has since been confined to the particular facts of the case (particularly the Ministry's delay in giving E sound advice). In the later *Steenhorst-Neerings* case, the Court declined to follow *Emmott* when called upon to rule on the compatibility with Community law of Dutch national rules restricting the right to back-dated social security benefits following a successful claim of sex discrimination.

Case C-338/91 *Steenhorst-Neerings v BBD*

S-N's claim was based (like Emmott's) on the equal treatment Social Security Directive 79/7 and it applied to discrimination in granting invalidity benefit between 1984 and 1988, which had been remedied in 1988 by bringing Dutch law into line with the Directive. Her claim was barred under national law, which imposed a statutory one year limit on the retrospective payment of invalidity benefit.

Following a reference under Article 177, the Court drew the following distinction: *Emmott* concerned national rules fixing time limits for bringing an action, which operated to prevent individuals from asserting their rights under the Directive. The purpose of such a limitation was to ensure that the legality of administrative decisions could not be challenged indefinitely. The one year rule in the instant case did not affect the individual's right to rely on the Directive; it merely limited the retroactive effects of claims made in order to obtain the relevant benefits. It could be justified as a basis for 'sound administration, most importantly so that it may be ascertained whether the claimant satisfied the conditions for eligibility and so that the degree of incapacity, which may well vary over time, may be fixed. It also reflects the need to preserve financial balance in a scheme in which claims submitted by insured persons in the course of a year must in principle be covered by the contributions collection during that same year'.

In essence, therefore, the effective extent of S-N's retroactive claim was limited; it was not completely blocked as in *Emmott*. Nevertheless, this decision (and distinction) was also criticised in some quarters as being 'poorly reasoned' and contrary to the principle of effective remedies. However, in a similar UK case involving disablement benefit, C-410/92 *Johnson v Chief Adjudication Officer (No 2)*, *Steenhorst-Neerings* was approved and followed by the Court of Justice.

The position was summed up by Hoskins as follows:

The effect of an *Emmott*-type limitation period is that a plaintiff will receive all or nothing, depending on whether he/she has commenced proceedings within the limitation period. The effect of a *Steenhorst-Neerings*-type limitation is that a plaintiff may never receive his/her full rights under Community law. Even if an applicant brings a claim for retrospective benefit payments within the relevant time period, he/she will only be able to claim payments backdated for one year, even if he/she has been discriminated against for a number of years.

These cases and further similar ones decided in the 1990s throw light on a delicate balancing act to be performed by the national courts. Since *Von Colson*, the Court of Justice has stressed the need for adequate and effective remedies for the enforcement of Community rights at national level. For example, compensation must be commensurate with the loss. At the same time, national procedural autonomy is to be respected, subject to the requirements of *equivalence* – regarding the treatment of purely domestic and Community rights – and *effectiveness*, in that national procedural rules must not make access to a remedy based on Community law 'impossible in practice' or 'virtually impossible' or, in a later phrase, 'excessively difficult'.

National limitation periods have been recognised by the Court as a vital feature of the principle of legal certainty and 'reasonable' time limits are acceptable. The reasonable time limit in *Steenhorst-Neerings* and other cases has, however, resulted in a dilution of the adequate and effective remedy requirement and, as time limits vary from Member State to Member State, in the uniformity of Community law. Nevertheless, the Court has squared this circle by stating in the *Preston and Fletcher* case (see below): 'Since the setting of reasonable limitation periods was an application of the fundamental principle of legal certainty, it was compatible with the principle of effectiveness.' In Case C-188/95 *Fantask A/S v Industriministeriet*, the Court, accepting a Danish five year limitation period for the recovery of debts, acknowledged:

> ... in the interests of legal certainty, which protects the taxpayer and the authorities concerned, that the setting of reasonable limitation periods for bringing proceedings [was] compatible with Community law. Such periods cannot be regarded as rendering impossible or excessively difficult the exercise of rights conferred by Community law, even if the expiry of those periods necessarily entails the dismissal, in whole or in part, of the action brought.

The Court's intervention into national procedural autonomy in *Emmott* was praiseworthy in terms of access to justice, but the Court has since been more careful when setting aside time limits where they 'deprive the applicant of any opportunity whatsoever' to rely on. In Case C-2/94 *Denkavit International v KKFM*, Advocate General Jacobs argued strongly in favour of reasonable time limits and their contribution to legal security even in cases of unimplemented Directives. He saw a State liability *Francovich* claim as the better way of protecting individual rights in such circumstances – protection of the individual this way would place great emphasis on the defaulting State's culpability. He was of the view in *Fantask*, with what may be read as a measure of support from the Court, that:

> It seems to me that the judgment in *Emmott*, notwithstanding its more general language, must be read as establishing the principle that a Member State may not rely on a limitation period where a Member State is in default both in failing to implement a directive and in obstructing the exercise of a judicial remedy in reliance upon it, or perhaps where the delay in exercising the remedy – and hence the failure to meet the time-limit – is in some other way due to the conduct of the national authorities.

Also as is apparent, and as Arnull has pointed out:

> ... the Advocate General added that a broad view of the *Emmott* rule could not be reconciled with the approach to national time limits which had been taken in the *Steenhorst-Neerings* and *Johnson* cases. The distinction drawn by the Court in these

cases between the types of limit applicable there and that applicable in *Emmott* was, he thought, not convincing: '... a five-year time-limit for instituting proceedings, if applied to recurring taxes or benefits, could equally be viewed as a rule limiting to five years the extent to which a claim may relate back ...'

What the case law in this area now shows is that the balance between respect for national procedural rules and the principle of effectiveness, that is, the need for Community rights not to be 'excessively difficult' to pursue, has now been better achieved so far as case law can do this. However, each case depends on its particular facts, on the nature and purpose of the national procedural rule, and on its effects. As the Court of Justice stated in Joined Cases C-430 and 431/93 *Van Schijndel and Van Veen v SPF*:

> ... each case which raises the question whether a national procedural provision renders application of Community law impossible or excessively difficult must be analysed by reference to the role of that provision in the procedure, its progress and its special features, viewed as a whole, before the various national instances. In the light of that analysis the basic principles of the domestic judicial system, such as protection of the rights of the defence, the principle of legal certainty and the proper conduct of procedure, must, where appropriate, be taken into consideration.

Case C-78/98 *Preston and Others v Wolverhampton Healthcare NHS Trust and Others and Fletcher and Others v Midland Bank plc*

The applicants were women who worked or had worked part time in the public and private sectors. The pension schemes at issue were contracted-out schemes amended between 1986 and 1995 to allow part time workers previously wholly or partially excluded to join them. P, F and the others claimed entitlement to retroactive membership of their schemes for the periods of part time employment completed by them before the amendments were made.

Section 2(4) of the Equal Pay Act 1970 provided that any claim in respect of [a sex] equality clause had to be brought within six months following cessation of employment, if it was not to be time-barred. Section 2(5), as amended, provided that, in an action to secure equal treatment as to entitlement to membership of an occupational pension scheme, the earliest date with effect from which it could be declared that the employee had a right to be admitted to the scheme was two years before the institution of the proceedings.

In response to questions put by the House of Lords, the Court of Justice ruled that:

(a) Community law did not preclude a national procedural rule which required that a claim for membership of an occupational pension scheme, from which the right to pension benefits flowed, had, if it was not to be time barred, to be brought within six months of the end of the employment to which the claim related, provided, however, that the limitation period was not less favourable for actions based on Community law than for those based on national law.

(b) However, as regards those claimants who had worked regularly, but periodically or intermittently for the same employer under successive legally separate contracts, the Act's setting of the starting point of the six month limitation period at the end of each such contract did render the exercise of the right conferred by Article 119 (now 141) excessively difficult. Such workers were unable to secure recognition of periods of part time work for the purposes of calculating their pension rights unless they had instituted proceedings after the end of each contract.

When considering this case, other points to note are as follows:

(a) Occupational pension benefits are 'pay' within the terms of Article 141 (formerly 119): Case 170/84 *Bilka-Kaufhaus*, in which the Court held that exclusion of part time workers from a supplementary occupational pension scheme amounted to indirect pay discrimination if the exclusion affects a greater number of women than men and which the employer cannot explain by objectively justified factors unrelated to sex.

(b) In Cases C-57/93 *Vroege* and C-128/93 *Fisscher*, the Court of Justice in 1994:

    (i) followed *Bilka-Kaufhaus* on the above point;

    (ii) ruled that the Maastricht Protocol on Article 119, 'clarifying' the *Barber* judgment on the limitation of retroactive entitlement to occupational pension benefits to periods of service *from* the date of that judgment (17 May 1990), applied only to benefits and not to the right to join or belong to an occupational pension scheme. This meant that discriminatory conditions governing membership of such a scheme (for example, the need for full time service) were governed by *Bilka-Kaufhaus*, where no temporal limitation was laid down, and not *Barber* or the Protocol;

    (iii) ruled that the direct effect of Article 119 could be relied upon in order retroactively to claim equal rights as regards access to an occupational pension scheme as from the date of the Court's ruling in Case 43/75 *Defrenne (No 2)*, that is, 8 April 1976, in which Article 119 was held to be directly effective (vertically and horizontally) for the first time: see also Case C-246/96 *Magorrian v Eastern Health and Social Services Board*.

(c) In *Preston and Fletcher*, the Court also ruled that: 'The workers concerned will be able to secure retroactive membership of the relevant schemes and payment of the resulting benefits only if they first pay contributions to cover all the periods of part time employment of which they seek recognition.'

(d) Many part time workers will not have lodged the necessary claim for membership within six months of completing their employment. Others will have difficulty confirming employment and pay records going back to 1976.

Remedies: Damages and Interim Relief

All the cases in the previous section, while concentrating on national procedural limitations, obviously illustrated their impact on the particular remedy sought – whether it was a form of restitution with respect to illegal charges (*Comet*, etc) or the retrospective payment of social security benefits (*Emmott, Preston and Fletcher*, etc).

This section (and the next on State Liability) will switch the emphasis to the provision of *adequate and effective* remedies, although the question of the disapplication of limiting national procedural rules is an important feature in some of the cases. We will be mainly concerned with the involvement of the English courts in the fields of sex discrimination, competition policy, and, in *Factortame/Brasserie du Pêcheur*, free movement, 'new' remedies and the development of the State liability principle.

In Case 158/80 *Rewe v HZA Kiel*, the facts of which were similar to those in *Comet* above, the Court stated that:

> ... it was not intended to create new remedies in the national courts to ensure the observance of Community law other than those already laid down by national law. On the other hand ... it must be possible for every type of action provided for by national law to be available for the purpose of ensuring observance of Community provisions having direct effect, on the same conditions as would apply were it a question of observing national law.

Four years later, in the sex discrimination Case 222/84 *Johnston v CC of the RUC* (see Chapter 14), the Court of Justice stressed that the existence of effective judicial protection was a general principle of Community law to be found in the constitutional traditions of the Member States. It will be recalled that the equal treatment claim in this case was eventually settled by a payment of £250,000 to 30 former RUC policewomen.

The basis of the Court's ruling in *Johnston* was Article 6 of the Equal Treatment Directive 76/207, which obliged Member States to introduce into their legal systems the measures necessary to enable alleged victims of discrimination 'to pursue their claims by judicial process'. Article 6 has been reworded following amendment of the Equal Treatment Directive by Directive 2002/73. Article 6(1) now states that:

> Member States shall ensure that judicial and/or administrative procedures, including where they deem it appropriate conciliation procedures, for the enforcement of obligations under this Directive are available to all persons who consider themselves wronged by failure to apply the principle of equal treatment to them, even after the relationship in which the discrimination is alleged to have occurred has ended.

The extension of the protection of the Directive in the face of 'adverse treatment by the employer' (see the new Article 7) after the end of the employment relationship was established by the Court in Case C-185/97 *Coote v Granada Hospitality*.

Remedies provided by national law must not only be 'such as to guarantee full and effective legal protection' but also have a 'real deterrent effect': see Case 79/83 *Harz v Deutsche Tradax*. In this case and its companion equal treatment Case 14/83 *Von Colson* (see Chapter 8), the plaintiffs' entitlement to damages for sexual discrimination was secured on the basis of the principle of indirect effect. Although at national level, they were initially awarded only nominal damages, the Court held that 'if a Member State chooses to penalise breaches [of the Equal Treatment Directive] ... by the award of compensation ... that compensation must in any event be adequate in relation to the damage sustained'.

The Court's rulings in *Von Colson* and *Marshall (No 2)* (see below), in which a national statutory ceiling on the recovery of compensation was overridden in the face of the Community law requirement to provide an effective remedy, lie at the heart of the introduction in 2002 of a new Article 6(2) of the Equal Treatment Directive, to be read in conjunction with a new Article 8(d):

Article 6(2)

> Member States shall introduce into their national legal systems such measures as are necessary to ensure real and effective compensation or reparation as the Member States so determine for the loss and damage sustained by a person injured as a result of discrimination contrary to Article 3, in a way which is dissuasive and proportionate to the damage suffered; such compensation or reparation may not be restricted by the fixing of a prior upper limit, except in cases where the employer can prove that the only damage suffered by an applicant as a result of discrimination within the meaning of this Directive is the refusal to take his/her job application into consideration.

Article 8(d)

> Member States shall lay down the rules on sanctions applicable to infringements of the national provisions adopted pursuant to this Directive, and shall take all measures necessary to ensure that they are applied.

The sanction, which may comprise the payment of compensation to the victim, must be effective, proportionate and dissuasive. The Member States shall notify those provisions to the Commission by 5 October 2005 at the latest and shall notify it without delay of any subsequent amendment affecting them.

In 1990, Collins wrote that:

Some very difficult questions have been raised in England on the availability of the damages remedy, and the relationship between the right to damages and the possibility of obtaining interim relief pending the determination of cases in which directly effective rights are claimed [but have] not yet been definitely established.

In the case which follows, interlocutory proceedings reached the House of Lords where difficult questions concerning injunctions and damages were considered by their Lordships but were not regarded as 'apt for decision' at that stage. The case involved a private law action brought against an undertaking in which the directly effective Article 86 (now 82) was used as 'a sword'.

Garden Cottage Foods Ltd v Milk Marketing Board (1984)

The plaintiffs regularly bought bulk butter from MMB, a statutory body holding a dominant position, for sale in the UK and abroad. As a result of a change of policy, the Board reduced the number of its sales outlets and cut off supplies to the plaintiffs, who alleged that the Board had acted in breach of Article 86 by abusing its dominant position.

At first instance, GCF's application for an interim injunction to compel the Board to resume supplies was refused principally on the ground that damages would be an adequate remedy. The Court of Appeal granted the injunction mainly because it was doubtful whether there was a cause of action in damages for breach of Article 86.

By a 4:1 majority, the House of Lords restored the decision at first instance. In the course of his speech, Lord Diplock stated that:

The rights which the Article confers on citizens in the United Kingdom accordingly fall within section 2(1) of the 1972 Act. They are without further enactment to be given legal effect in the United Kingdom and enforced accordingly. A breach of the duty imposed by Article 86 not to abuse a dominant position in the Common Market or in a substantial part of it can thus be categorised in English law as a breach of statutory duty that is imposed not only for the purpose of promoting the general economic prosperity of the Common Market but also for the benefit of private individuals to whom loss or damage is caused by a breach of that duty. If this categorisation be correct, and I can see none other that would be capable of giving rise to a civil cause of action in English private law on the part of a private individual who sustained loss or damage by reason of a breach of a directly applicable ['effective' – as used in this book] provision of the EEC Treaty, the nature of the cause of action cannot, in my view, be affected by the fact that the legislative provision by which the duty is imposed takes the negative form of a prohibition of particular kinds of conduct rather than the positive form of an obligation to do particular acts.

Therefore, although only an interlocutory ruling, this case supported the view that in principle a right of action for damages is available in English law under Article 82 (formerly 86) on the basis of the tort of breach of statutory duty. It is not an authority for saying that an injunction will never be granted in cases involving Articles 81 (formerly 85) and 82. An interim injunction was granted by the High Court in *Cutsforth v Mansfield Inns Ltd* (1986) to protect C from further financial loss resulting from the continued enforcement by M of tenancy agreements which the defendant had concluded with some of its public houses, and for which there was a 'serious case' as regards their infringement of Article 85(1) (now 81(1)).

The question of the recovery of compensation by a private party following an infringement of the directly effective competition rules came from the English courts to the Court of Justice in 2001 in *Courage Ltd v Crehan*. At the time when the Commission's modernisation and decentralisation programme was emphasising the importance of private actions to the enforcement of the competition rules (as seen in Chapter 17), the Court stated that:

> The full effectiveness of Article 85 [now 81] of the Treaty and, in particular, the practical effect of the prohibition laid down in Article 85(1) [now 81(1)] would be put at risk if it were not open to any individual to claim damages for loss caused to him by a contract or by conduct liable to restrict or distort competition.

The emphasis here is clearly on '*any individual*' and the 'full effectiveness' of the Community right – leaving to the English courts the matter of establishing the correct basis of the damages clam. As in *Garden Cottage Foods* the tort of breach of statutory duty would seem to be the most likely choice. The loss suffered falls within the scope of the statute (Article 81 as incorporated into UK law by section 2 of the European Communities Act 1972) and the statute gives rise to a civil cause of action. (An extension of State liability to private parties has also been put forward as the basis for such a claim.)

Case C-453/99 *Courage Ltd v Crehan*

The defendant C was a publican who entered into two 20 year leases with IEL, part owned by the plaintiff brewery CL. The leases contained a beer tie obligation under which C had to purchase *all* his supplies from CL. The brewery brought an action to recover the cost of unpaid deliveries and C counter-claimed for damages and contended that the tie was contrary to Article 85(1).

The Court of Appeal raised, among other things, the effect of the rule in English law that a party to an illegal contract could not claim damages from the other party. Was this a bar to the claim?

The Court of Justice ruled that:

(a) A party to a contract liable to restrict or distort competition within the meaning of Article 85 (now Article 81) can rely on the breach of that provision to obtain relief from the other contracting party.

(b) Article 85 precludes a rule of national law under which a party to a contract liable to restrict or distort competition is barred from claiming damages for loss caused by performance of that contract on the sole ground that the claimant is a party to that contract.

(c) Community law does not preclude a rule of national law barring a party to a contract liable to restrict or distort competition from relying on his own unlawful actions to obtain damages where it is established that that party bears significant responsibility for the distortion of competition.

The English contract rule therefore gave way to the Community principle of effectiveness except to the extent that unjust enrichment would result: 'a litigant should not profit from his unlawful conduct, where this is proven.' The Court continued in a contract law vein when considering the relevance of bargaining power

(Courage had a 19 per cent share of the UK beer sales market and no doubt a network of such arrangements) and of mitigation of loss in this context:

> In particular, it is for the national court to ascertain whether the party, who claims to have suffered loss through concluding a contract that is liable to restrict or distort competition, found himself in a markedly weaker position than the other party, such as seriously to compromise or even eliminate his freedom to negotiate the terms of the contract and his capacity to avoid the loss or reduce its extent, in particular by availing himself in good time of all the legal remedies available to him.

Another difficult and controversial question, that of the availability of damages against the Crown, arose in the pre-*Factortame* case of *Bourgoin v Ministry of Agriculture, Fisheries and Food* (1986). Following the decision in *Garden Cottage Foods*, the French plaintiff (and others) brought an action against the Ministry for an injunction and in tort for damages to compensate for substantial economic loss allegedly caused by the defendant. The basis of the claim was the Ministry's contravention of Article 30 (now 28) when placing an embargo on imports of the plaintiff's goods: as decided by the Court of Justice in Case 40/82 *Commission v UK (Re Imports of Poultry Meat)* – see Chapter 12. However, the fact that the defendant was a public body was taken to raise new questions not encountered in the *Garden Cottage Foods* case (Article 28 imposes obligations on Member States; Article 82 (formerly 86) imposes them on undertakings). Did Bourgoin have a remedy in damages against the national authorities?

The legal background to this case is to be found in English administrative law. The position was summarised as follows in the Report of the Committee of the JUSTICE–All Souls Review of Administrative Law in the United Kingdom (1988):

COMPENSATION: FINANCIAL LOSS CAUSED BY ADMINISTRATIVE ACTION

> SUMMARY OF ARGUMENT. Special provisions apart, the existing law in the United Kingdom stops short of providing for compensation for economic loss caused by invalid administrative action or by excessive delay in arriving at an administrative decision, or by the giving of wrong advice by a public official. It has been suggested that liability for damages is inappropriate in such cases on the principle that it is always open to the person affected to ignore an invalid administrative decision; but we consider that unrealistic. The administration is liable for such of its wrongful conduct as fits into one of the recognized common law categories such as trespass, nuisance, negligence, or breach of statutory duty. A particular difficulty occurs in the case of allegations of negligence in the exercise of statutory powers by a public body because such powers must necessarily often contain a large element of policy and that is a matter for the public body, not for the courts. But, generally speaking, the law of negligence is capable of dealing satisfactorily with cases of injury caused by negligence of the administration and in our view it should be allowed to develop on a case by case basis.

> For the many types of wrongful administrative conduct that do not fit into the recognized common law categories, the court has no power to award damages. 'Wrongful' includes those cases of action or omission by a public authority where a court would find that the conduct or any resulting decision should be declared illegal or be quashed or held void or voidable. For the present, the law takes no account of the fact that the administration is capable of inflicting damage in ways in which a private person cannot.

Reform is clearly needed to provide a remedy for the person injured by wrongful administrative action not involving negligence. In French law, there is a principle of general liability for injury caused by malfunctioning of the public service. There is no real likelihood that the common law will develop in that direction and we therefore suggest legislation to provide generally for compensation for material injury caused either by wrongful acts or omissions or by unreasonable or excessive delay of a public body. Decisions of courts and tribunals would be excluded.

Bourgoin v Ministry of Agriculture, Fisheries and Food (1986)

In September 1981, the Ministry effectively prohibited imports of turkeys from France purportedly on public health grounds. Having failed to justify the ban under Article 36 – now 30 – (see Case 40/82 above), the Ministry later complied with the judgment of the Court by allowing imports to recommence. However the effect was that the French producers missed not only the 1981 Christmas season but that of 1982 as well.

Calculating their losses at £19 million, they alleged that the Minister's action in imposing the embargo amounted to the torts of (a) breach of statutory duty and (b) misfeasance in public office. On the hearing of a preliminary issue as to whether the statement of claim disclosed a cause of action, Mann J at first instance and a unanimous Court of Appeal were prepared to find an arguable cause of action in misfeasance (if the Minister, although not acting maliciously, knew that his act was *ultra vires*, being in breach of the directly effective Article 30, and that it would injure the plaintiff).

Mann J was also of the opinion that an action for breach of statutory duty would lie. He reasoned that Article 30, like Article 86 (in *Garden Cottage Foods*), was directly *effective* and its breach must give rise to rights which national courts must protect in an effective manner. Although the rights under Article 86 were to be seen as rights in private law (enforceable against another individual, the Milk Marketing Board), Mann J felt unable to differentiate between the two Articles, and accordingly held that a statutory duty claim could similarly lie against the Ministry.

This latter ruling was reversed by a majority of the Court of Appeal who felt that in this respect, since no remedy other than the public law remedy of judicial review would be available for a breach of a similar domestic legal right, judicial review was a sufficient remedy, together with a declaration as to the invalidity of the national measure which introduced the embargo. (By way of analogy, both judges drew attention to the restrictive conditions under which the Community might incur liability for damages under Article 215(2) (now 288(2)), see Chapter 19). Oliver LJ (dissenting) agreed with Mann J particularly as regards the need for effective protection: '... in principle the "protection" of the individual rights under Community law involves, subject to the procedural requirements of the national forum, the payment of compensation in respect of the period between the commission of the wrong and its rectification.'

In view of the later decision concerning interim relief in the *Factortame* case (see below), it is noteworthy that Oliver LJ added that 'the fact remains that in the absence of a remedy in damages or immediate interim relief, breaches of the EEC Treaty occurring prior to the decision in those proceedings will remain uncompensated'.

As with *Garden Cottage Foods*, this case only dealt with preliminary issues and could hardly be said to be conclusive on the question of the appropriateness of breach of statutory duty as a basis for damages following a breach of directly effective Community law. In *Bourgoin*, leave to appeal to the House of Lords was granted but

THE FACTORTAME 'ANGLO-SPANISH' FISHING FLEET LITIGATION

Was an amendment of UK national law, designed to counter 'quota hopping', in breach of the directly effective Community rights of Spanish business interests?

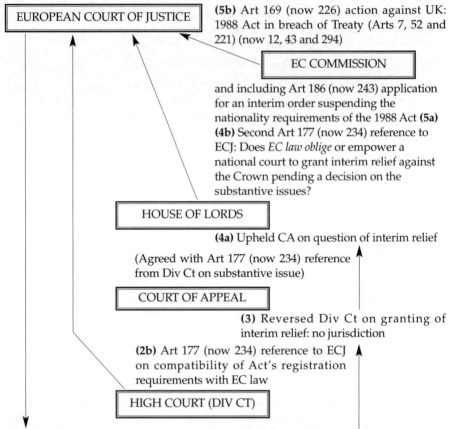

EUROPEAN COURT OF JUSTICE

(5b) Art 169 (now 226) action against UK: 1988 Act in breach of Treaty (Arts 7, 52 and 221) (now 12, 43 and 294)

EC COMMISSION

and including Art 186 (now 243) application for an interim order suspending the nationality requirements of the 1988 Act **(5a)** **(4b)** Second Art 177 (now 234) reference to ECJ: Does *EC law oblige* or empower a national court to grant interim relief against the Crown pending a decision on the substantive issues?

HOUSE OF LORDS

(4a) Upheld CA on question of interim relief

(Agreed with Art 177 (now 234) reference from Div Ct on substantive issue)

COURT OF APPEAL

(3) Reversed Div Ct on granting of interim relief: no jurisdiction

(2b) Art 177 (now 234) reference to ECJ on compatibility of Act's registration requirements with EC law

HIGH COURT (DIV CT)

DECISIONS

(5a) Interim relief granted: Case 246/89R. Nationality requirements suspended by Order in Council

(5b) Rules in 1988 Act contrary to EC law; discrimination on grounds of nationality, etc: Case 246/89

(4b) National courts had such a duty in cases involving EC law: Case C-213/89; applied by HL in *Factortame (No 2)*

(2b) Act's requirements not compatible with EC law: Factortame's directly effective rights upheld and prevail over national law: Case C-221/89

(2a) Granted interim relief; MS Act to be suspended.

Action for judicial review

FACTORTAME LITIGATION **(2)**

FISHING VESSEL
REGISTRATION REQUIREMENTS:

(1) *Merchant Shipping Act 1988*
For British ownership (eligible to fish against British quotas) –

NATIONALITY REQUIREMENTS;
RESIDENCE REQUIREMENTS;
MANAGEMENT AND CONTROL
FROM UK

the case was settled before the appeal was heard. The government paid £3.5 million in respect of damages, interest and costs.

It might be asked why, in the pursuit of effective remedies, Bourgoin did not seek interim relief as soon as the embargo took effect in late 1981. The answer must be that it was accepted at the time that, despite a requirement that effective protection be afforded Community rights, interim relief was not available against the Crown: section 21 of the Crown Proceedings Act 1947 in relation to civil proceedings.

The non-availability (as a matter of domestic law) of an interim injunction against the Crown or an officer of the Crown, together with serious doubts, following *Bourgoin*, as to any other than limited avenues to damages in tort against public authorities, is the background against which to examine the claims at national level in the *Factortame* 'quota-hopping' affair, discussed earlier in this chapter in the section on the supervision of Member States at Community level: see Case C-246/89R *Commission v UK (Re Merchant Shipping Rules)*.

In the Divisional Court of the QBD (see the diagram on page 578), Factortame and the other members of the 'Anglo-Spanish' fishing fleet brought judicial review proceedings challenging the nationality (and other residence and domicile) requirements of the Merchant Shipping Act 1988 on the grounds that, as in the case at Community level, they were in contravention of their directly effective Treaty rights, particularly their right of establishment under Article 52 (now 43). This question was referred to the Court of Justice by the Divisional Court for a preliminary interpretative ruling under Article 177 (now 234). As it would take perhaps two years for that ruling to be given and as in the meantime Factortame, not being able to fish against UK fishing quotas (or Spanish quotas either), claimed to be incurring heavy and irreparable financial loss, an application for interim relief pending final determination of the substantive issue was made to the Court.

This application required the relevant section of the 1988 Act to be suspended to enable Factortame and the others to continue to operate their vessels as if duly registered as British ships. (It was also considered on the facts that in the light of *Bourgoin* no remedy in damages would be available.) On the basis of then recent case law, the Divisional Court felt that it possessed the power in these circumstances to grant the application. This decision was reversed by the Court of Appeal, at which stage the Commission's application for interim relief under Article 186 (now 243) with respect to the Act's nationality requirements was made and, as we have seen, was granted by the Court of Justice. Compliance was achieved by means of the Merchant Shipping Act 1988 (Amendment) Order 1989.

In the national courts, following a further appeal, the House of Lords held that, under national law, the English courts had no power to grant interim relief by way of an order suspending the operation of a statute pending a determination of its validity by the Court of Justice, nor had they the power to grant an interim injunction restraining the Secretary of State from enforcing the Act. Their Lordships, however, asked the Court for a preliminary ruling as to whether there was an overriding principle of Community law that a national court was under an obligation or had the power to provide an effective interlocutory remedy to protect directly effective rights where a seriously arguable claim to such rights had been advanced and irremediable loss was at stake.

Just over a year later, in June 1990, in response to this Article 177 (now 234) reference, the Court, having drawn attention to the *Simmenthal* principle of the primacy of Community law and to the principle of co-operation in Article 5 (now 10) of the Treaty, designed to ensure the legal protection which persons derived from the direct effect of Community law, ruled that Community law was to be interpreted as meaning that a national court which, in a case before it concerning Community law, considers that the sole obstacle precluding it from granting interim relief is a rule of national law, must set aside that rule: Case C-213/89 *R v Secretary of State for Transport ex p Factortame Ltd.*

Amid considerable controversy regarding what was perceived by some in the UK as an unacceptable intrusion on UK sovereignty, the House of Lords just a month later applied the Court's ruling. This was on the basis of the facts before it and pending final judgment by the Court of Justice on the validity of the 1988 Act in the face of Factortame's putative rights under the Treaty.

R v Secretary of State for Transport ex p Factortame (No 2)

In July 1990, the House of Lords, using the powers established by the ruling of the Court of Justice, allowed Factortame's appeal and granted an interim injunction restraining the government from withholding or withdrawing registration under the 1988 Act to named fishing vessels on grounds of residence or domicile abroad. (It will be recalled that the Act's nationality requirements had previously been suspended by an amendment to the Act following a ruling by the President of the Court of Justice, see above.) The position was summed up by Lord Bridge as follows:

> Some public comments on the decision of the European Court of Justice, affirming the jurisdiction of the courts of Member States to override national legislation if necessary to enable interim relief to be granted in protection of rights under Community law, have suggested that this was a novel and dangerous invasion by a Community institution of the sovereignty of the United Kingdom Parliament. But such comments are based on a misconception.
>
> If the supremacy within the European Community of Community law over the national law of Member States was not always inherent in the EEC Treaty, it was certainly well established in the jurisprudence of the European Court of Justice long before the UK joined the Community. Thus, whatever limitation of its sovereignty Parliament accepted when it enacted the European Communities Act 1972, it was entirely voluntary. Under the terms of the Act of 1972, it has always been clear that it was the duty of a UK court, when delivering final judgment, to override any rule of national law found to be in conflict with any directly enforceable rule of Community law.
>
> Similarly, when decisions of the European Court of Justice have exposed areas of United Kingdom statute law which failed to implement Community directives, Parliament has always loyally accepted the obligation to make appropriate and prompt amendments. Thus, there is nothing in any way novel in according supremacy to rules of Community law in those areas to which they apply and to insist that, in the protection of rights under Community law, national courts must not be inhibited by rules of national law from granting interim relief in appropriate cases is no more than a logical recognition of that supremacy.

When considering its decision, the House of Lords had available to it unsworn evidence indicating that many of the owners of the 97 vessels involved (the 'Anglo-Spanish' fleet) had already suffered losses well in excess of £100,000 and that some feared imminent bankruptcy.

In reaching their unanimous decision, their Lordships took account of the two stage guidelines for the exercise of the court's discretionary jurisdiction to grant interim injunctions as laid down by the House in *American Cyanamid v Ethicon* in 1975. Such jurisdiction concerns the power to grant an injunction where it is just or convenient on such terms and conditions as the court thinks fit: section 37 of the Supreme Court Act 1981. Their Lordships also considered that on the basis of the decision in *Bourgoin*, the applicants would be unable to recover damages from the Crown if the Act were ultimately found to be contrary to the Treaty (their being unable to establish wrongful conduct on the part of the Secretary of State). It was therefore agreed that the application for an interim injunction against the Crown should go directly to the second stage of consideration, regarding the balance of convenience, and need not pass through the first stage, regarding whether damages were an adequate remedy.

On the question of the balance of convenience (the balance of interests in Community law), it was stressed that matters of considerable weight had to be put in the balance to outweigh the desirability of enforcing, in the public interest, what was on its face the law of the land. Each case was to be considered in the light of its circumstances; it was enough if the applicant could show that there was a serious case to be tried.

In this respect, it is noteworthy that in Case T-44/90 *La Cinq v Commission*, the CFI annulled a Commission refusal to order interim measures (see also Case 792/79R *Camera Care* in Chapter 17), stating that the complainant company need not show a clear and flagrant breach of the competition rules by another party, merely a *prima facie* case. On the question of damage to La Cinq if the interim measures were not ordered and the company had to await the outcome of the Commission's final decision, the Court stated that all the company's circumstances must be taken into account. Although the Court of Justice had held in Case 229/88R *Cargill v Commission* that damage is not serious and irreparable (a necessary requirement for the ordering of interim measures) if it is purely financial and can, if the complainant is successful in the main action, be fully recovered, La Cinq's position was that it ran the risk of going out of business altogether in the interim (cf the position of Factortame and the others) and suffering serious and irreparable damage whatever the outcome of the final decision (see the diagram on page 564).

It is important to recognise that the granting of interim relief in *Factortame* in 1990 meant that a new remedy had been created by the national court in order to ensure the effectiveness of Community law. This case therefore marked a significant development from previous rulings on supremacy and direct effect and a change of stance on the part of the Court of Justice which, in Case 158/80 *Rewe v HZA* (see above), had stated that 'it was not intended to create new remedies in the national courts to ensure the observance of Community law other then those already laid down by national law'. The House of Lords had stated that interim relief against the Crown was not available under national law. Nevertheless, this was a rule governing the grant of remedies which, according to other previous rulings of the Court, precluded the grant of an adequate and effective remedy. Accordingly, it was to be set aside. (Since *Factortame*, the House of Lords has changed its position concerning interim injunctions as a matter of English law irrespective of a Community dimension: see *M v Home Office* (1993), in which, in the Court of Appeal, Lord Donaldson MR stated that it would be 'anomalous and wrong in principle' if the courts' powers were limited in domestic law matters when the limitations had been removed by Community law in disputes concerning rights under that law. *M* is therefore authority for the availability of interim injunctions against ministers of the Crown as a matter of English law.)

That the applicants in *Factortame* had a serious case to be tried was later confirmed by the Court of Justice in response to the original Article 177 (now 234) reference from the Divisional Court of the QBD. The Court ruled that the nationality, residence and domicile requirements of the 1988 Act were contrary to Community law, in particular Article 52 (now 43) concerning the applicant's directly effective right of establishment: Case C-221/89 *R v Secretary of State for Transport ex p Factortame Ltd*. As in the case brought by the Commission, the Court stated that the system of national quotas under the Common Fisheries Policy did not affect the decision. However, although introduced on sound, conservational grounds, the national quota system does appear to lie at the heart of this problem. Nonetheless, as Lord Bridge had stated earlier in these proceedings:

> ... it is common ground, that in so far as the applicants succeed before the ECJ in obtaining a ruling in support of the Community rights which they claim, those rights will prevail over the restrictions imposed on registration of British fishing vessels by Part II of the Act of 1988 and the Divisional Court will, in the final determination of the application for judicial review be obliged to make appropriate declarations to give effect to those rights.

As regards a further State liability action for damages brought by Factortame and the other members of the 'Anglo-Spanish' fishing fleet against the British government, see the final part of this chapter.

Further difficulties have arisen in the UK regarding remedies despite the fact that the situation in question involved loss suffered as the result of a breach of an individual's directly effective rights and that damages to compensate for losses of the type in question were provided for under the relevant provisions of national law.

In Case 152/84 *Marshall* (see Chapters 8 and 14), directly enforceable rights regarding equality in retirement ages were established on the basis of Article 5 of the Equal Treatment Directive. Miss Marshall's case then returned to the national industrial tribunal where the issue was solely that of the amount of compensation to be recovered from her employers. The problem which she faced was that section 65(2) of the Sex Discrimination Act 1975 laid down at that time a maximum award of £6,250. Seeing its duty as that of providing an *effective* remedy, Miss Marshall's claim having arisen some eight years earlier, the tribunal held that the limit laid down by section 65(2) rendered the compensation (the only appropriate remedy) inadequate and in breach of Article 6 of the Directive (see below). It also awarded M £7,710 by way of interest, arguing that even if the 1975 Act did not allow it to do so (the relevant provisions may be said to be ambiguous), such a power existed under the Supreme Court Act 1981. The full award was £19,405. The AHA had already paid M £6,250 and paid her a further £5,445 but appealed against the award of interest.

Article 6 of the Equal Treatment Directive, as seen in Case 222/84 *Johnson*, requires all Member States to introduce into their national legal systems 'such measures as are necessary to enable all persons who consider themselves wronged ... to pursue their claims by judicial process'. The tribunal had taken the view that such judicial process, as construed in *Von Colson* (see Chapter 14), must include an adequate remedy, and that Miss Marshall, as an employee of the State, was entitled to rely on Article 6. The Employment Appeal Tribunal upheld the employer's appeal on the ground that

Article 6 of the Directive had been held in *Von Colson* not to have direct effect regarding the question of specific remedies. The case then proceeded to the Court of Appeal.

Marshall v Southampton and SW Hampshire AHA (No 2)

All three judges acknowledged the obligation based on Article 5 (now 10) of the Treaty which, as developed by the Court of Justice in *Von Colson*, falls on national courts to interpret domestic law so as to ensure that the objectives of a Directive are fulfilled. (In *Von Colson*, this meant that the German court was required to interpret German law in such a way as to secure an effective remedy as required by Article 6 of the Equal Treatment Directive: the indirect effect solution.)

However, the appeal judges stressed that, while the statutory level of compensation did not provide an adequate and effective remedy as required by Article 6 of the Directive, the limitation imposed in *Von Colson* that a national court should interpret national law so as to comply with Community obligations only in so far as it is given a discretion to do so under national law applied in this case. The Court was not in a position to disregard the statutory ceiling on damages and the word 'damages' could not be construed to include interest.

A further appeal in *Marshall (No 2)* went to the House of Lords, where the case was made the subject of another reference to the Court of Justice under Article 177 (now 234).

Case C-271/91 *Marshall v Southampton and SW Hampshire AHA (No 2)*

The Court ruled that where financial compensation was the remedy adopted by a Member State in order to achieve the objective in Article 6 of the Directive (the restoration of equality of treatment when it had not been observed), such compensation had to be effective, as implied by Article 6. As such, the compensation had to enable the loss and damage actually sustained as the result of a discriminatory dismissal to be made good in full in accordance with the applicable national rules.

The fixing of an upper limit to compensation could not constitute proper implementation of Article 6, since it limited the amount of compensation *a priori* to a level which was not necessarily consistent with the requirement of ensuring real equality through adequate reparation. Neither could full compensation leave out of account factors, such as the effluxion of time, which might reduce its value. The award of interest, in accordance with the applicable national rules, was therefore to be regarded as an essential element of the compensation.

The importance of Article 6 in attaining the fundamental objective of the Directive was such that, combined with the basic right to equal treatment in Article 5, it gave rise, on the part of a person injured as a result of discriminatory dismissal, to rights which that person could rely upon in national courts against the State or an emanation thereof.

An individual could not be prevented from relying on Article 6 in a situation such as that in the main proceedings (that is, in Case 152/84) where the State had no degree of discretion in applying the chosen remedy.

The Court's overriding consideration in this case was therefore to secure a compensatory remedy which guaranteed real and effective judicial protection and which had a definite deterrent effect on employers. The two national rules regarding remedies, the statutory ceiling on damages and the absence of a power to award interest, were to be overridden in the face of the requirement to provide an effective remedy. These rules, therefore went the same way as the limitation period in *Emmott* (a case, as seen, later restricted to its particular facts) and the interim relief rule in *Factortame*. However, in Case C-66/95 *R v Secretary of State for Social Security ex p Sutton* concerning the payment of interest on arrears of a social security benefit (the invalid care allowance), they distinguished *Marshall (No 2)*. Amounts paid by way of such a benefit were not compensatory in nature and did not constitute reparation for loss or damage sustained. The payment of interest on arrears of benefit was not an essential component of rights under the Social Security Directive 79/7.

Damages Claims based on *Francovich*

The Court of Justice pointed out in *Marshall (No 2)*, by reference to its judgment on State liability in *Francovich*, that the right of a Member State to choose among several possible means of achieving the objectives of a Directive did not exclude the possibility for individuals of enforcing before national courts *rights whose content can be determined sufficiently precisely on the basis of the provisions of the Directive alone*. As seen in Chapter 8, a Member State's liability under the Francovich principle, at least as regards its failure to transpose a Directive into national law within the time specified, depends on the following conditions:

(a) the result required by the Directive includes the conferring of rights for the benefit of individuals;

(b) the content of those rights is identifiable by reference to the Directive; and

(c) a causal link exists between the breach of the State's obligations and the damage suffered by persons affected.

The *Francovich* principle does not only apply where, as in that case, due to its lack of precision, the Directive is not directly effective. The Court in *Francovich* stated that it was necessary to provide full protection of the rights of individuals, *in particular*, where those rights were conditional on the Member States taking certain action and where, as a result of a Member State's breach of Community law, such individuals were unable to rely on their Community rights. In other words, although the direct effect of Article 5, (and later Article 6) of the Directive lay at the heart of Miss Marshall's success, it would appear that her case would *also* have met the three conditions necessary to establish a basis for the State's liability to pay compensation under the subsequent *Francovich* principle.

However, the State's failures in *Marshall* were not the complete failure of the Italian State in *Francovich*. They amounted to what Steiner (see Chapter 8) characterised as 'a partial failure, where implementation measures have been adopted, but they are faulty or inadequate'. Her general conclusion was that 'States should not, in this context, be liable in the absence of fault'.

By placing a statutory limit on the amount of compensation recoverable by a person discriminated against, contrary to the terms of the Equal Treatment Directive, would the UK also have rendered itself liable to pay compensation on the basis of the *Francovich* principle? Could liability similarly have been established to render the Ministry of Agriculture, Fisheries and Food liable on the facts in *Bourgoin*? Can inadequate implementation of a Directive be equated with the introduction or maintenance of national measures found to be in breach of Article 30 (now 28), or with the amendment of a statute with the declared purpose of safeguarding national rights under the Common Fisheries Policy contrary however to Article 52 (now 43)?

Answers to questions such as these have emerged, although, as yet, they apply more to the nature of the *Francovich* principle itself than to the question of how national courts will accommodate the damages requirement within domestic law. Since *Francovich*, further questions have been referred to the Court of Justice by national courts in the UK, Germany and elsewhere under Article 177 (now 234) and answers provided. The national courts have begun to apply those answers.

The references in Joined Cases C-46 and 48/93 *Brasserie du Pêcheur SA v Germany* and *R v Secretary of State for Transport ex p Factortame Ltd and Others* do not, like *Francovich* (see the concluding section of Chapter 8), concern the non-transposition of a non-directly effective Directive. In these cases, the Court of Justice was asked whether the State can be liable in damages for loss caused to individuals by *legislation* retained or adopted in contravention of directly effective rights. However, in a ruling that bears a close relationship to that in *Francovich*, the Court stated that where a Member State acts in a field in which it has a wide discretion, an individual's Community law right to reparation depends on three conditions:

(a) the rule of law infringed must be intended to confer rights on individuals;

(b) the breach must be sufficiently serious (this was not laid down as a condition in *Francovich*. It was assumed in *Dillenkofer*, below, that the breach in that case was 'sufficiently serious');

(c) there must be a direct causal link between the State's breach of its Community law obligation and the injured party's loss.

It will be seen that these conditions correspond in substance to those defined by the Court in relation to the *Community's* non-contractual liability to pay compensation under Article 288(2) (formerly 215(2)) in cases concerning legislative measures which involve 'choices of economic policy'.

The factual and legal background to the reference in *Factortame (No 3)* has been discussed in this chapter. This reference from the High Court arose from the damages claim promptly brought by Factortame and the other 96 members of the 'Anglo-Spanish' fishing fleet for losses sustained while the offending provisions of the Merchant Shipping Act 1988 were in force (from 1 April 1989, when the Act came into effect, until, according to the reference from the High Court, 2 November 1989 when, following the granting of interim relief by the Court of Justice regarding the Act's nationality requirement, the Act was repealed to that extent, or until 11 October 1990, according to Factortame, when, following the granting of interim relief by the House of Lords as regards the other, residence and domicile discriminatory conditions, the Act ceased to have harmful effects).

The reference in *Brasserie du Pêcheur* related back to the judgment of the Court of Justice in 1987 in Case 178/84 *Commission v Germany (Re Beer Purity Laws)* (see Chapter 12), in which it was held that the German beer purity rules were in breach of the directly effective Article 30 (now 28) of the Treaty relating to QRs and MEEQRs on imports. The French brewery's claim arose from its exclusion from the German market between 1981 and 1987; its beer, although meeting the requirements of French law, not satisfying the requirements of the relevant German provisions. Brasserie du Pêcheur claimed an interim sum of DM 1,800,000 and at the time, it was reported that the

Factortame claim might cost the UK government some £30 million. The Court's judgment in these joined cases proceeded on the basis of the following issues.

Joined Cases C-46 and 48/93 *Brasserie du Pêcheur SA v Germany* and *R v Secretary of State for Transport ex p Factortame Ltd and Others*

State liability for acts and omissions of the national legislature contrary to Community law

The argument (of certain Member States) that a right to reparation was unnecessary where directly effective provisions are breached was rejected. On the contrary, the Court stated that 'the right to reparation is the necessary corollary of the direct effect of the Community provision whose breach caused the damage sustained'.

By reference first to the non-contractual liability of the Community under Article 215(2) (now 288(2)) as an expression of the general principle that an unlawful act or omission gives rise to an obligation to make good the damage caused – and in particular the obligation on public authorities to make good damage caused in the performance of their duties – the Court stated that: 'It follows that that principle holds good in any case in which a Member State breaches Community law, whatever be the organ of the State whose act or omission was responsible for the breach [that is, whether it be the legislature, the judiciary or the executive].'

The conditions under which the State may incur liability for acts or omissions of the national legislature contrary to Community law

The Court stated that the conditions under which such liability arises depend, as laid down in *Francovich, on the nature of the breach of Community law giving rise to the loss or damage*. Account must be taken of the full effectiveness of Community rules, the protection of individual rights and the obligation on Member States to co-operate under Article 5 (now 10) EC. Further, 'the conditions under which the State may incur liability for damage caused to individuals by a breach of Community law cannot, in the absence of particular justification, differ from those governing the liability of the Community in like circumstances'.

The Court next reviewed its approach to liability under Article 215(2) with particular reference to 'the complexity of the situations to be regulated, difficulties in the application or interpretation of the texts and ... the margin of discretion available to the author of the act in question'.

The Court acknowledged its restrictive approach under Article 215(2) as regards the Community's legislative activities and justified it on two grounds:

(a) 'exercise of the legislative function must not be hindered by the prospect of actions for damages whenever the general interest of the Community requires legislative measures to be adopted which may adversely affect individual interests';

(b) 'in a legislative context characterised by the exercise of a wide discretion ... the Community cannot incur liability unless the institution concerned has manifestly and gravely disregarded the limits on the exercise of its powers [Case 83/76 *Bayerische HNL v Council and Commission*]'.

Noting that a national legislature does not necessarily have a wide margin of discretion within the Community sphere (for example, when, as in *Francovich*, implementing a Directive), where such a discretion is nevertheless to be found Member State liability must, in principle, correspond to that of the Community. The Court stated that, since the German and UK governments had a wide measure of discretion when legislating in the areas in question, both governed by Community law (that is, the German legislature when laying down rules relating to its beer market; the UK legislature as regards the registration of vessels and the regulation of fishing within the Common Fisheries Policy), both legislatures were faced with difficult situations involving choices of economic policy comparable to those faced by the Community institutions. (This finding has been queried by several academic commentators.)

In such circumstances, a Community law right to compensation depended upon three conditions:

(a) 'the rule of law infringed must be intended to confer rights on individuals';

(b) 'the breach must be sufficiently serious';

(c) 'there must be a direct causal link between the breach of the obligation resting on the State and the damage sustained'.

The Court stressed however that this test only applied in cases in which the State had a wide discretion (cf Article 215(2) *'Schöppenstedt* formula' cases). It would not apply where the State's margin of discretion was reduced, for example, where, in transposing a Directive, it must achieve the required result – as in *Francovich* itself.

Applying the three conditions to the present references, it was clear that the first condition was satisfied: both Article 30 (now 28) and Article 52 (now 43) are intended to confer rights on individuals. As to the second condition, the 'decisive test', under Article 215(2) and for State liability, was whether there had been a *manifest and grave disregard of the limits of the discretion*. On this question:

> The factors which the competent [national] court may take into consideration include the clarity and precision of the rule breached, the measure of discretion left by that rule to the national or Community authorities, whether the infringement and the damage caused was intentional or involuntary, whether any error of law was excusable or inexcusable, the fact that the position taken by a Community institution may have contributed towards the omission, and the adoption or retention of national measures or practices contrary to Community law [paragraph 56 of the judgment].

A breach of Community law will be sufficiently serious if it has persisted despite a judgment that has established the infringement (as in *Francovich*), or a preliminary ruling or settled case law of the Court has made it clear that the conduct constituted an infringement (paragraph 57) – but such a judgment was not essential for this purpose.

The Court stated that it would be 'helpful to indicate a number of circumstances which the national court might take into account' in the present cases: in *Brasserie du Pêcheur*, it was difficult to regard the breach of Article 30 by the German legislation relating to the *designation* of the beer marketed by the French brewery (as in effect 'non-beer') as an excusable error. The incompatibility of such rules was manifest in the light of earlier decisions of the Court, in particular *Cassis de Dijon*. However, the question of additives in beer was not settled until the German prohibition was held to be incompatible with Article 30 in Case 178/84 *Commission v Germany*, decided in 1987.

In *Factortame*, the 1988 amendments to the Merchant Shipping Act which made the registration of fishing vessels subject to a nationality condition constituted direct discrimination manifestly contrary to Community law: see Case C-246/89 *Commission v UK*. The conditions concerning the *residence and domicile* (of the Spanish operators) were defended by the UK in terms of the objectives of the Common Fisheries Policy but rejected by the Court in Case C-221/89 *Factortame (No 2)*. In order to determine whether the UK breach of Article 52 was sufficiently serious, the national court might take into account:

... the legal disputes relating to particular features of the common fisheries policy [conservation of stocks, size of national fishing fleets, national quotas and 'quota-hopping'], the attitude of the Commission, which made its position [regarding the UK 'nationality' breach] known to the UK in good time [that is, prior to the statutory amendment being put into effect], and the assessments on the state of certainty of Community law made by the national courts in the interim proceedings brought by individuals affected by the Merchant Shipping Act.

Additionally, if the allegation that the UK failed to adopt immediately measures needed to comply with the President's order in Case 246/89R *Commission v UK* regarding suspension of the nationality requirement (there was a delay of 23 days) and this needlessly increased the loss, this should be regarded in itself as a manifest and serious breach of Community law.

As to the third condition, it was for the national courts to determine whether there was a direct causal link between the breach and the damage sustained. The Court made clear that the three conditions were 'necessary and sufficient to found a right in individuals to obtain redress'. Where these conditions are satisfied, the State must make reparation in accordance with domestic rules on liability under conditions no less favourable than for similar domestic claims and such rules must not be such as in practice to make it impossible or excessively difficult to obtain reparation: see Case 45/76 *Comet* and Case 199/82 *San Georgio*. (Here, the Court recognised 'restrictions that exist in domestic legal systems as to the non-contractual liability of the State in the exercise of its legislative function', which might mean that, in its present state, national law was not in a position to satisfy these two requirements.) The need for proof of misfeasance in public office in English law – 'such an abuse of power being inconceivable in the case of the legislature' – would make obtaining effective reparation 'impossible or extremely difficult'.

The possibility of making reparation conditional upon the existence of fault (intentional or negligent)

The Court recognised that 'the concept of fault does not have the same content in the various legal systems'. In such cases as the present, the right to reparation depended *inter alia*, on the breach being sufficiently serious: 'So, certain objective and subjective factors connected with the concept of fault under a national legal system may well be relevant for the purpose of determining whether or not a given breach of Community law is serious [see the factors ... in paragraphs 56 and 57 above].' However, the obligation to make reparation 'cannot ... depend upon a condition based on any concept of fault going beyond that of a sufficiently serious breach of Community law. Imposition of such a supplementary condition would be tantamount to calling in question the right to reparation founded on the Community legal order'.

The actual effect of reparation

Reparation must be commensurate with the loss or damage sustained: see also *Marshall (No 2)*. The national legal system of each Member State is to set the criteria for determining the extent of reparation (subject to the usual Community conditions of equivalence and effectiveness). Questions of mitigation of loss and the availability of alternative legal remedies (such as interim relief) are relevant. The total exclusion of loss of profit 'in the context of economic and commercial litigation' was not acceptable. An award of exemplary damages could not be ruled out.

Extent of the period covered by reparation

The Court stated that 'to make the reparation of loss or damage conditional upon the requirement that there must have been a prior finding by the Court [as for example, in *Francovich*] of an infringement of Community law attributable to a Member State would be contrary to the effectiveness of Community law ...'. (In many cases, there will be no prior finding.) Therefore, the obligation to make good loss or damage cannot be limited in this way.

The request that the temporal effects of the judgment should be limited

There was no need for the Court to limit the temporal effects of this judgment: 'Substantive and procedural conditions laid down by national law [in similar domestic claims] on reparation of damage are able to take account of the requirements of legal certainty.' This was a point raised by the German government in the light of the French brewery not having made a *pre-Francovich* claim of any kind.

What are the key features of this judgment? Both cases concerned national legislatures; the German case being illustrative of, amongst other things, the maintenance of legislation clearly in breach of Community law; the English case involved an amendment of national law contrary to Community law. This inaction in the German case and action in the UK case led to an infringement of directly effective individual rights. In each case, the Court of Justice conceded that the national government possessed a wide measure of discretion when legislating in the economic policy area in question; that within the range of available choice, they were free to legislate without the fear of actions just because the interests of any particular group might be adversely affected. To this extent, State liability corresponds to Community liability under Article 215(2) (now 288(2)) of the Treaty. Only if the State 'manifestly and gravely' disregards its margin of discretion can there be a breach of Community law which is 'sufficiently serious' to attract the obligation to compensate injured parties.

It is the seriousness of the breach which triggers liability, and fault, which does not have 'the same content' in the various legal systems of the Member States, is merely one factor to be taken into account by a national court when assessing whether or not the breach is sufficiently serious. National courts are to decide a State liability case in the same way as they would when dealing with 'a similar claim or action founded on domestic law'.

It is at this point – at the *national* level – that the next big question arises. On what basis are State liability claims to be incorporated into domestic tort law (or the like) by national courts? Before examining this question, it is advisable to examine further post-*Francovich* decisions of the Court involving different factual and legal situations.

The Court of Justice has given several more interpretative rulings under Article 177 (now 234) in State liability actions. In the first, Case C-392/93 *R v HM Treasury ex p British Telecommunications plc*, a Community Directive had been incorrectly implemented by the UK government. Acknowledging that it was somewhat overstepping its powers under Article 177, the Court ruled that there was no sufficiently serious breach of Community law involved and no liability to compensate BT 'for any loss suffered by it as a result of the error committed by the State'. It did so on the following basis.

Case C-392/93 *R v HM Treasury ex p British Telecommunications plc*

While in principle it was for the national courts to verify whether or not the conditions governing State liability for a breach of Community law were fulfilled, in the present case, the Court had all the necessary information to assess whether the facts amounted to a sufficiently serious breach of Community law.

The 'necessary information' on which the Court based its ruling was as follows:

Council Directive 90/531 covers, amongst other things, the procurement (that is, purchasing) procedures of 'contracting entities' (BT, Mercury and the City of Kingston upon Hull, etc) operating in the telecommunications sector. Under Article 8(1) of the Directive, certain purchasing contracts awarded by these entities, in geographical areas where they are directly exposed to competitive forces, are exempt from the Directive. Under Article 8(2), the contracting entities are to notify the Commission, at its request, of circumstances in which they consider that the exemption applies.

BT claimed that the government, by taking upon itself (and not BT and other contracting entities) the question of exemption and notification, in regulations adopted in 1992, had incorrectly implemented the Directive. It was alleged that the government had deprived BT of the power conferred on it by the Directive to make its own decisions and, by inadequately providing for exemption for BT under Article 8(1), had caused it loss, in particular by preventing it from concluding profitable transactions and by placing it at a commercial and competitive disadvantage by subjecting it to the requirement, from which other operators in the sector were exempt, to publish its procurement plans and contracts in the Official Journal. (In the sector in question, BT in 1992 still controlled 90 per cent of the telephone business.)

The Court ruled that:

(a) It was not open to a Member State, when transposing the Directive, to determine which telecommunications services were to be excluded from its scope when implementing Article 8(1), since that power was vested in the contracting entities themselves (subject to Commission supervision).

(b) On the question of State liability for the loss claimed, the Court restated, with reference to *Brasserie du Pêcheur/Factortame*, the three conditions upon which reparation depends: the rule of law infringed must be intended to confer rights on individuals, the breach of the obligation resting on the State must be sufficiently serious, and there must be a direct causal link between the breach and the damage. The same restrictive conditions applied to the incorrect transposition of a Directive and for the same reason. However, when transposing the Directive into national law, the UK government had not manifestly and gravely disregarded the limits on the exercise of its legislative powers, and had not therefore committed a sufficiently serious breach such as to impose liability. The State had merely committed an 'error' which did not expose it to liability.

The reasoning behind the Court's ruling was as follows: (a) Article 8(1) of the Directive was imprecisely worded and was reasonably capable of bearing, as well as the construction applied to it by the Court, the alternative interpretation given to it by the UK, and shared by other Member States, in good faith; (b) no guidance was available to the UK from the case law of the Court as to the correct interpretation of Article 8, nor had the Commission raised the matter when the 1992 regulations were adopted by the UK. (Note the application of paragraph 56 of the *Brasserie du Pêcheur/ Factortame* ruling.)

The ruling in this case, concerning an incorrect implementation of a Directive by the national authorities, should be contrasted with that in *Francovich* itself, in which there was a failure to implement the Directive in question and a prior judgment of the Court in Article 169 (now 226) proceedings to that effect.

In the second State liability ruling subsequent to *Brasserie du Pêcheur/ Francovich*, the UK was alleged to be liable for loss caused by the conduct of the administrative authorities contrary to Community law in a situation not dissimilar from that in *Bourgoin* (1986).

Case C-5/94 *R v Ministry of Agriculture, Fisheries and Food ex p Hedley Lomas (Ireland) Ltd*

The Ministry refused to grant licences to Hedley Lomas for the export of live sheep to Spain. Although the EC Directive regulating the pre-slaughter treatment of certain animals, including sheep, had been transposed into Spanish law, the Ministry formed the view that information in its possession indicated a degree of non-compliance with the Directive such as to create a substantial risk that animals exported to Spain for slaughter would suffer treatment contrary to the provisions of the Directive regarding the avoidance of unnecessary suffering on the part of animals when being slaughtered.

The Commission investigated the situation in Spain and, after being given assurances, did not take any action under Article 169 of the Treaty. The Commission also informed the Ministry that it considered that the UK's general ban on export of live animals to Spain was contrary to Article 34 (now 29) of the Treaty and not capable of justification under Article 36 (now 30).

HL contended that there was no evidence that the Spanish slaughterhouse to which it wished to consign the sheep was acting contrary to the Directive. The company sought a declaration that the Ministry's refusal to grant an export licence was contrary to Article 34 (now 29) and damages. It was taken as common ground that the refusal constituted a quantitative restriction on exports but the Ministry argued that it was justified under Article 36 (now 30) on the grounds of the protection of the health and life of animals. Following a reference from the High Court under Article 177 (now 234), the Court of Justice ruled as follows:

(a) Recourse to Article 36 was no longer possible where Community Directives provided for harmonisation of the measures necessary to achieve the specific objective which would be furthered by reliance on this provision. This position was not affected by the fact that, in the present case, the Directive did not lay down any Community procedure for monitoring compliance nor any penalties for breach of its provisions: 'Member States must rely on trust in each other to carry out inspections on their respective territories.'

(b) A Member State could not unilaterally adopt corrective or protective measures designed to obviate any breach by another Member State of rules of Community law: Case 232/78 *Commission v France (Re Restrictions on Imports of Lamb)*.

(c) Applying the case law on State liability and in particular the three conditions necessary for a right to reparation to arise:

  (i) Article 34 (now 29) clearly imposed a prohibition on Member States; it was directly effective and created rights for individuals which national courts must protect: Case 83/78 *Pigs Marketing Board v Redmond*.

  (ii) Where the Member State at the relevant time was not called upon to make any legislative choices and had only considerably reduced, or even no discretion, the mere infringement of Community law might be enough to establish the existence of a sufficiently serious breach (here, the Court noted the absence of any proof of non-compliance with the Directive by the slaughterhouse in question).

  (iii) It was for the national court to determine whether there was a direct causal link between the breach of the State's Community law obligation and the damage sustained by the applicant.

(d) Subject to these three requirements, the State must make good any loss or damage caused by its breach of Community law in accordance with its domestic law on liability.

This decision surely puts the final nail in the coffin of the Court of Appeal's decision in *Bourgoin v Ministry of Agriculture, Fisheries and Food*, decided in 1986 (see earlier in this chapter). In *Bourgoin*, the import ban was unjustified; in *Hedley Lomas*, likewise the export ban.

Since *Brasserie du Pêcheur/Factortame*, *BT* and *Hedley Lomas*, further developments in the field of State liability have taken place both as regards new preliminary rulings and the application at national level of existing rulings. Several rulings involve Directives. The first, in Cases C-178/94, etc, *Dillenkofer and Others v Germany*, like *Francovich* itself, involved a complete failure to implement a Directive on time:

> Council Directive 90/314 on package holidays was to be implemented by 31 December 1992. It was not implemented in Germany until July 1994. In 1993, two German package tour operators became insolvent and as a result the plaintiffs either lost their holidays altogether or had to return at their own expense.
>
> Being unable to obtain compensation from other sources, the plaintiffs brought actions for reparation on the basis of the non-implemented Article 7 of the Directive: 'The organiser and/or retailer party to the contract shall provide sufficient evidence of security for the refund of money paid over and for the reparation of the consumer in the event of insolvency.'
>
> The Bonn court referred various questions regarding the operation and effect of the principle of State liability in the instant cases. The Court of Justice ruled;
>
> (a) Failure to transpose a Directive in order to achieve the result prescribed within the period laid down constituted *per se* a serious breach of Community law giving rise to a right to reparation for individuals suffering loss, if the result prescribed entailed the grant to individuals of rights the content of which was identifiable and a causal link existed between the breach of the State's obligation and the damage and loss suffered.
>
> (b) The result prescribed by Article 7 of the Directive entailed the grant to package travellers of rights the content of which was sufficiently identifiable.

In this case, Advocate General Tesauro, on the question of 'unlawful conduct on the part of the State', alluded to the fact that, in *Francovich*, the Court had not clarified the nature of such conduct. He stated that 'in that case there could be no doubt as to whether the omission on the part of the State was unlawful: the result sought by the Directive – in respect of which the State had *no margin of discretion*, at any rate, not in relation to the period within which the Directive was to be implemented – was not achieved' (emphasis added).

On this basis, the State's unlawful conduct in cases such as these is sufficiently serious because it amounts to an inexcusable breach of a clear Community obligation under Article 249(3) (formerly 189(3)). In *Dillenkofer*, the Court found a sufficiently serious breach and recognised that the State was not called upon to make 'legislative choices' (as conceded in *Brasserie du Pêcheur/Factortame*).

The second ruling on Directives concerned faulty implementation, not a failure to implement. Case C-283/94, etc, *Denkavit International and Others v Federal Finance Office* concerned an incorrect transposition by Germany of a Council Directive on corporate taxation. The Court of Justice itself in effect disposed of the claim by the plaintiff company for losses caused as a result in virtually the same terms as in the *British Telecommunications* case. The Court in essence again established a mere interpretative error on the defendant's part upon which liability in damages could not be based. This finding was explained in terms of the 'clarity and precision of the rule breached'.

Germany's interpretation of the relevant provision of the Directive had been adopted by several other Member States following discussions in the Council and, this being the first case concerning the Directive, the Court's case law provided no indication as to how the provision was to be interpreted: again, see paragraph 56 of the *Brasserie du Pêcheur/Factortame* ruling.

These cases established the basic features of State liability: its legal basis; the three conditions underlying liability and the right to damages, in particular the concept of serious breach; liability as a result of a legislative, administrative (or even judicial) act or omission; and the linking of State and Community liability in damages. They show that a legislative failure to implement a Directive is *per se* a sufficiently serious breach but that otherwise legislative or administrative breaches are only serious (a manifest and serious disregard by the Member States of their powers) if they fail the paragraph 56 tests involving such factors as discretion, clarity and good faith.

The later case law builds on those foundations, examining issues within the contours of the established principles, whilst showing a marked tendency to encourage national courts to deal with all the various factors themselves, that is, without a reference. For example, in Case C-127/95 *Norbrook Laboratories Ltd v Ministry of Agriculture, Fisheries and Food*, NL claimed for losses caused by a breach of the terms of two Directives by the Ministry. The Court of Justice merely stated that the scope of NL's rights were clearly and exhaustively laid down in the Directive – as opposed to the position in *BT* and *Denkavit*, above. The Ministry not being called upon to exercise any discretion, a mere infringement of Community law could be sufficient to establish a serious breach – as in *Hedley Lomas* – given a direct causal link.

Interesting questions concerning a Danish *failure* to transpose a Directive (a *per se* breach?) and causality arose in the following case.

Case C-319/96 *Brinkmann Tabakfabriken v Skatteministeriet*

B exported to Denmark a product which was neither a conventional cigarette nor conventional loose, rolling tobacco. It was taxed by the Danish tax authorities at the higher rate for cigarettes. It was claimed that this decision was wrong and that the German company should be compensated; its product having failed on the Danish market. Definitions of cigarettes and rolling tobacco were to be found in a Council Directive of 1979 but this had not been implemented by the defendant Ministry. However, the Danish authorities had in fact given immediate effect to the relevant provisions of the Directive containing the precise definitions of tobacco products.

The Court of Justice declared that, in the circumstances, the absence of an implementing national measure did not amount to a serious breach to be linked directly to the losses sustained by B. (The Court dealt with this issue, including causation, as it has done before, on the basis that it had 'all the necessary information' for it to do so: see *British Telecommunications*, above.) The precise wording of the Directive lent itself to ready application by the Danish tax authorities and this they had done in good faith. They had not committed a serious breach. The German product, which did not exist at the time the Directive was adopted, did not fit either of its definitions. The interpretation given by the Danish authorities, although contrary to that which applied in Germany, was not manifestly contrary to either the wording or the aim of the Directive. The Commission and the Finnish government agreed with the perfectly tenable Danish interpretation. The Court held that the Danish interpretation was incorrect but no serious breach had been committed.

Case C-140/97 *Rechberger and Others v Austria*, like *Dillenkofer*, dealt with Article 7 of the Package Travel Directive which provides that from 1 January 1995, the final date for transposition and the date of Austrian entry into the EU, purchasers of package holidays would be refunded money paid and repatriated in the event of the organiser's insolvency. Austria implemented the Directive in time, but placed both departure date and financial guarantee limitations within the national legislative provisions. *Dillenkofer* settled that Article 7 contained sufficiently precise individual rights, and in *Rechberger*, the Court held that the time limitation was not an interpretative 'error' but a serious breach – Austria having no legislative discretion in the matter. The financial limitation was held to amount to an incorrect transposition which was ineffective to achieve the Directive's result, but it was not specifically categorised as a sufficiently serious breach although some of the plaintiffs had suffered loss on account of this breach alone.

Case C-302/97 *Konle v Austria* and Case C-424/97 *Haim v KVN* both raised the same, new question: which public authority is responsible for the payment of damages, the conditions for liability having been established?

Konle involved discrimination against K, a German national, and breach by Tyrol regional legislation of K's rights under Article 56 EC on free movement of capital. The Court of Justice did not hold that a serious breach had been committed, this question being dependent in large part on interrelated and unresolved matters of Austrian national law. Resolution of the point therefore rested with the Vienna court. The Court of Justice did, however, hold that 'in Member States with a federal structure, reparation for damage caused to individuals by national measures taken in breach of Community law need not necessarily be provided by the Federal State in order for the obligations of the Member State concerned under Community law to be fulfilled'.

In *Haim*, H, an Italian national, was wrongly refused enrolment as a dentist under a German social security scheme by the competent professional association in the Nordrhein region, the KVN. This public law body, which was legally independent from the State, had acted, as an administrative agency, under German regulations adopted on the basis of Directive 78/686 (the Dentists Directive) and the directly effective Article 52 (now 43) EC on freedom of establishment. Only *later* did it transpire, following the Court's ruling in Case C-340/89 *Vlassopoulou* where the position under Community law was first made clear (a similar position to that in *Brasserie du Pêcheur*), that KVN had erred. It would therefore appear that neither the national legislature not the KVN had committed a *serious* breach.

On the question of liability, the Court held that reparation need not be provided by the Member State itself and could be provided by a public law body instead of, or in addition to, the Member State. The 'State' in State liability is taking on a wide meaning, as found in the direct effect cases.

In Case C-118/00 *Larsy v INASTI*, the defendant, the competent Belgian authority, was held to have wrongfully applied national procedural rules such that L's full pension rights were reduced contrary to clear, directly effective provisions of a 1971 Council Regulation. The defendant's misapplication of the national rules was readily apparent from an earlier ruling of the Court of Justice on the same issue. The Court held that in the circumstances INASTI had 'no substantive choice', and to the extent that the national procedural rules precluded effective protection of L's rights under Community law, INASTI should have disapplied them. A serious breach had been committed.

Finally, attention is drawn again to Case C-352/98P *Laboratoires Pharmaceutiques Bergaderm and Goupil v Commission*, a Community liability claim under Article 215(2) (now 288(2)) EC discussed in the previous chapter. It will be recalled that in *Brasserie du Pêcheur*, the Court of Justice stated that, generally, the conditions of State liability should correspond to those of *Community* liability. In *Bergaderm*, a full Court brought these conditions even closer together. It moved the assimilation process from the 'new' State liability conditions so as to redefine the 'old' Article 288(2) law. The Court (in *obiter* statements) linked liability with *discretion – at both levels*, and whether the measure challenged was of either a legislative *or* administrative nature. Liability for administrative acts (by which the administration applies general rules in individual cases or otherwise exercises its executive powers in an individual manner) was not treated in this way according to the earlier Community liability case law. The change recognises that administrative acts *may* involve the exercise of wide discretionary powers at both levels, not just at the State level.

Turning to applications by national courts of Court of Justice State liability rulings, no damages have been forthcoming in either *Francovich* or *Brasserie du Pêcheur*. The reason in both cases was the absence of the necessary causal link between the State's breach of its Community obligation and the individual's loss.

In *Francovich*, this finding by the Vincenza court was tested in a second reference in Case C-479/93 *Francovich v Italian State (No 2)*. The Court of Justice confirmed the national court's interpretation of Directive 80/987 (the non-implementation of which gave rise to the original claim and which had been belatedly but retroactively implemented in 1992) to the effect that individuals (here, employees) upon whom the Directive conferred rights did not include Francovich. The Court ruled that the Directive was to be interpreted as applying to all employees, other than those in certain categories listed in an Annex thereto, whose employers could, under the applicable national law, be made subject to proceedings involving their assets in order to satisfy collectively the claims of creditors. Francovich and his similarly placed colleagues were found to belong within a category of employees listed in the Annex. Francovich's losses were therefore not attributable to the Italian government's failure to implement the Directive. (The question of the scope of the Directive could presumably have been resolved at the very beginning.) However, further legislation was passed to provide compensation for those who have suffered loss.

The German Federal Court (GFC) applied the ruling in *Brasserie du Pêcheur* in October 1996. It stated that the crucial issue was proof that in the 1987 'Beer Purity' case Germany had 'blatantly overstepped the legal boundaries to which it should adhere'. Clearly separating the 'bier' designation rule from the additives rule, the GFC stated that as regards the former 'an adequately proven infringement of [the directly effective] Article 30 [now 28] by the German legislator can hardly be denied, as the incompatibility of such a regulation with Article 30 was quite clear in the light of existing precedents of the Court'. The question of the additives violation in the light of the relevant pre-1987 precedents was, in the GFC's view, 'considerably less conclusive'.

The German court then asked with which of these two issues was the brewery's claim linked. On the basis of documentary evidence provided by both parties, the court concluded that the prohibition of the French beer from the German market had been imposed because the beer contained additives. The court drew attention here to the label on Brasserie du Pêcheur's bottles – 'As always, brewed in accordance with the German Purity Laws' – as an attempt to mask the use of additives.

In consequence, the GFC ruled that there was no direct causal link between the clear (and sufficiently serious) breach of Article 30 by the national designation rule and the plaintiff brewery's loss. As to the additives rule, the court, while recognising that the Court of Justice had found the Federal government's public health arguments in 1987 to be without foundation, stated that the judgment in Case 178/84 *Commission v Germany* 'gave rise to no indication whatsoever that the legal standpoint of the Federal German Government had distanced itself in such a way from the European law guidelines that a blatant failure ... could be acknowledged'.

In conclusion, therefore, the GFC found 'the infringement as a whole, in as much as it is the direct cause of damage to the plaintiff, to be inadequately proven' (that is, the additives violation did not amount to a sufficiently serious breach). The brewery's claim accordingly failed and it was not necessary for the GFC to find a basis in German law for upholding the plaintiff's damages claim.

As regards the *Factortame* saga, in July 1997, the Divisional Court of the QBD, in an interlocutory decision in *R v Secretary of State for Transport ex p Factortame Ltd (No 4)*, went some way to applying the Article 177 (now 234) ruling of the Court of Justice in the 'quota-hopping' damages claim. It was held that breaches of Community law by the UK brought about by the introduction of the Merchant Shipping Act 1988 (operative from 1989 until 1991 when the Act was suspended) 'were sufficiently serious to give rise to liability for any damage that may subsequently be shown to have been caused to the applicants'. F and the other Spanish owners and managers were said to be entitled 'in principle' to compensation during that period. They had yet to prove their losses (estimated at £100 million) and therefore the causal link requirement had yet to be established.

The Divisional Court was satisfied that each of the nationality, domicile and residence conditions in the 1988 Act which excluded the Spanish concerns from fishing against UK quotas 'constituted a sufficiently serious breach of the relevant Articles of the Treaty': see in particular Article 7 (now 12) (discrimination on grounds of nationality) and the directly effective Article 52 (now 43) (freedom of establishment). Four factors formed the basis of this conclusion:

(a) Discrimination on the grounds of nationality was the intended effect of the domicile and residence conditions.

(b) The government was aware that the imposition of the conditions must necessarily injure the applicants.

(c) The government's decision to achieve its objective through primary legislation made it impossible for the applicants to obtain interim relief against the Crown (without the eventual intervention of the Court of Justice: see *Factortame (No 2)* in the House of Lords, above).

(d) The attitude of the Commission was hostile to the proposed legislation. (The Commission's view of the law is not always correct but the court stated that one acted against its advice at one's peril.)

A claim for exemplary damages was rejected, the court stating that the 1988 legislation was brought into force in the honest belief of a reasonable prospect of it being upheld by the Court of Justice.

As regards the question of the basis on which liability in damages is to be founded in national law, the court's conclusions on this point were as follows: 'In Community law, the liability of a State for breach of Community law is described as non-contractual. In English law ... it is best understood as a breach of statutory duty.' For this the court followed the judgment of Mann J in *Bourgoin v Ministry of Agriculture, Fisheries and Food* (1986), where he followed Lord Diplock's statement in *Garden Cottage Foods* (1984) that:

> A breach of the duty imposed by [the directly effective] Article 86 not to abuse a dominant position in the Common Market ... can thus be categorised in English law as a breach of statutory duty imposed ... for the benefit of private individuals to whom loss is caused by a breach of that duty.

Following Lord Diplock, Mann J had concluded that:

> ... I hold a contravention of Article 30 [of the Treaty] which causes damage to a person gives to that person an action for damages for breach of statutory duty, the duty being composed by Article 30 ... and section 2(1) of the [European Communities] Act of 1972 when read in conjunction.

On this basis, the Divisional Court stated that liability in damages in the *Factortame* case was similarly the tort of breach of statutory duty composed of Article 7 and Article 52 EC and section 2(1) of the 1972 Act which makes provision for the direct effect of Community law in the UK.

The government appealed against this decision to the Court of Appeal, which dismissed the appeal and affirmed the decision of the Divisional Court: *R v Secretary of State for Transport ex p Factortame Ltd (No 5)*.

A further appeal was made by the government to the House of Lords in *Factortame (No 6)*. Again, the appeal was dismissed; again unanimously. The leading speech by Lord Slynn gives an excellent account of the lengthy history of this litigation, which stretches back to the late 1980s, but he did not differ in his findings in any significant way from those in the lower courts.

R v Secretary of State for Transport ex p Factortame Ltd (No 6)

The House of Lords held:

The principles to be applied

(a) The decisive test for finding that a breach of Community law was sufficiently serious was whether the Member State concerned had gravely and manifestly disregarded the limits on the exercise of its power.

(b) It was not necessary to establish fault or negligence on the part of the Member State concerned going beyond what was relevant to show a sufficiently serious breach.

(c) The United Kingdom was entitled to consider how it would exercise the margin of discretion left to it under Community law in the application of the Common Fisheries Policy and in particular of the quota system, and also, subject to those limits how it would exercise its rights under international law to provide for registration as a British fishing vessel.

(d) In considering the three conditions of nationality, residence and domicile, which had always been treated separately, the less artificial approach was to consider the cumulative effect of those conditions, in order to decide whether the United Kingdom should be liable for compensation for its decision to adopt the legislation in question.

The conditions of nationality, domicile and residence

> The first question was whether in imposing a nationality requirement the United Kingdom had committed a sufficiently serious breach of Community law in manifestly and gravely disregarding the limits of that discretion. The Community rule prohibiting discrimination on grounds of nationality was a clear and fundamental provision of the Treaty. Moreover, the legislation was not adopted inadvertently by the United Kingdom Government but after anxious consideration and consultation, including with the Commission, who had communicated to the United Kingdom Government before the Bill received the Royal Assent, that the conditions were *prima facie* contrary to Community law. In an area so closely subject to Community control as the Common Fisheries Policy, the Commission's view, although not conclusive, was of importance, and if a Member State chose to ignore it, a court would be likely to find that the breach had been manifest and grave and thus sufficiently serious. The adoption of the nationality requirement therefore constituted a sufficiently serious breach for the purposes of the second condition of liability, and since it was agreed that the domicile requirement fell to be treated in the same way as nationality, that condition was also a sufficiently serious breach. In relation to the residence requirement, in so far as the aim of protecting the livelihood of British fishing communities could be justified, it was arguable that to require active fishermen to live in the communities concerned might be excusable. However, the terms of the Act were inappropriate to achieve this object because they were principally concerned with the nationality, domicile and country of residence of the shareholders in the companies owning the vessels. Accordingly, even when considered separately, the residence requirement was also a sufficiently serious breach as to entitle the respondents to compensation for damage directly caused.

Perhaps not surprisingly, after some 14 years of *Factortame* cases (three at Community level, seven at national level), damages have been settled at a reported figure in excess of £50 million. The question of the English law basis of liability to compensate (together with other matters such as causality and mitigation of loss) still remains without a clear answer, unless the Divisional Court's breach of statutory findings can be taken as such.

What is more certain is that the position regarding the statement by the Court of Justice in Case 158/80 *Rewe v HZA Kiel* (see above) that in general, the Treaty did not require the national courts to create new remedies for the breach of Community law has led, via promptings by the Court and the Commission, to the application in this country of 'old' remedies to new circumstances: interim relief in the first stage of the *Factortame* litigation, damages for breach of the competition rules in *Courage*, and, it would appear, a statutory duty tort law cause of action in the later *Factortame* State liability litigation.

Not that such tardy case law progress is the way forward for the Community. As Walter von Gerven has stated:

> Indeed, the need for harmonized legal remedies when it comes to protecting the individual's basic and therefore uniform Community rights is, it would seem, inherent in the concept of uniformity; in the absence of harmonized legal remedies, uniform rights cannot be adequately secured throughout the Community.

REFERENCES AND FURTHER READING

Article 169: Enforcement Actions

Borchardt, G, 'The award of interim measures by the European Court' (1985) 22 CML Rev 203.

Dashwood, A and White, R, 'Enforcement actions under Articles 169 and 170 EEC' (1989) 14 EL Rev 388.

Rawlings, R, 'Engaged elites, citizen action and institutional attitudes in Commission enforcement' (2000) 6 ELJ 4.

Rights and Remedies in National Courts

Barav, A and Green, N, 'Damages in the national courts for breach of Community law' (1986) 6 YEL 55.

Biondi, A, 'The European Court of Justice and certain national procedural limitations: not such a tough relationship' (1999) 36 CMLR 1271.

Convery, J, 'State liability in the United Kingdom after *Brasserie du Pêcheur*' (1997) 34 CML Rev 603.

Craig, P, 'Once more unto the breach: the Community, the State and damages liability' (1997) 113 LQR 67.

Deards, E, 'Curioser and curioser? The development of Member State liability in the Court of Justice' (1997) 3 EPL 117.

Deards, E, '*Brasserie du Pêcheur*: snatching defeat from the jaws of victory' (1997) 22 EL Rev 620.

Davidson, J, 'Actions for damages in the English courts for breach of EC competition law' (1985) 34 ICLQ 178.

Dougan, M, 'The *Francovich* right to reparation: reshaping the contours of Community remedial competence' (2000) 6 EPL 103.

Himsworth, CMG, 'Things fall apart: the harmonisation of Community judicial procedural protection revisited' (1997) 22 EL Rev 291.

Hoskins, M, 'Tilting the balance: supremacy and national procedural rules' (1996) 21 EL Rev 365.

Komninos, A, 'New prospects for enforcement of EC competition law: *Courage v Crehan* and the Community right to damages' (2002) 39 CML Rev 447.

Magliveras, K, 'Fishing in troubled waters: the Merchant Shipping Act 1988 and the EC' (1990) 39 ICLQ 899.

Oliver, P, 'Enforcing Community rights in English courts' (1987) 50 MLR 881.

Oliver, P, 'Interim measures: some recent developments' (1992) 29 CML Rev 7.

Report of the Committee of the JUSTICE–All Souls Review of Administrative Law in the United Kingdom, Administrative Justice: Some Necessary Reforms (1988), particularly Chapter 11.

Ross, M, 'Beyond *Francovich*' (1993) 56 MLR 55.

Steiner, J, 'From direct effects to *Francovich*' (1993) 18 EL Rev 3.

Temple Lang, J, 'Community constitutional law: Article 5 EEC Treaty' (1990) 27 CML Rev 645.

Temple Lang, J, 'The duties of national courts under Community constitutional law' (1997) 22 EL Rev 3.

Tridimas, T, 'Liability for breach of Community law: growing up and mellowing down' (2001) 38 CML Rev 301.

Tridimas, T, 'Bridging the unbridgeable: Community law and national tort laws after *Francovich* and *Brasserie*' (1996) 45 ICLQ 507.

Van Gerven, W, 'Bridging the gap between Community and national laws: towards a principle of homogeneity in the field of legal remedies?' (1995) 32 CML Rev 679.

Weatherill, S, 'National remedies and equal access to public procurement' (1990) 10 YEL 243.

INDEX